GIMP Bible

GIMP Bible

GIMP Bible

Jason van Gumster
Robert Shimonski

WILEY

Wiley Publishing, Inc.

GIMP Bible

Published by
Wiley Publishing, Inc.
10475 Crosspoint Boulevard
Indianapolis, IN 46256
www.wiley.com

Copyright © 2010 by Wiley Publishing, Inc., Indianapolis, Indiana

Published by Wiley Publishing, Inc., Indianapolis, Indiana

Published simultaneously in Canada

ISBN: 978-0-470-52397-1

Manufactured in the United States of America

10 9 8 7 6 5 4 3 2 1

For general information on our other products and services please contact our Customer Care Department within the United States at (877) 762-2974, outside the United States at (317) 572-3993 or fax (317) 572-4002.

Wiley also publishes its books in a variety of electronic formats. Some content that appears in print may not be available in electronic books.

Library of Congress Control Number: 2009943686

To my mother, who once made the mistake of telling me I could do anything I set my mind to do . . . only to have me terrorize her by trying to do everything.
— *Jason van Gumster*

This book is dedicated to my son, Dylan James.
— *Robert Shimonski*

About the Authors

Jason van Gumster got into animation when he realized that he wanted to create movies ... but that actors are generally intolerant of having pianos dropped on them. Using open source tools at nearly every step in production, Jason has produced animations and visual effects for television, film, and video games in his official capacity as a "Production Monkey" for Hand Turkey Studios, the company he helped start in 2005. He uses GIMP and the GIMP Animation Package on a daily basis for a variety of tasks ranging from creating graphics for the Web and television to drawing storyboards and creating images for both 3D and hand-drawn animations. Also the author of *Blender for Dummies*, Jason has given numerous live workshops and demonstrations on Blender internationally. Combining a unique educational background in animation and computer engineering with a penchant for the ridiculous, he strives to refine both the technical and creative aspects of production by taking on (and successfully completing) crazy projects like producing a 5-minute 3D animated short in a mere 48 hours with an international team communicating via the Internet. Based in Richmond, Virginia, Jason can often be found in cafés and diners drawing, espousing the virtues of open source software, or catching confused looks from strangers as he contorts his body to better visualize a scene he's animating.

Robert J. Shimonski is an expert digital media and technology consultant living in New York. Rob is also an author, and a regular contributor of tutorials and articles on digital editing, production, and development.

Having spent the past decade working with large, medium, and small companies as a technical consultant, Rob has helped develop digital art packages for many professional clients and businesses.

Rob has been working with GIMP for many years and has created graphics for corporate web sites, TV commercials, and professional magazines. Having worked with the many open source tools, Rob relies on GIMP for most of his graphics work.

Rob can be found online at www.shimonski.com.

About the Technical Editor

John Karnay is a published author and editor with over a dozen works to his credit. He has been writing and editing in the fields of technology, fiction, comic books, computer software, music, and video games for over 15 years. John is a computer software, audio engineering, graphic design, networking and IT specialist who has been working with and deploying Microsoft-, Apple-, and open source-based technologies for over 15 years. He also specializes in Spanish-to-English translation. John currently works in the video game industry as a producer, content writer and quality assurance manager and has over 30 game titles to his credit.

John resides in Jackson Heights, New York and spends his free time with his daughter Aurora and with his loving wife and partner, illustrator Gloria Rios.

Credits

Executive Editor
Carol Long

Project Editor
Sydney Jones

Technical Editor
John Karnay

Production Editor
Daniel Scribner

Copy Editor
Kim Cofer

Editorial Director
Robyn B. Siesky

Editorial Manager
Mary Beth Wakefield

Associate Director of Marketing
David Mayhew

Production Manager
Tim Tate

Vice President and Executive Group Publisher
Richard Swadley

Vice President and Executive Publisher
Barry Pruett

Associate Publisher
Jim Minatel

Project Coordinator, Cover
Lynsey Stanford

Proofreader
Heather Dweller

Indexer
Johnna VanHoose Dinse

Cover Illustration
Joyce Haughey

Cover Designer
Michael E. Trent

Acknowledgments

First (and most important) thanks go to the surprisingly small group of dedicated developers who voluntarily spend their free time coding GIMP. Most people don't realize that a program of GIMP's complexity is updated and maintained by only a handful of developers whose primary motivation is the fact that they enjoy doing it. Your patience and help with my questions and misplaced bug reports are sincerely appreciated. You are not and cannot be thanked enough.

Thanks, also, to the entire team at Wiley. Were it not for this talented group of professionals (and large quantities of coffee), this book would never have been produced. I'd especially like to acknowledge my project editor of unparalleled patience and tireless energy, Sydney Jones. I'd also like to thank Rob Shimonski not only for working as this book's initial technical editor, but also for stepping up and agreeing to write a portion of the book on incredibly short notice. It has been a pleasure to work with both of you. — Jason van Gumster

A book takes a lot of work to create and requires a very large team effort. I would like to thank the Wiley production team for all of their hard work. I would first like to thank my co-author Jason, who is truly a GIMP wizard. Special thanks goes out to Sydney for her untiring dedication to this project. I would also like to thank technical editor Johnny for keeping things on track. Lastly, I would like to thank Carol, who got me started on the project and kept everything locked on. — Robert Shimonski

Contents at a Glance

Introduction xxxi

Part I: Meet GIMP 1
Chapter 1: What Is GIMP? 3
Chapter 2: Thinking Digitally 41

Part II: Getting Started 59
Chapter 3: Working with Files 61
Chapter 4: A Brief Overview of GIMP's Tools 93
Chapter 5: Taking Advantage of Paths 109
Chapter 6: Working with Layers and Masks 135
Chapter 7: Using Channels 171

Part III: Manipulating Images 185
Chapter 8: Transforming Images 187
Chapter 9: Adjusting Colors 221
Chapter 10: Working with Text 281
Chapter 11: Painting in GIMP 297
Chapter 12: Enhancing Photos 323

Part IV: Exploring Filters and Effects 347
Chapter 13: Implementing Blur, Enhancement, and Distortion Filters 349
Chapter 14: Using Image Creation Filters 391
Chapter 15: Using Compositing Filters 427
Chapter 16: Enhancing Images with Artistic Filters 475
Chapter 17: Working with Specialized Filters 499
Chapter 18: Batch Processing with Automating Filters 513
Chapter 19: Using GIMP Animation Package 537
Chapter 20: Working with Video-Specific Functions in GIMP 567

Part V: Advanced Topics 599
Chapter 21: Finding and Installing Plug-ins 601
Chapter 22: Creating Custom Effects with Scripting 629

Contents at a Glance

Part VI: Appendices **647**

Appendix A: Downloading and Installing GIMP 649

Appendix B: Setting Up External Input Devices 663

Appendix C: Customizing GIMP 679

Appendix D: Additional Resources 691

Appendix E: What's on the Web Site 695

Index 697

Contents

Introduction xxxi

Part I: Meet GIMP   1

Chapter 1: What Is GIMP? 3
Knowing What GIMP Can and Cannot Do 6
Working with GIMP's Interface 7
　　Windows and Menus 7
　　Docks and Dialogs 9
　　Images and Canvases 16
　　　　Parts of the Image Window 16
　　　　The Concept of a "Canvas" 18
Setting Preferences 21
　　　　The Module Manager 21
　　　　GIMP Preferences 22
Customizing Keyboard Shortcuts 37
Summary 39

Chapter 2: Thinking Digitally 41
Digital Images vs. Traditional Photographs 41
Raster Graphics vs. Vector Graphics 44
　　Raster Images 44
　　Vector Images 44
Resolution and Image Size 46
　　Changing Image Size and Resolution 47
　　Confusing Terminology 49
Color Depth 50
Color Spaces and Color Modes 51
　　Color Spaces 51
　　Color Modes 52
Compression 55
　　Lossless Compression 55
　　Lossy Compression 57
Summary 58

Contents

Part II: Getting Started   59

Chapter 3: Working with Files 61

Opening Files 61
  Opening Images 62
    File ➤ Open 62
    Other Ways to Open an Image 66
  Creating a Blank New Image 68
  Generating an Image from Plug-in or Hardware 69
    Creating an Image from a Screenshot 70
    Creating an Image from a CMYK TIFF 72
    Using a Scanner to Import a Drawing or Photograph 73
    Letting GIMP's Automated Scripts Generate an Image 74
  Managing Open Images 75
Working in the Image Window 77
Copying and Pasting 79
  Fun Things You Can Do with Paste (Besides Eat It) 79
  Advanced Copy and Paste with Buffers 81
Taking Advantage of Undo 82
Saving Files 84
  GIMP's Native Format: XCF 85
  Other Formats 86
Summary 90

Chapter 4: A Brief Overview of GIMP's Tools 93

The View Menu 93
  Modifying Your View in the Image Window 93
  Using Display Filters to Color Correct GIMP to Your Monitor 96
  Showing and Hiding Information 97
  Snapping Controls 98
  Padding Color 98
  Showing and Hiding Parts of the Image Window 99
Selection Tools 99
  Rectangle Select 100
  Ellipse Select 101
  Free (Lasso) Select 102
  Fuzzy Select 102
  Select by Color 103
  Intelligent Scissors Select 103
  Foreground Select 103
Image Tools 104
  Informational Tools 104

Contents

Color Picker 104

Zoom 105

Measure 105

Transform Tools 106

Paint Tools 106

Color Tools 106

Summary 107

Chapter 5: Taking Advantage of Paths 109

The Advantages of Paths: Get Some Vector in Your Raster 109

Creating Paths 110

Drawing with the Paths tool 111

Creating a Path from a Selection 114

Managing Paths 118

The Paths Dialog 119

Importing and Exporting Paths 121

Importing Paths 121

Exporting Paths 123

Using Paths 123

Painting along a Path 124

Stroke Line 125

Stroke with a Paint Tool 126

Practical Example: Faking an Ink Drawing 129

Selecting with a Path 132

Summary 133

Chapter 6: Working with Layers and Masks 135

Managing Layers 136

A Quick Overview of the Layers Dialog 136

Adding, Duplicating, and Removing Layers 139

Creating a New Layer 140

Duplicating an Existing Layer 141

Deleting Layers 142

Arranging Layers in the Stack 142

Grouping and Merging Layers 143

Merging Layers 143

Grouping Layers 144

Manipulating Layers 146

Resizing Layers 146

Modifying the Layer Boundary Size 146

Scaling Layers 147

Offsetting the Content of a Layer 148

Aligning Layers 149

Contents

Working with Layer Transparency 152
    Additional Layer Transparency Features 152
    Using Layer Transparency for Selections 154
Blending Modes 156
Using Layer Masks 162
    Defining Layer Masks 162
    Modifying Layer Masks 163
    Effectively Using Features in the Select Menu 165
Summary 169

Chapter 7: Using Channels 171

Understanding Channels 171
    Red, Green, and Blue: The Default Color Channels 172
    A Fistful of Awesome: The Alpha Channel 173
Using Channels 175
    Creating Channels 176
    Taking Advantage of Channels Once They're Created 177
    Practical Application: Changing the Background 179
Summary 183

Part III: Manipulating Images   185

Chapter 8: Transforming Images 187

Adjustments Available in the Image and Layer Menus 187
    Sizing 188
        Fit Canvas to Layers 188
        Layer to Image Size 189
    Cropping and Guillotine 190
        Crop to Selection 191
        Autocrop 191
        Zealous Crop 193
        Guillotine 194
    Flipping and Rotating 195
        Flipping 195
        Rotating 196
    Liquid Rescale: Quite Possibly the Coolest Thing Ever 198
        Using Liquid Rescale 199
        Output Options 202
        Advanced Options 204
        Interactive Mode 206
        Advanced Techniques: Smart Zoom 208
Using the Image Tools 209
    Alignment Tool 209
    Crop Tool 213

Transformation Tool 215

    Moving 217

    Rotating 218

    Scaling 218

    Shearing 218

    Changing Perspective 218

Flip Tool 219

Summary 220

Chapter 9: Adjusting Colors **221**

Using the Color Menu 223

    Working with the Color Tools 223

        Features Available for All Color Tools 224

        Color Balance 226

        Hue-Saturation 227

        Colorize 229

        Brightness-Contrast 230

        Threshold 231

        Levels 232

        Curves 236

        Posterize 239

        Desaturate 241

    Inverting Values 243

    Using Automated Adjustments 243

        Equalize 244

        White Balance 245

        Color Enhance 245

        Normalize 246

        Stretch Contrast 247

        Stretch HSV 248

    Working with Separated Color Components 249

        Channel Mixer 249

        Composing, Decomposing, and Recomposing 252

    Remapping Colors 255

        Rearranging and Defining a Color Map 256

        Alien Map 257

        Color Exchange 258

        Gradient Map 260

        Palette Map 260

        Rotate Colors 260

        Sample Colorize 263

Contents

Analyzing Your Colors with Info Tools 266

    Histogram 266

    Border Average 267

    Colorcube Analysis 267

    Smooth Palette 268

Color Filter Plug-ins 269

    Color to Alpha 269

    Colorify 269

    Filter Pack 269

    Hot 272

    Maximum RGB 272

    Retinex 273

Exporting Color Separations with the Separate+ Plug-in 275

Summary 279

Chapter 10: Working with Text **281**

Uses for Text in Images 281

Adding and Editing Text 282

    Customizing Text from the Text Panel 286

        Font and Size 286

        Font Edging 287

        Changing Text Color 288

        Justification, Indentation, and Spacing 289

    Making Text Go Along a Path 290

    Using Text to Create a Path 292

Working with Text Layers 294

Summary 296

Chapter 11: Painting in GIMP **297**

Working with Brushes 298

    Adjusting Brushes 299

        Using Tool Options to Adjust Brushes 299

        Quickly Adjusting Brush Settings from the Image Window 302

    Creating New Brushes 303

        Using the Brush Editor to Create Procedural Brushes 305

        Creating Animated and Bitmap Brushes 307

    Paint Dynamics and Using Brushes with a Drawing Tablet 313

    GIMP Paint Studio — A Painter-Friendly Batch of Presets 314

Drawing Calligraphic Lines with the Ink Tool 315

Working with Gradients 317

Creating Pattern Fills 320

Summary 321

Chapter 12: Enhancing Photos **323**

Traditional Photographer Tools 323
   Blur/Sharpen 324
   Smudge 326
   Dodge/Burn 329
Using Cloning and Healing to Fix Problem Areas 331
   Clone Tool 331
   Perspective Clone Tool 335
   Healing Tool 338
Using the Exposure Blend Plug-in 341
Summary 345

Part IV: Exploring Filters and Effects   **347**

Chapter 13: Implementing Blur, Enhancement, and Distortion Filters **349**

Common Features among Filters 350
Using the Blur Filters 353
   Blur 353
   Gaussian Blur 353
   Motion Blur 354
   Pixelize 357
   Selective Gaussian Blur 359
   Tileable Blur 359
Enhance Filters 360
   Antialias 361
   Deinterlace 361
   Despeckle 362
   Destripe 363
   NL Filter 364
   Red Eye Removal 365
   Sharpen 365
   Unsharp Mask 367
Distortion Filters 368
   Blinds 368
   Curve Bend 369
   Emboss 371
   Engrave 372
   Erase Every Other Row 374
   IWarp 374
   Lens Distortion 377
   Mosaic 378
   Newsprint 380

Contents

Pagecurl 381

Polar Coordinates 382

Ripple 383

Shift 384

Value Propagate 384

Video 386

Waves 386

Whirl and Pinch 388

Wind 389

Summary 390

Chapter 14: Using Image Creation Filters 391

Light and Shadow Filters 391

Gradient Flare 392

Lens Flare 395

Lighting Effects 397

Sparkle 400

Supernova 402

Drop Shadow 402

Perspective 404

Xach-Effect 404

Lens Effect 405

Glass Tile 405

Noise Filters 406

Scatter HSV 406

Hurl 407

Random Pick 407

RGB Noise 408

Slur 409

Spread 409

Render Filters 411

Clouds 411

Difference Clouds 411

Plasma 412

Solid Noise 412

Nature 413

Flame 413

IFS Fractal 414

Pattern 414

CML Explorer 415

Checkerboard 415

Diffraction Patterns 416

Grid 416

Jigsaw 418

Contents

Maze 418

Qbist 420

Sinus 420

Circuit 420

Fractal Explorer 421

Gfig 421

Lava 422

Line Nova 422

Sphere Designer 423

Spyrogimp 424

Summary 425

Chapter 15: Using Compositing Filters 427

Working with Edge-Detect Filters 427

The Difference of Gaussians Option 430

Edge 431

Laplace 434

Neon 435

Sobel 436

Using the Filters in the Generic Menu 438

Convolution Matrix 438

Dilate and Erode 442

Using the Combine Filters 443

Depth Merge 443

Filmstrip 446

Selection 447

Advanced 449

Taking Advantage of Mapping Filters 450

Bump Map 450

Displace 453

Fractal Trace 456

Illusion 457

Make Seamless 459

The Map Object Filter 459

Options 460

Light and Material 461

Orientation 462

Extra Tabs: Box and Cylinder 463

Paper Tile 464

Small Tiles 466

Tile 467

Warp 468

Basic Options 469

Advanced Options 471

Contents

More Advanced Options 471

Using Warp to Map a Logo to a Photo of Rumpled Cloth 472

Summary 473

Chapter 16: Enhancing Images with Artistic Filters **475**

Artistic Filters 475

Apply Canvas 475

Cartoon 476

Cubism 477

GIMPressionist 479

Oilify 480

Photocopy 480

Predator 482

Softglow 484

Van Gogh (LIC) 486

Decor Filters 487

Add Bevel 487

Add Border 488

Coffee Stain 489

Fuzzy Border 491

Old Photo 492

Round Corners 493

Slide 494

Stencil Carve 495

Stencil Chrome 496

Summary 498

Chapter 17: Working with Specialized Filters **499**

Web Filters 499

Image Map 499

Semi-Flatten 501

Image Slice 501

Animation Filters 504

Blend 504

Rippling 505

Spinning Globe 506

Waves 507

Optimizing Filters 508

Alpha to Logo 508

3D Outline 508

Summary 511

Chapter 18: Batch Processing with Automating Filters **513**

Batch Processing Multiple Files 513

Using the Batch Process Plug-in 514

Using the Input Tab to Select Images 515

Contents

Using the Turn Tab 516

Using the Blur Tab 517

Using the Colour Tab 517

Using the Resize Tab 518

Using the Crop Tab 520

Using the Sharpen Tab 520

Using the Rename Tab 520

Using the Output Tab 522

Using the Contact Sheet Plug-in 524

Automating Tasks with GAP's Filtermacro 527

The Filtermacro Window 527

Adding Operations 528

Filter All Layers 530

Using Filter All Layers 531

Apply Constant 532

Apply Varying 533

A Quick Shortcut: Selection to AnimImage 535

Summary 536

Chapter 19: Using GIMP Animation Package 537

Using Still Image Sequences and Layers for Animation 538

Creating a Simple GIF Animation with Layers 538

Images to Layers and Layers to Images 542

Splitting a Layer Image into an Image Sequence 542

Converting an Image Sequence into a Single Layered Image 544

Managing the Frames of Your Image Sequence with GAP 546

The Easy Way: GAP's Video Navigator 546

Additional Frame Management Functions in the Video Menu 549

Convenience Features to Improve Workflow 553

Working with the Move Path Feature 553

Morphing 556

Onionskinning 559

Creating a Storyboard 562

Summary 566

Chapter 20: Working with Video-Specific Functions in GIMP 567

Playing Back Video 568

Video Options 568

Audio Options 572

Preferences 574

Encoding Video 575

Setting Video Options 576

Setting FFMPEG Parameters 578

Setting AVI1 parameters 583

Contents

Setting Audio Options 586

Configuring the Audio Tool 588

Using the Extras Tab 590

The Encoding Tab 592

Extracting Frames from a Video File 592

Using Extract Videorange 593

Setting Input Options 593

Setting Output Options 595

Using MPlayer-Based Extraction 596

Summary 598

Part V: Advanced Topics   599

Chapter 21: Finding and Installing Plug-ins 601

The GIMP Plugin Registry 602

Installing Plug-ins 604

Installing Scripts 605

Installing Compiled Plug-Ins 606

A Few Plug-ins Worth Mentioning 608

Exposure Blend 608

GIMP-GAP 609

Installing GAP on Linux 610

Installing GAP on Mac OS X 612

Installing GAP on Windows 612

GIMPshop and GimPhoto/GimPad 613

GIMPshop 613

GimPhoto/GimPad 614

GREYCstoration and G'MIC 615

Layer Effects 617

Liquid Rescale 621

Installing Liquid Rescale on Linux 621

Installing Liquid Rescale on Mac OS X 623

Installing Liquid Rescale on Windows 623

Separate+ 623

Installing Separate+ on Linux 624

Installing Separate+ on Mac OS X 626

Installing Separate+ on Windows 626

Summary 628

Chapter 22: Creating Custom Effects with Scripting 629

Multi-Lingual GIMP: Scripting Languages GIMP Understands 630

Scheme and Python — GIMP's Primary Scripting Languages 631

Other Scripting Languages Supported by GIMP 633

Taking Advantage of the Procedure Browser 634

Using the Scripting Console 634

Writing a Custom Script for GIMP 635

Building a Structure for Your Script 636

Writing the Meat of Your Script 639

Summary 645

Part VI: Appendices 647

Appendix A: Downloading and Installing GIMP 649

Installing GIMP on Linux 649

Debian/Ubuntu 650

Fedora 652

OpenSUSE 653

Gentoo 655

Mandriva 655

Installing GIMP on Windows 656

Regular Installation on Windows 657

Installing GIMP Portable 658

Installing GIMP on Apple Macintosh 660

Installing GIMP on OS X 661

Installing GIMP from MacPorts 662

Appendix B: Setting Up External Input Devices 663

Acquiring Images with a Scanner 663

Linux 664

Mac OS X and Windows 666

Printing Images 668

Using the Bundled GTKPrint Module 668

Printing with Gutenprint 671

Installing Gutenprint 671

Using Gutenprint 672

Configuring a Drawing Tablet 676

Appendix C: Customizing GIMP 679

Changing the Splash Image 679

Using a Different Theme 681

Linux 682

Windows 684

Mac OS X 687

Fixing the "Yellow Cursor" Bug 687

Changing Your GTK+ Theme 688

Contents

Appendix D: Additional Resources **691**

  On the Web 691

  Internet Relay Chat 694

Appendix E: What's on the Web Site **695**

  How the Site Is Organized 695

  Getting the Most out of the Site 696

Index **697**

Introduction

Thanks for picking up *GIMP Bible*, which I hope is the most comprehensive and up-to-date book on this very cool piece of Free Software. Whether you're a hobbyist interested in a free image editor, or a seasoned professional curious about what "that GIMP thing" is capable of, this book is designed to meet your needs and give you the information you're looking for. The idea is to cover everything that GIMP can do while also involving topics related to computer graphics in general. The primary purpose of this book is to show you how to be really productive with a program this complex. If you're anything like me, the more cool things you can make and the faster you can make them, the more fun you're having. And really, it's all about having fun. This is especially true for a program like GIMP, which is developed by volunteers all over the world, in their free time, because they really enjoy it.

That said, no piece of software is perfect and everyone has an opinion, myself included. Throughout the book, I may periodically voice my opinion about a feature in GIMP or a topic in computer graphics. However, when I do that, I try to make it a point to qualify that opinion and couple it with a relevant tip, trick, or workaround that's actually useful to you.

What to Expect

Unlike a lot of other books on the topic, *GIMP Bible* covers more than just the standard release of GIMP. GIMP's primary function is that of an image editor and GIMP is typically used a lot in photo editing. However, it's capable of quite a bit more, especially if you factor in the bevy of extensions and plug-ins that are available. For that reason, I also cover a variety of these very helpful plug-ins that are critical for digital artists who work in print, digital painting, video, and animation.

Another very important thing to note is that this book's goal is to be as up-to-date as possible, with a focus on the most recent features available. *GIMP Bible* is targeted to cover the features in the stable GIMP 2.8 release. Consequentially, much of this book was written using the GIMP 2.7 development series (the way GIMP versions work, odd decimals – 2.3, 2.5, 2.7 – are development versions and even decimals – 2.6, 2.8 – are stable). That being the case, there may be some minor inconsistencies between what you see on the screen and what you read in the text or see in the figures. The good news, however, is that by and large GIMP is still GIMP. What I mean is that while there may be some differences in how things look in GIMP, they should still work the same. A button may be moved or renamed, but it still performs the same function. Furthermore, to alleviate these issues, I will be diligently posting updates, errata, and tutorials to this book's companion website, www.wiley.com/go/GIMPBible.

Who This Book Is For

Because *GIMP Bible* is designed as a reference suitable for both beginners and experts in producing computer graphics, it doesn't presume to know your level of understanding of the field. Most terms and concepts related to computer graphics are explained in the text. That said, we've written this book with the assumption that you have at least a basic understanding of how your computer works. You should know how to start programs, open files, and install software on your operating system. The last of these is particularly important if you need to install some of the plug-ins and extensions covered within this book. On the hardware side of things, you should also be able to use peripherals like a mouse or drawing pad and understand the difference between system memory (RAM) and storage memory (hard drive or external media like USB sticks).

What This Book Contains

Looking through this book's table of contents, you can get a good idea of all of the concepts and topics that are covered. *GIMP Bible* is organized into seven parts, The following is a description of each one:

- **Part I: Meet GIMP** — This part serves as your first introduction to GIMP, providing a bit of its history and a first taste of the interface. The second chapter in this part should be particularly useful for complete beginners go computer graphics because it provides an introduction to many of the concepts and a lot of the terminology used throughout the rest of the book.

- **Part II: Getting Started** — This next part of the book really gets into the details of GIMP's interface and the features it provides. It starts with coverage of how GIMP handles files, and works forward through adjusting the image window. From there, the chapters in this part cover topics such as creating selections and taking full advantage of those selections with GIMP's Paths, Layers, and Channels dialogs.

- **Part III: Manipulating Images** — The focus of the chapters in this part is the application of GIMP's tools to manipulate existing images and create custom graphics. It starts with moving, rotating, and deforming elements of your images and continues to cover how much you can modify your image by simply modifying its colors. The final three chapters in this part really get into adding new content to your images in the form of text, paint strokes, and photo enhancement tools.

- **Part IV: Exploring Filters and Effects** — One of the most prominent features of GIMP is its incredibly wide variety of available filters. Filters are sets of processing steps that can be applied to your image in a single shot. Their effects range from barely perceivable and subtle to a complete overhaul of the appearance of your image. The chapters in this part cover every one of the filters that ship with GIMP, as well as a few useful ones that don't.

- **Part V: Advanced Topics** — Part of the beauty of GIMP is its extensibility. Anyone with a computer and a little bit of programming knowledge can add new features and functionality to GIMP in the form of extensions and plug-ins. Throughout the rest of the book, I cover some of these "third-party" extensions that don't come with GIMP by default. The chapters in this part cover the installation of these additions and then go into how you can easily write your own custom extensions to help improve your efficiency while working.

- **Part VI: Appendices** — Most of *GIMP Bible* is focused on creating computer art and graphics with GIMP. In order to use GIMP for that purpose, however, there are some technical steps that you may need to perform to get GIMP installed on your computer and to get your hardware playing nicely with it. The appendices provide you with those steps. They also cover supplemental information such as ways to customize the appearance of GIMP and additional resources online where you can learn more about GIMP, including this book's companion website, `wiley.com/go/GIMPBible.com`.

Conventions Used in This Book

As with any book on a technical topic, especially ones that deal with computer software, there are specialized methods and terminologies that specifically relate to the software or the field being covered. To deal with that, this book employs a few standards and conventions:

Terminology

Seeing as how this book is targeted at raw beginners as well as seasoned professionals (salty experts?) in computer graphics, I make it a point to define terminology and jargon specific to the field or unique to GIMP. You'll be able to notice this because defined words, like *megapixel*, will be italicized. The definition will immediately follow. If you run across a non-italicized word that you don't recognize, have a look in the index of this book and see where else it's used. That should give you enough context to figure it out on your own. And if that still doesn't work for you, send me an email (given in the "Contact Information" section later) and I'll do my best to clear things up for you.

Commands, Options, and Menus

Throughout this book I continually make reference to various commands, options, and menus in GIMP's interface. For many commands in GIMP, there's often more than one way to invoke them. So when I first give you a command, I'll also provide each of the ways to perform it, including a keyboard shortcut if one exists by default. If I reference a command more than once, then I typically just provide the fastest way to invoke that command.

Often commands are invoked by navigating a menu. In these cases, I use arrows to indicate drilling down through submenus to the final menu item, like Filters ➤ Map ➤ Make Seamless. Also, for both menu items and options that are in GIMP's interface, I use *title case* when referring to them. That is, I'll capitalize the first letter in each main word of the option or menu item, like Use Color from Gradient. Now, this choice may differ from the way it appears in GIMP, but capitalization in GIMP's interface is a bit inconsistent in parts. Because I use uppercase letters in this book in a consistent manner, you'll at least know what words to look for when going to GIMP's interface.

You may also notice that I may explicitly tell you whether to left-click, right-click, or (on occasion) middle-click. This is because working efficiently in GIMP requires that you have at least a two-button mouse. There's a lot of functionality in dialogs like the Layers and Channels dialogs that is most quickly accessed with a right-click. There are occasions in the book where I simply say click and don't stipulate which mouse button to press. In these cases any mouse button should do, but it's best to assume left-click.

Using GIMP on Multiple Platforms

GIMP runs on every major computing *platform*, or operating system on modern computers, including Linux, Unix, Mac OS X, and Windows. The cool thing is that regardless of the platform, GIMP typically looks and behaves the same. That said, there are a few things to bear in mind. For instance, Mac users may be used to pressing the Command key for operations like copy and paste. However, GIMP's current default is to use the Ctrl key across all platforms. Also, since printing, scanning, and screen capture subsystems vary from one operating system to another, there are minor differences in the way GIMP accesses them. These little inconsistencies across platforms can be a slight source of frustration for users who are used to working a certain way. For that reason, whenever one of these differences pops up, I make sure to point out how GIMP handles them on each platform. These differences are usually minor, though, so GIMP should look the same on all platforms. Since my preferred work environment (and GIMP's primary development) is in Linux, most of the screenshots in this book are taken from that platform. However, for the relatively few places where there are differences on Mac OS X or Windows, I do have platform-specific screenshots.

Another thing to note is that I occasionally need to refer to a location on your computer's hard drive. Since most operating systems do it this way, I notate the path using the standard forward-slash notation, like so: /usr/share/gimp. For those of you using Windows, you simply need to translate to using back-slashes and drive letters. And for you Unix folks, the things you call directories and sub-directories (such as usr or share in the previous example), I refer to as folders and sub-folders. How's that for compromise?

Versions and Actively Developed Software

Since this book covers plug-ins that don't ship with the official release of GIMP — plug-ins that you may have to download and install yourself — I've made it a point to try to use the most current stable version of each of these plug-ins. This is particularly true for larger plug-ins like G'MIC and Liquid Rescale, as well as extensions such as the GIMP Animation Package. Where it's helpful, I mention the version of the plug-in and how it may differ from previous versions. The companion website for this book (wiley.com/go/GIMPBible.com) also has links to the most current versions of any of these plug-ins, and provides any tips you may need to follow in order to get them installed.

And as I mentioned earlier, *GIMP Bible* was written while GIMP was under heavy development for the 2.8 series. It was an interesting challenge, but my hope is that doing this gives you the most thorough look at the new GIMP so you can take full advantage of all of the goodies the developers have packed into it for us. Where it's relevant, I'll mention how the behavior of GIMP 2.7/2.8 differs from the previous stable version and explain the benefits of the new behavior.

Features Used in This book

A common feature in Wiley's *Bible* series of books is the very useful icons. *GIMP Bible* uses these icons to highlight discussion topics and provide you with quick tips, warnings, and workarounds that relate to those topics. They're there to help and they can often give you a really cool or unexpected way to use a tool or perform a particular task. Skip them if you want, but you'll be missing out on the really good, juicy bits of information. In this book, you'll run across the following icons:

Warning

The Warning feature is probably one of the most important ones to look out for. The text by this icon gives you warnings of potential situations that may cause you to crash GIMP, or worse, lose data. The good news is that most of the time there's a workaround for these scenarios and the text next to the Warning icon provides you with it. ■

Note

Note features indicate bits of information that are handy to remember while you work. They provide additional information on how a particular feature or tool works. That information can, in turn, illuminate why that feature works in a particular way. If you want to get the most out of using GIMP, keep an eye out for these icons. ■

Tip

Tip features are the fun features. They give you hints at how to take advantage of GIMP or use it more efficiently. Also, in situations where a feature doesn't work as you might expect it to, Tip icons explain how you can bend that feature to your will. ■

Contact Information

This book was not written in a vacuum. A key tenet of the Free Software philosophy is the open exchange of information. Jason welcomes any reader's questions, suggestions, complaints, and (hopefully) the occasional compliment. The most effective way is through the blog and supplemental tutorials on this book's companion website at wiley.com/go/GIMPBible.com. This way if there's anyone else out there who has the same question you do, everyone can benefit from the answer. Of course, you can also reach me directly via email at author@gimpbible.com. While I will definitely read each and every email, because of the volume of email I receive, I cannot guarantee that I'll respond to all of them immediately. I do, however, promise to reply to any email that's sent to me. It just might take a while.

I only have one request: please limit your emails to content that relates specifically to *GIMP Bible*. If you have a bug report or feature suggestion for GIMP itself, please use the GIMP developer email list or bug tracker. Since I'm not an active GIMP developer, these are much more effective channels for those kinds of discussions.

Alright, enough talk. It's time to get elbow-deep in GIMPy goodness!

GIMP Bible

Part I

Meet GIMP

IN THIS PART

Chapter 1
What Is GIMP?

Chapter 2
Thinking Digitally

What Is GIMP?

IN THIS CHAPTER

Understanding GIMP's capabilities and limitations

Becoming familiar with GIMP's interface

Looking at preferences and customization

G IMP, GIMP, GIMP... oh what a name for an image editing program! With a name that's an acronym for GNU Image Manipulation Program, GIMP is the foremost application for raster graphics in the Free Software world. It's used for a variety of tasks ranging from photo editing and digital painting to batch image processing and traditional-style animation. If you have any interest in creating digital images, chances are good that you've at least heard of GIMP and perhaps even tried using it.

Whether you're a digital artist on a budget, an aspiring student, or just someone who needs a graphics program with more advanced features than those found in the simple paint program that may have come with your computer, GIMP is well-suited to helping you turn your ideas into images. You can start with a digital photograph, artwork from a scanner, or work from a blank canvas and create complete graphics from scratch. It's a great tool for getting the job done.

GIMP was born as a university project for two developers, Peter Mattis and Spencer Kimball, to fill the need for an advanced image editing program in the Unix and Linux environments when none existed. It has since grown to be an extremely influential force in the Linux world. In fact, the toolkit that was used to create GIMP's interface has been extended and expanded to become the basis for one of Linux's most popular desktop environments, GNOME. But although GIMP is included by default on nearly all popular distributions of Linux, you don't have to be a Linux user to take advantage of it. GIMP is a truly multiplatform program also available to Microsoft's Windows and Apple's Mac OS X users.

Perhaps GIMP's most valuable feature is its free and open nature. Not only is GIMP "zero money-out-of-pocket" free, but it's also "free speech" free. That is, GIMP is developed by an international team of volunteer programmers who have agreed to keep the program's source code freely available for anyone to see, modify, and extend. Not only does this produce solid, powerful software, but it also provides a level of customization that makes GIMP very appealing to independent artists, small graphics companies, and computer graphics researchers, to name a few. With GIMP, you have the advantages of your own in-house graphics program without having to hire a team of programmers to lay the groundwork for you. This means that if GIMP doesn't have a feature and you need it, you have the option to add that feature yourself (or hire only one programmer to do it). That's from an artist's point of view. From a developer's perspective, having GIMP as a base starting point allows you to focus on creating the unique features that *you* need.

What Are GNU and Free Software?

If you're coming from the world of Windows or Macintosh, then the concept of Free Software may not be something you're too familiar with. Simply put, *Free Software* is software that you can use, modify, and share with virtually no restrictions. Although it's often distributed free of charge — occasionally referred to as "free as in beer" — Free Software is not to be confused with "freeware." This is because of the all-important freedom to modify Free Software programs to do whatever you like. This is commonly referred to as being "free as in speech" and it's the primary thing that sets Free Software apart from software that's merely given away for free. For a program to be considered Free Software, users must be allowed unrestricted access to that program's source code. It is for this very reason that programs like GIMP can exist.

At this point, you may find yourself wondering why any software developer would ever give away their work for free. The answer to that question is surprisingly simple, but it varies from person to person. For some people, it's the idea that your computer (and everything on it) belongs to you and you should be allowed to use your computer as you see fit, without restriction. For others, it's a philosophy that stems from the belief that software is information and information should be freely available to everyone. And still other people approach it more pragmatically, noting that freely accessible source code is under the scrutiny of more eyes, ultimately leading to more stable software with fewer bugs and a lower probability of doing malicious things to your computer. Oftentimes, a Free Software developer's ideals involve a combination of these perspectives. The one commonality, though, is that they do this because they enjoy it. It's fun!

At the core of most Free Software projects — GIMP included — is a software license called the *GNU General Public License,* or GPL. This license is a clever use of copyright law that says you're free to modify a program and redistribute it, so long as you also make the source code to your changes freely available. Because this is basically using copyright law against itself, the GPL is often referred to as a *copyleft* license. The GPL was originally written by the founder of the Free Software Foundation, Richard Stallman, for the GNU Project. GNU is an acronym that stands for "GNU's Not Unix" and it was Stallman's project, which he started in 1983, to create a Free Software operating system. By 1992, the GNU Project had all of the necessary elements for this operating system with the exception of one thing: a central core to interface with hardware and manage processes, known as a *kernel.* Serendipitously, it's right around this time that a Free Software kernel developed by a Finnish programmer by the name of Linus Torvalds began reaching a usable level of maturity.

This kernel, Linux, filled in that last gap and gave the GNU Project (and the world), a working Free Software operating system. Because of this, the operating system's proper name is GNU/Linux. However, for the sake of simplicity and common discourse, this book will simply refer to it as Linux. The GNU is implied.

Of course, it's not all roses and cake. GIMP is often suggested as a replacement for Adobe Photoshop and, as a result, has received a fair amount of criticism based on the comparison; some of it well-deserved. Probably one of the most controversial subjects is GIMP's interface, shown in Figure 1-1. It's been called everything: unconventional, obtuse, brilliant, and some things I can't repeat in this book. GIMP gets a bit of an unfair shake due to the proliferation of Photoshop; its interface isn't so much bad — it's just different. That's not to say that it's perfect, though. There are certainly some interface quirks you need to deal with. Part of the purpose of this book, however, is to help you work *with* GIMP's interface rather than against it. Hopefully with this book as your reference, you'll find that you will be limited only by your imagination when working with GIMP.

FIGURE 1-1

What you're greeted with by default when you open GIMP

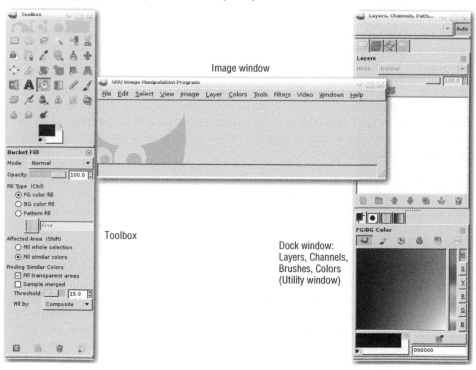

The remainder of this chapter lets you hit the ground running, introducing you to GIMP's inter-face and letting you play with it. Before doing that, though, you need to have GIMP installed on your computer. Fortunately, GIMP is completely free and available for you to download off the Internet. Regardless of whether you're running Linux, Mac OS X, or Windows, the place to find the latest and greatest version of GIMP is on its web site at www.gimp.org. Each operating system has its own set of installation instructions for GIMP. As a matter of fact, www.gimp.org actually links to other sites for downloading and installing on Mac OS X and Windows. Because of this, you may want to take a look at Appendix A in this book for clear instructions on installing GIMP for your specific operating system.

Knowing What GIMP Can and Cannot Do

So what exactly can this little program do? GIMP is an extremely capable piece of software that can do quite a few things other image editing programs can't do, but it's helpful to have a clear understanding of where its current limitations lie. This book focuses on the features planned for or available in GIMP's 2.8 series, and for general-purpose graphics work GIMP performs admirably. However, print professionals may miss some useful features that they would expect from a raster graphics program like Photoshop.

For example, GIMP supports RGBA (Red, Green, Blue, Alpha) images with 8 bits per channel, grayscale images, and images with a fixed color palette. However, it does not currently have native support for the more print-friendly Pantone or CMYK (Cyan, Magenta, Yellow, Black) color spaces or images with 16 or 32 bits per channel. This makes it less capable for use in print and film because the CMYK color space can't produce all of the colors available in RGB, and film image editing requires the refined detail of high bit-depth color.

That's not to say there aren't ways around this. GIMP can still do CMYK color separations and, with a plug-in, export images in CMYK. It can also read the raw image data from many digital cameras, although it can't save back to those formats. You may also be surprised to know that GIMP does support embedded color profiles and allows accurate on-screen print simulation using integrated color management tools.

GIMP also has an advanced layer system that allows for all sorts of complex compositing tricks and it supports an impressively extensive list of image formats, including Photoshop's native PSD format. That's not to say that the support is seamless. Because GIMP doesn't have adjustment layers like Photoshop, reading PSD files that utilize adjustment layers lets you see the data in that layer, but none of the adjustment layer tricks that were used.

Most of these limitations are technical and it's largely just a matter of time before GIMP overcomes them, thanks to the very active developer and user community around GIMP. And contrary to a fairly vocal minority, these limitations *don't* prevent GIMP from being usable for professional work. A few limitations, however, like support for the Pantone color matching system, are based on proprietary information and algorithms. This means that because of GIMP's developers' dedication to keeping its source code freely available, that feature cannot be legally implemented and distributed with GIMP. However, the flip side to this is that the ability to extend GIMP is not limited to a small group of privileged programmers. *Anyone* can add to, improve, and even change GIMP to suit their specific needs. It cannot be overstated how valuable this extensibility is. It's one of the beautiful things about Free Software. It's that potential for anyone's specifically added feature to benefit everyone who uses the program. Like other creative software in the Free Software world, GIMP has benefited greatly from the contributions of artists who had never written code before in their life, but because of its openness, they were able to add a new feature that they needed.

However, perhaps the best way to understand what GIMP is capable of is to see the results for yourself. GIMP was used to capture all of the figures in this book. Along with downloading and using the program yourself, this is probably the best way to get an idea of what GIMP can do.

Working with GIMP's Interface

So let's get started with this and get your hands dirty. When you start GIMP for the first time, one of the first things that you might notice is the number of windows that it opens. This is especially noticeable to Windows users who are used to programs occupying a single space on their taskbar. This multi-windowed environment comes from GIMP's origin in Linux and Unix, with their unique and varied means of window management. Fortunately for the users who find this to be troublesome, this situation has been somewhat rectified as of GIMP 2.6.1 for Windows and Linux users and will continue to improve in future versions of GIMP. I cover this improved window behavior in more detail later in this chapter in the "Setting Preferences" section. The purpose of this chapter is to get you familiar with the main parts of GIMP so you can get up and running and then right to work quickly. Refer to Figure 1-1 to see the default layout of GIMP when you load it for the first time.

Windows and Menus

When you launch GIMP, you're greeted with a splash window that displays while GIMP preloads plug-ins and extensions into memory. This should only take a few seconds. Once GIMP loads, you typically have three visible windows on-screen: the Main Toolbox, shown in Figure 1-1, on the left, an image window at the center, and a dock on the right that includes dialogs for layers, brushes, and palettes. Each of these windows serves a specific important purpose in GIMP, but as you may have guessed, the main image window with the menu along the top is where all of the action starts. Practically all editing operations can happen directly from image windows and their menu options. When you do not have images loaded, all you have is a gray box with a silhouette of Wilbur, the GIMP mascot, and the menu bar at the top. However, when you load your first image in GIMP, it's placed in this window. If you have more than one image open, each one gets its own image window with its own accompanying menu options.

You will find the same menu options are available by right-clicking anywhere within the image area of any image window. When you right-click your mouse, you invoke a menu like the one shown in Figure 1-2. For users of other programs that do not supply this option, this may seem a bit strange, but I personally love it because I don't have to move my mouse as far to get to the menu item I'm looking for.

FIGURE 1-2

The menu that pops up when you right-click in the image window

Another thing that's a little bit different in GIMP from other software is that most of its windows and dialogs are functionally *non-blocking*. This means that just because you have the File Open, File Save, or Preferences windows up, GIMP does not prevent you from changing tools in the Toolbox or even doing edits on your image. This is incredibly useful in terms of productivity. You can be doing a time-consuming operation on one image and GIMP won't prevent you from working on another image while that happens. You can customize your preferences on the fly and change them while you're working to suit your needs as you roll along. Basically, GIMP sticks to doing what you tell it to do and does everything in its power to get out of your way while you're working.

The menu options available to you in the image window give you access to nearly every available action in GIMP. Here's a quick heads-up on what you can expect to find in each menu item:

- **File** — This is where most of GIMP's file operations live. From here you can open, close, create, save, and export images. This menu also gives you the ability to acquire images like screenshots and images from a scanner. You can find more on the items accessible via the File menu in Chapter 3.

- **Edit** — The Edit menu is where a lot of the basic work gets done on your images. From here you can copy, paste, undo, and do basic actions like filling and stroking.

- **Select** — From this menu, you can control your selections within the image window. Not only do you have control over what's selected, but you can also control what GIMP does with that selection.

- **View** — This menu has a big influence on how you interact with the image window. Not only can you control zoom from here, but you can also show and hide features like guides and layer boundaries as well as turn on snapping.

- **Image** — This is where a good portion of the "heavy lifting" happens when you're working on an image. Chapter 2 has a lot more detail on the options here, but this menu allows you to perform basic transforms, size adjustments, cropping, and even a little bit of minor layer management.

- **Layer** — Of course, the really extensive layer management tools are in this menu. Nearly all of the functionality of the Layers dialog can be accessed from here, although it may be a bit more difficult. Chapter 6 is all about layers and covers this menu extensively.

- **Colors** — If there's anything color-related that you need to do, chances are good that it's going to happen by way of this menu. A whole bevy of color operations live here and each one is helpful for enhancing your images. You can find out more about this menu and adjusting colors in GIMP in Chapter 9.

- **Tools** — This menu is basically the functionality of your Toolbox all in one menu.

- **Filters** — Probably one of the largest, most extensive menus in all of GIMP, the Filters menu has an almost excessive number of potential ways to perform semi-automated effects on your images. This menu is so extensive and has so many options that all of Part IV is devoted to its contents.

- **Video** — The Video menu isn't available in most default installations of GIMP. It's included as part of the GIMP Animation Package, or GAP, and has some incredibly useful functions for modifying video and animation frames from within GIMP. Chapters 19 and 20 cover this functionality in depth.

- **Windows** — GIMP offers the potential to have quite a few open windows on your screen simultaneously. It's in your best interest to be able to manage those windows effectively. This menu is your tool to do just that.

- **Help** — No matter how long you've used a program as full-featured and complex as GIMP, there's a good chance that you'll need help with something somewhere along the line. This menu is your route to finding the help you need.

Another important thing to note is that you're not limited to just the three default windows that appear when you first load GIMP. Nearly every part of GIMP's interface can be detached and turned into its own window, including the main menu! Take a look back at the right-click menu in Figure 1-2 and notice the dashed lines at the top of it. If you left-click this dashed line, it will create another floating window just for this menu. To remove this window, simply click the dashed line again. Furthermore, notice that each of the submenus also features this dashed line. They can also be detached and turned into their own windows. You might find yourself asking why you'd ever want to do something like that, but imagine that you're performing the same operation over and over again. Simply clicking the same option more than once in a persistent menu is a lot faster than having to navigate from the base of the main menu every single time.

Warning

It's important to note that if you close the last remaining image window, GIMP quits and you will have to relaunch it. This isn't the case with the Toolbox or dock window. You can freely close either of these. The Toolbox can be returned by going to Windows ⇨ Toolbox (Ctrl+B) and the dock window can be brought back at Windows ⇨ Recently Closed Docks ⇨ Layers, Channels, Paths, etc. ∎

Docks and Dialogs

Of course, menus aren't the only thing that can be detached. Each of GIMP's other two main windows are composed of a set of dockable dialogs that work as panels and can be detached, shuffled, and re-attached at will. This is most valuable in the dock window on the right-hand side with the layers, palettes, and brushes dialogs. By default, this window has two docks, separated by docking bars, as shown in Figure 1-3. The top dock holds dialogs for Layers, Channels, Paths, and GIMP's Undo History. The lower dock holds Brushes, Patterns, Gradients, and the Color Palette dialog. In each dock, the individual dialogs are accessible by the tabs at the top of the dock or by picking the dialog from Windows ➪ Dockable Dialogs. If the icon in the tab isn't enough to remind you what the dialog is, you can hover your mouse over the tab for a few seconds and wait for the tooltip that describes the dialog to pop up.

FIGURE 1-3

The right-side utility window with the two default docks

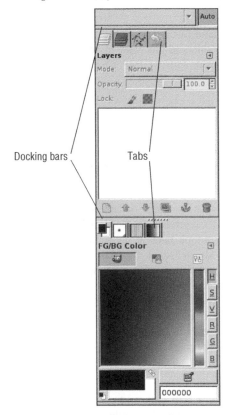

Docking bars   Tabs

You can resize the docks by left-clicking and dragging the docking bar that separates them. This is useful with more complex GIMP files that have a fairly high number of layers because it allows you to see as many of them as possible at the same time. You may notice that the docking bars at the top and bottom of the dock window are not draggable. However, if you hover your mouse over any of these docking bars for a couple seconds, a tooltip appears saying "You can drop dockable dialogs here." To see how this works, left-click the tab for the Layers dialog and drag it up to the top docking bar. When your mouse pointer hovers over the docking bar, it should become highlighted. Release the left mouse button and you'll see that you've created a new dock at the top of this window. Notice that because this new dock has only the Layers dialog, there are no tabs at the top, just the word "Layers." You can move the Layers dialog back to its original position by left-clicking that word, Layers, and dragging it to the dock below. You should notice that as you drag your mouse around the dock, certain parts get an outline or highlight. This is so you can tell exactly where you're placing the dialog. You can even use this to customize the order of the tabs in a particular dock. Just left-click the tab in question and drag it forward or back in the arrangement of tabs.

You can also completely detach any dockable dialog and let it float independently in its own window. As an example of how to do this, left-click the Layers tab at the top dock and drag it off the window. When you release your mouse button, a new window is created with the Layers dialog in it. From here, you can re-dock the Layers dialog the same way you would if you'd put it in its own dock. Alternatively, because you've created a new window with its own new dock, you could also take some of the other dialogs and dock them here. This is a great way to customize your GIMP layout to match your specific work style.

Clicking and dragging aren't the only ways to customize your GIMP layout. Many of these functions can be controlled from a Tab menu at the top of each dockable dialog. In Figure 1-3, notice a left-pointing triangle in a box at the top right of each dock. This is the Tab menu. Clicking it gives you a menu similar to the one you see in Figure 1-4.

FIGURE 1-4

Options available in the Tab menu

This menu allows you to do most of what you can do by mouse-clicking and dragging, as well as offers some specific controls for the dialog that you're currently working in. Following is a brief explanation of what each option does.

- **Dialog-specific context menu** — Not all Tab menus have this one. However, for some dialogs, like Layers, Channels, and Paths, the first item of the Tab menu is a submenu to address specific features available to that dialog.

- **Add Tab** — This menu item brings up a submenu from which you can choose another dialog to add to the dock you're working in.

- **Close Tab** — Clicking this item removes the current dialog from the dock.

- **Detach Tab** — This item performs the same function as left-clicking and dragging the dialog off to create a new window and dock.

- **Lock Tab to Dock** — Enabling this option prevents you from detaching the current dialog from the dock. This is a good way to keep you from accidentally removing or moving a dialog.

- **Preview Size** — Like the dialog-specific menu, this option is only available on some dialogs, like Layers and Channels, which utilize small versions of the image you're working on. The options in this submenu allow you to control the size of those small images.

- **Tab Style** — By default, GIMP uses icons for all of the tabs. However, some people like having a little bit more clarity. The options available in this submenu allow you to customize how the dialog appears in the tab. You can have it show an icon, text, or both. Some dialogs, like Brushes and Patterns, also offer specialized options for Status, which shows an icon of the currently selected brush or pattern in the dialog.

- **View as List/Grid** — These options are only available on some dialogs and are mutually exclusive; you can use only one or the other. The best way to see it in action is to look at the Brushes dialog. By default, this is set to View as Grid. However, from the Tab menu, you can change it to View as List to get a little bit more information about each brush.

- **Show Button Bar** — By default, at the bottom of each dialog in the dock is a button bar with a set of quickly accessible buttons for doing common tasks with that dialog, such as saving presets or adding a new layer, channel, or brush. This menu item shows or hides the button bar for the dialog you're currently working in.

- **Show Image Selection** — At the very top of Figure 1-3 is a wide drop-down button with an image preview in it. This is the Image Selection drop-down and it allows you to pick the image that you want the dialog to give you information about. It's not available for all dialogs, but for the ones that use it, this menu item toggles its visibility.

- **Auto Follow Active Image** — By default, the Image Selection drop-down will automatically switch based on whichever image window is active, or in *focus*. However, there may be an occasion when you want to, for example, see the layers of one image while you're working on another. Toggling this option off will allow you to do just that. You can also do the same thing by clicking the Auto button next to the Image Selection drop-down.

- **Move to Screen** — If you're using GIMP in Windows, you may not see this option. This menu item takes advantage of a multi-display feature of the X Windowing System used on Linux and Unix machines. It allows you to do cool things like run GIMP on one computer and control it from another. In a case like that, each computer is considered a screen. This submenu allows you to send a GIMP dockable dialog to another screen. As of this writing, this feature is currently experimental and may crash GIMP. There's a chance it may not be in GIMP 2.8.

If you look in the Add Tab item of the Tab menu, you can get a good idea of the different dockable dialogs available to you. You can see this same menu if you go to an image window and click Windows ⇨ Dockable Dialogs. Each of these dialogs has a specific use and purpose that can really help your productivity when used effectively. The following list is a quick run-down of each dialog and what it can be used for.

- **Tool Options** — For whichever tool you have selected, this dialog will show available options for it. By default, this dialog is the dock beneath the tools in the Toolbox window.

- **Device Status** — This dialog is most useful for users with a drawing tablet. It not only shows if you're currently using the mouse, stylus, or eraser, but also which tools are assigned to each of these. If you have a drawing tablet, check out Appendix B to see how to configure GIMP to recognize it.

- **Layers** — From this dialog, you can see the layers in the file you're working on as well as add, rearrange, merge, and remove layers. Because this dialog is so frequently used, there's a default keyboard shortcut for it: Ctrl+L. Chapter 6 covers layers in detail.

- **Channels** — This dialog serves dual purposes. Its primary use is to allow you to select and visualize the individual color channels in your image. However, if you are using selection masks, this dialog is also where those masks call home. You can find more on channels and this dialog in Chapter 7.

- **Paths** — Paths are curves that you can create in GIMP and use to create selections, masks, and even draw with. This dialog allows you to manage the paths you create. You can find out more about paths in GIMP by looking at Chapter 5.

- **Colormap** — If you're working with an image that has an *indexed color palette*, such as a GIF, where the image consists of a small number of discrete colors rather than the full RGB color range, you can use this dialog to see these colors and modify them.

- **Histogram** — When working with images, a histogram is a chart that shows the distribution of the values in that image. This is a good statistical way to check the color balance of your image. Note that you cannot edit the histogram from here. To do that, you'll need to use the Levels tool from the Color menu. For more on this, see Chapter 9.

- **Selection Editor** — This is a cool little dialog that comes in handy when you're making selections in GIMP. Not only does it display any current selection, but it also offers a quick way to outline that selection or save it to a channel or a path.

- **Navigation** — The Navigation dialog offers a quick and painless way to zoom in and see specific parts of your image. It's particularly helpful on very high-resolution images.

- **Undo History** — This dialog shows a list of each of the actions you perform on an image in chronological order and allows you to undo and redo them. Two things to note here, though. First, when you close a file, its undo history is not saved with it; you lose that data. Also, you cannot arbitrarily undo just one action in a series of actions. If you undo something, you basically go back to the last action you did before it.

- **Pointer** — The Pointer dialog is a lot more useful than you might think. It gives you immediate and exact feedback about where your mouse is in your image. This is useful not only for picking colors, but also for determining where something is, down to the pixel.

- **Sample Points** — This dialog is similar to the Pointer dialog, but it allows you to pick four specific points in an image you're working on and gives you feedback about them in real time as you work. This is helpful if you know a specific part of your image is supposed to maintain certain color values and you want to monitor that.

- **Colors** — These are the colors GIMP can use. From this dialog, you can set your foreground and background colors from a variety of color selectors, including the GIMP default, watercolor, wheel/triangle, CMYK, color swatches, or a set of sliders.

- **Brushes** — This dialog is extremely useful when you are painting in GIMP. It allows you to select, edit, and manage your GIMP brushes. Because it's used frequently, its default keyboard shortcut is Shift+Ctrl+B. You can find more information on brushes in Chapter 11.

- **Patterns** — When doing color fills and other automated tasks, patterns can be quite helpful. This dialog helps you manage your patterns from within GIMP. You can access it quickly by using the keyboard shortcut Shift+Ctrl+P. You can find out more about creating patterns in Chapter 11.

- **Gradients** — Gradients are very helpful tools when you are creating images in GIMP and this dialog, which you can quickly access with the Ctrl+G shortcut, is where you manage and modify preset gradients. Chapter 11 shows some tricks on how to get the most out of gradients.

- **Palettes** — Like with the Colormap dialog, this one is specifically useful for images with an indexed color palette. From here, you can choose from a set of preset palettes or create your own.

- **Fonts** — This dialog is specifically meant for the Text tool (see Chapter 10), but it's a good, quick way to see what fonts you have available from within GIMP. Also, if you've added a new font to your system while working, this dialog will allow you to update the list of available fonts without having to restart GIMP.

- **Buffers** — Buffers are pretty useful little things in GIMP. You can take a selection and save it as a buffer by navigating to Edit ➪ Buffer ➪ Copy Named. This adds the buffer to the list in this dialog. From there, you can create a new image with the buffer or paste it back into the image whenever you like. Note, however, that like the Undo History, buffers do not get saved with a file. So if you close GIMP, those buffers are gone forever.

- **Images** — Often when working in GIMP, you may have a large number of images open at the same time. Some image windows may be minimized and others may be hidden or overlapped by larger image windows. This dialog helps you manage the image files that you have open and provides you with a quick way to bring a specific image window into focus.

- **Document History** — This is similar to the Images dialog, except rather than showing the images you're currently working on, this dialog shows the images that you've worked on in the past. This is also like the File ➪ Open Recent menu, but much more extensive and it allows you to remove items from the list or clear it altogether.

- **Templates** — When you create a new image in GIMP, you can custom-set new parameters for the width, height, and default layout of an image or you can choose from a series of preset templates. This dialog allows you to create, modify, and remove templates from that list. It also allows you to quickly create a new image based on any of the available templates in this dialog.

- **Error Console** — The Error console will give you detailed feedback of all the errors, if any, that occur while you're running GIMP. This is helpful for two purposes. The obvious use is if you run into a bug and need to report some detailed information to the GIMP developers. A less obvious reason, though, is for feedback if you're writing your own scripts to automate processes in GIMP. You can read more about this in Chapter 22.

Figure 1-5 shows what each of these dockable dialogs looks like.

FIGURE 1-5

The dockable dialogs available to you in GIMP

Another useful feature while you're working in GIMP is the ability to quickly get these docks out of your way and simply let you work on the image. You have two primary ways to do this.

The fastest way is to simply press Tab when an image window is your focused window. Pressing Tab hides the Toolbox and any other visible docks. To bring them back, just press Tab again. The other way to get the docks out of your way is to expand the image window to full screen. To do this left-click View ➪ Fullscreen or use the F11 keyboard shortcut. If you're having trouble getting the Fullscreen option to work, make sure you actually have an image open in the image window. An image window without an image cannot be made full screen.

Images and Canvases

In any GIMP project that you work on, it's important to understand the workspace that an image window provides. Despite this window's rather minimalistic look, it provides you with an astounding amount of information. Figure 1-6 shows an image window with an image loaded in it.

FIGURE 1-6

The image window

Parts of the Image Window

As previously mentioned, you can right-click anywhere on an image window and get the same menu as those across the top of it. However, that's just the start. The bar that stretches across the bottom of the window is functional and informational. First you see the Pointer Coordinates box, which gives you real-time feedback about the exact position of your mouse in the image.

By default, these coordinates are given in pixel units. However, you can use the drop-down button next to the Pointer Coordinates to select any other types of units you would like to use, including real-world measurements like centimeters and inches as well as typographical units like points and picas. Of course, for non-pixel units, it's helpful to know what resolution your image is and you should probably disable Dot For Dot in the View menu (View ⇨ Dot For Dot). There's more information on this in Chapter 2.

Notice also that when you change units they don't just change in the Pointer Coordinates. The rulers that are along the top and left sides of the image window also adjust for the new units you've chosen. These rulers are pretty useful. Besides giving you a visual cue as to where your mouse cursor is in the image window, they also allow you to create *guides*. Guides are useful for helping you line things up in your image either horizontally or vertically and they're even more useful if you have Snapping enabled (View ⇨ Snap To Guides). To add a guide, left-click either of the rulers and drag your mouse over the image. When you release your mouse, a blue dashed line — the guide — appears over your image. Pulling from the top ruler gives you a horizontal guide and pulling from the right-side ruler gives you a vertical guide. You can adjust the location of any guide by left-clicking it again and moving it around. GIMP lets you know that you can select a guide, because it changes the guide from a blue dashed line to a red one when your mouse gets near it. To remove a guide, simply drag it off of the image.

Tip

To adjust or remove guides, make sure you're using the Move tool (M). You can find more on this tool in Chapter 4. ■

Next to the Units drop-down at the bottom of the image window is a Zoom field. This field lets you know how much you're zoomed in or out of your image and the drop-down arrow to the right of it allows you to choose among specific presets. You can also left-click in this number field and explicitly type in any arbitrary zoom percentage that you would like to use.

To the right of the Zoom button is the main Status Area of the image window. When you're not working in the image window, this Status Area shows the active layer and roughly how much of your computer's RAM is being used by keeping this image open. When you are working in the image window, though, the Status Area gives you helpful information on the tool you've selected, including feedback on what you're doing with it or extra tips on how to utilize it better. Also, when you're doing a time-consuming operation like a filter or even saving a large file, the Status Area shows a progress meter that indicates how soon the operation will complete.

Tip

The amount of system RAM you're using to work on an image does not necessarily reflect the size of the image file when you save it. Chances are good that the saved file will be much smaller than the "working version." The main reason for this is that when images are saved, they are compressed to save space. To work on the images, though, GIMP has to decompress them and let the full uncompressed image sit in memory. Chapter 2 has more information on image compression. Another reason for the difference in saved file size and the amount of RAM usage is that GIMP also stores additional information in memory while you work, such as the Undo History and any buffers you have stored. This information is not included in a saved file, but it's quite useful while you're working. ■

Looking at the corners of the image window, you should notice an icon at each one. Each of these icons is actually a button that gives you quick access to some useful functions. Figure 1-7 shows the four icons at each corner of every image window.

FIGURE 1-7

Clockwise from the top left: icons for the Menu button, the Image Window Resize toggle button, the Navigation Control button, and the Quick Mask toggle button

Menu [▶]   [🔍] Image Window Resize

Quick Mask [ ]   [✛] Navigation Control

The easiest is the top-left icon of a right-facing triangle in a box, shown in Figure 1-7. This is another quick way to access the menu for the image window. Some people who work with a drawing tablet find this to be a quicker way to navigate the menu. You can also bring up this menu by pressing Shift+F10.

The top-right icon features a small magnifying glass. This is the Image Window Resize toggle button and it's disabled by default. If you enable it, the image you're working on will also resize when you resize the image window. This can be helpful for tablet users or if you're just focused on a certain area and are more comfortable zooming in by adjusting the window size. The default behavior is that when you resize the image window, the image itself does not change in scale and you have to use the Navigation Control button or scrollbars to navigate to parts of your image.

Speaking of the Navigation Control button, that is the crosshairs icon on the bottom-right of the image window. If you left-click this icon, a small preview of your overall image will appear and you'll be able to navigate to specific parts of the image you're working on. Incidentally, this is the exact same functionality that you have with the Navigation dockable dialog mentioned earlier in this chapter.

The last icon is the dashed rectangle at the bottom-left of the image window. Left-click this button and it enables GIMP's Quick Mask (Ctrl+Q). This is a quick way to see exactly what you have selected and it's particularly useful if you have partial or fuzzy selections. Right-clicking this button allows you to choose whether the Quick Mask highlights selected or unselected areas. You can also customize the color and opacity of the Quick Mask from this menu. Chapter 6 gives you more information on creating and using masks.

The Concept of a "Canvas"

Like many other image editing programs, GIMP makes use of a *canvas* in the image window. Think of the canvas as your working area; the "drawing surface" that you're working on. The image, in contrast, is the final graphic that you're creating. It's the canvas plus the image data. This means that modifications to the canvas won't stretch, distort, or scale your final output, but that same kind of modification to the image will cause those distortions. To adjust the size of your canvas, click Image ➪ Canvas Size from the image window's menu and you'll get a dialog that looks like the one in Figure 1-8.

FIGURE 1-8

The Set Image Canvas Size dialog

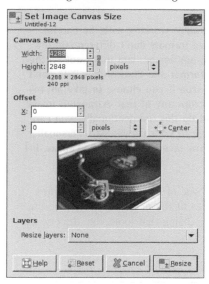

As Figure 1-8 shows, the Set Image Canvas Size dialog allows you to enter values for the new width and height of your canvas in any of the units available in GIMP. Take special notice of the chain-link icon that's to the right of the Width and Height values. This constrains, or links, the Width and Height values so adjusting one causes the other to automatically change its value to make the canvas maintain the same proportions. If you would rather explicitly enter your own values for Width and Height, simply left-click this chain-link icon and GIMP breaks the link so the values are no longer constrained to one another. If you're used to Photoshop, this is the same as enabling and disabling the Constrain Proportions check box.

Beneath the Width and Height values for the canvas is a set of offset values. Adjusting these numbers shifts your image data on the canvas in the X and Y directions. Rather than typing in numbers here, though, you may find it easier to simply left-click and drag the preview image below these values. If you need to center the image data on the canvas, there's a convenient Center button to the right that automatically adjusts the X and Y offset to ensure that everything is centered up.

The Layers portion of the Set Image Canvas Size dialog enables you to automatically resize the layers of your image to match your new canvas size. Unlike many other programs, layers in GIMP have their own explicit sizes that you can adjust independently of the image or the canvas. If you're not used to this concept, it can be a bit disorienting. Chapter 6 goes into this and other layer-related topics in more detail. The default behavior for resizing layers in the Set Image Canvas Size dialog is to do nothing keep the layers to their own sizes. However, if you do want to resize your layers to match the new canvas size, you can use the Resize Layers drop-down menu to stipulate which layers to do this to. Besides the option to not resize any layers, you can choose to resize all layers, only the layers which are currently the same size as your image, only the visible layers, or only layers that are linked together.

Warning

If you change your canvas size to be smaller than the image data that you're working with, be careful. Chapter 3 goes into image formats more deeply, but most standard image formats don't differentiate the canvas from the image, so if you export to something like JPEG or PNG, any image data that's not on the canvas will simply be cropped away and not saved. GIMP's native XCF format and Photoshop's PSD don't have this problem, but it's still worth taking note of. This is particularly true if you choose to take advantage of the Resize Layers functionality. Resizing the layers permanently crops any of that extraneous image information that's not within the canvas size. If you make a mistake and do this unintentionally, you can always use the Undo (Ctrl+Z) function, but this will also undo the change to your canvas size. Personally, I typically keep the default behavior and choose not to let GIMP resize my layers to match the canvas. If I want to do that, I do it separately. ■

In contrast to adjusting the size of your canvas, changing the size of your image is something quite different. Resizing the image will actually scale the data to fit the new size you've chosen. To see this in action, click Image ⇨ Scale Image and you get a dialog that looks like the one in Figure 1-9.

FIGURE 1-9

The Scale Image dialog

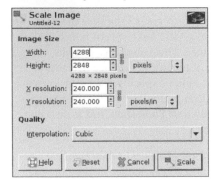

This dialog looks similar to the Set Image Canvas Size dialog, but because you're scaling the whole image, there's no need for any offset values. Instead, you're provided with resolution values and an Interpolation setting for controlling how GIMP adds or removes pixels when scaling your image. For more on image resolution, have a look at Chapter 2. The Interpolation setting is pretty important to the final outcome of your scaled image and like most things in computer graphics, it's a trade-off between the time it takes your computer to generate a result and how good that final result ultimately looks. GIMP offers four different types of interpolation:

- **None** — As its name implies, this doesn't interpolate anything. It just scales and moves the individual pixels. Of the available options, it's the fastest, but the results typically don't look very good.

- **Linear** — Linear interpolation is a basic form of interpolation that's a fair balance between speed and quality.

- **Cubic** — This interpolation method usually yields the best results. It's slower than Linear interpolation, but the results are usually worth it.

- **Sinc (Lanczos3)** — This is the newest interpolation method added to GIMP. It competes with Cubic interpolation for slowness, but the results are generally a bit less fuzzy.

After scaling your image or changing the size of your canvas, you may want to have the image window fit the size of your newly resized image. There's an option for doing this by default in the image windows category of GIMP's Preferences. However, if you don't want GIMP to do it automatically after a resize, you can do it manually by clicking View ➪ Shrink Wrap or using the Ctrl+R keyboard shortcut.

Setting Preferences

GIMP has a remarkably customizable interface, and not just in appearance. You can also control a fairly large chunk of its behaviors in two primary places: the Preferences command and the Module Manager. Both of these options are at the bottom of the Edit menu. Of the two, the Module Manager has the simpler set of options, as you can see in Figure 1-10.

FIGURE 1-10

The Module Manager dialog

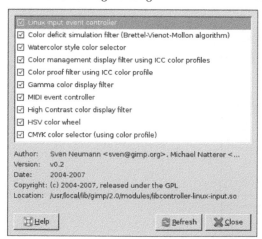

The Module Manager

The Module Manager is simply a set of check boxes that enable or disable the modules that GIMP has available to it. Modules are typically related to color selection, display filters, and event controllers for external input devices. Typically GIMP has all modules enabled. You may want to disable a module if you know you're not going to use it and you want GIMP to start up faster or utilize less of your system's RAM. For example, if you don't have any MIDI devices on your workstation or you rarely use the Watercolor Style Color Selector, you can disable them here.

At the bottom of the dialog is detailed information about the module you have highlighted, including the module's author, its version, when that was completed, the module's copyright and license information, and where it lives on your computer. If you download a new module for GIMP or write one yourself and place it in the folder where GIMP looks for modules (this is configurable in the Preferences; more on this in a bit), or if you decide delete a module from your computer, you can update the list of available modules by clicking the Refresh button. Note that the Refresh button does *not* restart GIMP; it just updates that list. So if you've enabled or disabled a module, you'll still have to close GIMP and start it up again for the change to take effect.

GIMP Preferences

The bulk of GIMP's customization happens in the Preferences dialog (Edit ➪ Preferences). When you click this item in the Edit menu, you get a window that looks like the one in Figure 1-11. On the left of the window is a list of categories that you customize in GIMP. Some of these categories have subcategories for more refined control. On the right of the window are the specific preferences that you can adjust in each category. The Preferences dialog should open by default to the Environment preferences.

FIGURE 1-11

The Preferences dialog

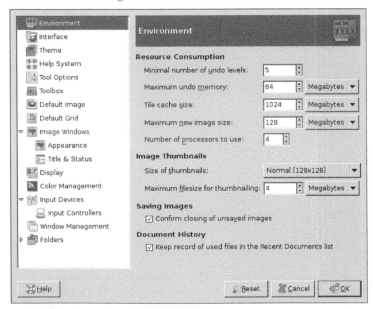

Tip

Changes you make in the Preferences dialog are instantaneous. Unlike what you may be used to in other programs, there is no Apply button here. If you change the size of your icons or the size of the default grid or whether or not GIMP displays tooltips, those changes take effect immediately. You can set them back to what they were by clicking the Reset or Cancel buttons at the bottom of the dialog. The cool thing about this, though, is that you can get immediate feedback on the changes you make. You can test preferences or, because the Preferences dialog is non-blocking, simply change them on the fly without having to wait. How's that for cool? ∎

Environment

Figure 1-11 shows the Environment preferences, which is the default preferences category that shows when you first open the dialog. These preferences give you a large amount of control over how GIMP performs on your computer. In particular, they control how much system memory that you allow GIMP to use while you work. If you're running GIMP on an older machine with a limited amount of RAM, you may want to reduce the Minimal Number of Undo Levels and decrease the Maximum Undo Memory.

To get a rough idea of how GIMP's undo system works, think about it like this: Each time you perform an action in GIMP, it saves a copy of the last version of your image before that action and stores it in RAM. And each action that you perform causes GIMP to save another copy. It will keep doing this until it gets to the limit that you stipulate in the Maximum Undo Memory value. Bear in mind that this is a bit of an over-simplified explanation of the undo system. It's a bit more efficient than saving full copies of the image, but the concept is still pretty much the same.

Other key settings that you can change to fine-tune GIMP's performance to your computer are the size of GIMP's tile cache and the number of processors it uses (helpful for newer multicore computers). The tile cache is how much system RAM you'll allow any open image in GIMP to use. Typically the default value works well here, but if you have a lot of memory on your machine, you should be able to set this value to at least half the amount of RAM you have pretty comfortably. If an image needs to take up more space than you allowed here, it swaps the overflowing data to your hard drive. Because your hard drive reads and writes data much more slowly than your system memory does, this has a heavy negative impact on performance. Keep this in mind if you're trying to reduce the Tile Cache Size.

The Image Thumbnails settings control the size of the thumbnails that get displayed when you open files in GIMP. You can find more on opening files in Chapter 3, but basically GIMP can give you a preview of an image before you load it. These settings control the size of that preview. The Maximum Filesize For Thumbnailing sets an upper threshold for which files GIMP automatically creates previews. Basically, if a saved image takes up less space than this value, GIMP builds a thumbnail without asking. The idea here is that it takes GIMP more time to process and create a preview of larger files. This setting is so you don't have to wait for that thumbnail to be created if the file is too large.

The other two settings in this category are pretty self-explanatory. If the Confirm Closing Of Unsaved Images option is enabled, GIMP will pop up a warning dialog if you try to close an image that you haven't yet saved. The Document History option controls whether or not GIMP keeps a chronological record of all of the images you've worked on.

Interface

Figure 1-12 shows preferences settings for GIMP's user interface.

FIGURE 1-12

User Interface settings in the Preferences dialog

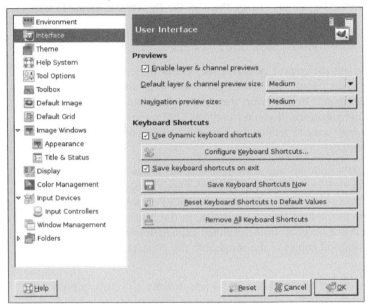

The first part of this category deals with how previews show up in GIMP's interface. By default, previews are enabled because they tend to make it easier for you to choose layers and channels. However, if you don't need previews or need to run GIMP on a slower machine, you can disable previews from here. If you have previews enabled, though, you can change the default size of these previews from this section. Earlier in this chapter, you saw an option in the Tab menu of dockable dialogs that allows you to adjust the size of previews. The option in that menu overrides the default value that you set here in GIMP's Preferences.

The other half of this category is devoted to keyboard shortcuts. There's more detailed information on this topic at the end of this chapter covering how you assign shortcuts, but it's worth mentioning here that what this category gives you is the ability to restore the "factory default" keyboard shortcuts by clicking the Reset Keyboard Shortcuts to Default Values button.

Theme

GIMP's interface is themeable, including its icons and interface colors. GIMP doesn't offer a way to interactively create or modify these themes; they're a combination of images and text files that are saved on your hard drive. See Appendix C for more information on using themes. However, GIMP ships with two different themes for use — Default and Small — and you can download custom GIMP themes from a few places on the Internet. Some of those resources are listed in Appendix D. Figure 1-13 shows the Theme settings in the Preferences dialog.

FIGURE 1-13

Theme settings in the Preferences dialog

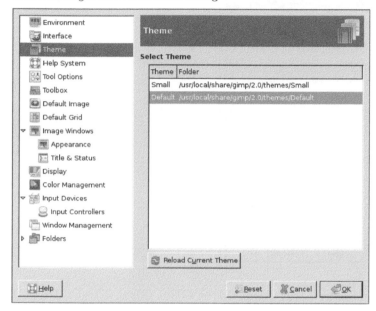

To change the theme, simply left-click the theme you want to use. If you've created a new theme for GIMP to use, all you need to do is put it in the folder that GIMP looks in for themes (more on this later) and it should appear in this list. If you modify the theme that you're currently using, the Reload Current Theme button reloads that theme into GIMP so you can see the results of your changes without actually restarting.

Help System

The Help System settings, shown in Figure 1-14, control how you can get interactive help while working in GIMP.

If you're a GIMP master genius, you can go here to disable the Show Tooltips and Show Help Buttons options. This gets GIMP out of your way and lets you work. Of course, GIMP is a complex program. So even if you disable the help buttons, you might consider keeping tooltips active. If you keep the help buttons active, though, you can bind them to use a local copy of the GIMP user manual installed on your hard drive or you can have GIMP jump on the Internet and let you look at the online version of the manual. The former is great when you need quick access or if you don't have an Internet connection. The latter is helpful because the online manual tends to be a bit more up-to-date than the installed version of the manual. You can even choose between the integrated GIMP Help Browser or the more familiar interface of your web browser of choice.

FIGURE 1-14

Help System settings in the Preferences dialog

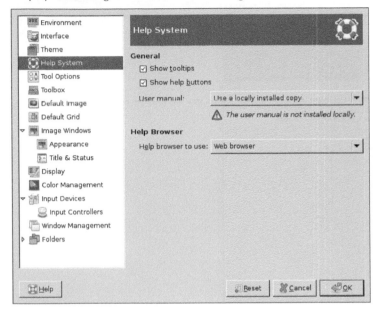

Tool Options

Figure 1-15 shows the preferences available for your tool options. The General settings are pretty straightforward, controlling when to save your tool options and allowing you to reset them back to GIMP's defaults.

The Snap Distance setting works for when you have Grid or Guide snapping enabled. The value here is in pixels, so when you're moving an object around, if it comes within this threshold (default is 8 pixels) of a guide or the grid, that object will be snapped to align with it. The Default Interpolation setting under Scaling lets you choose which interpolation you want GIMP to go with by default when doing scaling and other transformations, such as Rotate or Perspective. Look at the end of the "Images and Canvases" section of this chapter for more information on these interpolation methods.

The check boxes under Paint Options Shared Between Tools allow the various tools to share the same settings. For instance, if you have the Brush check box enabled, all of the tools that use brushes, such as the Paintbrush, Pencil, Airbrush, and Eraser, will use the same brush settings. If you're using the Paintbrush and then use the Eraser, they'll both use the same settings. And if you change brushes while erasing, when you go back to the Paintbrush, the brush you used for erasing will still be in use. However, if you disable this check box, each "brushable" tool retains its own independent brush settings between uses. Many artists tend to prefer this behavior because they rarely use the same brush to paint as they do to erase. However, it's usually more useful to keep the Pattern and Gradient check boxes enabled because that's something you typically want to stay consistent from tool to tool.

FIGURE 1-15

Tool Options settings in the Preferences dialog

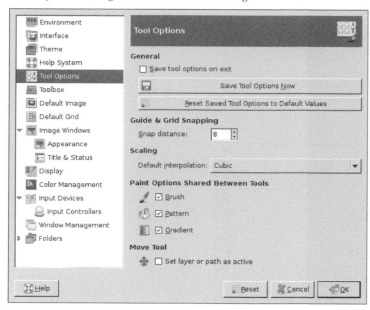

The Set Layer Or Path As Active option at the bottom of this category is particular to the way the Move tool works. More on this is in Chapter 4, but when you're using the Move tool, if you click the image data for any layer, you can move it. You're not restricted to just the active layer. So while moving, GIMP temporarily makes the layer with the data you're moving the active layer. With this option disabled, after you finish the move, GIMP reverts the active layer to the layer you were on before the move. If this option is enabled, GIMP simply keeps this newly moved layer as the active layer.

Toolbox

The Toolbox options, as shown in Figure 1-16, control the visibility of some features in the Toolbox. You can enable and disable the foreground and background color widget, the active brush, pattern, and gradient icons, as well as a preview of the active image.

The lower half of the Toolbox settings gives you control over which tools get shown in the Toolbox and what order they're shown. The eye icon next to each tool shows whether the tool is visible in the Toolbox. If you want to hide the tool, just left-click on its eye icon. If no eye icon is visible, then the tool is hidden and you make it appear by clicking the space where the icon would be. Beneath the list of tools are three additional buttons. The green up and down arrows allow you to control the order of the tools in the Toolbox. To use them, click the tool you want to move and then click these arrows to adjust that tool's location. You can also simply drag and drop a tool to a new location. The third button beneath the list of tools resets the order and visibility to the defaults.

FIGURE 1-16

Toolbox settings in the Preferences dialog

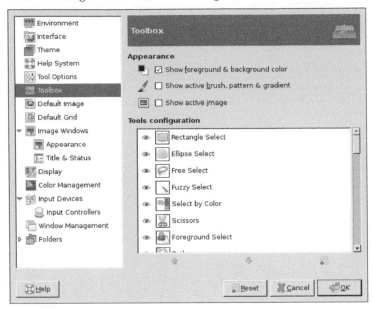

Default Image

The options in this category allow you to define the default settings that GIMP gives you when you create a new image. These settings, as shown in Figure 1-17, are basically the same settings that appear in the Create New Image dialog. There's more detailed information on this in Chapter 3, but if you read the "Images and Canvases" section about the Set Image Canvas Size dialog (refer to Figure 1-8), most of these settings should be familiar to you.

Default Grid

Figure 1-18 shows the Default Image Grid settings. These options control how the Image Grid appears on new images that you create. By default the image grid is hidden, but you can make it visible by clicking View ⇨ Show Grid in the image window. These settings are the exact same as you'll find in the Configure Grid dialog (Image ⇨ Configure Grid). Just know that changes to these values do not affect any of the images you currently have open in GIMP. These settings are specific to new images that you create. Most of these settings are self-explanatory, but it's worth noting that, like the Set Image Canvas Size and Scale Image dialogs, the Width and Height values have the little chain-link icon that constrains these values to change proportionally to one another.

FIGURE 1-17

Default New Image settings in the Preferences dialog

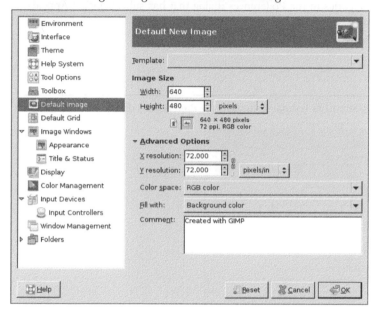

FIGURE 1-18

Default Image Grid settings in the Preferences dialog

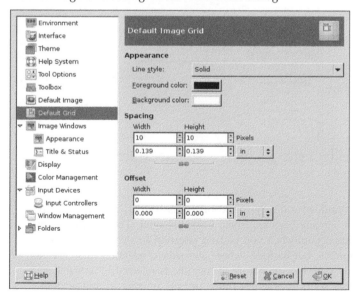

Image Windows

The Image Windows options control the behavior and appearance of the image windows in GIMP. This is one of the few categories in the Preferences dialog that has subcategories: Appearance and Title & Statusbar Format. Figure 1-19 shows the settings available for each of these categories and subcategories.

FIGURE 1-19

Image Windows, Appearance, and Title & Statusbar Format settings in the Preferences dialog

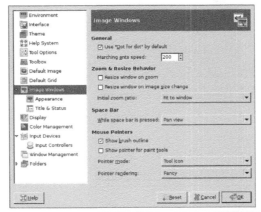

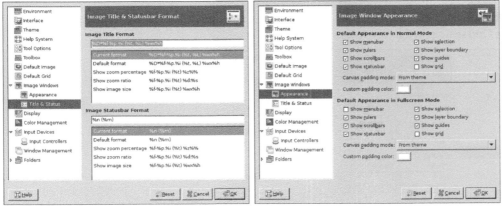

Most of the settings in the Image Windows category speak for themselves or, as in the case of Use "Dot For Dot" By Default, have already been explained in this chapter. The Marching Ants Speed refers an interface feature that occurs when you make a selection in the image window. Selection tools are covered in Chapter 4, but basically when you make a selection, that selection is outlined by a moving dashed line. The moving nature of this line is referred to as *marching ants*. The Marching Ants Speed value controls how fast those ants are moving in milliseconds. The smaller the value, the faster the ants move.

A couple other notable settings in this category are the Space Bar and Mouse Pointers settings. The Space Bar option controls what you want GIMP to do when you press the space bar in the image window. By default, this is set to Pan View, allowing you to move the view around and see image details better. Alternatively, you can make space bar a shortcut for the Move tool or disable the space bar altogether. The Mouse Pointers settings allow you to customize how your mouse cursor appears when working in GIMP. The defaults work nicely, but for more precision, you can change the Pointer Mode to Crosshair Only.

In the Image Window Appearance options, you basically have an array of check boxes to enable and disable viewable features in the image window. Most of these features are explained earlier in this chapter under the section "Windows and Menus," though it's worth pointing out the options on Canvas Padding. From that drop-down menu you can choose light or dark checks, the color defined by the theme, or a custom color from the color picker below it. Also notice that you can customize the image window's appearance to be different depending on whether it's in Normal or Fullscreen (View ⇨ Fullscreen or F11) modes.

At first glance, the Title & Statusbar Format options seem to be daunting because of all the letters and percent signs. Fortunately, several presets are built in to allow you to customize the Title bar of the image window as well as the text that shows up in the Status Area. Of course, to completely customize things, you need to know what each of these variables means. Table 1-1 gives a description of each.

TABLE 1-1

Variables for Title and Status

Option	Variable
%f	Image filename
%i	View number, for if it is displayed more than once
%s	Source scale factor
%Cx	"Clean indicator" — Show x if file does not need to be saved
%m	RAM used by image
%w	Image width (pixels)
%H	Image height (real-world units)
%%	A "%" sign
%F	Full path to file
%t	Image color mode
%d	Destination scale factor
%l	Number of layers

continued

TABLE 1-1	*(continued)*
Option	**Variable**
%n	Name of active layer/channel
%W	Image width (real-world units)
%u	Unit symbol
%p	Unique ID number
%ℓ	Zoom factor
%Dx	"Dirty indicator" — Show x if file needs to be saved
%L	Number of layers (long form)
%P	ID of active layer/channel
%h	Image height (pixels)
%U	Unit abbreviation

Display

Figure 1-20 shows the preference settings for Display in GIMP. The Transparency settings here are a bit of misnomer and would probably be better suited to be in the Image Windows settings, but it's not a huge issue for them to be here. What the Transparency settings do is control how GIMP displays transparent portions of an image you're working on in the image window. By default, GIMP does this by displaying a mid-tone checkerboard wherever there's a transparent portion of your image. From these settings you can choose darker or lighter checks, or remove the checkerboard altogether and just show a plain black, white, or gray background. You can also control how big the checks are on the checkerboard, should you decide to keep it.

Below the Transparency settings are settings for controlling how GIMP reacts to the resolution of your monitor. Chapter 2 has more information on resolution, but the short story is that having a proper resolution here is particularly important for print work. If the resolution is set properly, your images on-screen at 100% zoom should be the exact same size that they are when printed out. Generally speaking, most modern monitors can report their native resolution to your computer's operating system and GIMP can automatically get the information from there. However, in the event that the automatic values are incorrect or you have an older monitor, GIMP offers you the ability to manually enter a resolution or find out the proper manual settings by clicking the Calibrate button and measuring distances on-screen.

Color Management

Color management in GIMP is designed to get your graphics to appear on your monitor in colors that are comparable to what you'd see if those images were printed. Take special note, however, that this color management is not intended for use in printing directly from GIMP. Specialized printing tools are available that handle that better and it's in your best interest to use those. Of course, that doesn't mean you should forgo accurate colors while you work, though. By default, GIMP ships with color management disabled. If you enable color management, you'll need to define some *color profiles*, or color definition standards that allow consistency between different graphics programs. Color profiles are defined in files that end with the .icc or .icm extension. Use the profile drop-downs in this set of preferences to make GIMP aware of where these profiles are on your computer. Figure 1-21 shows what the Color Management settings may look like after choosing your profiles.

FIGURE 1-20

Display settings in the Preferences dialog

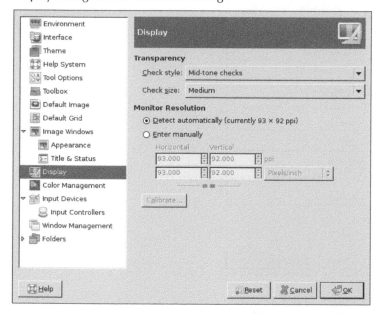

If you're doing color management, the *rendering intent* options are something you'll want to pay special attention to. The reason you need to define a rendering intent is because there are often situations where the color you want to produce is outside of the range, or *gamut*, of the color profile you want to use. So to deal with these out-of-gamut colors, the International Color Consortium (ICC) defined four standardized methods that GIMP provides to you as options:

- **Perceptual** — This method takes all of the colors from your image and scales their gamut until it fits in the gamut of the desired color profile. This is the intent that's usually used for photographs.

- **Relative colorimetric** — In this rendering intent, out-of-gamut colors are brought into the gamut of the destination profile by keeping their value the same, but adjusting the saturation. The typical application for this is when using spot colors.

- **Saturation** — This rendering intent is basically the opposite method to the relative colorimetric intent. This method tries to keep a color's saturation the same while adjusting its lightness to get it to fit in the destination gamut. This gets used most for business graphics.

- **Absolute colorimetric** — Use this method when you need to get an exact color to print. It's similar to the relative colorimetric intent, but it keeps the white point of your source image.

FIGURE 1-21

Color Management settings in the Preferences dialog

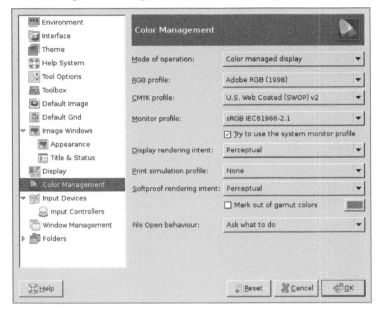

GIMP also gives you the ability to mark out-of-gamut colors with a color of your choice — gray by default — so you know where the color adjustments are going to take place in your image and you can adjust accordingly. Color management is a pretty heavy topic that's worth reading up on some more. There's a little bit more on how GIMP specifically handles colors and color management in Chapter 9.

Input Devices

As you may note in Figure 1-22, the Input Devices section and its subcategory, Additional Input Controllers, in GIMP's preferences are deceptively sparse. This is the area where you define and set up Extended Input Devices like drawing tablets and MIDI controllers.

It's from these sections that you can customize the behavior of buttons on a drawing tablet or make GIMP aware of an external controller like the 3Dconnexion's SpaceNavigator or perhaps a musical keyboard. Configuration for some of these things can get pretty involved and specific. Details are included in Appendix B.

FIGURE 1-22

Input Devices and Additional Input Controllers settings in the Preferences dialog

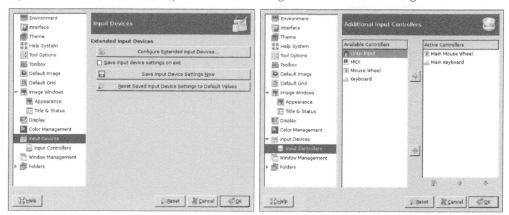

Window Management

The Window Management options are settings that for years some GIMP users have clamored for, particularly GIMP users who work in Microsoft Windows. One of the complaints some users have with GIMP's interface is that it has so many floating windows. In the Windows operating system, this gets exacerbated by the fact that each GIMP window, including the Toolbox and docks, gets its own window and subsequent tab on the taskbar. This is cluttered and ugly and drove Windows users batty ever since GIMP was introduced on that platform. With the release of GIMP 2.6.1, GIMP for Windows was able to set a window-type "hint" on its Toolbox and dock windows. You can define what that hint is from this section of the Preferences, as shown in Figure 1-23.

If you set the hint for the Toolbox and other docks to Utility Window, GIMP cleans itself up from your taskbar and gives you a single window interface that you can interact with, similar to Photoshop and other programs of this type. The GIMP developers are still refining this feature, but it works suitably well in both Windows and Linux and it's gone a long way toward making users happier. These drop-down menus also give you the ability to set the Toolbox and docks to Keep Above. This prevents image windows from obscuring the Toolbox or dock windows. The other settings in this section are pretty self-explanatory. Particularly useful is the Save window positions on exit option. It ensures that every time you open up GIMP, all of your tools and docks are exactly where you left them.

Tip

A slight bug in the Utility Window feature of GIMP is that when you try to minimize GIMP to your taskbar, the image windows will minimize, but the Toolbox and docks will remain on-screen. GIMP developers are working on a solution to make this work more cleanly, but in the meantime, an easy way to work around this issue is to press Tab in the image window prior to minimizing it. Pressing Tab, as explained earlier in this chapter, hides the Toolbox and docks. So now when you minimize, they're not left hanging. ■

FIGURE 1-23

Window Management settings in the Preferences dialog

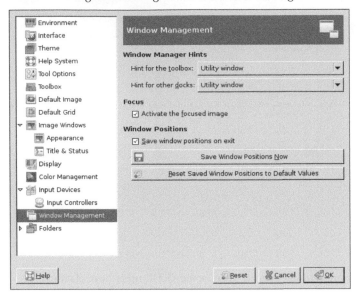

Folders

The final section in the Preferences dialog is Folders. Folders are typically where GIMP keeps data that can be used to customize and extend it. So if you create a custom brush or pattern or plug-in or theme, the best way to make GIMP aware of its existence is to put that thing you created into the folder where GIMP is looking for that data. As the left side of Figure 1-24 shows, GIMP has folders for storing brushes, patterns, palettes, gradients, fonts, plug-ins, scripts, modules, interpreters, environment variables, and themes.

Notice that the main Folders settings page has only two options: Temporary Folder and Swap Folder. These are folders that GIMP uses to hold transient data while you work. When you close GIMP, the information in these folders is cleared. It's a good idea to make sure that these folders are on a hard drive in your computer that has a fairly substantial amount of free space.

Also in Figure 1-24 are the settings for the Brush Folders. The interface here is pretty straightforward. The arrow buttons on the left move the selected folder up and down in the list of folders. The top folder in the list is the highest priority folder. If a brush by the same name exists in folders below it, it is superseded by the brush in the upper folder. You can also use this to add and remove folders from the list with the new page and trashcan icon buttons, respectively.

FIGURE 1-24

Folders settings and settings for the Brush Folders in the Preferences dialog

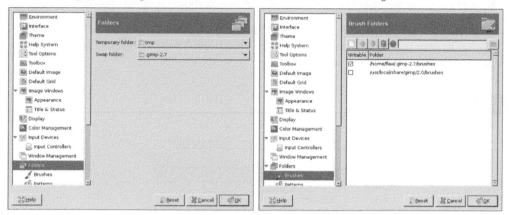

Customizing Keyboard Shortcuts

GIMP makes it very easy to customize keyboard shortcuts so you make your work environment comfortable for you. You can go about doing this in two primary ways. The fastest is to enable the Use Dynamic Keyboard Shortcuts option under the Interface settings of the Preferences dialog. By doing this, you're able to take nearly any menu command in GIMP and assign it a keyboard shortcut on the fly. As an example, here's how you would use this feature to get around one of my least favorite keyboard shortcuts in GIMP on a laptop: zooming in. By default, you can zoom out by pressing the minus, or dash (-) key while working on an image. And to zoom in, GIMP's default button is the plus key (+). This works great on a full keyboard with a numeric keypad. However, most laptop keyboards don't include the numeric keypad. So to get the plus sign, you have to press Shift+equal (=). This multi-key sequence can be bothersome if you're used to pressing one key and you want to quickly zoom in and out. To get around this, make sure you have dynamic keyboard shortcuts enabled and then use the menu in an image window to navigate to View ⇨ Zoom ⇨ Zoom In. Don't click Zoom In, though. Notice that to the right of it in the menu, you can see its shortcut, currently set to +. Well, with your mouse hovering over Zoom In, simply press the equal sign on your keyboard. You should see the keyboard shortcut hint instantly change from + to =. Now if you get out of the menu, you can immediately use that new shortcut. How's that for convenient?

So the generic steps to do this would be as follows:

1. Verify that dynamic keyboard shortcuts is on (Edit ➢ Preferences ➢ Interface ➢ Use Dynamic Keyboard Shortcuts).

2. Use the menu to navigate to the action on which you want to assign or change the shortcut.

3. With your mouse hovered over the action, press the shortcut you want to use.

4. Get out of the menu and enjoy the use of your new keyboard shortcut. Woohoo!

Of course, that's a kind of "quick 'n' dirty" way of assigning keyboard shortcuts. There is another way that has its own dialog. To access it, click Edit ➤ Keyboard Shortcuts. When you do that, you'll get a dialog like the one in Figure 1-25.

The Configure Keyboard Shortcuts dialog

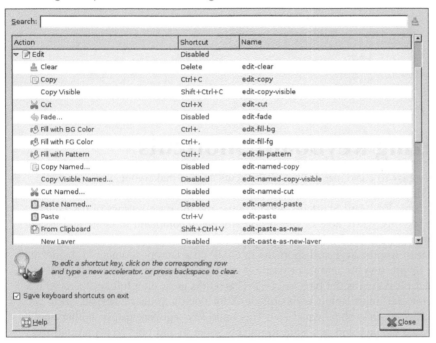

Using this dialog is pretty simple. Just navigate through the available actions or use the search bar at the top to type in the name of a specific action you're looking for. Then, when you find the action that you want, left-click it, and the item in the Shortcut column will say "New accelerator... " When you see that, press the new keyboard shortcut that you want to use and it is instantly applied. One of the nice things about using this interface to configure your shortcuts rather than the dynamic keyboard shortcuts is that this dialog will notify you if the shortcut you're trying to apply is already in use. Keeping you aware of conflicts helps ensure that you don't accidentally supplant another shortcut that you use more often.

Summary

GIMP is heavy-hitting Free Software that, despite the assertions of some detractors, is a popular and effective tool for digital artists. This chapter's purpose was to let you hit the ground running and not only get familiar with GIMP's capabilities, but also start getting to know its interface. The goal here is to get you familiar with GIMP and to get GIMP familiar with you by way of customizing it to work with you rather than against you. Onward!

Thinking Digitally

Before getting knee-deep in all of the detailed ins and outs of GIMP, it's well worth your time to familiarize yourself with some of the details and terminology of digital media. If you're a seasoned professional, much of this chapter might be a review for you. However, it never hurts to have a good reference that you can point to as a refresher or as a means of explaining things to someone else.

As with any other creative medium, the more you know about how digital imagery works, the more you can take advantage of its strengths and circumvent its deficiencies. You may even be able to find novel ways of using its perceived shortcomings to your advantage. Fortunately, there aren't so many differences between digital work and traditional, meatspace (what some people refer to as "the real world") work. Digital graphics borrows a lot of terminology from the analog world and quite a few techniques have been ported to our digital realm. And these days it's extremely common for artists to shift from analog to digital almost seamlessly, using the most effective tools in each medium to create images that would be difficult to create in either one by itself. This is especially true in commercial photography and illustration where deadlines are tight and efficiency is paramount.

By the time you finish this chapter, you should have a fairly complete understanding of what goes into a digital image as well as the differences between different digital graphic types. Have at it!

IN THIS CHAPTER

Comparing digital images to traditional photographs

Understanding the difference between types of digital images

Working with the attributes of digital images

Digital Images vs. Traditional Photographs

What's the difference between a digital photograph and a traditional photograph that's developed on film? Well, an obvious answer would be that you typically view the former on a screen and the latter on paper. However, it goes a lot further than that. From a purely visual standpoint, traditional photographs seem to have a lot more to offer than their digital counterparts. The reason for this has a lot to do with how the images are captured and stored. In film media, you're literally capturing light and chemically recording it to acetate. An incredibly immense amount of light information is captured this way, including some things not immediately visible to the naked eye because of an overabundance or deficit of light. Once the film negative has been developed, you can use it (within reason) to reveal some of those difficult-to-see parts. Furthermore, because you've recorded the light, it's pretty easy to enlarge an image to a size many times larger than the size of the negative without degrading the quality of that image.

Digital photos are different. For one, the sensors on digital cameras generally capture a smaller range of light than film does, so it's more difficult to reveal hidden detail in an image. Another difference is that digital images are, well, *digitized*. That is, where traditional film captures and records raw light information, digital cameras record samples of that light information. Two sorts of sampling take place. The first type deals with the area of the image itself. In digital images, the entire image area is divided into a grid. Each block in the grid is defined as a *pixel*, or "picture element." That pixel stores only one thing: a single color. Then for each of these pixels, the color itself is a sample of possible colors within a finite range. This range of colors is referred to as the *bit depth* of the image and though the size and granularity of that range can be somewhat refined by increasing the bit depth, digital images are still limited to a much smaller range than traditional photographs. Figure 2-1 illustrates how a digital image is sampled into pixels of a finite number of colors.

FIGURE 2-1

Digital images are sampled into a grid of pixels, each storing a single color defined by the image's bit depth. (Photo credit: Chris Hoyer)

All of this adds up to mean that it's more difficult to drastically increase the size of an image, and it's often impossible to pull a "hidden" image out of an over- or under-exposed portion of a photograph. If part of your image is white because it's blown out, those white pixels are white pixels and there's no way to pull more definition out of that.

Now, digital cameras have improved and are continuing to improve to increase the size of the available image area. This is the *megapixel* rating that most cameras advertise. A megapixel is one million pixels, so a camera that can take an image that is 1280 x 1024 pixels in size is a 1.3 megapixel (1280 x 1024 = 1,310,720) camera. These days, most good-quality digital cameras can take in excess of 10-megapixel images and even cameras on mobile phones can take 3.2-megapixel images.

To deal with the issue of limited bit depth in digital images, a relatively new technology called *high dynamic range*, or HDR, has grown in popularity. The technique starts by taking a series of photos where you *bracket* the exposures. That is, you take the photo at a base exposure that you consider to be normal, and then take one or more photos in both shorter and longer exposure times. Bracketing is actually a technique that traditional film photographers have used for years because film cameras don't have an LCD screen to give you the instant feedback that digital cameras do. Photographers compensated by bracketing their shots around the exposure that they thought was correct. Digital photographers use this same technique, but instead of throwing out the extra exposures, they use the whole set of bracketed images. Using this range of images, you can capture a larger range of the available light than the camera's sensor can take in a single shot. Incidentally, it's also a higher range than what can be displayed on a typical computer monitor. With a bit of adjustment, though, you can use these images together in a process called *tone mapping* to create an image that shows better than visible detail. All of this editing and adjustment can be done in GIMP. However, it's not uncommon for these images to be packed into a single HDR file format such as DPX or OpenEXR, and unfortunately at this time GIMP cannot read these files natively. Figure 2-2 compares a normal exposure photograph with one that's been treated with HDR. I go more into using this bracketing technique in Chapter 9.

FIGURE 2-2

On the left is an image taken with a single exposure and on the right is the same image tone mapped with bracketed exposures. (Photo credit: Chris Hoyer)

Although digital images have these shortcomings, their digitized nature offers some advantages over traditional photographs. The most readily noticeable of them is the instant nature of digital photography. There's no need to wait for the film to develop or to risk losing all of your images to mistakes in the darkroom. Additionally, digital images can be stored, copied, and archived multiple times on a variety of digital storage media such as hard drives, CD-ROMs, and USB thumbdrives without further degradation to image quality. This means that they can last much, much longer than film images, which are subject to the problems of aging. It also makes it a lot easier for you to share, modify, and reuse images for purposes ranging from simple scrapbooking to putting your friend's face on video footage of a famous celebrity.

Raster Graphics vs. Vector Graphics

In the previous section, you started to learn about the differences between traditional photographs and digital images. However, it doesn't stop there. When it comes to digital images, there are actually two classifications: raster images and vector images. Both of these image types output in pixels to your computer monitor or to a printer, but that's about the only similarity.

Raster Images

Raster images are what most people are familiar with. In their rawest form, they're described as a *bitmap*; each pixel in the image has its own color and that color is mapped to a grid that forms the full size of the image. This is what's described in Figure 2-1 and is the type of image that gets created by digital cameras. Raster images are at their best when you have high-detail images with large variations in color. For this reason, they're particularly good when you need an image that looks natural or realistic. Because raster images can have a high level of variety, it feels very natural to draw and paint. You have paint strokes that can have nearly unlimited variety. At its core, GIMP is designed to edit raster images.

The downside is that these images are difficult to increase in size or reuse output for media other than screen or print. Some resampling algorithms can help, but once you pass a certain threshold, the image becomes excessively blocky, or *pixelated*. This is because of the finite nature of pixels. The best you can do to upscale an image is increase the size of each pixel. Of course, you can compensate for this by starting with really large images (hence the reason why camera manufacturers have been racing for higher and higher megapixel ratings), but the trade-off here is that these large images end up taking a large amount of hard drive space and become increasingly time-consuming for the computer to process.

To this end, when working in GIMP it's in your best interest to consider the final output medium of your image ahead of time. It's very frustrating to spend hours modifying an image with a size that's best suited for a postcard only to find out that it's supposed to go on a billboard.

Vector Images

In contrast to rasters, vector images are described and stored more procedurally as a sum of mathematical functions. When you want to see what the image is, the computer translates those functions to fit whatever pixel size you stipulate. And because you're just storing the mathematical functions, the amount of disk space that a vector image takes up can be incredibly small. The reasons previously discussed make vector images an excellent choice when you have an image that has to look good regardless of size or output. Vectors can easily be scaled to any size with no noticeable degradation of quality. You can use the same vector image on letterheads, billboards, or even embroidered on a shirt. It's for this very reason that the majority of company logos and illustrations are created with vector drawing tools. Figure 2-3 compares what happens when you scale up a raster image versus when you scale up a vector image.

FIGURE 2-3

Scaling a raster image (left) produces pixelated results, whereas scaling a vector image (right) keeps edges and colors crisp and clean. (Photo credit: Melody Smith; Image credit: gopher on openclipart.org)

The unfortunate thing about vector graphics is that they don't have nearly the same capacity as raster images to store images with a lot of color variation. The more variation that you add to an image, the less efficient a vector image becomes and you start running into a point of diminishing returns on the advantages that vectors give you. If you were to attempt to get the same color variation of a raster image in a vector format, you would quickly notice that the file size becomes unmanageably large and your computer takes excessive amounts of time to process the image. This is because the math becomes a lot more complex with that much variation and the computer still has to translate all of those functions on the fly. What often happens is that the high-variation image looks *banded* or *posterized* when you try to use a vector format. Figure 2-4 shows what a vector image looks like when you try to include a lot of color variation.

In a nutshell, the best times to use raster tools are for images with high color variety like photographs and high-color paintings. Vector tools are best suited for images with a limited number of defined colors and a need to scale to any size, such as logos. Although GIMP is primarily a raster graphics application, it can import vector images and convert them into raster images for further refinement. Additionally, GIMP's paths and its text tool are actually vector-based. This makes it incredibly easy to edit and reuse these elements without drastically increasing file size. Chapters 5 and 10, respectively, cover these tools in greater detail.

FIGURE 2-4

A raster image converted to vector. Notice how the colors get flattened out and simplified. (Photo credit: Melody Smith)

Resolution and Image Size

One of the things that even some seasoned artists get mixed up is the difference between image size and image resolution. To put it simply, a digital image's size refers to its exact dimensions in real-world units, whereas the resolution attempts to relate those real-world units to the pixel size of that image. Real-world units include standard measurements like inches and millimeters, but they also include typographical units like points and picas. They can actually even include pixels if your final output is destined for a web site or computer monitor.

Resolution is typically defined by a *pixels per inch*, or ppi, value. Modern computer monitors tend to have a standard ppi that they display best. Usually that range is between 72 and 100ppi and the monitor's drivers report that resolution to your computer's operating system. For older monitors that don't do this or for standard-definition television, the convention is to use 72ppi. For print, the conventions are a bit more varied. High-quality printing, like what is used for magazine covers and photographs, is typically done at 300ppi or higher. The typical low bar for professional printing is at about 150ppi, but this is used only if you know that the print quality of the final output can't exceed a certain level, such as with newspaper printers.

What this all boils down to is that if you want to have a high-quality print of your digital image at 9 x 12 inches, the image size should be no less than 2700 x 3600 pixels (9" x 300ppi = 2700px; 12" x 300ppi = 3600px). By default, GIMP includes the image size in pixels in the title bar of the image window. As explained in Chapter 1, you can customize this as well as the status bar of the image window by going to the Title & Status section of the Preferences dialog (Edit ➢ Preferences ➢ Image Windows ➢ Title & Status). For a more complete view of the size and resolution of any given image in GIMP, use the Image Properties dialog, as shown in Figure 2-5, by clicking Image ➢ Image Properties in the menu or pressing Alt+Enter.

FIGURE 2-5

The Image Properties dialog. The image's size and resolution are shown in the first three values listed.

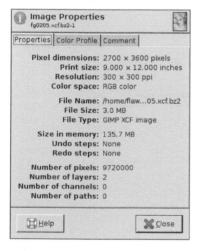

Tip

In GIMP, if you need to use non-pixel units like inches, millimeters, or picas, it's recommended that you disable Dot for Dot from the View menu (View ➢ Dot for Dot). The Dot for Dot feature makes a pixel in your image the same size as a pixel on your monitor. When you're just working in pixels, this is great. However, assume you're working on a print image with a resolution of 300ppi. This resolution is higher than your monitor natively displays, so if you have Dot for Dot enabled, the image at 100% will appear larger than its actual print size. If you disable Dot for Dot, then GIMP adjusts the image's display resolution so what appears on-screen matches the size of what gets printed. ■

Changing Image Size and Resolution

When you create a new image in GIMP (File ➢ New or Ctrl+N), you have to set the size and resolution of your image before you actually get started on your work. While you're working, it's not uncommon for specifications to change, so you may need to change your image's size or resolution. You do this from the Scale Image dialog (Image ➤ Scale Image). The thing to note here is that if you change the image's size, GIMP will have to resample the image. As an example, consider increasing the size of the image. If you're doing this, you're effectively increasing the number of pixels used to create that image. In order to do that, GIMP has to take your existing image data and use that to make an attempt at guessing the colors of the new pixels using a process called *interpolation*. GIMP does this by using one of the four interpolation algorithms that you can choose from at the bottom of the dialog, as explained in Chapter 1. The potential problem, though, is that because you're starting with only a fixed number of pixels, there's only so much you can scale up an image before it starts getting blocky and pixelated. Now, if you're just changing the image's resolution and maintaining the same image size in pixels, there's no need for GIMP to do any resampling or interpolation. GIMP just makes a note of this resolution change in the file and that note is recognized when the image is sent to the printer. In fact, if you're only interested in changing the image's resolution, you're best off using GIMP's Set Image Print Resolution dialog (Image ➤ Print Size). This dialog is nearly identical to Scale Image, except the Width and Height are in real-world units and there is no Interpolation setting. Figure 2-6 shows GIMP's Create a New Image, Scale Image, and Set Image Print Resolution dialogs.

FIGURE 2-6

GIMP's Create a New Image (left), Scale Image (center), and Set Image Print Resolution (right) dialogs allow you to set both the size and resolution of your image.

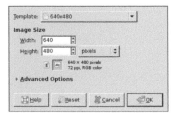  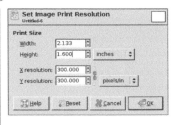

Tip

A neat feature that's been added for GIMP 2.8 is the ability to enter simple expressions in most of GIMP's numeric input fields. And even better, these expressions recognize different units. This means that rather than going to the units drop-down in the Scale dialog, switching to percentage, entering a value, and switching back, you can simply type "50%" in the Width field and GIMP does the rest of the work for you. From there you can do even more complex expressions. For example, say you're using the Rectangle Select tool and you want your selection to start an inch to the left of center, but you want to push it to the right by 15 pixels. Rather than setting up guides or measuring anything out, you can go to the Rectangle Select tool's options and in the X position field, type 50% - 1in + 15px, and GIMP positions your selection accordingly. ■

A common thing that you may find yourself doing is enlarging images. Though it's always best to start with as large of an image as possible, you won't always have this luxury. You can be faced with a situation where all you have is a small, low-quality image that's been downloaded from the Internet. Fortunately, there's a trick or two that you can use to enlarge an image while reducing the chance of getting jagged pixelation or making compression artifacts — discussed later in this chapter — more apparent. The following steps provide a rough outline of the process using GIMP's default values. It's a good idea to play with and adjust these values to your tastes for the images you work on.

1. **Scale your image up to the desired size (Image ➢ Scale Image).** Don't go too crazy, but I've had decent results pushing images up by 400% and 500%. After that, results can vary drastically depending on the type of image you start with.

2. **Apply the Despeckle filter (Filters ➢ Enhance ➢ Despeckle).** This does a good job at removing some of the noise and artifacts that get amplified when you enlarge. You can find more information on the Despeckle filter in Chapter 13.

3. **Apply the GREYCstoration filter (Filters ➢ Enhance ➢ GREYCstoration).** This step removes more of the extraneous noise that is prevalent in small images that have been compressed a lot. Depending on the settings, this filter can take away the realism in a photograph, so you may want to scale your image up by another 200% before applying this filter and then bring it back down to this size afterwards. Chapter 13 has more details on this filter.

4. **Apply the Unsharp Mask filter (Filters ➢ Enhance ➢ Unsharp Mask).** There's a more thorough description of this filter in Chapter 13, but basically this filter helps to make edges in you image more crisp.

Figure 2-7 shows a comparison between an image that's been enlarged 500% with these steps and an image that's just been enlarged with the Scale Image dialog. The difference between the two isn't monumentally huge, but the version enlarged with these steps has a bit more definition to it and fewer artifacts.

FIGURE 2-7

Enlarging an image by 500%. The image on the left just used the Scale Image dialog, and the image on the right was done with the previous steps. (Photo credit: Chis Hoyer)

Confusing Terminology

It's worth knowing that some of the preceding terminology has a tendency to get confusing in common discussions and documentation. A large reason for this is based in the fact that digital imaging terminology has roots in print terminology. For example, it's not uncommon to hear people use *dots per inch*, or dpi, when they actually mean ppi. This is because ppi is a relatively new term that is much more specific to digital images than dpi. The term *dpi* comes from print and refers to the number of ink dots that go into making a specific color. As an example, say you have a standard color printer. That printer uses four colors to generate any color in its spectrum: cyan, magenta, yellow, and black (CMYK). For each pixel in your digital image, the printer has to mix these four colors to produce the color of that pixel. If the printer can use more dots per pixel, it can get you more accurate colors. So if a printer manufacturer says its printer is capable of printing at 1200dpi, that's not actually the same as being able to accurately print a 1200ppi image. It means that if you have a 300ppi image, that printer can put 16 dots in the space of one of your image's pixels ((1200dpi x 1200dpi) / (300ppi x 300ppi) = 16).

The other point of potential confusion is that people have a tendency to use the term "resolution" when they are referring to size. This is particularly apparent when speaking in relative terms: "Can I get a high-resolution version of that photo?" or "Editing this image is going to be difficult because it's such a low resolution." Clearly both of these examples are talking about how large the image is in pixels, although they're using the word *resolution*. This can be a bit confusing, but it's usually pretty easy to figure out what someone means based on context. And if not, you can always specifically ask them whether they're talking about the image's size or its resolution. In an effort to maintain clarity, I've made it a point to avoid using phrases like these in this book.

Color Depth

As I explained earlier in this chapter, a digital image's color depth, or bit depth, defines the range of colors that a pixel could be set to. To define any color in GIMP, it uses a standard based on a combination of three primary colors: red, green, and blue (RGB). Each of those colors is considered a *channel* and all colors are generated by varying the intensity of each of these three channels. Currently, GIMP only supports colors with 8 bits per channel. Recall that information in a computer consists entirely of bits, each holding either a one or zero. GIMP uses a combination of 8 of these bits to define a channel. This means that there are 2^8, or 256, different combinations per channel. Or stated in another way, there are 256 levels of intensity for each of the red, green, and blue channels. This may not seem like a very large number, but consider the fact that your colors are based on a combination of these three channels. This means that you have 256^3, or 16,777,216, different colors to work with in GIMP.

Although most digital cameras still use 8-bit color, more and more cameras are coming out that support 12, 14, and even 16 bits per channel. Unfortunately, GIMP cannot currently edit images at these color depths, so you'll have to convert them to 8-bit or use another program, such as CinePaint. CinePaint originally started as a fork of GIMP 2.2 called FilmGIMP with the intended purpose of supporting higher-bit-depth images. It has since grown on its own development path and is actually used at large production houses like Sony Imageworks and Industrial Light & Magic for cleaning up individual frames in movies. That said, thanks to some intense work on getting GIMP to work on the GEGL (Generic Graphics Library) image processing library, it will only be a matter of time before the GIMP developers gift us with full support for high color depths of up to 32 bits per channel.

Color Spaces and Color Modes

By using red, green, and blue to define colors, GIMP is said to use an RGB *color space* natively. A color space defines an individual color by combining a set of primary elements. Those elements could be primary colors, like GIMP's native RGB, or a combination of a color with how bright and saturated that color is. When working on a digital image, you can stipulate the color space you're working in by setting an image's *color mode*. The color mode can be a color space, but it can also be used to let you explicitly limit the available colors to work with in your image. This section explains these terms so you can best take advantage of them.

Color Spaces

A color space specifically refers to the base values that are used to create colors in an image. We're taught in grade school that the wavelengths comprising visible light are a small range of a much larger electromagnetic spectrum that includes x-rays and radio waves. We're then usually shown how a prism can be used to separate that chunk of visible light into the various constituent colors. Well, it turns out that digitally re-creating any of those infinite color possibilities in an efficient way can be particularly challenging. In order to accomplish this task, some standards were created to model the visible light spectrum. Each model defines a color space that consists of a set of base components that can be combined to re-create a portion of the visible spectrum. This subset of colors is referred to as that color space model's *gamut*. Following is a list of some of the most common color spaces:

- **RGB (red, green, blue)** — This is the default color space for computer displays. It's an additive color model that uses red, green, and blue light as the primary colors. A combination of all three of these colors at full intensity will yield white light. RGB is also a subset of the RGBA (red, green, blue, alpha) color space, where the last channel, the *alpha channel*, determines the transparency of a given pixel. GIMP supports the RGBA color space natively.

- **HSV (hue, saturation, value)** — This is a direct transformation of the RGB color space and is often used interchangeably with it. It works by picking a color (the hue) and adjusting how much of that color is used (the saturation), and how dark or bright it is (value). This color space tends to be very intuitive for artists. Because GIMP supports RGB, it also gets the HSV color space "for free."

- **CMYK (cyan, magenta, yellow, black)** — CMYK is the primary color space for printing in color. Unlike RGB, CMYK is a subtractive color model based on pigments rather than light. This means that a combination of the base colors here will yield a dark result rather than a bright white one. CMYK has a smaller gamut than RGB, but because it has an explicit black component, the blacks in CMYK tend to be richer. You may wonder why this color space uses a K for black rather than a B. The most obvious explanation is to avoid confusing it with the B for blue in RGB. However, there's a bit more history to it than that. In traditional printing, the black printing plate is referred to as the "key" plate because the most critical visual details are in the black values. GIMP does not natively support CMYK colors, but it does have CMYK color sliders in the Foreground/Background Color dialog and it can also produce color separations for this color space.

- **YUV (luma, chrominance)** — YUV is a complex color model that has its roots in video technology and is actually a variety of similar color spaces such as YPbPr and YCbCr. The way it works is by mixing a *luma*, or brightness, with a pair of values (U and V) that define a color value, or chrominance. GIMP does not currently have any native support for YUV or similar color spaces.

As you can see, each color space is typically defined by the technology used to reproduce those colors. Many of these color spaces overlap and conversion from one to another is relatively painless. However, because the gamut of each color model covers a different space of the visible spectrum, that conversion will not always be 100% accurate. Because GIMP's only native color space is RGB, this is something to be aware of, especially if you're working on something that you intend to send to a printer. It's definitely in your best interest to do periodic print tests to ensure the accuracy of your colors. Figure 2-8 shows how GIMP allows you to pick colors using the RGB, HSV, and CMYK color spaces in the Foreground/Background Color dialog.

FIGURE 2-8

From left to right, GIMP's HSV/RGB, Watercolor, Wheel, and CMYK color palettes in the Foreground/Background Color dialog

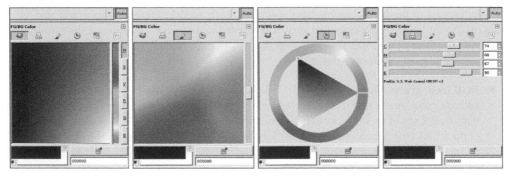

Color Modes

Although GIMP's only native color space is RGB, you do still have a couple other options. Technically, they could qualify as subsets of the RGB gamut, but they're important for determining how GIMP handles colors in a given image. What I'm referring to are the color modes that can be assigned to an image. To change the color mode that your image is using, click Image ➢ Mode and choose one of the following options:

- **RGB** — This is the default way that GIMP handles color. You have three 8-bit channels at hand to combine as you please and create more than 16 million colors.

- **Grayscale** — The Grayscale color mode limits an image to only a brightness, or intensity level. Images in this mode produce your typical "old black-and-white" images. If you choose to use this mode, be aware that this consists of a single 8-bit channel, so you have only 256 levels of gray to create your image. On the flip side, because you only have one channel, file size is usually smaller.

- **Indexed** — This provides you with a fixed color palette of a small set of defined colors. For an index, you are allowed an absolute maximum of 256 individual colors. The main use for this color mode is for image formats like GIF that support only an indexed color palette, or if you are absolutely certain that you're only using a handful of predefined colors to create your image.

Warning

If you're changing the color mode from RGB to either Grayscale or Indexed, you're making a fundamental change to your image that limits some of your functionality. Most obviously, you will not be able to pick an arbitrary color and simply use it. The only colors available to you are the ones that are defined by that color mode. ■

When you take an RGB image and change its color mode to Grayscale or Indexed, GIMP will do a conversion to that new mode. In the case of Grayscale, it happens automatically. For the Indexed color mode, however, GIMP pops up the dialog shown in Figure 2-9 to facilitate the conversion.

FIGURE 2-9

The Convert Image to Indexed Colors dialog

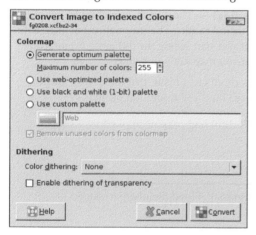

On this dialog, the first thing you have to choose is the color map that you would like to use. For this, you have the following options:

- **Generate optimum palette** — This option takes your image and creates a limited color palette from it, based on an algorithm that picks the best colors to use. GIMP will create a palette that has up to 256 colors in it. If you wish, you can reduce that number by lowering the value next to Maximum number of colors.

- **Use web-optimized palette** — When the World Wide Web first came out, not all computers had high-color displays and video cards, and the ones that existed weren't particularly consistent. One color on a Windows computer could look quite different on a Mac. With a bit of research, it was determined that a handful of colors — 216 to be exact — looked close enough to the same on both platforms. These colors are considered "web-safe" and constitute this indexed palette. Incidentally, even with the modern displays we have now, the color inconsistency between machines still persists, so this option is actually not obsolete if you're working on graphics for the Web.

- **Use black and white (1-bit) palette** — This palette makes each pixel in your image either black or white, based on a simple contrast threshold.

- **Use custom palette** — This option allows you to pick one of many predefined palettes available to you in GIMP (including the web-safe one). You can also create your own custom palette for choosing here from the Palettes dialog.

When you use any of the last three options, GIMP gives you the ability to further optimize those palettes by tossing out colors from them that are not present in your image. The Remove unused colors from colormap option controls this and it's enabled by default.

Besides the color map, your other option when converting to an indexed palette is *dithering*. Dithering is a sort of basic color mixing based on the limited number of colors available in your palette. GIMP offers the following dithering algorithms that you can choose from:

- **None** — This is the simplest setting. No dithering is done; the colors are simply distinct blocks of solid color.

- **Floyd-Steinberg (normal/reduced color bleeding)** — These two settings are largely the same and typically produce the most natural dithered results. The "normal" version should work adequately in most situations. However, if you start seeing the dithering overextending its bounds, the "reduced color bleeding" version may suit you better.

- **Positioned** — The positioned dithering setting produces a result that looks very much like you would see in an image that's been printed on a low-resolution printer.

Figure 2-10 shows enlarged versions of each of GIMP's dithering options applied to a simple gradient.

FIGURE 2-10

From left to right, a gradient with no dithering, Floyd-Steinberg (normal), Floyd-Steinberg (reduced color bleeding), and positioned dithering

GIMP also provides the ability to dither colors to transparency. This can be helpful if you're creating a transparent GIF for the Web, but you want to try to avoid overly jagged edges to the transparent parts of your image. To enable this, click the Enable dithering of transparency check box under the dithering options.

Compression

Another key attribute of digital images is compression. As explained earlier in this chapter, the absolute, most raw form of a digital image is a bitmap; a grid of pixels with defined colors based on three or four channels. Assume you've taken a digital photograph with a cheap 1.3-megapixel camera that takes pictures at an 8-bit color depth. 1.3-megapixel images have 1,310,720 pixels (1280 x 1024 = 1,310,720). Each pixel has a color that's stored by 24 bits (8 bits x 3 color channels = 24). This means that to store that image in a simple bitmap form takes about 3.75 megabytes (24 bits x 1,310,720 pixels = 31,457,280 bits and 31,457,280 bits / 8 bits per byte / 1024 bytes per kilobyte / 1024 kilobytes per megabyte = 3.75 MB). That may be a lot of space for a "dinky" 1.3-megapixel image, but it's still pretty manageable. However, what if you get a newer, better camera that shoots 10-megapixel images (3872 x 2592 pixels) with 12 bits per color channel? Using the same math, a bitmap image from this camera takes about 43 MB. This is a much, much bigger file and not only will it take more computing power to process, but storing and copying this image gets to be a larger challenge.

You may be thinking, "Now hold on. I have a totally awesome hard drive that stores a terabyte of data. What's a measly 43 MB? I could store that file over 24 thousand times on this drive!" That's true. However, what if you want to e-mail that photo to a friend or burn a bunch of these photos to a CD or put a set of them on one of those cool digital picture frames? If the photo took up less space, your e-mail to your friend would go through faster and you could put even more photos on that digital picture frame. This is the reason why compression algorithms exist for digital images. Their purpose is to reduce the amount of storage space that a given image takes up, hopefully without an overtly adverse effect on the quality of the image. When it comes to compressing images, there are two basic types: lossless compression and lossy compression.

Lossless Compression

Most people have zipped one or more files into a compressed archive before. This is a perfect example of lossless compression. The idea here is to reduce file size without destroying or degrading the integrity of the source data. That is, when you reverse the compression process, decoding the file to reproduce a copy of the original, there should be no difference between the decompressed file and the original file that it came from. If *image fidelity*, or how closely your compressed image resembles the uncompressed version, is important to you, you should find lossless compression to be particularly attractive.

The basic idea behind this type of compression is to temporarily reduce superfluous or redundant data; ordering it and organizing it so it takes up less space. Imagine your image is a plastic bag stuffed with wadded napkins. If you take those napkins, flatten them, fold them, neatly stack them in the bag, and then remove all of the extra air from bag, chances are good that it'll take up much less physical space. You have successfully compressed your napkin bag. And it's lossless compression because you can, with some work, unseal the bag and wad up the napkins exactly as they had been. Figure 2-11 illustrates this concept.

FIGURE 2-11

Lossless compression is like organizing the contents of a bag full of wadded napkins.

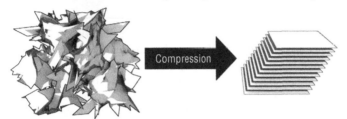

Lossless image compression techniques have continued to improve, yielding very impressive *compression ratios*. Taking the 10-megapixel image example earlier in this section, that 43 MB uncompressed image file could be compressed down to as small as 6 MB, depending on the content of the image and the compression codec you choose. Probably one of the most commonly used lossless image compression formats is the PNG (pronounced "ping") format, used everywhere from the Web to animation and video production. Another lossless format that's slowly gaining traction is JPEG 2000. It uses a fairly novel lossless compression algorithm based on wavelets that make it particularly nice for losslessly compressing photographic information. It's not likely to supplant PNG any time soon, but it will definitely become more helpful and useful over time.

A Note on Formats and Codecs

Whether you're talking about images, video, or audio, if you're compressing or encoding your digital media, there's a differentiation to keep in mind between a file format and a compression format. The file format is the home where the media data lives. Using the "napkin bag" example, consider the bag to be the format. It wraps around the data, giving it a home and giving the computer a single point of reference. It also offers the possibility of *metadata*, or notes on the information compressed inside of it. This would be akin to writing "300 napkins" on the outside of the bag with a marker.

Wrapped by the file format is the digital media; your napkins. The compression algorithm you use, called a *codec* (short for **co**mpressor/**dec**ompressor), stipulates how you're compressing your data. When working with images, it's most common to see codecs bound to image formats. That is, you're not likely to see PNG compression in a JPEG file or vice versa. There are a couple image formats, such as TIFF and Targa, that allow you to choose different types of codecs. The TIFF format gives you the option of a few compression formats, like LZW and even JPEG, while Targa lets you choose to use RLE compression. In both cases, using compression is completely optional. You can just as easily use the format with uncompressed image data. This is also how things work with video and audio data. Video file formats like QuickTime and AVI can support a vast shopping list of different codecs that you can use to encode your audio and video data. For more on how GIMP supports encoding video, have a look at Chapter 20.

Lossy Compression

Lossless compression is great when absolute image fidelity is required. However, lossless compression can help only up to a point. On an image that's suitably busy with content, like an outdoor photograph, there's not a lot of that superfluous or redundant data to squeeze out. In cases like that, lossless compression formats don't give you the drastically smaller file sizes that you would want. Enter lossy compression. Simply put, lossy compression reduces the file size by permanently and irreversibly removing image data from your file. This would obviously never fly as an option for compressing other types of information. Imagine using lossy compression on a report you've written in a word processor. Your file would be smaller, but you might suddenly be missing every other line of text in the report!

So why is this unacceptable in most types of data, but perfectly tolerable when it comes to images? Allow me to introduce you to a wonderfully imperfect viewing tool that we call "the eye." It's remarkably easy to trick the eyes. If you can give them a good enough hint at what goes on in an image, they do a pretty decent job at filling in the blanks for you. Lossy compression uses this fact to its advantage. These algorithms don't just randomly toss out image data; they try to do it intelligently in a way that most eyes won't notice.

For instance, if the human eye has difficulty differentiating between two shades of green, a good lossy algorithm will mark those pixels as the same color and then count them as redundant information in the image. By doing this, you can dramatically reduce the file size of large images, regardless of the complexity of the content. That imaginary 43 MB image that we've been working with through this chapter could be squeezed down to 2 MB or less by using a lossy algorithm like JPEG, which is the most prevalent format of this type.

That said, there are some caveats to using a lossy compression format. First of all, there is the risk of obliterating your image fidelity by over-compressing the image. As you increase compression, you reduce the quality of your image, often introducing *compression artifacts* to your image. These artifacts often manifest as blocky chunks of color that look out of place or the wrong color. In the case of JPEG compression, you can quickly start noticing these artifacts in large uniform areas of color as well as along the edges defined by two different colors. Figure 2-12 shows the same image with various levels of lossy compression and points out artifacts.

Another potential "gotcha" of lossy compression is the concept of *generation loss*. This is what happens if you save an image in a lossy format and then open and re-encode it to that lossy format again. Because you're using that lossy compression algorithm on an image that's already had information removed from it, repeated encodings quickly degrade the quality of your image and its fidelity in relation to its original uncompressed version. It's called generation loss because each time you re-encode the image counts as a generation; a step along its path toward being a heavily degraded image. The meatspace analogue to this is using a copy machine to repeatedly make copies of copies of documents. The results are similar to what you get in Figure 2-12, although not quite as pronounced. In order to get compression artifacts as pronounced as those in the 10% quality example of Figure 2-12, it would take over a dozen generations.

FIGURE 2-12

An image saved uncompressed, and gradually compressed more and more with JPEG compression at quality levels of 90%, 50%, and 10% (Photo credit: Melody Smith)

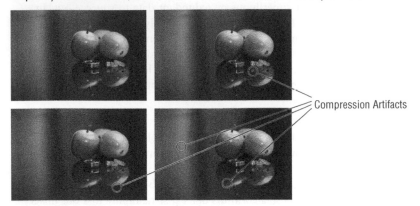

Compression Artifacts

When dealing with compression you have a natural trade-off between file size and image fidelity. The more you compress an image, the less it will look like its original source. Additionally, there's another, admittedly milder trade-off between file size and processor use. The more you compress an image, the harder your computer's processor has to work to encode and decode that image from its compressed format. Those things said, unless you have a distinct need to use an uncompressed format, it's usually in your best interest to at least use a lossless compression format. Chapter 3 has detailed information on the various image formats that GIMP supports and the types of compression that they use.

Summary

Working with images in GIMP requires you to have an understanding of some of the mechanics of digital images. By knowing how digital photographs relate to traditional film photographs, you can best see how to work around the some of the shortcomings of digital media while at the same time fully utilizing their advantages. GIMP natively supports 8-bit raster images in the RGBA color space, but it still uses vector graphics technology for some of its tools and it can provide some support for the CMYK color space used for print. In future versions of GIMP, there will be more support for high-bit-depth images. In the meantime, images can be assigned a specific color mode such as RGB, grayscale, or indexed color from the Image ➤ Mode menu. This can help reduce file size, but it can also effectively reduce the number of colors available to an image if you choose the grayscale or indexed options.

Another large part of digital media is the ability to compress image data, and compression can be either lossless or lossy. Lossless compression will reduce file sizes without degrading image fidelity, but lossy compression can get smaller files if you're willing to permanently sacrifice some fidelity. Ultimately it's a matter of weighing out the trade-offs and relating them to what your final output is supposed to be.

Armed with this knowledge, diving into GIMP and getting some real work done should be a cinch!

Part II

Getting Started

IN THIS PART

Chapter 3
Working with Files

Chapter 4
A Brief Overview of GIMP's Tools

Chapter 5
Taking Advantage of Paths

Chapter 6
Working with Layers and Masks

Chapter 7
Using Channels

Working with Files

IN THIS CHAPTER

Opening files in GIMP

Moving data from one file to another

Undoing mistakes

Saving your work

GIMP's purpose is to help you create and edit digital images. With a few exceptions (such as tying GIMP to code on a web site to create or modify image data on the fly — yes, this is actually possible), those digital images are stored as files. That being the case, GIMP has to provide you some tools to manage those files and the data that resides within them. This chapter shows you the full variety of tools and options that GIMP puts in your hands.

You may notice while going through this chapter that GIMP's file management tools, like the Open Image dialog, don't use the native File Open dialog used by most of programs on your computer. There are arguments on either side of this, but the good thing for you as the user is that GIMP's tools typically do more than the native one, so you get more helpful features. And just as importantly, you get the same GIMP on any computer you use, regardless of the underlying operating system. I carry a thumb drive around with me that has a functioning copy of GIMP for Windows and Mac on it so I can plug it in and edit images from virtually any computer I sit behind without installing anything. Not only is that extremely cool, but it's quite reassuring to know that I don't have to make any mental adjustments that are dependent on the machine I'm using.

Opening Files

So you want to modify an image in GIMP. Nearly all of GIMP's file management tools are accessible from the File menu (big surprise, huh?). The options that are relevant to opening and creating new images are in the upper third of this menu, shown in Figure 3-1. Through these options, you can start fresh with an empty canvas or generate a new image file from a plug-in or data received from hardware like a scanner or digital camera.

You can also open files from your hard drive or even directly from an Internet URI (uniform resource identifier; a fancy way of saying "Internet address").

FIGURE 3-1

GIMP's File menu and all of the available options therein

Opening Images

The quickest and easiest way to get an image into GIMP is to open one that already exists. The fastest way to do this is to use drag and drop. If you already have GIMP open, you can select an image's icon from your operating system's file management tool (Explorer in Windows, Finder in Mac, and usually Nautilus or Dolphin in Linux) and drag it into a GIMP image window. If there's no image in the window, GIMP opens the specific image file that you dragged in. If you drag the image icon into an image window that is already populated with an image, GIMP adds your dragged-in image as a new layer. This also works if you have an image available in a web browser like Mozilla Firefox. Just left-click the image and drag it to an available GIMP image window.

Of course, if you want more options or flexibility, you need to use the Open Image dialog for opening an image file. Do this by clicking File ➤ Open or pressing Ctrl+O. This brings up GIMP's file chooser, the Open Image dialog, shown in Figure 3-2.

File ➤ Open

Starting at the top of the dialog, a series of buttons indicates the *path* or location on your hard drive where you're currently looking. Clicking the left-most button, with the icon of a pencil and a piece of paper, toggles the visibility of the Location text entry field. This is where you can explicitly type out the path to a location on your drive if you know exactly where you want to look. Each of the buttons to the right of this icon represents an individual folder in the path. Because they show the path that you took to get to the folder you're currently in, these buttons are referred to as *breadcrumbs*. You can click any of these breadcrumbs and you'll be taken directly to that folder along the path.

FIGURE 3-2

The Open Image dialog

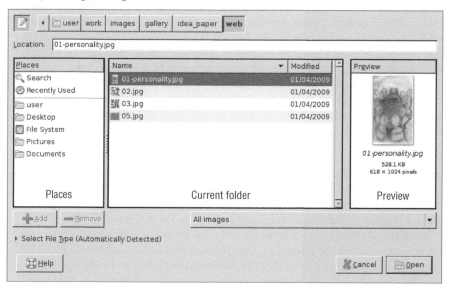

Below this are three panels: Places, Current Folder, and Preview. The best way to think about them is that as you move from left to right, you're refining the granularity of where you're looking. The Places panel gives you quick links to specific folders on your hard drive(s). This is great when you have a handful of folders where you always have your images saved. The Places panel also gives you quick access to files you've recently worked on in GIMP with the Recently Used option, as well as a rudimentary Search option that allows you to type in all or part of the name of a file and let GIMP hunt your drive for you.

Warning

Be a careful when using the Search option in Places. It doesn't let you specify which folder to begin searching it, so it hunts through all of the media drives you're currently using. If you have a really large hard drive or networked storage, this can be quite time-consuming. It's easy to cancel a search by clicking any of the other options in the panel, but it's worth knowing that GIMP's search might take a while to find what you're looking for. ∎

To add a custom location, called a *bookmark*, to the Places panel, you have to use the next panel to the right; the Current Folder panel. This panel shows a listing of the contents in the folder in which you're currently looking. Items with file folder icons are, as you may have guessed, folders. Not only does the icon indicate this, but if you click one of these items, the Preview panel to the far right will put the caption "Folder" under the name. Double-clicking a folder allows you to see a listing of its contents and adds a breadcrumb to your path at the top of the dialog. To add a bookmark in the Places panel, simply left-click the folder you want to add the Current Folder panel and click the Add button beneath the Places panel. Alternatively, you can right-click that folder and choose Add to Bookmarks from the context menu that pops up.

Once you have the bookmark added to the Places panel, you have the ability to give it a custom name by right-clicking that bookmark and choosing Rename from the menu that pops up. The cool thing here is that the custom name you use doesn't change the original folder's name at all. This is useful if you're the sort of person who has a different folder per project, but within each project folder you use the same names for subfolders. This way, rather than having a bunch of bookmarks in Places that all say "images" because that's the name of the folder, you can customize them to say "web site images," "animation stills," and "work-in-progress photos." Through the same right-click menu that you use to rename a bookmark, you can also remove it from the panel. This means you have two ways of removing a bookmark. After selecting the bookmark, you can either right-click and select Remove or click the Remove button beneath the Places panel.

While looking in the Current Folder panel, notice that, other than the folder icon, GIMP shows either an icon that looks like a sheet of paper or a thumbnail of the image. Initially, GIMP may not show a thumbnail for any of the images in a given folder. However, if you click an image file, GIMP generates a preview of the image and displays it in the Preview panel to the right, along with some statistical information, such as its file size, the image's size in pixels, what color mode it uses, and how many layers the image has. This preview gets stored and reused by GIMP as a thumbnail. Creating thumbnails for large files can be time-consuming, so by default, GIMP does not automatically create thumbnails for images that are larger than 4MB in size. For these images, once you click them in the Current Folder panel, the Preview panel shows a large version of the paper icon and gives you the ability to create a preview manually by clicking it. Figure 3-3 shows what the Preview panel looks like when this happens. You can also update the thumbnail on an image that's been edited elsewhere by clicking it in the Preview panel.

Tip

If 4MB is too small for you, GIMP gives you the ability to change the maximum file size for thumbnailing in its preferences. Go to Edit ➤ Preferences and look in Environment under Image Thumbnails to change this setting. You can find more information on customizing GIMP's preferences in Chapter 1. ■

By default, GIMP doesn't display hidden files or folders in the Current Folder panel. This usually keeps the listing in the panel clear of extraneous files. However, if the image you want to edit is in a hidden folder, or is a hidden file itself, you can show it in the listing by right-clicking the Current Folder panel and selecting Show Hidden Files from the context menu that appears. To open any given image from the Current Folder panel, simply double-click it or click the Open button in the bottom-right corner of the dialog. You can also select more than one file in the Current Folder dialog by holding Ctrl and clicking the files you want to select. GIMP also allows you to select a series of images by clicking the first image in the series and then holding Shift and clicking the last image. When you have your multiple images selected, clicking Open brings each of them up in their own individual image window. Regardless of how many images you have selected, clicking the Cancel button always closes the dialog without opening any files at all.

FIGURE 3-3

If an image is larger than 4MB, GIMP asks you to create the preview manually so you don't spend forever waiting for previews to be automatically generated.

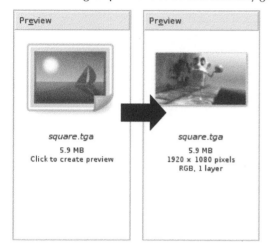

When looking for a specific file, it's often helpful if you change how the Current Folder panel sorts its listing. By default, it's sorted in ascending alphabetical order (0, 1, 2 … A, B, C …) and you can tell this from the downward-pointing triangle next to Name at the top of the panel. If you click Name, the arrow reverses direction and the files are sorted in reverse alphabetical order. You can also click the Modified button to sort the files by the date that they were last edited. A thing to note here is that regardless of sorting style, folders are always listed before regular files.

Beneath the Preview and Current Folder panels is a drop-down menu that controls which types of files get listed in the Current Folder panel. By default, GIMP has this set to All Images. However, if you know that you're looking for an image of a specific type, you can click this drop-down and choose the image type you want. Of course, sometimes, someone sends you an image that doesn't follow the standard naming convention of having an image name and a period followed by a short extension that's usually three or four characters long to indicate the type of file it is. For example, you may get "funny pic" as opposed to "funny pic.jpg." For those cases, you can select All Files from this drop-down and all of the files in the current folder are listed. The neat thing here is that even if the file is named weirdly — or even incorrectly — GIMP is very smart about figuring out what the image type is once you click the Open button.

Of course, on the rare occasion that GIMP can't figure this out automatically, you can force a file to be interpreted as a particular file type. You do this by expanding the Select File Type panel at the bottom of the dialog. By default this is collapsed and is set to Automatically Detected, but

Figure 3-4 shows what this panel looks like when you expand it. Here you can pick any of the file formats that GIMP understands and attempt to force that to be the file's type. This is a pretty useful function. However, more often than not, if GIMP can't read the image file, it's either in a format GIMP doesn't understand or the file itself is corrupted.

FIGURE 3-4

The Select File Type panel at the bottom of the Open File dialog, expanded

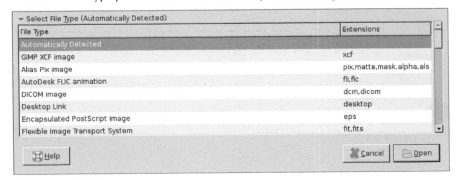

Other Ways to Open an Image

Besides using the File ➢ Open function, GIMP has a few other pretty slick ways to open files. One is the Open as Layers option in the menu. When you choose this option (File ➢ Open as Layers or Ctrl+Alt+O), GIMP provides you with a dialog that looks just like the Open Image dialog. However, there's a difference, and it happens when the image is loaded. Rather than opening your selected files in their own image windows, GIMP loads them as additional layers in the image window from which you chose File ➢ Open as Layers. Chapter 6 has more on working with layers, but this is a great way to load a set of images quickly into a single image window. An example of when this is useful would be if you've taken photographs with bracketed exposure settings and you want to tonemap them to get a higher dynamic range (HDR) in your final image. This gets all of those bracketed photos in the same file for you to play with in GIMP. For more on HDR techniques, have a look at Chapter 9.

Another pretty neat way that GIMP lets you open files is with its Open Location feature (File ➢ Open Location). Selecting this item in the File menu gives you a dialog like the one in Figure 3-5. This seemingly Spartan dialog gives you the ability to pull any image off of the Internet and load it directly into GIMP. All you need to do is type or paste the URI of the image into this dialog's text field and click the Open button. Upon doing this, GIMP fetches the desired image from the provided address and loads it into an image window for you to edit and modify.

Tip

When entering a URI, remember to include the prefix at the beginning of the URI scheme. For Internet addresses, this is typically `http://` for web sites and `ftp://` for FTP locations. ∎

FIGURE 3-5

The Enter Location dialog

Enter location (URI):

☐ Help   ✖ Cancel   ☐ Open

Warning

It's great that GIMP has the Open Location feature, but you should remember that images on the Internet are still subject to copyright and you may need to get permission from the image's original creator before making any changes to it in GIMP. ■

The last way to open an existing image in GIMP is to load one that you've opened in GIMP before. The quickest way to get at this is through the Open Recent item in the File menu (File ➤ Open Recent). This pops out a submenu that lists the last 10 images you had open in GIMP. Clicking any of the images in this list recalls that image back into an image window. Looking at this submenu on the left of Figure 3-6, you may notice that each of these 10 images has a keyboard shortcut associated with it. So if you want to open the image you most recently worked on, you navigate to it through this menu or simply press Ctrl+1. If you want to go further back in time, you can look at a more comprehensive list by opening the Document History dialog, shown on the right of Figure 3-6. This has a more complete list of the files you've opened in GIMP than the Open Recent submenu does. However, this dialog also gives you the ability to remove specific images from GIMP's history or clear it entirely.

FIGURE 3-6

On the left, the Open Recent submenu; on the right, GIMP's Document History dialog

Creating a Blank New Image

Another way to get an image in GIMP is to create that image yourself. You can provide yourself with a blank canvas and either paint or paste whatever your creative mind can muster. Fortunately, this is a fairly painless endeavor. Click File ➢ New or press Ctrl+N and you get a New Image dialog like the one in Figure 3-7.

FIGURE 3-7

GIMP's New Image dialog

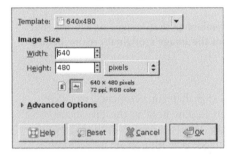

The New Image dialog allows you to choose the size of the canvas that you'll be working on in GIMP. The easiest way to start is to choose from the Template drop-down at the top of the dialog. The choices in this menu are a variety of common image sizes that you may run into for print, web, and television work. GIMP ships with around 20 predefined templates that specify an image size, resolution, and color space. You can actually add and remove templates to and from this menu with the Templates dockable dialog, as explained in Chapter 1. If you decide that none of the templates fit what you want to work on, you can manually determine your own size and details. By default, this dialog shows only options for changing image size and orientation. You can also choose the units you want to use with the drop-down to the right of the Width and Height text entry fields.

The thing to note, however, is that if you change your units from pixels to any of the real-world units, you'll want to pay attention the images's resolution. Usually it's set to 72ppi, the standard resolution for images destined for televisions or computer monitors. However, if you want to create something that you intend to print, you'll want to set the resolution to something higher, like 300ppi. Resolution is not one of the options available to you in the basic New Image dialog. To control that and other options, you need to expand the Advanced Options at the bottom of the dialog by clicking its arrow. Figure 3-8 shows the New Image dialog with the Advanced Options visible.

The first thing you can control with these options is the image's resolution. You actually have the ability to set horizontal (X) and vertical (Y) resolution independently if you click the chain-link icon to the right of the X and Y Resolution fields. This unlinks the two fields and allows you to adjust one without affecting the other. However, the situations where you'd want to do this are pretty rare. Typically, you'll want to keep this link enabled. Beneath the resolution options are a few more options. Most important of these is probably the Color Space setting. From this drop-down menu, you can set your image's color mode to be either RGB or grayscale.

GIMP's New Image dialog with Advanced Options visible

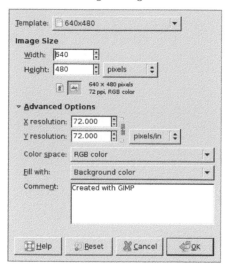

Below the Color Space drop-down is another one that allows you to control the initial Fill color for your new image. You can choose the current foreground or background colors in GIMP's color picker, a flat white, or Transparency, which is basically the same as having no fill on your new canvas. If you're creating something that you know is going to have any transparency to it, the last one is probably the best choice. The final field at the bottom of the dialog is the Comment field. This is where you can include notes on your image or simply indicate that you're the one who created it. This comment field is an additional bit of metadata that's embedded along with the image data. Most image formats support it in one form or another.

If at any time you want to put these settings back to their default values, simply click the Reset button at the bottom of the dialog. However, once you've gone through and adjusted the options for a new image to your liking, click the OK button at the bottom right of the dialog to get an image window for this new image and you'll be ready to rock.

Generating an Image from Plug-in or Hardware

So far you have seen how GIMP can open an image that already exists and you can create a blank canvas to build a new image from scratch. These aren't your only options, though. You can generate an image for GIMP to work on from a variety of different sources. All of this is controlled from the Create menu (File ➤ Create). An example of this menu is shown in Figure 3-9. Some of the options in this menu will vary depending on what hardware you have on your computer and what GIMP plug-ins you have installed.

FIGURE 3-9

The Create submenu in the File menu gives you options to get external image data into GIMP.

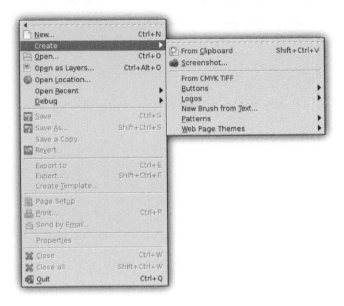

The first item in this menu, From Clipboard, is incredibly useful. It creates a new image with any image data you may have copied to your computer's clipboard. In case you weren't aware of this, nearly every modern operating system has the concept of a clipboard. It's kind of a communal temporary storage area for anything you highlight and copy. If you highlight text on a word processor document and right-click ➤ Copy or press Ctrl+C, that text gets stored on the clipboard. The same is true for image data. You can select an embedded image in a word processor document or an image on a web site and copy it to your system's clipboard. Once you've done that, you can create an image window with this image data instantly by clicking File ➤ Create ➤ From Clipboard or pressing Shift+Ctrl+V. This is useful when you want to take a selection from within one GIMP image and create a whole new image from it. The process is as simple as making a selection, copying (Ctrl+C), and creating from clipboard (Shift+Ctrl+V).

Creating an Image from a Screenshot

Say you're helping someone work on a web site by being their guinea pig and testing the site in your web browser for them. In doing so, you notice that parts of the site aren't lining up properly. Rather than go through the potentially arduous task of trying to describe the issue to this site's designer, you can take a screenshot and show exactly what you see. You can do this in GIMP by using the Screenshot feature (File ➤ Create ➤ Screenshot). When you choose this menu item you get a dialog like the one in Figure 3-10.

FIGURE 3-10

The Screenshot dialog allows you to take snapshots of all or parts of your computer screen.

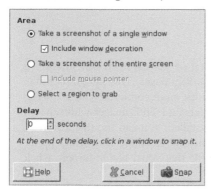

The Screenshot dialog allows you to capture a single window, your entire screen, or an arbitrary region that you select. The first two options are pretty straightforward. If you choose the Take a Screenshot of a Single Window option, GIMP changes your mouse cursor to crosshairs and the next window you click in is captured and that screen capture gets its own image window. When using this option, you also have the ability to choose whether the screenshot captures the window's borders and title bar, called *window decorations*. The Entire Screen option works as advertised, capturing your complete desktop as a single image and pulling that into a new GIMP image window. If you want to include the mouse cursor to point something out, there's a check box to enable that option. If you choose the third option, Select a Region to Grab, then when you click the Snap button at the bottom of the dialog, GIMP changes your cursor to crosshairs like you'd see if you were just capturing a single window. The difference here, though, is that this time you can click and drag your mouse to draw a box with that cursor. Anything within that box will be captured and brought into GIMP.

Occasionally, you may have to do some setup before you want to do the screen grab. This often happens if you need to take a screenshot of a program's menu. Normal menus go away if you click your mouse somewhere off of the menu, so there's no way you could bring up the menu and then go into GIMP and try to take an immediate screenshot. To do that, you need to use the Delay feature of the Screenshot tool. Simply increase the number in the Delay field to the number of seconds you would like GIMP to wait before taking the screenshot. Normally, 5 seconds is more than enough time. Then when you click the Snap button, you'll have that much time to go and open the menu you want to capture.

Incidentally, all of the figures in this book that are of GIMP's interface were taken with this tool.

Note
If you try using the Screenshot tool on a Mac, you may find that GIMP doesn't give you the expected results. Usually it only gives you a solid black image. This is largely because GIMP on Mac requires that you run in X11 and X11 can't see all of what Mac OS X sends to the screen. This makes GIMP's native

Screenshot tool almost completely ineffective. Fortunately, there's an alternative. In Mac versions of GIMP, the Create menu has another option: Grab. If you navigate to File ➤ Create ➤ Grab, you find three options: Screen, Selection, and Timed Screen. These correspond to GIMP's native Entire Screen, Region, and the Entire Screen option with a delay value. They should work as expected. ■

Creating an Image from a CMYK TIFF

Chapter 21 covers a few GIMP plug-ins that are worth installing on your system. One of them is the Separate+ plug-in, which helps GIMP work better with CMYK images. This plug-in doesn't give you native CMYK color space, but it does allow you to work more comfortably in a CMYK environment. One of its features is that it allows GIMP to understand TIFF images with separated CMYK channels. Once you have this plug-in properly installed, you can use this feature by choosing it from the Create submenu (File ➤ Create ➤ From CMYK TIFF). This brings up a File Chooser where you can select the separated CMYK TIFF file that you'd like to import. Click Open and the Separate+ plug-in does the rest for you.

Understand that this isn't the same as converting a CMYK image to RGB and it's definitely not the same as working directly in the CMYK color space. What it does is take each channel of the CMYK image and treat it as a layer mask for a layer that has a color of either cyan, magenta, yellow, or black. These layers are mixed using "Darken only" blend mode. This means that you have full access to all of GIMP's tools, but to get the results to work properly, you need to use those tools on every channel and you have to work in each channel in grayscale. Figure 3-11 shows what the Layers dialog looks like when you use this part of the Separate+ plug-in.

FIGURE 3-11

GIMP's Layers dialog after importing a separated CMYK TIFF image with the Separate+ plug-in

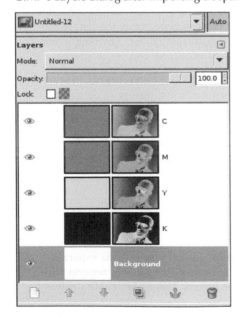

Tip

You might be tempted to convert this imported image to a flattened RGB image, work on it that way, and export that image back to CMYK, but this isn't necessarily a good idea. The reason for this is because conversions between RGB and CMYK are not symmetric. If you were to take a CMYK image and do a CMYK ➤ RGB ➤ CMYK conversion to it without making any additional changes between steps, the resulting image will likely have different colors than the original. There are a bunch of reasons for this, but the main one has to do with the fact that CMYK is based on four colors whereas RGB is based on three, and mapping between the two is a non-trivial task. ■

Using a Scanner to Import a Drawing or Photograph

The details of getting GIMP to recognize your scanner are explained in more detail in Appendix B, but once you have that set up, getting GIMP to use a scanner or even a webcam is surprisingly straightforward. Unfortunately, the process varies a bit depending on the operating system you're using.

Scanning in Windows and Mac

Fortunately, the process for getting images in GIMP for Windows and Mac users is pretty consistent. Basically, you navigate to File ➤ Create ➤ Scanner/Camera and a Select Source dialog pops up. Any scanners or webcams that you have installed on your computer appear here, as shown in Figure 3-12. When you select the device you want to use and click Select, the software that controls that device should load and allow you to either scan or snap a picture, depending on your selection. When it completes its image capture, it feeds directly to GIMP and resides in its own image window for you to edit at will.

FIGURE 3-12

The Select Source dialog that appears in Windows and Mac

Scanning in Linux with Xsane

Scanning in Linux uses a different system than the one you'll find in Windows or Mac OS X called Xsane. I know, I know; that sounds an awful lot like *insane*, but Xsane is actually a graphical interface for SANE, which is short for Scanner Access Now Easy. It's what's used in Linux to control your scanner. Appendix B has more on getting SANE to work on your Linux machine, but once you have that working, the Xsane interface is not all that different from what you find in other operating systems. To see it, navigate to File ➤ Create ➤ Xsane ➤ Device dialog. After you click this menu item, GIMP calls Xsane to check your system for installed devices. If you have more than one device installed, you may have to select from a list like the one in Windows and Mac OS X. Otherwise, Xsane pulls up its interface once it finds the device. From there, you can scan as many images as you like. Each time Xsane completes scanning, it sends its output directly to a new GIMP image window. When you're done scanning, choose File ➤ Quit in the Xsane interface to close Xsane and begin editing your scanned images in GIMP. Figure 3-13 shows how you bring up the Xsane interface from GIMP.

FIGURE 3-13

Bringing up Xsane from GIMP to scan in Linux

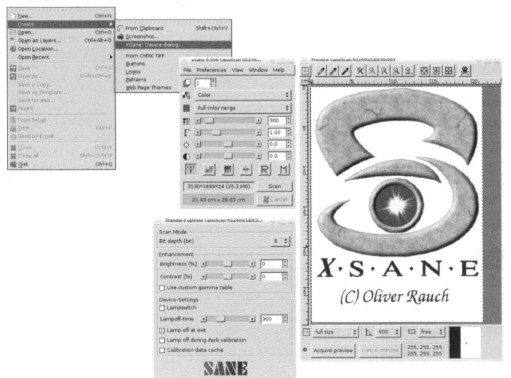

Letting GIMP's Automated Scripts Generate an Image

You can also let GIMP generate some frequently used images for you. These are created with a set of scripts that come bundled with GIMP, each affectionately referred to as a *script-fu*. These scripts add to submenus under Create, as shown in Figure 3-14.

Each script-fu has its own set of options and interface, many of which have parallels with some of the filters explained in Chapter 17. For the most part, though, they consist of picking some colors, adjusting some sliders, and possibly entering text for a button or logo. Then when you click OK, the script-fu does its automatic kung-fu action and generates one or more images for you. Figure 3-15 shows the results of each script-fu with default settings. You can also write your own script-fu to be included in this menu if you find yourself repeatedly creating the same type of image. You can find more on writing scripts in Chapter 22.

FIGURE 3-14

Script-fus available in File ⇨ Create, including buttons, logos, patterns, and web page themes

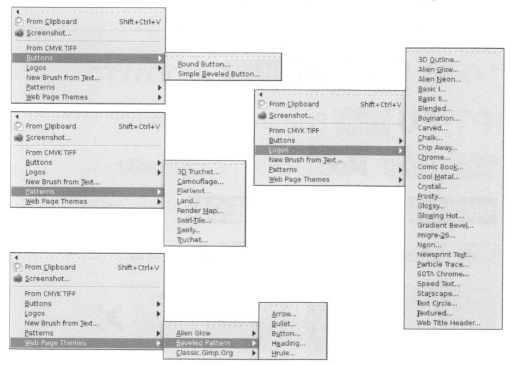

Managing Open Images

To help you manage the files that you have open, GIMP provides the Images dockable dialog, shown in Figure 3-16. Think of this an "asset bin" that shows each of the files you have open in your current session.

The Images dialog shows previews of each of the images that are open in GIMP. I've had editing sessions where I've had well over 20 images open in GIMP at the same time. Managing all of those image windows can get to be pretty daunting. If you're not careful, you can easily spend more time moving, minimizing, and maximizing those windows than actually modifying any images. The Images dialog is incredibly helpful in scenarios like this. The default view type shows your images in a list. However, you might want to use a grid view with as large of a preview as possible. To set up this configuration, use the Tab button in the upper right-hand corner of the dialog and make the following two selections:

1. **View as Grid** (Tab Button ➤ View as Grid).
2. **Gigantic Preview Size** (Tab Button ➤ Preview Size ➤ Gigantic).

FIGURE 3-15

Examples of each script-fu run with just its default settings

This gets you an Images dialog that looks like the one on the right of Figure 3-16. Now all you have to do is double-click the preview image that corresponds with the image you want to work on and that image window will come into focus at the top of your stack of windows.

FIGURE 3-16

The Images dockable dialog, your asset bin for your current GIMP session. On the left is the default list view. On the right is a grid view with larger preview images.

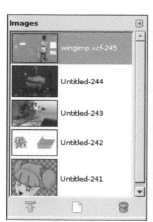

Working in the Image Window

Once you have an image window to play with, this is where the fun really starts. Chapter 1 has a thorough description of each part of the image window, but there are few helpful notes on navigating within the image window and using various tools in it. One of the first things to notice is what your mouse cursor changes to when it gets into this window. Unless you've changed your preferences, the cursor has two parts: a pointer that indicates exactly where your cursor is pointing and an icon that indicates the type of tool you're using. This icon should look similar to the corresponding tool icon in the Toolbox. Figure 3-17 shows what the cursor looks like in the image window for each tool you select. You can control whether you see these icons from the Preferences dialog (Edit ➤ Preferences ➤ Image Windows ➤ Mouse Pointers). Many artists prefer to show just the brush size outline for painting tools like the paintbrush, pencil, and eraser. It keeps less in your way as you paint.

A variety of controls are at your disposal for navigating around your image in the image window. You can certainly use the zoom value at the bottom of the window and the scrollbars to move in and around your canvas. However, GIMP offers some faster ways to navigate by using your mouse in combination with your keyboard. A good way to see this in action is to zoom in on your image. You could do this with the Zoom tool (Z), but rather than move your mouse from the image window to get to that tool, you can much more quickly press Ctrl and scroll your mouse wheel. Ctrl+scroll forward zooms in and Ctrl+scroll back zooms out. Another cool thing about zooming this way is that GIMP zooms in on the location your mouse cursor is over. So if you have a portrait and you want to zoom in on the subject's eye, you can put your mouse cursor over the eye and Ctrl+scroll directly to the eye.

FIGURE 3-17

Mouse cursors hint to you which tool you're currently using in the image window.

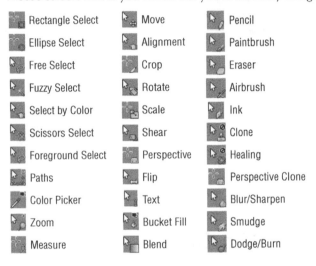

Rectangle Select	Move	Pencil
Ellipse Select	Alignment	Paintbrush
Free Select	Crop	Eraser
Fuzzy Select	Rotate	Airbrush
Select by Color	Scale	Ink
Scissors Select	Shear	Clone
Foreground Select	Perspective	Healing
Paths	Flip	Perspective Clone
Color Picker	Text	Blur/Sharpen
Zoom	Bucket Fill	Smudge
Measure	Blend	Dodge/Burn

Once you've chosen your new zoom level, you can *shrink wrap* your image window, or automatically resize it to fit your newly zoomed content, by clicking View ➤ Shrink Wrap or pressing Ctrl+R. In the event that you've zoomed in so far that the image is larger than the space available on your screen, GIMP will only shrink wrap within the constraints of your screen size. This means that you may still need to navigate within your zoomed view. For this, you could still use the scrollbars, on the side and bottom of the image window, but rather than move your mouse, you can again take advantage of your mouse wheel. Just scrolling the mouse wheel moves your view up and down the image vertically. To move your view horizontally, press Shift+scroll.

If you've used another image editor like Photoshop, you may be used to the Hand tool, which allows you to click anywhere in the image and drag it around your screen, like sliding a piece of paper around on your desk. GIMP has this functionality, but doesn't tie it to a specific tool in the Toolbox. You can use it by either middle-clicking and dragging your mouse around the image window or by holding down the space bar while moving your mouse. This is actually superior to the Hand tool because you always have access to it, regardless of which tool you're currently using. You can drag the canvas around whether you're painting, selecting, adding text, or anything else. It's incredibly powerful. Table 3-1 is a quick reference to these navigation shortcuts, which are good to remember while working in GIMP.

TABLE 3-1

Navigation Shortcuts for Quickly Moving around the Image Window

Shortcut	Description
Mouse wheel forward/back	Move view up/down
Ctrl+mouse wheel forward/back	Zoom in/out
Shift+mouse wheel forward/back	Move view left/right
Middle-click and drag	Move view freely
Spacebar+move mouse	Move view freely
Ctrl+R	Shrink-wrap window

Copying and Pasting

When working with images in GIMP, you'll find that you need to get image data from one image window to another, or even duplicated within the same window. All of this functionality happens with GIMP's copy and paste functions. GIMP offers a bit more than your standard word processor's copy and paste capabilities. As is standard in most modern programs, you can copy and paste data in GIMP by selecting it and clicking Edit ➢ Copy or Edit ➢ Paste, respectively. The standard Ctrl+C and Ctrl+V keyboard shortcuts for copy and paste also work as expected in GIMP. You also have Cut functionality, which copies the selected data to the clipboard while removing it from the image, by clicking Edit ➢ Cut or pressing Ctrl+X.

The real fun, though, comes from what GIMP can do that's beyond the standard behavior. For instance, a regular copy in GIMP is limited to the current active layer. So if you make a selection and click Edit ➢ Copy (Ctrl+C), you copy only the information on that layer to the clipboard, even if it's obscured by image data on another layer above it. However, if you want to copy data from all layers to the clipboard, you can click Edit ➢ Copy Visible and GIMP will take everything that's visible from your selection, merge it, and put it in your clipboard for future use. I use this functionality so frequently that I've actually mapped the Shift+Ctrl+C keyboard shortcut to it.

Fun Things You Can Do with Paste (Besides Eat It)

As explained earlier in this chapter, GIMP can access your computer's system clipboard and create a new image window from image data in that clipboard if you click File ➢ Create ➢ From

Clipboard. If you already have an image window available, though, you can paste that clipboard data directly into an active image by clicking Edit ➤ Paste or pressing Ctrl+V. Doing this creates a "floating selection" layer in the image that consists entirely of your pasted image data. You can see the floating selection in the Layers dialog, as shown in Figure 3-18.

Pasting image data in GIMP creates a floating selection layer on the image you're editing.

Once you have this floating selection, you have three choices:

- **Anchor the floating selection** — This merges the floating selection with the layer that was active when you performed the paste action. To anchor the selection, either click the anchor icon in the Layers dialog or press Ctrl+H. If you're using one of the selection tools or the Move tool you should also notice that your mouse cursor gets an anchor icon on it when you move it off of the selection. If you left-click when this happens, this also anchors the floating selection.

- **Create a new layer with the floating selection** — Do this if you want the floating selection to become its own real layer. To do this, click the New Layer icon at the bottom left of the Layers dialog or press Shift+Ctrl+N.

- **Delete the floating selection** — If you decide that you don't really need the image data in the floating selection, you can remove the selection by clicking the trashcan icon at the bottom right of the Layers dialog or clicking Layer ➤ Delete Layer from the menu.

There's more you can do than just a raw paste to a floating selection, though. Suppose you've used GIMP's selection tools (covered more in detail in Chapter 4) to select a portion of your image and you want to paste your clipboard data, but only in this selected area. For that, you want to use Paste Into (Edit ➤ Paste Into). This treats your current selection as a mask for your pasted data. Now if you move (M) the floating selection around, it only appears where your selection exists.

Note
Something to keep in mind here is that this selection mask persists only if you choose to anchor the floating selection. If you create a new layer with a floating selection that was created by Paste Into, it creates a new layer with all of the image data from the clipboard, not just the data in your selection. If you absolutely need a new layer for this pasted data, the workaround for this is to invert the selection (Ctrl+I) and delete the extraneous data (Delete). ■

If you want to take the image data in the clipboard and create a new layer, skipping the floating selection step, you can use the Paste As menu and click Edit ➤ Paste As ➤ New Layer. That's not the only handy function in this menu. Including this one, there are actually four useful things that you can paste a selection as:

- **New Image** — This is the exact same function found in File ➤ Create ➤ From Clipboard. It takes the image data that's currently residing on your system clipboard and creates a new image in GIMP.

- **New Layer** — As explained previously, this pastes the clipboard data directly into a new layer, skipping the floating selection step.

- **New Brush** — This item takes your clipboard image data and generates a GIMP brush out of it, accessible from the Brushes dialog. This is a very speedy way to create a new brush from a selection. The steps are as follows: make a selection, copy (Ctrl+C), paste as brush (Edit ➤ Paste As ➤ New Brush), and fill out the name field in the dialog that pops up. Easy!

- **New Pattern** — The same idea as the New Brush item, but this one creates a pattern that's accessible from the Patterns dialog.

Advanced Copy and Paste with Buffers

But wait, there's more! GIMP also offers you the ability to store and name multiple copies of data with named *buffers*. The way this works is by using the Buffer submenu under Edit. The process for creating a buffer goes pretty much like a regular copy or cut, except you navigate to Edit ➤ Buffer ➤ Cut Named, Edit ➤ Buffer ➤ Copy Named, or Edit ➤ Buffer ➤ Copy Visible Named. When you do this, a dialog pops up with a text field for you to provide a name for the buffer. Upon clicking OK, you have a named buffer created. Using this technique, you can create multiple selections and copy them to their own individual buffers for multiple reuses for as long as you have GIMP open. To make use of these buffers, click Edit ➤ Buffer ➤ Paste Named. This brings up the Buffers dockable dialog, which holds a list of each of your named buffers in it. Simply double-click the buffer you want to use, and it is pasted as a floating selection in your image window. You can also call up the Buffers dockable dialog whenever you want from the Windows ➤ Dockable Dialogs menu. Figure 3-19 shows the basic steps to creating a named buffer.

Note
When you close GIMP, your saved buffers are cleared out, so you cannot use them between GIMP sessions. If you want to reuse your buffers again in the future, the best solution is to create a GIMP file that has each buffer on its own layer. Then you can open that file and use those selections whenever you like. ■

FIGURE 3-19

From left to right, the Edit ➪ Buffer submenu, the dialog for naming your buffer, and the Buffers dockable dialog

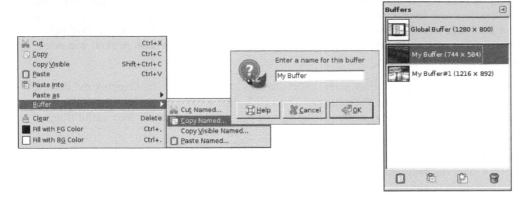

Taking Advantage of Undo

While working in GIMP, as with any other program, you're bound to make an error. You'll use the wrong filter settings or draw a stray line or change the color temperature to some painful yellow color. In these situations, you'll be glad for GIMP's very powerful undo functionality. GIMP has multiple levels of undo, which are limited only by the amount of RAM you have available on your computer. This means you can effectively click Edit ➢ Undo or press Ctrl+Z with impunity. Each time you perform an action in GIMP, be it a simple selection or an advanced filter or script, GIMP adds that action to its Undo History. You can see this by looking at the Undo History dockable dialog, available by default as a tab in the same dock as your Layers. Figure 3-20 shows this dialog.

With the action added to the Undo History, it appears at the bottom of the list in the dialog. You can reverse that action's effects by undoing it (Edit ➢ Undo or Ctrl+Z). When you do this, notice that the newest action in the history is no longer highlighted. The action above it is. If you Undo again, the next action is reversed and highlighted. In fact, if you click any action in this history, GIMP undoes everything back to that point. You can have GIMP re-perform steps by using Edit ➢ Redo (Ctrl+Y).

Warning

If you go back in the Undo History and perform a new action, GIMP removes all actions after that point from the history. Think about it like time travel. You went back in time and changed something, so everything that happens after that point is completely new. To put it another way, you can't just undo any arbitrary action in the Undo History without having an effect on the actions made after it. If you go back in the history and change one thing, you'll have to manually redo all of the subsequent actions after that. ■

FIGURE 3-20

GIMP's Undo History

Tip

You can increase or decrease the number of undos in the Undo History by clicking Edit ➤ Preferences and looking in Environment under Resource Consumption. The first two items there control your levels of undo. By default, GIMP has a minimum of five undo levels and will keep adding actions to the Undo History until it takes up 64MB of RAM. After that point, if you perform another action, the oldest action you have in the history is removed.

It's worth noting here that these values in the Preferences dialog are for each image window you have open. If you plan on having only one image open at a time, setting this value very high won't pose too much of a problem. However, if you intend on having multiple large images open in GIMP, a more conservative Maximum Undo Memory would be advisable. ■

On occasion, you may find that you've worked for a long time on an image and you feel dissatisfied with the whole process. You're not pleased with any of your edits. However, you may have performed so many actions that undoing as far back in the history as possible doesn't get you back to where you started. Fortunately, GIMP has a feature called Revert to help with this. To use it, click File ➤ Revert. This reloads your image from the hard drive, effectively taking it back to its original state. The only caveat here is that Revert takes you back to the last time you saved the file, not to its state when you first loaded it into GIMP. This means that if you save somewhere along the way while editing, Revert takes you back only that far.

Tip

To deal with the Revert issue, a good habit to use is to save multiple versions of your file as you work on it. The File ➤ Save a Copy function is a good, fast way to do this. Now you can save works in progress while retaining at least some form of the Revert functionality. You see more on saving in the next section. ■

Saving Files

So you've finished editing your image and you want to save it so you can share it with others and possibly work on it more in the future. For this, you'll have to use GIMP's various save functions. For the most part, saving an image in GIMP is nearly the same as opening one. All Save functions live in the File menu, as shown on the left of Figure 3-21. When saving, GIMP presents you with a File Chooser dialog (shown on the right of Figure 3-21) that's specific to saving.

FIGURE 3-21

On the left, the Save items in the File menu; on the right, GIMP's standard Save dialog

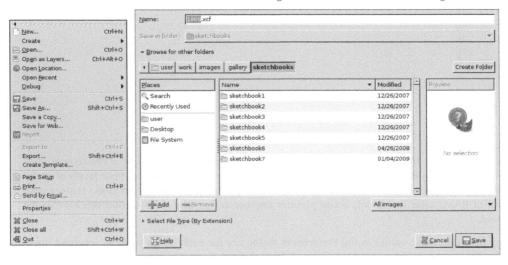

Two primary differences exist between the Save dialog and the Open dialog: the Name text field, and the Create Folder button on the upper-right side. Both are pretty self-explanatory. The Name field is where you type the name of the image you want to save. As of GIMP 2.7, you can only save images in GIMP's native XCF format. However, GIMP is capable of applying lossless gzip or bzip2 compression, which helps save disk space. The major difference between the two compression formats is that bzip2 tends to yield a smaller file, but it can take longer than gzip to compress and decompress. There's more on the XCF file format in the next section, but if you want to use either of these compression formats, simply add either .bz2 or .gz to the end of the filename in the Name field. You can also stipulate the file type by using the Image Type drop-down menu at the bottom right of the Save Image dialog. If you type a file extension on the name, like .jpg or .png or .bmp, GIMP will automatically figure out the type of file format you want to use. You can find more on specific file formats in the next section. If you'd rather be more explicit, you"re welcome to use the Image Type drop-down menu that"s beneath the Current Folder and Preview panels.

The Create Folder button above the Preview panel does as advertised. It creates a new folder in the Current Folder panel and immediately offers to let you give that new folder a custom name.

Once you give that folder a name, though, be aware that GIMP doesn't give you the ability to move or delete folders or files from within its Save dialogs. If you want to do these things, it's best to use your system's file manager to perform those tasks.

So what do GIMP's save options actually do? The following list should shed some light on that question:

- **Save (Ctrl+S)** — This is the standard save behavior. GIMP pops up the Save Image dialog and creates an XCF image file; storing it in a specified location on your hard drive. If you've already saved the file, choosing this option simply overwrites the existing copy.

- **Save As (Shift+Ctrl+S)** — If you've already saved the file, but you want to save it with a different name or in a different location on your hard drive, this is the option you want to choose. Choosing this option always brings up the Save Image dialog.

- **Save a Copy** — Choosing this option allows you to save a copy of your image somewhere on your hard drive, but it doesn't load that newly saved version back into GIMP. This allows you to save incremental versions of your project without obliterating the possibility of reverting the file all the way back to its pristine beginning.

- **Save for Web** — This option is available only if you've installed the Save for Web plug-in. It provides a function similar to Photoshop's Save for Web feature, optimizing your image's file size and appearance for use as a JPEG, GIF, or PNG on a web site. For more information on plug-ins, check out Chapter 21.

GIMP's Native Format: XCF

As you may have noticed when opening files, GIMP supports an enormous variety of image formats. However, of all these formats, there's one that GIMP supports the best and that's it's native format, XCF. The XCF format is actually named after the eXperimental Computing Facility, the computing lab at the University of California, Berkeley where GIMP's creators, Spencer Kimball and Peter Mattis, wrote the first version of GIMP. XCF has the most complete support of GIMP's features, including layers, paths, active channels, transparency, and even guides. This means that if you're planning on saving your edits and working on an image in future sessions, XCF is the format you want to choose. It's for this very reason that the only image format that you can save directly to is XCF.

Note
XCF supports GIMP's features, but some data, such as named buffers and the Undo History, are not stored in the XCF format. The addition of this support is unlikely to happen in the near future, so it's good to keep this in mind when saving. Some data, like undo, is retained only for the extent of the current GIMP session. ■

Another advantage of using XCF is its load speed. In many ways, the XCF file format is a direct copy of the image data GIMP has in memory, stored straight to your hard drive. Because there's no translation necessary, this makes opening and saving XCF files incredibly fast; much faster than any other file format that GIMP supports.

The only real disadvantage to using the XCF format is that it's not well-supported in a variety of other graphics applications. Because this format is essentially a memory dump of the raw data GIMP works with, it's difficult to translate for other applications to read. That said, there's been quite a bit of progress in this arena. There is now an official specification for the XCF format and GIMP developers have been working with developers of other Free Software graphics tools like Krita and Inkscape to design a unified format that can more easily be used for unified data exchange. In the meantime, however, if you intend on sharing your work with artists who use other applications, you may want to choose a different format, such as Photoshop's ubiquitous PSD format.

Other Formats

Of course, the XCF format isn't the only format that GIMP can read and write. GIMP supports an impressive list of image formats, some of which aren't even really image formats at all! For example, GIMP can save an image as straight C source code, for developers who want a raw way to incorporate a raster image in their software. GIMP also supports a variety of old and "outdated" image formats. This is particularly helpful when you're faced with an old image format for which other programs have discontinued support.

However, I already told you that as of the most recent version of GIMP, it can only save to the XCF format. How do you get files out of GIMP in other formats? You do this with GIMP's new Export feature. Refer back to Figure 3-21. The File menu on the left shows three items below the Save items: Export to, Export, and Create Template. The following explains what each of these items does:

- **Export to** — This functionality is only really available once you've already exported the image once. When you export your image to a non-XCF format, GIMP remembers where you exported it to and what format you used. This way, you can quickly hit Ctrl+E while you're working and regularly update your exported file.

- **Export** — Choose this option and you get a File Chooser window that's nearly identical to the Save Image window. The main difference is that you have at your disposal the full array of image formats that GIMP supports for exporting your image. You can stipulate the image type using the Image Type drop-down at the bottom of the window. Alternatively, if you know the file extension for your desired image type (such as .tif, .jpg, .png, etc.), you can type that directly at the end of the filename in the Name field and GIMP will figure it out for you. Table 3-2 covers all of the image formats that GIMP supports.

- **Create Template** — If you discover that the image size and color mode you're using are something you'll be using repeatedly in the future, you may want to save the file as a template for future work. Bear in mind here that this will not save the image in the image window or even your guides, if you have any. Templates store only the file's color mode and image size. Once the template is saved, though, you can always access it when you're creating a new image or directly from the Templates dockable dialog.

  Probably the most attractive image format for working with other artists is Photoshop's PSD format. GIMP can both open and export files in this format, but there are a few things to keep in mind. The most important thing to realize is that GIMP does not have all of the features that Photoshop has and cannot therefore show those on PSD files it opens. For example, Photoshop has *adjustment layers*, which are quick ways of adding procedural, non-destructive filters to a layer. GIMP does not yet have a feature analogous to this one, so if you try to open a PSD file that has adjustment layers, GIMP will read each layer's image data just fine, but the effects created by adjustment layers will be ignored. This means that if you're working in a team where other artists are using Photoshop, you should keep this limitation in mind. There are ways to re-create the effects of adjustment layers in GIMP, but they require a bit more work. Fortunately, loading GIMP-saved PSD files in Photoshop is much less troublesome.

Note

Looking back at Figure 3-21, you may notice that there's an additional option there called Send By Email. This is actually a feature provided by a plug-in and it's not available on all platforms. It basically opens up a dialog which allows you to create a simple e-mail with your image attached and send it to someone. There's a caveat with the current version of this plug-in, though. It requires that you have sendmail, a fairly common mail transfer agent (MTA), installed and configured on your system. Most modern Linux installations don't include a properly configured sendmail daemon, so there's a good chance that this feature won't work for you even if it does show up in the menu. Hopefully future versions of this plug-in will integrate more smoothly with whatever your preferred e-mail client is. ■

Table 3-2 has a full list of the formats GIMP supports, along with some notes on each one.

TABLE 3-2

Image Formats Supported by GIMP

Format	Extension(s)	Read	Write	Compression	Notes
GIMP XCF	xcf	Yes	Yes	Lossless RLE	GIMP's native format.
Alias Pix	pix, matte, mask, alpha, als	Yes	Yes		
AutoDesk FLIC	fli, flc	Yes	Yes		Animation format, similar to GIF. Requires gray-scale or indexed color.
bzip	xcf.bz2, bz2, xcfbz2	Yes	Yes	Lossless bzip2	GIMP's native format, zipped.
Colored HTML	xhtml	No	Yes	None	Produces HTML code that creates this image.
C source	C	No	Yes	None	
Desktop link	desktop	Yes	No	None	Configuration file for desktop icons in Linux.

continued

TABLE 3-2	(continued)				
Format	**Extension(s)**	**Read**	**Write**	**Compression**	**Notes**
DICOM	dcm, dicom	Yes	Yes		"Digital Imaging and Communications in Medicine" image.
Encapsulated Postscript	eps	Yes	Yes		A format often used for printing.
Flexible Image Transport System	fit, fits	Yes	Yes		Used primarily for scientific data.
G3 fax	g3	Yes	No		Stored fax data.
GIF	gif	Yes	Yes	Lossless LZW	Web standard image format.
GIMP brush	gbr, gpb	Yes	Yes	Lossless PNG	Image format used for GIMP brushes. Based on PNG.
Animated GIMP brush	gih	Yes	Yes		Animated Brush for GIMP.
GIMP pattern	pat	Yes	Yes	Lossless PNG	Image format used for GIMP gradients. Based on PNG.
GIMP XJT compressed	xjt, xjtgz, xjtbz2	Yes	Yes		Older GIMP format.
gzip	xcf.gz, gz, xcfgz	Yes	Yes	Lossless gzip	GIMP's native format, zipped.
HTML table	html, htm	No	Yes	None	Creates an HTML table where each cell is colored as a pixel in the image.
JPEG	jpg, jpeg, jpe	Yes	Yes	Lossy JPEG	Common format for photographs. Limited CMYK support in GIMP.
KISS CEL	cel	Yes	Yes		Image file for use in Kisekae UltraKiss programming.

TABLE 3-2 *(continued)*

Format	Extension(s)	Read	Write	Compression	Notes
MS Windows Icon	ico	Yes	Yes		Commonly used for icons in Windows.
MS WMF	wmf	Yes	No		Microsoft Windows metafile.
Paint Shop Pro	psp, tub, pspimage	Yes	No	Lossless	Native image format for Paint Shop Pro. Supports layers.
PBM	pbm	No	Yes		Portable Bitmap image. Commonly used in Unix and Linux.
PDF	pdf	Yes	No		Portable Document Format. Made popular by Adobe. Used largely in printing.
PGM	pgm	No	Yes		Portable Graymap image. Commonly used in Unix and Linux.
Photoshop	psd	Yes	Yes	Lossless	Limited read support for Photoshop features that GIMP doesn't share.
PNG	png	Yes	Yes	Lossless PNG	Portable Network Graphics. An excellent modern format for single-layer graphics work.
PNM	pnm, ppm, pgm, pbm	Yes	Yes		Portable Network Map. Related to PBM and PGM.
Postscript	ps	Yes	Yes		Related to EPS, but larger. Used specifically for print.
PPM	ppm	No	Yes		Portable Pixmap image. Related to PBM and PGM.
Raw image	n/a	Yes	Yes		Raw image data in a specific format usually used by cameras.

continued

TABLE 3-2	(continued)				
Format	**Extension(s)**	**Read**	**Write**	**Compression**	**Notes**
SGI IRIS	sgi, rgb, bw, icon	Yes	Yes		Raster image format commonly used by older Silicon Graphics workstations.
SUN Rasterfile	im1, im8, im24, rs, ras	Yes	Yes		Raster image format commonly used by older SUN workstations.
SVG	svg	Yes	No		XML-based vector image format used in may Free Software tools.
Targa	tga, vda, icb, vst	Yes	Yes		Older image format with an alpha channel. Commonly used in television. Limited CMYK support in GIMP.
TIFF	tiff, tif	Yes	Yes	Lossless LZW	Common print image format. Limited CMYK support in GIMP.
Windows BMP	bmp	Yes	Yes	None	Bitmap file format commonly used in Microsoft Windows.
X bitmap	xbm, icon, bitmap, xpm	Yes	Yes	None	Bitmap file format commonly used by the X Windowing System used by Unix and Linux.
X window dump	xwd	Yes	Yes	None	A memory dump of the image data seen by the X Windowing System in Unix and Linux.
ZSoft PCX	pcx, pcc	Yes	Yes	Lossless RLE	Old PC Paintbrush image format.

Summary

Annnnnnd ... scene! This chapter had a good chunk of information in it. You saw the full myriad of ways to get images into GIMP. You learned that you could open images in their own image windows, as layers in other image windows, and as multiple layers in the same image. You also discovered that you can have GIMP give you a blank canvas to start with or use a scanner, webcam, screenshot, or even a little script-fu to have GIMP build an image for you. Once you loaded an image into an image window, you discovered all of the quick and handy methods to work your way around there, zooming, panning, and scrolling at will. You also found out how to share image data between image windows by using GIMP's more-than-standard copy and paste features. This chapter also showed you how to use Undo to reverse mistakes and give you more freedom while working. Once you finished editing your pictures in GIMP, you got to see how to save that image to your hard drive for sharing with others or continuing work on it in the future. And, wow, that's a huge list of image formats that GIMP supports, isn't it?

Next step, working with tools!

A Brief Overview of GIMP's Tools

I n any industry that requires you to "build" something, you require a toolset to do the work. Within it, the individual tools have specific purposes. GIMP is no different. GIMP comes with many tools — so many, in fact, that it takes a while for those new to the interface to become acquainted with what is available, and to learn how to use each one in a production environment.

In this chapter you learn about using many of GIMP's tools to enhance, manipulate, and edit your work. You get started by examining the View menu.

IN THIS CHAPTER

Using selection tools to pick out parts of your images

Making modifications with image tools

Using enhancement tools for tweaking and cleaning up images

The View Menu

This section covers the View menu in GIMP's image window. You can adjust the "view" of your work within the image window with the many menu items that are available. This section looks at how to modify your work within the image window using operations such as Zoom, Snap to Grid, and much more.

Modifying Your View in the Image Window

Sometimes when you are working with GIMP, you want to see parts of your work more clearly, enlarged or shrunk down to specific sizes. No matter what you decide you want or need, GIMP can accommodate your needs.

In the image window, click the View menu and look at the many options available to you in the tools offered here. You can adjust the view, which is how you see your image while working. For example, you can start with the View ➤ New View menu selection, which opens a new image window in which you can work. This new window displays an *instance* of the same image, meaning that you can use it to work on a detailed portion of your image while still seeing the overall image without constantly zooming in and out.

You can use View ➤ Dot for Dot to enable (check) or disable (uncheck) Dot for Dot mode. If this option is disabled, the image is represented and displayed at its correct size, which is the size it will be when printed. One of the primary things to remember when working within this mode is that the image in the image window needs to be identical to the current screen resolution set in your operating system's settings. You can also set this within GIMP's preferences.

Zooming is one of the most important features available in the View menu. Here, you can snuggle up to your edited work. The zooming capabilities of GIMP run deep and most if not all of the options available within the Zoom submenu are extremely helpful. Zooming to an arbitrary magnification on a specific part of your image is typically faster with the Zoom tool or with Ctrl+scroll on your mouse. The Zoom submenu, however, is very useful for zooming to specific sizes like 100% or fitting to the image window.

You can access the Zoom submenu by going to View ➤ Zoom in the image window. When you first view this selection, you see a percentage (for example, 33%) that shows you the scale currently set for the image window. You can adjust the percentage beforehand and then go to View ➤ Zoom ➤ Revert Zoom to restore your previous zoom level. You can then expand the Zoom menu by selecting View ➤ Zoom ➤ Revert Zoom or using the backtick (`) keyboard shortcut. If you changed the zoom settings, this option restores your previous zoom level.

Other options available in the Zoom submenu are Zoom Out, Zoom In, Fit Image in Window, and Fill Window, as well as preconfigured setting options and an Other option, which allows you to specify settings manually.

To zoom in and out, you can use the View ➤ Zoom ➤ Zoom Out and View ➤ Zoom ➤ Zoom In menu options. Both allow you to move in and out (quickly and accurately) of your image window's contents, giving you a quick and easy way to scan your work, or to perform other editing tasks, such as cropping.

Other options for zooming are View ➤ Zoom ➤ Fit Image in Window (Shift+Ctrl+R) and View ➤ Zoom ➤ Fill Window. Both are helpful when you need to resize the view of your work. The Fit Image in Window operation zooms the image so the full canvas fits the dimensions of the image window, adding padding if necessary. The Fill Window option tries to ensure that the entire space of the image window is filled with your image, often requiring you to scroll either vertically or horizontally to see all parts of the image.

If you need to zoom manually, use the View ➤ Zoom ➤ Other menu option, which allows you to configure the zoom ratio in the dialog shown in Figure 4-1. This tool is helpful when you want to apply very specific zoom ratios to your work. As well, you can use preconfigured zoom ratios for quick changes to your image window. Access them directly in the View ➤ Zoom submenu. One of the most useful ratios in this menu is the 1:1 ratio, which can be quickly activated by pressing 1 on your keyboard.

Tip

You can speed up your editing process by using a wheel-mouse. For example, you can quickly zoom in on a feature of your image by placing your mouse cursor over it and using Ctrl+scroll up. If you Ctrl+scroll down, you zoom out. ∎

FIGURE 4-1

Using the Zoom Ratio dialog to adjust specific zoom settings for viewing your image within the image window

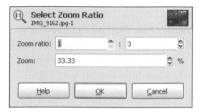

You can also view your image within the image window using the Shrink Wrap (Ctrl+R) and Fullscreen (F11) options within the View menu. Use View ➤ Shrink Wrap to shrink the image window to fit exactly around your image, or use View ➤ Fullscreen to expand the image window to the full size of your currently used desktop, whether running OS X, Linux, or Windows. Particularly with Windows, the image window can be obscured by the Toolbox and Dock when in Fullscreen mode. To rectify this, you can either hide these docks by pressing Tab or change them from Utility Windows to Normal Windows in the Preferences window (Edit ➤ Preferences) under Window Management.

The last option covered in this section is the View ➤ Navigation Window option shown in Figure 4-2. Here, you can move to any location on your image within the image window. This is very helpful if you are working on an extremely large image and do not want to use the scroll bars to navigate back and forth.

FIGURE 4-2

Using the Navigation dialog to access any area on your image in the image window. This tool is helpful when used on large images.

Using Display Filters to Color Correct GIMP to Your Monitor

In traditional photography, color correction is the process of using colorized filter sets (often referred to as color gels) to modify the light source of your image. You might want to do this when multiple light sources are used in one image; you can apply a filter to keep all light sources the same to avoid any problems in the final print. For example, if you were to take footage of an object inside a green room, you may want to apply a green filter to your light source to keep the "balance" of the light to avoid any aesthetic problems when viewing your final image. You adjust the color of the light source on a scale called Color Temperature.

The real purpose of the View ➤ Display Filters menu item is to modify how your image is displayed on your monitor. Display Filters don't actually change your image file in any savable way. However, by using them (particularly the Color Management or Color Proof filters), you can ensure that the image on your screen is being displayed with accurate colors. This way, if you're doing color correction, you can be reasonably sure that the colors you see on your monitor will match the colors seen on other displays and even in print. To learn more about color correction, please refer to Chapter 9. Figure 4-3 shows the Color Display Filters dialog where you can add any available filter to your work.

FIGURE 4-3

Color-correcting your work is easy when using Color Display filters. You can use any of the available filters to augment and enhance your viewable image.

Note

If you want the best results, do less editing and more hardware preparation and planning. For example, the simple process of "white balancing" your digital camera prevents the need to use most filters or enhancements. The thing to remember here is, for higher-quality final products, it makes sense to make sure the image being created is optimized to its full potential before importing and then editing it with GIMP or any other digital image editing software. Also note that some cameras apply automated color correction, which is similar to manually applying filters in GIMP, except the camera does it with sensors and code that automates the process. ■

Showing and Hiding Information

When you need to show (or hide) information in your current image window view, you can use the View menu options such as Show Selection, Show Layer Boundary, Show Guides, and Show Grid.

When working with the View ➤ Show Selection option, you can toggle the marching ants outline of your selection within the image window — when checked it shows the outline, and when unchecked it removes it. The View ➤ Show Layer Boundary option is similar to Show Selection, except it toggles the visibility of the active layer's boundary.

You can select to show guides and a grid for easier editing when using your rulers. Use View ➤ Show Guides (Shift+Ctrl+T) and View ➤ Show Grid to toggle them on and off. You should take note that if you haven't added any guides to your image (click and drag from the rulers in the image window to add), then you won't see any change if you toggle Show Guides. Figure 4-4 shows the use of the Show Grid view. The grid is useful if you're working on an image that requires precision, such as anything you may draw on graph paper.

FIGURE 4-4

Working in the image window using Grid view. This view is configured in the View menu by selecting Show Grid. Using this grid makes it easier to use your rulers.

You can also use the View ➤ Show Sample Points option in the View menu. This allows you to toggle the showing of sample points within your image window. You can define sample points in your image to help produce balanced photos. The Sample Points dialog doesn't modify your sample points; it only displays the color values for those (up to four) sampled pixels. Add a sample point by Ctrl+clicking either ruler in the image window and dragging your mouse to a location on your image. After you add them, you can change the location of sample points by clicking and dragging them. If you haven't added any sample points, toggling the Show Sample Points item doesn't hide or reveal anything.

Snapping Controls

Snapping controls let you align your part of work to various features of GIMP's image window, such as guides or the canvas edges, with little effort.

Sometimes when you are working within the image window, you need to adjust and align your image to the active guides, grid, active path, or canvas edges of your work. These controls make it easier to make accurate adjustments to parts of your image without the need to zoom in. You don't have to be precise with your movement. Just drag your layer or selection near the snapping feature (guides, grid, edges, and so on) and the nearest boundary or center point of your layer/selection snaps to it.

When you need to align your image in the image window to the guides you can use the View ➤ Snap to Guides option (enabled by default) within the View menu. Here, if your guides are visible (View ➤ Guides option enabled), you can visually align your image to the current guide configuration. In fact, even if your guides are hidden, your selection or layer will still snap to them if you have Snap to Guides enabled. The View ➤ Snap to Grid option works identically to the Guides option, except it aligns the image to the image grid as defined in the Preferences window under Default Grid (Edit ➤ Preferences; Default Grid). As previously covered, you can make the grid visible by choosing View ➤ Show Grid.

You can also use View ➤ Snap to Canvas Edges to align your image to the canvas edges, which may or may not be visible if your image fits the canvas completely. Use View ➤ Snap to Active Path to snap the image in line with the active path, if you have any paths in your project. This is a valuable feature if you're trying to place items along a path or defined by a path. Have a look at Chapter 5 for more information on editing paths.

Note

You may see a Use GEGL menu item at the bottom of the View menu. GEGL is the next-generation graphics library for future versions of GIMP. This feature is covered in more detail in Chapter 9, but at this point it's not recommended to work with this feature enabled because GEGL has not yet been optimized for performance in the latest version of GIMP. ■

Padding Color

There are five menu items within the Padding Color submenu. Select View ➤ Padding Color ➤ From Theme to use the current theme's background color, or View ➤ Padding Color ➤ Light Check Color and View ➤ Padding Color ➤ Dark Check Color to set the padding color to match either the light or dark color used in the checkerboard pattern used to indicate transparency in the image window. When a manual color adjustment needs to be made, you can use the View ➤ Padding Color ➤ Select Custom Color option.

You can find one final Padding Color option in the View ➤ Padding Color submenu. Select the As in Preferences option to reset the padding color back to what's defined in the Appearance section of the Preferences window (Edit ➤ Preferences; Image Windows ➤ Appearance).

Showing and Hiding Parts of the Image Window

Other ways to work with and manipulate your view are with the Show Menubar, Show Rulers, Show Scrollbars, and Show Statusbar options, all found in GIMP's image window View menu. All of these options allow you to adjust the view of the image window. Sometimes when using smaller screens to edit your work, you may need to remove some of the image window's interface features while working. This way you can use more of the desktop's viewable space while editing.

The View ➤ Show Menubar menu option allows you to toggle the visibility of the menu bar on the top of the image window. Some GIMP users prefer to access the menus by right-clicking the image window; for them it makes sense to hide the menu bar since they use it so rarely. View ➤ Show Rulers toggles the rulers on and off (found on the top and leftmost portion of the image window). View ➤ Show Scrollbars toggles the visibility of the scrollbars found on the bottom and leftmost portions of the image window, and View ➤ Show Statusbar toggles the visibility of the bottom portion of the image window, where processing requests are shown as well as helpful information and other tool icons.

Selection Tools

When working with digital images, you must select the pixels you want to modify. Only then can you perform operations, such as filling the pixels with a solid color, running a filter on them, or erasing all content from those pixels. GIMP's selection tools are in the Tools menu (Tools ➤ Selection Tools) and are accessible from the Toolbox. GIMP has seven tools to help you select pixels in your images: Rectangle Select (R), Ellipse Select (E), Free Select (F), Fuzzy Select (U), Select by Color (Shift+O), Intelligent Scissors Select (I), and Foreground Select.

Tip
You can also use GIMP's Paths tool, covered in Chapter 5, for selecting. ∎

The selection tools in GIMP are designed to be most beneficial for specific situations. However, these tools share many common settings. One common feature lets you move any selection area around the image window without modifying the pixels within that area. To do this, Alt+click and drag your mouse cursor in the image window using any of GIMP's selection tools. Most common settings are accessible from the Tool Options dialog when you have a selection tool active. The following is a list of options that are available to all selection tools:

- **Mode** — When making a complex selection, you often need to combine selection tools. These modes facilitate that:
  - **Replace** — (The default) If you make a selection in your image window and use a selection tool in this mode, your new selection replaces the old one.
  - **Add (Shift)** — In this mode, your new selection is combined with any selection already made on your image.
  - **Subtract (Ctrl)** — Use this mode with your selection tool to remove pixels from an existing selection.

- **Intersect (Shift+Ctrl)** — This mode creates a selection from the overlap between an existing selection and the selection created by your active selection tool.
- **Antialiasing** — Enable this option to smooth the edges of your selection. You can read more about antialiasing in Chapter 7.
- **Feather Edges** — *Feathering* softens the edges of your selection. If you click this check box, GIMP reveals a slider control that enables you to adjust your selection's feather radius (in pixels).

Rectangle Select

Activate the Rectangle Select tool by clicking its icon in the Toolbox (by default, it's the very first icon) or by using the keyboard shortcut, R. Then, click and drag in the image window where you want to make your selection and then release your mouse button.

Square control handles appear at the corners of your selection, indicating that your selection is editable. Click and drag these handles to adjust the height and width of your selection. If you hover your mouse cursor along an edge of your selection rectangle in the space between the corner handles, you see an edge handle. Click and drag it to adjust the edge's position. Figure 4-5 shows an image with a rectangular selection ready for editing.

FIGURE 4-5

When you use the Rectangle Select tool, your selections can be tweaked with the help of control handles.

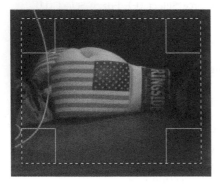

If you hold down Shift while adjusting the size of your selection box, your entire selection area maintains its proportions as you move that handle. If you're making a new selection with the Rectangle Select tool, hold Shift to keep the width and height of your selection box equal. Holding Ctrl while adjusting a selection causes it to resize relative to the center of your selected rectangle. Use Shift+Ctrl to make a proportional selection adjusted relative to its center.

The following list describes the settings in the Tool Options dialog that are specific to the Rectangle Select tool:

- **Round Corners** — Enable this check box and use its radius slider to adjust the radius of your corners.

- **Expand from Center** — Enable this check box and your selection grows and shrinks relative to its center.

- **Fixed** — When you enable this check box, you can lock the proportions of your selection box. The drop-down menu to the right of this label gives you four options:

  - **Aspect Ratio** — By default, if you're making a new selection, this option locks your selection box to the proportion of a square. If you're editing a selection, its proportions are maintained. You can type the aspect ratio you want to use in the text field below this drop-down. Enter your ratios in the format of *(width):(height)*, such as 2:1 or 4:3.

  - **Width** — Choose this option to constrain your selection to the Width value in the text field.

  - **Height** — This option constrains the height of your selection to the value entered in the text field.

  - **Size** — Use this option to lock your selection to an exact set of dimensions. Use the text field to enter a size in the format of *(width)x(height)*, such as 640 × 480.

- **Position** — If you need pixel-perfect accuracy, use the X and Y fields to move your selection around your image. These values treat the upper-left corner of your image as the origin and relate the upper-left corner of your selection to that.

- **Size** — Use these Width and Height fields to set the size of your selection. If you use the Fixed Size option, these fields are unavailable.

- **Highlight** — If you enable this check box, anything outside of your selection box is darker.

- **Guides** — This drop-down menu, with the default value of No Guides, gives you the ability to add guide lines to your selection box.

- **Auto Shrink** — Click this button and GIMP attempts to guess the feature of your image that you're trying to select. It adjusts the size of your selection rectangle to reflect that.

- **Shrink Merged** — By default, the Auto Shrink feature works on only the active layer. Enable this check box and GIMP looks at all the layers in your project to guess your selection.

Ellipse Select

To make a selection on an organic form, the Rectangle tool isn't necessarily the best tool for the job. This is where the Ellipse Select tool comes in handy. It's the second tool in the Toolbox and you can activate it there or use its keyboard shortcut, E.

The options for using the Ellipse Select tool are the same as for the Rectangle Select tool, except it doesn't have a Round Corners setting.

Free (Lasso) Select

The Free Select tool is the ideal tool for making complex selections. Enable this tool from the Toolbox by clicking the lasso icon or from the image window using its keyboard shortcut, F.

The Free Select tool enables you to use your mouse to draw a selection area in the image window. Left-click in the image window to add a control point. Then when you move your cursor, a line connects your cursor to that control point. Left-click again to create another control point. You can edit any control point by clicking and dragging it to a new location. Control points become highlighted as you move your mouse cursor close to them, indicating that you can select them. Close the tool by left-clicking your first control point or double-clicking your last control point.

If you need to make an organic or irregular selection, use the free-hand selection form of the Free Select tool by left-clicking and dragging your mouse cursor in the image window to define your selection. When you release your mouse button, control points appear at the beginning and end of the line, indicating that your line is treated as a single segment. From here you can close your selection, or continue building your selection using polygonal or free-hand selection.

Fuzzy Select

GIMP's Fuzzy Select tool lets you select large regions of your image based on contiguous colors. Activate Fuzzy Select from the Toolbox by clicking the magic wand icon or use its keyboard shortcut, U, while you're working. To use the Fuzzy Select tool, left-click in your image on a color region that you want to select. GIMP selects all pixels of similar hue that connect to the one you click. If you hold down the mouse button and drag your mouse left and right, you can adjust the sensitivity of the Fuzzy Select tool, which enables you to select pixels that are roughly the same color. The Fuzzy Select tool has some unique settings in the Tools Options dialog:

- **Select Transparent Areas** — This option, enabled by default, allows the Fuzzy Select tool to take the Alpha channel in an image into account, so you can select transparent areas.

- **Sample Merged:** By default, the Fuzzy Select tool works on only your active layer. If you enable this check box, the Fuzzy Select tool takes the colors from all of your layers into account when making a contiguous selection.

- **Threshold:** Increase this slider value to increase the range of pixels considered the same color as the one you clicked.

- **Select by:** With this drop-down menu, you can tell the Fuzzy Select tool which color space component to use to determine which pixels are similar to the one you clicked.

Select by Color

The easiest way to select all pixels that are similar to a particular color in your image is to use the Select by Color tool. Activate this tool from the Toolbox by clicking the icon that looks like a hand pointing at three colored squares or by using Shift+O. The usage and tool options for the Select by Color tool are the same as for the Fuzzy Select tool.

Intelligent Scissors Select

If you want to select a person, pet, or building, the Intelligent Scissor Select can assist you. The Scissors Select tool looks for edges in your image and attempts to snap to them while you make your selection. Enable the Scissors Select tool from the Toolbox by clicking its icon or by using its keyboard shortcut, I.

Using the Scissors Select tool is a two-step process. First you create a rough selection by clicking in your image window where you want your selection to start. This creates your initial control point. Then, if you click and drag in the image window, GIMP snaps to strong edges in your image. If you don't want to snap to these features, hold down your mouse button while holding down Shift. When you release your mouse button, GIMP creates a new control point at that location and attempts to connect your control points along the strong edges in your image. If GIMP guesses the connection incorrectly don't try to edit your control points until you finish building your rough selection. When you're done building your rough selection, click the first control point.

After you create your rough selection, you can tweak the control points. Click and drag any control point to a new location. If you have the Interactive Boundary check box enabled in the Tool Options dialog, GIMP updates the segments between the control points you're editing as you move them. If you click a segment of your selection area, GIMP creates a new control point, which helps GIMP. After you finish editing control points, press Enter or click within your selected area and GIMP finalizes the selection for you.

Note

While editing your selection area with the Scissors Select tool, be careful *not* to click the center of your selection area. If you do this, there's no way to get back to the editable state without restarting the process. ■

Foreground Select

Foreground Select provides you with a quick way to isolate features of your images and select them. This tool implements a Simple Interactive Object Extraction (SIOX) algorithm. To activate this tool, click its icon in the Toolbox or navigate to Tools ➤ Selection Tools ➤ Foreground Select. There's not a default keyboard shortcut for this feature.

Using the Foreground Select tool is a two-step process that involves first making a rough selection and then refining that selection. Your mouse cursor icon is the same icon used by the Free

Select tool. When you make your selection, the Foreground Select tool behaves as the Free Select tool does. Use the polygonal and free-hand selection forms to define a rough selection around the foreground element. After you close this selection, the Foreground Select tool's behavior is different from the other selection tools. Anything not in your selected area is overlaid with a blue mask and your mouse cursor changes to a circle. Click and drag your mouse cursor over the foreground element to mark the pixels of your foreground element. Just draw a line over enough pixels to include the full variation of color you need. You don't have to do your foreground marking with a single paint stroke. You can paint multiple strokes. As you make your marks, the blue mask updates after each stroke, showing what your final selection looks like. If the Foreground Select tool picks up pixels from your background that you don't want included in your selection, you can fix that by Ctrl+clicking and dragging over those pixels. While you're working, you can use some of the settings in the Tool Options dialog to refine the selection process:

- **Contiguous** — This option, enabled by default, causes the Foreground Select tool to choose only the elements that you mark as the foreground.
- **Interactive Refinement** — Use these radio buttons to tell the Foreground Select tool whether you want to mark foreground (the default) or background elements.
- **Brush Size** — This slider controls the size of the paint brush you use when marking foreground and background elements.
- **Smoothing** — Adjust this slider to help the Foreground Select tool account for irregularities and variations when making your selection.
- **Preview Color:** Use this menu to change the mask color.
- **Color Sensitivity:** The sliders here enable you to tweak the color components that the Foreground Select uses for picking your selection.

After you refine your selection of foreground pixels, press Enter; GIMP converts your Foreground Select mask into a selection.

Image Tools

After you select all or part your image, the next task is to do *something* to the image. You could be getting information about the image, or manipulating it as a whole. The tools covered in this section give you these facilities.

Informational Tools

GIMP offers three tools (Color Picker, Zoom, and Measure) that don't modify your image. Despite that, these tools are important for getting information from your image or adjusting your view of the image.

Color Picker

The Color Picker is one of GIMP's simplest tools, but it's incredibly helpful, especially when used in concert with any of the painting or creation tools. In other programs, this tool is sometimes referred to as the Eyedropper tool. Whether you enable it from the Toolbox or use its keyboard shortcut (O), it's extremely simple to use. Click your canvas within your image window and the color of the pixel you click becomes your foreground color. Any tool that adds color to your image uses the foreground color as its base color. If you Ctrl+click your image, the color you click is assigned to the background color. Shift+click on your image to open the Color Picker information dialog, which gives detailed information on the selected pixel.

The Color Picker has some unique settings in the Tool Options dialog:

- **Sample Average** — When you enable this option, GIMP lets you sample the pixels around where you click (based on the radius value) and pick the average of those colors for the foreground color.

- **Sample Merged** — By default, the Color Picker works on only your active layer. Enable this check box and it works on all layers in your image.

- **Pick Mode** — The radio buttons here give you choices for setting the foreground and background colors:

  - **Pick Only** — Enable this option and the Color Picker updates only the Color Picker Information dialog. Your foreground and background colors do not change.

  - **Set Foreground/Background Color** — These options are the default behavior for the Color Picker and you can toggle between them by holding Ctrl.

  - **Add to Palette** — If you're working on an indexed color palette, use this option to add a clicked color to your palette.

- **Use Info Window** — Shift+clicking in your image with the Color Picker opens the Color Picker Information dialog.

Zoom

Activate the Zoom tool by clicking the magnifying glass icon in the Toolbox or by using its keyboard shortcut, Z. The Zoom tool lets you draw a box around a part of your image that you want to zoom in on. To do this, simply click and drag your mouse cursor in the image window. This creates a rectangle. After you release your mouse button, GIMP zooms your image window to fit the box you've created.

Measure

When you are working on digital images, you sometimes have to measure the distance between points on the image or the angle of a line. This is where the Measure tool is helpful. Enable this tool with its keyboard shortcut (Shift+M) or by clicking the caliper icon in the Toolbox. To use the Measure tool, click and drag your mouse in the image window. This creates a pair of crosshairs as endpoints connected by a line. As you move your mouse cursor, the image window's status area updates with the length and angle of that line, and width and height of a bounding box that would be drawn around that line.

You can also use the Measure tool to add guides to the image window by Ctrl+clicking an end point on your measurement line. Alt+clicking an end point adds a vertical guide. Use Ctrl+Alt+click on an end point to add horizontal and vertical guides in your image window.

Transform Tools

GIMP's Transform tools let you manipulate your image, layer, or selection as a whole. They are listed in the image windows menu under Tools ➤ Transform Tools. Many of the functions provided by these tools can be accessed from the Image or Layer menus. However the menu features tend to be clunky.

Note

This portion of the book was written with an early development version of GIMP 2.8 which did not yet have the unified Transform tool. For updates to this section, please see this book's companion web site at www.wiley.com/go/GIMPBible. ■

Paint Tools

Most of the advanced techniques in digital image manipulation involve modifying the pixels in your image. Use the tools discussed in this section to change the pixel information. These tools are found in Tools ➤ Paint Tools. The only exception to this is the Text tool, found at Tools ➤ Text. You can find out more about Text tool by reading Chapter 10.

The tools in the Tools ➤ Paint Tools submenu can be logically broken down into two general categories: creation tools and enhancement tools. The creation tools use your foreground and background color as their base colors and are generally applied over top of existing image data. They usually replace existing pixels with new colors. Tools included in this category are Bucket Fill, Blend, Pencil, Paintbrush, Eraser, Airbrush, and Ink. All of these tools are covered in Chapter 11.

The tools in the enhancement category are designed to tweak, modify, and enhance existing pixels in your image. They typically work best with photographs and are great ways to modify an image. Included in this category are Clone, Healing, Perspective Clone, Blur/Sharpen, Smudge, and the Dodge/Burn tool, which are covered in Chapter 12.

Color Tools

Another common practice in image manipulation is the process of color correction. Although they're available in Tools ➤ Color Tools, the tools to perform color correction aren't actually in the Toolbox by default. You add them by going to the Preferences window (Edit ➤ Preferences) in the Toolbox section and unhiding them. Color Balance, Hue-Saturation, Colorize, Brightness-Contrast, Threshold, Levels, Curves, Posterize, and Desaturate are all accessible there. For more information on using these tools, look at Chapter 9.

Summary

You learned a lot about how to operate GIMP in this chapter. Mainly, this chapter introduced you to the many tools you can build upon within the rest of the book's chapters.

In the next chapter, you learn how to take advantage of paths. You not only discover how the vector nature of paths can be a helpful advantage to you while editing, but learn how to use them and get the most out of them. Ready? Get set. Go!

Summary

Taking Advantage of Paths

G IMP's primary purpose is to be an awesome raster graphics editor. It serves this purpose and does it quite well. However, even in raster editing, in some circumstances having the ability to use vector tools is a definite advantage. This is where GIMP's paths come in. They provide you with the vector advantages you need without making GIMP a full-on vector illustration program.

Paths are curves, specifically Bézier curves like the ones commonly found in vector drawing programs such as Inkscape or Adobe Illustrator. They're a very powerful way to define reusable forms that you can employ for selection, creating solid shapes, or making line drawings. You can also use them as a control structure for text, defining a form for the text to flow along.

This chapter builds on the brief section in Chapter 4 on the Paths tool. You will not only discover how the vector nature of paths can be an advantage to you while editing, but also how to get the most out of them in the process. By the time you're done, you'll be creating, editing, and deleting paths with the best of them.

IN THIS CHAPTER

Understanding what paths are good for

Using paths to good advantage

Removing paths from your file

The Advantages of Paths: Get Some Vector in Your Raster

So where exactly is it useful to have vector drawing tools in a raster graphics package like GIMP? Well, vectors give you two primary benefits:

- **Resolution-independence** — Vector graphics are not bound to any particular image size or resolution. This means that you can take a symbol drawn with vectors and use it in an image sized for either a web site or a billboard and there's no jagged stair-stepping at the edges or other degradation of quality.

- **Easy modification** — Because vectors are basically mathematical curves with only a few control points, they're much easier to change and edit. This makes them well-suited for building selections around objects with irregular edging. Paths can often be much more forgiving to use than the Free Select (or Lasso, for you Photoshoppers) tool.

These advantages make vector graphics ideal for use with logos and text, because they tend to get reused frequently in a variety of output media. It's best to keep this flexibility for as long as possible. In a commercial design environment, it's not uncommon for a client to request for text to be larger or the logo to be enlarged and moved or rotated. If you can do these operations with a vector, your output won't suffer from quality loss from resizing or transforming.

GIMP provides vector drawing capabilities with the Paths tool (B). In GIMP, a path is defined by a specific kind of curve called a *Bézier curve*. The most prominent features of Bézier curves are its control points, called *anchors*. These anchors lie along the surface of the curve and each one has a pair of *handles* associated with it. The handles control how smoothly the curve approaches and leaves each anchor. Handles can be either in alignment with one another, ensuring a smooth transition of the curve through the anchor, or they can be "broken" to move independently, making the curve have a sharp point at the anchor. You can also control whether a path forms a *closed* solid shape or is simply a line, known as an *open* path. With these controls, you can easily use a path to create a smoothly curved line or a line with a variety of sharp points all over it. You can even use it to create geometric shapes and straight lines. Figure 5-1 shows a couple of example paths with their anchors and handles visible so you can see how they work.

FIGURE 5-1

Paths can be used to create a wide variety of lines and shapes.

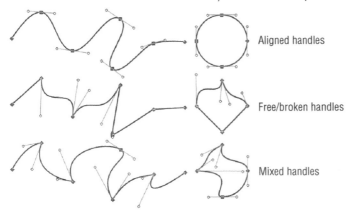

Aligned handles

Free/broken handles

Mixed handles

Creating Paths

When it comes to creating and editing paths, nearly all of the functionality resides in the Paths tool. You can activate this tool by clicking its icon in the Toolbox or by pressing its keyboard shortcut, B. If you've used other image editing programs, you may recognize this as the Pen tool. For familiarity, the icon in the Toolbox depicts a fountain pen manipulating a Bézier curve.

Drawing with the Path tool

Drawing with the Path tool is remarkably straightforward. With the tool active, click in the image window and a new anchor appears where you've clicked. Click again and you'll add a new anchor. If you click and drag your mouse, GIMP immediately gives you control of the handles for the anchor you add. When you control the handles in this way, their default behavior is to be aligned to one another. However, if you would like to break them and freely control the far handle, press and release Shift while dragging your mouse. From this point, if you decide that you want to have the handles aligned, press and hold Shift while you're dragging your mouse. When you release Shift, the handles revert to their free behavior. Figure 5-2 illustrates how this works.

FIGURE 5-2

Drawing a new path with the Path tool

 Paths tool

 Left-click creates a new anchor

Left-click and drag   While click-dragging,   While click-dragging,
creates an anchor   press and release Shift   press and hold Shift
with aligned handles   to break handles   to align handles

Tip

The semi-toggle nature of the Shift button when drawing paths may seem a bit strange at first, but it's surprisingly helpful. It's a great way to control both handles without releasing the mouse button. An example workflow would be to place your first anchor and then click and drag from the location of your next anchor. Use this moment to control the angle of the far handle. Once you have it set, press and release Shift to control the placement of the handle near your mouse. If you have to tweak the far handle, hold Shift momentarily to fix it and then release to go back to adjusting the near handle. This is a particularly helpful trick for tablet users. ■

If you want your path to form a closed shape, move your mouse cursor over the first anchor in the path and press and hold Ctrl. When you do this, your mouse cursor should change to include a small chain-link symbol in the upper right. Confirm closing the path by left-clicking. If you need to add more anchors anywhere along your path, Ctrl+click any segment between two anchors in the path. Anchors can be deleted by Shift+Ctrl-clicking them.

You can adjust any individual anchor by clicking it and dragging it to a new location. If you need to move multiple anchors simultaneously, you first have to select each one. Do this by Shift-clicking the anchors you want to move. Selected anchors appear as outlined circles and unselected anchors appear as circles filled with a solid purple color. With your anchors selected, move them by clicking any one of them and dragging the group to its new location.

GIMP gives you the ability to construct your path out of a set of individual *components*. Each component is an individual set of anchors forming their own curve. To create a new component, Shift+click anywhere in the image window and a new anchor that isn't linked to your existing component appears. Subsequent clicks draw a curve from this new anchor. With multiple components floating around, things can get to be a bit of a visual mess. Fortunately, GIMP allows you to manage this. Alt+clicking any component and dragging your mouse around the screen moves that component. If you Alt+click anywhere else in the image window, you'll move all of the components in the path. By using multiple components to build a path, you have quite a bit more control when using paths to create selections. In fact, you'll see later in this chapter how overlapping components can produce holes in your selections made with paths.

You may notice that some of your anchors don't appear to have handles. This happens when you create your path by just clicking new anchor points and not dragging your mouse to control the handles immediately. To reveal and edit handles on an anchor, Ctrl+click it and drag your mouse away from that anchor's center. When you do so, one of the handles will follow your mouse. You can control the opposite handle by pressing and holding Shift while you're still dragging out the near handle. Release Shift to relinquish control of that opposite handle. Alternatively, you can release your mouse button, go back to the anchor, and Ctrl+click it to draw that other handle out. Figure 5-3 illustrates how this process works.

FIGURE 5-3

Editing existing anchors and handles.

  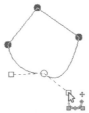

Ctrl+click to reveal an anchor's handle

Press Shift while editing to reveal the opposite handle

Or Ctrl+click from the anchor to reveal the opposite handle separately

---

Tip

For a quick edit, you can actually click and drag any segment between two anchors. When you do this, GIMP modifies the handles on each anchor to generate the curve shape you want. If you hold Shift while doing this, those handles will be aligned on their anchors. Note that where you click the segment is important. If you click halfway between the two anchors, you'll have equal control over both near handles. However, if you click nearer to one anchor than the other, your control of each handle is proportionate to the distance you are from it. So if you click closer to one anchor, you'll have immediate control over its handle, but much less control over the other anchor's handle. ■

Tip

There will be occasions when you want to draw a path with only linear segments. To avoid accidentally pulling out handles from your anchors in these cases, there's a check box called Polygonal in the Tool Options for the Paths tool. If you click this check box and enable it, as shown in Figure 5-4, new anchors that you create will not grow handles if you click and drag on them. Doing so will only move that anchor around. ■

FIGURE 5-4

You can enable the Polygonal option in the Paths tool's options in the Toolbox.

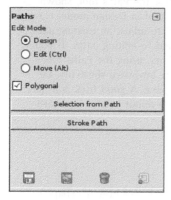

Table 5-1 has a quick reference for the various mouse and keyboard shortcut combinations that the Path tool uses.

TABLE 5-1

Mouse/Keyboard Shortcut Reference for the Path Tool

Shortcut	Behavior
Click empty space	Add anchor
Click+drag empty space	Add anchor and adjust handle (press and release Shift to break handles)
Click+drag anchor	Move anchor (or anchors if multiple anchors are selected)
Click+drag handle	Move handle independently
Click+drag path segment	Adjust path curvature by editing two handles simultaneously (click segment center for equal control of both handles)
Shift+click empty space	Add unconnected anchor
Shift+click anchor	Select anchor
Shift+click+drag handle	Move handles aligned
Shift+click drag path	Same as click+drag path segment, but with aligned handles
Ctrl+click+drag anchor	Reveal handle and move it independently
Ctrl+click first anchor	Close path component
Ctrl+click path segment	Add anchor in the path segment where you click
Alt+click+drag empty space	Move complete path
Alt+click+drag path component	Move path component (connected anchors)
Shift+Ctrl+click anchor or handle	Delete anchor or handle

Tip

This table has a pretty daunting list of mouse/keyboard combinations that may be tough to remember. Your life can be simplified a bit by using the radio buttons in the tool options for the Paths tool, shown in Figure 5-4. The combinations in Table 5-1 all work when you have the Paths tool in Design mode. However, if you know that you don't want to create new anchors and you just want to adjust an existing path, you can switch to Edit mode in the tool options and your controls will be limited to editing paths. If you just want to move path components without editing them or creating new anchors, using the Paths tool's Move mode will simplify things for you so you don't have to remember as many keyboard shortcuts. Of course, once you have the shortcuts down, you can edit paths at an incredible pace. A good trick is to pay attention to the status bar at the bottom of the image window. It gives you hints about helpful keyboard shortcuts to use while editing. ■

Creating a Path from a Selection

Although drawing your own custom path gives you the ultimate control over how it's shaped, it's often helpful if you're given a head start. Perhaps you're given a symbol or a logo to work with, but it's a very small raster image and you've been asked to enlarge it. If you try to simply scale it up, chances are good that it will be blurry and possibly pixelated. However, if you could get it in paths, resizing might be simpler. Fortunately, because most logos and symbols are solid colors, it's pretty easy to do this quickly. Note that this example uses a few concepts discussed later in this chapter, including the Paths dockable dialog and converting a path to a selection. If you want to find out more about these things, flip forward a few pages to preview them.

1. **With the Fuzzy Select (U) or Select by Color (Shift+O) tools, select one of the solid colors in the logo.** This gives you a base selection to work with. You may have to go in and clean up the selection, but it really depends on the image you're starting with.

2. **Change the path to a selection (Select ➤ To Path).** BAM! Your selection is now a path and free of the constraints of raster images. This step is where all of the fun of this technique lies.

3. **Perform steps 1 and 2 on other colors in the logo.** When finished, you should have a separate path that defines each color in the logo. You can see each of these paths in the Paths dockable dialog, which is covered in more detail later in this chapter.

4. **Scale the image up to the desired size (Image ➤ Scale Image).** In doing so, you also scale up the paths. Because they're vector, though, the lines remain crisp and the curves remain smooth.

5. **Add a new layer (Add ➤ New Layer or Shift+Ctrl+N).** This is where you will be putting your reconstructed logo.

6. **For each path in the Paths dialog, convert the path to a selection (Select ➤ From Path or Shift+V) and Bucket Fill (Shift+B) that selection with the proper color.**
   You may need to use the color picker (O) to select the matching color from the old logo in the lower layer before completing the Bucket Fill. And remember, to fill the whole selection with the Bucket Fill too, use Shift+click in the selected area.

7. **You've done a quick logo enlargement without losing much, if any, quality.**
   Figure 5-5 has an example of this process in action.

FIGURE 5-5

Using a selection to create a path so you can cleanly enlarge a simple logo

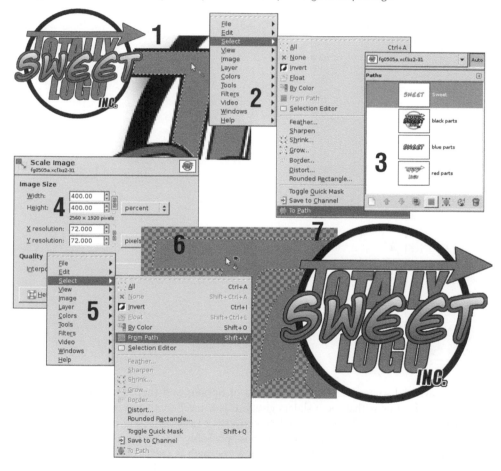

The default settings for the Select to Path feature work well in most instances. However, occasionally you may find that GIMP creates too many or too few anchors to match your selection exactly. You could also want to create a path that's a simplified, smoother approximation of your selection. For any of these scenarios, you can use the Advanced options for the Select to Path feature. Because it's not a frequently used set of options, you won't find the advanced options in GIMP's main menu. Instead, the way to access these options is from the Paths dockable dialog. At the bottom of the dialog is a red Select to Path button. If you Shift+click this button, you get a dialog like the one in Figure 5-6.

FIGURE 5-6

Advanced options for creating a path from a selection

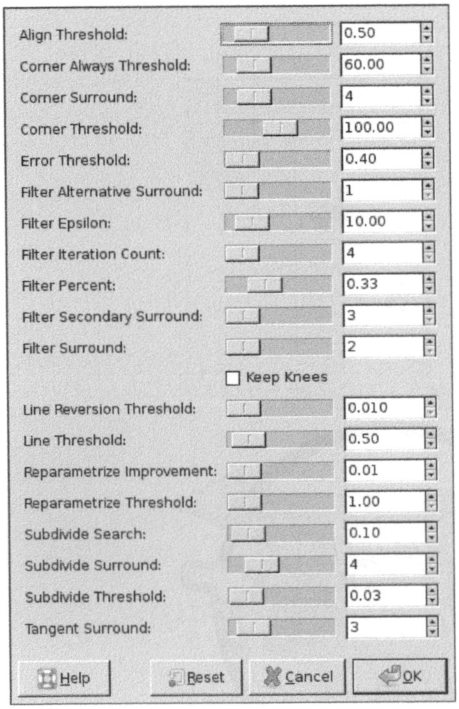

Align Threshold:	0.50
Corner Always Threshold:	60.00
Corner Surround:	4
Corner Threshold:	100.00
Error Threshold:	0.40
Filter Alternative Surround:	1
Filter Epsilon:	10.00
Filter Iteration Count:	4
Filter Percent:	0.33
Filter Secondary Surround:	3
Filter Surround:	2
☐ Keep Knees	
Line Reversion Threshold:	0.010
Line Threshold:	0.50
Reparametrize Improvement:	0.01
Reparametrize Threshold:	1.00
Subdivide Search:	0.10
Subdivide Surround:	4
Subdivide Threshold:	0.03
Tangent Surround:	3

Help   Reset   Cancel   OK

This is an impressive and somewhat overwhelming list of options and they're in "programmerese." The reason for this is that these sliders give you low-level control over how the path is generated and they directly influence how GIMP converts a raster selection into a vector curve. The online GIMP manual says that these options "probably [are] only useful to GIMP developers." However, if you want real control over how the path is created and you don't want to spend a lot of time adding or deleting anchors to adjust your path, knowing how even a handful of these options affect the final output can be a great help.

Before getting into the details of each setting, though, it's helpful to understand the process that GIMP uses to convert a selection to a path. Assume for a moment that you've made a single contiguous selection, say with the Rectangle or Ellipse Select tool. GIMP starts by choosing a start position on the selection and from there it generates a series of points along the edge of your selection. With these points as an initial state, GIMP attempts to filter out points that don't add any detail, such as points along a straight line. It also tries to determine whether a point more clearly defines the shape of the selection as a corner anchor or an anchor with aligned handles. GIMP also tests its decisions to see if the created path accurately fits the original selection. If not, it generates an alternative set of points and checks if those are a better fit. GIMP will iteratively continue this refinement process, called *reparameterization*, until it reaches a threshold whereby continuing doesn't yield a large enough change. At that time, GIMP treats the remaining points as anchors and presents you with a path from your selection. This appears to be a lot of steps, but it typically happens almost instantaneously. Now, on to the individual settings:

- **Align Threshold** — The ToolTip for this option states "If two endpoints are closer than this, they are made to be equal" and the values range from 0.2 to 2.0. Basically this has to do with the start and end of the path created from your selection. At low values, there's a greater chance that you'll have two anchors near each other at that point. At high values, you may not even have any anchors there and the shape is defined by surrounding anchors.

- **Corner Always Threshold** — Measured in degrees, this defines whether a point creates a corner. Looking at the points before and after the point it's evaluating, if those other points form an angle that is smaller than this value, GIMP marks this point as a corner. This setting has an influence regardless of whatever is set for Corner Surround. If you set this to its maximum value, all points are considered corners.

- **Corner Surround** — When determining whether a point is a corner, you can control how many points before or after it GIMP uses to make this determination. On complex selections, lower values should give you more accurate results, although you'll have more anchors at detailed parts of the selection.

- **Corner Threshold** — Similar to Corner Always Threshold, but this setting is dependent on the value you set for Corner Surround. Increasing this threshold to 180 degrees not only makes all points into corners, but also dramatically increases the overall number of anchors used to create your path.

- **Error Threshold** — Consider this value to be an accuracy setting for the path. The lower the number you use here, the more accurately your path matches your selection. Higher numbers are less accurate, but they're a handy way of quickly simplifying a complex selection to a nice, clean shape.

- **Filter Alternative Surround** — Increasing the value for this option increases the number of anchors you have at curved portions of your selections.

- **Filter Epsilon** — This option controls which points GIMP uses when filtering the points it creates. Basically, GIMP takes the vectors made by Filter Surround and Filter Secondary Surround and evaluates their angles. If the angle is less than this value, the alternative points should be a better fit and GIMP uses the angle from Filter Alternative Surround. Otherwise, it stays with Filter Surround. Lower values should yield you more accurate results.

- **Filter Iteration Count** — This value determines how many times GIMP will run a smooth operation once it determines where the anchors are. Increasing this value reduces accuracy, but it can help smooth out excessively rough selections.

- **Filter Percent** — When determining whether to create a new point, GIMP uses this value with the last point it created. Very high and very low values give you a lot of anchors. Values in the middle range give a smaller, more acceptable number of points.

- **Filter Secondary Surround** — This is the number of adjacent points that GIMP will use to determine whether a segment is a straight line. Higher values tend to spread your anchors out a bit more.

- **Filter Surround** — Increasing this value reduces accuracy, but it also helps reduce the roughness in jagged selections.

- **Keep Knees** — Knees are kind of like "helper points" that GIMP uses to determine the shape of the path created from the selection. Normally these knees get removed after the path is calculated. However, if you'd like to keep them as control anchors, enable this check box.

- **Line Reversion Threshold** — This value controls whether a segment is considered a line or a curve. Higher values increase the likelihood that a segment will be considered a line rather than a curve.

- **Line Threshold** — Increasing this value reduces the accuracy of your path and increases the likelihood that a segment will be considered a line rather than a curve.

- **Reparametrize Improvement** — Increasing this value sacrifices some accuracy for greater speed when creating the path. If you set this value to 0.0, GIMP may take quite a while to generate your path for you.

- **Reparametrize Threshold** — Beyond a certain point, reparameterization stops being useful. This value is where you adjust that threshold. Increasing it from its default value should reduce the number of anchors in your curve, but the curve may fit less accurately.

- **Subdivide Search** — GIMP creates paths from selections through an iterative process. So it may find a segment that doesn't match the selection. If that segment is off the selection by larger than the percentage you set here, GIMP tries to subdivide the segment somewhere else to get a better result.

- **Subdivide Surround** — If GIMP does subdivide a segment to try to get a better result, it uses this number of adjacent points on the path to decide whether or not the new subdivide point is an improvement.

- **Subdivide Threshold** — This value, measured in pixels, is how far a segment can be away from a straight line and still be considered an improved subdivide over the last point.

- **Tangent Surround** — To accurately determine how a segment should curve, it's important for GIMP to calculate the tangent of points along that path. This value determines how many points GIMP uses to help calculate that value. Higher values should yield more accurate results, but with slightly more anchors in the final path.

Managing Paths

In the previous example, notice that GIMP is able to handle multiple sets of paths. When you use the Paths tool, unless you tell GIMP otherwise, all of those curves you draw, called *components*, are considered part of a single path. That path can be managed as a single complete unit from the Paths dockable dialog, shown in Figure 5-7.

FIGURE 5-7

The Paths dockable dialog allows you to manage all of the paths in your current project.

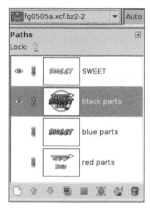

The Paths Dialog

By default, the Paths dialog is available in the dock window as the third tab in the upper dock. If you don't see it there, you can always bring it up by clicking Windows ➤ Dockable Dialogs ➤ Paths in an image window. As Figure 5-7 shows, the Paths dialog is a comprehensive list of each of the paths you have in your image. Each path entry in this list has four controllable bits of information associated with it:

- **Visibility** — This eye icon is a button that controls the visibility of the path. By default, GIMP keeps this functionality disabled. To make a path visible for editing, just click this first icon.

- **Chaining** — Chaining is a concept that works on layers, channels, and paths, linking them together and making them *transform locked*. This means that if you've clicked this second space and enabled the chain icon on two paths and a layer, then when you move the layer, the paths move with it. If you've used a path to create a selection on a layer, and then want to move the layer, it's a good idea to enable this feature, chaining the path and layer together.

- **Preview** — This shows a small thumbnail of your path. Often it's easier to remember the shape of the path you created rather than its name or anything else. Double-clicking this preview image automatically enables the Paths tool and reveals the anchors for that path, regardless of whether the path is visible or what tool you have when double-clicking.

- **Name** — Each path has a unique name associated with it. For better organization (and the sake of your own sanity while working), it's a very good idea to give your paths names that make sense for your image. It's not helpful if you look at the Paths dialog and see "Path," "New Path," "New Path #1," and "New Path #2." So whenever you create a new path, make it a point to give it a good name. You can always change that name by double-clicking it in this dialog.

119

Above the list of paths is a label that says Lock, followed by a button. Locks are a new feature in the latest version of GIMP and they can be found in the Paths dialog as well as dialogs for Channels and Layers. After the Lock label is one or more buttons. In the case of the Paths dialog, there is only one button. Click this button and the active path becomes locked, or uneditable. Click it again and you unlock that path. This is useful if you have a path set and you want to see it, but don't want to accidentally modify it with any stray clicks.

- **New Path** — Clicking this button creates a new path. When you click this, GIMP pops up a dialog like the one in Figure 5-8 that allows you to give your new path a name. Give your path a logical name that makes sense.

FIGURE 5-8

The naming dialog that pops up when you create a new path

- **Raise/Lower Path** — These buttons allow you to re-order the paths in the list. Clicking the raise button takes the selected path and moves it up in the list. Clicking the lower button moves it down. If you Shift+click either of these buttons, it raises the path to the top of the list or lowers it to the bottom. Of course, you can also re-order your paths by clicking and dragging a path directly to its new location in the list.

- **Duplicate Path** — Clicking this button makes a duplicate of the currently selected path. Do note that when you do this, GIMP appends a number to the end of the path's name. So if you want to give this duplicated path a custom name, double-click that name and change it. Alternatively, you can right-click any path and choose Copy Path from the menu that pops up. Then to add duplicates of that path, right-click the Paths dialog and select Paste Path.

- **Path to Selection** — This button is a controller that allows you to use the closed components of the current path to make a selection. If you just click this button, your current selection is completely replaced with this new one. If, however, you would like to use your current selection along with a selection created by your path, you have a few more options that are quickly accessible from this button.

  - **Add (Shift+click)** — Choosing this option increases your overall selected area by adding your path selection to what you already have selected.

  - **Subtract (Ctrl+click)** — This option takes your current selection and deselects portions that overlap with closed components of your path.

  - **Intersect (Shift+Ctrl+click)** — On some occasions you want to select only the areas that are covered by *both* your current selection and the closed components of your path. This option does just that.

Tip

Each of these selection functions is also available by right-clicking in the Paths dialog. ■

- **Selection to Path** — Click this button to convert your current selection into a path. Shift+click this button to show the advanced options for doing this conversion. Details on these advanced options are covered earlier in this chapter.

- **Paint Along the Path** — One of the cool features about paths is that they allow you to use any brush in GIMP and paint a line that goes along that path, sometimes referred to as *stroking* the path. This is a great way to create outlines, edges, and even some cool neon effects. There are a lot of controls that you can have with this and they're discussed in the next section of this chapter. If you've already painted along a path, Shift+clicking this button reuses those settings.

- **Delete Path** — As advertised, clicking this button deletes the selected path.

Occasionally you may find that you need to consolidate your paths. Perhaps you've created two paths that you would like to work together to create a single selection. Well, rather than convert one to a selection and then add or subtract the other from that selection, you can merge the paths into a single one. To do this, make the paths you want to merge visible by clicking the visibility eye for each. Then right-click in the Paths dialog and choose Merge Visible Paths. Doing this consolidates all components from the visible paths into a single path in the Paths dialog. You can still move the components individually by Alt+clicking and dragging any of them.

Warning

Be careful when you're merging paths. Currently, there's no quick way to separate components in a path. You can always use Undo (Ctrl+Z) if you immediately realize that you didn't mean to merge paths. However, if you don't realize this until later or if you just decide later on that you'd like the path components to be separate, things are going to be a bit troublesome. The way to separate components into individual paths is by duplicating the path and manually Shift+Ctrl+clicking each anchor in the component you want to remove from the new path. And then you need to go back to the original path and remove the anchors from the other component in that path. Alternatively, you can export your paths to a vector graphics program like Inkscape and separate your paths there. Either way, this process can be a bit of a bother, so keep that in mind when you're merging paths. ■

Importing and Exporting Paths

GIMP also gives you the ability to import vector curves from other programs using the SVG file format. SVG is an abbreviation for Scalable Vector Graphics and it's an open vector image format used in a variety of programs. As an open format, SVG is easily supported in proprietary commercial software like Adobe Illustrator, as well as most Free Software programs like Inkscape, Scribus, and OpenOffice.org. In fact, even Mozilla Firefox can display SVG images!

Importing Paths

GIMP's paths were actually redesigned in GIMP 1.3.21 specifically with SVG support in mind, so importing is painless. To import SVG paths into GIMP, right-click in the Paths dockable dialog and choose Import Path. As Figure 5-9 shows, the File Chooser is pretty much the same one you see when opening a new file, with the exception of two check boxes at the bottom of the dialog.

FIGURE 5-9

The File Chooser dialog for importing paths into GIMP

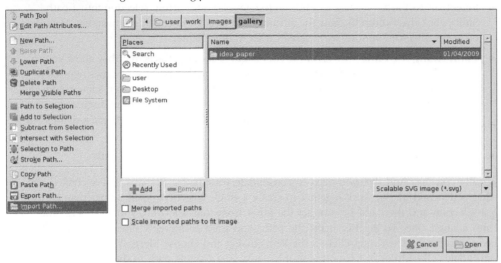

The two additional options you have are as follows:

- **Merge imported paths —** Enable this option to import all of the curves in the selected SVG file to a single path in the list. If you leave this option disabled, each individual curve object in the SVG file will get its own path element in the list.

- **Scale imported paths to fit image —** Although SVG is a vector format, SVG files have a size and resolution associated with them so artists can relate them to real-world units. By default, GIMP uses these values to calculate the size of the paths when they're imported. If you enable this option, GIMP scales the paths so they fit the image size. This means that SVG images that are smaller than your image canvas will be scaled up while larger images will be scaled down. Be aware, though, that GIMP does *not* maintain the proportions of the SVG curves if you enable this option. It will squash or stretch the curves to fit the available size, regardless of the original proportions. If you want to maintain proportions, it's best to import the SVG curves at their original size and then scale the paths once they're in GIMP.

Tip

To scale a path, choose the Transform tool and click the Path button in the Tool Options panel. This way you can arbitrarily rescale your path to whatever size you need. ∎

Note

The SVG file format actually supports much more than curves. You can create vector text and shapes like rectangles, ellipses, and stars. Unfortunately, GIMP does not support these vector forms directly. To import these into GIMP as paths, you first need to convert them to curves in the vector drawing program you're using. Once you do that, however, GIMP can import them just fine. ∎

Exporting Paths

Just as you can import SVG curves as GIMP paths, you can also export paths as curves in an SVG file. This is a great way to have interoperability between GIMP and your vector drawing tools and even 3D software like Blender, which support SVG curves. To export paths from GIMP, right-click in the Paths dockable dialog and choose Export Path. Doing this pops up a Save dialog like the one shown in Figure 5-10.

FIGURE 5-10

The Save dialog that GIMP pops up for exporting paths

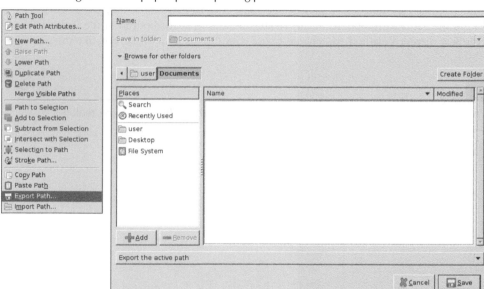

This dialog looks like the standard Save dialog with the exception of an additional drop-down box at the bottom. From this drop-down, you have two options:

- **Export the active path —** Choosing this option exports on the path that you have selected in the Paths dialog. All components of this path are included as a single object in the SVG file.

- **Export all paths from this image —** This option takes all of the paths in the image and includes them in the exported SVG file. Each path is treated as its own individual object, so you don't have a mess of overlapping curves when you open the file in your vector drawing tool.

Using Paths

Once you have one or more paths created, you can do a whole slew of things with them. Earlier in this chapter, there's the example of how you can use paths to cleanly enlarge a logo. Of course, that's just one application. Paths are best suited for creating shapes, drawing lines, making complex selections, and deforming other parts of the image. Paths are where this starts, but when it comes to using them in these situations, there can be overlap with some of GIMP's other tools, particularly the Paintbrush and Bucket Fill tools.

Painting along a Path

Have you ever had trouble drawing a smoothly curving line or needed to draw a clean line with a very specific curve? This is where paths have a distinct advantage over your typical freehand drawing and painting tools. You can take your time and meticulously lay out the shape of a line first. When it's all properly laid out, you create that line in a single operation. This is done with GIMP's Stroke Path function (Edit ➢ Stroke Path). You can also more quickly access this feature from the Paths tool's options in the Toolbox as well as at the bottom of the Paths dialog. Regardless of which method you choose to use, GIMP pops up a dialog box like the one in Figure 5-11.

FIGURE 5-11

GIMP's Stroke Path dialog. On the left is the standard dialog and on the right is the same dialog with the Line Style options expanded.

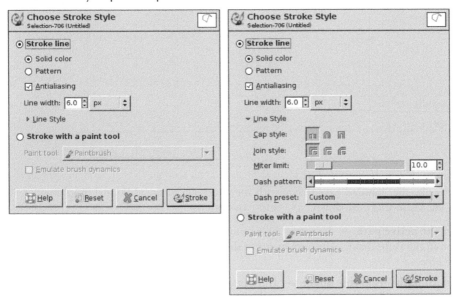

For as simple as the Stroke Path dialog appears, it's packed with a remarkable amount of versatility. Ultimately, though, you have two main options: stroking a line with some procedural preset or stroking with a paint tool.

Stroke Line

GIMP's default behavior is to use the Stroke Line option. This uses a set of procedural options to generate your desired line. At its simplest, you have two settings for painting along the path this way:

- **Line Width** — Allows you to control the width, or thickness, of the line you're creating in any of the units that GIMP supports. A thing to remember is that this is the total width, centered along the path. So if you're using a line width of 10 pixels, your stroke will be out 5 pixels on either side of the path.

- **Solid/Pattern** — Because you can only choose to paint with either a solid color or a pattern, this counts as a single setting. If you choose Solid, your line will be drawn with the current foreground color. If you choose Pattern, GIMP uses the active pattern to fill the width of your line. The cool thing here is that the Stroke Path dialog is *non-blocking*, so you can leave it open and still change the foreground color or active pattern to whatever you'd like before you click the Stroke button.

The real power of using this procedural Stroke Line method is the variety of options you have access to when you expand the Line Style options. Here you can really control the nature of the line that gets drawn. This is great for technical drawings and illustrations where you need specific dash patterns or you need greater control over how the line looks at its tips or at anchors along the path that creates that line. Each of these options can have a dramatic effect on how your line looks, regardless of whether you're using a solid color or a pattern:

- **Cap Style** — If you're using an open, rather than closed, path, these options control how the line you draw terminates when it gets to the end of the path.

  - **Butt** — When the line reaches the end of the path, it stops drawing right there, squared off.

  - **Round** — Occasionally you may want your lines to end more organically rather than ending with a harsh, squared-off edge. Choosing this option terminates your line with a semi-circle that has a diameter equal to your line width.

  - **Square** — This is kind of a hybrid between the preceding two options. You get a squared-off end, but it's extended from the tip of the path by half of the line width that you set.

- **Join Style** — These options control how GIMP draws your line at corners. This specifically applies to anchors on your path and is most visible on linear anchors without any handles on them.

  - **Miter** — This is the default behavior, simply drawing a hard-edged corner at sharp, linear anchors.

  - **Round** — Choose this option to soften corners a bit. It draws a radius at corner anchors, rounding them and making them less harsh.

- **Bevel** — This choice is used more in technical drawings when you want to keep hard edges, but you want something a bit smoother than the straight miter look. The size of the bevel is determined by keeping the same line width as much a possible, rather than the additional thickness that occurs on a corner with standard miter joins.

- **Miter Limit** — Even if you choose the Miter join style, you can actually still use a bevel join style under certain circumstances where the corner is extremely sharp. If you reduce this value to 0.0, GIMP always bevels the corners. If you set it to 100.0, GIMP never bevels, regardless of how sharp the corner angle is.

- **Dash Pattern** — One of the really cool things you can do with GIMP's stroke is draw dashed lines This control allows you to see the dash pattern you're using. You can also use it to create your own custom pattern. Just click the line to toggle a portion of it as empty or full. GIMP will then use this as its pattern when painting along your path.

- **Dash Preset** — In case you don't want to spend time creating your own custom dash pattern, GIMP comes with about 10 preset patterns ranging from a solid line to alternating dots and dashes. Click this drop-down to select the pattern you want to use and it will be loaded into the dash pattern setting. Then you can either choose to use this pattern or use it as a starting point to edit your own.

- **Antialiasing** — Aliasing is an effect that is unique to digital images, readily recognizable as that stair-stepped effect you see along hard edges in an image. Antialiasing is a means of subtly blurring those edges to reduce that stair-stepping, thereby making it look more natural. Enable this option to keep the edges of your line from being jagged and aliased. In most circumstances you'll want to keep this enabled because lines typically look better with antialiasing. However, on very thin lines, sometimes antialiasing hurts more than it helps. In these circumstances, click this check box to disable it.

Figure 5-12 shows some examples of the kinds of lines you can draw with just the Stroke line options in this dialog.

FIGURE 5-12

Some lines that can be drawn with the procedural options under Stroke Line in the Stroke Path dialog

Stroke with a Paint Tool

The Stroke Line options give you a lot of control with procedural options. However, you can have nearly limitless versatility if you stroke your path using one of the paint tools. Looking back on Figure 5-11, the Stroke with a Paint Tool options seem pretty basic and innocuous; just a drop-down menu and a check box. This is deceptively simple because when you choose to paint along your path this way, your options are any of the options available to you in any of the available paint tools. Your versatility here is almost limitless.

The really unique thing here is that not only can you stroke the path using standard drawing tools like the Pencil, Paintbrush, and Ink, but you can also use some of the more specialized painting tools like Clone, Heal, and Smudge. This gives you a ton of additional flexibility and options when painting along a path. If you need to, review the options for paint tools in Chapter 4 to see all of your available options. Figure 5-13 shows some examples of what can be done with a couple brushes and a little bit of creativity.

FIGURE 5-13

Using the various options in GIMP's paint tools to get highly customized strokes along a path

Warning

Currently, there's a bug in GIMP when you try to use Stroke with a Paint Tool using a tool that requires you to set a source, such as Clone, Heal, and Perspective Clone. If you try to use this painting tool with Stroke Path, you'll get an error dialog that says "Set a source image first" regardless of whether or not you've actually already set a source with that tool. This bug was confirmed in December of 2008. Hopefully it will be fixed soon. In the meantime, there is a workaround you can use. Create a new layer and stroke your path there with a regular paint tool. Then use Layer ➤ Transparency ➤ Alpha to Selection to turn your stroke into a selection. Then hide your new layer and go back to the original layer. From here you can use the Clone tool in the selection defined by your stroke. It's a few steps for a workaround, but at least it works. ■

It's worth it to take a moment here and look at the Emulate brush dynamics check box at the bottom of this dialog. When you're using the paint tools by themselves, brush dynamics are most useful if you have a drawing tablet because when they're enabled, they nicely emulate the effects that occur when drawing with "real" media in meatspace. However, you can really take advantage of them when using the Stroke Path feature. This is a great way to use your precisely created paths to generate lines that look closer to hand-drawn. If you want tapered strokes, this is the way to do it. To take the most advantage of this, though, you need to understand how the stroke function relates your path to the brush dynamics values. For the painting tools that support them, five brush dynamics settings are available:

- **Pressure** — When used with a tablet, pressure is controlled by how hard you press the pen to the tablet surface. When related to paths, pressure relates to where the path starts and stops. GIMP assumes that at the beginning and end of a stroke is where you would have the least pressure, and the most pressure is at the middle of the stroke. So if you have pressure associated with brush size, then as the stroke moves along your path, it will be small at the start, increase in size, and then get smaller at the end.

- **Velocity** — On a tablet or a mouse, velocity relates to the distance the cursor travels in a period of time. The faster you move your mouse or tablet pen, the higher the velocity. When related to paths, GIMP assumes that the lowest velocity is at the beginning of the stroke and increases as you get to the end. So if you relate this to opacity, then at the beginning of the path, your stroke would be solid at the start of the path and become more and more transparent as it nears the end of the path.

- **Direction** — This is a new setting that was added for GIMP 2.8. When using a tablet, this setting relates to the direction that you draw a line. As you change the direction of a line, you see a change in whatever you bind this setting to. When it comes to painting along a path, the change in direction is most apparent as you cross through anchors, especially anchors with broken handles.

- **Tilt** — The tilt feature relates to the angle of the drawing pen used on a tablet. The tilt of the pen rotates the brush that you're drawing with. Currently, a path doesn't have any tilt influence associated with it, so this setting isn't particularly useful when painting along the path.

- **Random** — Just as with a tablet, the Random setting independently adjusts its value over time, so it results in a highly variable stroke. You can use this like Jitter, to get uneven strokes, or you could associate Random with color and the color of your stroke will randomly bounce between your foreground and background colors as it moves along your path.

The really interesting thing is that just like you can combine brush dynamics when painting, you can also combine them when stroking a path. This can give you a high variety of natural-looking linework. Figure 5-14 shows the results of binding pressure, velocity, direction, tilt, and random brush dynamics to the size of a brush stroked along a path, as well as an example combining them.

FIGURE 5-14

Using brush dynamics when stroking a path

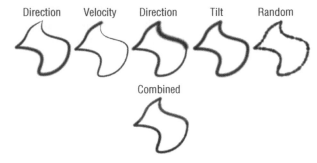

Tip

In GIMP, you can stroke a selection directly by choosing Edit ➤ Stroke Selection from the image window menu. When you do this, you get a dialog with all of the exact same options available to you when stroking a path. This means you can immediately stroke a selection without first converting it into a path, which is useful if you don't want to clutter up your Paths dialog with paths that you're never going to reuse. ■

Practical Example: Faking an Ink Drawing

All of these settings are interesting, but seeing them in action can really get the ideas and possibilities flowing through your brain. One of the interesting things you can do with paths and painting along them is quickly take a photograph of just about anything and make it look like an ink drawing. Have a look at Figure 5-15. Let's say you want to take this photo and make it look like it was drawn and inked with a brush. This takes fewer steps than you might think.

FIGURE 5-15

A standard photograph. It looks nice, but let's try to "art it up." (Photo credit: Melody Smith)

Use the following steps to take this from a photo to an ink drawing:

1. **Create paths.** It depends on the image you're using, but use a combination of any of the techniques explained in this chapter to define the shape of the subject with paths. If there are nice solid colors that allow you to get clean selections, use the Fuzzy Select tool (U) to build a selection and turn that into a path. For this example, I did a little bit of that, but most of it was done by tracing the shapes I want with the Paths tool (B). For sections where you know you'll want thicker or thinner lines, create new paths in the Paths dialog. It will make things easier on you down the road.

2. **Add a layer and fill it with white (Layer ➤ New Layer or Ctrl+Shift+N).** Now that you've created your paths, you need a drawing surface to work on. This is your base. It's mainly there to separate your line strokes from the original image. If you make your paths visible in the Paths dialog by clicking the eye icon next to each path, the Paths dialog and image window should look like Figure 5-16.

3. **Add a new transparent layer (Layer ➤ New Layer or Ctrl+Shift+N).** This is where you will be creating the strokes for your ink drawing.

FIGURE 5-16

Paths created from your original image on a white surface

4. **Select one path and click the Stroke Path button (Edit ≻ Stroke Path).** When the Stroke Path dialog appears, select Stroke with a Paint Tool. You have a bunch of choices for which paint tool to use, but I'd recommend using either the Paintbrush or Ink tools. The Paintbrush offers a bit more control over brush dynamics, but Ink tends to be more procedural and look a bit cleaner. You may want to play with both to see what suits your tastes best.

5. **Enable Emulate Brush Dynamics.** This is what's going to give you that brushed ink feeling.

6. **Activate the tool you've selected (Paintbrush or Ink) and adjust its settings in the Toolbox.** The Stroke Path dialog is non-blocking, so you can adjust the settings on these tools without closing it. If you choose Paintbrush (P), it would be best to use one of the hard Circle brushes. Also, expand the Brush Dynamics section and enable the Size check box next to Velocity. If you're using the Ink tool (K), the main thing to adjust is the Size slider. Figure 5-17 shows tool settings for Paintbrush or Ink that would work well for this example.

FIGURE 5-17

Paintbrush and Ink settings that would work on this example image

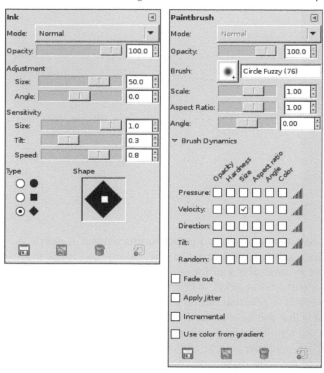

7. **Click the Stroke button in the Stroke Path dialog.** This creates a nice ink-like line along your path. Now, on this first go, the line may not behave the way you want. It may be too thick in places or terminate strangely. In that case, just Undo (Ctrl+Z) and repeat steps 4–6 until you get settings that you're comfortable with.

8. **Repeat steps 4–6 for each path that you've created.** Depending on how fine you need lines to be, you may have to do a couple iterations to get the thickness that you want, but each time you do it, it should be easier to guess the settings that you want.

9. **Woohoo! Done!** From this point, you can save your image and move on or you can go down to your white layer and perhaps try to create a parchment texture to make your ink drawing look like it's had some wear and tear. You have all sorts of options to play with! Have fun!

Figure 5-18 shows the finished result of the image that started as Figure 5-15.

A digital ink drawing, quickly created from a photograph. How sweet is that?

Selecting with a Path

Because you can create a path out of a selection, as explained earlier in this chapter, it makes sense that the reverse is also true. Because paths are often easier to edit, modify, and tweak than some of the other selection tools, they're an invaluable tool for making complex and irregular selections. To create a selection out of a path choose Select ➤ From Path (Shift+V) from the menu in the image window or click the Path to Selection button in the Paths dockable dialog. The advantage of using the Paths dialog is that you have greater control over how the selection is made. Pressing Shift+V or using Select ➤ From Path completely replaces your current selection with a selection defined by the path. If you want the path to add or subtract from the current selection, the way to go is to right-click in the Paths dialog and choose the option you need from there.

Once you've created a selection out of your path, you can treat it like any other selection in GIMP and adjust its feathering, fill it with a color or gradient, or use it as a mask for a color operation or filter. If you did the logo-enlarging example near the beginning of this chapter, you already used this feature. Like how I snuck that in there on you?

Note
When you're exporting your projects from GIMP, be aware that most file formats don't support saving paths embedded in them. Path data is simply discarded in these formats, so if you want to keep your paths, it's highly recommended that you first save to GIMP's native XCF format. After you've done that, export your image into whatever other file format you need to deliver to other people. ∎

Summary

This chapter was all about paths: the way to take advantage of vector tools in a raster graphics program like GIMP. You discovered that you can create paths by drawing them yourself or you can generate them from any selection that you've made. The chapter covered the Paths dockable dialog in detail and showed how you can let GIMP interoperate with vector drawing programs by importing and exporting paths in the open SVG file format. You also found out how to use paths effectively by painting along them or using them to build complex selections.

With any luck, you've got another valuable graphics weapon in your arsenal. Time to add another one!

Summary

Working with Layers and Masks

IN THIS CHAPTER

Creating and modifying layers

Organizing your layers into groups

Applying masks to layers

One of the primary features that defines an advanced image editing application is a robust layer system. As a tangible comparison, think of a *layer* as a single sheet of acetate. By drawing on multiple sheets and stacking them on top of one another, you have a lot of flexibility in the process you use to create your images. With the additional power of the digital medium, you have even more control and flexibility because you can have one layer influence the look of the layers beneath it, rather than simply being stacked above. It's through layers that digital artists do complex compositing and image enhancement. Digital painters use layers to logically separate their work so, for example, they can freely adjust colors without messing up their line work.

Going hand-in-hand with layers is the concept of a *mask*. In traditional art, a mask is an object used to block part of the work so it isn't affected when new paint is applied. As an example, airbrush artists often mask off large sections of their painting surface, leaving only the section that they're interested in working on. Traditional photographers use masks in the darkroom to limit what parts of the photographic paper get exposed to the image in their film negative. In GIMP, each layer can have a mask that dictates which parts of the layer are visible, and at what opacity. The really cool thing, though, is that masks in GIMP give you this control in a non-destructive way. The image data on the layer is still there for future use; it's just hidden by the mask. This gives you a lot more control than you may have by simply using the Erase tool (Shift+E).

This chapter covers GIMP's layer system, showing you how to create, modify, and organize layers in your digital graphics projects. You also learn how to make layers most effective by using them in conjunction with masks.

Managing Layers

In GIMP, you can manage your layers from the image window in the Layer menu or you can use the Layers dockable dialog. The Layers dialog should be available to you by default in the Dock, but if it isn't there, you can bring it up by going to Windows ➤ Dockable Dialogs ➤ Layers or pressing Ctrl+L. Most layer functions can be accessed via either method, but the most comprehensive controls are in the Layer menu. However, the Layers dialog gives you the quickest access to some of the most-used layer functions. Access these controls by right-clicking within the Layers dialog. Figure 6-1 shows the Layer menu in the image window as well as the Layers dialog and its right-click menu.

Note

If you don't have an image actively open, right-clicking the Layers dialog doesn't bring up a menu at all. It makes sense because having no image means you have no layers. If you have no layers, none of the options that would appear in the Layers dialog apply. ■

Generally speaking, if you have the Layers dialog open, it's fastest to use it for layer management. Then you use the Layer menu in your image window for less frequently used layer operations.

You can manage your layers from a menu in the image window (left) or from the Layers dockable dialog (right).

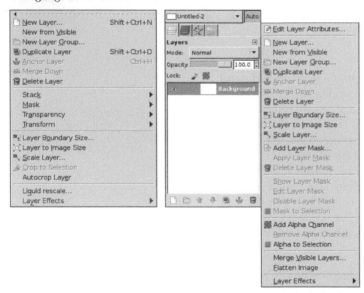

A Quick Overview of the Layers Dialog

The majority of this chapter is devoted to detailed explanations of how to interact with the Layers dialog. However, to get the most of these sections, it's helpful to first do a run-down of what's in that dialog. If you load an image into GIMP that already has a set of layers (several are available to you on this book's companion web site), you should have a Layers dialog like the one that appears in Figure 6-2.

GIMP's Layers dialog gives you quick access to functions for managing layers in your project.

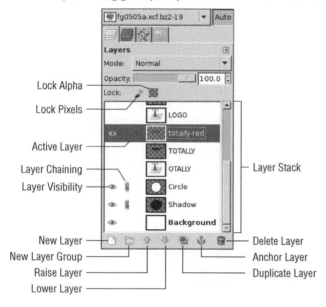

The largest feature in the Layers dialog is central space dedicated to the layer stack. Remember, each layer in GIMP is treated as a sheet of acetate that is stacked on top of the layers beneath it. In the stack, you have one highlighted layer that's your *active layer*. With a few rare exceptions, most tools and filters operate only on this layer. You change active layers by clicking the layer you want to work on. If you want a tool (for example, the Transformation tool) to influence multiple layers at the same time, you need to *chain* them together by clicking the chain-link icon for each layer that you want to be bound together.

Tip

The default behavior for setting an active layer is to click that layer in the Layers dialog. However, on complex images with many layers (or layers without clear names), it can be difficult to know which layer affects each element in your image. In those situations, its nice to be able to click a specific element in your image and have GIMP automatically change layers for you. You can enable this behavior in the Preferences window (Edit ➢ Preferences) in the Tool Options section. At the bottom is a check box under the Move Tool heading labeled Set Layer or Path as Active. Enable that check box and when you're using the Move tool, you can set the active layer by clicking on elements in the image window. ■

Note

An important distinction that differentiates GIMP's style of chaining from the chaining methods in other programs, like Photoshop, is that GIMP's chaining is persistent regardless of whatever the active layer is.

That is, in other programs, if you click the chain-link icon for multiple layers, those layers are chained to the current active layer. If you switch active layers, you can chain a different set of layers to that one, so each individual layer can be chained to a distinct set of layers. This is *not* how chaining works in GIMP. GIMP doesn't track chaining sets per layer. Instead, GIMP maintains a global list of chained elements. Though this may seem strange at first, there's a definite advantage to this technique because it allows you to chain together more than just layers. You can actually chain a layer to a channel or a path and transform operations (rotate, scale, and so on) affect *all* chained elements. Of course, if you need to get something like the behavior of other apps, you should use layer groups, covered later in this chapter. ∎

Each layer also has a visibility icon that you can toggle on or off. This is useful if one of your layers is obscuring the ones below it and you want to hide that layer so you can more clearly see what's going on. Each layer also has a name and an icon associated with it. In most situations, the icon is simply a thumbnail version of the actual content of that layer. The only exceptions to this are text layers, which give you a text icon instead. (You can find more on text layers in Chapter 10.) You can rename layers easily by double-clicking and typing a new name directly in the dialog. When you finish typing, press Enter to confirm the name change. You can also rename by right-clicking the layer and choosing Edit Layer Attributes from the context menu that appears. Regardless of the method you choose, it's definitely a good idea to use logical names that make sense for the image you're working on. This makes it much easier for you or someone else to modify your image in the future.

Tip

If you Shift+click the visibility or chaining icon for a layer, it disables the visibility or chain links on all other layers. If you Shift+click the icon again, it makes all layers visible or chains them all together. For chaining, this is a great, quick way to remove all chain links, and for visibility this is extremely useful for isolating a single layer so you can focus your work directly on that one. ∎

Each layer also features a pair of locks. However, rather than clutter up the layer stack with these icons, the developers chose to place them above the stack area. To enable a lock on the active layer, click the icon of the lock you want to use. GIMP remembers the lock on that layer until you disable it. As the previous figure shows, layers have two kinds of locks:

- **Pixel Lock** — Enable this lock on a layer and no tool or operation that modifies pixels will work on that layer. You're basically limited to selecting pixels on the layer or simply hiding it. Locking pixels is extremely useful if you've modified a layer and want to prevent yourself or someone else from accidentally messing it up while editing the rest of the image.

- **Alpha Channel Lock** — Locking the alpha channel is a little bit confusing. You would think that enabling this lock would prevent you from modifying the alpha channel of your layer at all, meaning that GIMP wouldn't let you paint opaque pixels in transparent areas or erase pixels from opaque areas. Unfortunately, only the latter scenario is true. This means that if you have a layer with transparent parts, when this lock is enabled those parts remain transparent, regardless of what you paint (or paste) on the layer. Figure 6-3 illustrates this concept.

Tip

If you paint or paste on a layer with a locked alpha channel, that doesn't mean that the transparent pixels aren't being modified. They are. As proof of this, you can re-create the rightmost image in Figure 6-3 and, after disabling the Alpha Channel Lock, use the anti erase option of the Erase tool (press Alt while erasing), and the line you drew will be revealed in the transparent areas. ∎

FIGURE 6-3

If you have a layer with transparency (left) and draw a line across that transparent area, the normal behavior is to modify the layer's alpha channel and display that entire line (center). However, if you lock the alpha channel of that layer, your line appears only in the non-transparent parts (right).

  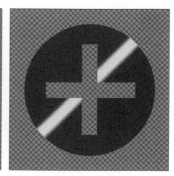

Adding, Duplicating, and Removing Layers

If you have an image open in GIMP, you've already created your first layer. Remember that GIMP works on files only in its native XCF format, so when you open an image from a format that doesn't support layers, like JPEG or PNG, GIMP treats that image as an XCF file with just one layer. GIMP does the same thing when you create a new image with Ctrl+N or File ➤ New. Doing this gets you a Layers dialog like the one shown in Figure 6-1. That particular image has one layer, named Background.

Besides the default layer you get on a new (or newly opened) image, GIMP gives you many ways to create additional layers. This was covered briefly in Chapter 3 in the discussion of copying and pasting. When you paste a selection in GIMP, it creates a special layer called a *floating selection*. You can do anything with that floating selection that you can do with any regular layer, including transform and paint operations. Only two caveats exist:

- **Selection tools work only on the floating selection.** When you use a tool like Rectangle Select or Fuzzy Select, the new selection limits what can be seen of the floating selection layer, showing only what's in the selected area. Think of it like a quick way of masking the floating selection.

- **You cannot select any other layers until you either anchor the floating selection or make it a regular layer.** *Anchoring* the layer merges it with the last active layer in your image. Do this by pressing Ctrl+H, clicking the Anchor icon in the Layers dialog, or going to Layer ➤ Anchor Layer in the image window. Alternatively, you can make the floating selection a new layer of its own by pressing Shift+Ctrl+N, clicking the New Layer button in the Layers dialog, or going to Layer ➤ New Layer in the image window.

Creating a New Layer

Knowing how to handle a floating selection layer is actually pretty useful because it includes the basics of how to control regular layers in GIMP. For example, in the previous bullet point on floating selections, you were given three methods for converting that floating selection into a regular layer. If you don't have a floating selection available, you can use these exact same methods (Shift+Ctrl+N, Layer ➤ New Layer, or the New Layer button in the Layers dialog) to add a new layer to your image. The only difference is that when you create a totally new layer GIMP pops up a dialog like the one shown in Figure 6-4.

FIGURE 6-4

GIMP's Create a New Layer dialog

This dialog gives you quite a bit of control over your layer before it's even created. Right at the top, you're encouraged to give your layer a custom name. This is highly recommended. Use a name that's logical and makes sense for the project you're working on. There's not much worse than opening an old GIMP project and seeing each of the layers named New Layer #1, New Layer #2, and so on.

Below the Layer Name field is a pair of fields to designate the dimensions of your new layer. If you're used to other image editing software, this may be a somewhat alien concept. Unlike other programs where the layer size is essentially infinite, in GIMP, layers have an explicitly defined width and height. Those boundaries are displayed with a yellow-and-black dashed line. Though this may seem strange at first, it's actually pretty useful, particularly if your layer is larger than your image canvas or if your layer is moved off of the canvas area. In other programs, you can't easily see the boundaries of your layer, so you never really know if the layer has any components that are off the canvas. In GIMP, you never have this problem. If your layer is active, you can see its boundaries. By default, the Width and Height fields of the New Layer dialog are the same dimensions as your image.

Tip

If you don't want to see the layer boundaries at all, you can toggle their visibility by going to View ➤ Show Layer Boundary in the image window. Just be aware that this doesn't remove the boundary itself; it only hides it from being displayed while you're working. ∎

A set of radio buttons below the layer dimensions allows you to control how the layer is filled. You have four choices; the first three fill the layer with a solid color. That color can be your current foreground or background color, or it can be solid white. The fourth option, Transparency, doesn't actually fill the layer at all. It's like laying down a blank sheet of acetate that you can make fresh marks upon. Unless you know for certain that you want the new layer to be based on a solid color, Transparency is probably the best choice. Once you've set these options to your liking, click OK and GIMP adds a new layer at the top of your stack in the Layers dialog.

Tip

As a convenient shortcut, if you want to create a new layer without seeing the New Layer dialog, you can Shift+click the New Layer button in the Layers dockable dialog. This creates a new layer with the same dimensions as your image and sets the fill type to be the same option you chose the last time you created a new layer. ■

Another convenience that GIMP provides you with is the ability to create a new layer that's pre-filled with the visible content on all layers by using the Layer ➤ New from Visible menu item. This single menu item replaces going through the three steps of Edit ➤ Select All (Ctrl+A), Edit ➤ Copy Visible (Shift+Ctrl+C), Edit ➤ Paste as ➤ New Layer. This is particularly useful if you want to apply a filter to your entire image, but don't want to destroy your layer structure by flattening or merging all layers. More on merging and flattening is covered later in this chapter.

Duplicating an Existing Layer

Periodically you may want to test a series of edits on a layer without obliterating that layer's contents, or you may want to use an existing layer as the basis for a mask or effect on lower layers. For either of these scenarios, you can take advantage of GIMP's layer duplication feature. To use it, first make sure that the layer you want to duplicate is the current active layer in the Layers dialog. From here you have four (yes, four) different ways that you can duplicate that layer, depending on which GIMP window you're in and what's most convenient for you. If you're in the Layers dialog, you can right-click the layer you want to duplicate and choose Duplicate Layer from the context menu that appears. Alternatively, you can click the Duplicate Layer button at the bottom of the dialog. It's the third button from the right. If you're in an image window, you can duplicate the active layer by choosing Layer ➤ Duplicate Layer. Of course, the absolute fastest way is to use the keyboard shortcut Shift+Ctrl+D. When you perform any of these operations, the new layer is made active and placed directly above the original one in your stack.

Transparent Layers versus Solid Layers

An important thing to be aware of in GIMP is that a layer can be solid or transparent. That is, you can control whether an individual layer in GIMP has an alpha channel. If the layer has an alpha channel, when you use the Erase tool (Shift+E) on it, erasing reveals the layers below or the checkerboard background if that layer is at the bottom of the stack. However, if the layer has no alpha channel, erasing pixels merely paints them with your chosen background color.

You can quickly distinguish between layers with and without an alpha channel by looking in the Layers dialog. Layers with names that are in bold are solid and have no alpha channel. This is the default behavior for the bottom layer (typically named Background) if you open an image in GIMP that's in a

continued

---

continued

format that doesn't support alpha channels, such as JPEG. If you duplicate that layer (Shift+Ctrl+D), the newly created layer is also without an alpha channel. This can make it difficult to erase parts of a layer and reveal other layers beneath it.

Fortunately, you can toggle whether a layer has an alpha channel by right-clicking that layer and choosing either Add Alpha Channel or Remove Alpha Channel, depending on what you need. These functions are also available in the image window within the Layer ➤ Transparency submenu. For the most part, layers are most useful when they have an alpha channel, so you'll usually want to use the Add Alpha Channel function. Layer transparency is covered more later in this chapter.

Deleting Layers

Of all the layer operations, removing layers is probably the simplest and most straightforward. Of course, like the Duplicate Layer feature, GIMP gives you multiple ways to delete a layer, depending on what suits your specific workflow the best. Assuming the active layer is the one you want to delete, the fastest method is to click the trashcan-shaped Delete Layer icon at the bottom of the Layers dialog. Alternatively, you can right-click the undesirable layer and choose Delete Layer from the context menu that appears. If you're in the image window, you can delete the active layer by going to Layer ➤ Delete Layer.

Do note that when you delete a layer, it's gone permanently. You can potentially retrieve it by using Undo (Ctrl+Z), but if you deleted the layer a few steps back or your Undo Memory (set in Edit ➤ Preferences under Environment) is really small, that layer is gone forever.

Arranging Layers in the Stack

The order in which the layers appear in the stack is very important. For example, if you're working on a diagram image that has callouts to specific elements within that diagram, you usually want to have the layer with all of your callout arrows above all other layers. Otherwise, the arrows are obscured by other content in your image. The same is true if you're editing an image and you want it to have a new color in the background. Assuming you control that background with a single layer, you definitely want to have that layer at the bottom of the stack so it shows up behind everything else in your image.

The fastest way to move a layer around is to use drag and drop in the Layers dialog. Simply click the layer you want to move and drag it to its new location in the stack. As an alternative, you can also use the green arrow buttons at the bottom of the Layers dialog. Clicking the up arrow raises the active layer in the stack, and clicking the down arrow lowers the layer. As a convenient shortcut, if you Shift+click the up or down arrows, GIMP moves your active layer directly to the top or bottom of the stack, respectively. You can also raise and lower layers in the stack from the image window using the Layer ➤ Stack submenu. Though this is the slowest of the three methods of moving your layers around, this submenu does offer an additional feature not found elsewhere in GIMP: reversing layer order. To use it click Layer ➤ Stack ➤ Reverse

Layer Order. Once you click this menu item, your layer structure is flipped, placing your topmost layer at the bottom of the stack, the bottom layer up at the top, and all of the middle layers (if you have them) in reverse order.

Grouping and Merging Layers

Earlier in this chapter you saw how you can get a set of layers to work as single unit by chaining them together. Though chaining is a great way to quickly and temporarily bind layers together, it has some shortcomings. For instance, as explained previously, GIMP chains elements globally, so you can't use chaining to group a logical set of layers together. Furthermore, chaining influences only transform operations on layers. If you want to apply a color modification or filter to multiple layers at the same time, chaining doesn't help you at all. The color adjustment or filter still applies only to the current active layer. If you want to perform these operations on multiple layers, you need to use GIMP's layer merging or layer grouping features.

Merging Layers

Of the two methods available to you, merging layers is the tried-and-true technique that's been in GIMP the longest. The functionality of merging is pretty simple: layers are permanently and irreversibly combined to form a new single layer. Once the layers are merged, you can apply the filter or color correction operation to it and the full content of that single layer is affected. You have several different ways to merge layers together, depending on your project's needs:

- **Merge Down** — Access this functionality by right-clicking the layer you want to merge in the Layers dialog and choosing Merge Down from the context menu or, if the active layer is the one you want to merge, choose Layer ➤ Merge Down from the image window. Either way, once you activate this function, the active layer is combined with the next visible layer beneath it. It's important to note that it's the next visible layer. Hidden layers are skipped. If there are no visible layers beneath the one you select, the Merge Down option is grayed out.

- **Merge Visible Layers** — The Merge Down feature is great, but if you want to merge more than two layers together at once, it can be an extremely tedious process to go through and use Merge Down on each and every layer. Fortunately, there's a way around this: Merge Visible Layers. This option is actually not available in the Layer menu of the image window. Instead, you can find it at Image ➤ Merge Visible Layers (Ctrl+M). It's also accessible from the right-click menu in the Layers dialog. Once you click it or use the keyboard shortcut, a dialog like the one in Figure 6-5 appears with some options for controlling the merge operation:

  - **Final, Merged Layer Should Be** — Because layers can be different sizes, you have to decide how GIMP handles the final size of the new merged layer. You have three options:

    - **Expanded as Necessary** — This is the default behavior. The dimensions of the final merged layer are increased to accommodate the content of all the merged layers regardless of whether it all fits your image canvas.

- **Clipped to Image** — If the elements of your merged layer go beyond the boundaries of your image canvas, the merged layer is cropped to fit the canvas. Note that if you choose this option, the clipped content cannot be retrieved unless you undo the merge operation.

- **Clipped to Bottom Layer** — This option is just like the previous one, but rather than cropping the layer to fit your canvas, the newly merged layer is cropped to fit the dimensions of whatever the bottom layer has.

- **Discard Invisible Layers** — If you know that you're not going to need the hidden layers after doing this merge operation, you can activate this check box and any hidden layers are deleted when the merge is complete. Enabling this option means that once you complete the merge, you only have one layer available in the stack.

- **Flatten Image** — At first glance, this appears to be a shortcut operation that's like running Merge Visible Layers with the Clipped to Image option and the Discard Invisible Layers check box enabled. However, there's one more thing flattening does that merging avoids: a flattened image does not have an alpha channel. This is actually like running Merge Visible Layers and then removing the final layer's alpha channel. This is useful if you know you're exporting to an image format that doesn't support alpha. You can access this function just like the Merge Visible Layers feature: right-click in the Layers dialog or choose Image ➤ Flatten Image from within the image window.

FIGURE 6-5

The Layers Merge Options dialog appears when you run the Merge Visible Layers operation.

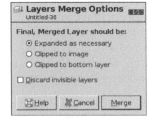

Warning

Remember that merging and flattening are permanent operations. Once you do them, you can reverse them only if they're still in your Undo History. Once you run out of Undo Memory, there's no way to retrieve your original layers. For this reason, you may want to duplicate your layers before merging them, or use Layer ➤ New from Visible to get a merged layer without destroying your originals, or duplicate the entire image (Image ➤ Duplicate or Ctrl+D) and perform your merge or flatten on the duplicate. Alternatively, you can use GIMP's new layer groups, described in the next section. ■

Grouping Layers

The merging and flattening functions are great, fast, and reliable. However, they're also destructive. Unless you work with duplicates of your original layers, there's no way to tweak or adjust those originals after you've merged them. This can make image editing a pretty frustrating task, especially if you're likely to require multiple revisions of a single image. To help alleviate this, GIMP developers introduced layer groups for the 2.8 series. Simply put, a layer group is a logical organization of multiple layers that behave as a single unit. This gives you the benefit of chaining, but with a retained logical structure, making it easier to understand what's going on in an image.

Note

Currently, you cannot perform pixel operations directly on a layer group. This means you can't paint on a layer group or select it and run a filter or color adjustment operation on it. At this point in time, layer groups are primarily an organizational tool. For this release of GIMP, the developers want to make sure that the basic functionality and structure of layer groups are in place and behaving properly before pushing forward with more dynamic features. This means that although you can't do pixel operations on a layer group, you're completely free to do transform operations like move, rotate, and scale. However, once the GEGL graphics library is fully integrated with GIMP (the target for this is GIMP 2.10), you should be able to do color adjustment and filter operations on a layer group. You can read more about GEGL in Chapter 9. In the meantime, the merge functions and the Layer ➤ New from Visible feature should work as effective stand-ins. ■

To create a new layer group, either click the New Layer Group button in the Layers dialog, right-click within the Layers dialog and select New Layer Group, or go to Layer ➤ New Layer Group in the image window. This creates a new layer group above the active layer. By default, the new group is called Layer Group. You can rename it just like any regular layer by double-clicking it or choosing Edit Layer Attributes from the right-click context menu in the Layers dialog.

By default, new groups are empty. To populate a group, you need to move layers into it by clicking a layer and dragging it over the layer group's name in the Layers dialog. When you release your mouse button, your dropped layer appears indented as part of your new layer group. If you do this a few times, you can get a result that looks like the one in Figure 6-6.

FIGURE 6-6

Using layer groups to organize the structure of your GIMP XCF files

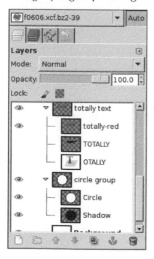

Layer groups can be stacked, renamed, and transformed just like any regular layer can. In addition to that, you can also expand and collapse layer groups from the Layers dialog by clicking the triangle icon next to the layer group name. This gives you a hierarchical organizational structure that can help make your project files much easier to understand. You can also nest your groups, allowing for even more structural control. Furthermore, the controls for visibility, chaining, and locks propagate to the layers that are members of a group. As an example, this means that if you set the visibility of a layer group to be hidden, all of the members of that group are hidden as well, regardless of whether those individual layers have their visibility enabled or disabled. The same goes for locks and chaining. Of course, you still retain the ability to chain any layer to any other layer, so you're free to chain a grouped layer to anything else and GIMP respects that link. This means that even with the structure imposed by layer groups, you still have the flexibility to use chaining anywhere you need it.

Warning

When you delete a layer group, not only are you deleting the parent group, but you also delete each of its constituent layers. Keep this in mind if you decide that you no longer need a layer group for organization, but you want to retain the layers within that group. To do that, you need to move the member layers out of the group via the same drag-and-drop method you used to move them in. Once you do that, you're free to delete the layer group without worrying about the loss of your layers. ∎

Manipulating Layers

Layers are a central structural concept in GIMP, so nearly every operation that you can perform is relative to your active layer. This includes the Transformation tool and color adjustments as well as filters and paint tools. Now, of course, there are some exceptions to this rule. You've already seen in this chapter how you can batch groups together using chaining and layer groups, and Chapter 4 covers quite a few tools, such as Crop, Clone, and Healing, that utilize the Sample Merged option, which allows you to use all visible pixel data, regardless of what layer it's on. All that said, you still have more ways to directly manipulate the content of a layer that aren't necessarily specific to any one tool. This section is dedicated to those operations.

Resizing Layers

Throughout this chapter it's been re-emphasized that unlike the layers in some other image editing software, GIMP's layers have an explicit size. This gives some distinct advantages, but it also means that you still need to maintain an awareness of what size your layers are in relation to your image and canvas size. To that end, you're able to adjust the dimensions of your layers. Just like you have two ways to adjust the dimensions of the image, you have two different ways to adjust layer size.

Modifying the Layer Boundary Size

Just like you can adjust the size of your image's canvas without distorting or scaling the pixels of that image, you're also able to modify the dimensions of a layer without scaling it. You do this by using the Layer Boundary Size menu item available in the Layers dialog's right-click menu or at Layer ➤ Layer Boundary Size in the image window. When you activate this feature, GIMP provides you with a dialog like the one shown in Figure 6-7.

FIGURE 6-7

GIMP's Set Layer Boundary Size dialog

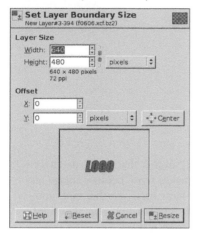

This dialog is remarkably similar to the Image ➤ Canvas Size dialog discussed in Chapter 1. In fact, the only difference is that the Set Layer Boundary Size dialog doesn't have a Resize Layers section, which makes sense because you're only resizing a single layer in this case. Go though, set your width and height to a larger or smaller value, adjust the offset to get the layer's content positioned where you want it, and click the Resize button to increase or decrease the boundaries of the active layer.

Of course, if you're trying to adjust the layer's boundaries to match the dimensions of your image, there's a faster way. You can use the Layer to Image Size menu option that appears directly below the Layer Boundary Size option on both the right-click menu of the Layers dialog and on the image window's menu under Layer ➤ Layer to Image Size. This shortcut method doesn't pop up any window. It simply modifies the layer's dimensions to match those of the image canvas.

Warning

Be careful when using the Layer to Image Size feature, especially if your layer is larger than the dimensions of your canvas because the Layer to Image Size operation behaves like a cropping tool when the layer is larger than the image. It simply crops the layer down to fit the desired space, removing any image content that may have been on your layer but not visible on the canvas. ■

Scaling Layers

Just as you can modify the boundaries of a layer without scaling its contents, you're also able to scale an individual layer independently of the overall image or other layers that it isn't chained to or grouped with. You do this with GIMP's Scale Layer feature, accessible from the right-click menu of the Layers dialog or from the image window at Layer ➤ Scale Layer. Doing so brings up a dialog like the one shown in Figure 6-8.

FIGURE 6-8

The Scale Layer dialog

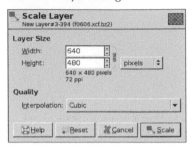

This dialog is identical to the Image Scale dialog available in GIMP except that the Scale Layer dialog doesn't include fields for adjusting image resolution. This makes sense because image resolution isn't really something you would want to adjust on a per-layer basis. To that end, you can set the size that you want to scale your layer to, decide which interpolation type you want to use, and then click the Scale button. From there, GIMP handles the rest.

Offsetting the Content of a Layer

One of the neat things that the Layer menu offers that isn't available in the Image menu is the ability to offset the content of the layer, optionally wrapping "bumped" pixels to the opposite side of the layer. This feature is often used in conjunction with the Clone tool by texture painters who want their textures to tile seamlessly. To see this feature in action, launch it by going to Layer ➤ Transform ➤ Offset or pressing Shift+Ctrl+O. This provides you with a dialog like the one in Figure 6-9.

FIGURE 6-9

GIMP's Offset Layer dialog

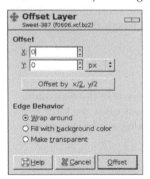

To use this dialog, enter the number of units by which you want to offset your layer's content in the X and Y directions. By default, the units are set in pixels, but you can use the drop-down menu to the right of these fields to change to any of the other units that GIMP supports. Entering positive values in the X and Y fields offsets the layer's content to the right and down, respectively. Negative values push the content left and up. Below the X and Y entry fields is a button labeled Offset by X/2, Y/2. If you click this convenient button, the X and Y fields are filled with values for half the width of the layer and half the layer's height.

Below the offset values are three choices under the label of Edge Behavior. These options determine what GIMP does with the layer's content as it reaches the layer boundary. Your choices are as follows:

- **Wrap Around** — This is the default setting. As the layer's content approaches the outer dimensions of that layer, those pixels are wrapped to the opposite side of the layer.

- **Fill with Background Color** — Rather than wrap the content around, this option simply fills the missing space with the current background color.

- **Make Transparent** — This option is the same as Fill with Background Color, but rather than use the background color, this option just makes those empty pixels transparent.

Figure 6-10 shows the results of the three different edge behaviors on a layer where the content is pushed to the right.

FIGURE 6-10

From left to right, the original layer image and the offsets of that content using Wrap Around, Fill with Background Color, and Make Transparent edge behaviors

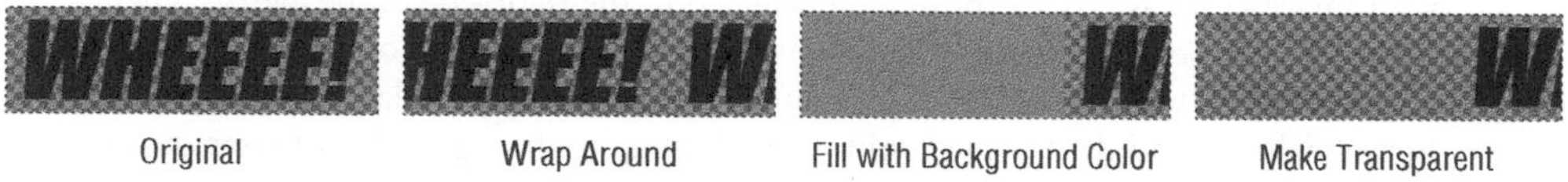

| Original | Wrap Around | Fill with Background Color | Make Transparent |

Aligning Layers

One of the few tools that doesn't work directly on the active layer is the Alignment tool (Q). This tool was briefly covered in Chapter 4, but there's more in-depth coverage of the Alignment tool and its options in Chapter 8. That said, there is a menu-based way to align the various layers in your image. You can find it by going to your image window and choosing Image ➤ Align Visible Layers. This brings up the dialog shown in Figure 6-11.

FIGURE 6-11

The Align Visible Layers dialog

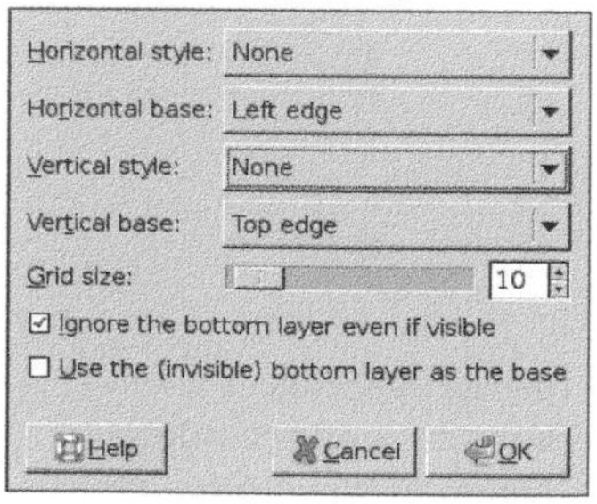

Horizontal style:	None
Horizontal base:	Left edge
Vertical style:	None
Vertical base:	Top edge
Grid size:	10

☑ Ignore the bottom layer even if visible
☐ Use the (invisible) bottom layer as the base

Help Cancel OK

All of the control for this feature comes from the four drop-down menus at the top of this dialog. They control the type of alignment you're using and to what part of the layer you're aligning (an edge or the layer's center). These controls are repeated horizontally and vertically so you have fully independent control of alignment in both directions. The breakdown for the controls in this dialog are as follows:

- **Horizontal/Vertical Style** — The style options control how you're aligning your layers. You have four basic options:

  - **None** — As you'd expect, choosing this option tells GIMP not to do any alignment in that direction. This is useful if you want your layers to keep their position in one direction, but align them in another. For example, if you want to align your layers with the top of the image, you'd set Horizontal Style to None and Vertical Style to Collect.

  - **Collect** — The Collect option gathers your layers to either the left edge or top edge of the image canvas, depending on whether you choose it for the Horizontal or Vertical Style. Unlike the Alignment tool (Q) the Align Visible Layers feature doesn't give you a direct way to align your layers to an arbitrary layer or any canvas edge other than the left or top edges. For example, if you want to align your layers to the right edge of your image, you need to set Horizontal Style to Collect and Vertical Style to None. You also need to set the Horizontal Base to Right Edge. Click OK after configuring those options, and all of your layers seem to disappear. Don't worry; they haven't. They're just off of your image's canvas. To get those layers aligned to the right side of the canvas, chain all of your visible layers together and move them to the right side of the layer using the Transformation tool. Hold down Ctrl while moving to keep your layers locked to their horizontal axis, and the layers should naturally snap to the right edge of your canvas when they get near it. Figure 6-12 shows this example in action.

FIGURE 6-12

Aligning layers to the right side of your image canvas using the Align Visible Layers feature

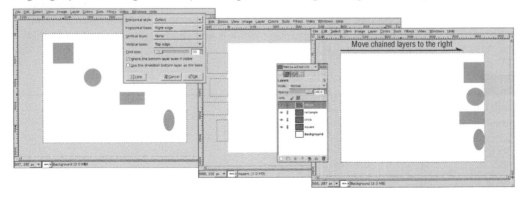

- **Fill** — Whereas a the Collect style gathers all your layers to a specific edge, the Fill style attempts to spread your layers out evenly, without overlapping, and according to their order in the layer stack. Horizontally, you have the option to fill your layers

from left to right or from right to left. Vertically, filling happens from top to bottom or vice versa. As an example, say you have a bunch of layers and you want them to be spaced evenly along the diagonal line from the top left of your canvas to the bottom right according to their order in the layer stack. To do this, set your Horizontal Style to Fill (Left to Right) and your Vertical Style to Fill (Top to Bottom) and click OK. You should have something that looks like Figure 6-13.

FIGURE 6-13

Organizing your layers by filling them from the top-left corner to the bottom right

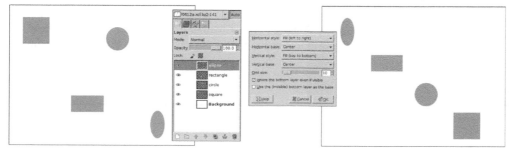

- **Snap to Grid** — This style option aligns your visible layers to an invisible grid over your image. Take special notice that this grid is different from the one you can see if you click View ➤ Show Grid in the image window. You can set the size of this grid to any dimensions that you need for this specific alignment task. To do that, use the Grid Size slider at the bottom of the Align Visible Layers dialog. The default value is a grid with intersections every 10 pixels.

- **Horizontal/Vertical Base** — The base is the part of the layer to which you're aligning. It's important to note here that GIMP uses the layer boundaries to determine where the left, right, top, and bottom edges are. That means if you have a large transparent area around the content of your layer, your alignment results won't be what you expect them to be. If that's the case, you may want to run Layer ➤ Autocrop Layer on your visible layers before activating the Align Visible Layers feature. If you're adjusting the Horizontal Base, your options are the left edge of each layer, the right edges, or the horizontal center of each one. If you're adjusting the Vertical Base, you choose between the top edges, bottom edges, or vertically center line of each layer.

- **Grid Size** — This slider controls the size of the grid that's used if you use the Snap to Grid alignment style. If you don't use Snap to Grid, the value here is ignored.

- **Ignore the Bottom Layer Even if Visible** — In most cases, the bottom layer in your image is a background layer and you typically won't want it moving when you're aligning layers. However, it's often helpful to keep this bottom layer visible while you're aligning. Keep this check box enabled and that bottom layer stays put even if it is one of your visible layers.

- **Use the (Invisible) Bottom Layer as the Base** — By default, the Align Visible Layers feature treats your image canvas as the base reference for alignment. However, you may want to align your visible layers to a different base, such as another layer. To do that, take the layer that you want to behave as your base and move it to the bottom of the layer stack. Then set that layer's visibility to be hidden. Once you have that done, run Image ➤ Align Visible Layers and enable this check box before you click OK. Doing so tells GIMP to use that hidden bottom layer as your base instead of using the image canvas.

Working with Layer Transparency

One of the most valuable benefits of layers is the fact that each one can have varying levels of transparency so you can reveal parts of layers below. As mentioned earlier in this chapter, you can add or remove an alpha channel from any layer by right-clicking that layer in the Layers dialog and choosing Add Alpha Channel or Remove Alpha Channel from the context menu. These options are also available in the image window at the top of the Layer ➤ Transparency submenu, shown in Figure 6-14.

FIGURE 6-14

The Layer ➤ Transparency menu

However, a layer doesn't have to have an alpha channel to be transparent. Above the layer stack and lock controls in the Layers dialog is a slider labeled Opacity. By default, all layers have 100% opacity. However, if you adjust this slider, you can adjust the overall opacity of the active layer. This is especially useful when working with blending modes — discussed later in this chapter — because you can use the Opacity slider to control the strength of the blending mode. Of course, your ultimate flexibility comes from making use of the alpha channels on each layer. And beyond merely adding and removing alpha channels to and from layers, GIMP provides you with a handful of other helpful features that relate to the layers' alpha channels.

Additional Layer Transparency Features

Looking back at Figure 6-14, three additional operations are available below the Add and Remove Alpha Channel functions. These features allow you to control the nature of your alpha channel; controlling what's transparent and by how much. Descriptions of each function follow:

- **Color to Alpha** — Of these three functions, this is the only one that's available if your layer doesn't already have an alpha channel. As its name implies, it allows you to designate a specific color in your layer as being transparent. The cool thing is that it does this pretty intelligently. Rather than doing simple *binary transparency* (for example, "This color is transparent, but anything that isn't this exact color is opaque"), the Color to Alpha feature actually accounts for the mixing of colors. This is especially useful when you have semi-transparent elements in your layer. Figure 6-15 shows this feature in action.

FIGURE 6-15

If you have a white layer that has a fuzzy paint stroke on it, using the Color to Alpha feature on the layer and choosing white as your color keeps the fuzzy parts of your paint stroke semi-transparent.

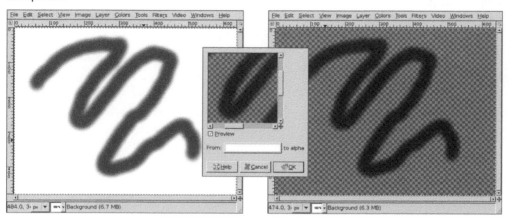

- **Semi-Flatten** — The Semi-Flatten feature is of specific use when you're saving to an image format that supports only binary transparency, like GIF. GIF images don't have an alpha channel. Instead, you pick a single color from the GIF palette and declare that color to be transparent. In many cases this works just fine. However, if parts of your image are semi-transparent or have antialiased edges, binary transparency looks really ugly. A trick that digital artists used to employ when working with GIF images for web sites is determine the background color of their web site and use that specific color to mix with the semi-transparent portions of their images. This makes the edges of transparent images appear to be antialiased when they really aren't. The Semi-Flatten feature of GIMP automates this process for you. To use it, first set your background color in GIMP to match the color you want to mix in the semi-transparent areas. For example, if you're making a GIF for a web site, this color would likely be your web site's background color. Once you have your color picked, choose Layer ➤ Transparency ➤ Semi-Flatten from the menu in the image window and GIMP does the rest for you from there. Do note that this only affects semi-transparent pixels. Any complete transparent pixels in your layer are left alone.

- **Threshold Alpha** — This feature works similarly to Semi-Flatten, but rather than mix a color with semi-transparent pixels, the operation simply declares that a pixel is either transparent or opaque. You can control how sensitive this operation is to transparency by adjusting the Threshold slider in the dialog that appears when you run it from Layer ➤ Transparency ➤ Threshold Alpha. Figure 6-16 shows what this dialog looks like. Lower Threshold values make even the lightest of semi-transparent pixels completely opaque, and higher Threshold values make even opaque pixels completely transparent.

FIGURE 6-16

The Threshold Alpha dialog

Using Layer Transparency for Selections

Another helpful use of alpha channels on each layer is for generating and building quick selection masks. The fastest way to do this is to go to the Layers dialog, right-click the layer you want to use, and choose Alpha to Selection from the context menu. This tells GIMP to select pixels in your image based on the active layer's alpha channel. This is much more useful than trying to select transparent areas with the Fuzzy Select tool because it allows you to accurately select semi-transparent pixels as well.

The context menu in the Layers dialog gives you only one selection option relative to a layer's alpha channel. However, you can actually build even more complex selections with the additional options available at the bottom of the Layer ➤ Transparency submenu in the image window. If you need a quick refresher on what that submenu looks like, take a moment and look back at Figure 6-14. As the figure shows, in addition to Alpha to Selection, you have three other options:

- **Add to Selection** — A disadvantage of the Alpha to Selection feature is that it completely replaces any selection you've made prior. There may be situations where you already have a base selection made and you want to add the selection from a layer's alpha channel to it. This is precisely what Add to Selection is for.

- **Subtract from Selection** — Where you can add, you can also often subtract. This continues to hold true for selections. If you have a selection created and you don't want the opaque portions of one layer to be affected, you can use this function and remove those pixels from your existing selection.

- **Intersect with Selection** — This feature is pretty interesting. On some few, admittedly rare, occasions you really only want to select the pixels that are overlapped by your current selection and the selection created by a layer's alpha channel. This area is referred to as an intersection, and this operation is the way to get those pixels selected.

These selection features give you a lot of power over selection and let you make very accurate selections that fit your layers. Not only is this helpful for creating masks (covered later in this chapter), but you can use these features to create some of the most commonly used special effects in graphic design. For example, you can use a layer's alpha channel to generate a drop shadow. The basic steps for doing this are as follows:

1. **Build your selection.** This example, shown in Figure 6-17, uses a single text layer so all that is necessary is the single use of Alpha to Selection. However, you can easily build a more complex selection with the alpha selection features available in the Layer ➤ Transparency submenu.

2. **Create a new transparent layer (Shift+Ctrl+N).** This new layer is where your drop shadow is going to live. Name this layer **Drop Shadow**.

3. **Set your foreground color to black and use the Bucket Fill tool (Shift+B) to fill the selected area in your new layer with black.** To do this quickly, Shift+click within the selected area and even isolated selections will be filled. At this point, your original image is completely obscured by black. Don't worry; it's part of the process. After you fill your selection, deselect everything by going to Select ➤ None or pressing Shift+Ctrl+A.

4. **Perform a Gaussian blur on your new, black-filled layer (Filters ➤ Blur ➤ Gaussian Blur).** Use the preview and play around with the blur values until you get a shadow with your desired softness. It depends on the size of the image you're working on, but I often find that values of 25 are typically a good place to start. Once you confirm the blur operation, you have the basic foundations of your drop shadow. All that remains now is making it pretty.

5. **In the Layers dialog, lower your drop shadow layer so it's below the layer that you're shadowing.** This basically gives you a shadow that's directly beneath your original layer. If you want to give it a somewhat more directional shadow, use the Transformation tool or Layer ➤ Transform ➤ Offset to shift the shadow around. You can also adjust the Opacity slider for your drop shadow layer to reduce the intensity of the shadow.

6. **You're done!** You should have something like the final result shown in Figure 6-17.

Plug-ins and filters have been created to automate this process and create drop shadow effects more quickly. However, even with all those shortcuts, many artists still prefer to do it this way because it offers more custom control over the effect and it works regardless of the software package you're using.

FIGURE 6-17

Using Alpha to Selection to create a drop shadow

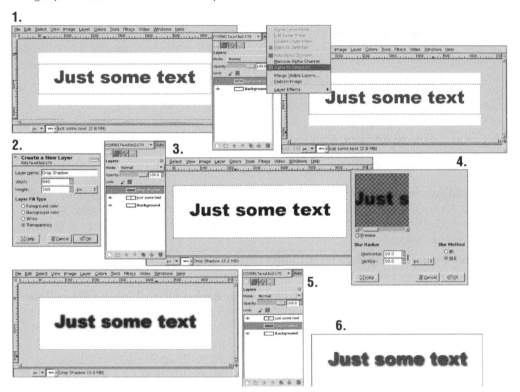

Blending Modes

The default behavior for a layer is to sit on top of the layers beneath it, replacing lower layers' pixels with its own. If a layer has an alpha channel, some of the lower layer pixels may make it through and be seen. Additionally, you can use the Opacity slider in the Layers dialog to control how much influence the active layer's pixels have over the layers beneath it. This default behavior is referred to as GIMP's Normal Blending Mode. At its core, a *blending mode* is a simple rule that relates the active layer's pixels to the pixels of the layers underneath it. The Normal mode is basically a replacement rule. Of course, GIMP offers quite a few modes to choose from. To access the blending modes for a layer, you need to look in the Layers dialog. The first item in the dialog is a drop-down menu labeled Mode. This is where you choose the mode for your active layer. Click this drop-down to reveal more than 20 different blending modes to choose from:

- **Basic modes** — These two modes offer very basic blending functionality.
  - **Normal** — This blending mode simply takes the active layer's pixels and uses them in place of the pixels of the lower levels. If you have a completely opaque layer set to this mode, it effectively prevents you from seeing any of the content from lower layers.

- **Dissolve** — The Dissolve blending mode is kind of the weirdo of the group. It influences only semi-transparent pixels. It takes a generally smooth transition and dithers it by randomly making some of the semi-transparent pixels opaque and making others completely transparent. Figure 6-18 shows what happens when you use the Dissolve blending mode on a layer with a black-to-transparent gradient.

FIGURE 6-18

If you place a layer with a black-to-transparent gradient (left) above another layer (center) and you use the Dissolve blending mode, GIMP dithers the semi-transparent pixels (right). On the far right is a detail shot of an area highly affected by the Dither blend mode. (Photo credit: Melody Smith)

- **Lighten modes** — As the name implies, these modes have the effect of taking the pixels from lower layers and making them brighter and closer to white. Figure 6-19 shows the results of using each of these blending modes on a test pattern laid over a photograph of a sheep.

  - **Lighten Only** — This mode is a simple comparison. For every pixel in your image, GIMP compares the value in the active layer to the value of the next visible layer below it and keeps the lighter of the two values. Completely black pixels have no influence, revealing the pixels of the lower layers. Completely white pixels remain white.

  - **Screen** — The way GIMP determines the final color of a pixel in Screen mode is a bit more complex than the simple comparison of Lighten Only, but the results are similar. White pixels remain completely white and black pixels have no influence at all. However, the middle values yield a slightly more subtle outcome than Lighten Only does, resulting in an image that's a bit more washed out.

  - **Dodge** — In traditional photography, *dodging* is a process that's performed in the darkroom to increase the time that specific sections of the photographic paper are exposed to light passed through the negative. This typically pulls more detail out of darker parts of the photograph, making it easier to see. In digital imaging, the Dodge blending mode performs a similar task. You don't get the washed out results that you see in Lighten Only and Screen, but light pixels in your Dodge layer have a much greater influence on the brightness of pixels from lower layers.

  - **Addition** — As the name implies, this blending mode adds the value from the upper layer's pixel to the value of the lower layer's pixel. In many ways, this blending mode produces results that look like a combination of using the Screen and Dodge blending modes at the same time.

On the top row, the left image is a test pattern and the right image is a photograph that the test pattern is stacked on top of. The second row is the result of each of the lighten modes applied to the test pattern on top of the photo. (Photo credit: cgtextures.com.)

Test pattern   Photograph

Lighten Only   Screen   Dodge   Addition

- **Darken modes** — In contrast to the previous set of blending modes, these modes darken pixels of lower layers, pushing them closer to solid black. Figure 6-20 shows each of these blending modes using the same test pattern and photograph.

From left to right, applying each of the darken modes to a test pattern on top of a stock photograph

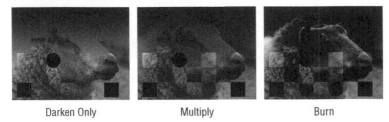

Darken Only   Multiply   Burn

- **Darken Only** — The Darken Only blending mode is the exact opposite of the Lighten Only mode. That means that each pixel from the blending layer is compared to the pixel in the layer below it and the darker of the two pixels is retained. Completely white pixels have no influence on the image and completely black pixels remain completely black.

- **Multiply** — In some ways, it's convenient to think of the Multiply mode as the dark version of the Screen mode. Like Darken Only, white pixels have no influence and black pixels stay black. However, the in-between values provide a result that's like looking at the lower levels through dark tinted glass.

- **Burn** — In traditional photography, the process of *burning* is the opposite of dodging. Burning prevents portions of the photographic paper from receiving light so parts of the image that are too bright can be brought down to a more acceptable level. In digital work, the result is roughly the same. Where you have darker pixels on your upper layer, the pixels in the lower layer get much, much darker.

- **Overlay modes** — The modes in this section are very helpful for compositing where you want to use one layer to intensify the brights and/or darks of the layers below. Figure 6-21 shows each of the overlay modes applied using the same test pattern and photograph as before.

FIGURE 6-21

From left to right, each of the overlay modes

  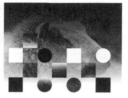

| Overlay | Soft Light | Hard Light |

- **Overlay** — In the lighten and darken modes, completely black or completely white pixels have no influence on the value of pixels from lower layers. For overlay mode, the non-influencing pixels are at 50% gray. Pixels lighter than that brighten the lower layer, and pixels darker than 50% gray darken the lower layer.

- **Soft Light** — This blending mode has no real relation to the Hard Light blending mode described next. In fact, as of this writing, the results from Soft Light are identical to the results from the Overlay mode. In other software, Soft Light and Overlay are similar, but Soft Light tends to soften edges and desaturate colors.

- **Hard Light** — This mode is like an intense version of the Overlay blending mode. 50% gray is still the baseline where pixels in lower layers are not influenced. However, the difference is that as pixels approach being fully white or black, their intensity is increased. This results in an image with very bright and very dark portions along with parts of the image that are largely unchanged.

- **Mathematical/Mixing modes** — These blending modes provide some of the most drastic results, often changing a pixel's color to something completely different. The results can also be a bit disorienting because, with the exception of Grain Merge, dark pixels on your blending layer produce brighter results and light pixels produce darker results. It's like the Bizarro World of blending modes. Figure 6-22 show the results of each of these blending modes.

FIGURE 6-22

Each of the different mathematical/mixing modes

Difference   Subtract

Grain Extact   Grain Merge   Divide

- **Difference** — This blending mode is a quick and easy way to invert some of the pixels in the lower layers. Darker pixels in your blending layer cause there to be less of an inverting effect. Completely white pixels in the blending layer totally invert the pixels of lower layers.

- **Subtract** — The Subtract mode is simply the opposite of the Addition mode. Whereas the Addition blending mode adds pixel values together to get an overall brighter result, the Subtract mode subtracts pixel values, yielding a much darker result, often with heavy black areas. The interesting thing to note here is that the brighter your blending layer is, the darker the overall result will be.

- **Grain Extract** — This mode is designed to isolate film grain that may be in a photographic image, but can also be used as a somewhat more subtle version of the Subtract mode. 50% gray pixels on your blending layer have no influence on the value of pixels in lower layers.

- **Grain Merge** — Grain merge does the exact opposite operation of the Grain Extract blending mode. The results of this mode actually fall between what you get if you use the Overlay or Hard Light modes. In fact, in future versions of GIMP, it's likely that this blending mode will be moved to the overlay modes section.

- **Divide** — In some ways, this mode is the opposite of the Multiply mode. Everywhere Multiply mode would make your image darker, Divide mode makes it much brighter. However, the results of Divide tend to be a lot more intense, producing results that look similar to results from Dodge mode.

- **Color modes** — Whereas all the other blending modes mostly deal with brightness and contrast levels to influence pixel color, these modes deal directly with the hue and saturation to affect the color of individual pixels. Specifically speaking, these blending modes work using the Hue Saturation Value (HSV) colorspace discussed in Chapter 2. The images in Figure 6-23 show how these blending modes work with the test pattern and example photo. Unfortunately, these results may be a bit tough to see in the grayscale figures of this book. For that reason, I highly recommend you play with them yourself to see how they work. You can also see some of these figures in full color on this book's companion web site at `www.wiley.com/go/GIMPBible.com`.

The results of using the various blending modes in the color modes category

   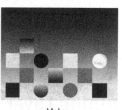

Hue   Saturation   Color   Value

- **Hue** — This mode takes the hue from the blending layer and combines it with the saturation and value of the lower layer. If your blending layer is an entirely grayscale image (therefore having no real hue value), the hue is taken from the lower layers as well. This can generally result in a subtle noise or grain over your image.

- **Saturation** — The Saturation mode takes the saturation value from the blending layer and mixes it with the hue and value of pixels on lower layers. Of course, if your blending layer is completely grayscale, the result usually desaturates your lower layers. However, it's really not a good idea to use this to desaturate your images, because it can often result in a few color artifacts.

- **Color** — This mode takes the hue and saturation of the blending layer and mixes it with the value of pixels in lower layers. Just like the Saturation blending mode, if your blending layer is grayscale, the resulting effect turns lower layers grayscale as well.

- **Value** — This mode is basically the inverse of the Color blending mode. It uses the value of pixels in the blending layer and mixes it with the hue and saturation of the lower layer. This result can drastically influence the colors in your result.

Tip

The list of blending modes that are available to you is long and potentially daunting. However, there's a useful hint to note about how they're organized. If you look at the name of the first blending mode for each section, it gives you a good idea of what the other modes in that section do. Furthermore, the ordering of the modes in each section goes from the most subtle, softly influencing mode to the mode with the strongest, most harsh influence of that section. ■

Tip

If a blending mode gets you close to the effect you want, but it's a bit too harsh, you can reduce its strength by adjusting the Opacity slider in the Layers dialog. Lowering the Opacity on a layer reduces the intensity of the blending mode that's used by that layer. ■

Using Layer Masks

Having an alpha channel on each layer is a powerful way to add customized transparency on a per-layer basis. However, the problem with alpha channels on each layer is that it's easy to forget that there's layer content hidden by the alpha channel and it's somewhat difficult to edit that alpha channel directly. You have the anti erase feature of the Erase tool (Shift+E), but that's pretty much the extent of it.

Fortunately, there's another way to give customized transparency to a layer: layer masks. A layer mask is like an easily editable alpha channel that's bound to a specific layer. The cool thing is that you can also hide or disable the layer mask and edit your layer's content directly without being obscured behind transparency. It's the preferred method for non-destructively adding transparency to any layer. It even works on layers that can't or don't have alpha channels.

Defining Layer Masks

A layer mask is basically a selection defined by a grayscale image. White pixels are 100% opaque and black pixels are completely transparent. This is the same way channels work in GIMP. You can find more on channels in the next chapter. Defining a layer mask for the active layer is really quite simple. You can either right-click the desired layer in the Layers dialog and choose the Add Layer Mask option or you can choose Layer ➤ Mask ➤ Add Layer Mask. Either way, GIMP gives you a dialog like the one that appears in Figure 6-24.

FIGURE 6-24

The Add Layer Mask dialog

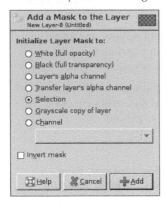

As the figure shows, this dialog provides you with a handful of options to generate your new layer mask:

- **White (Full Opacity)** — This initiates your layer mask to be completely opaque. This is the equivalent to having a completely opaque layer with no alpha channel. This is a good option to choose if you want to adjust the layer's transparency by editing the mask after you create it.

- **Black (Full Transparency)** — This is the opposite of the White option, rendering your layer completely transparent.

- **Layer's Alpha Channel** — If your layer already has an alpha channel, you can use it as a starting point for your layer mask by choosing this radio button. An important thing to note about this option is that it leaves your layer's alpha channel intact. This means that the transparency generated by the layer mask is combined with the alpha channel's transparency. This effectively makes semi-transparent parts of the layer even more transparent than you likely want them to be. If you choose this item, you may want to remove the layer's alpha channel.

- **Transfer Layer's Alpha Channel** — This option is just like the Layer's Alpha Channel option, but it takes the liberty of removing the layer's alpha channel for you, preventing you from doing extra work and ensuring that the transparent parts of your image maintain the same level of transparency. Between this option and the Layer's Alpha Channel option, this one is probably the one you want to use.

- **Selection** — If you currently have a selection in your image, this option takes that selection and treats it as the starting point for your layer mask. Selected areas are set to be opaque.

- **Grayscale Copy of Layer** — This option takes your layer and makes a grayscale version of it to be your layer mask.

- **Channel** — If you've created any custom channels (covered in Chapter 7), you can use one of those channels as the starting point for your layer's layer mask. To take advantage of this feature, click its radio button and choose your custom channel from the drop-down menu beneath it. If you have no custom channels, this drop-down remains blank.

At the bottom of the dialog, there's also a check box labeled Invert Mask that allows you to initialize your layer mask as the inverse of the option you've chosen in the radio buttons. This is particularly useful for the Selection option. You may have a selection made in your image window, but rather than designate the selected area as opaque, you may want to make that area transparent and all other areas opaque. Enabling this check box allows you to do just that, without the need to invert your selection ahead of time.

Once you decide how you want to initialize your layer mask, click Add and the layer mask is created for the active layer. You can tell that a layer has a layer mask because it has a second thumbnail next to the layer's main thumbnail in the Layers dialog. Also, in the image window, the border for your active layer changes color. Rather than the standard yellow dashed border that normal layers have, layers with a layer mask have a green dashed border. Figure 6-25 shows the Layers dialog displaying a single layer with a newly added layer mask.

Modifying Layer Masks

Once you've created your layer mask, you can tweak it further to customize your layer's transparency. To do this, you need to edit the layer directly. You have three ways to make a layer editable:

- **Click the layer mask** — By simply clicking the layer mask thumbnail in the Layers dialog, you activate it for editing. You can tell that the mask is editable because it has a white border around it. If the white border is around the layer's thumbnail, the mask won't be editable until you click it.

When you create a layer mask, it's immediately visible on your layer in the Layers dialog

- **Right-click the layer** — If you right-click the layer with your layer mask and click the Edit Layer Mask menu item, it sets your mask to be editable.

- **Use the Layer ➢ Mask submenu** — The same functionality can be achieved using the Mask submenu of the Layer menu in the image window.

You edit a layer mask by painting on it. Remember that it's a grayscale image, so the hue from any colors you choose is disregarded when you paint. To see how things work, with the layer mask editable, choose the Paintbrush tool (P) and set your foreground color to black. Now anywhere you paint in the image window is made transparent. You should be able to see lower layers through your active layer, or the checkerboard backing if you don't have any lower layers. This is basically like using the Erase tool (Shift+E) on a layer with an alpha channel. However, the layer mask gives you more flexibility. For one, you can temporarily disable the layer mask so you can see the fully opaque layer by itself. To do this either right-click the layer in the Layers dialog and choose the Disable Layer Mask menu item or go to Layer ➢ Mask ➢ Disable Layer Mask in the image window. When you do this, the border for the layer mask's thumbnail turns bright red. Those menu items are toggles, so you can re-enable your layer mask by going back to either menu and clicking Disable Layer Mask again.

You also have the ability to see exactly what your layer mask looks like. Access this functionality the same way you would disable the mask. Either right-click your layer or go to Layer ➤ Mask in the image window and choose Show Layer Mask. This reveals the layer mask in the image window and changes the color of the border around the layer mask's thumbnail image in the Layers dialog to green. From here you're able to edit your mask by painting upon it directly. When you're done or if you want to see the results of your edit, you can hide the layer mask by toggling the Show Layer Mask menu item again.

With the mask created and edited to your liking, you have another handful of options available to you. For one, you can use your layer mask like an alpha channel and use it to build complex selections. Do this by going to the Layer ➤ Mask submenu and looking at the bottom. Figure 6-26 shows this submenu. If you recall the Layer ➤ Transparency submenu shown in Figure 6-14, you should notice quite a few similarities. In fact, when it comes to the selection tools, the only difference is the name of the first item, Mask to Selection. It performs the exact same way as Alpha to Selection, but it just uses your layer mask as a base instead of the layer's alpha channel.

FIGURE 6-26

The Layer ➤ Mask submenu's selection options are nearly identical to the options available in the Layer ➤ Transparency submenu.

The only other options available to you for layer masks are to apply or remove a mask permanently. The first option, Apply Layer Mask — accessible in the Layers dialog's right-click menu as well as the Layer ➤ Mask submenu — takes your layer mask, assigns it to an alpha channel for its layer, and then removes the mask from your project. If the layer doesn't have an alpha channel GIMP goes ahead and creates it for you. Of course, if you decide that you no longer need your layer mask, you can permanently remove the mask by using the Delete Layer Mask function in the Layers dialog's right-click menu or by going to Layer ➤ Mask ➤ Delete Layer Mask.

Effectively Using Features in the Select Menu

One of the most powerful ways to initialize a layer mask is with a selection. GIMP's built-in selection tools, like the Rectangle Select tool or the Fuzzy Select tool, which were covered in Chapter 4, give you a lot of power in this realm. However, a good chunk of features in the image window's Select menu give you even more control. Figure 6-27 shows the contents of this menu.

FIGURE 6-27

GIMP's Select menu gives you a large variety of features to complement the selection tools in GIMP's Toolbox.

A quick run-down of each of these operations follows:

- **Selection creation functions** — The operations in this section are entirely devoted to creating selections and are some of the most frequently used functions in GIMP.

  - **All (Ctrl+A)** — Selects all pixels within the area of your image canvas.

  - **None (Shift+Ctrl+A)** — If you have any pixels selected, this option guarantees that they become deselected.

  - **Invert (Ctrl+I)** — This operation simultaneously selects unselected pixels while deselecting pixels that were initially selected.

  - **Float (Shift+Ctrl+L)** — This convenience operation is the same as taking your selection, copying it (Ctrl+C), and then pasting it (Ctrl+V) back to your image, creating a new floating selection layer. It's pretty handy and helps reduce the overall number of steps you take when copying and pasting image data.

  - **By Color (Shift+O)** — This is the only option in this menu that calls a tool from GIMP's Toolbox. As expected, this calls forth GIMP's Select by Color tool.

  - **From Path (Shift+V)** — If you've created any paths as covered in Chapter 5, you can use this option to quickly convert the active path into a selection.

  - **Selection Editor** — This menu item is a convenient way to quickly bring up GIMP's Selection Editor dockable dialog, which can be really helpful in seeing and editing your selection mask.

- **Selection modification functions** — Once you have a selection created, the options in this section can be used to modify and enhance that selection to get exactly what you're looking for. Most of these functions bring up a dialog with additional options.

  - **Feather** — The effect of this function softens the edge of your selection by the units defined in the dialog that appears when you choose it (shown in Figure 6-28).

FIGURE 6-28

The Feather Selection dialog

- **Sharpen** — This menu item performs the inverse operation of the Feather feature, reducing the fuzziness of your selection. There is no dialog for this feature.

- **Shrink** — If your selection is too large or you want to inset your selection a bit, you can use this feature to do just that. The dialog that appears, shown in Figure 6-29, allows you control how many pixels (or any other GIMP-supported unit) you want to shrink your selection by. The Shrink from Image Border check box prevents your selection from sticking to the border of your image.

FIGURE 6-29

The Shrink Selection dialog

- **Grow** — The Grow function is the exact opposite of the Shrink feature. Select it and use the dialog that appears, shown in Figure 6-30, to define by how many units you want your selection to increase in size.

FIGURE 6-30

The Grow Selection dialog

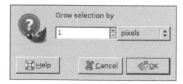

- **Border** — Occasionally, you may want to take your selection and quickly convert it into a border. The dialog that appears for this option, shown in Figure 6-31, allows you to define your border width. If you want the border to be a bit fuzzy, enable the Feather Border check box. The Lock Selection to Image Edges option controls how the border selection works if it encounters one of the image edges. If you use the default behavior of leaving this check box disabled, the selection that runs along an edge receives border treatment. If you enable this check box, the border selection disregards selections that run along the image edge.

FIGURE 6-31

The Border Selection dialog

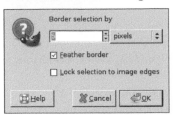

- **Distort** — This feature is actually a really clever plug-in. If you've made a simple rectangular selection and you want to rough it up a bit, you can call this operation and make your selection edges less rigid. You can customize exactly how rough you want to make your selection using the dialog that appears (shown in Figure 6-32).

FIGURE 6-32

The Distort plug-in dialog

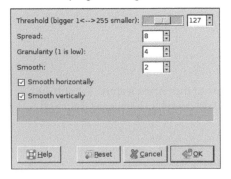

- **Rounded Rectangle** — GIMP's Rectangle Select tool is extremely useful, but it's limited to always having sharp corners. In a lot of design scenarios, it's more pleasant to have rounded corners. This Script-Fu plug-in allows you to round off those corners based on a percentage of the selection. The dialog that appears when you choose the function is shown in Figure 6-33. Not only does it give you radius control over the rounded corners, but it also gives you the option to make the corners concave instead of the default convex style.
- **Additional selection features** — These last three options are additional features that relate more to channels and paths rather than layers or layer masks. Review Chapter 5 to cover the path-related feature and look forward to the next chapter to see how these tools help with channels.

- **Toggle Quick Mask (Shift+Q)** — The Quick Mask is an incredibly cool feature that allows you to quickly paint a selection like you'd paint the transparency of a layer mask. There's a lot more on this feature in Chapter 7.

- **Save to Channel** — Any selection that you make can be saved as a custom channel and reused later. This menu item performs that exact function.

- **To Path:** Just like you can create a channel from a selection, you're also able to generate a path from one. This menu item provides you with that functionality. Look back at Chapter 5 to find out more about paths.

FIGURE 6-33

The Rounded Rectangle dialog

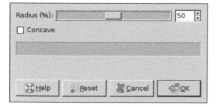

Summary

Whew! What a chapter! You were exposed to layers, one of the fundamental building blocks of nearly all serious image editing programs. Not only did you see how to create and edit your layers, but you also learned how GIMP's new layer groups can be used to facilitate better non-destructive organization of your GIMP projects. You also found out that GIMP layers can have their transparency edited with an Opacity slider in the Layers dialog as well as with more advanced feature like per-layer alpha channels and layer masks. Speaking of layer masks, this chapter showed you how awesome they are and also introduced you to GIMP's additional selection features (from the Select menu in the image window) that you can use to more effectively define your layer masks. Fun stuff across the board. Next stop: Channels.

Using Channels

I n most image editing applications, the channels feature is usually the most misunderstood and underutilized tool in the kit. Part of this has to do with the fact that most image formats are flattened and the only channels that they have available to them are red, green, and blue. Although these channels can be very helpful in tweaking your image's colors, there's much more to channels than the component colors that make up the image. This is especially true in a powerful image editor like GIMP.

The purpose of this chapter is to introduce you to channels and demonstrate all of the cool ways that they can be used to enhance your digital images. You see how they can not only give you precise control of colors, but how to use them in GIMP to create and store selections, enhance the contrast in black-and-white images, and control the overall transparency of your final output.

Understanding Channels

The fastest way to see and control channels in GIMP is through the Channels dockable dialog, shown in Figure 7-1. By default, it's the second tab after the Layers dialog and it shares a number of the same interface paradigms. It has a large central panel that displays a list of elements and a series of buttons beneath this panel.

On a typical flat image format like JPEG or PNG, you will see three or four separate channels: Red, Green, Blue, and possibly Alpha, if the image format supports it. Shorthand abbreviations for these channels are RGB and RGBA, respectively. Notice that all of these channels are enabled and visible by default. The eye icon to the left of the channel name indicates its visibility, and the fact that the channel is highlighted tells you that it's active. You can toggle between active and inactive by clicking the channel. To toggle the visibility of a channel, click the eye icon. Click the eye next to the blue channel and your image takes on a much more yellow hue. Follow that by clicking the eye on the green channel to hide it as well, and your image is distinctly more red.

The Channels dockable dialog in GIMP is where most of the channel controls live. On the left is an image with RGB channels and on the right is an image with RGBA.

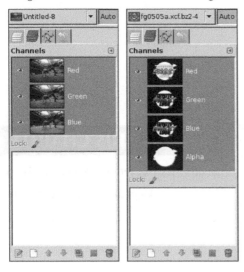

Red, Green, and Blue: The Default Color Channels

At its most distilled form, a channel is a grayscale representation of some property of your image where white indicates full intensity and black indicates none at all. In other words, a channel is a mask that controls a single visual property of the image. In the case of RGB channels, each channel controls the amount of that particular color that gets into your image. As covered in Chapter 2, RGB is GIMP's native color space. GIMP uses the RGB channels to mix the red, green, and blue primary colors and generate a full-color image. To get a better idea of how this works, open an image in GIMP and bring up the Channels dialog. Left-click the red channel and drag it to the Layers tab. Wait until the dock switches you to the Layers dialog and drop the preview into the layer list panel. This creates a new layer for you with the contents of your red channel. This way you can see the grayscale image that represents your red channel.

Here's where things get interesting. You can use the RGB color channels as masks and control the color of parts of your image by painting. To see how this works, open a new image (File ➤ New or Ctrl+N) or revert one you have open (File ➤ Revert) and use the following steps:

1. In the Channels dialog, deactivate the Green and Blue channels by clicking them. This should make Red your only active channel.

2. Choose the Paintbrush (P) from the Toolbox and use the color picker or color dialog to change the paint color to white.

3. Paint a few places in the image. When you do this, notice that if you paint on dark areas of the image, you see red color coming up at full intensity. Painting on light areas should result in a less noticeable change. The reason for this is that the RGB color spectrum is an *additive* color space, so if an area is white, it already has a full red intensity.

4. Change your paint color to black.

5. Now when you paint, you're *removing* red from those parts of the image, yielding a blue, green, or cyan color in light areas and less noticeable changes in dark areas.

A Fistful of Awesome: The Alpha Channel

In addition to the Red, Green, and Blue channels, you may notice that some images have a fourth channel, called the *Alpha channel*. Like the other three channels, this one is a grayscale image, but rather than representing a primary color, the values in the alpha channel represent the image's transparency. In this channel, the lighter the pixel is, the more opaque it is. Darker pixels are more transparent, with white being completely opaque and black being completely transparent. This mechanism gives you an incredible amount of control when compositing two images together. In particular, it gives much better antialiasing at the edge between opaque and transparent pixels. Recall from Chapter 5 that aliasing is the stair-stepped effect you sometimes see along hard edges in a digital image. When working with transparency, you see aliasing frequently in image formats like GIF, which have *binary transparency*, meaning that a pixel is either transparent or it is opaque, with no middle ground. You choose a specific color in that image's palette and declare it to be transparent. Unlike GIF's binary transparency, an alpha channel is a grayscale mask with 256 levels between opaque and transparent. This allows you to have smoothly antialiased edges between opaque and transparent pixels. Figure 7-2 shows the difference between an aliased edge and an antialiased one.

FIGURE 7-2

On the left, a close-up of an aliased edge; on the right, an edge with antialiasing

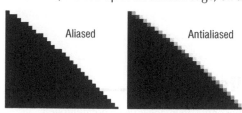

The superior control over transparency is what makes the alpha channel so awesome. Now, at this point you may be tempted to deactivate all channels but alpha and paint on it like described previously for the Red, Green, and Blue channels. Unfortunately, this is an incompleteness in GIMP and at this point it's not that simple. If you deactivate the other channels and attempt to paint black pixels directly to the alpha channel, nothing will happen. The easiest way to make transparent pixels in GIMP is to use the Eraser tool (Shift+E). You can find more details on this tool in Chapter 4, but the quick version is that when you paint with the Eraser tool, the pixels you paint become transparent, revealing the layers below, or GIMP's checkerboard background that indicates complete transparency. The cool thing about using the Eraser tool is that it doesn't destroy the underlying pixel information. If you've accidentally erased something that you didn't mean to, you can "anti erase" by holding Alt while using the Eraser tool. This is made possible, in part, because GIMP stores alpha channel data in a straight, or *non-premultiplied* format, meaning the transparency of a pixel is stored separately from its color.

Note

GIMP's native file format, XCF, stores a non-premultiplied alpha, but not all formats do this. The PNG and TIFF formats actually allow you to choose between storing premultiplied or non-premultiplied alpha. You can see this control in the dialogs that pop up when you attempt to export to (Shift+Ctrl+E) either of those formats. Figure 7-3 shows these save dialogs. The option you're interested in here is the Save Color Values from Transparent Pixels check box. With this option enabled, you get non-premultiplied alpha and you should be able to successfully anti erase the alpha channel when you re-open the file in GIMP. With this option disabled, anti erase will only give you a solid color (usually black or white) where you use anti erase in the reopened file. ■

FIGURE 7-3

On the left, the save dialog for PNG images; on the right, is the dialog for TIFFs

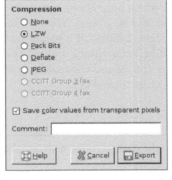

A Brief Explanation of Premultiplied Alpha

Because most programs are pretty smart about guessing whether or not an image is using premultiplied alpha, most digital artists could go their entire lives without knowing what it is or how it works. However, for those instances where things go awry or where the program guesses incorrectly, understanding premultiplied alpha can be helpful. The way it works is pretty straightforward. Each of the primary color channels is multiplied by the value of the alpha channel. As an example, assume you have a completely green pixel that's 50% transparent. Using normalized values for RGBA, the non-premultiplied channel values for each would be (0, 1, 0, 0.5). The premultiplied version of the same pixel would be (0, 0.5, 0, 0.5). Basically, the value of green — 1 in this case, because it's at full intensity — is multiplied by the value of the alpha, 0.5. That's basically all premultiplied alpha is.

The reason why premultiplied alpha exists is actually to improve performance when compositing images atop one another. Programmers discovered that if you try to composite using an image with straight, non-premultiplied alpha, there's usually an additional calculation (typically division) that has to be done per pixel to get the composite to look correct. If they use premultiplied alpha, that additional per-pixel calculation isn't required and the composite can be calculated more quickly. For still images, this isn't as important. However, if you're working as a video editor or film compositor where you often have thousands of frames of film or video that you have to composite, these calculation savings can add up and save quite a bit of time when rendering.

The quickest way to tell whether a program has incorrectly guessed if you're using premultiplied alpha is to look at the edge of the image that borders between opaque and transparent pixels. If the program guessed wrong, there will usually be a white or black halo in this area or an ugly bit of aliasing.

The Eraser tool is an excellent way to edit the alpha channel of your images, but suppose you absolutely need the ability to control your alpha channel by painting grayscale pixels. Fortunately, it's possible to do this as well with a layer mask. Chapter 6 discusses this in more detail, but the basic steps go like this:

1. In the Layers dockable dialog, right-click the layer you want to work on and choose Add Layer Mask.

2. In the Add Layer Mask dialog that pops up, choose White (full opacity) and click Add. This creates your new layer mask and selects it as the active surface in your layer.

3. Choose the Paintbrush (P) tool and set your foreground color to some level of gray or black. Because the mask is already set to white, everything on your layer is opaque. By choosing a gray or black paintbrush, you're choosing the transparency that you want to paint.

4. Paint the areas you would like to make transparent.

5. When complete, depending on the file format that you're saving to, you can either leave the mask as is, or apply it to the image's alpha channel by right-clicking the layer with the mask and choosing Apply Layer Mask.

Using Channels

The most effective use for channels is to assist in selecting. This makes sense, considering the fact that they're selection masks for the primary colors in GIMP's native RGB color space. The typical workflow is to use one of the RGB color channels as a quick base for a more refined selection mask. You may be thinking that this sounds a lot like the Select by Color tool explained in Chapter 4. In a way, you're correct, but you have a lot more flexibility with channels. Not only can you use paint tools to refine selections with channels, but you can also save your selections and reuse them later by using custom channels. That's right; you can create your own channels. Pretty cool, huh?

Creating Channels

From the Channels dockable dialog, you have a few different ways to create a new channel. The fastest way is to click the New Channel button at the bottom of the dialog. Refer back to Figure 7-1 to see what the buttons at the bottom of the dialog look like. The New Channel button is the second button from the left and its icon looks like a blank piece of paper. You can click this button or right-click in the Channels dialog and choose New Channel from the menu. When you click this button GIMP pops up a dialog like the one in Figure 7-4 that allows you to name your channel and control the color and opacity of its mask. The controls for the name and opacity are pretty obvious. To change the mask color, click the color swatch on the right of the dialog and choose the color from the picker that appears. This dialog also gives you the option of creating a blank channel or initializing the channel's mask from whatever you currently have selected. Enable this option by clicking the Initialize from Selection check box.

FIGURE 7-4

The New Channel Options dialog that appears when creating a new channel

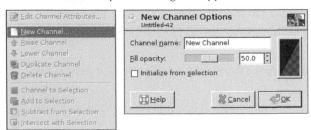

Alternatively, if you already have a channel that you would like to use as your starting point, you can duplicate that channel. If you're duplicating a custom channel, the process is as simple as clicking that channel and then clicking the Duplicate Channel button at the bottom of the dialog. To duplicate any of the primary channels, you'll have to use the right-click menu and choose Duplicate Channel from that list of options. It's also possible to simply click the primary color channel that you would like to duplicate and drag it to an empty portion of the channel list panel.

One more way to create a channel is to do it directly from the Select menu in the image window. To do this, use whatever selection tools you want to create a selection. Once you have the selection that you'd like to save, choose Select ➤ Save to Channel from the menu.

To get a quick idea of what your custom channel will look like prior to saving it, you can use GIMP's Quick Mask feature by pressing Shift+Q or clicking Select ➤ Toggle Quick Mask. This temporarily adds a Quick Mask channel to your channel list and indicates it in the image window by covering masked areas with a semi-transparent red hue. The Quick Mask is pretty slick because when it's enabled, you can paint on it like any other mask and quickly paint a desired selection. This is especially nice if you're using GIMP with a drawing tablet. When you toggle the Quick Mask off, it automatically converts the Quick Mask to a selection and you can keep working from there. Alternatively, you can make your Quick Mask a custom channel by duplicating it in the Channels dialog. For a more thorough review on masking, have a look at Chapter 6.

Taking Advantage of Channels Once They're Created

When you have a new custom channel, you can do a few things to it directly from the Channels dialog:

- **Edit channel attributes** — Clicking this button pops up a dialog similar to the one shown in Figure 7-4, allowing you to edit properties of the channel, including its name, the opacity of the mask, and its color. You can also quickly bring up this dialog by double-clicking the preview image for your custom channel. If you just want to change the name of your channel, the fastest way to do that is by double-clicking the channel's name in the Channels dialog.

- **Raise or lower a channel** — The up and down arrows at the bottom of the Channels dialog raise or lower the selected channel in the list. Shift+clicking either arrow pushes the selected channel to the top or bottom of the stack. For a little bit faster re-ordering, you can click any channel and drag it to its new position in the list.

- **Duplicate a channel** — As discussed previously, clicking this button takes the selected custom channel and creates a copy of it in the list of channels.

  - **Create a selection from a channel** — Channels are basically custom selection masks, so it makes sense to have quick access to the ability use a channel to create a selection. Clicking this button uses the selected channel to create a selection in the image window, replacing any selection you currently have. If you want to take your current selection and add or subtract the channel's selection mask, you need to press a modifier button (Shift or Ctrl) while you click this, as explained next.

  - **Add to selection (Shift+click)** — This adds the channel's selection mask to your current selection. Generally speaking, this increases the number of pixels you have selected. You can also access this functionality by right-clicking the Channels dialog and choosing Add to Selection from the menu.

  - **Subtract from selection (Ctrl+click)** — Doing this reduces the number of selected pixels by subtracting the channel selection mask from your current selection. This function is also accessible from the Channels dialog right-click menu.

  - **Intersect with selection (Shift+Ctrl+click)** — An intersection of selections is where your current selection and the channel's selection mask overlap. Choose this option by Shift+Ctrl+clicking the selection button or pick it from the Channels dialog's right-click menu.

- **Delete a channel** — As advertised, clicking this button removes the selected channel from the list.

When you create a new channel, unlike the primary channels, there's an additional space between the visibility (eye) icon and the thumbnail preview of the channel. This space is for the channel chaining icon. Clicking this space enables channel chaining for this channel and makes the chainlink icon visible. Figure 7-5 shows the Channels dialog with a couple custom channels chained together.

The Channels dialog with two channels chained together

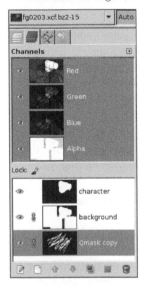

By chaining channels together, you're linking them and forming a group. When you perform an operation like sheer, scale, or rotate on one of these chained channels, GIMP automatically performs the same operation on all of the others that are chained. This is very similar to the layer chaining discussed in Chapter 6. Also notice that just like the Paths and Layers dialogs, the Channels dialog also offers locking control on custom channels. As you can see in Figure 7-5, the Lock label is in the space between the RGBA channels and your custom channels. Lock your current active channel and any channels chained to it by clicking the button next to the Lock label.

Note

When used as selection masks, you may notice that custom channels slightly overlap the functionality of using paths as selection masks as described in Chapter 5. There's a pretty important difference between the two, though: paths don't give you the ability to partially select pixels. When you create a selection from an antialiasing path, pixels are either selected or they aren't, kind of like the binary transparency of GIF images. However, since channels are grayscale masks, you have very fine-grained control over how much your selection influences each pixel. As an example, assume you have a logo that has a fuzzy, semi-transparent drop shadow and you select it by using the logo's layer transparency

(Layer ➤ Transparency ➤ Alpha to Selection). If you convert that selection to a path, you lose all of the opacity information from that selection. However, if you create a custom channel with that selection, you retain all of the transparency information for each pixel in the selection. ■

Practical Application: Changing the Background

The best way to understand how to use channels effectively is to see a practical example. One of the most commons applications for monkeying with your channels is replacing the foreground or background of an image. The following steps are an example of how you can use channels to do just that. These steps have figures with them, but don't pay a lot of attention to the specific values used in these figures. Every image you work on will be different, so the important thing is to focus on the major steps. Another thing to note is that many of these steps utilize color adjustment tools. You can find more details on these tools in Chapter 9. Figure 7-6 shows what you may start with.

FIGURE 7-6

The starting image, after duplicating the source layer to give you a workspace (Photo credit: Chris Hoyer)

1. Use the Select by Color tool (Shift+O) to select the most prominent color in the background. If you click the color and drag your mouse, you can interactively adjust the threshold of the color you're selecting. Don't worry too much if you pick up some color from the foreground. That will be fixed in future steps.

2. Enable the Quick Mask (Shift+Q) and show your Channels palette. This gives you a much clearer view of what you're selecting. To make it even more clear, hide the RGB channels by clicking the eye icon next to each one. Your Quick Mask channel should look similar to the one in Figure 7-7.

FIGURE 7-7

The selection mask after doing a rough Select by Color

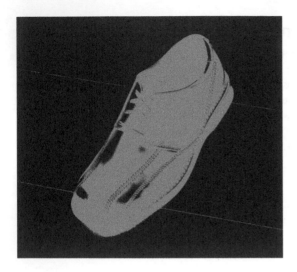

3. Increase the contrast of your selection. Looking at Figure 7-7, notice that in a few spots the selection is fuzzy or outlying dots are selected when they don't need to be. Increasing the contrast of your selection mask will remedy this. You can do this with either the Brightness-Contrast tool (Color ➤ Brightness-Contrast) or the Levels editor (Color ➤ Levels). I prefer the greater control that the Levels editor provides, but use what you're most comfortable with. Once you complete this step, you should have something like Figure 7-8.

4. Use the Paintbrush (P) to tweak the mask. Paint with white on the places you want to include in the selection and paint with black on the parts that you don't want to be selected. Remember that you're selecting the background, so the mask is covering the foreground elements. This technique is especially helpful for facial features like eyes that have similar colors to the background. While painting, it may be helpful for you to unhide the RGB channels so you have a visual reference to the selection you're painting. With this step complete, your mask should be much more clear, like the one in Figure 7-9.

5. Toggle off the Quick Mask (Shift+Q) and Invert your selection (Ctrl+I). By toggling off the Quick Mask, you automatically replace your selection with the one you just painted. Inverting the selection causes you to have your foreground element selected rather than the background.

FIGURE 7-8

The selection mask with increased contrast, reducing partial selections

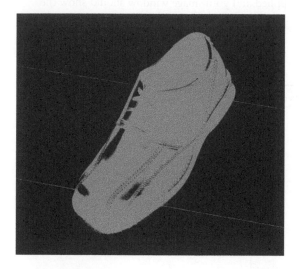

FIGURE 7-9

A cleaned-up quick mask after a quick paint job

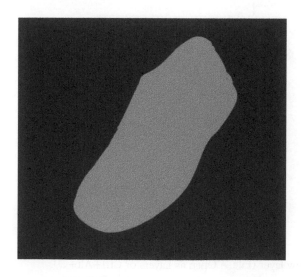

6. Add a Layer Mask from your selection (Layer ➤ Mask ➤ Add Layer Mask). When you choose this option, a dialog pops up asking you what to initialize the layer mask to be. Click the Selection radio button and then click Add. If you switch to the Layers dockable dialog, you should see the layer mask applied and your image window should show the checkerboard where your background once was. Figure 7-10 shows the process of adding a layer mask from your selection.

FIGURE 7-10

Creating a layer mask from your selection, and the results of doing so

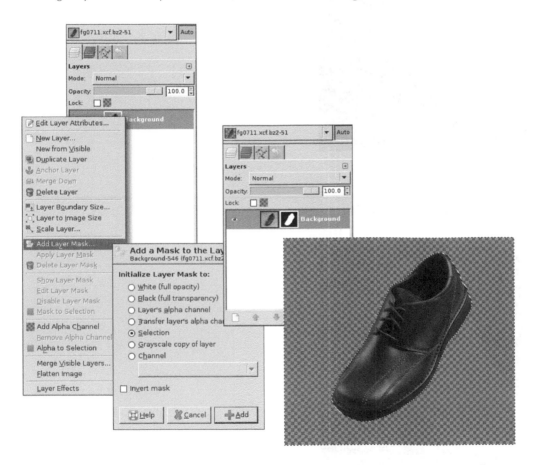

7. Add a new background image as a new layer (File ➤ Open as Layers or Ctrl+Alt+O). This places your new background image as the topmost layer in the stack. Pull the layer beneath your masked layer and your new background will appear behind your foreground subject, giving you something like the image in Figure 7-11.

An image that used channels to replace its background. Easy! (Background photo credit: cgtextures.com)

Summary

In this chapter, you found out that channels are an overlooked feature of digital images that, when wielded effectively, can be used to enhance images with an incredible amount of control. You discovered that GIMP doesn't allow you to paint directly on the alpha channel, but the anti erase option of the Eraser tool is an excellent way to overcome this issue. You saw that the Channels dockable dialog can be used to manage a set of custom channels, or selection masks that you can use, reuse, and mix together. Using all of this, you were shown how to use channels and the Quick Mask in GIMP to remove a background from an image quickly.

Next up, making *really* drastic changes to your images in GIMP. It's awesome, I promise.

Part III

Manipulating Images

IN THIS PART

Chapter 8
Transforming Images

Chapter 9
Adjusting Colors

Chapter 10
Working with Text

Chapter 11
Painting in GIMP

Chapter 12
Enhancing Photos

Transforming Images

Transform operations are some of the most commonly used functions in image manipulation. Technically speaking, a *transformation* involves moving the existing pixels in an image according to a given rule. Occasionally a transformation involves adding or subtracting pixels from the image. Assuming you've already used the Move tool, you've already performed a basic transform operation by moving a layer around. Other transformations include scaling, cropping, and rotation. Because these operations are used so frequently, GIMP provides a couple different ways to access them quickly. The main access methods are either by way of the Image and Layer menus in the image window or by directly using tools accessible in the Toolbox.

This chapter covers each of these methods in detail, pointing out useful situations for each one and tips about situations where one operation is more useful than others.

Adjustments Available in the Image and Layer Menus

As you may have already noticed from Chapter 6, the Image menu and the Layer menu in the image window share quite a bit of similar functionality. Don't make the mistake of assuming that this is overlapping functionality, though. There's a difference between transforming the entire image and transforming a single layer. When you apply a transformation to a layer, it has no influence on any of the other layers in the image unless you've chained layers together. On the other hand, if you apply a transformation to the image, that transformation influences everything in the image: layers, channels, paths ... everything. Figure 8-1 shows both the Image and Layer menus with their Transform submenus expanded.

FIGURE 8-1

On the left, the Image menu with its Transform submenu expanded; on the right, the same thing with the Layer menu

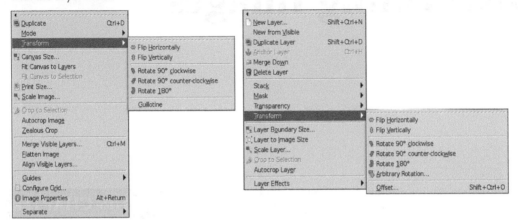

This section covers operations that are within both of these menus. Where necessary, I describe how the same function might perform differently depending on which menu you call it from.

Sizing

Chapter 1 goes into a pretty heavy description of the Scale Image and Canvas Size operations from the Image menu. It shouldn't surprise you that the Scale Layer and Layer Boundary Size operations, as described in Chapter 6, work and behave the same as their respective Image menu counterparts. That said, a couple shortcuts exist that can make your life easier by automatically resizing your images or layers. You do this with the Fit Canvas to Layers and Layer to Image Size operations.

Fit Canvas to Layers

Activate this option by clicking Image ➤ Fit Canvas to Layers. When you do so, GIMP looks at all the layers in your image and adjusts the extents of your image's canvas to fit and show the full contents of all layers. This operation is extremely useful if you bring in image data from another source as a new layer and that layer is larger than your current image. Rather than go through the hassle of checking the layer's size and then manually changing the canvas size to match, you can run this function and GIMP does it all for you. I actually used this function quite a bit when assembling screenshots for this book, using the following process:

1. **Take some screenshots of a couple windows (File ➤ Create ➤ Screenshot)**. Each screenshot gets its own image window. This is good for giving me raw data, but if I want to composite the screenshots in a single image, I need to do some more work. Note that when dealing with screenshots, you want to work in pixels as your units. If you do that, then the resolution (i.e., ppi, or pixels per inch) of your image is irrelevant because

you're working directly in pixels. This is useful if you're getting screenshots from a bunch of sources (other than just GIMP) that may take screenshots at different resolutions.

2. **Get the image contents of one screenshot into the image window of the other screenshot.** The easiest way to do this is to go to the Layers dialog in the Dock and drag the layer from one screenshot (each screenshot should have only one layer) to the image window of the other screenshot. Alternatively, you could use the following process:

   a. Go to the image window of one screenshot, select all (Ctrl+A), and copy (Ctrl+C).

   b. Go to the other screenshot's image window, paste (Ctrl+V), and convert the floating selection to a new layer (Shift+Ctrl+N).

3. **Use the Move tool (M) and drag the new layer into position.** Don't worry if you move the layer off the canvas. At this point, the important thing is to get the layer where you want it to be relative to the bottom layer. The layer's boundary outline is really useful for this. In fact, as of GIMP 2.8, layers automatically snap their boundaries to the canvas edge. This is a great way to ensure your layer is lined up without using guides. You end up with something that looks like Figure 8-2. Once you have things where you think they need to be, move on to the next step.

4. **Fit the canvas size to encompass all layers in the image (Image ➤ Fit Canvas to Layers).** That's pretty much it. Once you're here, you can readjust your layers to your liking. You may even want to use the Align tool or add a drop shadow. Whatever you do, once you're done, it's a smart move to re-run the Image ➤ Fit Canvas to Layers operation to make sure everything's visible.

FIGURE 8-2

Moving a second layer off the canvas area, but using the layer boundary and canvas edge as guides

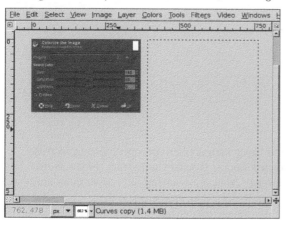

Layer to Image Size

While working with layers you frequently run into situations where the layer you're working on isn't large enough for the operation you want to perform. For instance, say you've added some text and you want to give that text an outline. The easiest way to do this would be to make a selection using your text layer's alpha channel (Layer ➤ Transparency ➤ Alpha to Selection) and then paint along that selection with the Stroke Selection operation (Edit ➤ Stroke Selection). A problem arises, however, if these are the only two steps you use. For some fonts there's not a lot of space around your text in its text layer, so when you stroke the selection, it's likely that you'll get something that looks like the text in Figure 8-3. Notice how the outer portion of the outline is cropped off by the boundaries of the text layer.

FIGURE 8-3

When you create an outline on some text layers, your outline may be constrained by the boundaries of your layer.

This is text

You could get around this by creating a new transparent layer (Shift+Ctrl+N) and adding the stroke there, but if you ever decide to edit that text, you would have to delete and replace that layer. However, as explained in Chapter 10, text layers in GIMP are still editable even if you paint on them or perform other operations on them. Of course, editing removes all of those additional operations, but the benefit is that you don't end up with superfluous layers that you have to delete. So to resolve that cropped outline problem, you need to increase the size of the text layer to accommodate the extra space that the outline requires You could do this manually with the dialog that appears when you run Layer ➤ Layer Boundary Size, but that's a bit slow and it involves some guesswork on your part to make sure you create enough space. A faster way is to run Layer ➤ Layer to Image Size. As long as your text isn't close to the edge of your canvas, this should quickly give you enough space to get a non-cropped outline, as shown in Figure 8-4.

FIGURE 8-4

Text without the cropping problems shown in Figure 8-3

This is text

Cropping and Guillotine

The previous section showed how the Image and Layer menus offer you operations to increase the size of an image canvas or a layer to predefined values. It makes sense that these menus would also provide you with a way to do the reverse: cropping your image or layer in an automated way. You can perform four operations: Crop to Selection, Autocrop, Zealous Crop, and Guillotine. All of these functions are available in the Image menu, but only the first two appear in the Layer menu.

Warning

Even though these operations are in the Image menu and they affect all of the layers in your image, you should know that GIMP uses the current active layer as its starting point when it runs these operations. I go

into more detail later in this section, but as an example, if you use the Autocrop Image operation and your active layer has content that's smaller than other layers, GIMP crops the image to fit that layer's content rather than cropping to fit all of the visible content in the image. There's a way around this and I go into it in the next section. ■

Crop to Selection

As explained in Chapter 4, GIMP has a very powerful Crop tool (Shift+C). However, in some instances it's not the fastest or most ideal tool for the job. As an example, say you're working on a photograph of a group of people and you've gone through the effort of using the Free Select tool and the Quick Mask to select a single person from that group to tweak some colors. If you want to crop the image and isolate that person, you could switch to the Crop tool, but it's much faster to use either Image ➤ Crop to Selection or Layer ➤ Crop to Selection. This way you don't have to spend time with the Crop tool trying to get it to fit your selection.

The Crop to Selection operation is particularly useful when you have softer selections. For instance, say you've feathered a selection (Select ➤ Feather) or used the Quick Mask with a soft-edged brush or a brush at less than 100% opacity. In these cases, the marching ants that show your selection may not fully encompass all of the pixels that have been selected. That makes it a lot harder to estimate visually what's been selected if you're just using the Crop tool. Figure 8-5 shows the Crop to Selection function in action.

FIGURE 8-5

Using Crop to Selection to crop an image based on a selection you've already made (Photo credit: Melody Smith)

Original

Crop to Selection

Selection mask

Autocrop

Crop to Selection is a really handy feature, but GIMP offers some other more automated ways to crop images. One of the handiest tools for this is the Autocrop feature. Basically, what Autocrop does is remove empty space from an image or a layer. To understand this, the simplest example is to imagine an image with a gray background and a black circle somewhere in the middle of that space. If you Autocrop that image, all extraneous gray is cropped away, leaving you with only an image of your black circle, as shown in Figure 8-6. The cool thing is that GIMP's Autocrop doesn't just work on colored pixels. It also accounts for pixels that are made transparent, whether by erasing or using a layer mask. For an automated tool, you get a lot of flexibility out of it.

Using Autocrop to clear away empty space

Original image   Autocropped image

You can use Autocrop from either the Image menu or the Layer menu by going to Image ➤ Autocrop Image or Layer ➤ Autocrop Layer, respectively. A very important thing to note here is that even if you're calling Autocrop from the Image menu, GIMP uses the current active layer to determine which pixels count as empty space. To illustrate this, say you took the circle in Figure 8-6 and added a new layer to turn it into a cartoon cat like the one in Figure 8-7. The space covered in the new layer to create the eyes, whiskers, and ears is larger than the circle in some parts and smaller in others. You may expect that if you run Image ➤ Autocrop Image the result would be your full cartoon cat on a smaller gray background. However, this is not what happens. If the original circle layer is active, Autocrop chops off a lot of your additions. If your new "cat bits" layer is active, part of your original circle is cropped.

Autocropping an image still uses the active layer to determine what pixels to crop off.

Original image

New layer

Autocrop to
original layer

Autocrop to
new layer

You have four possible solutions to deal with this situation:

- **Merge visible layers** — The easiest one is to simply merge your layers by right-clicking in the Layers dialog and selecting Merge Visible Layers, or from the image window go to Image ➤ Merge Visible Layers. Because this leaves you with just one layer, the Autocrop Image operation works as desired. The disadvantage to taking this route, however, is that it destroys your layer structure and makes it more difficult to edit your image in the future.

- **Create a temporary layer from visible elements** — Another solution is to use the Layer ➤ New from Visible feature. This creates a new layer based on the visible elements in your image. Once you do this, select the new layer and run the Autocrop Image operation on it. After that, you can delete this extra layer from the Layers dialog. This method is fast and it preserves your layer structure, but it does require you to go through the somewhat annoying step of creating a temporary layer.

- **Use a group layer** — GIMP 2.8 introduced the very slick feature of group layers. As explained in Chapter 6, a group layer is a special layer that encompasses multiple layers within it. To create a new group layer, click the Group Layer button in the Layers dialog. With the group layer created, you can drag each of your element layers (the circle and the cat bits) into the group layer. Once you've done that, select the group layer and run the Autocrop Image operation on it. With this method you get to keep your layer structure and you don't have to create any temporary layers.

- **Use the Crop tool with Auto Shrink and Shrink Merged enabled** — This is discussed later in this chapter in the "Crop Tool" section.

Tip

The Autocrop feature is implemented in GIMP as a plug-in. A side effect of this is that it's counted as a filter operation. Though this may seem a bit odd, the benefit is that it's actually really easy to quickly re-run the operation by going to Filters ➤ Repeat "Autocrop Image" or using the Ctrl+F keyboard shortcut. ■

Zealous Crop

The Zealous Crop feature is similar to Autocrop, but it takes an additional step. Whereas Autocrop crops only from the borders of your image, Zealous Crop also deals with empty space between elements in your image. As an example, take the cartoon cat head from Figure 8-7 and say you've added a rectangular section at the bottom of the image for the cat head to rest upon, as shown in Figure 8-8. You could go through the laborious process of visually lining up the block and the head. However, this is where Zealous Crop can simplify things for you. Just run Image ➤ Zealous Crop and GIMP automatically removes the empty space around and between the cat head and the block at the bottom of the image.

Take note that, as opposed to Autocrop and Crop to Selection, the Zealous Crop feature is available only in the Image menu, so you can't really Zealous Crop an individual layer. That said, Zealous Crop still has the limitation of Autocrop in that it uses only your current active layer to calculate where the empty space is. This means that if you have a multi-layer image that you want to use Zealous Crop on, you should merge layers before performing this operation. The other two techniques that you can use with Autocrop don't work as desired with Zealous Crop.

This is because Zealous Crop doesn't currently move elements in other layers (including layers that have been grouped). It would be nice if in the future Zealous Crop takes advantage of group layers, but it currently doesn't work that way.

FIGURE 8-8

Using Zealous Crop to remove empty space between elements.

Original image

After Zealous Crop

Guillotine

The last automated cropping tool in GIMP is the Guillotine function. Guillotine uses the guides in your image window to slice your image into component parts. This is an extremely useful tool if you're doing web or interface design. As an example, take a look at Figure 8-9. This is a simple mock-up for some company's web site. Guides have already been placed where the designer wants to slice the image.

To perform the actual slicing operation, simply run Image ➤ Transform ➤ Guillotine. When you do so, GIMP goes through the image, moving from the top left to the bottom right, and creates a new image window for each block outlined by the grid. From there, you can go into each image window, make any changes you feel are necessary, and export to whatever image format you want. The really cool thing about Guillotine is that it actually maintains your layer structure for the visible elements in each sliced component. For example, the central content block of the design in Figure 8-9 has a bunch of filler text. Obviously that's not something you'd really want to include in the final design, and because GIMP doesn't flatten the image when it performs the Guillotine, you can just hide the filler text layer in the image slice that it created.

Tip

If you're working on a design like the one in this example that features empty space around the actual design, it's probably a good idea to Autocrop the image prior to running Guillotine. This way GIMP won't create a bunch of superfluous slices of solid color that you'll ultimately end up getting rid of anyway. ∎

FIGURE 8-9

You can use the Guillotine operation to slice this web site design into its component parts.

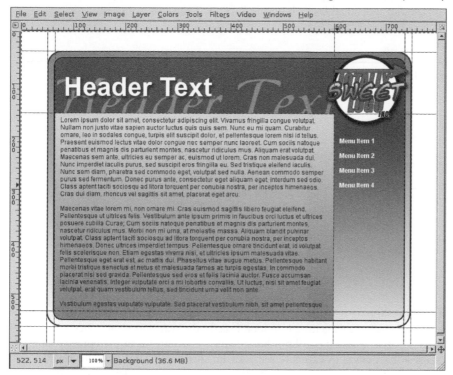

Flipping and Rotating

So far, with the possible exception of Zealous Crop, this chapter has covered only features that involve increasing or decreasing the boundaries of a layer or an image canvas. Of course, transforming pixels involves a lot more than that. Two critical transform operations that any serious image editing application requires are flip and rotate. GIMP offers convenient menu items to perform either of these functions quickly for the entire image or for individual layers. To access the flip or rotation menu items, look in the Transform submenu of either the Image or the Layer menu, as shown in Figure 8-10.

Flipping

The ability to flip an image quickly is a surprisingly underutilized feature by people who are new to digital image editing. Flipping is particularly useful for digital painters. It's a common practice for traditional artists to turn their work upside down or look at it in the mirror as a means of testing their composition. Doing this tricks your brain into looking at the shapes and colors of your composition rather than the content of the image. The digital equivalent to this is quickly flipping your image horizontally or vertically, or both. As a matter of fact, I use flipping often enough when I'm working that I created custom keyboard shortcuts so I can perform this action quickly in the middle of painting. If you look at Figure 8-10, you can see that I set these short-cuts to Ctrl+Alt+F for flipping an image horizontally and Shift+Alt+F for flipping the image vertically. You can also flip individual layers from the Layer ➤ Transform submenu.

FIGURE 8-10

You can find flipping and rotating controls for the whole image or individual layers in the Transform submenu.

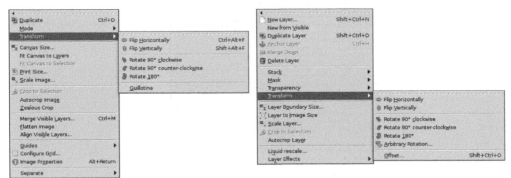

Another common use for flipping is to create a symmetrical image. To do something like this, you work on one half of your image, getting it to look exactly the way you want. Once you finish, duplicate the layer you're working on, flip it horizontally, and move it to the opposite side. After that, run Image ➤ Fit Canvas to Layers to see your finished work. This is useful if your are painting portraits, editing photographs of architecture, or, as shown in Figure 8-11, drawing gears.

Rotating

The ability to rotate an image or layer is a feature that's available for nearly every application used to edit images. In fact, most image viewers even have some rudimentary form of rotation. As shown back in Figure 8-10, the Transform submenu of both the Image and Layer menus allows you to do basic rotations in 90° increments as well as a full 180° rotation. If you want to rotate the entire image, including all layers, choose the rotation angle you want from the Image ➤ Transform submenu. This is particularly useful if you get a photograph from an older digital camera that doesn't store rotation information. So if you get an image that's sideways, this is the quickest way to fix it. However, if you want to rotate only one layer, you need to select that layer and use the Layer ➤ Transform submenu.

One additional task that you can do with individual layers that's a little bit more difficult to do with the whole image is rotate by an arbitrary value. To do this, select the layer that you want to rotate and go to Layer ➤ Transform ➤ Arbitrary Rotation. This actually activates GIMP's Rotate tool and calls up a dialog like the one in Figure 8-12.

FIGURE 8-11

Quickly drawing a symmetric gear using GIMP's flip feature

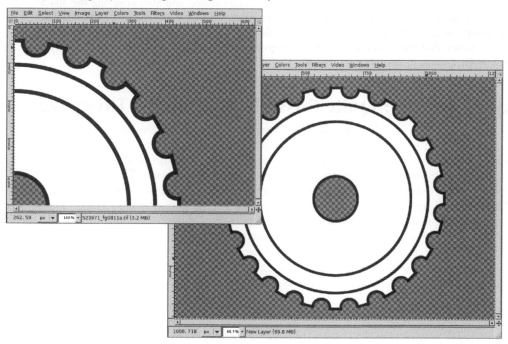

FIGURE 8-12

The Rotate dialog gives you direct control over how your layer is rotated.

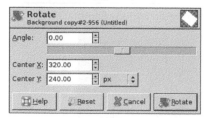

With this dialog, you can use the Angle slider to control the specific angle that you want to rotate your layer to. You can also use the Center X and Center Y values to control where the axis of rotation is. By default, GIMP places a center point indicating the axis of rotation at the absolute center of the layer. However, by adjusting these values or simply clicking the axis of rotation in the image window and dragging it to a new location, you can change the axis to another location. This is particularly useful if you need to rotate relative to another part of your image. The next section covers the Rotate tool as well as other transform tools in more detail.

Tip

Rotating all layers in your image by an arbitrary value takes only a couple more steps. Basically, before you do the rotation, you chain all layers together by going to the Layers dialog and Shift+clicking the space where the chain icon lives on any layer. When you use Shift+click, all layers are chained together. After that, rotate the layers by going to Layer ➤ Transform ➤ Arbitrary Rotation. Once you've completed your rotation, you may notice that the layers no longer fit the given image canvas. You can fix this quickly by using the Image ➤ Fit Canvas to Layers operation. ∎

Liquid Rescale: Quite Possibly the Coolest Thing Ever

In August of 2007 a research paper entitled "Seam Carving for Content-Aware Image Resizing" was published by Shai Avidan and Ariel Shamir. This paper and its accompanying video described a completely new way to change the size and scale of images while preserving the most important information in the image. You can watch the video yourself at www.youtube .com/watch?v=vIFCV2spKtg. Their research hit the graphics world like a ton of bricks and had legions of digital artists salivating in anticipation of getting such a feature in their tool of choice. A couple months later, the preliminary release of the Liquid Rescale plug-in was made. This kind of speedy development is one of the beautiful things about Free Software. Photoshop didn't get the Content Aware Scaling feature until the release of Photoshop CS4, nearly a year later. To do anything in this section, you're going to need to install the Liquid Rescale plug-in. If you don't already have it installed, have a look at Chapter 21.

To get an idea of some of the things Liquid Rescale is capable of, have a look at Figure 8-13. Using the same base image, the Liquid Rescale plug-in can adjust the image's scale to fit all kinds of proportions, ranging from a CD sleeve to a wide panorama. It can even intelligently zoom in on the subject without horribly squashing or stretching any of the important elements. This is the power that Liquid Rescale has over conventional image scaling.

FIGURE 8-13

Liquid Rescale can effectively resize your image without distorting it. (Photo credit: Melody Smith)

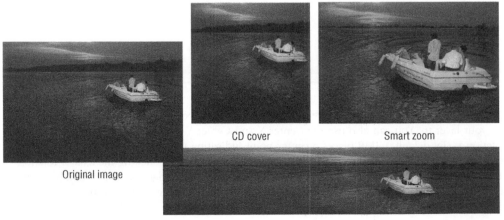

CD cover

Smart zoom

Original image

Panorama

The released paper that Liquid Rescale is based on has all of the technical details about how it works. You can find it on the Liquid Rescale web site (http://liquidrescale.wikidot.com) if you're interested. The short explanation goes like this: conventional scaling algorithms don't take into account the content of an image; a pixel is either enlarged or reduced and an interpolation algorithm is used to fill in or remove extra pixels. In contrast, the content-aware resizing algorithm that Liquid Rescale uses first analyzes the image in an attempt to determine the most visually relevant parts. These are the portions of the image that should be modified the least. Liquid Rescale uses this analysis to generate a *seam map*, which does the actual scaling using a technique called *seam carving*. A *seam* in this case is either a horizontal or vertical string of pixels. The scaling algorithm creates a seam by using the seam map and connecting the pixels with the least important information in the image. From there, Liquid Rescale either removes the seam to scale the image down or adds a new seam with interpolated pixels to scale the image up. The cool thing is that horizontal and vertical seams work independently, so you can easily increase the width of your image while simultaneously decreasing its height.

Using Liquid Rescale

For the most part, using Liquid Rescale is a straightforward process. The first thing you need to know is that although the Liquid Rescale plug-in can be called only from the Layer menu, it actually does have an effect on the whole image. For instance, if your rescaled result is larger than your canvas size, Liquid Rescale increases the image's canvas for you. However, if your result is less than the original image size, Liquid Rescale actually crops the other layers to fit the available space. In this way, it's a bit like the Zealous Crop feature. For this reason, it's a good idea to save backups of your image or, better yet, create a duplicate image (Ctrl+D or Image ➤ Duplicate) for doing your Liquid Rescale work.

Once you've got your image all set up and ready to rock, it's time to use the plug-in. Select the layer you want to rescale and then go to Layers ➤ Liquid Rescale. You should get a dialog like the one that appears in Figure 8-14.

As with most scaling and sizing utilities, the real meat of the Liquid Rescale plug-in is the Width and Height fields on the left side of the dialog, beneath the preview image. Simply enter the width and height that you want to rescale the image to. Because one of the nice features of the seam carving algorithm is the ability to scale the vertical cleanly and independently of the horizontal, the chain link button next to the Width and Height fields is disabled by default.

Note

Although GIMP 2.8 allows you to use units, percentages, and expressions in numeric entry fields (for example, 8in, 50%, or 6cm+12px), that same feature isn't automatically extended to entry fields in plug-ins. Hopefully this is something that will be fixed in the future, but in the meantime, know that numeric entry fields in plug-ins are only in the units shown in the drop-down menu. ∎

There are three buttons to the right side of the Width and Height fields. The topmost one resets the Width and Height values to the original values that were there when you first opened the Liquid Rescale plug-in. The next button down, with the floppy disk icon, allows you to recall width and height values from the last time you ran Liquid Rescale. This is handy if you're using Liquid Rescale to make a set of images all the same size. The last button in this column has an icon with a set of gears. Click this button to activate Liquid Rescale's interactive mode. The interactive mode is a good way to get fast feedback on your rescaling. It's covered in more detail later on in this chapter.

The Liquid Rescale dialog

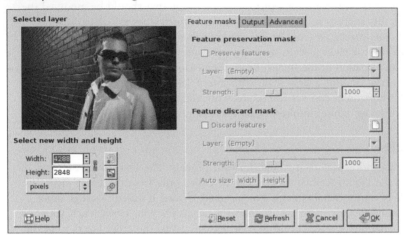

The quick-and-dirty way to run this plug-in is to load Liquid Rescale, enter your desired width and height, and then let it do all of the hard work for you. In quite a few instances, this is all you need to do and everything will turn out awesome. However, in a few circumstances — particularly those involving recognizable subjects like humans — the seam carving algorithm could use a little help. This is where the Feature Masks tab comes in handy. Liquid Rescale allows you to define a layer as a mask to indicate which pixels in your image are most important to you and which ones you'd prefer to get rid of. The former is referred to as a *feature preservation mask*, and the latter is a *feature discard mask*.

You can define these masks ahead of time using GIMP's standard selection and painting tools, but you don't have to. The Liquid Rescale plug-in takes full advantage of GIMP's non-blocking, non-modal interface. If you already have the Liquid Rescale dialog open and you want to create a feature preservation mask to prevent the subject of a photograph from getting distorted, just click the button with the paper icon in the Feature Preservation Mask section. Clicking this button does two things. First, it enables the Preserve Features check box so Liquid Rescale knows that you're using a feature preservation mask. Second, it creates a new layer at 50% opacity and sets your foreground color to bright green. Now you can use GIMP's paint tools to paint over the parts of your image that you don't want Liquid Rescale to distort. When you finish painting your mask, go back to the Liquid Rescale dialog and click the Refresh button at the bottom. This updates Liquid Rescale with your newly created preservation mask. If you need to make any further changes to the mask, you don't have to close the Liquid Rescale dialog. Just paint your updates and click the Refresh button again when you're done. The Strength slider beneath the Layer drop-down controls how much influence your preservation mask has. The default value usually yields acceptable results, but if you've painted a mask that's thin in parts, it may be helpful to increase the Strength slider to ensure those pixels are preserved. Figure 8-15 shows how much difference a feature preservation mask can make. Note that for Figure 8-15, I've converted the feature preservation mask to a black-and-white image so you can see it better, but the standard green paint on a transparent layer works fine.

FIGURE 8-15

Using a feature preservation mask prevents Liquid Rescale from running seams through important parts of your image, reducing distortion. (Photo credit: Melody Smith)

Original image

Plain Liquid Rescale

Feature preservation mask

Liquid Rescale with feature preservation mask

Of course, because you can define a preservation mask, Liquid Rescale also offers you the ability to define a feature discard mask. You can create this mask the same way you create the feature preservation mask; the only difference is that Liquid Rescale sets your foreground color to bright red instead of bright green. This is actually pretty convenient because it allows you to view your preservation and discard masks simultaneously without confusion about which is which. The Strength slider for the discard mask works as it does for the preservation mask, but the discard mask section does have an additional pair of buttons next to the label Auto Size.

When you're discarding pixels, the default behavior of Liquid Rescale is to generate a smaller finished image. There are ways around this, but if you want to remove a feature from an image, it makes the most sense to subtract those pixels from the overall image size. Rather than calculate the new, smaller image size yourself, you can click the Width or Height button to have Liquid Rescale attempt to calculate the exact final size of your image if the features in your discard mask were removed. If you know that you intend on rescaling your image horizontally, click the Width button. If you plan on discarding those pixels by rescaling vertically, click the Height button. Of course, the results from these buttons may not be perfect, but they do give you a good starting point if you want to set a custom size. Figure 8-16 shows how using a discard mask along with a preservation mask can remove some people from a group without distorting the people left in the image.

FIGURE 8-16

Using a feature discard mask to remove the males from this photo while preventing the ladies from being distorted in the rescaling process (Photo credit: Melody Smith)

Original image

Feature discard mask

Feature preservation mask

Final image

Output Options

Besides the Feature Masks tab that shows by default, the Liquid Rescale dialog offers two additional tabs, Output and Advanced, that allow you to tweak and customize the results that the plug-in produces. The first of these tabs is the Output tab, shown in Figure 8-17.

FIGURE 8-17

The Output tab in the Liquid Rescale dialog

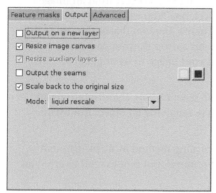

The check boxes in this tab enable you to control how Liquid Rescale delivers its results to you. The options available are as follows:

- **Output on a New Layer** — If you have an interest in keeping the original, unscaled version of your image, enable this option. This way, your newly rescaled image gets its own layer and you don't have to use Undo to get back your original.

- **Resize Image Canvas** — Because Liquid Rescale applies to a specific layer, you don't have to adjust the image canvas to accommodate your rescaled layer. It's typically fine to keep this check box enabled. However, if you prefer to resize your canvas yourself, feel free to disable it.

- **Resize Auxiliary Layers** — If you're using any masks with the Liquid Rescale plug-in, you have the option of resizing those masks along with your image. This is particularly useful if you intend on doing multiple passes of liquid rescaling on your image. If you would rather the mask layers remain in their original state, uncheck this box.

- **Output the Seams** — If you want to see the seam map that Liquid Rescale used on your image, enable this option. If you do that, then when you run Liquid Rescale, one or two layers (depending on whether you scaled in just one direction or both) are added to your image, showing you the seams that the plug-in used. This is helpful if Liquid Rescale doesn't behave as you expect. You can output the seams and check to see if, for example, it's recognizing your preservation mask. The two color swatches to the right of this option indicate the range of colors used to show your seams. The first swatch is the starting color and the second swatch is the ending color. Click either to customize them to your taste. Be aware that if you're scaling in both directions, the seam layers may look a bit wonky. One set of seams relates perfectly to your original image (it's a good idea to enable Output on a New Layer if you're using this feature) and the other set of seams appears to relate more with the resulting image. This is because Liquid Rescale does horizontal and vertical scaling independently. So whichever seams it does first (horizontal is the default) matches your original image.

- **Scale Back to the Original Size** — If your goal is to remove an object from an image without reducing the size of that image, enable this check box. You can also use this feature to implement a kind of smart zoom on your image. (There's more on that at the end of this section.) If you enable this option, Liquid Rescale reveals a drop-down menu where you can choose the scaling algorithm that it uses to return your image to its original size. The following are descriptions of each mode:

  - **Liquid Rescale** — As expected, this mode uses the seam carving algorithm to return your image to its original size. This is useful if you're removing an object from your image.

  - **Standard Scaling** — This mode uses the regular scaling method available through GIMP. It's not all that great for dealing with object removal, but it does tend to give you better results if you're doing a smart zoom.

  - **Width/Height Only (Uniform Scaling)** — If you scaled your image only horizontally or vertically, using one of these scaling modes may yield better results than the Standard Scaling option.

Advanced Options

The last tab available in the Liquid Rescale dialog is the Advanced tab, shown in Figure 8-18. The settings in this tab really get to the nitty-gritty of what makes this plug-in work. They allow you to control how the seam map is generated and tweak how Liquid Rescale uses that map to scale your image.

FIGURE 8-18

The Advanced tab in the Liquid Rescale dialog

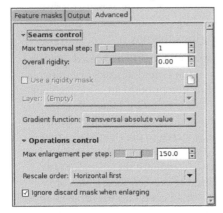

As the figure shows, the Advanced options have two sets of controls: Seams Control and Operations Control. The Seams Control section dictates how the seams in the seam map are constructed. The following bullets explain what each setting controls:

- **Max Transversal Step** — When Liquid Rescale creates a seam, by default, it moves one pixel at a time, using that pixel's immediate neighbors to determine the next step in creating the seam. Because the seam can't loop back upon itself, the algorithm has only three pixels to choose from as the next pixel; the pixel directly ahead and the pixels on either side of that one. The resulting default behavior is that seams can't deviate more than 45 degrees from their baseline. If you increase the Max Transversal Step, you allow seams to move at a larger angle, but there's a greater risk of scaling artifacts. If you do increase this value, it's highly recommended that you also adjust the Overall Rigidity or use a rigidity mask.

- **Overall Rigidity** — A seam's *rigidity* defines how much of an inclination that seam has to be perfectly straight. Maximize this value and your seams will be straight lines. Reduce it and the seam's direction is dictated more by the value of its Max Transversal Step.

- **Use Rigidity Mask** — The Overall Rigidity value is global for all seams over all areas of your image. However, in some areas of your image you may want straighter seams and in other parts you want seams to be a bit more flexible. To facilitate this, you can paint a rigidity mask. To create the mask, you use the exact same steps that you would to create a feature preservation or discard mask. Wherever you paint, Liquid Rescale generates more rigid seams. Liquid Rescale sets the base color of the rigidity mask to blue so you can differentiate it from the green and red feature masks. One thing to bear in mind here is that rigidity masks behave somewhat like preservation masks and repel seams a bit. To compensate for that, you may want to make sure your discard mask overlaps your rigidity mask.

- **Gradient Function** — When generating a seam map, Liquid Rescale has the capability of using a handful of different gradient functions to determine which parts of an image are the most visually relevant. The default value of Transversal Absolute Value tends to give the most favorable results, but if you're not getting the results you want, try choosing a different Gradient Function. The only odd option in this drop-down menu is Null. As its name implies, the Null setting tells Liquid Rescale not to do any sort of automatic feature detection. This means that Liquid Rescale relies entirely on your feature preservation mask to determine which pixels to avoid and which ones are expendable.

Below the Seams Control are the settings for Operations Control. These settings control how the seam map is used in the actual rescaling of images. There aren't that many settings here, but they're really quite powerful:

- **Max Enlargement per Step** — If you're enlarging your image, this value is very important. Measured in percent, this is the most that Liquid Rescale can enlarge your image in a single pass. If your desired new size is greater than this percentage, Liquid Rescale enlarges up to this percentage's value and then repeats the process of enlarging until it gets to your desired value. This setting is particularly useful if your image has a very large preservation mask. If the preservation mask takes up an overly large section of your image, Liquid Rescale won't have enough pixels to give you a clean enlargement in a single pass. For those kinds of situations, it's a good idea to play with smaller Max Enlargement per Step values.

- **Rescale Order** — This drop-down menu is relevant only in situations where you're rescaling in both the horizontal and vertical directions. It stipulates whether Liquid Rescale does its first scaling operation in the horizontal or vertical direction. For example, if you have an image that's taller than it is wide, you may want to do the vertical direction first.

- **Ignore Discard Mask When Enlarging** — If you have a discard mask on your image and you're trying to enlarge your image, the standard seam carving algorithm actually works in reverse on the areas you've painted. This means that rather than removing the seams in the space of your discard mask, Liquid Rescale actually chooses this space as the first place to add seams. Of course, this is probably not what people want when they paint a discard mask, so this check box is enabled by default to rectify that situation. It doesn't force Liquid Rescale to discard these pixels when enlarging, but at least they won't be the first ones that get duplicated.

Interactive Mode

If you click the gears icon in the standard Liquid Rescale interface, the dialog changes to look like the one in Figure 8-19. This is Liquid Rescale's interactive mode. Though it has a few limitations relative to the standard, non-interactive mode, this mode is a good way to see how Liquid Rescale handles different width and height values for your image.

FIGURE 8-19

The Liquid Rescale dialog in interactive mode. On the left is the default appearance and on the right is the dialog with the Map section expanded.

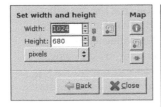 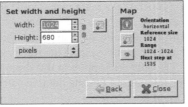

When you activate interactive mode, Liquid Rescale uses whatever width and height values you have in the standard interface and applies them directly. Personally, I prefer to start with the original size, but you're free to work the way that you're most comfortable. Once you're in interactive mode, GIMP automatically updates each time you change the values in the Width or the Height field. Like the non-interactive interface, the dialog for interactive mode also has a button to reset the Width and Height fields. Interactive mode supports most of the features available in non-interactive mode, but there are a few things that it can't do (or at least, can't do automatically):

- The Ignore Discard Mask When Enlarging feature doesn't work in interactive mode. This means that if you have a discard mask and your first move is to enlarge your image, the pixels within the discard mask will actually be among the first to be scaled. This is typically not what you want, so for that situation, you're better off in non-interactive mode.

- Interactive mode won't automatically create a seams layer like the non-interactive mode does. Fortunately, interactive mode provides a way for you to do this manually from the

Map section of the dialog. How to do that is covered a little bit later in this segment of the chapter.

- Interactive mode doesn't provide any automated facility for doing the Scale Back to the Original Size feature available in non-interactive mode. You can kind of get around this by using the Map Reset button (covered later in this section) and manually scaling back to the original size, but results are typically not all that great and you don't get the variety of scaling modes available in the non-interactive interface.

Although interactive mode has its limitations, it provides some information that isn't available in the non-interactive mode. This information is featured in an additional section of the interactive interface's dialog called Map. Expand this section by clicking the topmost button with the info (the letter "i" in a blue circle) icon. Look back at Figure 8-19 to see what the Map section looks like when it's expanded. This section shows some statistical information about the seam map that Liquid Rescale created for your image. Each element is described in the following list:

- **Orientation** — All seam maps have an orientation dependent on the direction that you're scaling. So if you're scaling horizontally, the map's orientation is horizontal.

- **Reference Size** — This is the value that the seam map was initialized with. The reference size is relative to the seam map's orientation. So looking back at Figure 8-19, the image's initial width is 1024 pixels and because the seam map's orientation is horizontal, the reference size is 1024.

- **Range** — If you keep the scaling within this range, Liquid Rescale won't have to regenerate a seam map. The side benefit of this is that as long as you stay within this range, rescaling happens almost in real time. When you first bring up interactive mode, there's a chance that the start and end range will be equal to the reference size. This means that whatever you do, a seam map needs to be generated. I typically get good results by setting the width or height (depending on the map's orientation) to the value noted by the Next Step At value. Do note, however, that if you change the direction that you're scaling, Liquid Rescale needs to generate a new seam map and all information pertaining to orientation, reference size, and range is lost.

- **Next Step At** — Liquid Rescale marks seams at defined increments, or *steps*. This value indicates the location of the next seam step. It is almost always outside of or at the very extent of the Range.

In the Map section, two other buttons besides the info button reveal the expanded information. The button directly beneath the info button is the Map Reset button. It shares the same icon as the button for resetting the width and height of your image; however, its function is very much different. It actually resets the seam map that Liquid Rescale uses to calculate seams and perform rescaling. Clicking this button is like telling Liquid Rescale, "*This* is my new start size. Please generate a new seam map." At the bottom of this column of buttons is a button with an eye icon. Click this button and Liquid Rescale creates a layer on your image with a visual representation of the seam map that Liquid Rescale is using. This is a handy way of seeing where Liquid Rescale plans on adding or removing seams. Do note, however, that unlike the Output the Seams check box in the non-interactive interface, this button only dumps the seams in the current direction that you're scaling.

Be aware that if you use interactive mode on large images, you might be doing a lot of waiting while your computer processes the changes. This kind of kills the interactive experience. A good way to deal with this is to create a duplicate version of your image and scale it down to a more manageable size with GIMP's standard Scale Image feature. It's difficult to give a recommended size for this because GIMP can run on a very wide range of hardware. However, an image size near 1024x768 tends to yield decent performance while giving you something decent to look at. Then you can use Liquid Rescale in interactive mode to test out some rough dimensions.

Advanced Techniques: Smart Zoom

The most obvious applications of the Liquid Rescale plug-in are cleverly reducing or enlarging images and intelligently removing features from an image. However, there's another use for Liquid Rescale that can be filed under the heading of "image enhancement." Sometimes referred to as a *smart zoom*, this technique cleanly enlarges a portion of an image without adversely affecting the rest of it. For a quick reference, look back to Figure 8-13. In that figure, the upper-right version of the image was quickly enhanced to increase the size of the boat and the people on it without obliterating that really nice sunset. Now, you could attempt to replicate this effect by cutting out the boat and scaling it independently of the background, but you'll run into complications requiring you to make a really clean selection or spend hours with the Clone tool getting the larger boat to cleanly fit in with the rest of the image. Liquid Rescale can do this for you much faster.

To do this technique, you need to utilize a feature preservation mask and Liquid Rescale's Scale Back to the Original Size feature in the Output tab. The details of the process are explained in the following steps:

1. **Select the layer you want to work on and run Liquid Rescale (Layer ➤ Liquid Rescale).**

2. **Paint a feature preservation mask on the part of the image that you would like to zoom in on.**

3. **Enable the Scale Back to the Original Size check box in the Output tab.** Set the scaling mode to Standard Scaling.

4. **Chain the Width and Height fields together by clicking the chain link icon to the right of them.** This ensures that your enhanced area is scaled proportionally. If you don't do this, that area may be stretched or squashed in an undesirable way.

5. **Set the Width or Height value to a size smaller than the current size.** You may want to use percentages here instead of pixels. As a rule of thumb, the inverse value of the percentage gives you a rough indicator of how much you are zooming in on your subject. For example, if you set the width and height percentages to 50%, you can expect your enhanced area to nearly double in size. You may need to come back to this step a couple times to play with the numbers to get the desired result.

6. **Click OK and let Liquid Rescale do the heavy lifting for you.** If you're working on a large image this step might involve you stepping away to make a sandwich.

That's it! With just those few steps you can bring more attention to a less prominent portion of an image. And if you work in multiple passes, you can use this technique with the standard Liquid Rescale tools to modify the overall image size as well as perform this kind of smart zoom.

Figure 8-20 shows an image before and after applying this technique, and the feature preservation mask used to highlight the portion of the image to zoom in on.

FIGURE 8-20

Using Liquid Rescale to do a smart zoom on part of an image (Photo credit: Chris Hoyer)

Original image   Preservation mask   Smart zoom + Liquid Rescale width

Using the Image Tools

There's a lot of power to be had in the Image and Layer menus, but oftentimes these tools don't give you the immediate feedback that you might want as an artist. To accommodate that, GIMP offers a few tools that are easily accessible from the Toolbox. Like the operations available in the Image and Layer menus, you're able to use these tools to move, crop, rotate, scale, and flip elements in your image. However, unlike most of the menu operations, these tools allow you to perform transforms interactively with immediate, real-time feedback. Additionally, you also get a few other operations, such as adjusting perspective and shearing image data.

Alignment Tool

GIMP's Alignment tool (Q) is incredibly useful for arranging a bunch of layers in your image. Figure 8-21 shows the Toolbox with the Alignment tool selected and its Tool Options visible.

When you choose the Alignment tool, select the layers that you want to align. Select the first layer by left-clicking it. You can tell a layer is selected by looking at the corners of the layer. There should be a small rectangular violet dot at each corner. Add more layers to your selection by Shift+clicking them. You can also draw a selection rectangle by left-clicking and dragging in the image window. Any layer with its borders entirely within your selection area is selected. Press and hold Shift before drawing your selection rectangle if you want to add these layers to your selection. As a neat little additional feature, you can also use the Alignment tool to align guides. To do this, you can click or Shift+click any guide the same way you would select a layer.

Warning

Currently there's no way to deselect any layers, so if you select the wrong layer for aligning, you'll need to restart your selection process. ■

Tip

Unlike the Move tool, the Alignment tool does not disregard transparent pixels. This means that if you have two layers with transparent areas that overlap and you click in that overlap area, the Alignment tool selects only the topmost layer. To select the lower layer, you need to click part of that layer that isn't overlapped by another layer or draw a selection rectangle around that layer's area. ■

FIGURE 8-21

GIMP's Toolbox with the Alignment tool selected and its Tool Options visible

With your layers selected, your next step is to determine what you want to align these layers to. The drop-down menu under the Relative To label gives you six options:

- **First Item** — This is the default behavior for the Alignment tool. With this option selected, the Alignment tool aligns or distributes your selected layers relative to the first layer you selected.

- **Image** — You can also align your layers relative to your image's canvas. If you need to align one or more layers along your image's center line, this option makes it really easy.

- **Selection** — If you used one of the selection tools to select some pixels prior to choosing the Alignment tool, you use this option to align your layers to the boundaries of that selection. Note that the alignment is to the rectangular boundary of the selection, not the selection itself. If you have no pixels selected, the Alignment tool aligns your layers to the whole image.

- **Active Layer** — Choose this option to align your selected layers to the boundaries of the current active layer. This does not require you to include the active layer among the layers you've selected with the Alignment tool.

- **Active Channel** — Because a channel is essentially a custom selection mask, this option produces results similar to those you would get by choosing the Selection option. It just uses the selection defined by the active channel.

- **Active Path** — Like channels, paths can be used to create a custom selection, so this option behaves like using the Selection option on a selection defined by the active path.

Once you've determined what you're aligning your selected layers to, you can go ahead and do the alignment. In the Alignment tool's Tool Options, you have two sets of alignment buttons: one under the heading of Align and the other under Distribute. By default, both of these sets of buttons do the exact same thing. The first row of buttons controls horizontal alignment, aligning your layers to the left, center, or right of what you're aligning relative to. The second row of buttons controls vertical alignment, aligning to the top, bottom, or vertical center. Figure 8-22 shows the different types of alignments with a set of different-shaped layers.

Tip

The Alignment tool does not disregard transparency when performing alignment operations. It uses the entire layer size, regardless of the size of the content within the layer. For this reason, if you want to align your layers, you may want to run Layer ▷ Autocrop Layer on those layers before using the Alignment tool. ∎

The value that makes the Align and Distribute buttons behave differently is the Offset value at the bottom of the Tool Options. This value is the number of pixels a layer is displaced from its nearest neighbor in the direction you're aligning. When it's set to its default value of zero, the Distribute buttons behave just like the Align buttons. However, if you set the Offset value to any other positive or negative number, the Alignment tool displaces layers according to that number.

As an example, have a look at Figure 8-23. This figure starts with the same original 640 x 480 image as the one in Figure 8-22. Assuming you're aligning relative to the image canvas, if you select all the elements in this image and click the Distribute Left button with an Offset value of zero, all the shapes end up flush against the left side of the image. However, if you change the Offset to a value of 50 pixels, the leftmost object (in this case, the cube) starts 50 pixels away from the left side of the image. The next leftmost object then starts 50 pixels from the cube's left boundary, or 100 pixels from the left side of the image. This continues on to the last object farthest away from the left side. In this case, because that's the fourth object, it's 200 pixels (50 x 4) from the left side of the image.

Note

It's important to note here that the Alignment tool goes through each layer one at a time when it's aligning them. When doing so, the tool uses neither your selection order nor the layer order to determine which layer it's going to operate on next. That is entirely determined by what is closest to the alignment target. In the previous example, the order would be determined by which layers are closest to the left side of the image. If you choose to distribute relative to the center of the image, the Alignment tool operates on the layers closer to that target first. ■

FIGURE 8-22

Aligning layers horizontally and vertically relative to their image canvas

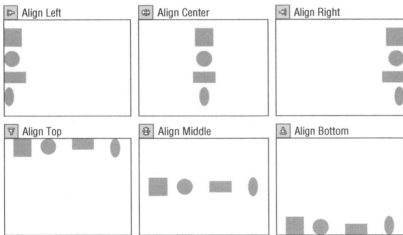
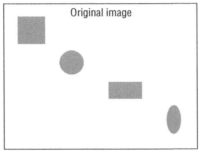

FIGURE 8-23

Distributing a set of layers 50 pixels from left side of the image

Original image   Distribute Left – offset = 0   Distribute Left – offset = 50

Crop Tool

The most straightforward of the transform tools is the Crop tool (Shift+C). Most of this tool's basic functionality is covered in Chapter 4; however, there are some details worth mentioning here. In contrast to the more automated cropping tools available in the Image and Layer menus, the Crop tool gives you the most complete amount of control and flexibility when cropping an image. Using it is pretty simple: select the Crop tool and then click and drag a crop box in the image window over the area that you want to keep.

Like the Rectangle Select tool, the Crop tool can be resized. Click and drag any of the boxes at the corners of the crop area to resize two sides at the same time. Bringing your mouse near any of the edges of the crop area allows you to adjust just that particular edge. If you hold down Shift while making your adjustments, the other sides of the crop box proportionally increase or decrease, maintaining the same aspect ratio. You can also move around the entire crop area by clicking and dragging within it.

Once you've determined the portion of the image that you want to keep, press Enter or left-click within the crop area to perform the crop action. By default, when you use the Crop tool, GIMP crops the entire image, including all layers you have, whether they're visible or not. That's the default behavior, but you can use the Tool Options for the Crop tool, shown in Figure 8-24, to customize the Crop tool's behavior.

FIGURE 8-24

The Tool Options for the Crop tool give you additional flexibility when cropping.

The Crop tool's Tool Options actually give you complete control over everything that it can do. Each of these options is described here:

- **Current Layer Only** — The Crop tool's default behavior is to affect all layers. However, if you enable this check box, you crop only the current active layer.

- **Allow Growing** — Another default behavior of the Crop tool is that the crop area is constrained to the width and height of your image canvas. This may not be what you want. Enable this check box and you no longer have those constraints. Then when you confirm the crop, the image canvas is expanded to include the off-canvas space that was in your crop area.

- **Expand from Center** — By default, when you adjust the dimensions of your crop area, you adjust only the edge or corner that you click and drag. This is done because the Crop tool treats the opposite corner or edge as the reference point: the point that doesn't move. If you enable this option, GIMP treats the center of your crop area as the reference. So if you adjust one corner, all of them move, and if you adjust an edge, the opposite edge moves proportionally.

- **Fixed** — Click this check box and your crop area becomes constrained according to one of the four rules. Note that rather than enabling this option from the Tool Options, you can also quickly enable this option by pressing Shift while adjusting your crop area.

  - **Aspect Ratio** — This is the default behavior. If you already have a crop rectangle created, that rectangle's aspect ratio is what's used. If you want to use a specific aspect ratio, just type the desired value in the text entry field below this drop-down menu (such as 1:1 for a square box or 16:9 for the standard HD television aspect ratio). The portrait and landscape buttons to the right of the text entry field allow you to swap the horizontal and vertical components of the aspect ratio you entered. As you adjust the size of your crop area with your mouse, its aspect ratio is displayed in the image window's status area.

  - **Width/Height** — These options limit the width or height of your crop area to the value you specify in the text field below.

  - **Size** — This option works like the Aspect Ratio option, except you specify a specific size in pixels in the text entry field. It defaults to 100×100, but changing that is as easy as clicking in the text field and typing the dimensions you want.

- **Position** — The numeric entry fields here stipulate where the upper-left corner of your crop area is located relative to the upper-left corner of your canvas. They can accept negative values, but only if you enable the Allow Growing option described earlier. The Position units default to pixels, but the drop-down menu on the right allows you to define other units.

- **Size** — Though these inputs look identical to those of the Position settings, they control something different. They actually define the absolute width and height of your crop area. Unless you have Allow Growing enabled, the size can't be set to make the crop area larger than your canvas.

- **Highlight** — By default, the Crop tool uses an effect called a *passepartout* (pronounced "pass-par-too"), darkening the region that isn't within your crop area. This typically makes it easier to visualize what your final crop will look like prior to confirming it. However, if it makes it difficult to see your image, you can disable the effect by clicking this check box.

- **Guide Style** — One of the main reasons why people crop images is to improve the overall composition of them. If you're improving composition, it's often helpful to have a set of guides that relate to some basic composition rules. You have the following options:

- **No Guides** — This is the default. You see all of your crop area without obstruction, but you don't have any guides to assist with composition.

- **Center Lines** — Choose this option and guides are drawn horizontally and vertically along the center of your crop area, breaking it up into quadrants.

- **Rule of Thirds** — This option adds guides in your image according to the rule of thirds; a composition rule where you break up your image into thirds horizontally and vertically. For good composition, the center of interest in your image should appear at one of the four locations where these guides intersect.

- **Golden Sections** — This option creates guides similar to the ones created by the Rule of Thirds option. The guides are defined a bit differently, but the idea is the same. Your center of interest should be at one of the locations where these guides intersect.

- **Diagonal Lines** — In composition, having elements that create diagonals tends to give the image more energy. Choose this option to see diagonal guides. Then you can crop your image to try to have elements in the image correspond to these guides.

- **Auto Shrink** — Click this button to get your crop area to fit content in your active layer. It's a lot like running Layer ➤ Autocrop Layer. The thing that makes this button different is that it only evaluates what's already within your crop area. To get Auto Shrink to behave exactly like Autocrop Layer, you'd have to set your initial crop area to encompass your entire layer.

- **Shrink Merged** — This option influences how Auto Shrink works. By default, Auto Shrink only evaluates the current active layer. However, if you enable this option, Auto Shrink tries to take all visible layers within the crop area into account.

Transformation Tool

In older versions of GIMP there were separate tools for moving, rotating, scaling, shearing, and changing the perspective on layers. In GIMP 2.8, all of these tools were consolidated into a unified Transformation tool. In a way, this new tool works like a supercharged version of the Crop tool. With the Transform tool selected from the Toolbox click in your image window and it becomes active for you to transform. While you're working, the Transform tool provides you with a real-time preview of the result of your transform. If you don't like your transformation and you want to reset things to their original state to start over, press Esc. Once you're satisfied, press Enter and the full transform operation will be finalized. Unlike the Crop tool's relatively simple controls, the Transform tool's controls are more numerous and somewhat more complex. Despite that, the Tool Options for the Transform tool, shown in Figure 8-25, are pretty straightforward.

Note

Due to the tight publishing deadlines for this book, this section on the unified Transformation tool was written before the tool was implemented in GIMP, using design specifications provided by GIMP developers. Please refer to this book's companion Web site for updates and errata to this section. ∎

A description of each of these settings follows:

- **Transform** — The first option for the Transform tool, appropriately labeled Transform, dictates just what it is that you're transforming.

- **Layer** — This first button is the default mode. This means that the tool influences the current active layer. You can have it simultaneously work on other layers and even paths if you chain them together in the Layers and Paths dialogs. If you have a selection made and you use the default Layer transform mode, it automatically turns your selection into a floating selection, allowing you to transform it independently of your active layer.

- **Selection** — If you want to transform the selection without modifying the pixels within that selection, you need to click this second button.

- **Path** — This option allows you to use the Transform tool on the current active path, if one exists.

FIGURE 8-25

Tool Options for the Transform tool

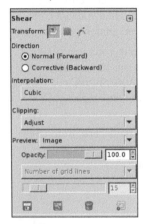

- **Direction** — Most of the time, you never need to change this from its default value of Normal (Forward). In the Normal direction, the Transform tool works as expected. If you instead choose the Corrective (Backward) direction, the Transform tool appears to respond as you expect, but when you confirm the transform operation, it behaves with inverted values from what you set. This feature is primarily used when fixing the rotation of images.

- **Interpolation** — The options in this drop-down menu are exactly the same ones that are found in the Scale Image dialog. Look back to Chapter 1 if you need to review what each one does.

- **Clipping** — Often when you transform a layer, the result is larger than the initial layer boundaries. The options in this drop-down menu tell GIMP what to do when this happens.

  - **Adjust** — This is the default behavior. The layer boundary size is enlarged to accommodate the entire result of your transform operation.

  - **Clip** — Choose this option to simply trim off any parts of your transformation result that don't fit within the space defined by the original layer dimensions.

- **Crop to Result** — This option is most commonly used when fixing the rotation of a photograph. When you choose this option, GIMP finds the rectangular area of your result that doesn't include any transparent pixels and crops the layer to that space.

- **Crop with Aspect** — This option does the same thing as Crop to Result, but it also maintains the aspect ratio of the original layer size. If your transformation isn't too drastic, you can use this option and scale the result to match the original layer size. This is especially useful if you're digitally fixing the rotation or perspective of an image.

- **Preview** — While you're working on your transformation, GIMP tries to give you as much useful feedback as possible. This drop-down and its associated sub-options let you control how much feedback GIMP gives you.

  - **Outline** — If you're working on a large image or you have a slower computer, the default Preview setting may not be the best option for you. Choose this one, and a simple outline of your transformation result is all you'll see.

  - **Grid** — The outline is useful, but it often doesn't give you enough information about what's happening within the actual area that you're transforming. Choose this option and a grid of guides is drawn to show how the transform is happening. At the bottom of the Tool Options is a slider that you can use to control the number of grid lines GIMP uses for this. If you want to ensure that the grid is made of squares rather than rectangles, use the drop-down menu above the slider to change it from Number of Grid Lines to Grid Line Spacing. Then the slider controls the space between grid lines (in pixels) rather than the number of lines themselves.

  - **Image** — The default preview behavior is to use your actual image so you can see what the result will look like. It works really well, but by default it's difficult to see how your newly transformed layer relates to the original. You can easily get around that, though, by using the slider beneath this drop-down to reduce the opacity of the preview.

  - **Image + Grid** — This option combines both the Grid and Image options so you can get a really detailed idea of what your transform operation is doing. With this option set, you can also control the preview opacity as well as the number of grid lines or the spacing between them.

Now we get into the real fun of actually using the Transform tool. When you activate this tool on your layer, you get a *control frame*. Like I mentioned before, this is pretty similar to the Crop tool, but with a lot more options. Each portion of this control frame has a function that relates to transformation.

Moving

The simplest of the transforms is Move. Simply click in the central transparent area of the control frame and drag the layer to a new location in your image window. Hold down Ctrl while moving and the layer is constrained to moving horizontally, vertically, or in 45-degree diagonals. If you have guides on your image, you can move those around by simply clicking them and dragging them to a new location. Be careful not to click the crosshair at the direct center of the layer. Doing this moves the rotation axis rather than the layer itself.

Rotating

With the Transform tool, you have a lot more flexible — and more immediate — control over rotation than what's available in the Image or Layer menus. For one thing, as I just mentioned, you can change your axis of rotation by clicking and dragging the crosshair at the center of the control frame. To rotate, though, click and drag the circular control in the upper left of the control frame. Think of this as a handle that you grab onto and rotate your layer around its axis of rotation. If you hold Ctrl while doing this, the rotation is constrained to increments of 15 degrees.

Scaling

To scale your image, click and drag one of the squares at the corners of the control frame or the rectangular area along the edges of your layer. You can use this to quickly enlarge or reduce the size of your layer. Most of the time when scaling, you'll want to maintain the same aspect ratio as the original layer. You can do this with the Transform tool by holding down Shift while you're scaling. Also, like the Crop tool, you can scale from the center of the layer by holding down Ctrl. If you want to scale from the center while simultaneously retaining aspect, hold down both Shift and Ctrl while you're scaling.

Shearing

The process of *shearing* shifts two opposing sides of a layer in opposite directions, forming a basic parallelogram shape. It's a nice quick-and-dirty way to make a static image look speedy. Also (and I'm sure there are some typographers out there who will hate me for writing this), but when you use shearing on a text layer, you can quickly fake italics if you have a font that doesn't have italics versions of each character.

To perform the shearing, click and drag the diagonal controls on any of the four sides of the control frame. If you choose the controls at the top or bottom, you can shear your layer side to side. Choosing the side controls lets you shear up and down. By default, you're not able to shear in both directions at the same time. This is referred to as a *free shear*. In order to do that, you need to hold down Shift while shearing. Then you'll be able to free shear all you want. And like Scaling, the shear controls also allow you to shear from the center by holding down Ctrl.

Changing Perspective

The perspective controls give you by far the most latitude when transforming your layer. It's useful to use them when you want your layer to look like it pushes back into the distance. Say you have an image like the one in Figure 8-15 and you want to put a logo on that brick wall. If you want to do that, you need to change the perspective of that logo image so it matches how the bricks converge in the distance. Changing a layer's perspective requires you to click the triangular corner shapes in the control frame. By default, you can move each of these controls independently to squash and stretch your image to match your desired perspective. If you hold down Ctrl while transforming one of these corner controls, you activate a constraint. That constraint attempts to make the perspective tool follow basic perspective rules. Specifically, it tries to keep two sides of the layer parallel while only producing angles on the other two sides. This is the easiest way to get proper perspective on an image or photograph where elements converge on a *vanishing point* the farther they go in the distance. Figure 8-26 shows the result of using the perspective transform to place a logo on the brick wall from Figure 8-15.

Tip

One of the advantages of unifying all of GIMP's transformation tools into a single Transform tool — besides saving space in the Toolbox — is the fact that now you can do multiple transforms in a single pass. You can move a layer, scale it up, rotate it slightly, and adjust its perspective all in one go. This is definitely a workflow improvement. The other cool thing is that while you're still working on your transformations, if you use Undo (Ctrl+Z), it doesn't undo the entire transform. GIMP just reverses the last thing you did from within the Transform tool. Once you confirm the transform operation, however, the aggregate result of all your transformations is undone, taking you back to before you first used the Transform tool. ∎

FIGURE 8-26

The perspective controls on the Transform tool allow you to effectively place a logo on a brick wall that goes to the distance. (Photo credit: Melody Smith)

Flip Tool

The Flip tool (Shift+F) is a much faster way of flipping layers than navigating all the way through Layer ➤ Transform ➤ Flip Horizontally/Vertically. Also, like the Transformation tool, you can use it to affect more than just layers. The Tool Options for the Flip tool, shown in Figure 8-27, allow you to choose whether the Flip tool affects layers, selections, or paths.

FIGURE 8-27

The Tool Options for the Flip tool let you control what you're flipping as well the direction of the flip.

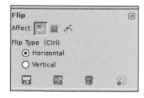

Remember that if you click the middle button next to the Affect label to choose to flip selections, it doesn't flip the pixels that are within the selection, only the selection area itself. If you want to flip the pixels within your selection, that happens by default. For flipping layers or paths, the

Flip tool works on the current active channel. However, if you chain together multiple layers and paths, you can get the Flip tool to work on them together.

You can use the radio buttons for Flip Type to control which direction you do the flip, but it's much faster leave this set to one value and use Ctrl+click in the image to flip the other way. The default behavior is for a click in the image window to cause a horizontal flip and a Ctrl+click to cause a vertical flip.

Summary

Oh, wow, what a chapter. Here you learned a whole mess of ways to drastically modify the look of your images. You saw the variety of transform tools available to you in the Image and Layer menus. They provide you with a variety of automated methods for quickly cropping and rotating images in layers. You were also introduced to the incredibly cool Liquid Rescale plug-in and its incredibly powerful abilities to scale an image without horribly distorting the content within that image. In the last half of the chapter, you had an in-depth look at the transformation tools available in GIMP's Toolbox, including Alignment, Crop, Flip, and the new unified Transformation tool. These are some of the most powerful tools available in GIMP for manipulating the locations of pixels in your images. The next chapter gets into adjusting the color values of those pixels. Have at it!

Adjusting Colors

When editing images, one of the most common tasks is *color correction*, the term used for adjusting, tweaking, and enhancing the colors in a particular image. This is especially true when it comes to digital photography. Often it's impossible to get the color or lighting exactly the way you want when you're out shooting. In those situations, rather than spending all of your time moving lights around or adjusting your position or waiting for the sun to come back out, it may be faster to get the shot as close as possible to what you want and do the corrections later in GIMP. This is the core of the *post-production* portion of the creative process in digital imagery. Color correction a very powerful way to enhance a good image to make it great and even make some poor images at least passable, especially when used with the rest of GIMP's tools. Of course, post-production can never be a replacement for good photography. It's best to get it right (or as close to right as possible) in the camera first. Many professionals who work in image editing and visual effects groan when they hear the phrase, "We can fix it in post," because they're often expected to turn horrible images into beautiful works of art. Post-production isn't magic and some images are simply not salvageable. That said, in the right hands, the tools covered in this chapter can produce some dramatic changes and enhancements to any image.

Because the figures in the book are printed in black and white, it's difficult to illustrate all of the effects that these color correction tools have within these pages. For this reason, you may find it helpful to have GIMP open with a test image in the image window when you're looking through this chapter. That way you can experience the effects of these tools first-hand. The example figures from this chapter are available for download on the companion web site for this book (wiley.com/go/GIMPBible.com). That way if you don't have a copy of GIMP immediately available, you can still see the results of these tools. You can also find good color examples of these tools in the official GIMP documentation at http://docs.gimp.org.

Using GEGL

Historically, one of the biggest criticisms leveled at GIMP is its limitation of only using 8 bits per color channel. Modern digital cameras are capable of using 12-bit and even 16-bit color. GIMP's limitation is a severe handicap preventing you from editing these images at their native bit depth. Fortunately, the developers are working to remedy the situation by integrating *GEGL*, the Generic Graphics Library, to handle GIMP's core color operations. Among its other useful features, GEGL is capable of processing images using a 32-bit floating-point buffer for each color channel. This ensures that GIMP can not only work with current modern cameras, but also technology developed in the future.

That all said, full GEGL integration into GIMP is still incomplete. Rough integration was introduced in GIMP 2.6, but disabled by default. This allowed developers to work on advancing GIMP without sacrificing existing functionality. To enable the GEGL core for color operations go to Color ➤ Use GEGL and toggle on that option. This ensures that color processing is handled internally at 32 floating-point bits per channel using GEGL. Of course, all of these operations are converted to 8-bit color when they're displayed and saved out of GIMP.

In addition to the Color ➤ Use GEGL option, the View menu has also acquired this functionality in GIMP 2.8. Go to View ➤ Use GEGL and this causes the view projection in the image window and layer blending modes to be handled by GEGL. In addition to these two Use GEGL options, a GEGL Operation tool lets you see GEGL at work. Access this tool from the image window by going to Tools ➤ GEGL Operation. A dialog like the one shown here opens. From this dialog, you can play with the GEGL operations and get a glimpse of what's coming in future versions of GIMP.

The GEGL Operation dialog (left) lets you play with a handful of GEGL operations (on the right) before it gets fully integrated in GIMP.

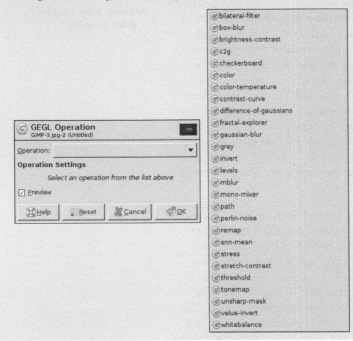

Because GEGL integration is incomplete, the existing integration isn't optimized. Operations that are normally snappy and nearly instantaneous may take much longer to execute when you enable the Use GEGL options (particularly View ➤ Use GEGL). Part of this is simply because 32-bit floating-point values are larger than 8-bit values and therefore take longer to process. This performance hit is one of the reasons I recommend against doing production work with GEGL enabled. Hopefully as GEGL gets fully integrated in GIMP 2.10, these performance issues will be addressed and rectified. In the meantime, it's there for you to see and experiment with, but it's not something for day-to-day image editing.

Using the Color Menu

To do any color correction in GIMP, go to the Color menu in the image window. GIMP's native color correction tools are available in this menu, shown in Figure 9-1. This section explains each operation available in this menu.

FIGURE 9-1

The Color menu in the image window is where you find GIMP's native color correction operations.

Working with the Color Tools

Even though they're not shown in the Toolbox by default, the color operations at the top of the Color menu are tools just like the Transformation tool or Rectangle Select tool. To verify this, you can look in the Tools ➤ Color Tools menu, shown in Figure 9-2. For even faster access to these tools, you can add them to the Toolbox by going to Edit ➤ Preferences and choosing to the Toolbox tab. There you can add any of these color tools to the Toolbox.

FIGURE 9-2

The first items in the Color menu are actually GIMP tools available in Tools ➤ Color Tools and can be added to your Toolbox via Edit ➤ Preferences for fast access.

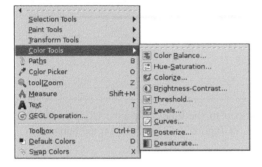

Features Available for All Color Tools

Regardless of what part of GIMP's interface you use to activate these tools, a dialog opens for adjusting the results produced by them. Furthermore, you can enable a live preview when working with the color tools in the image window so you can see the color adjustments happening in real time. If you have a slower computer or a large image, disable the preview so your computer doesn't lag while you're adjusting values in the dialog.

Also, with the exception of the Posterize and Desaturate tools, each of these tools enables you to save presets that store your color correction settings for each one. This is useful if you've shot or otherwise created a series of images with a consistent lighting style and need to apply the same color correction to every one. GIMP doesn't ship with any presets by default, but to create your own for each tool click the plus-sign icon next to the Presets drop-down menu. This brings up a dialog that allows you to name a preset that will be immediately available to you in the Presets drop-down for that tool. Figure 9-3 shows how this process works using the Brightness-Contrast tool.

After you create your presets, GIMP enables you to manage those presets by exporting them, importing them, or deleting them altogether. For example, you may want to take your presets with you for using GIMP on other computers. To access the preset management functionality, click the triangle icon to the right of the Add Preset plus sign. This gives you a menu with the following options:

- **Import Settings from File** — If you've exported settings from another copy of GIMP and you want to use them in your current session, choose this option. It brings up a File Browser where you can go through your hard drive and find the exported settings file for the current color tool and bring it into GIMP.

FIGURE 9-3

Adding a custom preset for one of GIMP's color tools

- **Export Settings to File —** This option takes the current settings in your color tool dialog and saves them to a file on your hard drive. When you choose this option, a File Browser appears where you can name the file and determine where on your hard drive it's going to live. The settings file itself is just a simple text file. As an example, the following text shows settings exported from the Brightness-Contrast tool:

```
# GIMP brightness-contrast tool settings

(time 0)
(brightness 0.206349)
(contrast 0.216931)

# end of brightness-contrast tool settings
```

- **Manage Settings —** This option brings up a separate window that you can use to manage your settings. The window gives you the same import and export functionality found in this menu, but you can also select specific settings to export or delete them altogether.

Figure 9-4 shows the preset import/export menu and the Manage Saved Settings window.

FIGURE 9-4

On the left is a color tool with the import/export menu visible and on the right is the Manage Saved Settings window where you can select and delete presets.

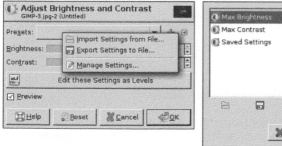

Tip

The color tools affect only the active layer. To affect multiple layers, you need to merge them together first. Also know that you cannot apply a color tool directly to a layer group. This functionality may arrive in future versions of GIMP, but in the meantime your best solution is to make use of the Layer ➤ New from Visible menu option to create a separate merged layer that you can color adjust independently of your other layers. ∎

Tip

Although you can't apply a color tool to more than one layer at a time, you can apply it to a portion of your active layer using GIMP's selection tools. Just select the pixels you want to color correct and then run whichever color tool you want. It affects only the pixels within your selection. If you choose to adjust colors this way, you may want to feather your selection (Select ➤ Feather) so the color change won't be too abrupt. ∎

Color Balance

The Color Balance tool is an excellent tool for making subtle changes to the coloring in your images. Use it, for example, if you want to make your shadows warmer or if your highlights have too much yellow. If you haven't added the Color Balance tool to the Toolbox, activate it by going to Color ➤ Color Balance and you are presented with a dialog like the one shown in Figure 9-5.

FIGURE 9-5
_____

The Color Balance tool's configuration dialog

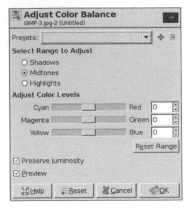

The following controls are available to you in the Color Balance dialog:

- **Select Range to Adjust** — Of all the color tools, the Color Balance tool is unique in that it's the only one where you can define which pixels you want to adjust without first making a selection. You use radio buttons to tell the Color Balance tool to work on just Shadows (darker pixels), Midtones, or Highlights (lighter pixels). Click the range you want to adjust and use the sliders below to adjust that range. When you're done, you can then click another range and adjust its color balance or complete the process by clicking OK. This way you can adjust your Shadows, Midtones, and Highlights in one session with the Color Balance tool without having to recall it for each value range.

- **Adjust Color Values** — These sliders pit the Cyan, Magenta, and Yellow color values against their respective Red, Green, and Blue complements. Reducing the red in your image naturally increases the cyan. Increasing the green levels reduces the amount of magenta in your chosen value range. Each slider has a range from −100 to 100 and starts at zero with the original pixel colors that exist when you first activate this tool. At any point while you're working, you can click the Reset Range button beneath these sliders to set them all back to zero. Note, however, that the Reset Range button affects only sliders for your current value range. To return all ranges (Shadows, Midtones, and Highlights) to their original levels, click the larger Reset button at the bottom of the dialog.

- **Preserve Luminosity** — This check box, enabled by default, prevents the Color Balance tool from modifying the luminosity, or lightness value, of your pixels. If you disable this check box, the results from the Color Balance tool are typically much brighter as you push toward the Red, Green, and Blue sliders and darker as you push them to Cyan, Magenta, and Yellow.

Note

When it comes to the various color models in digital graphics, there are actually subtle technical differences between the terms luminosity and lightness. GIMP's interface doesn't really differentiate between the two and often uses the term lightness when some features are implemented as luminosity. This is actually not a problem that's unique to GIMP, and even spans out to commercial software like Photoshop. Because it's more descriptive and technically accurate, I'll be using luminosity throughout the text unless I'm talking about a specific interface item named Lightness. ∎

Like all tools in this section, the dialog for this tool offers a check box where you can toggle a live preview in the image window. The Color Balance tool is pretty fast, though, so you should be just fine with keeping the preview enabled.

Hue-Saturation

The Hue-Saturation tool would probably be better named the Hue-Saturation-Luminosity tool, because you use it to adjust the hue, saturation, and luminosity of pixels in your image. You can adjust these values for all colors in your image or tweak them for a specific color range. If you haven't added this tool to the Toolbox, activate it from Colors ➤ Hue-Saturation. When you do this, you get the dialog shown in Figure 9-6.

The largest feature on this dialog is the rough color wheel at the top. It consists of six color swatches and a Master button in the center of the wheel where you define the color range that you want to work on. By default, the Master button is depressed, indicating that when you use the Hue, Lightness, and Saturation sliders at the bottom of the dialog, you are going to adjust those values for the full color range in your image. You can also use the radio buttons next to each color swatch to adjust the hue, luminosity, and saturation for the pixels in that specific range. The cool thing is that this color wheel control lets you adjust all color ranges without closing and re-opening the dialog. So you can, for example, reduce the luminosity of the whole image using the Master button and then go in and increase the luminosity of just the pixels in the Yellow color range.

FIGURE 9-6

The Hue-Saturation tool's dialog

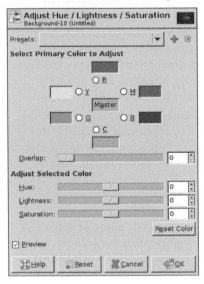

Below the color wheel control is a slider named Overlap. This slider controls how much overlap there is between colors adjacent to one another on the color wheel. It's a percentage value where zero dictates no overlap between colors and 100 indicates the greatest amount of overlap. Increasing the overlap value prevents overly abrupt changes from occurring when you tweak a single color range.

In the sliders at the bottom of the Hue-Saturation dialog, the most prominent results can be seen with the Master button activated and adjusting the Hue slider. It has the effect of rotating the color influence for all colors in your image. For example, if you push the Hue slider to its maximum value of 180 degrees, red pixels become cyan, yellow pixels become blue, green pixels become magenta, and so on. The Lightness slider controls how bright or dark the pixels in your image are and the Saturation slider controls the color intensity, with its minimum values resulting in a completely grayscale image. The Lightness and Saturation sliders have a range from −100 to 100. Like with the Color Balance tool, the zero position on these sliders represents the values for your pixels when you first bring up the Hue-Saturation tool. At any point while working with this tool, you can set these sliders back to zero by clicking the Reset Color button below them. Also like the Color Balance tool, this affects the sliders only for the range you're currently working on. To reset the values for all ranges, use the larger Reset button at the bottom of the dialog.

Figure 9-7 shows an example of what this tool can do. In the original photograph, the background of the image consists of largely bluish values and the shoes in the foreground consist of mostly warm colors. The Hue-Saturation tool was used to darken and desaturate the background while maximizing the saturation and intensity of the warmer tones. Of course, this is difficult to see in grayscale, but notice how much darker the background elements are in the final image when compared to the foreground. See this book's companion web site for the color version and the exported settings for this specific image.

FIGURE 9-7

Using the Hue-Saturation tool to make the foreground elements of a photograph "pop." The original photo is on the left and the color-adjusted one is on the right. (Photo credit: Chris Hoyer)

Colorize

The Colorize tool pushes your image to a monotone tint based on a color of your choice. Although it works great on full-color images, the real benefit of this tool is adding color to grayscale images. If you want a portrait of your mother to look like one of those old-timey sepia-toned photographs, this is the way to do it. Figure 9-8 shows the dialog that you get when you use this tool.

Note
Like the other color tools, the Colorize tool requires your image to be in the RGB color mode. If you open a grayscale image in GIMP and you want to colorize it, you have to go to Image ➢ Mode ➢ RGB. Once you do that you're free to colorize your image (or select portions of it). ■

The dialog for the Colorize tool presents you with sliders for Hue, Saturation, and Lightness; just like the ones used in the Hue-Saturation tool. Use these sliders to determine what color to tint your image, how saturated that color should be, and the overall luminosity of the final result from this tool. Of these three sliders, the Hue slider is the least intuitive. If you recall from the Hue-Saturation tool, think of this slider as a linear progression around the color wheel. From left to right, the range of the slider goes from 0 to 360 degrees, using the following color sequence: red, yellow, green, cyan, blue, magenta, and back to red. For a visual reference, look at the vertical hue strip on the right of the color dialog. From bottom to top, it follows the same sequence. By default, the slider starts in the center, tinting your image in a greenish cyan color.

The other two sliders work as expected. The Saturation slider goes from a completely desaturated grayscale at zero to full color intensity of your chosen hue at 100. The Lightness slider has a range from −100 to 100, with the −100 value being completely black and the 100 value being at full white.

FIGURE 9-8

The dialog for the Colorize tool allows you to configure the monotone color of your image.

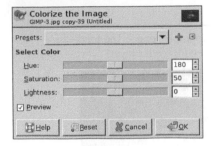

Brightness-Contrast

The Brightness-Contrast tool is one of the simplest color tools. As Figure 9-9 shows, the dialog for this tool has two control sliders, one for Brightness and one for Contrast. The Brightness slider has a range from −127 to 127. Negative values make your image darker and positive values lighten it. The Contrast slider has the same range of values as the Brightness slider and works like the contrast adjustment on your television or monitor. Negative values reduce the extreme light and dark values in your image until it's an even gray, whereas positive values push the image to the point where your image consists of only very dark pixels or very light ones.

Tip

The Brightness-Contrast tool has an extra handy feature. With the tool active, you can control Brightness and Contrast sliders from within the image window. If you click and drag within the image window, moving your mouse side to side adjusts contrast and moving it up and down adjusts brightness. ■

FIGURE 9-9

The Brightness-Contrast tool's dialog

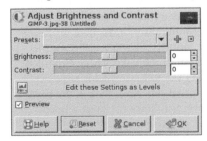

Of course, the Brightness-Contrast tool gives you only the most basic and rudimentary controls. Often you'll need the more advanced controls available in the Levels tool. It's for this reason that the Brightness-Contrast tool has a button at the bottom of its dialog labeled Edit These Settings as Levels. Click this button and you can take your roughed-out settings from this tool and further refine them in the Levels tool. Figure 9-10 shows the results of using this tool on the same example image used in Figure 9-7.

FIGURE 9-10

Two adjustments to an image using the Brightness-Contrast tool. On the left, the Brightness and Contrast values are used to isolate the light foreground. On the right, the overall contrast is reduced so the image can be used as an unobtrusive background.

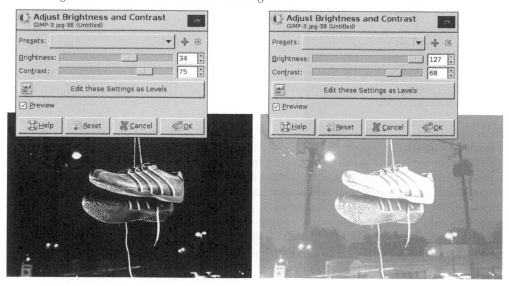

Threshold

Simply put, the Threshold tool takes each pixel in your image and decides whether that pixel is black or white, based on a threshold range that you define in the Threshold tool's dialog shown in Figure 9-11. The primary purpose for this tool would be to define a selection mask based on the luminosity of pixels in your image. As an example, the Threshold tool could be used to define the initial rough selection mask in the background replacement example given at the end of Chapter 7. You can also use this filter to clear up scanned or faxed text as well as blueprints.

The dominant feature in this dialog is the large histogram at its center. This histogram is a graph of the number of pixels in your image for each luminosity value. Darker values are on the left of the histogram and lighter values are on the right. By default, the Threshold tool shows the histogram on a linear scale. However, sometimes it's more useful to see the histogram on a logarithmic scale. You can switch between these two scales with the two buttons at the top right of the dialog.

FIGURE 9-11

The Threshold tool's dialog

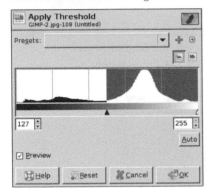

Beneath the histogram are two numeric entry fields. These numbers define the range for this tool. Pixels with luminosity values within this range are changed to be white, and pixels outside of this range are made black. You can adjust these values directly by clicking them and typing the number you want. However, an easier way is to simply click the histogram and drag left or right to define the range you want to use. You can then refine that range by clicking the black and white triangles beneath the histogram. The black triangle corresponds with the left numeric field and the white triangle corresponds with the right one. You can also have GIMP try to determine the optimal threshold by clicking the Auto button. This analyzes the histogram and determines the best range to use for isolating the brightest pixels. Figure 9-12 shows using the Threshold tool to define a rough mask of the example image.

Levels

The Levels tool is one of the most advanced color correction tools available to you in GIMP. In fact, using the Levels tool you can get the same effects achieved with the Color Balance, Colorize, Brightness-Contrast, and Desaturate tools as well as the Invert operation. As a matter of fact, the Levels tool allows you to achieve similar results in one step to using combinations of each of these other tools in multiple steps. It's not all-encompassing in functionality, but it's very powerful in the hands of someone who knows what they're doing. Its interface is similar to the one presented by the Threshold tool, only with even more controls. Additionally, the Levels tool and the Curves tool — covered later in this chapter — are the only color tools that have settings available in the Tool Options dialog.

The Levels tool is commonly used to give colorists more advanced color control than the previously mentioned filters. Rather than call each of those tools one at a time to, for example, darken an overexposed photo and enhance its saturation and contrast, a digital artist can do all of these operations right from within the Levels tool. Figure 9-13 shows the Levels tool dialog as well as its settings in the Tool Options dialog.

FIGURE 9-12

Using the Threshold tool to isolate the subject of a photo

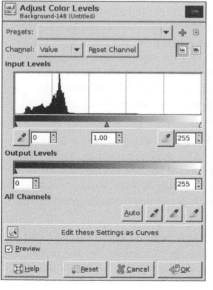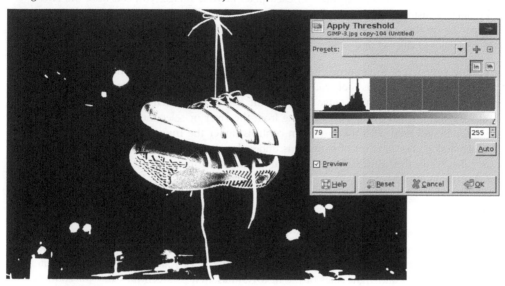

FIGURE 9-13

On the left is the Levels tool dialog and on the right are Tool Options available for the Levels tool.

Like the Threshold tool, the Levels tool features a large histogram across its center, which you can switch between displaying a linear or logarithmic scale. However, whereas the Threshold tool deals with only the luminosity value of each pixel in your image, you can have the Levels tool display a histogram for each of the Red, Green, Blue, and Alpha (if it exists) channels in your image. To do this, click the Channel drop-down menu above the histogram and pick the channel you want to display and modify.

As for editing your levels, the controls here are also similar to those in the Threshold tool, but a bit more advanced. With this tool, you're not just defining a threshold range; you're adjusting the intensity of values within that range for a specific channel. This happens in two steps. First you deal with the original pixel values coming from the layer or selection you're working on. Those values are adjusted with the histogram controls under the Input Levels heading in the Levels tool's dialog. The next set of controls is under the Output Levels heading. This control constrains the values that ultimately get returned to your final image. Each of these controls is explained in the next section.

Input Levels

Like with the Threshold tool, numeric entry fields beneath the histogram allow you to control input levels. However, unlike the Threshold tool, which has only two numeric entry fields, the Input Levels for the Levels tool has three. There are the *black point* (dark) and *white point* (light) limits on the left and right sides of the histogram as well as a central value for controlling the mid point for each channel. All values can be controlled by their numeric fields, but it's usually easier and more natural to click their corresponding black, gray, and white triangles directly beneath the histogram. Regardless of which channel you choose to work with (Value, Red, Green, Blue, Alpha), these controls work the same. The following list describes how manipulating each of these values affects your image:

- **Black point** — If you move the black point to the right, increasing its value, pixels that fall to the left of that range are zeroed out for that specific channel. For example, if you're working in the Value channel and move the black point to the right, any pixels with a value below that point are painted solid black. If you do that for the Alpha channel, pixels to the left of that range are completely transparent. Doing this for one color channel decreases the amount of that color in your image. You could also look at this like increasing the amount of that color's complement. For example, if you're working on the Green channel and you increase the black point, your image becomes less green and more magenta.

- **White point** — All pixels with values greater than the point controlled by this value are painted at full intensity for your chosen channel. Using the Alpha channel as an example, pixels greater than the white point are completely opaque. If you're working with one of the color channels, pulling the white point to the left increases the prevalence of that color in your image. So if you're working on the Red channel, decreasing the white point makes your image get a reddish hue.

- **Mid point** — The mid point control is an interesting little beast. Whereas the black and white points control the extreme shadows and highlights in your image, the mid point dictates the overall tone of the rest of the image. If you decrease the mid point, pushing it closer to the black point, the values in your chosen channel take greater priority. If you increase the mid point and push it closer to the white point, the influence of your chosen channel's value is reduced. This is easiest to see with the Value channel. Push the mid point to the right and your image gets darker. Push it left and your image gets lighter.

Tip

As a quick shortcut for editing the black point and white point for a channel, click the eyedropper button next to the numeric entry field of the point you want to adjust. After doing that, click the part of your image in the image window that has the value you want to use. For example, if you want to adjust the white point, click the white point eyedropper button and then click the part of your image that should be the lightest. ■

Adjusting the black, mid, and white points for each channel gives you the same controls you have in the Color Balance tool. Plus you have the benefit of working with the overall Value and — if you have it — the Alpha channel in your image. Not only that, but you can define exactly which values are considered shadows, midtones, or highlights.

Output Levels

Whereas the Input Levels control how you treat the pixels coming in from your original image, the Output Levels dictate the range of values returned to the image window when the Levels tool is done processing. This control is a lot more like the controls in the Threshold tool: you define a range with two numeric entry fields that each have a corresponding black or white triangle that you can click and drag along a gradient. Bringing these values closer together reduces the number of available values that your chosen channel can use for output. When working with the Value channel, this has the effect of reducing the overall contrast in your image. When working with a color channel, all colors are mapped to that reduced range.

In contrast to the levels controls in both the Input Levels and the Threshold tool, there's one special thing that you can do with Output Levels that you cannot do with the others. You can make the white triangle's value less than the value of the black triangle. When you do this with the Value channel, you effectively do the same thing as running Color ➤ Invert. If you do this with the Alpha channel, your opaque pixels become transparent and your transparent pixels become opaque.

All Channels

The four buttons in this section give you quick access to some convenient shortcuts for working across multiple channels at the same time. Breaking it down, you have the Auto button and three separate eyedroppers. The following list describes the functionality of each of these:

- **Auto** — Click this button and the Levels tool attempts to optimize the histogram of each of the available color channels. Ideally, a "well-balanced image" has a histogram with levels distributed across the full range. The levels don't have to be even, but if the histogram shows a large region of values that aren't assigned to pixels — especially at the far left or right of the histogram — that's a good sign that the image is too bright, doesn't have enough contrast, or is overly dominated by a single color channel. Clicking the Auto button adjusts the Input Levels of each of the color channels to balance their histograms. The Value and Alpha channels, as well as the Output Levels of all channels, are stretched to cover their full ranges. If you have a low contrast or over/under-exposed image, clicking the Auto button can often give you a quick fix for that.

- **Eyedroppers** — The three eyedropper buttons give you a quick way to simultaneously set the black point, mid point, and white point for each of the red, green, and blue color channels. To use any of them, just click the eyedropper icon that corresponds to the input level point that you want to adjust and then click the value in your image that you want to dictate as the value of that point for all three color channels.

Tip

When using any of the eyedropper buttons, whether they're the three under All Channels or the black point or white point eyedroppers under Input Levels, it's sometimes easy to click the wrong area of your image. To help mitigate that, go to the Tool Options dialog while you're using the Levels tool and adjust the Radius slider under the Sample Average check box. This value increases the area selected by the eyedropper and averages the values of all the pixels within the selection area to be the value you choose. To see the influence area of the eyedropper in your image window, click and hold your left mouse button while in the image window. This draws a square that shows you the selection area affecting the eyedropper. ∎

As much as the Levels tool can do, it actually isn't the most powerful color correction tool in GIMP. That esteemed distinction belongs to the Curves tool. If, while working on colors with the Levels tool, you find that you need the strengths available to you in the Curves tool, you can click the Edit These Settings as Curves button at the bottom of the Levels tool's dialog. This takes your current adjustments with the Levels tool and brings them into the Curves tool the same way you can migrate adjustments from the Brightness-Contrast tool to the Levels tool. Once you do this, you'll probably find the next section of this chapter useful.

Curves

As previously mentioned, the Curves tool is the most powerful and flexible color correction tool in the GIMP arsenal. Ironically, compared to the interface for the Levels tool, the dialog for the Curves tool, shown in Figure 9-14, seems rather unassuming. Don't let it fool you. This little tool is a big bucket of awesome.

The top of the Curves tool's dialog is just like the top of the Levels tool. You have your Presets controls, a drop-down menu for determining which channel you want to work on, a button for resetting that channel, and a pair of buttons to switch the histogram display between linear and logarithmic scales. After that, things get all kinds of different. The large square chart at the center of the dialog with a superimposed histogram in it is the primary control structure of the Curves tool.

Like the Levels tool, the histogram reflects the number of pixels at each value in your chosen channel. However, the controls for dealing with that histogram are very different. Rather than splitting input and output levels into two separate, one-dimensional controls, the Curves tool combines both of these levels in a single two-dimensional chart. In the Curves tool's chart, the input levels are the horizontal, x-axis values and the output levels are on the y-axis. You can verify this by adjusting the two end points, called *anchors*, on the diagonal line that goes from the bottom left to the top-right corner of the chart. Click the lower-left anchor and drag it up the left side of the chart. Assuming you're doing this from the Value channel, your image becomes lighter. If you take the anchor from the upper-right corner and pull it down the right side of the chart, the contrast on your image is reduced. This is the same as reducing the range in the Output Levels section of the Levels tool. Moving either of these anchors horizontally produces the same results as adjusting the Input Levels in the Levels tool. Figure 9-15 illustrates this direct correlation between the Curves tool and the Levels tool.

FIGURE 9-14

The deceivingly innocent interface for the Curves tool

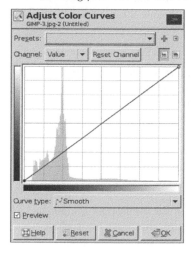

FIGURE 9-15

The input and output levels that you set with the Levels tool (left) directly correspond with the curve end points in the Curves tool (right).

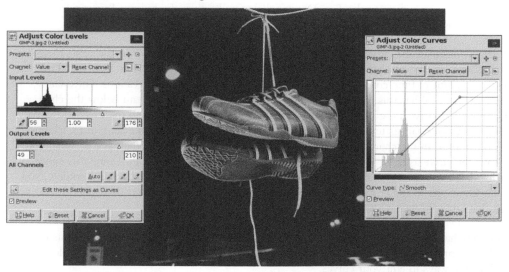

So far you've seen only how the Curves tool can replicate output from the Levels tool. That's great and all, but the real power of the Curves tool comes from the ability create additional anchors on the curve in the chart and use those anchors to shape the color characteristics of your image with a high degree of control. To add an anchor to your curve, simply click anywhere on the curve. Wherever you click, a new anchor is created. If you keep your mouse button pressed and drag your mouse, you can instantly move your new anchor around the chart. The curve segments between each anchor are interpolated as smooth Bézier curves like the ones used for GIMP's paths. For a review on Bézier curves, seeh Chapter 5. And as you already discovered earlier in this section, you can move any anchor with your mouse by simply clicking it and dragging it to a new location. To delete an anchor, click and drag it left or right until it disappears.

For more refined control of your anchors, you can also use the directional keys on your keyboard. To do this, you first need to know which anchor is currently active. You can make any anchor active by clicking it. When you do so, GIMP draws the anchor as a solid black circle. Inactive anchors are drawn as hollow circles. You can use the left and right directional arrows on your keyboard to cycle through the anchors in your curve. Use your keyboard's up and down directional arrows to increase or decrease that anchor's value in the vertical direction. If you hold down Shift while pressing the up and down arrows, the anchor moves in increments of 15 pixels.

One of the really convenient features of the Levels tool is the use of the eyedropper buttons to pick specific pixels in your image to define values for the black point, mid point, and white point of that image. The interface for the Curves tool doesn't have an explicit eyedropper button, but the functionality still exists. With the Curves tool active, simply click anywhere in your image. A vertical line appears in the chart corresponding to the value in the histogram of the pixels you're clicking. If you Shift+click in your image, an anchor is created for that value on your curve in the active channel. If you Ctrl+click your image, the anchor is created for that value in all channels, including the Value and Alpha channels (if your image has an alpha channel). Like the Levels tool, you can go to the Tool Options dialog and adjust the radius of your selection area with the Radius slider under the Sample Average check box.

The default behavior for curves is to smoothly interpolate from one anchor to the next. However, it's occasionally valuable be able to draw the curve that you want rather than spend an excessive amount of time constantly adding anchors and tweaking their locations. Fortunately, GIMP's Curves tool has this feature. To enable it, click the drop-down menu below the chart and change the Curve Type from Smooth to Freehand. When you switch to the Freehand curve type, your cursor changes to a pencil when you put it over the chart. From here, just click and drag your mouse in the chart to draw the shape of the curve you want. When you're done, you can leave the curve as is, or you can switch the Curve Type back to Smooth. Doing this converts your hand-drawn curve into a smoother curve with a series of anchors. Using this workflow, you can quickly rough in the curve you want with the Freehand curve type and then smooth and tweak that curve in Smooth mode.

As you may have noticed, the Curves tool has quite a few controls and as powerful as this tool is, it doesn't provide you with any real hints at how to use it. To help alleviate this, Table 9-1 lists all of the ways to edit your curves.

The Curves tool is incredibly useful and gives you a ridiculous level of control over your image's color characteristics. However, it's often difficult to understand what it can do without actually seeing it in action. To that end, Figure 9-16 shows some commonly used curve shapes and how they influence the final look of an image.

TABLE 9-1

Mouse and Keyboard Commands for Editing Curves in the Curves Tool

Keyboard or mouse input	Location	Function
Click	Chart (empty space or on curve)	Create anchor
Click	Chart (anchor)	Activate anchor
Click	Image window	Sample image (draw vertical line in chart)
Click+drag	Chart (empty space or on curve — Smooth curve type)	Create anchor and move to location
Click+drag	Chart (anchor — Smooth curve type)	Move anchor (moving anchor too far to the left or right will remove it from the curve)
Click+drag	Chart (Freehand curve type)	Draw a custom curve
Shift+click	Image window	Sample image and create an anchor for the current active channel
Ctrl+click	Image window	Sample image and create and anchor for all channels
Left/right directional arrow	Anywhere	Change active anchor
Up/down directional arrow	Anywhere	Increase or decrease the output level (vertical location) of the active anchor by 1 pixel in the chart
Shift+up/down directional arrow	Anywhere	Increase or decrease the output level (vertical location) of the active anchor by 15 pixels in the chart

Posterize

The main function of the Posterize tool is to attempt to reproduce your layer or selected area with a limited number of colors that you define. From a technical perspective, this feature is useful if you're using the image on a platform that displays a limited number of colors, such as embedded devices with low-color LCD screens. It's also useful if you're saving your image to an image format with a fixed color palette, like GIF. From an artistic perspective, the Posterize tool's effects can be a good starting place for creating a colored line-drawing effect or for reducing the results of compression artifacts. Whatever your reason for using it, when you click Colors ➤ Posterize, you get a dialog like the one in Figure 9-17.

FIGURE 9-16

Using some common curve shapes, you can enhance or reduce contrast, bring out detail from dark or light areas, or even invert all values in your image.

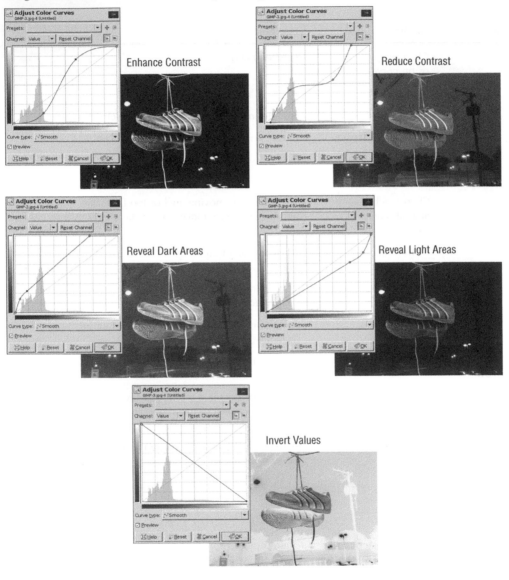

The Posterize tool's dialog is very simple, consisting of a single slider to control Posterize Levels. Reducing the value of the slider decreases the number of colors in your image, and increasing that value has the opposite effect. The range for the slider goes from 2 to 256. It describes the number of levels for each of the Red, Green, and Blue channels to determine the final color for a pixel. This means that the default level of 3 limits your image to 8 colors ($2^3 = 8$). A level of 10 limits it to 1024 colors ($2^{10} = 1024$). Figure 9-18 shows the results of using the Posterize tool on the example image with Posterize Levels of 3.

Tip

The Posterize tool may not pick the color that you would prefer at the Posterize Levels you choose. To have more control over the color, after using the Posterize tool, use the Select by Color tool to select the color you want to change and then use the Bucket Fill tool with the color you want. ■

FIGURE 9-17

The Posterize tool's dialog

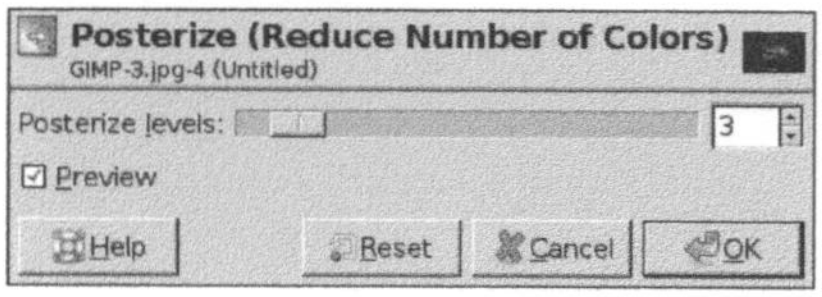

FIGURE 9-18

Use the Posterize tool to reduce the number of colors in an image

Desaturate

As its name implies, the Desaturate tool (Colors ➤ Desaturate) removes the color saturation from the pixels in your image, effectively turning it into a grayscale image. That being said, it's not the same as going to Image ➤ Mode ➤ Grayscale. For one thing, this tool — like the other color tools — works only on the active layer or your selected pixels within that layer. Changing your image's mode to Grayscale modifies all layers of your image, whether or not they're visible or selected. Furthermore, the Desaturate tool keeps your image in the RGB color space rather than reducing your image to a single channel per pixel. This means that you're free to paint in color or do some other color-related operation after using the Desaturate tool. You can't really do that after you change your color mode to Grayscale.

You be wondering, "But can't I just change the color mode back to RGB after I make the image grayscale?" Yes, of course you can. However, there's one more reason why you may want to use the Desaturate tool instead: it gives you more control. With the change to Grayscale mode, GIMP changes your pixels from RGB to Grayscale and that's that. But with the Desaturate tool, you get some options with a dialog like the one shown in Figure 9-19.

The dialog for the Desaturate tool gives you more control over how you remove colors from your pixels.

The Desaturate tool makes your image grayscale by calculating how bright each pixel is. The Desaturate tool's dialog gives you three different methods for making this calculation:

- **Lightness** — Of the three options, this one is the most straightforward. Lightness is determined by looking at the value for each of a pixel's three color channels and averaging the highest and lowest ones. So if you have an orange pixel created with a Red value at 221, Green at 142, and Blue at 5 (#DD8E05, in hexadecimal notation), the resulting gray value for this pixel would be 113 ($(221 + 5) / 2 = 113$).

- **Luminosity** — The problem with the Lightness method of calculating a gray value is that images desaturated this way tend to look a little bit "off." The reason for this is that the human eye doesn't treat each of the primary colors in the same way, perceiving some better than others. To create a grayscale image that's a bit more natural, this method weights each channel to match more closely how our eyes see color.

- **Average** — This third option is similar to the Lightness method, but rather than take the average of the highest and lowest channel values, this method averages all three color channels. Taking the previous orange example, the resulting gray value with the Average method is 123 ($(221 + 142 + 5) / 3 = 122.66$ and that value is rounded up).

Figure 9-20 shows the effects of each of these methods on the example photograph. As in this image, the difference in the results of each method can be very subtle, perhaps too subtle to notice in many cases, particularly in dark images. However, in other images, the differences can be stark and the results of the Lightness or Average methods my appear slightly off.

FIGURE 9-20

From left to right, using the Lightness, Luminosity, and Average methods for desaturating an image

Lightness   Luminosity   Average

Inverting Values

Occasionally you need to invert the values of pixels in your image. You could be refining a selection mask or inverting the influence of a layer's blending mode or simply producing a special effect to try to make your image look more interesting. Although these functions aren't explicit tools like the ones covered previously in this chapter, they still work the same way. The effect works on only the active layer or your current selection area on that layer. However, unlike the color tools, which can work only on RGB images, these functions can also work on images in the Grayscale color mode. GIMP provides you with two ways to invert colors in your image:

- **Invert** — Simply put, this function inverts all values in your image. In a grayscale image, white pixels become black pixels and blacks become whites. In color images, each hue is swapped with its complement; red pushes to cyan, green becomes magenta, and so on. Activate the feature by choosing Colors ➤ Invert in the image window.

- **Value Invert** — Rather than working in the RGB color space, this operation works in the HSL (Hue, Saturation, Luminosity) color space and inverts only the Luminosity value. On grayscale images, Colors ➤ Value Invert produces the same results as the Invert function. However, on color images, the luminosity of a pixel is inverted while maintaining its hue and saturation values.

Figure 9-21 shows the differences between the Invert and Value Invert functions.

Using Automated Adjustments

Quite often when working on images, there's no need to spend heavy amounts of time with the Levels or Curves tool. You can rely on an automated process where GIMP enhances the color or contrast on your active layer or selection. In many ways, the options in this submenu (Colors ➤ Auto) are an extension of the Auto button in the Levels tool. Having them available in this menu is a good convenience that you can use as a starting point or shortcut when doing color correction. Each of these functions works in its own particular way and the results can vary quite a bit from one image to the next.

FIGURE 9-21

From left to right: the original image, inverted, and value inverted (Photo credit: Chris Hoyer)

Generically speaking, these functions are often referred to as *color stretching* functions because they tend to stretch the histogram of each color channel in your image. This is the best way to understand how each method works. However, the actual visual results are more difficult to predict. The best way to see the effects of each function is to try them out for yourself and experiment. Thanks to the ability to have multiple layers and undo, you have this luxury.

For each of the functions in this section I've used the same image, which I tweaked ahead of time with the Curves tool to purposely have a lower-than-ideal contrast.

Equalize

The way the Equalize operation (Colors ➤ Auto ➤ Equalize) stretches your active layer's histogram is by trying to flatten it out. The idea is to get each color's histogram to equally distribute the number of pixels for each value. Of the automatic operations, this one tends to give the most dramatic results, drastically increasing the contrast in the active layer. This can land the results right "in the money," yielding you exactly the results that you want by bringing out otherwise-hidden details throughout your image. At the same time, often you would rather have some details in an image remain hidden, such as uneven skin complexion in a portrait. Figure 9-22 shows the results of using Equalize.

FIGURE 9-22

Using Colors ➤ Auto ➤ Equalize on a low-contrast image (Photo credit: Melody Smith)

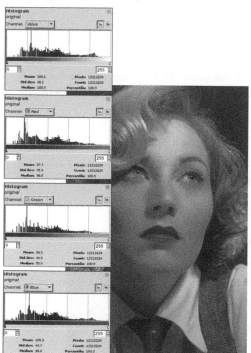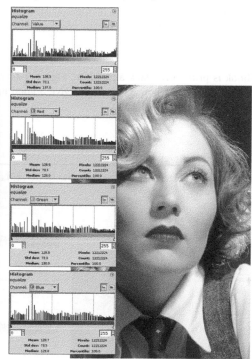

White Balance

The White Balance operation (Colors ➤ Auto ➤ White Balance) actually deals with more than just the white elements of your image. It's a color stretching scheme that accounts for the lights as well as the darks. In contrast (forgive the pun) with the other Auto operations, the White Balance operation actually discards the pixel values that occur with the least amount of frequency in your image. Specifically, the values in each channel that are only used by 0.05% of the pixels in your active layer are disregarded and the histogram is stretched to fill those gaps. This is a really effective way to remove noise or dust from your image. It's also effective at making sure that the brightest parts of your image are fully white and the darkest shadows in your image are completely black. Figure 9-23 shows the results of the White Balance operation.

Color Enhance

The Color Enhance operation (Colors ➤ Auto ➤ Color Enhance) produces some effects that can definitely punch up the visual impact of an image. Of course, you should take care because an increased punch isn't always what you want or need in an image. This function works by maximizing the saturation of colors in the pixels of your active layer without affecting the hue or luminosity. The work for this operation is done from the HSL color space, so its effects may be difficult to see from an image's histogram. However, as Figure 9-24 shows, this operation has no influence on the Value channel, only the Red, Green, and Blue ones.

Note

Because this book is printed in black and white, Figure 9-24 may not show the full impact of the Color Enhance operation. The histograms in the figure give a good hint, but the best way to see the results of this operation is to play with it yourself. ■

FIGURE 9-23

Using Colors ➤ Auto ➤ White Balance reduces the noise and artifacts in an image

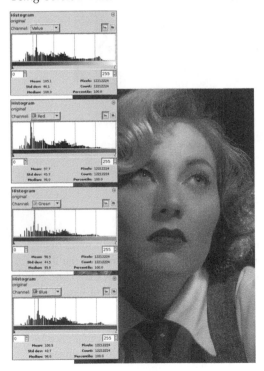
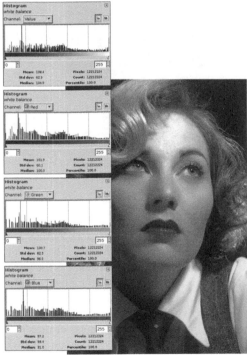

Normalize

If your image is washed out and low in contrast, the Normalize operation (Colors ➤ Auto ➤ Normalize) is probably a good place to start. This function has a minimal influence on the hue of a pixel. Its primary purpose is to ensure that the full range of each channel is filled. Basically, if the histogram on a channel has empty space on the left or right of it, the Normalize filter stretches the histogram to eliminate that empty space. The results are often more subtle than some of the previously covered Auto operations, but there's also a lower likelihood of getting an unfavorable hue shift when using this function. Figure 9-25 shows an example of how Normalize works on the example image.

Using Colors ➤ Auto ➤ Color Enhance

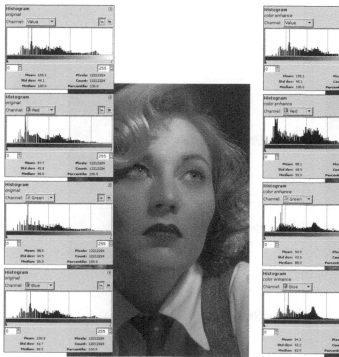

Stretch Contrast

The Stretch Contrast operation (Colors ➤ Auto ➤ Stretch Contrast) produces results that are similar to Normalize, but you really should use it only if your image has pixels that are tinted when they should be pure black or pure white. This is a situation that comes up frequently when digitally cleaning up old photographs. Many old photos aren't properly stored and protected, so as a result they lose their vibrancy over time, often shifting colors to appear reddish-brown. The Stretch Contrast operations can often fix this color shift with a single click.

However, if your only goal is to enhance the contrast of an image, Normalize might be the better choice because whereas Normalize works on all channels in your active layer simultaneously, the Stretch Contrast function operates on each channel individually. This helps to accommodate for color shift in older photos, but in images that already have good whites and darks, it may cause an undesirable color shift. Figure 9-26 shows the results of this operation on the example image.

FIGURE 9-25

Using Colors ➤ Auto ➤ Normalize to enhance the contrast of an image without getting a nasty hue shift

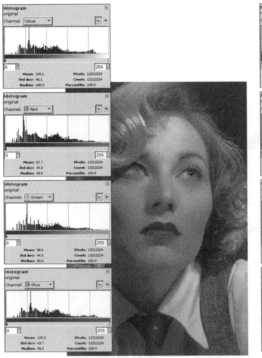

Stretch HSV

The Stretch HSV operation (Colors ➤ Auto ➤ Stretch HSV) works the same way as Stretch Contrast, but rather than working on each of the RGB color channels, this function first converts the image to the HSV color space. After the conversion, this filter stretches the histogram for the hue, saturation, and luminosity of the image and then converts back to RGB space. Often the results are nearly identical to the results of Stretch Contrast. However, this operation can often result in more saturated colors and it also has a greater likelihood of getting a color shift because it's maximizing your active layer's hue histogram. Figure 9-27 shows how this operation affects the example image.

FIGURE 9-26

Using Colors ➤ Auto ➤ Stretch Contrast can often fix an image that has an overall tint.

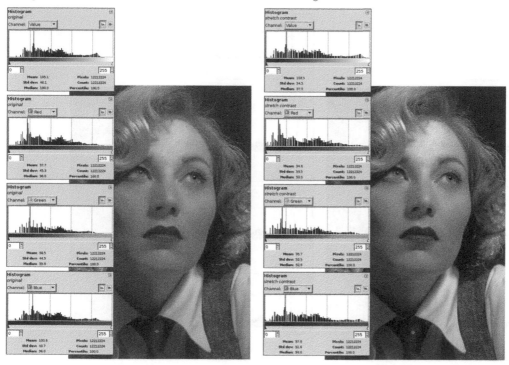

Working with Separated Color Components

It's often useful to work with your image using separated color components. The previously covered tools and functions in this chapter give you the opportunity to do this but often you want another level of control. For that, the functions in Colors ➤ Components are pretty helpful.

Channel Mixer

The Color Balance tool enables you to adjust your RGB channels for shadows, midtones, and highlights, but there's not really an integrated tool that gives you direct access to each of the red, green, and blue channels for the overall image. You technically could go to the Channels dialog and attempt to adjust the channels directly from there, but although that method gives you the ultimate in control, it's difficult to preview the results and make changes to one channel in relation to the other. This is where the Channel Mixer, shown in Figure 9-28, comes in. Launch this dialog by going to Colors ➤ Components ➤ Channel Mixer.

FIGURE 9-27

Using the Colors ➢ Auto ➢ Stretch HSV operation

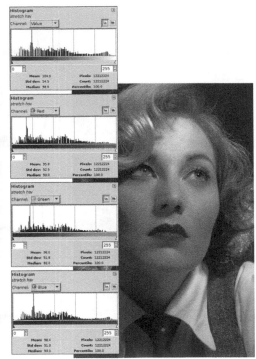

FIGURE 9-28

The Channel Mixer dialog enables you to adjust your RGB color channels relative to one another.

Like many of the other dialogs in GIMP, the Channel Mixer's dialog features a preview window that allows you to see the results of your changes to the values and options in the window. Below the preview windows is a set of options that provide the real controls to this feature:

- **Output Channel** — This drop-down menu is the color channel that you're currently working on. Whatever channel you choose is controlled by the sliders beneath it. By using this drop-down menu, you can — for example — reduce how much green influences the Red channel and then switch the Output Channel to Blue and increase the influence of red. This has the effect of leaning your overall hue toward a light-blue, cyan hue.

- **Red/Green/Blue values** — These sliders control the color influence for the channel you've chosen in the Output Channel drop-down. Think of each slider as a percentage value with a range from −200 to 200. By default, the slider that corresponds to the Output channel you've chosen is set to 100 and the other channels are set to zero. Pushing these sliders into their negative values has the effect of modifying that color's influence on the channel.

- **Monochrome** — Enable this check box and the Red, Green, and Blue sliders control the influence of the Red, Green, and Blue sliders on a final grayscale image. If the Desaturate tool doesn't give you quite the control you want in creating a grayscale image, call the Channel Mixer operation and enable this check box. This way if you have an image with most of its detail in the Green channel, you can use the Channel Mixer to retain that detail before converting that image to grayscale.

- **Preserve Luminosity** — When adjusting the sliders in this dialog, it's very likely that you'll push the values in the final image beyond their limits, often making the image look overly dark or completely blown out. This is apparent when you have the Monochrome check box enabled. Enable the Preserve Luminosity check box and GIMP compensates for those adjustments and attempts to prevent your image from losing detail in bright or dark areas.

- **Open/Save** — The Channel Mixer isn't a tool like the tools covered earlier in this chapter, so it doesn't have the presets infrastructure that those tools have. Instead, this dialog gives you the Open and Save buttons for importing and exporting Channel Mixer settings. Click the Save button to create a simple text file on your hard drive that you can later call up by clicking the Open button in a future session. The following code example shows the format of the text file created when you save your settings:

```
# Channel Mixer Configuration File
CHANNEL: BLUE
PREVIEW: TRUE
MONOCHROME: FALSE
PRESERVE_LUMINOSITY: FALSE
RED: 1.128 0.000 0.000
GREEN: 0.231 0.872 0.000
BLUE: -0.205 0.154 1.282
BLACK: 1.000 0.256 0.128
```

- **Reset** — Click this button to reset all drop-down menus, sliders, and check boxes to their default values.

Figure 9-29 compares the results of the Desaturate tool using the Luminosity values to the results from the Channel Mixer. The thing to note about this picture is that the cart is a bright blue, so increasing the Blue slider in the Channel Mixer with the Monochrome check box enabled makes those pixels brighter.

FIGURE 9-29

On the left is an image turned to grayscale with the Desaturate tool. On the right is the same image desaturated in a more controlled way using the Channel Mixer. (Photo credit: cgtextures.com)

Composing, Decomposing, and Recomposing

When working in a creative pipeline that involves other graphic arts professionals who may have used other software packages or have hardware requirements that limit them to working with a specific color space, GIMP's restriction to only working in the RGB color space can be a bit of an impediment. However, all is not lost. With the last three options in the Colors ➤ Components submenu, GIMP has at least a rudimentary means of interacting within these other environments. Contrary to the menu order, everything starts with Decompose.

Decompose

Decomposing an image basically means breaking down the image into a set of known quantities. Those known quantities are mapped to a grayscale image. Chapter 7's coverage of GIMP's channels covers this fact. Each of the red, green, and blue channels in GIMP is a grayscale representation of that color's influence on each pixel in your image. The alpha channel is a grayscale representation of the transparency of each pixel. Using this same logic and methodology, GIMP can export grayscale images to represent the channels of nearly any other color space. This is precisely what calling Colors ➤ Components ➤ Decompose does. When you do so, GIMP presents you with the dialog shown in Figure 9-30.

The most important feature of this dialog is the Color Model drop-down menu. With this menu, you choose which color model you want to decompose your image into. It gives you the following choices:

- **RGB/RGBA** — These two color models match GIMP's native RGB color space. Decomposing to either one of these is the same as creating images out of the Red, Green, Blue, and Alpha channels from the Channels dialog.

FIGURE 9-30

The Decompose dialog

Note
The Decompose operator will not let you decompose to RGBA if you do not have an alpha channel on your image. It simply reports an error in the image window's status area. To decompose to RGBA, make sure you have an alpha channel. ■

- **HSV/HSL** — As covered in Chapter 2, the Hue, Saturation, Value and Hue, Saturation, Luminosity color models cover the same gamut as the RGB color model. As covered earlier in this chapter, many of GIMP's color correction tools convert to the HSV or HSL color spaces to operate on your image's colors. Choose these options to create grayscale images to map to hue, saturation, and either value or luminosity. For the purposes of this discussion, Luminosity is similar to Value, it just more closely resembles the behavior of the human eye. Furthermore, the grayscale image created for hue may look pretty wild. This is because the hue values are mapped to a linearized version of the color wheel, starting with red at the top, rotating around through each hue, and returning back to red. This means that both white and black values in the hue image are mapped to the color red.

- **CMY/CMYK** — These two options represent the Cyan, Magenta, Yellow, and Cyan, Magenta, Yellow, Black color models, respectively. These two color models are used predominantly for print purposes. One thing to note here is that although the Decompose operation can create the proper grayscale values for these color models, it's not on a color managed system that a print shop may prefer. If you're decomposing to send separations to a printer (a person or a shop; not a machine), you may want to use the features provided by the Separate+ plug-in, covered later in this chapter.

- **Alpha** — This option is similar to the RGBA choice, but without the actual color information. Basically, if your image has an alpha channel, decomposing with this option just creates an image with a grayscale map of your image's alpha channel.

- **LAB** — A common color model used in Adobe Photoshop consists of a Luminosity component (L) for describing pixel brightness and then two additional components (A and B) to describe the pixel's hue. The A component describes the hues between green and red, and the B component covers hues between yellow and blue.

- **YCbCr** — Also sometimes referred to as the YUV color space, the last four options that begin with YCbCr describe the colors of your image's pixels similarly to LAB in that it has a Luminosity value (Y) and two component values (Cb and Cr). The difference is that in YUV colors, Cb and Cr — chrominance values — respectively describe the amount of blue and red in your pixels. All of the YUV color models are most commonly used in television. The

ITU numbers after the YCbCr prefix describes a color matrix defined by the International Telecommunication Union (ITU).

Below the Color Model drop-down menu is a pair of check boxes that dictate further details about your decomposed results:

- **Decompose to Layers** — By default, this check box is enabled, causing GIMP to generate a new image with a separate layer for each channel it extracts while decomposing. The image itself uses the Grayscale color mode, but each layer that's created is named according to the channel it represents in the Color Model you chose. If you disable this check box, GIMP creates a separate image window for each extracted channel.

- **Foreground as Registration Color** — This option is useful only if you're decomposing an image for use in print. A *registration color* is typically reserved for special printers' marks like registration crosshairs and crop marks. These marks are used in the printing process for aligning multiple color plates and determining where the paper's edge is going to be after cutting. For this reason, all extracted channels need to have registration marks on them. The standard for registration colors is to use black, but with this option enabled, whatever color you have set as your foreground color is considered the registration color. Any pixels that are your foreground color are included on all channels, regardless of whether that color belongs in the extracted channel.

Figure 9-31 shows an example of an image decomposed into RGB, HSL, and LAB channels.

FIGURE 9-31

To the left is the original image. On the right, from top to bottom are extracted channels using the Decompose function in RGB, HSL, and LAB color models.

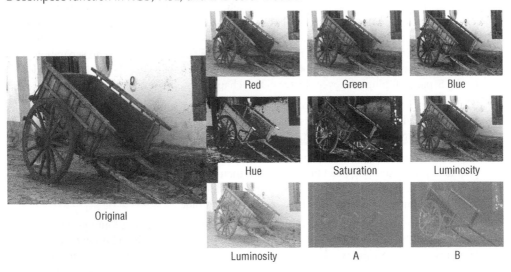

Red   Green   Blue

Hue   Saturation   Luminosity

Original

Luminosity   A   B

Compose and Recompose

Of course if you're able to extract channels out of a layer by way of decomposing, it follows that you'd be able to assemble an image in GIMP's native RGBA format given a set of grayscale images representing channels for various color models. You do this using either the Colors ➤ Components ➤ Compose or Colors ➤ Components ➤ Recompose menu options. The purpose of the Recompose operation is to regenerate your original image after a Decompose operation. GIMP doesn't provide you with any dialogs. It just uses the naming convention it created for each color channel it extracted and generates a new RGB image from that base. The Compose function gives you a bit more control because it presents you with a dialog like the one shown in Figure 9-32.

FIGURE 9-32

The Compose operation's dialog

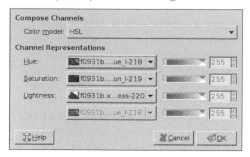

To use this tool, first pick the Color Model that your source imagery is coming from. For example, if you have grayscale images that correspond to the Hue, Saturation, and Luminosity channels, pick HSL from the Color Model drop-down menu. Once you do that, you then assign each grayscale image or layer to its corresponding channel. After you complete that, click OK and GIMP takes that channel information and composes a proper RGB image from it with correct coloring.

Tip

This feature is also an interesting way to experiment with different color balance situations with your image. You can get some pretty interesting effects, for example, by decomposing your image into the CMYK color model, but when you compose it to a new image using the RGB color model, your colors end up dramatically shifted to different tones. ∎

Remapping Colors

For all intents and purposes, a color channel is nothing more than mapping one of GIMP's primary colors — Red, Green, Blue, or Alpha — to the pixels of your image with a weight determined by a grayscale value. White values are full intensity and black values are at zero intensity for that channel. It's with that logic that the Decompose and Compose functions covered earlier in this chapter are able to extract channels for a variety of color models that GIMP doesn't natively support. Take it one step further and you can do some incredibly wild things with the colors in your image. The operations available to you in this submenu (Colors ➤ Map) are included to provide you with the facilities to do exactly that.

Rearranging and Defining a Color Map

Chapter 2 covers the process and dialogs that GIMP provides you with when converting an RGB image to an indexed color palette. In that process, GIMP gives you the option to choose how many colors are in the palette and exactly which color palette you use for the image, be it an optimized palette based on the predominant colors in your image or one of the preset palettes, like the Web-safe palette. Despite this level of control, you need additional tools for a few things. That's where these two menu items come in:

- **Rearrange Colormap** — This operation, accessed by going to Colors ➤ Map ➤ Rearrange Colormap, enables you to change the order of the colors in your Indexed colormap. The dialog that appears when you choose the operation (shown on the left of Figure 9-33) doesn't change the colors in your image, just the arrangement of those colors in the map. This is useful for programmers and web developers using an indexed image. Often it's useful to have a specific color — be it white, black, or the chosen transparent color — at a specific location in the index. The Rearrange Colormap interface allows you to do just that. Simply click the color swatch you want to move and drag it to the location in the map where you want it to go. This dialog also features a right-click context menu that allows you to change the arrangement of all colors at once by sorting them according to their hue, saturation, or value. You can also reverse the order of the colors in the map.

- **Set Colormap** — Quite a few of the tools and operations available in the Color menu don't work with indexed color because of the limited nature of an indexed palette. For example, say you're using an optimized palette on an indexed image that's predominantly blue and you want to use the Color Balance tool to make your image consist of warmer orange and yellow tones. Unless you switch to RGB mode, you're likely out of luck because those oranges and yellows probably don't exist on your indexed color palette. Fortunately, you can get around this by going to Colors ➤ Map ➤ Set Colormap. This brings up the dialog shown at top right of Figure 9-33. Click the large button at the center of the dialog and GIMP presents you with a second dialog (shown on the bottom right of Figure 9-33) that allows you to swap your image's current palette with another prebuilt palette that has the colors you desire.

Tip

The Set Colormap operation does a simple one-to-one swap of colors, trading the first position color in your image with the first position color in your target map, and so on. This means that the Set Colormap operation may assign the wrong colors to the wrong parts of your image on its first run. To deal with this, use the Rearrange Colormap feature to change the order of the colors in your palette. This gives you the ultimate control over changing colors in your palette. ■

FIGURE 9-33

On the left, the Rearrange Colormap dialog, and on the right, the Set Colormap dialog and the Palette Selection dialog for indexed colors

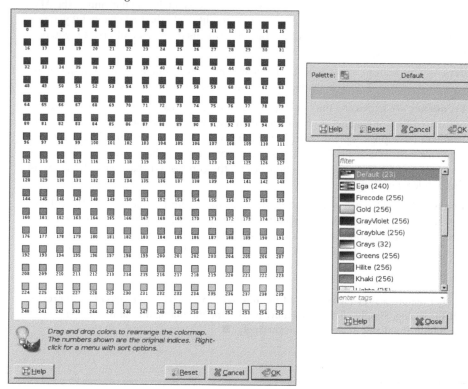

Alien Map

The Alien Map effect, called from Colors ➤ Map ➤ Alien Map, can dramatically modify the appearance of your image. It works by treating each channel the same way that Hue is treated throughout the rest of GIMP's color tools and operations. That is, rather than treating each channel linearly, the Alien Map function treats each channel somewhat like you're traversing the circumference of a circle. This is particularly true with the Phaseshift slider (covered shortly), which works by moving along both the sine and cosine curves related to that value. Figure 9-34 shows Alien Map's dialog and the results of the operation on an example image.

The Alien Map dialog features a large preview window at the top. Beneath the preview window is where all of the controls for this dialog live:

- **Mode** — Alien Map can work on your image using either the RGB or HSL color models. These two radio buttons allow you to switch between the two. When you make the switch, the slider and check box values in the rest of the interface change to reflect the chosen color model.

- **Modify Channel check boxes** — Regardless of which color model you choose, the check boxes to the right of the Mode selection allow you to cherry-pick which channels the Alien Map operation actually affects. This allows you to modify only the Red channel if you're working in the RGB color space, or to disable adjustments to the Hue of pixels if you're working in the HSL space.

- **Sliders** — The bottom of the dialog is dominated by a set of sliders for each of the channels you're adjusting. For each channel, you have a slider for two values:

  - **Frequency** — Increasing the frequency of a channel increases the number of pixels influenced by that channel. As frequency increases, the noisier your image appears and you have more pixels dotted throughout your image that have this channel's color. For a quick adjustment that isn't so crazy-looking, you can keep the Frequency value for the channel between 0.3 and 0.7. This punches up the contrast for that channel. Values for these sliders range from zero to 20.00.

  - **Phaseshift** — On each channel, this slider has the greatest influence over the colors generated by it. These sliders are measured in degrees and have a range from zero to 360. Each of those end values yields a result identical to the channel from the original image. Setting the Phaseshift value to 180 degrees inverts the value for that channel.

Tip

For most tools in GIMP that feature a preview window at the top, you can increase the size of your preview by increasing the size of the dialog. Simply click the window border for the dialog and drag it to be a larger size. The preview image within the dialog scales to fit accordingly. ■

FIGURE 9-34

Using settings from the Alien Map dialog (center) to dramatically change the colors of an image (Photo credit: cgtextures.com)

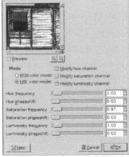

Color Exchange

Simply put, the Color Exchange operation (Colors ➤ Map ➤ Color Exchange) takes one color in your image and swaps it with another color. The interface shown in Figure 9-35 is entirely geared toward this purpose.

FIGURE 9-35

The Color Exchange dialog

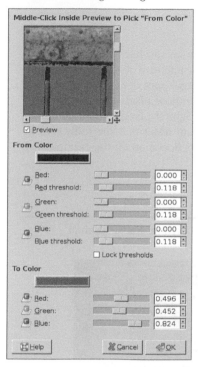

In contrast with many of the other preview windows in the dialogs of other GIMP operations, the preview in the Color Exchange dialog enables you to do more than just move around your image or zoom in on details. If you middle-click in the preview window, the value of the pixel you click is entered for the From Color swatch. Alternatively, you can set the From Color by clicking its corresponding color swatch lower in the dialog or by manually adjusting the Red, Green, and Blue sliders under the From Color heading. The Threshold sliders for each channel control whether you're swapping only pixels that exactly match the From Color, or all of the pixels that fit within a certain range around the chosen color. You can move the Threshold sliders independently, but it's often more useful to move them together by enabling the Lock Thresholds check box beneath the sliders.

Once you've determined the color that you're swapping, you need to tell GIMP what color to put in its place. That color is defined by the color swatch under the To Color heading. Either click the color swatch and use the color picker to designate the color you want or manually adjust the Red, Green, and Blue sliders below the swatch. After you make your color choices, click OK and the From Color in your image is swapped out for the To Color that you've chosen.

Tip

The Color Exchange operation uses thresholds to define the color range that you're modifying. This often leads to rough aliased edges around the colors you've exchanged. A cleaner solution would be to use the

Select by Color tool (Shift+O) to choose the color you want to exchange and then feather that selection prior to running Color Exchange. Of course, if you're going to do that, you could also take that feather selection and use the Bucket Fill tool with the color you want to swap in. ■

Gradient Map

For a feature that doesn't have a dialog, the Gradient Map operation can have a very dramatic effect on the look of your image. It works by first using the color intensity of each pixel to determine its brightness, much like the Average method of the Desaturate tool does. Then your active gradient — set in the Gradients dockable dialog — is mapped to those pixel values by associating the darkest pixels with the left side of the gradient and the lightest pixels to the rightmost values of the gradient. Depending on the chosen gradient, this can result in some really cool effects on your image. Figure 9-36 shows the results of using this operation on the example with a couple different gradients.

FIGURE 9-36

From left to right, using Gradient Map on the example image using the Skyline, Radial Eyeball Blue, and Nauseating Headache gradients

Palette Map

The Palette Map operation does the same thing as the Gradient Map, but rather than using a gradient as its source for mapping colors, this operation uses the indexed color palettes available in the Palettes dockable dialog. With palettes, you have a bit more control over the colors used in your image, at the expense of potentially more harsh, aliased edges. Figure 9-37 shows the results of the Palette Map operation with three different palettes.

Rotate Colors

In a lot of ways, the Rotate Colors operation (Colors ➢ Map ➢ Rotate Colors) is like a more advanced version of the Color Exchange operation previously covered. The problem with the Color Exchange operation is that it works on a threshold and basically gives you only a binary replacement of one color for another. This gives you aliasing issues and hard transitions at the edge of your color swap. It's hardly an ideal look if your primary goal is to transition an entire tonal range in your image to a new one. Fortunately, this is a perfect job for the Rotate Colors operation. Activate it by going to Colors ➤ Map ➤ Rotate Colors and then working within the dialog that appears, shown in Figure 9-38.

FIGURE 9-37

From left to right, using Palette Map on the example image using the Default, Gold, and Volcano palettes

FIGURE 9-38

The Rotate Colors dialog and the information within its tabs

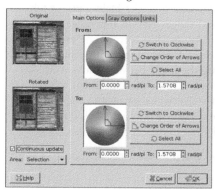
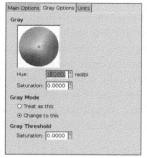
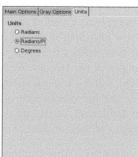

Along the left side of the Rotate Colors dialog is a pair of preview images. Unlike the preview images of other operations, these do not resize when you adjust the size of the dialog. Despite that, they still provide you with some rather useful visual feedback. The top preview image never changes, displaying the original image before rotating colors. The bottom preview shows the results of your adjustments and enhancements with the Rotate Colors controls.

Below the preview images are two controls that are especially useful if you're running GIMP on a slower computer:

- **Continuous Update** — This check box (enabled by default) shows real-time updates to the Rotated preview image as you adjust the controls in the Rotate Colors dialog. It's handy for seeing results as you work, but if you have a slower computer, performance could be laggy. Disable this check box and the Rotated preview is updated after values are changed instead of while they're being changed.

- **Area** — This drop-down menu controls what gets shown in the preview window:

  - **Entire Layer** — Choose this option to see your entire image in the preview, regardless of whether anything is selected. This way you can see how your color adjustments affect the whole layer that you're working on.

  - **Selection** — This is the default setting. If you have a selection made on your layer prior to running this filter, the Original and Rotated previews zoom in to cover only the selected area. If you have no selection, both previews show the entire layer.

  - **Context** — If you're working on a small selection within a large image, neither the Selection nor Entire Layer options are likely to give you an adequate view of how your color rotations look near your selected pixels. Your selection could be lost in a preview of the entire layer, but seeing only the selected pixels may lock you into a digital tunnel-vision of just those pixels in your image. The Context option for Area is a middle ground. It shows you the area defined by your selected pixels plus an additional range so you can get an idea of how your color adjustments look in the image as a whole without getting lost.

Main Options

The primary controls for this operation are the two large color wheels in the Main Options tab. Each wheel has a pair of arrows that you use to define a tonal range. To edit this range, click an arrow and drag it around the wheel to another location. The arc drawn from one arrow to the next defines the color range you've chosen. If you click and drag the arc, you can change the angles of the two arrows simultaneously without affecting the angle between them. You can also adjust these values numerically with the numeric text entry fields below each color wheel. The From field controls the angle of one arrow and the To field controls the angle of the other. By default, angles are defined in radians per pi. However, if you're more comfortable with degrees or straight radians, you can change units in the Units tab of this Rotate Colors dialog.

For convenience, three buttons next to each color wheel give you the following functions:

- **Switch to Clockwise/Counter-clockwise** — Click this button to force the direction of the arc, between arrows in the opposite direction. By default it's set to go counter-clockwise, defining the color range from red through yellow and ending at green. If you click this button, the range stays the same, but is ordered in reverse.

- **Change Order of Arrows** — Where the previous button changed the direction of the arc but left the range in place, this button inverts the range that the arrows cover. If you click this button with the default values, rather than starting at red and rolling left 90 degrees through yellow to green, your range starts at green and rolls left 270 degrees through cyan, blue, and magenta before finally landing on red.

- **Select All** — Click this button to ensure that you're involving the full color range available.

The upper color wheel is labeled From and it defines the color range that you want to change. The lower color wheel, labeled To, defines the range to which you're remapping the colors in the upper wheel. For example, if you have a photograph of some rusty metal and you want to make it look like green oxidized copper instead of brownish red, you would set the From range to cover your red and orange tones, and for the To range you'd assign green and cyan values. Examples for this feature are difficult to display in grayscale. To get a better idea of what this tool can do, check out the supplemental figures on this book's companion web site at www.gimpbible.com.

Gray Options

By default, the Rotate Colors feature doesn't have any influence over neutral values, including solid white, black, or any gray value in between where the color saturation is at zero. However, with the controls available in the Gray Options tab, you're given some flexibility with how neutral values are handled. Like the Main Options tab, this one features a color wheel as its primary control feature. The purpose of this wheel, however, is different; it's a color picker. Click the wheel to define specific values for the Hue and Saturation numeric entry fields beneath it. This is the color that you will associate with gray values when rotating colors. Luminosity is not included here because that value is determined by the image you're working on.

Below the color picker for your gray value are two radio buttons under the heading of Gray Mode. These buttons control how your chosen color relates to gray values while the other colors are being rotated. The following list describes your two choices:

- **Treat as This** — Click this option, and your gray pixels are treated as if they had the Hue and Saturation values defined with the color picker. This means that if you set your gray value to a red hue and you use the Rotate Colors operation to rotate red tones to blue tones, your gray pixels carry a blue hue when the operation completes.

- **Change to This** — Choose this option, and gray values take on the Hue and Saturation values you defined in the color picker, regardless of how other colors are rotated in your image.

The last control in this tab is a Saturation value under the heading Gray Threshold. Be default, the Gray Options influence only pixels that are absolutely gray. That is, if the pixel's saturation is anything other than zero, it's not considered gray. This, of course, allows for no wiggle room to include pixels that are only mostly desaturated. To compensate for that, this control defines a threshold within which pixels are considered to be gray. When you modify this value, a circle is drawn on the gray color picker at the top of the window to show how much of the color wheel you're considering as gray. Increase this value just a little bit to handle those nearly gray pixels. However, don't increase it too much. Like all other threshold values, this one does not taper at the edges, so it's prone to give your image harsh, aliased transition areas.

Sample Colorize

Whereas Rotate Colors is a supercharged version of Color Exchange, it's useful to think of the Sample Colorize operation (Colors ➤ Map ➤ Sample Colorize) as a supercharged version of the Gradient Map function. At its simplest, you're using a gradient map to modify or enhance the color profile of another image. This is particularly useful if you're starting with a completely desaturated image and you want to impart some color to it. However, unlike the Gradient Map operation, calling Sample Colorize brings up a dialog that affords you quite a bit more control. Figure 9-39 shows the Sample Colorize dialog.

FIGURE 9-39

The Sample Colorize dialog gives you a lot more control over how you add color to an image.

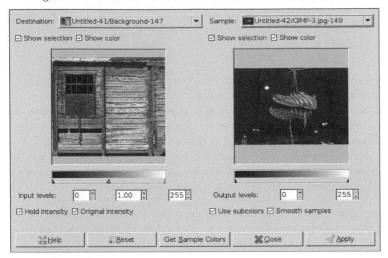

The way Sample Colorize works is pretty slick. On the left of the dialog is your destination image, defined by the Destination drop-down at the top. By default, this is the image you called the Sample Colorize operation from, but it can really be any image that you currently have open in GIMP. On the right is a sample from which you're deriving color information. The sample can be either another image or one of the gradients available in the Gradients dockable dialog. You choose which one by using the drop-down menu labeled Sample. It gives you the following options:

- **From Gradient/Reverse Gradient** — If you choose either of these options, the current active gradient in the Gradients dialog is loaded as your color sample. Because they're gradients, there's no image associated with them, so the preview is empty and gray. If you're using gradients, the real control is in the triangle sliders beneath the preview.

- **Image List** — After the gradient options in this drop-down is a list of all the layers in each of the currently open images in your GIMP session. You can use the color data in any available image as your sample source for colors. This is extremely useful if you want to have a series of photographs share the same tonal qualities or if you want your grayscale photo to match an existing color photo. One thing to note is that if you do actually choose an image as your sample source, click the large Get Sample Colors button at the bottom center of the dialog. After you click it, it takes some time to process, but GIMP creates a custom color gradient based on the colors in your sample image. That custom gradient is what you then use to colorize your destination image.

Above each of the preview images is a pair of check boxes that control what you see in those previews. Note that for the Sample preview, if your sample source is a gradient, neither of these check boxes has an affect on the (empty) Sample preview:

- **Show Selection** — If you're applying the Sample Colorize function to only a set of selected pixels in your active layer, keep this check box enabled to have the preview zoom in on those specific pixels. If you want to see the full image in the preview area, disable this check box. If your sample source is a gradient, then this option has no effect.

- **Show Color** — This check box toggles whether its corresponding preview displays in color or in grayscale. This is most useful on the Destination preview because it allows you to compare the image before and after colorization is applied.

Beneath each preview is a set of triangle sliders like the ones available to you in the Levels tool. In fact, they serve the same purpose. Under the Destination preview are sliders to control Input Levels. This is the range of values coming into the Sample Colorize function. You can tweak the black point, mid point, and white point of the image, controlling the range of pixels that get mapped from your color sample. The triangle sliders under your Sample preview control Output Levels, defining the range of the gradient that gets mapped to your destination image. You can adjust these sliders directly by clicking and dragging them with your mouse or you can type explicit values in their respective numeric entry fields.

The Destination image has two more controls beneath it, dictated by a pair of check boxes:

- **Hold Intensity** — This option — enabled by default — causes the destination image to match the average light intensity coming from the source image. Disabling this check box gives you a straight mapping from the sample, similar to the results you get from the Gradient Map operation.

- **Original Intensity** — This check box is available only if Hold Intensity is enabled. It's enabled by default and it tells Sample Colorize to ignore the values set for the Input Levels and just stick with the intensity of the original image. If you want the Input Levels sliders to have an effect on the final colorized result, disable this check box.

The Sample gradient also has its own pair of final control check boxes. These toggles control how the gradient is mapped to the destination image. The following is a description of each:

- **Use Subcolors** — Each pixel in your sample gradient is an RGB color comprised of three constituent primary channels. If you leave this check box enabled, the Sample Colors feature mixes those primary channels before mapping them to your destination image, ensuring that the colors match between the sample and the destination. However, if you disable this check box, the Sample Colors feature only uses the most dominant channel per pixel when mapping to the destination image. This yields more even tones in the destination image, but at the expense of matching colors with the sample.

- **Smooth Samples** — If your source image or gradient doesn't have many colors in it, the changes in the gradient may be harsh and abrupt. Keep this check box enabled and GIMP attempts to keep the transition from one color to the next relatively smooth.

One of the really cool features of the Sample Colorize operation is that once you choose your sample and configure it for your destination, the dialog remains open after you click the Apply button. This allows you to do multiple passes of colorizing your final image without repeatedly hunting down the Sample Colorize option in the image window. You can do cool things like apply a warm gradient to the lighter pixels in your destination image and a cooler gradient to the darker pixels.

Analyzing Your Colors with Info Tools

Before doing color correction on an image, it's a good idea to understand the nature of that image in an analytical sense. The functions available in the Colors ➤ Info submenu are well-suited to providing you with the raw data about your image that can facilitate that analysis.

Histogram

Probably the most useful of the informational tools is the histogram. As you may have noticed, the histogram is an integral part of many of GIMP's color tools, including the Levels, Curves, and Threshold tools. It's also the easiest way to see how the automated tools have modified the tonal qualities of your image. Because the histogram is so valuable, it's actually one of GIMP's dockable dialogs, briefly covered in Chapter 1. The Colors ➤ Info ➤ Histogram menu item is just a convenient shortcut that brings up the same dockable dialog you get by going to Windows ➤ Dockable Dialogs ➤ Histogram. As explained earlier in this chapter, a histogram is a chart that shows how many pixels in your image share a specific value for a given channel in your image. Figure 9-40 shows the Histogram for each of its available channels.

FIGURE 9-40

The Histogram dialog can show statistical data for each of the channels in your image, including a combined view of all channels.

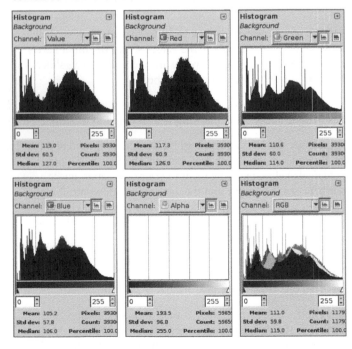

Like in the Levels and Curves tools, you can switch which channel the histogram displays by clicking the Channel drop-down menu. You also still retain the ability to display the histogram on either a linear or logarithmic scale with the two buttons on the right side of the dialog. The Histogram dialog also features a set of triangle sliders beneath the actual histogram graph, but this does not modify anything in the image. It merely defines a range for giving you statistical information at the bottom of the dialog.

The Histogram dialog displays information only for the active layer or the current selection of pixels within that layer. If you want to have the histogram show an analysis of all visible pixels, you first need to merge layers.

Border Average

Like the other color operations in the Info submenu, the Border Average operation (Colors ➤ Info ➤ Border Average) does not modify your image. However, it does change the foreground color used by your paint tools. Basically this tool traverses either the border of the active layer or your current selection and calculates the dominant color used for that perimeter. That color is assigned to your foreground color. To do this, the Border Average operation brings up a dialog, such as the one shown in Figure 9-41.

FIGURE 9-41

The dialog for the Border Average operation

This dialog features two primary controls:

- **Border Size —** When the Border Average function runs, it creates a border around your active layer or selection and samples the pixels within that border. The Thickness value set here in the dialog determines how wide that border is. Larger Thickness values increase the number of sampled pixels that Border Average uses to pick your new foreground color.

- **Number of Colors —** As the Border Average operation traverses the border it has created, it takes the colors it samples and organizes them into a series of *buckets* that it later uses to determine the dominant color along the border. The drop-down menu here dictates how many colors get included in each bucket. If you have a smaller Bucket Size, the Border Average operation yields more precise results about the nature of the colors in the selected border area.

Colorcube Analysis

As Figure 9-42 shows, the Colorcube Analysis function (Colors ➤ Info ➤ Colorcube Analysis) produces a histogram that looks remarkably similar to the Histogram dialog when set to the RGB pseudochannel. For the most part this is true; it just shows the information at a somewhat finer grain, using each of the six common hues in digital color (red, yellow, green, cyan, blue, magenta) and showing the results in an additive format where each color overlaps with the others to generate a new color. Where all of the colors overlap, you see white.

FIGURE 9-42

The results of running Colors ➢ Info ➢ Colorcube Analysis on a color image

Smooth Palette

Unlike the other operations in the Info submenu, the Smooth Palette operation (Colors ➢ Info ➢ Smooth Palette) actually creates an image as output. Specifically speaking, it creates an image that looks very similar in appearance to the gradients in the Gradients dialog. Basically, it takes all of the colors in your image and generates a linear palette from them. The main purpose of this filter is to create custom input for the Flame filter (Filters ➢ Render ➢ Nature ➢ Flame). However, it's also a pretty convenient way to generate a map of the colors used in an image. Then you can use the strip that's generated as your painting palette if you want to create an image with similar tonal qualities. Figure 9-43 shows the Smooth Palette operation's dialog and an example palette that it created.

FIGURE 9-43

On the left, the Smooth Palette dialog; on the right, a palette that this operation generated

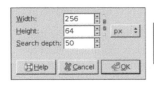 

The Width and Height values in this dialog dictate the final size of the generated palette image. The Search Depth field stipulates the number of shades included in the palette. It has a range from 1 to 1024. If you choose to generate a palette with a Search Depth that's greater than the default value of 50, it's definitely a good idea to at least increase the width of the generated palette image.

Color Filter Plug-ins

The last set of items in the Colors menu is actual filter plug-ins that ship with GIMP and explicitly work with color. For convenience and organization, they've been included with the Colors menu rather than cause undo clutter in the already lengthy Filters menu.

Color to Alpha

This filter performs the exact same function as can be found in Layer ≻ Transparency ≻ Color to Alpha. This feature is discussed more in depth in Chapter 6, but the thrust of it is that you use the dialog that appears (shown in Figure 9-44) to choose a color to be mapped to the alpha channel. The cool thing about this filter is that rather than do a binary transparency operation where one specific color is transparent and all others are opaque, this filter measures the influence of the chosen color in each color channel and uses that to produce varying levels of transparency on the active layer or selection.

FIGURE 9-44

The Color to Alpha dialog

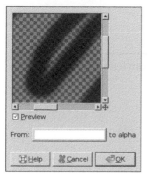

Colorify

The Colorify filter is like a quick-and-dirty version of the Colorize tool. Rather than present you with a handful of sliders to adjust the hue, saturation, and luminosity of the overlay color for your active layer or selection, the Colorify filter presents you with a dialog (Figure 9-45) that has a preview window and seven preset colors to apply to your image: the six core component colors and white. If none of those colors are to your liking, you can click the Custom Color swatch and choose the color you want with the color picker that appears. Ultimately the effect is about the same as Colorize. You get an image that appears like you're viewing it through colored glass.

Filter Pack

The Filter Pack filter is pretty interesting. It doesn't really provide any facilities that you can't get with any of GIMP's standard color correction tools, but it does offer a cleaner interface to perform color-correction activities. When you call Filter Pack from Colors ➢ Filter Pack, you get a dialog like the one in Figure 9-46.

FIGURE 9-45

The Colorify filter's dialog

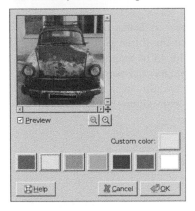

FIGURE 9-46

The Filter Pack dialog (left) and its various sub-windows for adjusting (in columns from left to right) Hue, Saturation, Value, and for performing advanced curves techniques

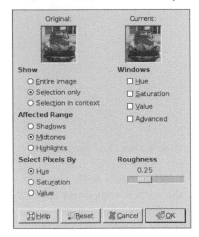

The best way to approach the Filter Pack plug-in is to work down the left column of the dialog and then work down the right. So the first thing you want to set is what gets shown in the preview images at the top of the dialog. Just like the Rotate Colors operation, you have the choice of showing the Entire Image, your Selection Only (if you have a selection), or the Selection in Context. Both the Original and Current preview images at the top are updated to reflect your changes.

After determining what you want to see in the previews, you can then decide which pixels you want to tweak first. The radio buttons under the Affected Range heading have the same effect as the Shadows, Midtones, and Highlights radio buttons in the Color Balance tool.

Unlike a lot of other filters and tools that can work in RGB space or HSV space, the Filter Pack filter works exclusively in HSV. Therefore, the next set of radio buttons under the heading Select Pixels By is how you tell Filter Pack which channel you want to work on: Hue, Saturation, or Value (Luminosity).

With all of the controls on the left side of the dialog set, you have your work environment for color correction established. Now you can really get into some color correcting. The way it works is pretty intuitive. On the right side of the dialog under the Windows heading, click the check box that corresponds with the channel that you want to modify. The first three options pop up sub-windows, each with an array of thumbnail previews of your image with various color adjustments applied to them. Click the image that most closely matches the final look you want. You can continue with this process until you're satisfied with the final look presented. If you're completely satisfied, you can click OK and Filter Pack processes your color corrections to give you your final results. Figure 9-47 shows the secondary dialogs that appear when you enable the check boxes for each of the Hue, Saturation, and Value channels.

FIGURE 9-47

From left to right, channel dialogs for Hue, Saturation, and Value

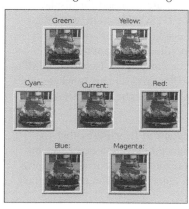

If you're *not* completely satisfied, you have two further options. For one, you may want to have more fine-grained control over the differences between the thumbnail choices that Filter Pack presents you with. You can compensate for that by adjusting the Roughness slider at the bottom of the Filter Pack dialog. Lower Roughness values reduce the amount of change between preview images.

Your other option for fine-grained control is in the Filter Pack's Advanced window. This window gives you even more control over the difference between the preview images presented to you in each of the filter's sub-windows. This window is dominated by a Curves tool–like control for tweaking intermediate levels between the previews. You can also use the Preview Size slider on the right of this sub-window to increase or decrease the size of the previews so you can better see what Filter Pack is doing. Figure 9-48 shows the Advanced sub-window for the Filter Pack feature.

FIGURE 9-48

The Advanced window for the Filter Pack gives you controls similar to the Curves tool.

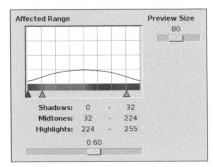

Hot

The Hot filter is most valuable when you're working on images that are destined for display on television in older standard definition (SD) formats like PAL or NTSC. The issue with older SD televisions is that historically they're not particularly good at displaying colors or values at full saturation or luminosity. So to compensate for that television editors and graphic artists have to work in "television-safe" colors, kind of like the Web-safe color palette. However, GIMP doesn't natively limit you to working only in the NTSC or PAL color spaces. This is where the Hot filter comes in. Launch this filter from Colors ➤ Hot and you get the dialog shown in Figure 9-49.

The options in this dialog allow you to adjust your image's histogram to fit within either the NTSC or PAL color spaces. Furthermore, it also gives you the chance to create a new layer in your image with the modified version of your image. This way you can compare it with the original and see if there are any glaring problems with the automated color conversion that this filter implements.

Maximum RGB

The Maximum RGB filter (Colors ➤ Maximum RGB) has the relatively simple dialog box shown in Figure 9-50.

This filter works by analyzing each pixel in your image and determining which of the three channels (red, green, or blue) is the most dominant or least dominant for that pixel. Which one it chooses to display is determined by the radio buttons in the dialog:

- **Hold the Maximal Channels** — The dominant channel is retained. The other two channels are discarded.

- **Hold the Minimal Channels** — The least dominant channel is retained and the other, more dominant channels are discarded.

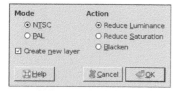

FIGURE 9-49

The Hot filter's dialog

FIGURE 9-50

The Maximum RGB filter dialog

Regardless of which channels are retained and which are discarded per pixel, the end result is an image that consists entirely of the primary colors red, green, and blue.

Retinex

Typically speaking, the human eye is much better at seeing in low light conditions than the electric sensor of a camera. Therefore, cameras don't always pick up the detail in low light that humans would find critical for correctly understanding what's going on in the image. The Retinex filter is an attempt to enhance dark images in a way that's more akin to the way the human eye works. The core of the filter is in the MultiScale Retinex with Color Restoration (MSRCR) algorithm. The term *Retinex* is a combined abbreviation of *retina* and *cortex*. It works well on underexposed photographs and is often used to show more detail in astronomical photographs and medical images like x-rays and MRIs. When you activate this filter by going to Colors ➤ Retinex, you get a dialog like the one in Figure 9-51.

FIGURE 9-51

The Retinex filter's dialog

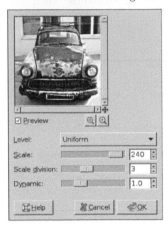

The key to the MSRCR algorithm is that it attempts to replicate the behavior of the human eye. That being the case, many of the settings in this filter's dialog are a bit obtuse and lean toward the technical side of things. Explanations of the inner workings of this algorithm are beyond the scope of this book, but if you're interested, there's a good reference paper online at www.dti.unimi.it/rizzi/papers/josa.pdf. Fortunately there aren't too many controls, so this filter is pretty conducive to a healthy amount of fiddling and playing with the controls to get a good feeling for how they behave. The default values tend to yield acceptable results, but the following descriptions of each control setting should help you attain better results:

- **Level** — The Level drop-down gives you three options that deal with the light intensity in the image.

  - **Uniform** — This is the default value. It treats both high and low intensity areas evenly and tends to yield the most natural results.

  - **Low** — The results of this option tend to look a bit like simple edge detection. The emphasis here is on the low-intensity details of the image at the expense of washing out the rest of it.

  - **High** — This option tends to emphasize the clearest part of the image, accentuating contrast and enhancing the colors. If the results from the Uniform option appear muddy, this option should appear cleaner.

- **Scale** — The lower this value is, the more rudimentary the filtering is in the results. At low values, you may still see details in the image, but there's often a glow or color shift around features that reduces the clarity of the image overall. Typically, the optimal setting for this option is a value of 240 and therefore that's also the default value.

- **Scale Division** — The Retinex filter is an iterative filter, meaning it runs its core algorithm multiple times when you click OK. This value controls how many iterations are used. The default value of three gives good results. Setting the Scale Division too high not only increases processing time, but it also tends to make your final image a bit noisy.

- **Dynamic** — Of the controls for this filter, this one is the most image-dependent. Higher values reduce the saturation and overall contrast of the results and lower values tend to blow out the details in the image.

The biggest thing to know about the Retinex filter is that it can sometimes take a while to finish processing. This is particularly true on larger images. That's something to keep in mind as you monkey around with the settings. Be careful when adjusting them (especially the Scale Division slider), or you may be waiting a while for GIMP to finish processing after you click OK. Figure 9-52 shows the results of the Retinex filter for each of the three Level options.

FIGURE 9-52

From left to right, the original photograph and that same photograph with the Retinex filter applied using Uniform, Low, and High levels (Photo credit: cgtextures.com)

Exporting Color Separations with the Separate+ Plug-in

Earlier in this chapter you saw how the Decompose operation could be used to take images from GIMP's native RGB color space and spit out color plates for channels in a variety of other formats, including HSL, LAB, and CMYK (pronounced in the GIMP community as "schmuck"). As part of that discussion, I recommended against using Decompose to produce your CMYK plates. The reason for that is because you typically want to go to CMYK only when you want to take an image to a printer using a traditional four-color process. That being the case, straight CMYK likely won't cut it. The reason for that is because GIMP's Decompose feature doesn't take any color management profiles into account. When it comes to getting computer graphics off of a computer monitor and on to some other media, color management becomes very important. It's through the color profiles used by *color management systems* (CMS) that hardware printers and software applications can agree on a display standard. Without color management, it's incredibly difficult to work with a digital color image and be guaranteed its colors on screen will be accurate to the printed result.

This is where the Separate+ plug-in comes in. If you don't already have Separate+ installed for GIMP, have a look through Chapter 21 and follow the installation instructions there for your operating system. Once you get Separate+ installed and working on your computer, come back here and have some fun.

At its core, the Separate+ plug-in does the exact same thing that the Decompose operation does. The only difference is that Separate+ uses industry-standard color profiles to dictate the color spaces that it decomposes to. Because Separate+ operates on an entire image and not just the active layer, the Separate+ functions are not found in the Colors menu. Instead, go to Image ➢ Separate to see the Separate+ submenu, shown in Figure 9-53.

FIGURE 9-53

See the items in the Separate+ submenu by going to Image ➢ Separate, as shown on the left here. On the right is the Separate+ dialog called when you go to Image ➢ Separate ➢ Separate+.

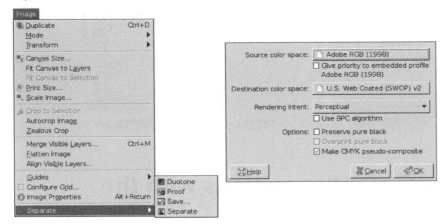

The real functionality you want to work with is at Image ➢ Separate ➢ Separate+. The two most important controls in this dialog are dictated by the buttons next to the Source and Destination Color Space labels. These define the color space that you're working with in GIMP and the color space that you want to print in, respectively. Assuming you've set up your color space properly through GIMP's Preferences window (as described in Chapter 1), everything here should be ready to go. However, if you've got a special situation and are either working in a different color space or you want to create color separations for a different destination color space, just click the button next to the color space you want to change, and choose your desired color space from the dialog that appears. It should look something like the one in Figure 9-54.

Beneath the Source Color Space button is a check box labeled Give Priority to Embedded Profile. Most photographs and other images intended for print typically come with their own color profile embedded in the file. To ensure the most color accuracy, it's usually a good idea to stick with the embedded profile. The only exception to this would be if GIMP can't handle the embedded color profile and you have to convert to something GIMP can handle before continuing to edit the image. If that's the case, you'll want to leave this check box disabled.

FIGURE 9-54

The dialogs that allow you to pick your desired Source (top) and Destination (bottom) color spaces

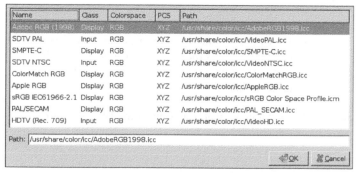

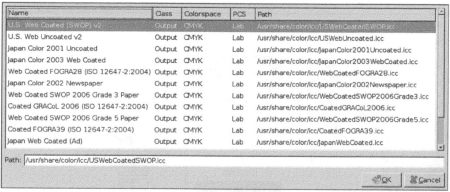

The next control in the Separate+ dialog is the drop-down menu labeled Rendering Intent. Your options in this menu match the same menu in the Color Management section of GIMP's Preferences. For a review of these Rendering Intent options, refer back to Chapter 1. Typically, you should use the same Rendering Intent here that you defined in those Preferences.

Beneath the Rendering Intent drop-down are four more check boxes:

- **Use BPC Algorithm** — BPC is an abbreviation for *black point compensation*. Typically it's okay to leave this check box enabled. If you're taking your image to a professional print shop, ask them whether they would prefer to have BPC enabled in your files or disabled.

- **Preserve Pure Black** — Enable this option to ensure that the blacks in your image are truly black rather than a concentrated mixture of the cyan, magenta, and yellow inks.

- **Overprint Pure Black** — Overprinting is when one color is printed over another. This is either done to get a third color or, in the case of overprinting black, compensate for possible registration and alignment errors when printing. The main situation where you want to enable this option is when you have pure black overlapping another color. For instance, if you have black text on a blue background, you'll want to overprint the black. However, if you have black text straight on the white paper, there's no need to overprint. This option is available only if you enable the Preserve Pure Black check box.

- **Make CMYK Pseudo-Composite** — When you run the Separate+ plug-in, it works like the Decompose operation and generates a new image with four grayscale layers; one for each color channel in the CMYK color space. Separate+, however, offers another possibility if you enable this check box. Rather than create the grayscale channels as layers, Separate+ creates a layer for each color and then uses the grayscale channel as a mask for that color. By doing that and compositing the layers on the same image, you get a rough composite of what the final color image looks like.

Figure 9-55 shows the color separations that Separate+ creates as well as the layer structure when you have Make CMYK Pseudo-Composite enabled.

FIGURE 9-55

The CMYK color separations for a photograph and the layer structure GIMP creates when doing a pseudo-composite (Photo credit: cgtextures.com)

Original   Cyan Magenta Yellow Black Pseudo-Composite

Once you've created your separations, you have a few options that you can play with. Probably the most useful thing you can do is save your color separations to an image format that a print shop can handle. Fortunately, you can do this easily by going to your separated image and choosing Image ➤ Separate ➤ Save. This brings up a File Chooser where you can export a separated TIFF image with the proper CMYK color profile embedded with it. Once the file is saved, you can verify that it works by trying to re-open it with File ➤ Create ➤ Separated TIFF. This should open your separated image with the proper color profile and color masks assigned to each layer.

The other useful operation you can do with the Separate+ plug-in is create a print proof based on your separated color channels. To do this, go to Image ➤ Separate ➤ Proof. This brings up a dialog like the one in Figure 9-56.

Separate+'s Proof dialog for testing to see how your separated image may look when printed

This dialog is kind of like the inverse of the Separate+ dialog. Use the buttons next to Monitor/Working Color Space and Separated Image's Color Space to choose the correct color spaces for your image and your working environment. Assuming you've properly configured everything in GIMP's Preferences, these buttons should default to the correct color spaces. You can also lend priority to the embedded color profile in your image. That shouldn't be necessary if you've just created the separated image on the same machine, but if you're dealing with a file created elsewhere, this option is incredibly helpful.

The only other options for creating a proof are in the drop-down menu labeled Mode. For most circumstances, Normal should yield the results that you want. However, if you need to simulate black ink or the white color of the paper you're printing on, this menu provides you with those options as well. Once you've made your settings, click OK and the Separate+ plug-in creates a new image with a reproduction of what should be produced by the printer.

Summary

This chapter was *huge*. Not only did you go through a comprehensive explanation of all the color correction tools and operations available in GIMP's Color menu, but you also got to see where some of them are more useful than others. In particular, you discovered that in the right hands, the Levels and Curves tools can be used to create almost any other color correction effect. You also saw the value that histograms have in correcting and analyzing the colors in your image. And at the end of the chapter, you were introduced to the Separate+ plug-in and discovered why it's superior to using the Decompose operation if you're taking your image to a printing professional. All in all, this chapter covered a ton of stuff. Next up, working with text. It's fun. I promise.

Working with Text

IN THIS CHAPTER

Knowing the benefits of text

Using the Text tool

Understanding how text layers work

A picture may be worth a thousand words, but that doesn't necessarily dictate that they'll be the best or most appropriate words for communicating any given subject matter. Sometimes you don't need a thousand words; you just need one or two properly chosen ones. Enter GIMP's text editing features. If you're working with digital images, somewhere along the line you're probably going to need to mix text with those images. This chapter gives you the rundown on exactly how you do that in GIMP. GIMP isn't necessarily a typesetting or layout tool, but its text features are extensive enough for you to do everything from labeling photos to using that text as a design element.

Another thing to note is that, along with paths, GIMP handles text as vector image data. This gives you the ability to edit, move, resize, and drastically modify your text over and over again, *non-destructively*. If you save your image in GIMP's native XCF format or the Photoshop PSD format, the text vector information is retained so you can continue to edit in future sessions. However, if you save in a pure raster format like JPEG or PNG, the text layers are rasterized and merged with the other layers in the image.

Uses for Text in Images

You can find countless uses for text in your images. Perhaps you've taken a photograph of an engine and you need to label its parts. Or maybe you're producing a flier for a local music venue. Possibly you're producing a web comic and your characters have dialogue. Or maybe you need to mock up a layout for an entire web site and you need to see how text will look on the page. You could even want to be a bit designerly and use the text itself as your primary design element for a banner or magazine ad.

Adding and Editing Text

Nearly all of GIMP's text editing features can be accessed, unsurprisingly, using the Text tool. To use this tool click the icon in the Toolbox that looks like the letter "A" (shown in Figure 10-1) or press the keyboard shortcut, T. Doing so changes your mouse cursor in the image window to a crosshair with the text insertion "i-beam" to the lower right.

The Text tool activated in GIMP's Toolbox

Once you have the Text tool activated, you have two options:

- **Click and drag to create an area where you would like your text to live** — Doing this creates an explicit place that your text is allowed to be. In layout programs, this is referred to as a text *frame*. Think of the frame as a window to the text you've typed. Any text you add to this frame wraps when you get to its maximum width. If you type more text than the frame allows space for, that additional text is simply not seen unless you resize the frame. Like the boxes created with the Rectangle Select tool and the Crop tool, you can resize this text frame by clicking and dragging any of its edges or corners. And you can move it by Alt+clicking and dragging in the middle of the frame. This text frame also establishes the dimensions of your text layer, discussed in more detail in the next section.

- **Click in the image window where you would like your text to be** — This is the easiest way to add text to an image in GIMP. If you use this method, the text frame will be dynamically resized to fit whatever text you type. This guarantees not only that no text will be hidden, but also that the frame is exactly the dimensions of your available text. Of course, choosing this method doesn't lock you into it. You're free to resize your text area whenever you please with the same methods mentioned earlier.

Note

If you manually resize a text frame created by the second method, there's no way to revert its behavior to dynamic resizing. ∎

Figure 10-2 shows an image window with a text frame created and filled with some text.

FIGURE 10-2

Text frames can dynamically resize or you can explicitly define their size by clicking and dragging an edge or corner.

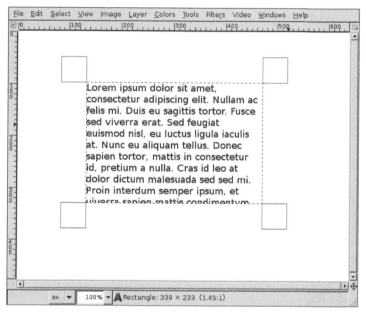

In earlier versions of GIMP, regardless of whether you explicitly create your text frame or have it dynamically resize, GIMP would automatically pop up a Text Editor window. This is where you would actually type in the text that you want to have appear in the text frame. While there are certainly advantages to having a simple text editor built into GIMP, this is not the ideal behavior that most artists want from their Text tool. It's usually much nicer to be able to add the text directly in the image window and interactively see how that text appears in your image with your desired font. Fortunately the GIMP developers understood this need and added this feature early on in the development for GIMP 2.8. This means that now, once you add your text frame, you can begin typing immediately and edit your text directly from the image window. Hooray!

If you've used the Text tool in previous versions of GIMP and enjoyed some of the additional features that the Text Editor window provided, you should be glad to know that the bulk of that functionality is still accessible when editing text from the image window. To access these features, simply right-click in the text frame that you're editing and you should see the context menu that's shown in Figure 10-3.

As the figure shows, you can perform standard Cut, Copy, Paste, and Delete operations on your text as well as a handful of other helpful functions. One of the most useful features is the ability

283

to load text from an external file. Say you've already typed all of your text and you just want to lay it out. Or perhaps you're creating a magazine ad and you receive the textual content of that ad, called the *copy*, from someone else who was hired to write it. Well, rather than retyping all of that text or trying to copy and paste all of it, you can simply load the text from a file. To do this, right-click your text frame and choose Open Text File from the context menu. This brings up a File Chooser where you can select the text file you want to use.

FIGURE 10-3

Additional functionality from the Text tool can be accessed from a context window invoked by right-clicking in an active text frame.

Besides being able to load text from an external file, you also have the ability to remove all text from the text frame by right-clicking and choosing Clear from the menu. This function is particularly useful when you have more text than can fit in the text frame. Rather than trying to select all of the text and then deleting it, this menu item does it all for you in a single step.

The Path from Text and Text along Path items in this menu will be covered later on in this chapter, but the last two menu items deserve immediate attention. They're actually a toggle; that is, you can only choose one or the other. Either you choose From Left to Right or you choose From Right to Left. These options control which direction text flows in the text editor. The default behavior should match the language you've set your machine to work at. So if you're using a Western language, it should be set to use From Left to Right. Of course, you can use these menu items to change the direction the text flows whenever you need.

Note

When you're adding text in the image window, be aware that keyboard shortcuts are specific to editing text. For instance, pressing Ctrl+A selects all of your text in the active text frame rather than creating a marching ants selection around your image canvas. Likewise, keyboard shortcuts like P for the Paintbrush tool won't work. To activate those tools, you need to go to the Toolbox or the Tools menu in the image window. ■

Despite the enormous convenience of being able to edit text directly within the image window, there are still advantages to using a Text Editor window instead. The biggest advantage is that you can see all of your text. This is particularly helpful if you've written or loaded more text than your text frame has space for. You can type and edit your text in the editor first and then get it to fit in the frame once you're done. To enable the Text Editor window, go to the Text tool's Tool Options in the Toolbox and enable the Use Editor check box. Upon doing so, you get a window like the one shown in Figure 10-4.

FIGURE 10-4

GIMP's Text Editor window is another place where you enter the text that appears in the text frame.

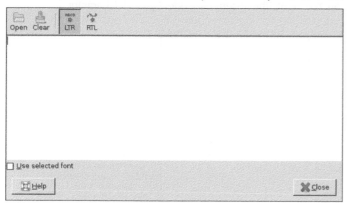

Through the Text Editor, you have all of the functionality available when editing text in the image window, plus a few additional features. You can load external text by clicking the Open button or remove it all by clicking Clear. The LTR and RTL buttons control whether your text flows from left to right or from right to left, respectively.

The text entry area is a very simple text editor, allowing you to type whatever text you would like to appear in your image and do some basic formatting of that text. You can access a context menu for this area by right-clicking within it. Like the menu available in the image window, this one provides your basic cut/copy/paste/delete options, but a few additional options are here, but not available in the image window:

- **Select All** — Pretty straightforward, this option selects all of the text that you've entered into the text area.

- **Input Methods** — This allows you to choose how text is interpreted from your hardware. For instance, if you have a Cyrillic mapping for your keyboard, you can choose that from the menu as your input method.

- **Insert Unicode Control Character** — This menu offers you the ability to enter some special characters to help you explicitly control your text flow, such as a right-to-left override character.

Figure 10-5 shows these two submenus of the right-click context menu in the Text Editor window.

Tip

Right-clicking the Text Editor window isn't the only way to access the Input Methods and Insert Unicode Control Character menus. These menus are specifically related to the language that you're writing in and they're accessible at the very bottom of the Tool Options panel for the Text tool, under the label of Language. Simply right-click in this text field and you get the exact same context menu that appears when right-clicking in the Text Editor. ∎

FIGURE 10-5

On the left, the Input Methods submenu; on the right, the Insert Unicode Control Character submenu

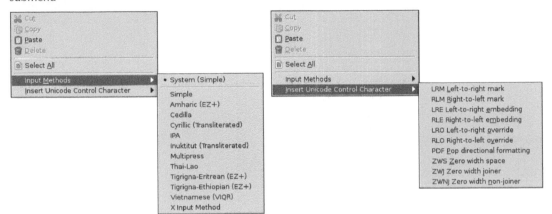

Below the text entry area for the text editor is a Use Selected Font check box. When you enable this option, whatever font you've chosen in the Text tool's options appears in the text area. The size of the font doesn't change in the text area, but being able to see the font here certainly helps get your basic text layout visible from within the text editor. This is a holdover feature from when you couldn't edit text in the image window, but it's still useful on occasion.

Note

Although you can do a lot with GIMP's text editor, it's still pretty basic. In its current form, it doesn't allow you to mix fonts or font attributes such as bold or italics. To do that with the current version of GIMP, you need to use multiple text layers. This can be a bit of a headache, but it should be addressed in future versions. ∎

Customizing Text from the Text Panel

By default, GIMP uses a standard Sans font when you first start using the Text tool. Sans is nice, but you're using an image editor; part of the fun is making things look interesting and awesome! Control of that is handled from the options of the Text tool, which appears by default at the bottom of the Toolbox window when you have the Text tool selected. Figure 10-6 shows the options available to you in the Text panel.

Font and Size

The two most useful — and most used — options in this panel are at the top, Font and Size. The Font option shows you the current font that you're using. The easiest way to change your font is to click the square font icon immediately to the right of the font name. This brings up a drop-down menu with a full listing of all the fonts you have installed on your computer.

Next to each font name is an icon that gives you a quick preview of what the font looks like with an uppercase and lowercase letter "a." Select the font you want to use from this list and it will immediately change in the image window. Alternatively, if you know the name of the font you want to use, you can click in the text field where the font name is and start typing the name of that font. When you do this, GIMP brings up a list of the fonts that match what you've typed and you can select your font from there or finish typing. Figure 10-7 shows this in action.

Note

The way GIMP handles fonts appears a bit strange. This is because GIMP reads each individual font file you have installed on your system. This is strange because different styles of a font, like bold or underlined versions, are often stored as separate files. Whereas most programs load the main font and offer buttons to access the bold or italic versions, GIMP loads each of these files individually and lists them in the Font drop-down. This is why your font list may appear to be much longer than you expect. The benefit of doing it this way, though, is that you're guaranteed to get an italic version of a font only if it actually exists, rather than having a standard font skewed to the right. (Typeface designers hate it when you do this.) ■

FIGURE 10-6

The Text panel allows you to control a variety of attributes on the text you enter in the image window.

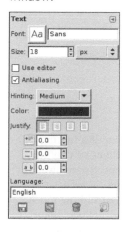

The next option is the text's Size. By default, this is defined in pixels and you can adjust the value by typing it in or using the up/down tumbler buttons on the right of that number value. If you want to describe the text size in different units, such as points, picas, inches, or any of the other units that GIMP recognizes, you can choose those units from the Units drop-down at the far right.

Below the Size entry field is the Use Editor check box. As described earlier in this chapter, this option toggles the visibility of the Text Editor window. By default it's disabled.

Font Edging

Below the Use Editor option is another check box, labeled Antialiasing, which, as you may expect, toggles whether or not the font is rendered with antialiasing. As discussed elsewhere in this book, aliasing is the pixelated, jagged-edge effect that often happens at the edges of objects in digital images. Antialiasing is a method to reduce those jagged edges. Enabling this option will antialias your text. If you're working with really small text, however, using this option might make your fonts look blurry and unreadable. In those cases, it's better to accept a bit of jagginess (it's a word, I swear) in exchange for readability.

FIGURE 10-7

Typing the name of the font you want brings up a list of installed fonts that match that name.

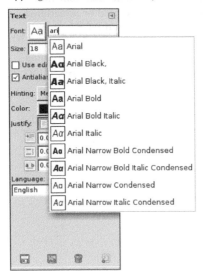

Below the Antialiasing option is a drop-down menu that controls how GIMP handles hinting. Specifically, *hinting* pertains to the font's edging. Many fonts offer modified outlines so they may render more clearly at smaller sizes and appear more readable. To make the font system aware of this ability, fonts that can do this are embedded with *hints* that let the system know what to do for each character if the font size is small. This drop-down allows you to control how much GIMP takes advantage of these hints if the font has them. You have four options: None, Slight, Medium, and Full. The default setting of Medium suits most cases, but if you're using smaller fonts, it may look better if you use Full hinting.

Changing Text Color

Below the Hinting drop-down is the option that allows you to change the color of your text. By default, the color is set to whatever you have chosen for your foreground color in the Colors dockable dialog. However, if you want to use a different color, click the color swatch in the Text options panel. This brings up the Text Color dialog. This window, shown in Figure 10-8, gives you all of the color picking options that you'd recognize from the Colors dockable dialog, with an additional feature: saved color history.

The way the saved color history works is pretty simple. If you choose a new color with this window and click OK, that color is added to the history swatches at the bottom of the dialog. The next time you choose a text color, that color will be available at the bottom of the dialog for you to choose. This is particularly useful if you're designing a flier or brochure and you need to use consistent colors throughout the design. You can also explicitly add colors to the history by clicking the arrow button to the left of the history swatches. And because this is a persistent history within GIMP, these swatches are available to you each time you run GIMP, regardless of whether you're re-opening the same image file.

FIGURE 10-8

The Text Color dialog gives you *just* a little bit more than the Colors dockable dialog.

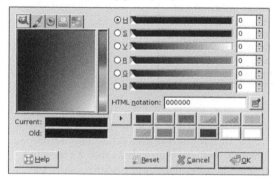

Justification, Indentation, and Spacing

The next control available in the Text tool's options is your text's *justification*, or alignment. This control has four available options:

- **Left Justified** — Click this icon to align the text to the left of the text frame.

- **Right Justified** — Clicking here aligns text to the right of the frame.

- **Centered** — When you click this icon, your text is centered within the text frame. If your text frame is automatically sizing to fit your content, you may not notice this unless you have more than one line of text.

- **Filled** — Choose this option to create filled justification. This means that GIMP increases the spacing between words so your text frame has text aligned to both the left and the right edges, like you might expect in a newspaper or magazine article.

Note
Using the Left Justified and Right Justified buttons is not the same as toggling between From Left to Right and From Right to Left when you're editing text. While text that's added using the From Right to Left option is right justified, that's not the only change that occurs. Unfortunately, it's difficult to see other changes without writing in a non-Western language that actually flows from right to left. ■

The next three options in the Text tool's options panel deal with spacing. The first option controls indentation on the first line of a paragraph. Positive values in this field indent the first line to the right. If you use a negative value in this field, GIMP gives you a *hanging indent*. That is, the first line of text aligns with the left of the frame while the rest of the paragraph is indented. Figure 10-9 shows an example of what changing the values in this field does.

FIGURE 10-9

If you set the indentation value to 50 pixels, you get a normal indent like the one on the left. If you set the value to −50 pixels, you get a hanging indent like the one on the right.

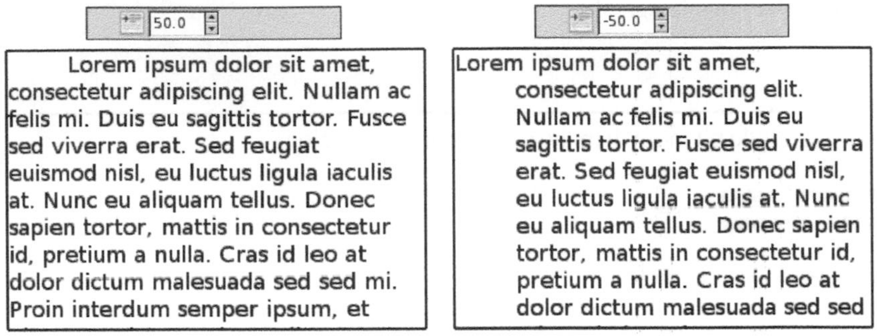

Lorem ipsum dolor sit amet, consectetur adipiscing elit. Nullam ac felis mi. Duis eu sagittis tortor. Fusce sed viverra erat. Sed feugiat euismod nisl, eu luctus ligula iaculis at. Nunc eu aliquam tellus. Donec sapien tortor, mattis in consectetur id, pretium a nulla. Cras id leo at dolor dictum malesuada sed sed mi. Proin interdum semper ipsum, et

Lorem ipsum dolor sit amet, consectetur adipiscing elit. Nullam ac felis mi. Duis eu sagittis tortor. Fusce sed viverra erat. Sed feugiat euismod nisl, eu luctus ligula iaculis at. Nunc eu aliquam tellus. Donec sapien tortor, mattis in consectetur id, pretium a nulla. Cras id leo at dolor dictum malesuada sed sed

The next numeric field controls line spacing. In typography, this is often referred to as *leading* (pronounced like "sledding"). Quite simply, this is the amount of space that GIMP places between each line of text in your text frame. If you use the default value of zero, GIMP relies on the spacing hints indicated by the font itself. However, you can adjust this value if you want more control. Use positive values to increase the spacing between lines and negative values to cram the lines closer to one another.

The last value in this last numeric field is letter spacing, called *tracking* by typographers. Adjust this value to increase or decrease the amount of space between each letter in your text field. Note that this setting is different from *kerning*, though the differentiation between the two settings is subtle. Letter spacing controls the total amount of space between each letter in a word. Kerning, on the other hand, is intended to account for how characters in a non-fixed-width, or proportional, font relate to one another. Because letters in a proportional font don't all have the same width and some letters hang into the space of adjacent ones, kerning is used to make the spacing look even. Kerning hints are typically embedded in font files and GIMP recognizes them. Currently, though, GIMP allows you to control only letter spacing and not kerning.

Note

You might notice that none of the spacing values have any units associated with them. This is because they use the units that you stipulate at the top of the Text tool's options panel for your font size. Pay close attention to this, because GIMP doesn't automatically convert units for you on these values. If, for example, you change from pixel-sized fonts to inch-sized fonts, your indentation setting of 10 pixels will suddenly become an indentation of 10 inches. Unless you're doing something weird and working at 1ppi, this is quite a dramatic change! ■

Making Text Go Along a Path

One of the cool things about text in GIMP is that you're not limited to keeping your text locked to the hard rectangular shape of the text frame. You can actually have your text flow along the length of a path. Following is an outline of the process you have to use to achieve this effect:

1. **Create your text.** Enable the Text tool (T) and enter text as described earlier in this chapter.

2. **Create a path.** Use the Paths tool (B) to create the path that you would like text to use to control its shape. Chapter 5 covers the usage of the Paths tool in depth.

3. **Activate your path in the Paths dockable dialog.** If this is your only path, it should be activated by default. If it isn't, simply click it in the Paths dockable dialog to activate it. For your sanity, it may also be a good idea to rename your path here by double-clicking it and typing a new name. This is purely optional, but it really helps you organize your project, especially if you have a lot of paths.

4. **Using the Text tool (T), select your text layer by clicking it.** This is simply to let GIMP know which text you intend to work on. If you skip this step, GIMP doesn't know what text to flow along the path.

5. **Right-click in your text frame and choose Text along Path from the context menu.** Depending on the complexity of your text and your curve, this might take a few seconds to process.

Figure 10-10 shows an example of the process used to make text flow along a path.

FIGURE 10-10

Making text flow along a path

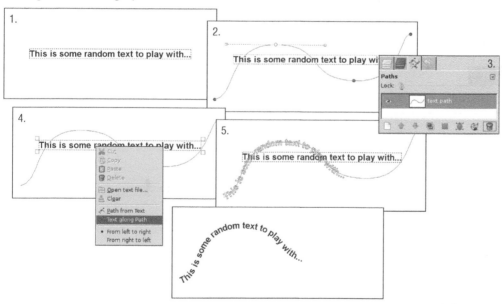

When this process completes, you have a new entry in the Paths dockable dialog for your text along the path you drew. You can then take this path and edit its individual points or use it to create a selection that you can fill with any color or pattern. You may notice that the way this works in GIMP is a bit different from the way it works in other programs. GIMP actually converts the text itself to a new path. This method has its advantages and disadvantages, but the pros generally outweigh the cons.

291

The advantage of working this way is that you can edit the content of your text independently of its "designed" look along the curve. It's often easier to type and edit text in the familiar rectangular frame format than along the shape of a path. Of course, the biggest disadvantage is that the text along the path is not directly editable as text. You don't have a "what you see is what you get," or *WYSIWYG* editing experience here. If you want to edit the content of your text, you need to use the Text tool on the original text layer and then repeat the previous process to flow the newly edited text along the path. This is also true if you decide to change the path that the text flows along.

Tip

If you do change the text or the shape of your path, it's a *very* good idea to delete the path that was generated when you first chose the Text along Path menu item. It's not critical that you do this, but it's certainly helpful in preventing you from getting confused about which new path you've created. ■

Note

When you use the Text along Path feature, the size of your text frame is actually pretty important for controlling the placement of the text along the path. If you have a lot of space beneath your text, the text is offset above the curve by that distance. Another thing to note is that *all* text is used, not just the text viewable in the text frame. This might be a bit disorienting, but it allows you to have tight control over the placement of your text along the path. ■

Figure 10-11 shows how you can control the placement of text on a path by adjusting the height of your text frame.

FIGURE 10-11

Adjusting the placement of text on a path by varying the height of the text frame

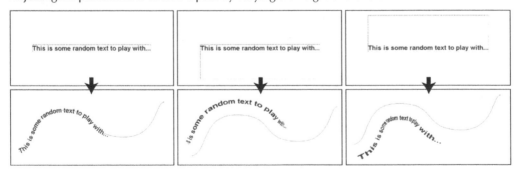

Using Text to Create a Path

Because the Text along Path feature basically generates a new path with your content, it makes sense that GIMP would offer you the ability to directly generate a path from a text layer. Not only does it make sense, but it's possible! To do this, use the last button at the bottom of the Text tool's options panel labeled Path from Text. Your next question might be, "Why would

I ever want to do this?" The most common reason for this is customizing text for a logo. You can use the Text tool to type the text of your logo, convert that to a path, and then use the Paths tool to customize its shape. The basic step-by-step process for this is as follows:

1. **Create your text**. Enable the Text tool (T) and type whatever text you want.

2. **Right-click within the text frame and choose Path from Text**. At first glance, it won't appear like anything has happened. However, if you look at the Paths dialog, you'll have a new path that shares the name of whatever your text layer is.

3. **Use the Paths tool (B) to edit the path to your liking**. Depending on how complicated you want to go, this can be pretty time-consuming. As an alternative, you could export the path as an SVG file and edit it in a dedicated vector graphics tool like Inkscape. You can find more on editing paths in GIMP in Chapter 5.

4. **Convert the path to a selection (Shift+V) and create a new layer (Shift+Ctrl+N)**. You may also want to hide your original text layer at this point.

5. **Fill in the selection**. This is the part where you get to be creative. You can be as complex or as simple as you like. Use the Bucket Fill tool to fill a solid color or pattern or break out the Blend tool to put a gradient in your selection. You could even paint something custom in the space with GIMP's various painting tools. Your options from this point are virtually limitless.

Figure 10-12 shows a simple example created from these steps.

FIGURE 10-12

Creating a customized logo by using the Path from Text feature

Working with Text Layers

Up to this point I've been referring to editing text frames to control the area. Really, though, these text frames are a specialized kind of layer. By default the name of the layer is the first few words of your text. You can reorder and adjust these layers the same way you can control regular orders, as discussed in Chapter 6, but because you're working with text, you can do a few additional things. The first thing involves recognizing the difference between a text layer and a regular layer. GIMP's interface gives you hints about this. For example, rather than creating a thumbnail image, GIMP indicates text layers by using an icon with a large T as the preview image for the layer.

One of the biggest differences between text layers and regular layers is the ability to interactively resize the text layer with your mouse using the Text tool (T) as well as change the text itself with the text editor. Regular layers can only be resized by cropping or choosing Layer ➤ Layer Boundary Size. Of course, that's not the only difference. When you have a text layer, you actually get a few additional options on the Layer menu in the image window, as shown in Figure 10-13.

FIGURE 10-13

Text layers have a few menu items that you don't find on regular layers.

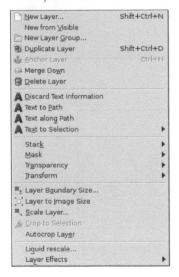

These new menu options, shown in Figure 10-13, are as follows:

- **Discard Text Information** — The wording in this menu item is a bit confusing. It doesn't actually clear the layer of text. Instead, it rasterizes the text layer, converting it into a regular layer.

- **Text to Path** — As described at the end of the previous section, this takes the text you've typed and converts it into a single path. This is just like clicking the Path from Text button in the Text tool's options panel.

- **Text along Path** — This menu item has the exact same functionality as right-clicking the text frame with the Text tool and choosing Text along Path from the context menu, creating a new path from your text that flows along the length of the active path. Note that this item is grayed out and unselectable if you don't actually have a path in the Paths dockable dialog.

- **Text to Selection** — This menu item actually hosts a submenu of items that relate your text to selecting in your image. These options are very much like the Transparency options available to regular layers, discussed in Chapter 6.

  - **Text to Selection** — This is the most straightforward option. It creates a new selection based on the text you've typed. If you already have something selected, choosing this menu item replaces that selection with one created by your text. You can choose this option to add a quick drop shadow to your text. Do this by using Layer ➤ Text to Selection, New Layer (Shift+Ctrl+N), Bucket Fill (Shift+B) with black, Deselect All (Shift+Ctrl+A), Filters ➤ Blur ➤ Gaussian Blur and then move this new layer beneath the text layer. You may choose the Move tool (M) after this and shift the shadow layer a few pixels down and to one side to get the shadow effect.

  - **Add to Selection** — This item is similar to Text to Selection; however if you already have something selected, it doesn't get replaced. Instead, your text is added to the existing selection.

  - **Subtract from Selection** — Alternatively, if you already have a selection, but you'd like to cut your text from that selection, choose this option. This is a fun way to get your text to look like it's cut from a solid color.

  - **Intersect with Selection** — Occasionally, if you already have a selection made, you may only want to select where that and your text overlap. Choosing this option gets you that result.

Once you've typed your text, any other layer modification will work on it. You can use the Transform tool to rotate, scale, skew, flip, or otherwise distort this layer to suit your tastes. There's one very important thing to note, though. Even if you perform one of these modifications, you still have the ability to edit your text. Just enable the Text tool (T) and click your text layer. Unfortunately, if you choose to do this, GIMP needs to undo these modifications and revert the text layer to its original non-distorted state. To protect you from accidentally reverting a text layer when you don't want to, GIMP pops up a warning dialog like the one shown in Figure 10-14.

FIGURE 10-14

The Confirm Text Editing warning dialog that appears if you try to edit text that's been distorted

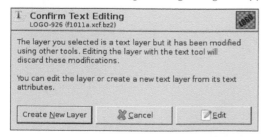

To edit your text, click the Edit button in this window and the text layer reverts to its original state before your deformations. Then once you finish modifying your text, you need to re-apply your deformations. Otherwise you can cancel the operation altogether or create a brand new text layer by clicking the Create New Layer button.

Summary

This chapter covered the usage of GIMP's Text tool and the options associated with it. You found out how to create text, adjust the font of that text, and control its layout in the image window. You also discovered how text relates to paths in GIMP as well as how text layers differ from regular layers. In the course of all of this, you saw that GIMP's Text tool is a powerful means of adding textual data to your images.

Now it's time to paint.

Painting in GIMP

IN THIS CHAPTER

Using GIMP's brushes

Getting fancy with the Ink tool

Working with gradients and patterns

GIMP's main purpose is to allow users to edit and manipulate existing images. It's not primarily designed to serve as a complete digital painting application for generating original art from scratch. That being the case, all of GIMP's painting tools are targeted toward facilitating photo retouching, image enhancement, and compositing. Despite that, these tools are generalized and powerful enough that you can still use them to create original digital paintings, and many GIMP artists do just that. They use these tools to create digital images for print or to set as desktop wallpaper. They're also commonly used to create textures that can be applied to 3D models used in film and video game animations.

In this process, a texture artist paints an image and that image is applied to the surface of 3D mesh object as a texture. This can take a plastic and sterile-looking computer-generated object and give it a unique life and grit that brings it into the realm of believability. Figure 11-1 shows an example texture painted in GIMP and the 3D character it was applied to.

This chapter explains how GIMP's various painting tools work and how you can get the most out of them. The chapter focuses on the painting tools that don't necessarily require you to have any image data to start with. This includes brush-based tools like the Pencil, Paintbrush, Eraser, and Airbrush tools as well as GIMP's very cool Ink tool and the more generalized Bucket Fill and Blend tools. GIMP has a few more brush-based tools: Clone, Healing, Perspective Clone, Blur/Sharpen, Smudge, and Dodge/Burn. However, these tools require that you already have image data to work with. For that reason, the detailed information on those tools is collected in Chapter 12. Because those tools are brush-based, they share some interface behavior with the brush-based tools covered in this chapter. If you're unfamiliar with the way GIMP's brush system works, it's worth it to read through the next section of this chapter before skipping forward to Chapter 12's tools.

FIGURE 11-1

On the left are three textures painted in GIMP (a color map, a bump map, and a specularity map) that are all applied to the surface of a character model in 3D software like Blender. (Image credit: Blender Foundation, from *Elephants Dream*)

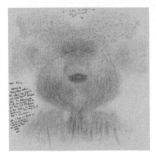
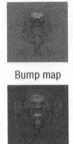

Bump map

Color map   Specularity map   Rendered image

Working with Brushes

Regardless of which brush-based tool you use in GIMP, they all have common features and settings that you can use when painting. These settings live in one of three dockable dialogs: Tool Options, Brushes, and Paint Dynamics. By default, the Tool Options dialog is docked with the Toolbox and the Brushes dialog is docked with the tabs in the lower half of the Dock window. You can bring up any of these dialogs from the Windows ➤ Dockable Dialogs menu in the image window, and the Brushes dialog is used frequently enough that it has a keyboard shortcut of Shift+Ctrl+B. Figure 11-2 shows these three dialogs together.

FIGURE 11-2

From left to right, the Tool Options, Brushes, and Paint Dynamics dockable dialogs are the places to go for adjusting brush-based painting tools in GIMP.

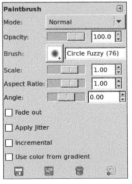
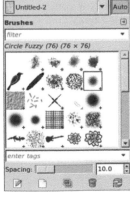

Drawing Straight Lines, or Where's My Line Tool?!

Using the paint tools in GIMP is as simple as clicking and dragging your mouse in the image window. However, a frequently asked question for users who are transitioning to GIMP from other digital graphics programs like Photoshop or Paint Shop Pro is "How do I draw a straight line?" Many other programs feature a Line tool of some sort for fulfilling this purpose and you may notice that GIMP seems to be missing this particular tool. In fact, GIMP provides a way of drawing straight lines that's much faster and more readily accessible. Rather than having an explicit line tool with its own drawing modes and rules, GIMP allows you to draw straight lines with *any* of its available paint tools (Pencil, Paintbrush, Eraser, Airbrush, Ink, Clone, Healing, Perspective Clone, Blur/Sharpen, Smudge, and Dodge/Burn).

To draw a straight line, first click the image canvas where you want the line to start. This creates a single dot stroke, which indicates the beginning of your line. Now hold down Shift. GIMP now overlays a line from your original dot to the location of your mouse cursor. Shift+click where you want the line to end and GIMP paints a straight line between those points using the active brush for your paint tool. If you hold Shift+Ctrl, the line is constrained to 15-degree increments about your starting point. This is a great way to get perfectly horizontal or vertical lines.

This method of drawing straight lines works from the end of your last stroke with your current paint tool. This means that you can quickly switch from hand-drawn, organic lines to straight lines without switching tools. It's an incredibly fast way to work and lets you think more about painting than working with an interface. The only thing to remember about this is that if you switch tools, GIMP forgets where your last stroke ended, so you need to create a new starting point for your line.

Tip

When painting with any of the brush-based tools in this chapter, you can quickly set the foreground paint color with a color picker by Ctrl+clicking your image where your desired color is. This is a handy shortcut that's much faster than switching to the Color Picker tool (O) and then switching back to your paint tool. This way GIMP also remembers your last paint stroke and you can draw a straight line without establishing a new start point. ■

Adjusting Brushes

The quickest way to adjust the brushes of your painting tools in GIMP is to use the Brushes dialog (Shift+Ctrl+B) and select the brush that you want to use. Of course, there may not be a brush that suits your specific needs when painting. Later in this chapter you see how to create your own custom brushes, but often that's not completely necessary. Most of the time, you can simply adjust some basic settings for the brushes that are already available. To do this, you work in the Tool Options dialog for the paint tool that you have selected.

Using Tool Options to Adjust Brushes

As explained in Chapter 4, all of GIMP's brush-based painting tools have the same basic options available in the Tool Options dialog, and below these standard options is a set of options specific to each brush (such as the Erase tool's antierase option or the Rate and Pressure sliders for the Airbrush tool). These tool options give you the most rudimentary controls over the appearance and behavior of your brushes with your selected tool. The list following explains each of the standard options available for your paint tools:

- **Mode** — These painting modes control how your paint strokes influence existing pixels on your active layer. The list of available modes is nearly identical to the layer blending modes covered in Chapter 6, although this drop-down includes a couple additional modes. The modes that are shared between this menu and layer modes behave in exactly the same way, so you can review Chapter 6 to see how they work. The modes listed here are exclusive to GIMP's painting tools.

Note

For the Behind and Color Erase modes to work, the layer you're painting on must have an alpha channel. If your layer's name appears in bold text in the Layers dialog, it doesn't have an alpha channel. To add an alpha channel to your layer, right-click it in the Layers dialog and choose Add Alpha Channel from the context menu that appears or select the layer, and go to Layer ➢ Transparency ➢ Add Alpha Channel from the image window. ■

- **Behind** — This mode affects only transparent and semi-transparent pixels. Painting with this mode causes your paint strokes to have greater influence the more transparent the pixel is. The result is the same as if you create a new layer (Shift+Ctrl+N), move it below your current layer in the stack, and then paint on your new layer. It appears as if you're painting behind your original layer.

- **Color Erase** — This mode is essentially the inverse behavior of the Behind mode. When you paint with this mode, any pixels that share the same color as your foreground color are made transparent. Think of it as a paintable version of the Color to Alpha feature covered in Chapter 9 (Colors ➢ Color to Alpha).

- **Opacity** — This slider lets you control the amount of influence your paint stroke has on existing pixels. Think of it as your paint tool's strength. This slider is valuable if you want to add a slight tint to existing pixels or if you only want to paint subtle strokes on your image.

- **Brush** — This setting is the most influential way of changing your paint tool's behavior. Brushes control the size, appearance, opacity, and even color of your paint strokes to a fine degree. Click the brush icon here and GIMP shows all the preset and custom brushes available in the Brushes dialog. Click the brush you want and start painting. You can find more on brushes, including how to create your own custom brushes, later in this chapter.

- **Scale** — This slider influences the size of your brush. At its default value of 1.00, the brush is its original size. With this slider, you can make your brush anywhere from one one-hundredth (0.01) of its original size to 10 times larger.

- **Aspect Ratio** — With this slider, you can stretch your brush vertically or horizontally. The numbers in this slider are calculated by dividing the brush's relative width by its height. The default value of 1.00 is a 1/1 ratio. Values greater than 1.00 make your brush shorter, and values less than 1.00 make your brush thinner.

- **Angle** — This slider has values in degrees and has a range from −180 to 180. It controls the angle that your brush is applied to the canvas. One thing to note is that if you've adjusted your tool's aspect ratio, you might expect your thinner or shorter brush outline to rotate as you change the Angle slider. However, this doesn't happen. If you do this, the brush is actually rotated within the constraints of the Aspect Ratio value, ultimately causing a shearing effect on your brush.

- **Fade Out** — Enable this option and your paint stroke gets progressively more transparent over a distance that you specify with the slider that appears when you click this check box. The default value is 100 pixels, but you can change it to any length and unit that you'd like.

- **Apply Jitter** — GIMP draws paint strokes by replicating your brush multiple times along the length of the stroke. The spacing between each replication is small enough that it appears as a single line. If you enable this check box and adjust the Amount slider that appears, not only can you increase the spacing between replicated brushes, but also the placement of the replications along your stroke. Increased Amount values give you larger spacing that's less in line with your drawn stroke. Jitter is a good way of creating a shaky line or creating a scatter brush effect.

Those are the settings available for all of GIMP's brush-based paint tools. However, each brush also has its own set of options that relate specifically to how they operate. These specific options are covered in Chapter 4, but here's a quick run-down of these additional options for the tools covered in this chapter:

- **Incremental (Pencil, Paintbrush, Eraser)** — With this check box disabled (the default behavior), the maximum strength of any one stroke is no greater than the brush's opacity. This means that if your Opacity is set to 30, that's the maximum influence your paint stroke has over pixels no matter how many times you run your mouse over them in a single stroke. However, if you enable this option, the brush's influence is increased each time you paint over those pixels. So even if you have a low opacity, it's possible to get a stroke to 100% by drawing over the same area multiple times in a single stroke.

- **Use Color from Gradient (Pencil, Paintbrush, Airbrush)** — By default, GIMP's paint tools use the foreground color as the color that you paint with. However, you can also use any gradient in the Gradients dialog (Ctrl+G) as your color source. Enable this check box and GIMP allows you to select the gradient, how long the gradient should stretch along your brush stroke, and the way the gradient is repeated along the stroke if it's repeated at all.

- **Hard Edge (Eraser)** — By default, the Eraser tool behaves like the Paintbrush tool, allowing you to do sub-pixel paint operations. This means that a pixel can be only partially influenced rather than completely influenced. However, this isn't always what you want. On occasion, you may want the Eraser tool to behave more like the Pencil tool, giving you all-or-nothing control over the pixels you paint over. Enable this check box and that's the result you get. This feature is also available on all of the paint tools covered in Chapter 12.

- **Anti Erase (Eraser)** — As covered in Chapter 7, this tool is exclusive to the Eraser tool. Basically, it allows you to selectively undo an erase operation or reveal areas of an image with a non-premultiplied alpha channel.

- **Rate (Airbrush)** — This option is similar to the Incremental check box. A rudimentary explanation for how a real-world airbrush works is that air is used to push paint particles from the airbrush to the painting surface. If you increase how fast the air goes (its rate), the painted surface gets more paint on it faster. Digitally, the Rate slider gives you the same result. Increase this value, and the influence of your brush (even at low opacities) gets pushed to 100% faster. The Rate slider is also available for the Blur/Sharpen and Smudge tools covered in the next chapter.

- **Pressure (Airbrush)** — When working with a real airbrush, you can increase the amount of paint that gets put on the painting surface by increasing the amount of air and paint that comes out of the brush. This is what the Pressure slider does in GIMP. Think of it as fine control for the Opacity slider.

Quickly Adjusting Brush Settings from the Image Window

Later this chapter covers how you can use GIMP's paint dynamics and a drawing tablet like the ones manufactured by Wacom to provide a more natural means of influencing these brush settings. For instance, Opacity can be bound to how much pressure you apply to the drawing tablet with its pen. Unfortunately, as useful as tablets can be, they're not always affordable for everyone. For people without tablets, painting can be made easier by binding a mouse action or keyboard shortcut to adjust these settings. That way you can adjust the scale or opacity of a brush without having to leave the image window and go to the Tool Options dialog.

As an example, say you want to use your mouse wheel to adjust the Scale setting for your brush. To bind this action, go to GIMP's Preferences window and look in the Input Controllers section (Edit ➢ Preferences; Input Devices ➢ Input Controllers). On the right panel, you should see two active controllers: Main Mouse Wheel and Main Keyboard. Double-click Main Mouse Wheel and you get a dialog like the one in Figure 11-3. You could bind the Scale value directly to the mouse wheel; because you can use your middle mouse button or spacebar to pan the image window, it's not as critical to use the mouse wheel for navigation. However, if you want to keep scrolling for navigation, you can instead bind Scale with scrolling combined with one or more modifier keys like Shift, Ctrl, and Alt. By default, you can see in the Configure Input Controller dialog that brush opacity is already bound to Alt+scroll and brush selection is bound to Shift+Ctrl+scroll.

Personally, I prefer to select my brushes from the Brushes dialog, so this binding is less useful to me. To change a binding — like Scroll Up (Shift+Ctrl) — double-click it or select it and click the Edit button at the bottom of the dialog. This brings up the Select Controller Event Action dialog. Use this dialog to pick the action you want scrolling to control. GIMP has a wide array of actions, so it's helpful to use the Search bar at the top of the dialog. For this example, look for the Increase Brush Scale action. Select that action, click OK, and it's bound to the Shift+Ctrl+scroll up event. Bind Shift+Ctrl+scroll down to Decrease Brush Scale, and you're ready to rock. This method also works for binding keyboard shortcuts to various actions. To make things easy, here is a generic step-by-step process for binding any action to any mouse scroll or key press event:

1. **Open the Preferences window and go to the Input Controllers section (Edit ➢ Preferences; Input Devices ➢ Input Controllers).**

2. **Configure the Active Controller that you want to modify by double-clicking it or selecting it and clicking the Configure button at the bottom of the window.** This brings up the Configure Input Controller dialog.

3. **Edit the event you want to bind by double-clicking it or selecting it and clicking the Edit button at the bottom of the dialog.** This brings up the Select Controller Event Action dialog.

4. **Select the action that you want to bind to your selected event by clicking it and then clicking OK.** The action list is long, so make use of the Search bar to find your desired action.

5. **When you're finished binding events to actions, click Close on the Configure Input Controller dialog and click OK in the Preferences window.** Your events are now bound to your desired actions. You should be able to see them working in the image window.

Figure 11-3 shows how this process works for binding Shift+Ctrl+scroll up to increasing your brush scale.

FIGURE 11-3

Binding a mouse scroll event to adjust your brush scale

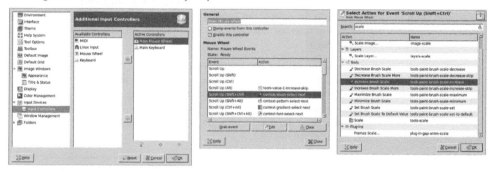

Creating New Brushes

The settings that are available to you in the Tool Options dialog give you a lot of control, but you're still bound to the initial size, shape, transparency, and even color of the brush you've selected for your painting tool. If you want absolute control, you need to be able to edit the brush itself. You manage this from the Brushes dockable dialog (Shift+Ctrl+B). Refer back to the central dialog in Figure 11-2 if you need a visual aid (or you don't currently have GIMP open on your computer). Before diving too heavily into editing brushes, it's worth taking a moment to understand the information that the Brushes dialog provides you. The first thing to note is that most brushes in this dialog have a small plus sign in the lower-right corner. This indicates that the actual brush is larger than its preview shows. You can see the full-size brush by clicking it and holding down your mouse button. This floats a small window that shows the brush at its full size.

Some of these brushes have a red triangle in the lower-right corner. These are animated brushes. They're covered in more detail later in this chapter, but to get a good idea of what an animated brush does, click one and keep your mouse button held down like you're previewing a large brush's full size. The preview window that appears for these brushes cycles through each of the frames of the animated brush so you get to see the sequence used by the animated brush.

Some of the brushes in the Brushes dialog carry their own color. This is particularly true of the notorious Pepper brush as well as the Sparks and Vine animated brushes. These brushes are based on image templates and carry color information with them. This means that if you change the foreground color while using one of these brushes, it's not going to affect the color of your paint stroke. The Pepper is always green with a reddish shadow.

Tagging and Filtering Resources

A new feature for GIMP 2.8 enables you to assign *tags*, or descriptive words, to resources such as brushes, paint dynamics settings, gradients, and patterns. One of the problems with having a large number of preset resources like these is that it can often be tough to find the exact resource that you're looking for. These tags, when combined with filtering, are a great way to organize and manage those resources. For instance, you can tag all of your animated brushes as `animated` and all of your gritty brushes as `grunge`. Then you can filter for brushes using either or both of those tags and have them display in the Brushes dialog.

Tags are assigned in the dockable dialog for each resource. Below the list of resources is a Tags text field. The quickest way to assign a tag is to select a resource and then type the tag you want to use. Each tag is separated with a comma. If a resource already has tags, you can see them listed in the Tags field. You can also click the down arrow on the right of the Tags field and see a list of available tags that you've already used. Tags assigned to the selected resource are highlighted and you can toggle whether or not they're assigned by clicking them.

At the top of the resource's dialog is another text field for filtering your resources. You can type a search term and if it matches any of the tags that you have assigned, those resources appear in the list or grid below. Clicking the down arrow to the right of this field also gives you a list of tags you've already used on your available resources. You can then click the tags to filter for. The following figure shows the Brushes dialog and a brush selected that's been assigned with a couple tags as well as the Brushes dialog that's been filtered with brushes tagged as `animated`.

On the left is the Brushes dialog with a selected brush that's been assigned tags for being animated and grungy. On the right is the same dialog filtering to show all brushes that have been tagged as animated.

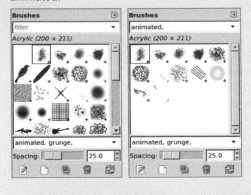

The quickest way to create a new brush is to select a region of an image and Copy (Ctrl+C) or Cut (Ctrl+X). This instantly places your copied region in the first location of the Brushes dialog grid. Click that first brush (the Clipboard brush) and that copied region is treated as its own brush. This is a great, quick way to create and use a temporary brush. If you want a more permanent brush from your selection you can go to Edit ➤ Paste as ➤ New Brush. This brings up a small dialog like the one shown in Figure 11-4 that allows you to name your brush and control the spacing between replications of that brush. Click OK and your copied region gets its own space in the Brushes window.

FIGURE 11-4

The New Brush dialog that appears when you have a selection copied to the system clipboard and you use Edit ➤ Paste as ➤ New Brush

The only downside to these techniques is that the Clipboard brush and your pasted brush are color-locked. They use only colors from your original selection and don't use your chosen foreground color at all. To get that effect, you need to use a different technique.

Using the Brush Editor to Create Procedural Brushes

If you double-click any of the brushes in the Brushes dialog, GIMP provides you with a Brush Editor window like the one shown in Figure 11-5. Note that if you double-click any of the preset brushes that ship with GIMP, all sliders in the Brush Editor are grayed out and unavailable for you to edit. To have editable settings in the Brush Editor, you need to have a custom brush of your own.

FIGURE 11-5

GIMP's Brush Editor allows you to procedurally create and modify brushes, but only for custom brushes (right). Preset brushes (left) cannot be edited.

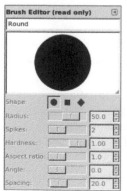 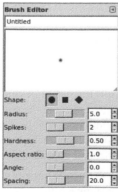

The easiest way to create a custom brush is by clicking the Create a New Brush button at the bottom of the Brushes dialog. Alternatively, you can right-click in the Brushes dialog and use one of the options provided there. For creating new procedural brushes, you have the following options:

- **New Brush** — This performs the same function as the Create a New Brush button. It creates a new brush named Untitled and pops up the Brush Editor dialog if it's not already available.

- **Duplicate Brush** — If the brush you've right-clicked is procedural, you can make a copy of that brush and use the Brush Editor to modify it.

- **Preset Starter Brushes** — The four options at the bottom of the right-click menu (Elliptical, Feathered; Elliptical; Rectangular, Feathered; and Rectangular) give you a head start on creating your custom brush. Rather than using the defaults in the Brush Editor that the New Brush operation gives you, these menu options act as presets so you can create your custom brush more quickly.

The Brush editor gives you a nice, procedural means of creating and editing *parametric* brushes. In fact, for full custom control, some GIMP artists create a specific custom brush that they continually edit with the Brush Editor as necessary while they're painting. When creating a custom brush with the Brush Editor, the first thing you should do is give your brush a name. Do this by typing in the text field at the top of the editor. The default name for new brushes is Untitled. It's definitely a good idea to pick a name that's more distinct than that. You have access to seven different control options:

- **Shape** — GIMP's procedural brushes can take three primary shapes: Circle, Square, or Diamond. Click any one of these shapes to define the starting point for your brush.

- **Radius** — The Radius slider defines, in pixels, the size of your brush from its center to its farthest outlying point.

- **Spikes** — This setting is a bit of a misnomer because it doesn't necessarily create spikes by itself. To really get a spike shape, use this slider in conjunction with the Aspect Ratio slider. Spikes are generated by replicating half of your brush and rotating it about the center point. If your Aspect Ratio is set to 1.0, increasing Spikes on a Circle brush does nothing, whereas increasing spikes on Square or Diamond brushes give it a more faceted appearance.

- **Hardness** — As its name implies, this slider defines how hard or soft the edge of your brush is. Higher values make your brush behave more like the Pencil tool and lower values are best suited to the Paintbrush tool.

- **Aspect Ratio** — Simply put, this slider controls the height of your brush. With the default value of 1.0, your brush's width and height are equal. As you increase the Aspect Ratio, your brush becomes shorter and shorter until it's a thin horizontal line. Use this slider in conjunction with the Spikes slider to control the thickness of each spike and use it with the Angle slider to rotate it off its flat horizontal appearance.

- **Angle** — This slider, with a range from 0 to 180 degrees, rotates your brush about its center by that amount. This is useful if you're creating a calligraphic brush.

- **Spacing** — As previously mentioned, GIMP makes paint strokes by replicating your brushes with such a fine spacing that it appears as a single stroke. However, on some occasions you might prefer more space between each replicated brush mark. Adjust this slider to tweak that spacing to your liking. Also note that this is the only brush editing slider that's quickly accessible from the Brushes dialog. You can adjust this value without actually opening the Brush Editor. The thing to know about the Spacing slider is that it's measured in a percentage relative to the diameter of the brush. When you set Spacing to 100.0, none of the brush replications that create your stroke overlap. Set the Spacing to its maximum value of 200.0 and a full brush diameter of empty space is placed between each replicated brush shape.

Like the sliders in the Tool Options dialog, you're able to use the Input Controllers interface in the Preferences window (Edit ➤ Preferences; Input Devices ➤ Input Controllers) to bind their action to any mouse wheel or keyboard event. So with a custom brush added to the Brushes dialog, you're actually free to modify the parametric settings in the Brush Editor while you paint.

Creating Animated and Bitmap Brushes

When working with the Brushes dialog, you may notice that not all brushes can be duplicated from the right-click menu. In fact, quite a few of them have that option grayed out because the Brush Editor allows you to duplicate only parametric brushes. For bitmap and animated brushes, the Brush Editor isn't particularly useful. Modifying these kinds of brushes is a more involved task, so the workflow of duplicate and tweak doesn't work as well. It's for this exact reason that the Open Brush as Image option is available at the top of the right-click context menu in the Brushes dialog. This is one of the easiest ways to see and edit an existing GIMP brush. It opens up the brush in a GIMP image window where you can tweak and adjust it to your liking. Of course, that also means that any image you create in GIMP could potentially be turned into a brush that one of the paint tools could use.

Creating a Bitmap Brush

Whether you've opened an existing brush as an image or created a new brush from scratch, turning your image into a brush that appears in the Brushes dialog follows the same process. You export the file into GIMP's .gbr brush file format and locate the file in a folder where GIMP looks for brushes. To review where GIMP is storing brushes, look in the Folders section Preferences window, specifically the section for Brushes (Edit ➤ Preferences; Folders ➤ Brushes). That's the path where you want to export your brush. Once you know where the file must go, export it (Shift+Ctrl+E) and use the File Chooser to navigate to that location on your hard drive. Make sure you type .gbr at the end of your filename or choose GIMP Brush (*.gbr) as the file type at the bottom of the file chooser. When you click the Save button, you get a dialog like the one in Figure 11-6, which enables you to give your brush a unique name and define the default spacing that it has when you paint with it.

Click the Refresh Brushes button at the bottom right of the Brushes dialog to get your brush to appear in the grid. By default, the brushes in the Brushes dialog are arranged in alphabetical order according to their names, so if you exported your brush to the correct folder, it should appear in its proper location here.

FIGURE 11-6

GIMP's brush saving dialog lets you name your brush and define its default spacing.

Note

If you went through the process outlined earlier of turning a selection into a brush by copying the selection (Ctrl+C) and pasting it as a new brush (Edit ➤ Paste as ➤ New Brush), you've actually already gone through all of the steps necessary to create a bitmap brush. The only difference is that with that process, GIMP helped automate things for you a bit. ■

Tip

It's important to note the color mode that you're using when you export your .gbr file. If you use the RGB color mode, GIMP treats your brush like the Clipboard brush; retaining all color information and disregarding the color you have chosen as your foreground color. If you want your brush to make use of the foreground color, convert it to the Grayscale color mode. When you do this, white pixels are completely transparent and non-white pixels use the foreground color, with black pixels using it at full opacity and gray pixels using the color on a semi-transparent scale. ■

Creating an Animated Brush

On the surface, creating an animated brush in GIMP is an incredibly simple task. It's very much like creating an animated GIF as covered in Chapter 19, where each GIMP layer is an individual frame in the animation. Though you can certainly create basic animated brushes with this method, GIMP gives you the opportunity to create animated brushes that are much more complex, responding to drawing angle and speed as well as using special features of drawing tablets like pressure and tilt.

First things first, though: a simple example. Use layers to define the frames, or *cells*, of your animated brush. Remember that the same base rules for bitmap brushes also apply for animated brushes. So if you want your animated brush to make use of your chosen foreground color, make sure that you've set the image's color mode to grayscale (Image ➤ Mode ➤ Grayscale) and use layers without alpha channels. However, if you're making a brush like the Sparks or Vine brush that ships with GIMP, keep your image mode in RGB and make use of alpha channels on each layer. Regardless of your methodology, you should end up with an image consisting of multiple layers, where each layer is an individual cell of animation. Once you have your cells created, you can export your brush for use in the Brushes dialog. Animated brushes go in the same folder as bitmap brushes. The only difference is the file format that you're exporting to. Instead of exporting to the .gbr file format, you want to export to GIMP's .gih (short for *GIMP Image Hose*, also known as the GIMP Image Pipe) animated brush format. When you click the Save button from the File Chooser, you should get a dialog like the one in Figure 11-7. This is where all of the magic happens for defining your animated brush.

FIGURE 11-7

The Export Image as Brush Pipe dialog (left) is where you define the behavior of your animated brush. On the right is the Layers dialog for an animated brush, where each cell is a number from 0 to 9.

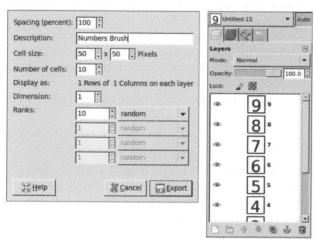

Tip

When creating brushes with the layer-based method, your layers don't actually have to all be the same size. You're free to vary them as much as you want. ■

The following is a description of each setting in this dialog:

- **Spacing (percent)** — This setting works like the spacing sliders in the Brush Editor and the Brushes dialog. It's the percentage of the brush's diameter that determines when the next replicated brush stamp is drawn in a stroke. A value of 100 ensures that replications don't overlap one another at all.

- **Description** — This is the name of your brush as it will appear in the Brushes dialog.

- **Cell Size** — These values are preset to be the width and height of the image you're using to create your animated brush. If you're using layers to create your animated cells, the cell size should be the same as your canvas size.

- **Number of Cells** — This is the number of cells in your animated brush. In the example brush in Figure 11-6, there are 10 cells, each with a numeral from 0 to 9, so the value in this field needs to be set to 10 to make all cells viewable.

- **Display As** — Using Layers isn't the only way that you can create animated brushes. You can use a grid-based technique like what's commonly used in 2D sprite-based video games. The Display As value isn't something you can set explicitly, but it does provide you information as to how GIMP will convert your image into an animated brush. For a solely layer-based animated brush, it should say "1 Rows of 1 Columns on each layer."

- **Dimension** — To create the more complex animated brushes, GIMP uses a data structure known as a multi-dimensional array and this value controls how many dimensions the array has, up to four. For a simple animated brush where each layer is a single cell, you're using a one-dimensional array, so leave this setting at its default value of one.

- **Ranks** — Ranks become very important when you're dealing with a complex animated brush that makes use of a multi-dimensional array. Each of the four values and drop-down menus corresponds to a dimension in the array. The numeric text field indicates the number of cells that belong to that rank and the drop-down menu dictates the order and method that GIMP uses for painting each cell of your animated brush. If you're only using a one-dimensional array, only the first Rank value is available. In that case, make sure the numeric text field has the same value as Number of Cells. Once you do that, you have a few options to control how each cell is painted:

  - **Incremental** — Simply put, each cell is painted in order and when the brush reaches the final cell, the sequence starts again.

  - **Angular** — This mode is pretty interesting. Each cell in your brush is assigned a direction. The first cell is in the upward direction. From there, GIMP divides 360 degrees by the number of cells in your brush and works clockwise, assigning each cell a direction. For example, if you have eight cells in your animated brush and you choose Angular, each cell would be painted in one of the 45-degree directions. With this you could pretty easily make a brush that paints footsteps in the direction of your brush stroke.

  - **Random** — As advertised, this mode takes the available cells and paints them in a random order along the brush stroke.

  - **Velocity/Pressure/Tilt** — These modes act similarly to the Angular mode. Although the Pressure and X/Y Tilt behaviors require a drawing tablet, they all basically work the same way. Your available cells are spread along the spectrum of speed, pressure, or tilt values and assigned to cover a range of that spectrum. As you move your mouse or press or tilt your tablet pen, GIMP evaluates what speed, pressure, or tilt you're using and paints the appropriate cell from your brush.

Using Layers isn't the only way to create animated brushes. An alternative method is to use the same technique that 2D video game artists use for sprite-based video games. You can use a single layer and break that layer up into a grid. Each grid square serves as a cell in your animated brush. To pull this off, you need to make sure your grid is evenly spaced. GIMP's guides really come in handy for this. Then, once you have your grid set up, use the same process to save a .gih file, but make sure that your Cell Size in the Export Image as Brush Pipe dialog is not the same as your image's canvas size. Instead, be sure that the Cell Size matches the size of each cell in your grid. Once you do that and define the Number of Cells value, the export dialog should have something different next to the Display As label. Rather than saying "1 Rows of 1 Columns on each layer" like in the previous example, it should have Rows and Columns values that match your grid. Assuming you're still using a one-dimensional array, the Dimension and Ranks values should remain the same. Figure 11-8 shows the exact same brush created in Figure 11-7, but this time created with a single layer and grid.

FIGURE 11-8

The Export Image as Brush Pipe dialog and the necessary image to re-create the same brush in Figure 11-7 using just a single layer rather than multiple ones. At the bottom is a quick image made with these brushes.

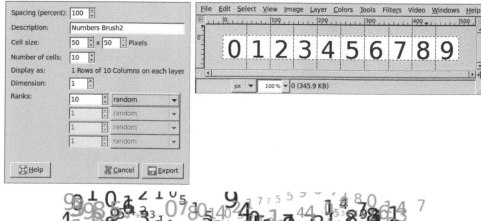

Note

You may notice that any animated brush you open as an image (right-click in the Brushes dialog and choose Open Brush as Image) appears as a set of layers, regardless of whether it was created with the grid method. It's for this reason that you should also save your brushes in GIMP's native XCF format in addition to exporting to the .gih format. That way you maintain your organizational structure and layer names if you ever want to tweak the brush in the future. ■

But wait, there's more! By using multi-dimensional arrays and possibly combining both the layer and grid techniques, you can make some extremely complex animated brushes. Say, for example, you want to be able to paint a marching line of ants (the bugs, not the marching ants that are used to outline a selection) in the direction of your paint stroke, but you want each ant to be one of three different colors. This is completely doable using a multi-dimensional array. To achieve this effect, you first need to figure out how many images you need and how you're going to organize them. For this example, the easiest solution is to use layers to define the direction of your ants and use a grid on each layer to vary the color. Figure 11-9 shows the layer structure and images needed to create this brush.

FIGURE 11-9

To create multi-colored ants marching in eight different directions, you can use this structure for your animated brush.

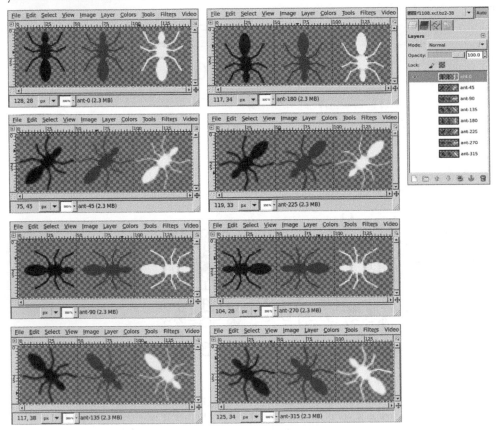

Once you have your layers and grids set up, it's time to export the `.gih` file. Press Shift+Ctrl+E to export and find GIMP's brushes folder in the file chooser. When you click Save, you get the Export Image as Brush Pipe dialog. Configure the dialog as shown in Figure 11-9. You've created a two-dimensional array with eight layers and three images in a grid for each layer. This means that you have a total of 24 cells (8 x 3 = 24). Enter this value in the Number of Cells field. Also make sure that your Cell Size values match the size of the images in your grid and not the canvas size. In this example, each ant fits a 50 x 50 pixel space, so even though the canvas is 150 x 50 pixels, the Cell Size should be set to be 50 x 50. Because you're using a two-dimensional array, set the Dimensions value to 2. Now, in the Ranks section, the first dimension is going to dictate direction. Set the value here to match your number of layers (8) and use the drop-down menu to set the drawing mode to Angular. For the second dimension, use the value to match the number of images per layer (3) and define the mode as Random. Once you click Export and refresh the Brushes dialog, your new animated brush should be available to you. Figure 11-10 shows the export dialog for the colored ants brush as well as an example of that brush stroked along a spiral path.

FIGURE 11-10

Using the proper values in the Export Image as Brush Pipe dialog (left) yields you an animated brush that can be re-used whenever you need it. The image on the right is the Colored Ants brush stroked along a spiral path.

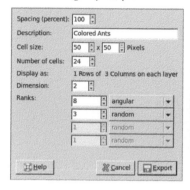

Paint Dynamics and Using Brushes with a Drawing Tablet

One of the really great additions to GIMP 2.8 is an enhanced paint dynamics engine. Earlier versions of GIMP had a rudimentary system of brush dynamics that would react to various inputs from drawing tablets such as pen pressure and tilt. These inputs would be bound to various brush settings like opacity, scale, and angle. The paint dynamics in GIMP 2.8 offer the same thing but with more options and improved performance. Furthermore, you don't necessarily have to have a tablet to take advantage of them (although it's certainly nicer if you do. See Appendix B for more information on getting your tablet to work with GIMP).

By default, all of GIMP's brushes have paint dynamics activated. You can see this by choosing a painting tool and painting a stroke across your canvas. You should notice that the faster you move your mouse while painting, the thinner the paint stroke gets. This is because the default dynamics preset, Basic Dynamics, binds Velocity to Size. To see this, open the Paint Dynamics dockable dialog (Windows ➢ Dockable Dialogs ➢ Paint Dynamics). This has a list of preset dynamics behaviors that you can use with any brush-based painting tool. Figure 11-11 shows the Paint Dynamics dialog as well as the Paint Dynamics Editor for Basic Dynamics and a custom dynamics setting.

As with the set of preset brushes that ships with GIMP, you cannot directly edit the default Paint Dynamics settings. However, you can create new dynamics behaviors by clicking the New Dynamics button at the bottom of the Paint Dynamics dialog or by right-clicking in the dialog and choosing the New Dynamics option from the context menu that appears. From here, you're presented with a grid that allows you to bind brush attributes (Opacity, Hardness, Rate, Size,

Aspect Ratio, Color, Angle, Jitter) to various input device values (Pressure, Velocity, Direction, Tilt, Random, Fade). Of these input device values, only Pressure and Tilt require that you have a drawing tablet to take advantage of them. Any of the other settings can be used with a regular mouse.

FIGURE 11-11

From left to right, the Paint Dynamics dialog, the Paint Dynamics Editor for the default Basic Dynamics preset, and the Paint Dynamics Editor for a set of custom settings

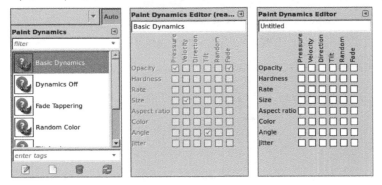

To bind a brush attribute to an input device value, just click the check box where they intersect. Looking back at Figure 11-11, you can see that the Basic Dynamics preset binds Opacity to Pressure and Fade, Size to Velocity, and Angle to Tilt. These default settings are often enough to get you through any painting project. However, many digital artists prefer to leave the Paint Dynamics Editor open and make adjustments to a custom paint dynamics preset as necessary. Other artists prefer to have a wide array of preset dynamics settings that they can call forth at will. For these users, the Paint Dynamics dialog features the resource tagging and filtering features that are also available in the Brushes dialog.

GIMP Paint Studio – A Painter-Friendly Batch of Presets

In Appendix D, one of the resource web sites that I point you to is one for GIMP Paint Studio, or GPS, a set of brushes and artist-friendly presets created by GIMP artist Ramón Miranda. Because GIMP is not designed with the primary intent of being a pure digital painting application, it can be an arduous and time-consuming process to put together a set of brushes and tool presets in GIMP that fit the needs of digital painters. Fortunately, we have GPS to help out with this. To get these presets, go to the GPS web site (http://code.google.com/p/gps-gimp-paint-studio/) and download it from there. It's also a good idea to download the PDF manual for GPS. It will aid you with the installation process and it gives some pretty good tips for getting the most of out of GPS.

One word of warning: GPS's presets cover a little bit more than just brushes and other tools. It also slightly rearranges your workspace to fit more closely to the classic digital painting environment. This means that some portions of this book and some of the figures may appear differently than the way they work in GPS. It's not a huge deal, but it's worth mentioning to help avoid confusion.

Also know that GPS won't turn you into a magnificent digital painter overnight any more than a pen or pencil will. You still need to know fundamentals of drawing, color, composition, and light. That said, the presets in GPS certainly help make the process go more smoothly. As an example, Figure 11-12 was painted by David Revoy as concept art for the Durian open movie project, hosted by the Blender Foundation. It was created using only GIMP and the GPS presets created by Ramón Miranda.

FIGURE 11-12

A character design painted in GIMP using presets provided by GIMP Paint Studio (Artwork credit: David Revoy www.davidrevoy.com)

Drawing Calligraphic Lines with the Ink Tool

The purpose of the Ink tool (K) is to simulate the behavior of drawing with an ink pen. It's like working with the Pencil tool, but with the added benefit of nicely antialiased edges. If you activate the Ink tool, one of the first things you may notice is that it doesn't share the same brush engine as the rest of GIMP's painting tools. The biggest thing to notice is that the Ink tool's brushes are completely parametric; they're generated procedurally and controlled entirely from the Ink tool's Tool Options dialog. Figure 11-13 shows the Tool Options dialog for the Ink tool.

FIGURE 11-13

The Ink tool's brushes are parametric and completely controlled from the Tool Options dialog.

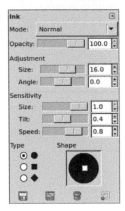

Most of the Ink tool's settings are roughly the same as those for GIMP's brush-based painting tools. You have all the same painting modes available in the Mode drop-down and you still have an Opacity slider to control the strength of the Ink tool. Beyond that, though, the Ink tool has a few settings that are unique to it. The first thing to notice is that the settings are broken down into three separate sections: Adjustment, Sensitivity, and Type. The second thing to notice is that it appears as if the settings in each of these sections are the same or very close to one another. For instance, a Size slider appears under both Adjustment and Sensitivity. And Angle, Tilt, and Shape all seem to be three terms that mean about the same thing. What gives?

The answer comes back to the point that the Ink tool is designed to simulate the behavior of drawing with an ink pen, like a fountain pen. The tips of these pens — called *nibs* — have some flexibility and give a bit as you draw with them, causing the size and appearance of your stroke to change as you go along. Bearing this in mind, it's best to think of the values under the Adjustment setting as the initial size and angle that the Ink tool's virtual nib has. Size gives you a range in pixels from 0.01 to 200 and Angle gives the angle of the nib between −90 and 90 degrees relative to an initial state of horizontal.

By the same token, the Type and Shape controls can also be deemed as initialization values. Like the brush-based paint tools, you can choose for the Ink tool to use an initial shape of Circle, Square, or Diamond. However, unlike those other tools, you can use the Shape controller to manipulate the angle and aspect ratio of the brush simultaneously. Simply click the white rectangle at the center of the Shape control and drag your mouse around. You should see the shape become thinner and rotate to match the location of your mouse cursor.

The values that really give the Ink tool its dynamic appearance are under the Sensitivity setting. Think of these as variable versions of the Paint Dynamics settings for the brush-based painting tools. You have three sliders: Size, Tilt, and Speed. All are in relative units with a range from

0.0 to 1.0. They define how much the Ink tool's nib varies over the course of a stroke. Setting them to 1.0 indicates that the full range is to be used. At reduced values, their influence is more slight. Both the Size and Speed sliders influence the size of the Ink tool's stroke and the Tilt slider influences the apparent tilt of the nib relative to horizontal. You can see the influence of these sliders when using a mouse, but the most pronounced results can be found by using the Ink tool with a drawing tablet. You can also get some very powerful results by combining the Ink tool with stroking paths and emulating dynamics along the path, as shown in Chapter 5.

Working with Gradients

One of the easiest ways to fill an empty layer in GIMP is to use the Blend tool (L). As explained in Chapter 4, this tool uses colors defined by a gradient and fills an area while smoothly transitioning from one color in the gradient to the next. Gradients are useful for all sorts of things. At their simplest, you can create a more interesting background for your image than a straight solid color. In more complex applications, you can use gradients and the Blend tool to define depth maps, simulate chrome reflections, and even produce effects like fire and lens flares.

Using the Blend tool, you can define the gradient's *vector* (size and direction) by clicking anywhere in the image window to define the starting point and dragging your mouse to the desired location of the gradient's ending point. Like any of the painting tools, if you hold Ctrl while defining the end point, the gradient's vector is locked to 15-degree increments relative to the start point.

The Tool Options for the Blend tool are covered in Chapter 4, so I won't repeat them here. However, this section covers how you can use the Gradients dialog (Ctrl+G) to get the most out of the Blend tool. Figure 11-14 shows the Gradients dialog.

FIGURE 11-14

GIMP's Gradients dialog enables you to view and customize gradients for use by the Blend tool.

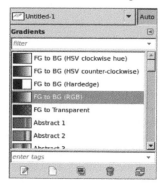

Like the Brushes dialog and the Paint Dynamics dialog, the Gradients dialog allows for resource tagging and filtering so your can more easily manage the large number of gradients available to you. Also as in those other dialogs, you cannot directly edit the preset gradients that ship with

GIMP. To edit an existing gradient, you must first duplicate it by clicking the Duplicate button at the bottom of the dialog or by right-clicking the desired gradient and choosing Duplicate Gradient from the context menu that appears. You can also build a gradient from scratch by choosing New Gradient from this same context menu. Either way you go, you should get a Gradient Editor dialog like the one in Figure 11-15.

The Gradient Editor is deceptively simple. Within the large gradient area of the editor, you can click and drag the triangular-shaped sliders around to define the start and end points for each color in the gradient. If the Instant Update check box is enabled (it is by default), you can see your changes to the gradient happening in real time. Notice that the sliders alternate in color. This is because each black slider defines a color and each white triangle controls the nature of the transition between colors. The space between black sliders is referred to as a gradient *segment*. You can select a segment by clicking it in the editor. This means clicking in the area where the sliders reside. Clicking the gradient preview doesn't do anything to select segments. You can select a group of segments by clicking one and then Shift+clicking another segment. Those two segments, as well as all segments between them, are then selected.

FIGURE 11-15

GIMP's Gradient Editor on the left and the right-click context menu for that editor on the right.

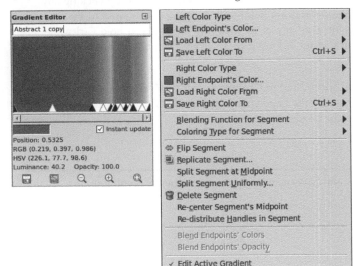

On complex gradients with a high number of colors, it's worth it to zoom in on the gradient area by using the zoom buttons at the bottom of the editor or by using Ctrl+mouse wheel in the gradient area. Then you can use the horizontal scrollbar to home in on a specific color in the gradient. Also, as you run your mouse over the gradient, the editor provides you with feedback in the form of the position of your mouse as well as the RGB, HSV, Luminance, and Opacity of the color directly under your cursor.

To change any of the values in the gradient, you need to use the right-click context menu for the Gradient Editor. If you need a review of its contents, refer back to Figure 11-15. Following is a description of each of the options in this context menu:

- **Left/Right Color Type** — This submenu allows you to define the color of the left or right end of your segment. This is the color controlled by the black slider. With this menu item you get a submenu that has the following options:

  - **Fixed** — This allows you to define a color using GIMP's color picker. It also allows you to use colors that you'd previously saved or used in the color picker. If you choose this option, you need to set the color using the Left/Right Endpoint's Color menu item to pull up that color picker dialog.

  - **Foreground/Background Color** — You can also have the color for a segment's endpoint be defined by the current foreground or background color. This gives your gradient some flexibility if you need something more generic that you can reuse in the figure with different foreground or background colors.

  - **Foreground/Background Color (Transparent)** — This option is the same as the Foreground/Background Color option, except it adjusts the alpha channel for your color so it's completely transparent.

- **Left/Right Endpoint's Color** — If you decided to have your segment's endpoint colors defined by a specific, fixed color, this is where you define that color. If the Left/Right Color Type menu is set to anything other than Fixed, this option is grayed out and unavailable.

- **Load Left/Right Color From** — This option brings up a submenu with an array of color presets. The first four are defined by neighboring segments as well as the foreground and background colors. The lower ten presets are values that you can define with the next menu option.

- **Save Left/Right Color To** — This option brings up a submenu similar to the previous one, but instead of pulling a color from the submenu, this option allows you to set the colors in the submenu. This is extremely useful if you need to reuse a color over and over again within a gradient.

- **Blending Function for Segment** — This option brings up a submenu that allows you to control the nature of the transition from the color at one end of your segment to the other. You can choose for the transition to be Linear, Curved, Sinusoidal, or Spherical in either an increasing or decreasing manner.

- **Coloring Type for Segment** — By default, colors on opposite sides of a segment transition from one to the other in RGB space. However, on occasion, you may want the transition to happen in HSV space, transitioning through unrelated hues as it traverses the segment. This is the menu that allows you to define such a transformation.

- **Flip Segment** — This menu item simply swaps the colors at opposite ends of the selected segment.

- **Replicate Segment** — Choose this option and your selected segment is split into multiple components with identical left and right colors.

- **Split Segment at Midpoint** — This option splits your selected segment into two equal parts. Unlike the Replicate Segments option, the color transition across the two new segments doesn't change.

- **Split Segment Uniformly** — This menu item behaves just like Split Segment at Midpoint, except it opens a dialog that allows you to define the number of new segments created within your original.

- **Delete Segment** — As advertised, this option removes the selected segment.

- **Re-center Segment's Midpoint** — The white triangular sliders on the Gradient Editor are the midpoints for each segment. If you want the midpoint for your selected segment to return to the center of that segment, this is the option to choose.

- **Re-distribute Handles in Segment** — If you have multiple segments selected in a row, this option takes both the black and the white sliders and spaces them out evenly.

- **Blend Endpoints' Colors/Opacity** — If you have a series of segments selected at the same time, you can smooth the transition across the whole bunch by using either of these options. Of course, if you only have one segment selected, these options are grayed out and unavailable.

- **Edit Active Gradient** — This check box is enabled by default. It causes the Gradient Editor to display whatever gradient you have selected in the Gradients dialog.

Creating Pattern Fills

Many people who are just starting with computer graphics are often under the impression that the Bucket Fill tool is only useful for filling a space with solid color. Although that's the primary use for the tool, as explained in Chapter 4, it's not the only use. You can also use the Bucket Fill tool to fill a layer or selection with a pattern. Furthermore, as you see in Chapter 12, patterns are also value assets for the Clone tool. GIMP ships with a wide array of preset patterns that you can use in your images. To see these patterns, open the Patterns dialog (Shift+Ctrl+P), shown in Figure 11-16.

FIGURE 11-16

GIMP's Patterns dialog gives you a wide choice of patterns for breaking up uninteresting portions of your image.

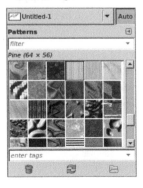

In many ways, the Patterns dialog is like a simplified version of the Brushes dialog. Like the Brushes dialog, the first item in the Patterns dialog is a Clipboard pattern. That pattern is populated with whatever you pulled from your last Copy (Ctrl+C) or Cut (Ctrl+X) operation. You can open any of the preset patterns as an image by right-clicking it in the Patterns dialog and choosing the Open Pattern as Image item from the context menu.

Besides using the Clipboard pattern, the fastest way to create a custom pattern is to use the Paste As menu. Just select what you want to work as a pattern, copy it with Ctrl+C and then go to Edit ➤ Paste as ➤ New Pattern. This brings up a dialog like the one in Figure 11-17 where you can pick both the filename and resource name for your pattern.

The New Pattern dialog that appears when you have data in the clipboard and you choose Edit ➤ Paste as ➤ New Pattern.

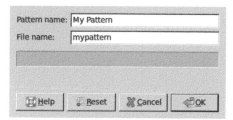

This automatically saves your copied data in GIMP's .pat pattern format and places that file in the appropriate patterns folder. You can do this manually by taking an image and exporting it to the .pat format. The only thing you have to do is make sure you save the pattern file in a folder where GIMP is looking for patterns. To see where your copy of GIMP looks for patterns, open the Preferences window (Edit ➤ Preferences) and look in the Patterns subsection of Folders.

Also note that GIMP has a *lot* of patterns. Fortunately, you can use resource tagging and filtering to help you organize and manage them, just like you can do with the Brushes, Paint Dynamics, and Gradients dialogs. Once you have a pattern created, you're free to use it anywhere it's taken advantage of in GIMP, particularly with the Blend tool and the Clone tool.

Summary

Although GIMP's primary purpose isn't to be a digital painting application, it can actually service that need surprisingly well. This is particularly true considering the features covered in this chapter, such as GIMP's improved Brush Editor and enhanced paint dynamics features. With the presets available through GIMP Paint Studio, GIMP has even more capability as a painting application. You also saw how the Ink tool's features work, giving you the feel of an ink pen with completely parametric configuration options. At the end of the chapter, you saw how to create and modify gradients and patterns for use with the Blend tool and the Bucket Fill tool, respectively. They're kind of the unsung heroes of digital art and now you know how to customize them to your liking in GIMP.

Of course, GIMP's main vision is to be a powerful image editor. The tools covered in the next chapter show how GIMP is exactly that.

Enhancing Photos

One of the explicitly mentioned elements of the official product vision for GIMP is to be a "high-end photo manipulation application [that] supports creating original art from images" (http://gui.gimp.org/index.php/GIMP_UI_Redesign#product_vision). The features and utilities covered so far in this book form the core toolset to service that particular vision. However, the tools covered in this chapter are uniquely geared toward working with photographic content and other images generated from sources outside of GIMP. Technically, these tools — Blur/Sharpen, Smudge, Dodge/Burn, Clone, Healing, and Perspective Clone — fall in the paint tools category, as you can see by going to the Tools ➤ Paint Tools submenu. But in contrast to the other paint tools covered in Chapter 11, these tools are specifically geared toward manipulating image data that already exists on your canvas. For example, with the Paintbrush or Ink tool, you can be presented with a blank canvas and all you have to do is pick color and have at it; painting a brand-new image from whole cloth if you will. If you try to do that with the Clone tool, however, the results are going to be far less impressive. In fact, on a blank canvas, there will be no perceptible results at all.

This chapter covers in more detail tools that were briefly discussed in Chapter 4 and gives you more hints at how to apply them in your work. Of course, because these tools fall in the paint tools category, they have many of the features of the other paint tools, including custom brushes, paint dynamics, and paint modes. That being the case, you may find it useful to review the first section of Chapter 11 before diving into the content here.

IN THIS CHAPTER

Understanding how GIMP's tools relate to traditional photographer tools

Getting the most out of cloning and healing brushes

Using the Exposure Blend plug-in for high dynamic range (HDR) tone mapping

Traditional Photographer Tools

The last three tools in GIMP's default Toolbox layout have names and functions that relate back to the days of traditional photography, where images were captured on film and photo manipulation happened in a darkroom (and dinosaurs roamed the earth). Replicating the effects that these tools produce used to involve a lot of time and trickery and there was no Undo if you messed up or simply didn't achieve the desired results. Fortunately, modern digital photographers and artists don't have to deal with these "character-building" exercises. What remains are digital versions of these processes that can be applied, reversed, and otherwise experimented with free of the expense of throwing away failed versions and restarting the whole process anew. We live in the future ... and it's awesome.

Blur/Sharpen

Also referred to as the Convolve tool, the Blur/Sharpen tool works as expected: it allows you to selectively blur or sharpen portions of your image with the control and flexibility afforded by GIMP's brush engine. The word *convolve* refers to a mathematical operation used to alter the appearance of an image. For more on convolution, have a look at Chapter 15 in the "Convolution Matrix" section. In the case of this tool, you have two convolve operations to choose between: blur and sharpen. When you blur, GIMP causes the pixels within the space of your brush to smooth out and share the color of pixels adjacent to them. Sharpening, the natural inverse procedure, attempts to increase the contrast between pixels, isolating their colors from their neighbors.

Note

It's important to know that the Blur/Sharpen tool was referred to as the Convolve tool in older versions of GIMP. In fact, hold-overs from that still exist because when you look at Edit ➤ Undo, if your last operation was using the Blur/Sharpen tool it will say Undo Convolve instead of Undo Blur/Sharpen. This may be fixed in future versions of GIMP, but until that point, it's worthwhile to know this tidbit so you're not confused by a menu item. ∎

The thing to note is that the Blur/Sharpen tool is for selected use. If you want to blur or sharpen your entire image in a single pass, you're better off using Filters ➤ Blur ➤ Gaussian Blur and Filters ➤ Enhance ➤ Unsharp Mask, respectively. You can find more on these filters in Chapter 13. To activate this tool, use the Shift+U keyboard shortcut, click its water-drop icon in the Toolbox, or choose it from Tools ➤ Paint Tools ➤ Blur/Sharpen. Regardless of the method you choose, your mouse cursor should change to include the Blur/Sharpen icon and reveal the brush outline for your chosen brush. Additionally, if you have the Tool Options dialog open, it automatically updates to show the options available for this tool. Figure 12-1 shows a screenshot of the Blur/Sharpen tool's cursor and its Tool Options.

The Blur/Sharpen tool shares mostly the same tool options as any of the other paint tools, including custom brushes and paint dynamics, with only a few exceptions. For one, the Mode drop-down menu at the top of the Tool Options dialog is grayed out and inaccessible. It simply doesn't make sense to apply a painting mode to a blurring or sharpening operation. Besides that change, the only differences are the two options at the bottom of the Tool Options:

- **Convolve Type** — Under this label, you have two radio buttons to choose between: Blur and Sharpen. This is the most basic way to switch between the two operating modes of this tool. By default, Blur is selected. Regardless of which one is selected, though, you can hold down Ctrl while you're working in the image window and you'll activate the functionality of the opposite Convolve Type. This way you can work quickly without having to constantly move your mouse to the Tool Options dialog each time you want to switch.

- **Rate** — This slider controls how intense the blur or sharpen effect is in the area covered by your brush. Like the Airbrush Tool, the Blur/Sharpen tool works progressively, meaning that you can run your brush over the same pixels in a single stroke and the effect is multiplied each time, so your painted area gets progressively more blurry or sharp with each pass. In contrast, if you reduce the Opacity slider for the Blur/Sharpen tool, that limits the maximum strength of your blur or sharpen effect, regardless of how many times you paint over the same pixels.

FIGURE 12-1

When you enable the Blur/Sharpen tool, your mouse cursor updates (left) along with your available tool options (right).

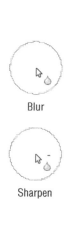

Blur

Sharpen

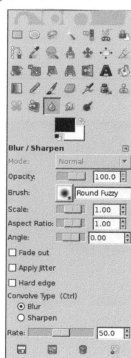

Although the Blur/Sharpen tool is primarily for subtle effects — especially on larger images — it's very handy for applying that last bit of polish when enhancing your photographs. For example, you may want to give an image enhanced *depth of field* (DOF). In photography, depth of field refers to how much of your image is in focus relative to your focal point. If you have a large depth of field, more of your image is in focus. With a smaller, or *shallow* depth of field, your background and foreground are out of focus while your subject remains in focus. Generally speaking, shallow depth of field often creates a more interesting image with more attention on the subject.

Achieving a shallow depth of field in a photograph requires the proper combination of lens aperture, available light, and format size of your camera. Getting this effect right in-camera can be a challenge, especially in low-light situations. Often your resulting image may not be as extreme as you would like, or worse, everything in your photo is in full focus. Fortunately, you can use GIMP to help with this and the Blur/Sharpen tool can play a large part. Figure 12-2 shows an image that has had its depth of field artificially shortened with the help of GIMP.

Tip

On large images, it's not advisable to use only the Blur/Sharpen tool if you're blurring a large area of the image. Blurring can be a processor-intensive task and you may find that your brush lags behind your mouse cursor, especially on larger brushes. In these cases, it's better to use your selection tools to isolate your subject and use the Gaussian Blur filter (Filters ➤ Blur ➤ Gaussian Blur) to blur out the foreground and background. Then you can go in with the Blur/Sharpen tool and clean up edges where your selection is abrupt. ■

FIGURE 12-2

With the help of the Blur/Sharpen tool, the background and foreground of the original image (left) were further blurred to enhance the subject of the photo.

Smudge

The Blur/Sharpen tool is great for general blurring, but on some occasions you want to mix colors from pixels adjacent to one another rather than blurring. You may want to extend part of your image or simulate motion blur without using a filter or you may want to do watercolor-like color mixing. To perform these tasks, you want to use GIMP's Smudge tool, activated by clicking its pointed finger icon in the Toolbox, going to Tools ➤ Paint Tools ➤ Smudge, or using the S keyboard shortcut. Figure 12-3 shows the Smudge tool's mouse cursor and its Tool Options.

Note

This book was written using a development version of GIMP prior to the release of GIMP 2.8. As of this writing, paint dynamics are disabled and not worked for the Smudge tool. This is a bug that will likely be fixed in the future, but if you're using the Smudge tool and you notice paint dynamics not working, this is why. ■

When you enable the Smudge tool, your mouse cursor updates to a paint cursor (left) and your Tool Options are updated to reflect the options for this tool (right).

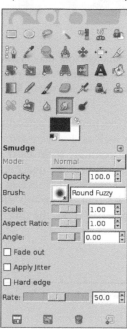

As the figure shows, with the exception of the Convolve Type radio buttons, the Smudge tool shares the same tool options as the Blur/Sharpen tool. If you've ever used finger paints or worked with chalk or charcoal, you should understand how the Smudge tool works. If you click and drag your mouse, the colors from the pixels where you initially clicked are drawn in the direction that you drag your mouse. An obvious application of this tool is digitally mixing colors on your canvas much as a traditional painter may do with real, physical paints. However, it's also incredibly useful when working with digital photographs. For instance, the Smudge tool is a great way to implement a "quick 'n' dirty" motion blur effect. GIMP's built-in Motion Blur filter (Filters ➤ Blur ➤ Motion Blur), covered in Chapter 13, is very useful, but the results tend to be very uniform. Though that may be a bit more realistic, it's often much less interesting to look at. The Smudge tool can give your motion blur a bit more flare. On larger images, it may actually be faster to use the Smudge tool than to wait for the Motion Blur filter to process. Figure 12-4 compares the two methods.

FIGURE 12-4

From left to right, the original image, that image with the Motion Blur filter, and the same image blurred with the Smudge tool (Photo credit: Melody Smith)

Tip

If you use a brush that's been scaled much larger when smudging, the Smudge tool may create spaced replications rather than a smooth blur within the space of the brush. To alleviate this, reduce your brush's scale or use a smaller brush and clean up the spacing after roughing out your initial smudges. ■

An even more interesting use of the Smudge tool is to warp, deform, and extend portions of an image. When used heavily, you can make a photograph look as if it were airbrushed, as you can see in the image on the far right of Figure 12-5. In contrast, when used sparingly, you can enhance and extend select parts of your image. For instance, the image in the center of Figure 12-5 shows the result of using the Smudge tool to just lengthen eyelashes. The effect in this figure is somewhat subtle. Check out this book's companion web site for an animated GIF that flips back and forth between the two images to make the difference more apparent.

FIGURE 12-5

From left to right, the original image, lengthening the eyelashes with the Smudge tool, and softening the same image to appear airbrushed (Photo credit: Melody Smith)

Tip

When using the Smudge tool to extend parts of an image, it's a good idea to duplicate the original layer prior to smudging and work on the duplicate layer. The reason for this is that it's pretty easy to pull the color from more pixels than you want when smudging. Trying to undo and redo the smudge can be a frustrating exercise. However, by duplicating the original layer, you can use the Clone tool (discussed later in this chapter) to repair these unintentionally smudged pixels. ■

Dodge/Burn

Of the tools available in GIMP, the Dodge/Burn tool is probably the most familiar to traditional photographers. Dodging and burning are briefly covered in Chapter 6's coverage of layer modes, but here's a quick review of the terminology. In traditional photography, a photographic print is created in a darkroom by shining light through the developed film negative on to a piece of light-sensitive photographic paper. In the course of doing this, the person creating the print has quite a bit of flexibility. By blocking off some parts of the photographic paper and reducing its exposure to the light being shined through the negative, those parts of the image would be lightened, or *dodged*. By the same measure, other parts of the image could be exposed to the light for a longer period of time and darkened, or *burned*. GIMP's Dodge/Burn tool gives you these same abilities, but with the advantages and additional flexibility of the digital medium. Activate the Dodge/Burn tool by clicking its icon in the Toolbox. It's a dark circle with a diagonal line coming from it. The icon is based on the actual dodging/burning tool used when creating a photo print. I like to think of it as an evil lollipop. You can also activate the Dodge/Burn tool by going to Tools ➤ Paint Tools ➤ Dodge/Burn or using the Shift+D keyboard shortcut. Your mouse cursor and the Tool Options dialog change to look like the cursor and options shown in Figure 12-6.

When you enable the Dodge/Burn tool, your mouse cursor updates to a paint cursor (left) and your Tool Options are updated to reflect the options for this tool (right).

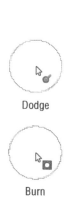

Dodge

Burn

The Dodge/Burn tool shares the same basic options available to other paint tools, but like Blur/Sharpen and Smudge, the Mode drop-down menu is disabled. Of course, Dodge/Burn has some additional options available that are specific to its functionality. In particular, it has two sets of radio buttons and a slider that you can adjust. The following explains each of these options for this tool:

- **Type** — Like the Blur/Sharpen tool, the Dodge/Burn tool is actually two tools with complementary functionality. These radio buttons allow you to choose which function is the primary function. While working, you can quickly access the non-selected function by Ctrl+clicking in the image window.

  - **Dodge** — Lightens the pixels within the area covered by your brush.

  - **Burn** — Darkens the pixels within the area covered by your brush.

- **Range** — To give you a bit of flexibility, the Dodge/Burn tool works only within one of these selected value ranges. The benefit of this is that you won't, for example, blow out your highlights while trying to lighten the shadows in your image. Like with GIMP's Color Balance tool (covered in Chapter 9), you have three ranges to choose from:

  - **Shadows** — The darkest pixels in your image.

  - **Midtones** — This range typically forms the bulk of the pixels in an image and in most cases, you're using the Dodge/Burn tool to create more contrast in this range. For this reason, the Midtones range is enabled by default.

  - **Highlights** — The lightest pixels in your image.

- **Exposure** — This slider has a range from zero to 100 and controls the strength of the dodge or burn effect.

Digital painters love to use the Dodge/Burn tool to add shadows and highlights to their images. This is because the Dodge/Burn tool darkens or lightens pixels without grossly distorting color or obfuscating detail. This is the primary advantage of using this tool over using the Paintbrush tool and trying to choose the proper color for subtle shadows and highlights. The Dodge/Burn tool basically figures out that stuff for you. These same principles that digital painters like can be leveraged by digital photographers to achieve the same results. The Dodge/Burn tool is great for reducing glare, enhancing shadows, and pulling somewhat lost detail from overly dark or light regions of the photo. Figure 12-7 shows an example where the Dodge/Burn tool was used to improve an image taken from a camera phone.

Note

There's one marked difference between GIMP's Dodge/Burn and the dodging and burning that's done in the darkroom. When you dodge and burn in the darkroom, you can often pull "hidden" detail out of parts of the negative that appear over- or underexposed. This is because film has a higher *dynamic range* than digital images do. To achieve something like this digitally, you need to take bracketed photos and use a process known as *tonemapping* to generate a high dynamic range image (HDRI). GIMP does not natively have this ability. However, a plug-in called Exposure Blend has been developed to fill this gap in GIMP's toolchest. See Chapter 21 for details on how to install this plug-in. Use of the Exposure Blend plug-in is covered later in this chapter. ■

FIGURE 12-7

The Dodge/Burn tool was used on the original image (left) to reduce the glare from my grand-mother's glasses, enhance contrast, and create a simple vignette effect around the image border.

Using Cloning and Healing to Fix Problem Areas

Although digital tools that are based on traditional photography workflow are great — especially when transitioning photographers to the digital medium — the really impressive tools are the ones that can't easily be replicated in a traditional darkroom setting. This is where the advantages of working digitally really start to shine. With tools like Clone, Perspective Clone, and Healing, you can repair old images, remove troublesome elements from photos, or even add new elements. Effects like these used to be tricks that would take enormous amounts of time to even attempt to replicate in traditional photography. In digital photography, these tools are used everywhere so often that they're almost taken for granted.

To get a good understanding of what these tools can do, think of them as a more advanced type of copy and paste that you can control with GIMP's paint system. With them, you can very quickly replicate part of any *drawable element* (image, layer, channel, mask) to any other drawable element in your current work session. It's very cool and very, very powerful.

Clone Tool

Say you've taken a portrait of someone and you notice a blemish on their face. No big deal; everyone gets them. However, chances are good that unless you're taking a "before" photo to market a skincare product, that blemish is something that should be removed from the final delivered image. One option to take care of this would be to try to paint it out. The disadvantage of that technique, however, is that you're painting a face and it's pretty easy to tell the difference between a solid paint color and the texture of the face. You could try to mottle things a bit by using a textured brush, but this only helps a little bit and if you don't match the skin tone exactly, it sticks out like a sore thumb. You could also try to make a selection around the blemish and fill that selection with a textured pattern. The downside there, of course, is that it's tough to find the perfect pattern that fits your subject's face.

What you need to use is texture and skin tone that exactly matches your subject. Fortunately, most people have generally even complexions, so there's a good chance that there's another portion of your subject's face that has the tone and texture that you need. You could copy that part of the face, paste it over the blemish, and soften the edges around it so your pasted selection flows with the rest of the face. In essence, this is exactly what GIMP's Clone tool does, but in fewer steps. To activate the Clone tool, click the icon in the Toolbox that looks like a rubber stamp. You can also go to Tools ➤ Paint Tools ➤ Clone or use its keyboard shortcut, C. Figure 12-8 shows the different mouse cursors for the Clone tool as well as its settings in the Tool Options dialog.

FIGURE 12-8

The various mouse cursors employed by the Clone tool (left) and the Clone tool's settings in the Tool Options dialog (right).

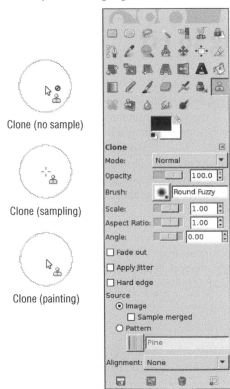

Clone (no sample)

Clone (sampling)

Clone (painting)

When you first activate the Clone tool, notice that although your mouse cursor shows your current brush and the rubber stamp icon, there's also the circular No icon as well. If you try to paint in your image window with this mouse cursor, you get no results and the status area of the image window gives you a message that says "Set a source image first." The typical usage for the Clone tool requires that you first select a sample target on your image or another GIMP layer. For this reason, the default Source in the Clone tool's Tool Options is set to the Image radio button. To set the source, Ctrl+click your drawable element. When you press Ctrl, your mouse cursor changes to crosshairs so you can more precisely select your desired source. Once you set your clone source, you can start painting.

Tip

Be mindful of the layer you're on when you set your clone source. GIMP's default behavior is to use as your source only the drawable element you Ctrl+click. If you want to use what's visible in your image, regardless of what layer was active when you set your source, enable the Sample Merged check box in the Tool Options dialog for the Clone tool. This treats your clone source as a location on your image and paints whatever is visible. This means you can maintain the same source location, but modify what's painted by hiding and showing different layers in your image. ∎

When you paint, you're subject to all the same options available for any other painting tool in GIMP. For example, you're free to adjust the Opacity and Brush type, and use any of the different settings in the Paint Dynamics dockable dialog (Windows ➤ Dockable Dialogs ➤ Paint Dynamics). The painting modes in the Modes drop-down menu of the Tool Options dialog are also available. The best way to think about them is as paintable layer blending modes. The pixels that you paint with the Clone tool have their colors modified according to the rules of each paint mode. If you're cloning a dark portion of your image and painting it on a lighter part using the Lighten Only mode, you're not going to see a lot of change in your image. In contrast, if you change the painting mode to Darken Only, that light area of your image is going to be heavily influenced by your cloned painting.

Of course, the Clone tool has another set of options that specifically correspond to how your paint strokes relate to your clone source. These options are in the last drop-down menu of the Tool Options for the Clone tool: Alignment. This drop-down menu gives you four options:

- **None** — This is the Clone tool's default behavior. Each time you click and drag your mouse to create a paint stroke, it's made relative to your clone source. GIMP maintains no memory of previous strokes, so with this behavior, the Clone tool replicates the same pixels with each stroke.

- **Aligned** — Using this behavior, the Clone tool uses your first stroke to define an offset from your clone source. Each subsequent stroke is relative to that offset. If you choose this option and paint your entire image canvas, it will be as if you used the layer offset feature (Layer ➤ Transform ➤ Offset).

- **Registered** — This option matches the pixel location in your clone stroke with the corresponding location on your clone source. If you use this option and your clone source is on the same layer as your clone stroke, you won't see any change in your image. However, you can see the power of this option when you clone from one layer to another. With this option, you can create a "filter brush" using the following steps:

1. **Duplicate your base layer (Shift+Ctrl+D) or create a new layer from your visible elements (Layer ➤ New from Visible).** Name this layer "Filter Source" or something similarly notable.

2. **Apply a filter to your Filter Source layer.** You can find more on GIMP's filters in Part IV of this book.

3. **Pick the Clone tool (C) and Ctrl+click anywhere on your Filter Source layer to set your clone source.**

4. **Set the Clone tool's Alignment to Registered.** Make sure the Sample Merged check box is disabled.

5. **Hide your Filter Source layer and go to the layer that you want to paint on.** This could be your original base layer or an altogether new layer.

6. **Paint.** Anywhere you paint, the pixels from your Filter Source layer will appear. This is a great way to localize the effect of any filter, tool, or color operation. As a matter of fact, a reverse of this process (duplicating a layer, modifying it, and cloning from the original) is the exact way that the eyelashes lengthened with the Smudge tool in Figure 12-5 were cleaned up.

- **Fixed** — This option offers what is probably the most unique behavior of the Clone tool's Alignment options. It simply repeatedly replicates the pixels under your brush area in your clone source. Although this offers you limited benefits when painting strokes, it's actually very helpful if you're *daubing* the Clone tool by just clicking different parts of your image. The best way to think of this is as if you're treating the Clone tool as a rubber stamp. Each click is a stamp of your clone source sample.

Tip

The official GIMP manual has a really good set of reference images that depict the different Alignment behaviors for the Clone tool. You can see them at `http://docs.gimp.org/en/gimp-tool-clone.html#id3285773`. ∎

Tip

Some other image manipulation programs have a tool called a History Brush. Using the Clone tool and the Registered Alignment option, you can re-create this functionality in GIMP. To do this, duplicate your image (Ctrl+D). Now, in the *original* image, go back in the Undo History dialog (Windows Dockable ➤ Dialogs ➤ Undo History) that you want to clone from. Once you do that, activate the Clone tool (C) with Registered Alignment and Ctrl+click in the original image to set your clone source. Now when you paint in your duplicated image, you get the results from that point in your image's history. The only disadvantage to this trick is that it obliterates the Undo History of your image, so be mindful of that when you do this. ∎

One of the disadvantages of using an image source with the Clone tool is evident when you paint pixels near your clone source's borders. When you're using the Clone tool, GIMP doesn't wrap or tile from your source drawable. If you attempt to clone pixels that don't exist on your source drawable (either off-canvas or beyond your source layer's boundary), the Clone tool simply doesn't paint anything at all. However, if you go to the Tool Options dialog for the Clone tool and set your source to be Pattern instead of Image, the Clone tool operates a little bit differently. When you choose Pattern as your source, there's no need to Ctrl+click anywhere. The

Clone tool uses the upper-left corner of your selected pattern (chosen by clicking the pattern button in the Tool Options dialog or by going to the Patterns dockable dialog) as your clone source and each of the Alignment options works in relation to that. The cool thing about using a pattern is that it's tiled. So if you're painting a cloned stroke and you reach the border of the pattern, it's simply repeated as if you're sampling from an infinitely large layer that's been Bucket Filled with that pattern.

Note

It's important to be aware of how the Clone tool handles transparency. When it comes to dealing with the alpha channel, cloning is a purely additive process. That is, if your clone source has a transparent region and you're painting on an opaque or semi-transparent layer, the result will never get more transparent. However, the result *can* become more opaque. If your clone source is semi-transparent and you're painting on a transparent or semi-transparent region, the alpha channels are added together to yield a less transparent result. ■

Using the Clone tool you can, as explained earlier, remove blemishes from a person's face in a portrait or do something more involved. As an example have a look at Figure 12-9. Using the Clone tool, all of the text from the signs of the vending stand in that photo have been removed. From this point you can use the image as is or add your own text and in place of the old ones.

FIGURE 12-9

Using the Clone tool on a photo of a state fair vending stand (left) to remove all of the text and graphics from its signs (right) (Photo credit: Chris Hoyer)

Perspective Clone Tool

The Perspective Clone tool works exactly like the Clone tool, but with an added twist: it can deform your cloned paint stroke to match the perspective in your image. This is great because you don't always have images and photographs that have been shot at orthographic angles. More to the point, the parts of an image that you often have to fix typically aren't parallel to the image plane. You have to deal with the perspective of the image. The Perspective Clone tool affords you this exact feature. By default, there's no keyboard shortcut to activate it, but you can select it from the Toolbox (it's the icon with the rubber stamp in front of a skewed light blue rectangle) or go to Tools ➤ Paint Tools ➤ Perspective Clone. As Figure 12-10 shows, this tool has some extra settings at the top of its Tool Options dialog and an extra mouse cursor.

FIGURE 12-10

The Perspective Clone tool has its own set of extra mouse cursors (left) and Tool Options (right).

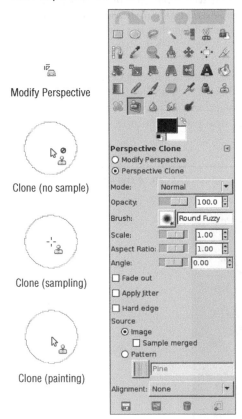

Modify Perspective

Clone (no sample)

Clone (sampling)

Clone (painting)

The only additional tool options that the Perspective Clone tool has are the two radio buttons at the top of its Tool Options: Modify Perspective and Perspective Clone. These radio buttons define the mode for the Perspective Clone tool. The default mode when you first launch the tool is Modify Perspective. This is because the Perspective Clone tool requires you to define the perspective that you want your cloned strokes to be mapped to. Setting the perspective it pretty easy; just like using the perspective controls on the Transform tool. You should note four boxes: one at each corner of your image. Click and drag these boxes to define the perspective that you want the Perspective Clone tool to use. Once you have the perspective that you want to use, change the tool's mode to Perspective Clone and you're ready to set your clone source and begin painting cloned strokes. If you ever want to re-adjust the perspective, just change modes by clicking the Modify Perspective radio button in the Tool Options dialog and fix the perspective as needed. Your clone source is maintained when you go back to the Perspective Clone mode.

In practical use, the Perspective Clone tool is helpful in a wide variety of applications. You can use an asphalt pattern to digitally pave a road in an image. You could duplicate cars on a street or add traincars to a train. You can even clean up or add grass to the yard of an unfinished house. Really, you can treat the Perspective Clone tool as a means of performing a perspective copy operation. Figure 12-11 shows the process used to produce the digital paving example.

FIGURE 12-11

The steps to take a single-car dirt road and change it to a two-lane highway (Photo credit: Rennett Stowe, `www.flickr.com/photos/tomsaint/3363940784/`)

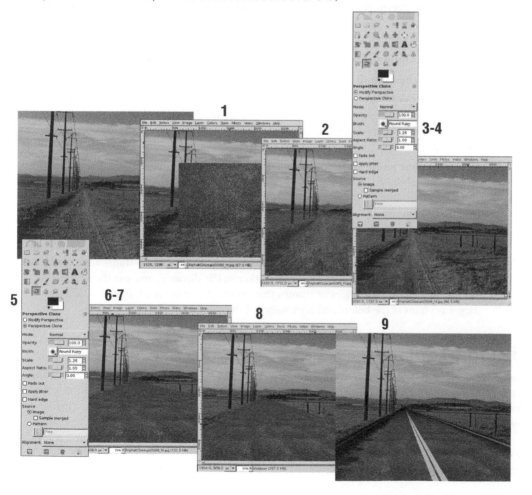

The following are the basic steps you use to re-create this image:

1. **Starting with the image you want to add the road to, load your asphalt texture as a new layer (Ctrl+Alt+O).** You could instead load the texture as a separate image, but it's more useful to have it on your base image.

2. **Use the Transform tool to adjust the perspective of your texture to match the perspective of the road.** The reason you need to do this is because the Perspective Clone tool is really designed to clone an object that's already in an image and subject to that image's perspective. If you try to use the flat texture or a pattern, the results will not be as expected. In fact, the results will be really unpredictable. You may find it easier to reduce the Opacity of your texture layer so you can see your base image through it as you adjust perspective.

3. **Set the size of your texture layer to match the size of your image (Layer ➢ Layer to Image Size).** This way you can paint your new road directly on your texture layer.

4. **Activate the Perspective Clone tool and modify the perspective to match the road.** It would be nice to be able to reuse the perspective results from the Transform tool, but that feature doesn't currently exist, so you'll need to "eyeball it" a bit.

5. **In the Tool Options dialog switch to Perspective Clone mode.**

6. **Ctrl+click the asphalt texture to set your clone source.**

7. **Paint your road.** You may want to play with Alignment modes to see what works best for you. None or Aligned typically give the best results. You don't have to be perfect here. The idea is to get the texture painted at the right perspective. You can clean up in the next step.

8. **Clean up your paint job.** For this, you can use a combination of selection tools and the Eraser tool (Shift+E). The idea is to get the sides of the road straight and even. At this point, you have the basic foundation. The next step is getting shadows right and making the image pretty.

9. **Add finishing touches.** This is where you can really play to get it looking like a road. Add some stripes using the Free Select tool and the Bucket Fill tool. Use those same tools with a soft brush to add shadowing at the road edges. Use a dark-to-transparent gradient with the Blend tool to make the road get darker in the distance, and use the Clone tool on the background for fences or stumps that get cut off by the road. Figure 12-12 shows larger versions of the before and after stages of this process.

Healing Tool

Though the Clone tool is extremely powerful and helpful, it's not a complete fix-all. One of the primary disadvantages of the Clone tool is that it makes an exact copy of the pixels from your clone source and doesn't account at all for the color of the pixels you're painting on. This is fine if your image has generally even tones, or when you have small fixes here and there, but it tends to fall over if you have to use a single source on a large area or where you have a lot of color variety. In these situations, even if you're using a soft-edged, low-opacity brush, there's a good chance that you're going to get the wrong color where you paint or, worse, you start seeing a pattern of your clone source where you paint. Fortunately, GIMP has the Healing tool to help remedy this. It works like the Clone tool, but it explicitly takes into account the pixels that you're painting over. This allows your image to maintain its color variation and reduce the amount of noticeable patterns. The most common use for this tool is removing blemishes and wrinkles from faces in portraits.

FIGURE 12-12

On the left is the original photograph and on the right is the same scene with a road added, courtesy of the Perspective Clone tool.

To use the Healing tool, activate it by clicking the crossed band-aid icon in the Toolbox, using the H keyboard shortcut, or going to Tools ➤ Painting Tools ➤ Heal. As Figure 12-13 shows, the settings in the Tool Options dialog for the Healing tool are a simplified version of the options available to the Clone tool.

The only difference between the Healing tool's Tool Options and those for the Clone tool is that the Healing tool doesn't give you the option to use a pattern as a clone source. Beyond that, the Sample Merged option and the Alignment modes work the same way. Usage of the Healing tool is also the same as usage of the Clone tool. Ctrl+click somewhere on your source drawable (image, layer, mask, channel) to set your clone source. After you do that, click and drag your image to paint healed pixels. Notice while you paint that the colors of the pixels you're painting on are intelligently mixed with your clone source. To use this to remove blemishes and wrinkles, Ctrl+click a smooth part of the skin and paint over the wrinkled area. As an example, take the photo of my dear old grandmother that was used in Figure 12-7. By using the Healing tool to reduce the wrinkles on her face and the Burn tool to darken her hair, I can do quite a lot to reduce her age, as shown in Figure 12-14. Now, the Healing tool alone isn't going to magically drop 60 years off of her fiery 80-year-old face. However, I can certainly make her look less mad at me by reducing her wrinkles.

On the left are the three different mouse cursors for the Healing tool and on the right are the Tool Options for the Healing tool.

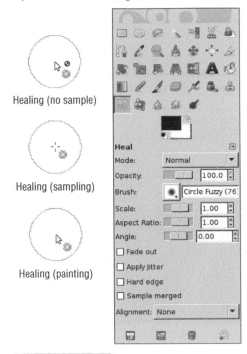

Healing (no sample)

Healing (sampling)

Healing (painting)

On the left is the original image and on the right is the same image after treatment with the Healing tool for wrinkles and the Burn tool for her hair.

Using the Exposure Blend Plug-in

When dealing with digital photography, you're eventually going to run across the phrase *high dynamic range*, or HDR. In fact, this very book has touched on the topic a few times. HDR refers to the fact that common digital image formats can't currently store as much light information as film. By its very nature, film has a high dynamic range and digital images do not. To overcome this, digital imaging has taken advantage of something many photographers have done for years. In traditional film photography, it's common to do *bracketing*, a process where photographers take a picture at an exposure that they expect will give the greatest range of darks and lights while retaining as much light information as possible. After taking that initial shot, they will often take the exact same photo at both a shorter and longer exposure time, bracketing around the original exposure time. That way if the initial guess about the light was off, there is another shot that's brighter or darker. This is because traditional cameras don't have the fancy LCD preview window that we're spoiled with today on modern digital cameras.

To attain the same amount of dynamic range as traditional film in a digital image, photographers still use bracketing. However, rather than choosing the brighter or darker exposure as a whole, the digital photographer can combine the three images, revealing details that are either blown out or obscured in darkness in the image taken at the normal exposure. The process by which this is done is referred to as *tone mapping* and it can be an extremely tedious way to drain all of your available time. Fortunately, the process can be automated to get the rough exposures right and then tweaked afterwards. In GIMP, the way to do this is with the Exposure Blend script. This script is listed in the GIMP Plugin Registry and you can find the most recent version and detailed documentation on its web site at `http://tir.astro.utoledo.edu/jdsmith/code/exposure_blend.php`. If you don't already have this plug-in installed, have a look at Chapter 21 for installation instructions.

To start using Exposure Blend navigate to Filters ➢ Exposure Blend ➢ Blend. When you click this menu item, you get the dialog that appears in Figure 12-15.

Once you have the dialog up, you can load your bracketed images. First load the image that you intend on using as your normal, or reference, exposure by clicking the topmost button in the dialog and finding the image in the file chooser that appears. Do the same for the short exposure and long exposure images. With the three images chosen, you can play with some settings. The defaults generally yield pretty reasonable results, but if you want to play with these settings a bit, the following is a quick description of each one:

- **Blend Mask Blur Radius** — The process of tone mapping involves using differences between the bracketed images to generate layer masks that reveal image information from the brighter and darker images. To keep this from being too abrupt, the masks are blurred. This value, set in pixels, controls how blurry the mask is. The default value of 8 pixels is usually pretty good for most high-resolution images. However, on lower-resolution images, this might cause a strange glow at the edges of objects. To fix that, reduce this value.

- **Blur Type/Edge Protection** — The options in the drop-down control the type of blur used for the masks and how much that blur tries to maintain the consistency of edges. The choices are actually a bit of misnomer. All of the blurs are Gaussian blurs, but the Selective option is a specific type of Gaussian blur that pays attention to edges. The default Gaussian blur without edge protection generally gives good results, but in images where you start seeing glow around edges, you may want to play with one of the other three options.

- **Dark/Bright Mask Grayscale** — These options control which of the three images you want to use as the layer mask for the dark and bright image. Typically you'll want to stick with using the defaults here, but if you need to squeeze out some extra detail from some parts, changing these values can help.

- **Dark Takes Precedence** — When Exposure Blend finishes, you'll have three layers, two with masks, as shown in Figure 12-16. By default, the bright exposure layer is at the top of the stack. However, this may yield results that are brighter than you want. You can manually move the dark exposure layer up or you can send it straight to the top here by enabling this check box.

- **Auto-Trim Mask Histograms** — Enabling this option is basically the same as opening the Levels dialog and clicking the Auto button on each of the exposure masks.

- **Scale Largest Image Dimension to** — Type in an image size here in pixels, such as 800x600, and the tone-mapped image that comes out of Exposure Blend is proportionally scaled to be no larger than those dimensions. This is useful if you want to test some settings before applying them to full-sized images.

FIGURE 12-15

The Exposure Blend dialog

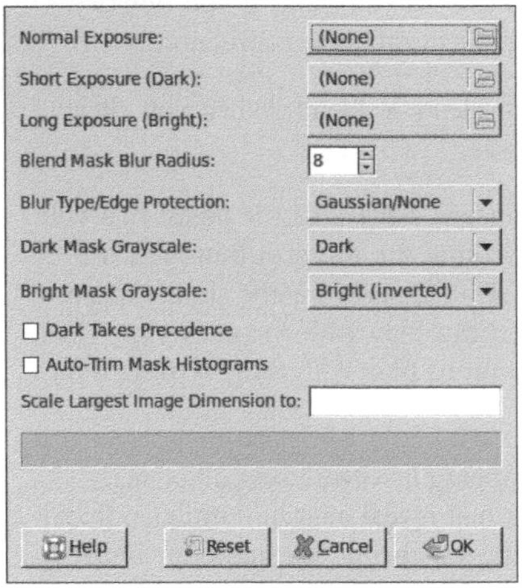

Normal Exposure:	(None)
Short Exposure (Dark):	(None)
Long Exposure (Bright):	(None)
Blend Mask Blur Radius:	8
Blur Type/Edge Protection:	Gaussian/None
Dark Mask Grayscale:	Dark
Bright Mask Grayscale:	Bright (inverted)
☐ Dark Takes Precedence	
☐ Auto-Trim Mask Histograms	
Scale Largest Image Dimension to:	

Help   Reset   Cancel   OK

Once you have all the settings adjusted the way you like, click the OK button and Exposure Blend will do its magic. If the source files you're using are large, this step might take a while, especially if you're running GIMP on an older computer. When it's complete, though, you have an image window with your processed results in it. The cool thing is that Exposure Blend doesn't give you a flattened image as your result. You actually get three layers, as shown in Figure 12-16. The bottom layer is the normal exposure and the two layers above it are the bright and dark exposures, masked to reveal content that's not apparent in the normal exposure.

FIGURE 12-16

When you run Exposure Blend, the result is an image with three layers. The normal exposure image is at the bottom and the other two are masked above it.

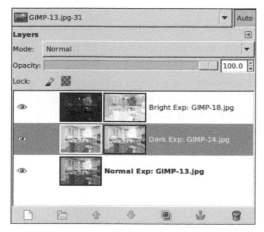

What makes this so cool is that now you can manually tweak things with all of the tools available to you in GIMP to get more customized results. You can reorder the exposure layers, tweak the masks in the Channels dockable dialog, or paint directly on each layer. If you want to re-run Exposure Blend on your images to regenerate your masks or adjust their blur, you don't have go through the process of selecting your images all over again. Instead, choose Filters ➤ Exposure Blend ➤ Reset Blend Details. This brings up a dialog like the one shown in Figure 12-17, which allows you to adjust all of the settings without needing to reselect your exposure images.

FIGURE 12-17

The Reset Blend Details dialog allows you to adjust tone mapping settings without reselecting your exposure images.

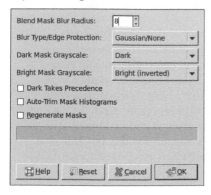

Because the process of bracketing requires that you take multiple photos, there's a chance that all of those exposures will be slightly offset from one another, especially if you take the photos without a tripod. Fortunately, Exposure Blend also includes features to help you align these images. Choose Filters ➤ Exposure Blend ➤ Align Exposures and you'll find four options:

- **Bright** — This sets the bright exposure layer to the difference blending mode to help you accurately align the bright exposure layer with the normal exposure layer. Use the arrow keys on your keyboard with the Move tool (M) to move the layer one pixel at a time to nudge it into place.

- **Dark** — This does the same as the Bright menu option, but for the dark exposure layer.

- **Off** — Choose this option after you've aligned your layers to set everything back to the resulting tone-mapped image.

- **Trim Image to Overlap Area** — If you adjust your layers to get them to line up, parts of the exposure layers no longer cover the normal exposure layer. You can recognize this as a strip along the perimeter of you image that looks markedly darker or brighter than the rest of the image. To rectify this, you can crop these protruding bits. This menu option in Exposure Blend does this automatically for you.

Figure 12-18 shows the difference between an image that's been tone mapped with Exposure Blend and the original, normal exposure image.

FIGURE 12-18

On the left, a digital photograph created with a single exposure; on the right, the same image tone mapped with Exposure Blend

And with that, you've got a nicely tone-mapped image from a set of three bracketed photographs. It's important to note here that you're not technically saving an HDR image. If you save in GIMP's native XCF format, the layers and their masks give you high dynamic range data, but it's not really an HDR format. And if you flatten the layers to save to another format like PNG or JPEG, the result is not HDR; it's a regular image that's been tone mapped with bracketed photos. It's a subtle distinction, but it's definitely worth keeping in mind. To have an HDR image, GIMP would have to support more than 8 bits per channel and be able to save to an HDR-aware format such as OpenEXR. There is not currently support for this in GIMP, but hopefully future versions that have tighter integration with GIMP's new imaging library, GEGL, will add this support.

Summary

This chapter covered the use of GIMP's painting tools that are extremely useful in photo retouching work. You saw how the Blur/Sharpen tool could be used to direct viewers to specific parts of your image and how the Smudge tool can drastically modify an image by extending it and softening its appearance. You saw how the Dodge/Burn tool relates to the traditional photographic printing techniques, but with the added flexibility of the digital medium. Then you got to play with GIMP's Clone, Perspective Clone, and Healing tools, allowing you to fix small parts of an image or change an image drastically. At the end of this chapter you saw how the Exposure Blend plug-in can be used to get a larger dynamic range in your image by taking advantage of bracketed photos.

Next up, *all* of GIMP's included filters. Sweet!

Part IV

Exploring Filters and Effects

IN THIS PART

Chapter 13
Implementing Blur, Enhancement, and Distortion Filters

Chapter 14
Using Image Creation Filters

Chapter 15
Using Compositing Filters

Chapter 16
Enhancing Images with Artistic Filters

Chapter 17
Working with Specialized Filters

Chapter 18
Batch Processing with Automating Filters

Chapter 19
Using GIMP Animation Package

Chapter 20
Working with Video-Specific Functions in GIMP

Implementing Blur, Enhancement, and Distortion Filters

This chapter marks the beginning of an entire section of this book devoted to GIMP's extensive and impressive list of filters. Simply put, a filter is a small program that takes image data as input, performs one or more processing steps on that image data, and returns a modified version to you. The filter may require additional input from you in the form of settings and parameters to help customize and control those processing steps. In the case of most GIMP filters, the active layer (or your current selected pixels in that layer) serves as the image data that's fed to the filter.

This chapter covers some of the most commonly used filters in image editing. The Blur filters are designed to obscure details, but in using them you can focus the viewer's attention on more important parts of your images. In GIMP's array of Enhance filters, you're given tools that allow you to accentuate specific details or *all* details in your images. The filters in the Distorts submenu can take your image data and dramatically transform it into something that only hints at what your original image was. It's really quite exciting.

IN THIS CHAPTER

Introducing GIMP's filters

Increasing depth and focus by – ironically – using blur

Using automated ways of cleaning up images

Deforming your images and actually making them look better

Filters Anonymous: A Serious Note on Filter Abuse

With this chapter and the seven others that belong in Part IV, you get to explore the incredible world of GIMP filters. A word of warning, especially if you're new to computer graphics: filters are incredibly powerful tools that can produce some seriously cool effects on your images. Why is this a cause for warning? Well, just because you *can* do something, that doesn't mean it's always a good idea. It's a common thing that you see among people who are just starting out with digital imagery. They have hard drives just chock full of over-processed images where they've taken a perfectly passable photograph that may need just a little bit of work and run nearly every one of the available filters and plug-ins at their disposal. The final result may look cool or interesting because of how drastically different it is from its original state, but that doesn't necessarily mean that it's a good image.

Now, that's not to say that there isn't a time and a place for heavy processing every now and again. I'm sure on some occasions even using a lens flare makes sense and doesn't look too cheesy. But it's really worth it to sit down and try to understand what an image *needs* rather than what's going to make it look "cool." Furthermore, *anybody* can go to the Filters menu and create one of these special effects with the click of a few buttons. It's a "canned effect" and by itself, it usually lacks the punch that you'd want to give an image. A good digital artist knows how to make the most of a filter by using it minimally where it's needed and combining that with skillful use of more manual tools to get a powerful and unique final image.

Filters are a little bit like alcohol. When used with moderation, they can be a lot of fun and do a lot to enhance the look of your images. However, when used in excess, there's a good chance that you're going to puke all over your image and make it a muddy mess. Use filters responsibly.

Common Features among Filters

Most of the filters in GIMP share some common features. The most obvious of these features is the fact that they're all accessible from the Filters menu in the image window, shown in Figure 13-1.

In this menu, the first four items are incredibly useful:

- **Repeat Last (Ctrl+F)** — Click this menu item to launch the last filter you ran, using all of the same settings from the last time you used it. Using this function's keyboard shortcut, you can quickly apply the same filter to multiple selections, layers, or even images. An important thing to note about this feature is that it remembers only the last filter you used in your current GIMP session. If you close and restart GIMP, this item is grayed out and inaccessible.

- **Re-show Last (Shift+Ctrl+F)** — This option works just like the Repeat Last feature, but instead of blindly reusing the same filter settings, it shows you that filter's dialog — if it has one — and allows you to make changes before re-running it. This is a great feature when you're trying various settings on a filter on a particular image. You can preview the changes it makes within the filter's Preview pane. You can run the filter, Undo (Ctrl+Z) the processed effect(s) if you don't like the results, and then re-show that filter's dialog (Shift+Ctrl+F) to try out new settings. Some filter effects do not have a Preview pane, so the effect is previewed within the image window. You can view the effect, Undo (Ctrl+Z) and then try something new (Shift+Ctrl+F).

- **Recently Used** — The submenu that this option reveals shows a list of all the filters and plug-ins you've used in your current GIMP session. Click any one of them and that filter's dialog window appears with its last-used settings. This menu item and its associated submenu appears only if you've run plug-ins or filters in this session. Otherwise it's hidden.

- **Reset All Filters** — Typically when you re-show a filter, whether by using the Re-show Last feature or just by choosing it from its window a second time, that filter is shown with its last-used settings. In most cases, this is the desired behavior and it's great for keeping a speedy workflow. However, on occasion, it's more useful to start fresh with a filter using its default values. This is especially true on some of the more complex filters. Click this menu item to return all filters in your GIMP session to their default values.

Note

The Repeat Last, Re-show Last, and Recently Used menu items actually work on more than just the operations that are accessible from the Filters menu. Any installed plug-in that registers within GIMP can be called from these functions. For example, the Autocrop Layer feature found in Layer ➢ Autocrop Layer is actually implemented as a plug-in. When you run it, it's added to the Recently Used submenu and is repeatable using the Repeat Last and Re-show Last functions. This is convenient if you want to autocrop a lot of layers without navigating through the menu because you can just use the Ctrl+F shortcut. However, it can be disorienting to see operations that aren't really filters listed at the top of the Filters menu. Fortunately, now you know why that happens and it should be less troublesome for you. ∎

FIGURE 13-1

All of GIMP's bundled filters and many of the plug-ins you can download are included in the Filters menu of the image window.

Another common feature that many of GIMP's filters have is a small preview window. Figure 13-2 shows three typical versions of the preview windows you may run into.

FIGURE 13-2

From left to right, a basic preview window, one with panning ability, and one with zooming ability

As the figure shows, you can have a basic preview window that shows only a thumbnail view of your image, a slightly more advanced version with panning navigation, or a deluxe preview window that allows both panning and zooming. Most preview windows are of the middle variety; they show a 100% zoom version of your active layer or selection and you're allowed to pan around that space by clicking and dragging your mouse within the window's space. You can also click the Navigation crosshairs in the bottom right of the preview window to move the preview area interactively around a thumbnail version of your image. This works just as the same button in the image window works.

Tip

The common panning-only preview window can be pretty frustrating to work with on larger images because it shows only a small square of the available pixels in the image. Though there's no easy way to zoom this preview, you can increase its viewable size. Simply resize your filter's dialog window and make it bigger by clicking and dragging one of its borders. The preview window should adjust to accommodate for the newly available space. You're still not zoomed out on your image, but this does provide you with greater context. ■

The panning-only and panning/zooming varieties of preview windows have one additional control on them. Right-click in the preview window and a small context menu appears. If your active layer or selection has an alpha channel, you can dictate how the preview window displays transparent regions using these two menu items:

- **Check Style** — This controls the checkerboard style that's used to represent the transparent regions of your image in the preview window. You can choose light, medium, or dark checks, or you could forgo the checkerboard altogether and set transparent areas to be solid white, gray, or black.

- **Check Size** — If you do choose to show the checkerboard pattern in the preview window, this second menu item controls whether those checks are small, medium, or large. On images with a lot of detail, it's often beneficial to have larger checks so the view isn't cluttered and noisy.

Using the Blur Filters

It may seem a bit ironic that in a medium that has an implied goal of communicating visual information some of the most commonly used tools are filters designed to make details more difficult to see. Strange as that may be, it's definitely true. Filters in the blur category are useful for everything from creating glows and drop shadows to implying motion and even assisting with image restoration. As a matter of fact, quite a few other filters in GIMP, such as some edge detection filters, call filters from Filters ➤ Blur as a step in their processing. From an artistic perspective, blurring part of an image is an excellent way to guide viewers to focus their attention on specific parts of your composition.

Blur

This first item on the Blur submenu is the simplest of the set. Run it by going to Filters ➤ Blur ➤ Blur. When you call this filter, it runs immediately; there is no dialog window for it. Each pixel in your active layer or selection has its color values mixed with the color values of the pixels adjacent to it. It runs very fast, even on larger images. However, if you *are* using this filter on a very large image, it's likely that the results will be too subtle for you to notice. It's not uncommon to see people running this filter multiple times on larger images. In contrast, when you run this filter on smaller images, the results are much more pronounced. The best applications of this filter are for slightly softening an image or a quick-and-dirty means of antialiasing an image with extremely harsh edges or color transitions. However, if you find yourself running the Blur filter and then pressing Ctrl+F another dozen times, you may want to consider using one of the other filters in the blur category. Figure 13-3 compares the results of running the Blur filter on an image once versus calling the Blur filter 20 times in a row.

FIGURE 13-3

From top to bottom, the original image, blurred once, and blurred 20 times

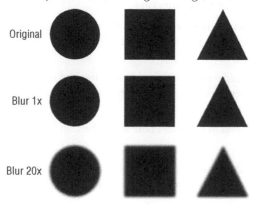

Original

Blur 1x

Blur 20x

Gaussian Blur

The Gaussian Blur algorithm is probably the most commonly used blurring algorithm in computer graphics, and for good reason. It works quickly, produces consistent results, and is easy to control. It's the go-to filter that digital artists rely on when they need to blur any part of an image. When you run the Gaussian Blur filter in GIMP (Filters ➤ Blur ➤ Gaussian Blur), you should get a dialog window like the one shown in Figure 13-4.

FIGURE 13-4

The Gaussian Blur dialog gives you refined control over blurring your image, including the amount of blur in horizontal and vertical directions and the blurring method used.

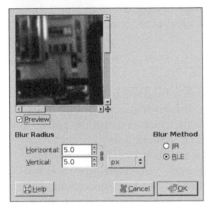

Below the preview window in the Gaussian Blur's dialog are two primary controls for the nature of your blur:

- **Blur Radius** — These two numeric entry fields control the strength of your blur. By default, they're chained together so changing one value changes both. However, you can unchain the fields and blur your image more in one direction than in the other. The default unit for the Blur Radius is pixels, but you can use the units drop-down next to the Vertical text field and use any of the other units that GIMP supports.

- **Blur Method** — The Gaussian Blur filter offers two different methods for implementing the blur. They produce identical results, but depending on the content of your image, one may run faster than the other:

  - **IIR** — An abbreviation for infinite impulse response, this Gaussian Blur method is most effective on images with a lot of variety in them, such as photographic content. It's also a good option to choose if your Blur Radius values are set high.

  - **RLE** — The run-length encoding (RLE) method of Gaussian Blur works best on images with large sections of flat (or near-flat) color.

Figure 13-5 shows the results of using the Gaussian Blur filter on an example image. You can also look back to Chapter 6 to see how the Gaussian Blur can be used to create a drop shadow effect.

Motion Blur

By unchaining and isolating the Horizontal or Vertical Blur Radius values in the Gaussian Blur filter, you can create a rudimentary motion blur effect in either the horizontal or vertical directions. However, what if you want to have motion blur at an arbitrary angle? Or what if you

FIGURE 13-5

The Gaussian Blur filter can very easily blur an image into obscurity.

Original   5px blur   25px blur   100px blur

want to get a blur effect that looks like the camera is quickly zooming in on your subject? These effects are difficult or impossible using just the Gaussian Blur filter. Fortunately, GIMP includes the Motion Blur filter and it can easily create these effects as well as a couple more. Activate this filter by going to Filters ➤ Blur ➤ Motion Blur and you get a dialog like the one in Figure 13-6.

FIGURE 13-6

The Motion Blur filter's dialog

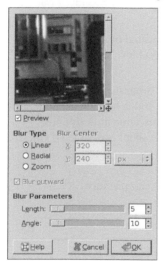

Beneath the preview window in this dialog are three primary controls for dictating the nature of the blur that the filter produces: Blur Type, Blur Center, and Blur Parameters. The following is a description of each control and the options available within each one:

- **Blur Type** — The Motion Blur filter gives you multiple varieties of blurred motion:
  - **Linear** — This is similar to using the Gaussian Blur filter. The difference, however, with this blur is that you can blur in any arbitrary direction, not just horizontally or vertically.

- **Radial** — Imagine spinning your image's canvas around a single point, as if your image were on the top of an umbrella that someone was spinning around. That spinning sensation is replicated with the Radial motion blur.

- **Zoom** — This blur effect attempts to replicate the look of quickly moving toward or away from a single point on the canvas. Whereas the Linear blur moves in a direction parallel to your image plane, the Zoom blur moves perpendicularly.

- **Blur Outward** — This check box is available only if you choose Zoom as your Blur Type. By default it is enabled, meaning that pixels are pushed away from your chosen Blur Center. Disable this check box and the Zoom blur pulls pixels toward the Blur Center.

- **Blur Center** — This is relevant only if you're using Radial or Zoom blur. It defines the coordinates for the single point that you're either rotating about or zooming toward or away from. By default, the X and Y values are set as the center of your canvas. Change these values and the Motion Blur filter adjusts itself to your newly defined center. Unfortunately you can't simply click the preview or the image to define these values, but you can find the coordinates of the Blur Center you want to use by using the coordinate display in the status area at the bottom of the image window.

- **Blur Parameters** — These two settings define the intensity of your blur. Depending on the Blur Type you've chosen, they may behave slightly differently or may be grayed out and not available at all:

  - **Length** — When using Linear or Zoom blur, this value (measured in pixels) dictates how far a pixel is displaced from its original position when you blur. This slider is disabled if you choose Radial blur.

  - **Angle** — If you're using Linear blur, this value stipulates the arbitrary angle that you're blurring in. It's measured in degrees, so a value of 0, 180, or 360 is horizontal and a value of 90 or 270 is vertical. If you're doing a Radial blur, this value indicates how far you're rotating a pixel from its original position. The Angle slider is disabled if you choose Zoom blur.

Figure 13-7 shows each of the possible blurs that the Motion Blur filter can produce.

FIGURE 13-7

The Motion Blur filter can create (from left to right) a linear blur, a radial blur, or a blur that zooms in or out.

 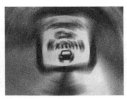  

Linear blur   Radial blur   Zoom blur—outward   Zoom blur—inward

Pixelize

When you want your image to be pixelated, you can simply use GIMP to apply the correct filter. Before I get into how to do this, you should first review what a pixel is and how it is used, as well as how it affects digital images.

By definition, a pixel is considered the smallest component of an image or picture as seen on a computer screen and is usually represented by a dot. The pixels per inch (ppi) is used to represent pixel resolution of an image. The greater the number of ppi, the greater the resolution of the viewable image will be. These dots, when viewed at the correct image size, accurately represent an image on your computer screen. The image contains a specific number of pixel blocks that are used to create the tonality. Digital image pixel tonality (which simply means darkness to lightness) is expressed as a number between 0 and 255 when working with a 24-bit RGB image file. As with a standard hex chart, colors are represented by these numbers. The number 0 produces pure black and 255 produces pure white. Because every image contains a very specific number of pixel blocks used to describe the tonality, you should know that the more pixels used, the finer the resolving capability of the image.

To figure out pixel dimensions, you can use a simple mathematical equation. If you need to guesstimate or assess the size of an image, you can calculate this quickly using the image dimensions. The following formula shows how this is calculated:

> Number of pixels = physical dimension x pixels per inch (ppi).

You should also consider how this applies to a sample image file. The pixel dimensions of a digital image are an absolute value. A practical example would be to apply this formula to an image file and calculate the exact number of pixels based on the image's physical dimension multiplied by the pixels per inch (ppi). You should also note that I am discussing RGB images; CMYK files will be slightly greater in size.

Now that you understand what a pixel is and how it relates to your image size and resolution, you can apply the Pixelize filter to a sample image to see how it can be pixelated. When working with computer graphics, pixelation is an effect you can apply to cause an image (such as a bitmap) or a section of an image to appear at a larger size, thus distorting it.

Tip

If you enlarge a photo, it may become distorted if you make it bigger than what it can resolve correctly to. This is commonly seen when you enlarge a picture and can see the pixel structure clearly, as shown in Figure 13-8. ∎

Instead of enlarging an image to cause pixelation, you can apply GIMP's Pixelize filter. Much like the previous example, to pixelize (or blur) an image, all you need to do is select it and then apply the appropriate filter. To do this, choose Filters ➤ Blur ➤ Pixelize. To pixelize an image, apply the filter as shown in Figure 13-9.

After you apply the Pixelize filter to your image in the image window, it should distort as shown in the Preview section of the Pixelize filter dialog box. This applies what appears to be a "blurring" effect, although all the filter is really doing is enlarging the image beyond its intended size (and ratio) to cause a blurring effect. Note that you can also change the pixel option (seen as px) to other units, such as cm (centimeters), ft (feet), in (inches), yds (yards), and so on.

FIGURE 13-8

You can take an image file and enlarge it, creating a pixelation effect, or use the Pixelize filter. Enlarging the image from its intended resolution brings out the pixels so that you can see them clearly.

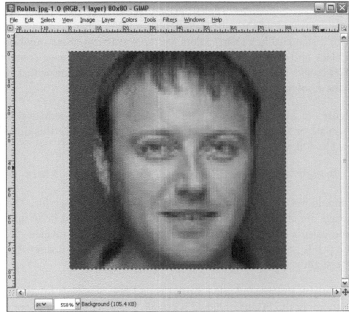

FIGURE 13-9

Viewing the Pixelize effect in Preview mode

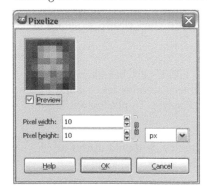

Selective Gaussian Blur

Just like Gaussian Blur filter, which was covered earlier in the chapter, the Selective Gaussian Blur filter applies the exact same effect except you have different control over the application of the filter. For example, if you want to apply a Gaussian blur to a background image (layer) to make the foreground image stand out better, you use this filter. This effect is referred to in photography as '*depth of field*'. It gives the image in the foreground some depth. If you need to apply a blur effect that gives you some depth, you can use the Selective Gaussian Blur filter. Run it by going to Filters ➤ Blur ➤ Selective Gaussian Blur.

The filter acts on only specific pixels, instead of all of them like the Gaussian Blur filter covered earlier. It does this by blurring only the value of the surrounding pixels (that is, background image) and making it less than the defined delta, which can be configured within the Selective Gaussian Blur filter dialog box as shown in Figure 13-10.

FIGURE 13-10

Applying Selective Gaussian Blur to a foreground image

Within the Selective Gaussian Blur dialog box, you can adjust filter parameter settings such as Blur Radius and Max. (maximum) Delta. When adjusting the blur radius, you are simply selecting the blur intensity value for your selection. Blur Radius should not be confused with similar effects such as Radial Blur, which apply a spinning blur to your image and can be configured with the Motion Blur filter.

You can also adjust the maximum delta, which is the numbered difference (0 and 255) between the selected pixel value in comparison to the surrounding pixel values.

Tileable Blur

You can configure and use the Tileable Blur filter to soften the seams between tiled images. Many times, graphic designers apply a background image that is made up of smaller, identical images, which causes a "tiling" effect. When you want to create a seamless tile-like background, you use GIMP's Tileable Blur filter.

This filter (when applied) blends, blurs, and distorts the image's seams so that the tiling effect isn't so dramatic; it will appear to have smoother edges and connections from one tile to another either vertically or horizontally. The softened seams give you work a more aesthetic look.

You can find this filter by going to Filters ➤ Blur ➤ Tileable Blur. Figure 13-11 shows the Tileable Blur dialog box.

FIGURE 13-11

The Tileable Blur filter can be used to soften seams between tiles.

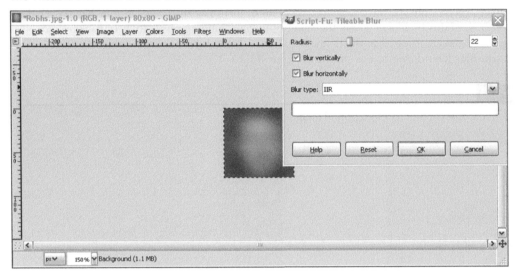

The Tileable Blur filter provides many options you can use to adjust your image. For example, you can set the Radius setting to adjust your blur effect. If your tiled background needs to be "seamless," you may want to set a Radius setting of 50. If you want a smaller blur radius, you can adjust the Radius setting to 5, for example.

You can also use the Blur Vertically and Blur Horizontally options to set a horizontal or vertical tileable blur. The Blur Type option allows you to choose between two different compression algorithms by default. One is infinite impulse response (IIR) and the other is run-length encoding (RLE). IIR can be used for scanned images and photographic images. RLE can be used for computer generated images.

Enhance Filters

Enhance filters are used to compensate for image imperfections. Such imperfections include dust particles, noise, interlaced frames (coming usually from a TV frame-grabber), and insufficient sharpness. The filters covered in this section include Antialias, Deinterlace, Despeckle, Destripe, NL Filter, Red Eye Removal, Sharpen, and Unsharp Mask.

Antialias

When working with GIMP, you may need to apply an edge treatment to your images, or the selections you make within them. You can use the Antialias filter to perform this function. If you do not use this filter on work that requires it, visual distortion may occur.

Antialiasing is the process of smoothing an image that is composed of hard elements with jagged edges. For example, a bitmap image is made up of tiny squares. If enlarged, an image may not appear smooth, but instead may have jagged edges. If you make a selection within the image window and use the Antialias filter, GIMP smooths out the edges by using the selected layer's alpha channel. Run it by going to Filters ➢ Enhance ➢ Antialias. Figure 13-12 shows the process of applying the Antialias filter within the image window.

FIGURE 13-12

When using the Antialias filter, note the status bar on the bottom of the image window processing the image while configuring the effect.

Antialiasing effects are covered in Chapter 19, so flip to it if you need to learn more.

Tip

One of the things you can do after applying the Antialias filter is go to the Edit menu in the image window and select Fade Antialias. This brings up the Fade Antialias dialog box, which allows you to modify the paint mode and opacity of the last pixel manipulation you applied. Another helpful tip is to use Blur filters when only a small section of your image needs to be antialiased. ■

Deinterlace

The Deinterlace filter is an important part of your toolset. Because many digital video cameras sold today only record about 60 frames per second with the NTSC standard (50 images per second with the PAL standard) in half vertical resolution, the result is that when images are recorded while moving, they appear distorted. If an important movement was missed while recording, it's likely that the resulting image will appear "split." The Deinterlace filter works by taking a subset of the images and replacing lines between previous and following lines of the image. The result is an image or selection that appears blurred. Run it by going to Filters ➢ Enhance ➢ Deinterlace. Figure 13-13 shows the difference between blurring with odd or even fields. You should try both and see which one provides the better result.

It should be noted that the Deinterlace filter is extremely useful in digital videography and isn't used much in regular photography. The Deinterlace filter gets used with GIMP Animation Package (GAP) to deinterlace video footage. GAP is covered in Chapter 19.

FIGURE 13-13

Using the Deinterlace filter to create a blurred image

Despeckle

The Despeckle filter (Filters ➤ Enhance ➤ Despeckle) is used to remove any defects in your image, such as scratches from an image that has been scanned, or dust speckles. Any blemish that appears on your image may (or may not) be fixed with Despeckle. It's important to try to pinpoint the exact area you want to apply the filter to by selecting it; otherwise you may affect the entire image, thus distorting it as demonstrated in Figure 13-14.

In addition to the Preview option (which allows you to view the effect before applying it), other options are available within the Despeckle filter dialog box. They are as follows:

- **Median (Adaptive)** — Use Adaptive when you want to have the radius adapt to the image selection (or entire image).

- **Median (Recursive)** — Use Recursive when you want to have the filter repeat the Despeckle filter action to make it stronger.

- **Radius** — The Radius option sets the size of the action window from 1 (3 x 3 pixels) to 20 (42 x 42). You can use this to smooth imperfections and smooth the image.

- **Black Level** — Use the Black Level to remove any pixel on the image darker than the value you set. This setting ranges from 0 to 255.

- **White Level** — Use the White Level to remove any pixel on the image lighter than the value you set. This setting ranges from 0 to 255.

Viewing the application of the Despeckle filter on an entire image

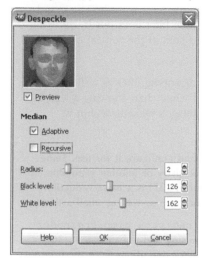

Destripe

Destripe (Filters ➤ Enhance ➤ Destripe) is used to remove small defects due to dust or scratches on a scanned image, and also the moiré effect on images scanned from a magazine. Select isolated defects before applying this filter to avoid unwanted changes in other areas of your image. Figure 13-15 shows the Destripe filter dialog box.

Enhancing an image with the Destripe filter. Because the image has a high pattern strength, stripes can also be created by the Destripe filter, so use caution and test the outcome before you apply the filter.

Although the Destripe filter dialog box doesn't offer a lot of options, the toolset is extremely powerful when you need to fix (or remove) striping in your image, which is usually created by low-quality scanners, or images with patterns that feature extremely fine lines. The Destripe filter removes stripes by creating a pattern within the image that interferes with the image and removes the stripes that may have been in your image. The Destripe filter does this by applying what is called a "negative pattern" to the image from a calculated sum of the vertical elements contained within.

The Destripe filter options allow you to adjust the width of the destriping filter as well as create a histogram. A histogram is a usually represented as a black-and-white chart showing a legible interference pattern and can be created to show specifics of the image's makeup within it.

Note

Some plug-ins are not available by default with GIMP when you install it and configure it for use. Some plug-ins (or filters) require you to download them from the GIMP Plugin Registry or another reputable source. For example, GREYCstoration (http://registry.gimp.org/node/137) is a noise reduction plug-in that you can download and install. It allows you to remove noise or grain as well as small artifacts.

Another popular plug-in is G'MIC. The G'MIC plug-in for GIMP (http://registry.gimp.org/node/13469) defines a set of various filters, including artistic filters, image denoising and enhancement, 3D renderers, and much more. The G'MIC plug-in is able to update its list of filter definitions from the Internet and you can customize your own. G'MIC was created by the author of the GREYCstoration algorithm and was intended to replace it. For more on plug-ins have a look at Chapter 21. For more information on GREYCstoration, refer to Chapter 2. ∎

NL Filter

The NL (non-linear) Filter (Filters ➤ Enhance ➤ NL Filter) is used much like the Despeckle filter, but it works on the entire image, instead of just a selection of it. You can use either filter for selections or entire images, although each works best for its intended function. The filter does not work if the active layer has an alpha channel; then the menu entry is inactive and grayed out. Run it by going to Filters ➤ Enhance ➤ NL Filter. Figure 13-16 shows an example of how the NL Filter can enhance your work.

Multiple options are available within the NL Filter dialog box. Aside from adjusting the Alpha and Radius settings based on which filter mode you select, you can select between three distinct modes. They are as follows:

- **Alpha Trimmed Mean** — This mode allows you to adjust the intermediate values of the alpha and provides an effect somewhere between smoothing and "pop" noise reduction.

- **Optimal Estimation** — This mode creates a smoothing effect over the image. The variance of the surrounding hexagon values is calculated for each pixel and the amount of smoothing applied is based on the inverse variation.

- **Edge Enhancement** — When you do not want a smoothing effect, you can apply Edge Enhancement. This mode is the direct opposite of a smoothing filter and creates a more defined edge within the image.

FIGURE 13-16

Use the NL Filter in GIMP to smooth out your image or create other types of enhancement effects. The NL Filter has three main operating modes: Alpha Trimmed Mean, Optimal Estimation, and Edge Enhancement.

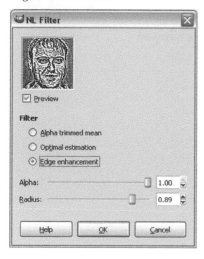

Red Eye Removal

Sometimes you take pictures, or have images that show what is called the "red eye" effect — the reddening of the eyes based on the lighting and how the picture was taken. You can remove this easily without disturbing the quality or integrity of your image. The Red Eye Removal filter is easy to use and is a filter you use constantly when working with images that contain eyes (or pupils).

This handy filter allows you to zoom in and correct any redness that appears in the image subject's pupils. To do this you must first open the filter and crop a selection you want to adjust (or enhance). Run it by going to Filters ➤ Enhance ➤ Red Eye Removal. Figure 13-17 shows the Red Eye Removal filter dialog box with an image selection that needs correction applied to it.

To operate the filter, simply click the (+) for zooming in or (−) for zooming out. You can move the scrollbars or click and drag in the preview window to bring the pupils into view. Next, you can adjust the threshold, which discolors the pupils thus removing the redness. You can also manually select the eyes (pupils) and then apply the filter, which makes zooming easier to do on larger images.

Sharpen

Many times when correcting an image, you will find that it lacks life and may appear out of focus, or dull. Most digital images need some form of correction, and sharpening the image is a favorite tweak among many digital photographers and artists. Lifeless images do not stand out to the viewer and can be easily corrected. Maybe the edges or seams are blurred or perhaps the picture is of low quality. To enhance (or sharpen) the image you can apply the Sharpen filter (Filters ➢ Enhance ➢ Sharpen) to your image.

FIGURE 13-17

Adjusting the Red Eye Removal filter so that redness within the pupils can be removed

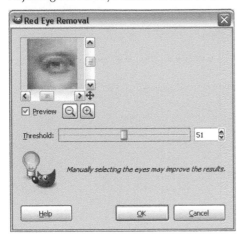

The filter works by accentuating the image's edges. It can, however, distort the image if too much sharpness is applied. Figure 13-18 shows an image with the Sharpen filter applied.

The Sharpen filter can also be used in conjunction with the Unsharp Mask filter, which is covered next. You may find that the Unsharp Mask filter provides the same results, so either can be used.

FIGURE 13-18

Viewing an image with the Sharpen filter applied. If too much sharpness is applied, the image may become distorted, so use the Preview option to help you make your adjustments if a more natural blend is required for your final proof.

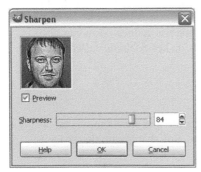

Tip

You can also use the Smart Sharpen (Redux) plug-in, which you can download from GIMP Plugin Registry at `http://registry.gimp.org/node/108`.

Smart Sharpen (Redux) utilizes a redux version of "smart sharpening." You can also download the Refocus (`http://refocus.sourceforge.net/`) plug-in if you want to script your sharpening options. ■

Unsharp Mask

Similar to the Sharpen filter, the Unsharp Mask filter (Filters ➤ Enhance ➤ Unsharp Mask) applies sharpness correction to your image or selection. It applies a more natural-looking enhancement to your image. Whereas the Sharpen filter sometimes creates (or increases the amount of) noise in your image, the Unsharp Mask filter enhances your images or selections without creating noise or blemishes. Figure 13-19 shows the Unsharp Mask dialog box with an image preview that shows a cleaner-looking image once the filter is applied.

FIGURE 13-19

Using the Unsharp Mask filter to create a great-looking image without the noise, distortion, or blemishes sometimes created by the Sharpen filter, or other applications, such as a scanner's sharpen software tools

A few options are available within the Unsharp Mask filter. They are as follows:

- **Radius** — You can adjust the Radius option by using the slider and moving it from left to right. Or, you can simply key in the number you want within the input box. The numbers range from 0.1 to 120. This slider (or numerical setting) allows you to set the number of pixels on either side or any edge found on your image that will be affected.

- **Amount** — This slider and the input box allow you to set the sharpening strength. The numbers range from 0.00 to 5.00.

- **Threshold** — The Threshold option operates just like the Radius and Amount options do. Threshold allows you to adjust pixel values so that you can refine the sharpening effect to avoid noise or blemishes in your composition or work.

Note

Some plug-ins are not available by default with GIMP. Some require you to download them from the GIMP Plugin Registry. If you are looking for a denoising tool, you can download the Wavelet Denoise plug-in (http://registry.gimp.org/node/4235). This filter/plug-in is a tool to reduce noise in each channel of an image separately. It provides you with a user interface to work within, gives you selectable denoising effects per channel, allows you to perform noise-profiling, and much more. ∎

Distortion Filters

Distortion (also known as Distort) filters are used for taking a clean image and creating distortion effects within it. The Distort filters transform your image in many different ways. The filters covered in this section include Blinds, Curve Bend, Emboss, Engrave, Erase Every Other Row, IWarp, Lens Distortion, Mosaic, Newsprint, Pagecurl, Polar Coordinates, Ripple, Shift, Value Propagate, Video, Waves, Whirl and Pinch, and Wind.

Blinds

The Blinds filter creates a "'venetian blind" effect within your image. Typical window blinds allow light in and out based on horizontal and vertical slats. You may want to apply this to an image to produce an effect that gives the viewer a distorted view of the original image. Run it by going to Filters ➤ Distort ➤ Blinds. Figure 13-20 clearly shows how the Blinds filter distorts an image, just like a set of window blinds distorts the incoming sunlight.

FIGURE 13-20

Using the Blinds filter on your image to create a distorted view of the original picture

The Blinds filter dialog box contains many options you can work with. You can adjust the orientation of the effect with the Orientation option. Here you can adjust the distortion of the blinds

to appear horizontally, or as in Figure 13-20, vertically. As well, you can adjust the Background option so that the batten color is that of the toolbox background. The Transparent check box option allows you to create a transparent background within your image, but your image must have an Alpha channel.

You can also adjust the displacement by using the slider option. The slider (or input box) allows for the widening of the battens and simulates the opening and closing of window blinds. The Number of Segments option allows you to select the number of battens that are viewable within the image.

Curve Bend

The Curve Bend filter (Filters ➤ Distort ➤ Curve Bend) is extremely useful when you want to create a flexure effect on your image. The Curve Bend filter can help create concave images, and give the image swerve, arc, and many other features that provide the viewer something interesting to look at.

This filter allows you to produce curves and other distortions that, when applied to the active layer or selection, give you many different effects to select from within GIMP's Distort menu.

In the Curve Bend filter dialog, you can configure many options to include smoothing, antialiasing, setting curves, and many others covered in more detail shortly.

It is important to take some time and go over all the options within this filter, because it's one that offers many features. You will find this filter extremely dense. For example, even the preview options are more detailed than those for some of the other filters and provide you with a more "flexible" approach in working with your image — pun intended! Take note that the preview options in this dialog take some time to process. Hence the two options for viewing: Preview Once, which allows a manual option to preview, and Automatic Preview, which shows you changes as you make them. Again, this is extremely processer (system resource) intensive, and may be slow or choppy when you are working. You can configure multiple options within the Curve Bend filter dialog box. They are as follows:

- **Options** — Within the options section of the Curve Bend filter dialog box, you can adjust the rotation of the image, the smoothing, and the antialiasing, as well as work on a copy of the image instead of the original. You can adjust the rotation of the image by selecting the input box and keying in the rotation amount from 0 to 360 degrees counterclockwise from the image's starting point. When selected, the Work on Copy option creates a new layer within the Layers dialog box as shown in Figure 13-21. This layer is called curve_bend_ dummylayer_b and allows you to see changes to your images without changing or affecting the original layer. Once you click OK, it alters the image unless you decide to undo, or reverse it.

- **Modify Curves** — The Modify Curves option is where you can make the magic happen. This option is laid out in grid form and when used in conjunction with the Rotate option, allows you to create some very cool-looking distortion effects. The horizontal line present in the middle of the grid is where you can start to bend and twist your work. Each point along the line you decide to alter is called a *node*. You can grab each node with your mouse

FIGURE 13-21

Using the Curve Bend filter to apply distortion effects to your image. Here, you can use the Work on Copy option to create a new layer called curve_bend_dummylayer_b, which allows you to view changes to your image without affecting the original until you commit the changes by clicking OK in the Curve Bend dialog box.

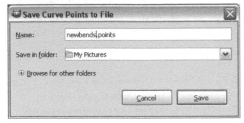

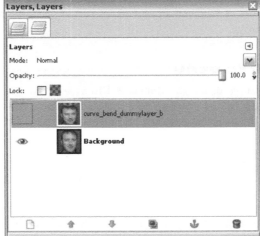

and further bend your work along the grid. The one limitation you should know about when working with this grid is that you can create only two curves on the grid at one time. Each one is defined with a name: one is the upper border and the other is the lower border. These are activated by selecting the appropriate radio button.

- **Curve for Border** — The Curve for Border option allows you to configure the upper and lower sections of the image. It allows you to select whether the active curve should be applied to the top or bottom of the image. The curve border is tricky to configure because it's based on the active curve, which can change based on how you rotate your image, so be aware of the changes you make and check them often within the preview of the dialog box.

- **Curve Type** — The Curve Type option allows you to automatically set a smooth, well-rounded curve when you move the nodes within the Modify Curves section of the Curve Bend filter dialog box. You can set the Smooth option or the Free option. The Free option allows you to draw (freehand) the curve you need. Your curve replaces the active curve.

- **Copy, Mirror, Swap, and Reset** — These buttons give you many options. Select Copy to copy the active curve you are working on from one border to the other border of the image. Mirror allows you to copy (or mirror) the active curve to the other border of your image. Slightly different from the Copy option, the Mirror option produces a mirror effect, which is the reverse of what you would see with the Copy option. Swap produces an interesting result: it interchanges upper and lower curves within your image, swapping one for the other. Upper defines the top portion of the image and Lower defines the bottom side of the image. Reset simply resets the active curve to its default or original position point.

- **Open or Save** — The Open button option allows you to load a curve from a file and the Save button allows you to save the curve dimensions you created to a file (discussed next) so you can apply it to other images (or new ones) you load into the image window.

You can save your Curve Point options to a file and then open that file to apply your presets to new images. Figure 13-22 shows the loading of a newbends.points file, which speeds up your work. You can find these files by clicking the top of the Load Curve Points from File dialog box, either in your profile or My Documents, for example.

FIGURE 13-22

Loading curve points from a saved file, which can be applied to new images. This saves you a lot of time and produces a great deal of accuracy when trying to give multiple images an identical effect.

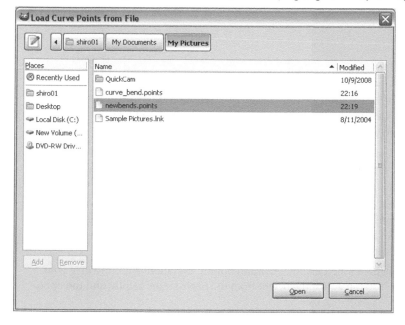

Emboss

Embossing is the application of the Emboss filter to your image in the active layer. It can only be used with RGB images, so others, such as CMYK or grayscale, will not work and the Emboss option in the Filter menu is grayed out and unusable.

This filter is helpful in creating different lighting effects within your image. Run it by going to Filters ➢ Distorts ➢ Emboss. Figure 13-23 shows the Emboss filter dialog box where you can adjust the effect to your liking.

FIGURE 13-23

Viewing the Emboss filter when editing an RGB file. Here you can see that nifty effects can be created, such as taking a full-color image and turning it into what appears to be a hand drawing.

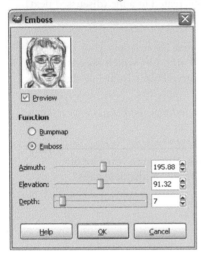

The Emboss filter affects the active layer of your image or a selection of it. You can create "bumps" and "hollows" in your work, or bright and dark areas. Multiple options are available within the Emboss filter dialog box. They are as follows:

- **Function** — You can set two function controls: Bumpmap and Emboss. With the Bumpmap option, you can configure smoothing options that preserve your original image colors. The Emboss option creates a grayscale image out of the original RGB file.

- **Azimuth** — You can adjust the amount of lighting used in your image based on the points of a compass by configuring the Azimuth slider or numerical input box. These numbers range from 0 to 360, just like the circumference of a circle. This works counterclockwise, with east being 0 degrees and west being 90 degrees.

- **Elevation** — Configured much like the Azimuth option, Elevation is used to give your image some depth. You can adjust the height from the horizon, the zenith, and the opposite horizon.

- **Depth** — Configured much like Azimuth and Elevation, the Depth option is used to provide the element of depth when used in conjunction with the Elevation option. It does this by utilizing lighting to create depth. When you increase the value of Depth, light decreases and vice versa.

Engrave

Engraving it a very old technique that has been used for centuries and was started with rocks! It involves etching or carving designs into a plate (or other flat surface), which can then be used to produce a lithograph. Today in the digital realm, the effect is the same but you do not need to use rocks and stones; instead you apply the Engraving effect with the click of a mouse.

The Engrave filter (Filters ➤ Distorts ➤ Engrave) is used to produce an engraving effect on your image. The image can be made into a black-and-white graphic and can only be used on layers (or floating selections) with an alpha channel; otherwise, it is inaccessible within the Distort menu. When you add a layer, the option appears and you can launch the filter. Figure 13-24 shows the addition of a layer so that the Engrave effect can be used.

FIGURE 13-24

Creating a new layer so that the Engrave option can be used on your selection

Figure 13-25 shows the Engrave filter dialog box. Here you can adjust the amount of effect to be applied to your image.

FIGURE 13-25

Using the Engrave filter dialog box to apply engraving distortion effects to your current image or selection

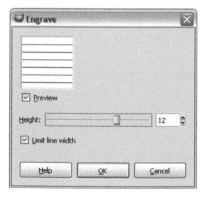

You can adjust a couple of options within the Engrave filter. For one, you can use the Height slider (or input box) to apply the height of the engraving lines from 2 to 16. You can adjust the line width between individual engraving lines by selecting the Limit line width check box. If enabled, lines that are thin will not be drawn on areas of contiguous or juxtaposed colors.

Erase Every Other Row

The Erase Every Other Row filter (Filters ➤ Distorts ➤ Erase Every Other Row) is an easy-to-use effect that allows you to do exactly what it says; erase every other row within your image's active layer, which changes the rows to the background color. You need to set your background color before applying this effect; otherwise the default will be solid white. Figure 13-26 shows the dialog box where you can make your adjustments.

FIGURE 13-26

Using the Erase Every Other Row filter to set what you erase to the background color in the image window

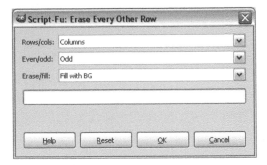

You can also adjust a few Erase Every Other Row options. Rows/Cols (columns) allows you to adjust the use of either rows or columns. The Even/Odd field allows you to set either even or odd rows or columns. The Erase/Fill field allows you to set the background as the color of your current background, or erase, which removes it. Fill with BG (background) relies on the color you set for your background.

You also need to rely on the alpha channel when using this effect. If the active layer has an alpha channel, your erased rows or columns will not be viewable because they will be transparent. Click OK to process the filter, or Reset to set the settings within the Erase Every Other Row filter dialog box to their original (default) settings.

This filter is helpful when interlacing effects are desired. For example, you can use the Erase Every Other Row filter to do the inverse of the Deinterlace filter.

IWarp

The IWarp filter allows you to distort sections of your image to create fading effects using enhanced animation tools. Run it by going to Filters ➤ Distorts ➤ IWarp. Figure 13-27 shows the IWarp filter, which can help you create animations with your images.

FIGURE 13-27

Using the IWarp filter to create animations with your images. In the left image distortion, the deform mode selected was Move, which was used to move elements of the image around. In the right graphic, the Shrink mode was used, creating a very different effect with the same tool.

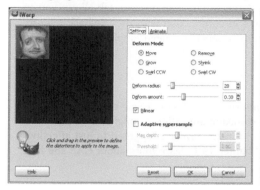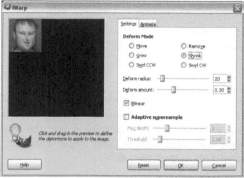

As you can see, the IWarp filter dialog box includes many features and options. This is arguably one of the most difficult filters to grasp and work with because of its flexibility and the depth and breadth of its contents.

Also, learning how to apply animation correctly can be challenging, but not impossible. To use the IWarp filter, you can select Deform Mode, and then click the preview and drag the mouse pointer. You can see the handy tip within the dialog box that explains how to use the preview function, which is much different than the other distortion effects previously discussed. The Reset button on the bottom of the dialog box resets your settings as well as the preview you worked with.

You can use multiple options within the IWarp filter dialog box and they are found on two separate tabs: Settings and Animate. The following options are located within the Settings tab:

- **Deform Mode** — This allows you to move, grow, swirl (counterclockwise and clockwise), remove, and shrink your image easily. Move mode allows you to stretch sections of your image, and Grow mode allows you to inflate or grow sections of your image based on where you select from within it. Using the Swirl mode (CCW or CW) allows you to create a swirling effect in your image. Remove mode allows you to remove any distorted effects previously applied. You can also use the Reset button to do this, but it resets the entire image, whereas Remove mode can be selective. Shrink mode is handy when you want to shrink or collapse sections of your image. Selecting each mode and working with it in the Preview section gives you a good grasp of what these modes allow you to do.

- **Deform Radius and Deform Amount** — Deform Radius allows you to use the slider or input box to adjust the radius of the pixels in the image from 5 to 100. Deform Amount gives you the same slider and input box options and helps you to set the shape of your image in pixels ranging from 0.0 to 1.0. Bilinear provides a smoothing effect to your image. You can check the box to activate it.

- **Adaptive Supersample** — Use Adaptive Supersample when you want to adjust your image so that it looks better by allowing for more sampling content (or a higher sample rate) to be used within your image. Check the check box to activate it. You can then to adjust the slider (or input boxes) of Max (maximum) Depth and Threshold.

The second tab in the IWarp filter dialog box is the Animate tab. The Animate tab allows you to apply animated effects to your image. This filter works in conjunction with the Playback plug-in. When these filters are used together, they allow you to produce animated graphics. The Animate tab is shown in Figure 13-28.

Note

The IWarp filter is used explicitly for simple styles of animation, similar to a GIF. Grow causes a growing animation. Swirl causes a swirling animation. Shrink causes a shrinking animation. It might be helpful to clarify that these effects occur as an animation over the course of many layers as opposed to just affecting a single image the way other tools in GIMP might. Reference Chapter 19 to learn more about GAP and how to make animated GIFs with GIMP. ■

FIGURE 13-28

Working with the Animate tab to produce effects and apply options such as Reverse and Ping Pong

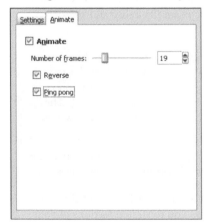

The Animate tab has multiple options. They are as follows:

- **Animate** — By selecting this check box, you allow GIMP (and the IWarp filter) to utilize the Playback plug-in to produce animated effects.
- **Number of Frames** — The Number of Frames slider and input box option allow you to set the number of images that appear in your final work. For example, selecting 5 produces an animation using five different images (and their corresponding layers) that you config-ure. The frames are stored as layers. When you save your work, it is saved in GIMP's native XCF format.

- **Reverse** — You can set the Reverse option by checking the check box. This creates an animation out of the original that plays in reverse.

- **Ping Pong** — Ping Pong is identical to Reverse, except it starts 0playing forward, then when it reaches the end of the animation, it plays in reverse until it gets back to the beginning — much like a game of ping-pong!

Figure 13-29 shows one layer of the final work. This gives you the option to get creative when using multiple images and layers. You can create a really interesting animation once you get the hang of working within the filter. For example, you can use the Layers dialog and edit each layer of your work (such as changing colors) to create a less generic looking animation.

FIGURE 13-29

Viewing one layer of a multi-layer animation created by IWarp

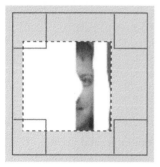

Lens Distortion

The Lens Distortion filter (Filters ➤ Distorts ➤ Lens Distortion) gives you a strong toolset to enhance and distort your images within GIMP. If you need to create a concave image, or bend the image to create a movement effect, the Lens Distortion effect is what you use. This filter, as shown in Figure 13-30, allows you to create effects, as well as correct an already distorted image that may have been taken by a camera with this exact same Lens Distortion effect.

The Preview option (Select the check box) gives you the same abilities as the Red Eye Removal filter but provides you more flexibility in working within your image or selection. Multiple options are available within the Lens Distortion filter dialog box. They are as follows:

- **Main** — The slider and input box fields of the Main option allow to control the exact amount of spherical correction needed to create convex and concave effects within your image or selection.

- **Edge** — The Edge option works identically to the Main option and specifies how much correction needs to be applied to the image's edges.

- **Zoom** — The Zoom option works the same way as the Main and Edge options. It allows you to control the amount of image enlargement and reduction.

FIGURE 13-30

Using the Lens Distortion filter to simulate a camera filter, produce distortion in a clean graphic, or give some depth to your image

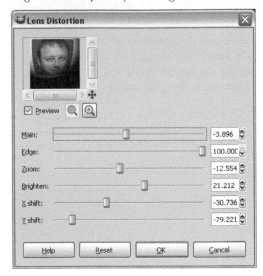

- **Brighten** — The Brighten option works the same way as the Main, Edge, and Zoom options. You use the slider (or input box) to adjust the amount of brightness introduced into your image. This option works only if you set the Main or Edge options to anything but zero.

- **X Shift and Y Shift** — The X Shift and Y Shift sliders allow you to specify the effect produced by setting the Main and Edge options to anything but zero and then control each axis until the effect gives you the result you want.

Mosaic

Traditional artists define a mosaic as art consisting of a design made of small pieces of colored stone or glass, or other elements. The Mosaic filter produces this effect by cutting the active layer (or selection) into chunks that resemble common shapes and then separating them so that the picture or image appears much like a traditional mosaic painting.

The Mosaic filter also takes each piece it creates and adds a little depth to it to create an aspect ratio. Run it by going to Filters ➤ Distorts ➤ Mosaic. Figure 13-31 shows the use of the Mosaic filter to produce a painting-like image based in traditional art concepts.

Mosaic filter options run deep and wide, just like the sliders that control them. Following are the multiple options you can use within the Mosaic filter dialog box:

- **Antialiasing** — Covered earlier in this chapter, Antialiasing is used to reduce the stepped aspect of your image borders. You can adjust your image in the Mosaic filter and apply antialiasing functions to create a better-looking image.

FIGURE 13-31

Distorting your image with the Mosaic filter to produce a painting-like image based in traditional art concepts. This filter allows you to control tiling options as well as lighting and color.

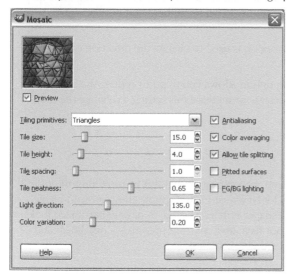

- **Color Averaging** — The Color Averaging option is used to provide a gradient to your image so that "inside" tiles (those within borders) can be averaged to a single color. This provides flexibility when trying to clean up and adjust the tiles you created or will create once you click OK. You can use the Preview pane to find the right gradient for your work.

- **Allow Tile Splitting** — The Allow Tile Splitting option gives you control over the splitting of tiles with multiple colors in your image, therefore providing better detail and flexibility in image distortion.

- **Pitted Surfaces** — The Pitted Surfaces option can give you a pitting or "pitted" look, which is similar to a porous, grainy surface image.

- **FG/BG Lighting** — The FG (foreground)/BG (background) Lighting option does exactly what it says; it gives you control over which tiles are lit and provides depth effects. Between each seam edge (or join), the lighting can be used to give a "raised" feel to your tiles.

- **Tiling Primitives** — The Tiling Primitives option is a fancy name to specify what type (or shape) your tiles form to. For example, you can create squares, hexagons, octagons, and triangles. Once you view the selection in the preview pane, you can select which tiling effect best suits your composition or work.

- **Tile Size** — The Tile Size slider and input box allow you to set the size of tile surface between seams and edges. You can create large or small tiles based on your needs.

- **Tile Height** — Just like the Tile Size option, the Tile Height option allows you to specify the height of each tile in your work.

- **Tile Spacing** — Just like Tile Size and Tile Height, Tile Spacing provides you with an option to create larger seams between tiles.

- **Tile Neatness** — There will come a time when you want to leave a more distorted look to your tiles. You can do this with the Tile Neatness option. You can specify the "neatness" level between 0 and 1. Setting the option to 0 provides a random shape and size selection that varies. When set to 1, many of the tiles will appear at the same size, although this may not look like a true mosaic image; using a setting in between these two numbers gives you a "messier" view of your work.

- **Light Direction** — The Light Direction option is used to change the direction of artificial light created by the Mosaic filter.

- **Color Variation** — The Color Variation option allows you to set or reduce the amount of color used within the image. You can decrease or increase this setting to change the coloring of your work.

Newsprint

GIMP's filter set to create distortion is in fact deep, and extremely helpful in providing multiple ways to enhance as well as distort your work. The Newsprint filter option allows you to create images that look like they were printed in a newspaper article. The way a newspaper image looks is extremely unique, because you normally do not have any coloring present — just black and white. If colors are used, many times they appear drab, or lifeless.

The way the filter works is simple. You can allow the Newsprint filter to "halftone" your work using a clustered-dot dither. Dithering is the process of taking a sample of the current pixel coloring scheme, taking a result from the comparison, and then applying that across all other pixels. Clustered-dot dither takes these consecutive results and makes a judgment based on how close (or adjacent) the pixels are, whereas dispersed-dot dither takes these consecutive results and makes a judgment based on how far apart they are from each other. Dispersed-dot dithering is the reverse of clustered-dot dithering.

The result of using dither and the Newsprint filter is to create an even look and feel across all pixels in the image and avoid the loss of spatial resolution. Run it by going to Filters ➢ Distorts ➢ Newsprint. Figure 13-32 shows an example of an image manipulated with the Newsprint filter.

Newsprint filter options include the ability to reset the entire filter to factory defaults, as well as to control resolution, screen type, and antialiasing features. You can use multiple options within the Newsprint filter dialog box. They are as follows:

- **Resolution** — The Resolution option helps control the cell size of your image, giving you more flexibility in your work and the best clarity options for your image. Multiple sliders and input boxes allow to refine your work. The Input SPI slider and input box are used to configure the resolution in samples per inch (SPI). This is automatically initialized to the input image's resolution. The Output LPI option is identical to the SPI slider and input box options, except Output LPI is configured by lines per inch (LPI). The Cell Size adjustment is used to configure the cell size in pixels.

FIGURE 13-32

Viewing an example of an image manipulated with the Newsprint filter

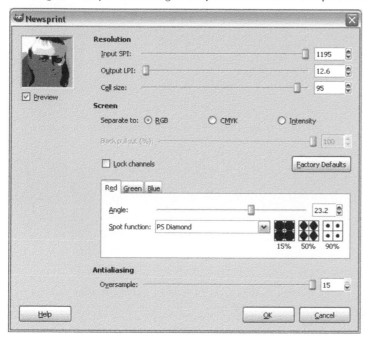

- **Screen** — The Screen option is used to select between RGB options and CMYK options and to configure intensity. This allows you to select the color space you want to work with.

Pagecurl

The Pagecurl filter is simple to use and self-explanatory in nature. It creates a page curl effect similar to a magazine with a one of its pages turned up. It curls a single corner of the image so that it looks like a turning page. To create this effect, GIMP relies on using a new alpha channel and layer. Run it by going to Filters ➤ Distorts ➤ Pagecurl. Figure 13-33 shows the Pagecurl Effect dialog box.

You can configure multiple options within the Pagecurl Effect filter dialog box. First, you can select where the page curl takes place — at the upper left, lower-left, upper-right, or lower-right corner of the image. The Curl Orientation option allows you to select either Horizontal or Vertical. You can also adjust the Shade under Curl option, which provides a deeper shadow effect in the corner of image directly under the page curl. If you select the drop-down menu, you can adjust the gradient. You can also adjust the curl opacity, which allows for more visibility into the corner that is curled.

FIGURE 13-33

Viewing the Pagecurl Effect dialog box, where you can create an interesting effect with the corner of an image

Polar Coordinates

Polar coordinates (sometimes referred to as polar coords) are used to configure a swirl-like distortion effect within your image that can be seen in the Preview pane of the dialog box shown in Figure 13-34. Run the Polar Coordinates filter by going to Filters ➤ Distorts ➤ Polar Coordinates. Figure 13-35 shows the Polar Coordinates filter dialog box.

FIGURE 13-34

Viewing the Polar Coordinates dialog box, where you can adjust your image so that it appears "swirled"

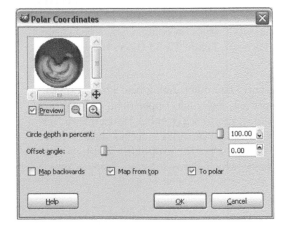

This filter is simple to use and understand. Need a distorted swirl effect? Use this filter. You can also use this filter for mapping an image, whether mapping filters or by applying the image to a 3D object. The Polar Coordinates filter options are as follows:

- **Circle Depth in Percent** — Shows the percentage you can set to create depth within your image. You can use the slider or the input box to change the percentage and check it in the preview pane.

- **Offset Angle** — The Offset Angle helps to control the angle from which the circle-based swirl will originate. It does this within a scale of 360 degrees (0 to 359°). You can also select check boxes for Map Backwards, Map from Top, and To Polar. If the Map Backwards check box is selected, mapping begins from the right side. If Map From Top is selected, then the bottom row of the image appears on the outside and the top row is placed in the middle. If To Polar is selected, the image is mapped onto a circle. If unchecked, a rectangle is used.

Ripple

The Ripple filter is also another tool that is very easy to use and understand. Just like a ripple that forms from skipping stones across a calm body of water, this tool creates wave-like ripples. This filter operates by displacing the active layer's pixels to create the illusion of a rippled image. Run it by going to Filters ➤ Distorts ➤ Ripple. Figure 13-35 shows how the Ripple filer effect can be used to take a static image and apply the appearance of motion.

FIGURE 13-35

The Ripple filter effect used to create motion in a picture or image that has none

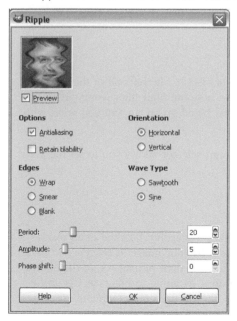

Once you have launched the filter, you can use multiple settings within it to create distorted effects. They are as follows:

- **Options** — The Options section allows you to adjust antialiasing and retain tilability. Antialiasing improves the image's edges so that they have a consistent look and feel. To retain tileability, you only need to check the check box to enable it. This ensures that GIMP preserves the image if it is tiled. This creates an interesting effect on tiled images.

- **Edges** — The Edges option allows you to adjust the Wrap, Smear, and Blank settings of the image. Ripples cause pixel displacement, so this radio button option allows you to keep the integrity of your edges (or seams in tiles) so that the tiling imagery is not completely disrupted by the ripple effect. When using the Wrap option, you can instruct GIMP to wrap the pixels to reduce the damage to your seams that Ripple can and will affect. Selecting Smear does the opposite of Wrap; it blurs the seams. Blank can be used when you want to replace spaces or spots in the image that are missing an entry in the pixel. It fills this blank space with a black-colored pixel.

- **Orientation** — The Orientation option allows you to select whether the image has a horizontal or vertical orientation in relation to the picture within the image window.

- **Wave Type** — You can select two different wave types in the Wave Type option section of the Ripple filter dialog box. You can configure a sawtooth-type wave or a sine-type wave. Sine waves are commonly used to refer to analog, and sawtooth waves usually represent digital signals.

- **Period** — You can also adjust (with a slider or input box) the period, which is related to wavelength and numbered from 0 to 200 pixels.

- **Amplitude** — You can also adjust (with a slider or input box) the amplitude, which is related to wave height and numbered from 0 to 200 pixels.

- **Phase Shift** — Phase Shift can be configured just like the Period and Amplitude options, but can be set from 0 to 360 degrees.

Shift

The Shift filter (Filters ➤ Distorts ➤ Shift) does exactly what is says. It shifts all of the pixels in the image horizontally or vertically. Figure 13-36 shows how the Shift filter works on an image. Here, you can see how a simple image can be shifted based on an amount you select with the Shift Amount pull-down or input box option.

Whether you shift horizontally or vertically, the Shift Amount selector allows you to set the pixels (or other selectable units of measurement) to be shifted.

Value Propagate

The Value Propagate filter works on colored borders. It takes a snapshot baseline of all pixels in the image, and then from this difference, applies a pattern to your image in reference to the types of pixels that were discovered. This finds a mean value and then propagates, or distributes, this value across the remaining pixels within the image. Run it by going to Filters ➤ Distorts ➤ Value Propagate. Figure 13-37 shows the Value Propagate filter in use on a graphic to create a distorted view of the original image.

FIGURE 13-36

Viewing a distorted image within the Shift filter dialog box

FIGURE 13-37

Using the Value Propagate filter to adjust all of the pixels in your image so that if (for example) you wanted a lighter-looking picture, you would attempt to create a larger value of white pixels within the image

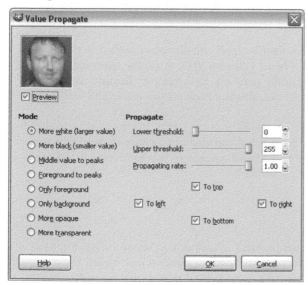

The Value Propagate filter options are dense, but simple to understand. If you understand how the tool works, all you need to do is use the remaining sections to modify (and refine) your work. You can use multiple options within the Value Propagate filter dialog box. They are as follows:

- **Mode** — The Mode section allows you to select multiple options to refine your work. For example, you can select More White (Larger Value), which supplies a larger amount of white colored pixels to your image. The rest of the options are extremely easy to understand as well. If you want More Black (Smaller Number), you need to adjust your mode option and check to see if your image turns out correctly in the preview pane. There is no reason to fear experimentation when working with filters, because you are creating art and it's ultimately up to you how you want your image to appear. If you are looking for specific effects like producing an image that is more opaque, you would make that radio button selection under the Mode section.

- **Propagate** — The Propagate section allows you to adjust lower and upper thresholds as well as an average propagation time.

- **Propagating direction** — These check box options allow you to select the direction of propagation, either to the top, bottom, left, or right side of your image.

Video

The Video filter option is very handy and extremely easy to use. It supplies a way to create RGB files with a low dot-pitch value. Run it by going to Filters ➤ Distorts ➤ Video. (See Figure 13-38.)

To create a video-like screen you can use this filter to apply the distortion needed to create the simulated lines you would normally see on a home video on VHS, or on the television. This is helpful when you want to make a picture really stand out to the viewer. Because most folks are extremely familiar with what the TV looks like, this is a great way to create an effect that simulates that same look and feel.

There are many screen emulations available for use and you should be aware of the differences between each. If you do not like the type of video-based emulation, you can research and use other options, plug-ins, and tools to enhance your work.

Waves

The Waves filter (much like Ripple) is another tool that is very easy to use to create distorted views of your image. Just like a wave that forms from skipping stones across a calm body of water, this tool creates wave-like ripples. This filter operates by displacing the active layer's pixels to create the illusion of a rippled image or a wave. Run it by going to Filters ➤ Distorts ➤ Waves. Figure 13-39 shows an image twisted to display a wave effect.

FIGURE 13-38

Viewing the Video effect on an image located within the image window of GIMP

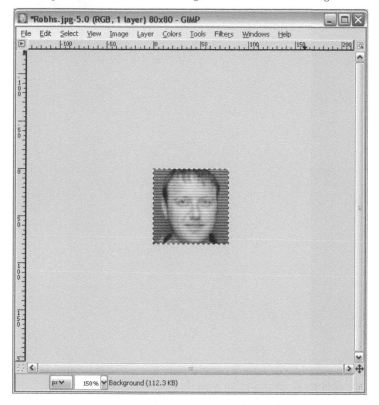

The Waves filter options are similar to Ripple as well. You can use multiple options within the Waves filter dialog box. They are as follows:

- **Mode** — The Mode section contains two main modes: Smear and Blacken. The Smear option allows areas in the selection or image to be rendered as empty space within and on all sides. The Blacken option sets all empty areas as colored pixels.

- **Reflective** — The Reflective check box causes a reflective effect within your wave. Use this to mirror the wave on all sides of the top of the curve.

- **Amplitude** — You can also adjust (with a slider or input box) the Amplitude, which is related to wave height and will vary the height of the waves created in your image.

- **Phase** — Phase can be configured just like the Amplitude option, and helps to focus the shift to the top of wave.

- **Wavelength** — You can also adjust (with a slider or input box) the wavelength. Wavelength adjusts the distance between the tops of all waves in your image.

FIGURE 13-39

Viewing a distorted image within the Waves filter dialog box. Use this filter to create swirling and smearing effects.

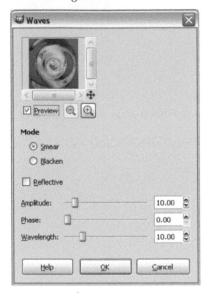

Whirl and Pinch

If you haven't seen enough distortion already, you have a couple more filters to work with. This filter, Whirl and Pinch, focuses the distortion effect so that you do not affect the entire work (or image) as a whole. Just like most other filters, this filter can be applied to small portion or segment of an image by using any of the selection tools in the Toolbox. This way if you want to put a whirl effect on a select area rather than the whole image, you can do so. This filter is a faster way of achieving these effects than other methods we have covered (like using the Displace filter) to create your desired effects.

Whirl and Pinch (Filters ➤ Distorts ➤ Whirl and Pinch) distorts your image so that all waves have a common center. It creates a "whirlpool" effect that you can apply to your images. Pinching is used to fix issues resulting from using "fish-eye" type lenses on your camera. (It is also known as "barrel distortion.") Figure 13-40 shows how an image can be whirled and swirled for different distortion effects.

You can use multiple options within the Whirl and Pinch filter dialog box. They are as follows:

- **Whirl Angle** — The Whirl Angle option turns the effect clockwise or counterclockwise.

- **Pinch Amount** — The Pitch Amount option sets the depth, meaning if you wanted a whirlpool effect, you would want the center to seem sucked in. This slider (or input box) can be used to adjust the setting so that depth can be created.

- **Radius** — The Radius option is used to set the width of the whirlpool effect. You may want to spread the pool out a bit to make it concave, so you can set the Radius option to control this.

Viewing an image distorted by the Whirl and Pinch filter

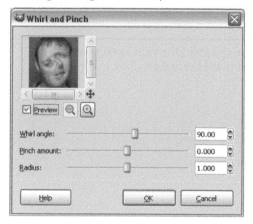

Wind

Have you had enough distorting yet? Well, if you have room for one more, another awesome tool to create digital art is the Wind filter. When you use the Wind filter to distort your image, you can create motion blur.

This tool can be used just like any blurring filter. It's versatile because it can give you very creative distortions. The Wind filter can render very thin black and white lines by detecting the image's edges and stretching the image to create motion blur.

Run it by going to Filters ➤ Distorts ➤ Wind. Figure 13-41 shows the Wind filter dialog box. Within it, you can adjust the style, direction, and edge affected of the blur motion you create. Use the Preview pane to adjust it and, as shown in the image, create an interesting distortion effect.

You can use multiple options within the Wind filter dialog box. They are as follows:

- **Style** — The Style option can be used to produce a "moving" effect. Just like real wind, Mother Nature blows leaves off trees, or provides a light breeze to relax by; the same goes for the style in which this effect is put to use. That being said, you should try the Wind and Blast options, which are similar to a light breeze or a hurricane, respectively.

- **Direction** — The wind comes from the eastern, western, northern, or southern directions. Although real wind can come from any direction (including up and down), the Direction settings within the Wind filter allow you to bring the wind in from the left or right side of the preview pane.

- **Edge Affected** — The Edge Affected option is exactly what it sounds like. The edge that is affected is the leading edge, trailing edge, or both edges.

- **Threshold** — You can adjust the slider from 0 to 50. The higher the number, the less the effect on the overall image.

- **Strength** — You can set the wind source in two directions. You can apply a strength factor to show stronger wind from either direction by adjusting the Strength option.

FIGURE 13-41

Using the Wind filter to create a blurring distortion effect. Here the Left Direction option was selected to show that the distortion effect follows the selection within the Wind dialog box.

All your setting changes appear in the preview window without affecting the image until you click OK. The Wind filter then produces a final image, which should look as if wind moved the image left or right.

Summary

Wow, this chapter covered a lot of filters and how to use them, and there are many more filters to come in the next chapter. In this chapter you learned a lot about blurring, enhancing, and distorting your images using GIMP.

You also learned about the Blur, Enhance, and Distort menu options as well as all the tools contained within them, such as Gaussian Blur, Destripe, and Ripple, to name a few. While working within GIMP's many filter sets, you will find many new ways to work with and alter your graphics, photographs, or scanned images.

The next chapter covers image-creation filters, which you can use to give depth to your images by using light and shadow effects, as well as using render filters for natural image creation.

Using Image Creation Filters

The first section of this chapter covers the fundamentals of light and shadow effects and how they affect your digital images when filtered with GIMP. GIMP's Filters menu runs deep and this chapter covers many of the plug-ins you can use. Of course, you can find many more online within GIMP's Plugin Registry and expand your toolset. I point you in the right direction to get them, so no worries.

GIMP includes three groups of filters that directly relate to lighting and shadow effects. First, you can work with filters that render illumination effects within your image. Second, many script-based shortcuts are available that apply multiple effects for lighting and shadowing features. Third, you can use specific filters such as the Lens Effect filter you'll learn about in this chapter, to apply glass-like effects to an image to emulate many popular digital camera lenses.

IN THIS CHAPTER
Giving your images depth with light and shadow effects
Understanding the possibilities that a little noise can provide
Using render filters for natural image creation

Light and Shadow Filters

Light and Shadow filters are useful when you need to change the lighting effect in a digital image. Your work may require the use of shadow effects as well. GIMP includes many filters for adjusting, changing, and filtering out light. All these tools are found within the Filters ➢ Light and Shadow menu, where they are broken into three groupings of filters. Use them to render illumination effects in your work. The first set of filters you can use includes Gradient Flare, Lens Flare, Lighting Effects, Sparkle, and Supernova. You can also use Drop Shadow, Perspective and Xach-Effect to create many different shadow effects in your work. These are basically scripts that run various other effects to produce any type of shadow you can think of. GIMP also incorporates many glass-effect filters, which can alter your image in a way as if it were being seen through a photographic lens. These are Lens Effect and Glass Tile. Let's take a look at the first set of filters in the Light and Shadow category.

Gradient Flare

When thinking about how to apply lighting enhancements to your image or selection, you should consider using the Gradient Flare filter effect. Staring directly into the sun is not recommended, but using this effect gives you an effect similar to looking into the sun or some other form of blinding light source. Although you cannot stare into the sun for too long, you can create the same effect on an image without any of the harmful side effects.

The filter does this by creating a glow around the source of the blinding light, as well as halo and radiation effects. The Gradient Flare filter effect is comprised of three main components with many configurable options: Glow, Rays, and Second Flares. Although it's not recommended that you abuse this filter, try them to get accustomed to how they work.

This filter is located in the image window menu under the Light and Shadow menu. Run it by going to Filters ➤ Light and Shadow ➤ Gradient Flare. Figure 14-1 shows the Settings tab options found within the Gradient Flare filter dialog.

FIGURE 14-1

Adjusting the gradient options within the Settings tab of the Gradient Flare filter

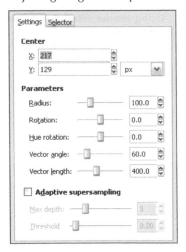

The two main tabs — Settings and Selector — allow you to configure the Gradient Flare filter quickly and easily. The presets (found in the Selector tab) are covered shortly. For now, let's go

over the Center, Parameters, and Adaptive Supersampling sections so you get an idea about how to use this specific GIMP plug-in. The Settings tab allows you to set the following parameters manually:

- **Center** — The Center section allows you to adjust the X and Y options.

- **Parameters** — The Parameters section allows you to adjust the Radius, Rotation, Hue Rotation, Vector Angle, and Vector Length slider boxes and input boxes to adjust the look of the effect. Obviously the Radius slider adjusts the position of the effect from center, and Rotation rotates the effect. Hue Rotation adjusts the color or tint of the filtered effect. Vector Angle turns the Second Flares and Vector Length adjusts the variance of Second flares. When we discuss the Gradient Flare filter later in the chapter, Second Flares will be covered in more depth.

- **Adaptive Supersampling** — When you check Adaptive Supersampling, you select antialiasing options to set the depth and threshold of the effect.

The next tab over is the Selector tab, as shown in Figure 14-2. This tab allows you to select from multiple presets. The preconfigured glare is useful and can be adjusted to your liking.

FIGURE 14-2

Using the Gradient Flare filter to adjust the lighting on items in your image, such as intensifying the glare that may be coming from a windshield

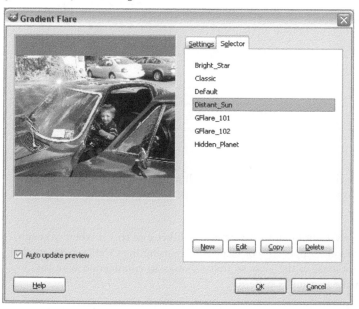

In the Selector tab, you can select from Bright_Star, Classic, Default, Distant_Sun, GFlare_101, GFlare_102, and Hidden_Planet. You can also use the New, Edit, Copy, and Delete buttons to

create new preset profiles you design, edit any of the current (or future) presets, and copy one (if you need a backup before editing). You also have an option to delete unwanted or unused profiles.

The Gradient Flare Editor (as shown in Figure 14-3) is a great tool for tweaking the glow of the glare and adjusting the beams, flares, and rays. The tabs let you adjust General, Glow, Rays, and Second Flares options.

FIGURE 14-3

Using the Gradient Flare Editor to further tweak your Glow, Rays, and Second Flares

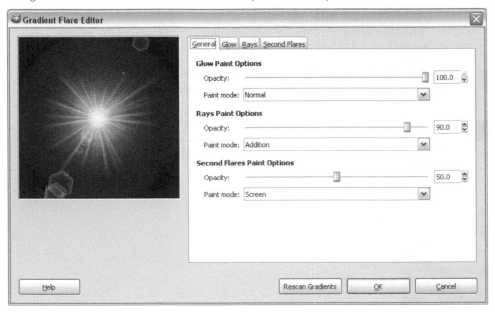

In the General tab you can adjust the Glow Paint options, which allows you to contain the opacity of the glow from 0 to 100. You can adjust this using the slider or input box adjustment options.

The Paint Mode option under Glow Paint Options is worth a look because this is where you can really get the most out of this tab's effect options. For example, try using the Overlay paint mode while adjusting the light and dark areas of the glow so that it works in conjunction with the picture's natural dark areas to make a seamless pattern.

Once you click OK, the Editor closes. Next, you can apply the effect by clicking the OK button in the Gradient Flare filter dialog. In the image window, you see the application of the new lighting effect take place. The final product, as shown in Figure 14-4, shows a glow coming off a glass and metallic surface, which gives the impression that it's a very sunny day and the light is very bright, causing a reflection on the edge of a car.

Tip

You can quickly try different views of the Gradient Flare filter by going to the Filters menu and selecting Repeat "Gradient Flare." You can also use the shortcut keystroke Ctrl+F on your keyboard. This reapplies the effect and may give you different flares (which, as an example, may follow the natural ones on the screen). If you're intensifying an effect, this can help you line up the rays better and give you options for variety. Or, you can use the Rescan Gradients button at the bottom of the Gradient Flare Editor dialog. These are quick ways to try for a different effect if you are unhappy with the first one selected. ■

FIGURE 14-4

Applying the Gradient Flare to the windshield of a car

Lens Flare

If you want to intensify a light source (such as a light bulb), you can use the Lens Flare filter included with GIMP's plug-ins. This filter helps produce a glare where one is not present and is much more limited than the Gradient Flare filter. However, the Lens Flare filter is easier to use when this specific effect is needed.

To open it, go to the image window and click Filters ➤ Light and Shadow ➤ Lens Flare. Figure 14-5 shows the application of the Lens Flare filter effect within the Lens Flare filter dialog box. Here, you can use the crosshairs in the preview section of the dialog to place the origin of the intensity.

You can also zoom in using the horizontal and vertical scroll bars and zoom button options. The right side of Figure 14-5 shows how easy it is to zoom in to a light and meticulously apply the flare. You can also use the Center of Flare Effect X and Y input options to apply the effect.

The differences in your final images are quite dramatic. Figure 14-6 shows the stark differences between the before and after images. Other than applying this effect, you have more functionality (and flexibility) when using the Gradient Flare filter.

FIGURE 14-5

On the left, creating a glare where one doesn't already exist using the Lens Flare filter dialog crosshairs; on the right, zooming in to place the Lens Flare crosshairs direclty on the light source for best effect

FIGURE 14-6

On the left, viewing an image before rendering the Lens Flare filter, and on the right, viewing an image after rendering the Lens Flare filter

Lighting Effects

Digital photographers and editors all know that the secret to getting great shots is to make sure that you set your lighting correctly. Whether a flash on your camera, or lights you set up to illuminate the area in which you intend to take your shots, knowing how to reduce shadows (unless intended) will inevitably save you loads of time while editing.

When working with green screen elements, for example, lighting the background is important for getting a great shot. With the Lighting Effects filter, found in GIMP's Filter menu, you can create great lighting effects that light up an entire background evenly without creating shadows. This is done with artificial light sources that were not present in the original photo shoot. Now you can apply any type of lighting desired, without having it in the original.

To use this filter, from the image window choose Filters ➤ Light and Shadow ➤ Lighting Effects. Figure 14-7 shows the Lighting Effects filter dialog box.

FIGURE 14-7

Using the Lighting Effects filter in GIMP to adjust the lighting on the face of a guitar amplifier

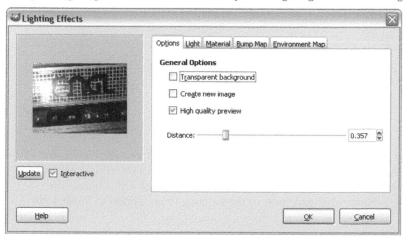

When shooting and working with lighting, you should try to get the shot you intend before applying effects. If you need to adjust the lighting in an image, the Lighting Effects filter is for you. When working with slow systems (low on hardware resources), you may want to uncheck Interactive for quicker previews. The Update button can then be used to process your changes for preview.

Next, you will find the Options tab, followed by the Light, Material, Bump Map, and Environmental Map tabs. In the Options tab, you can adjust the General Options by checking the Transparent Background, Create a New Image, and High Quality Preview check boxes. These options set the options for new image creation, whether the final image will be a new image (not replacing the old one), one with a transparent background, or one that shows the final image at its highest quality in the preview pane. Take note that using this last option taxes your hardware resources to their limits, so use caution when applying it.

You can also adjust the Distance slider and input box to set a very specific amount of light originating from the center of the image. This helps you refine the effect as you need to.

The next tab is the Light tab as shown in Figure 14-8. This tab provides options to adjust the exact amount and focus of the light effect you apply.

FIGURE 14-8

GIMP's Light Settings options give you six light setting choices to choose from. You have multiple options and you can save your own using the Lighting Preset Save option at the bottom of the dialog box.

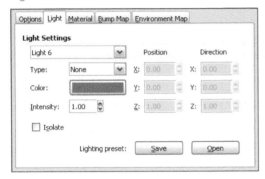

You can adjust the color of lighting preset by selecting the color bar (or swatches) with your mouse. You can adjust the lighting color by clicking the color swatch and choosing your desired color from the color picker that appears. After you adjust the color, click OK. To save the current light source color scheme, click Save next to the Lighting Preset option to finish your adjustments.

Now, you can check to see how this color scheme works with your image in the preview pane, or apply it. This filter asks a lot of your hardware to process and generate a preview, so be patient. If you have multiple lights, the Isolate check box singles out just the current light you're working on so you can differentiate it from the other lights. Click OK to process the effect, or move to the Material tab.

Tip

You can use the Isolate check box within the Lighting Effects filter dialog box to toggle between viewing all six preset light sources together in the preview pane, or just the one you are currently adjusting. Use the preview options of Interactive and Update to use less CPU resources, because using all of these options together on a low-quality workstation may freeze up your system, or take forever to process. A low-quality workstation would be one that does not meet or exceed the recommended system requirements needed to run GIMP.

If you like the new coloring, you can then adjust the Material Properties options found within the Material tab shown in Figure 14-9. ∎

FIGURE 14-9

Making Material Properties adjustments to your final work within the Lighting Effects filter

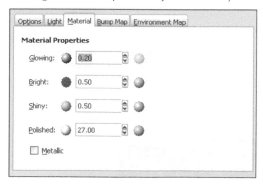

Try each option for the best results on your finished work. Check the preview pane to see how these options directly affect your work. Next, click the Bump Map tab. By checking the Enable Bump Mapping check box, you apply a new distorted filter effect to your image as shown in Figure 14-10.

FIGURE 14-10

Using a bump map to apply a distorted lighting effect to your image

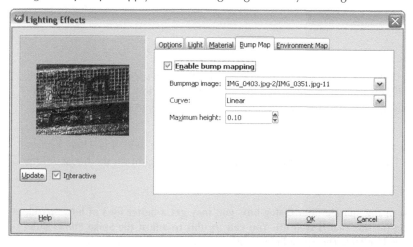

The bump map found in this filter differs from the one generated by the Bump Map filter. The latter only accounts for a single light source while using the bump map here takes into account up to all six of the available lights.

To apply another distorted view of your image using lighting effects, click the Environment Map tab and check the Enable Environment Mapping check box. This filter lets you use lighting to bend your image. It does this by faking reflections.

Try each tab and its lighting effects to find which ones give you what you are looking for. Figure 14-11 shows the before and after shots of the amplifier's chrome face front with additional lighting added to enhance it.

FIGURE 14-11

On the left is the unmodified photo. On the right, the same amplifier after the Lighting Effects filter was applied to add light to a section of the image that requires glow effects, recoloring, bump mapping, and environmental mapping features.

Sparkle

The Sparkle filter effect (Filters ➤ Light and Shadow ➤ Sparkle) can be used to give your image some glitter and shine. If you find an image is dull, or the lighting has low contrast (such as a foreground object is light colored, and the background is well lit), you can create an interesting effect with Sparkle.

Figure 14-12 shows the use of the sparkle effect on the front of a house, which is white, against a blue sky background. The Sparkle effect applies what appears to be a glint on the house siding.

Tip

If you click the Inverse check box in the Sparkle filter dialog box, you may get a better idea of how Sparkle affects a picture with good lighting (or one that is well lit). You can try this to adjust the Spike Points slider when looking for shine, or the twinkle effect. The Spike Points option allows for 0 to 16 and this adjusts the larger spikes.

This helps to define spike points if you cannot see them clearly in very well-lit foreground and background images. Flip Inverse off to revert to the original color. ∎

FIGURE 14-12

Using the Sparkle effect to add glitter, shine, brilliance, and glimmer to your digital image

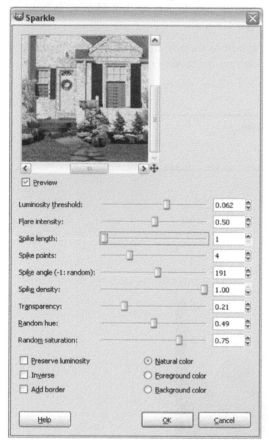

To use Sparkle, zoom in with the preview pane options and adjust the many slider and input box options available to you (such as Random Hue) and adjust the intensity of the effect. This filter simply adds sparkles to your image and can be manipulated in many ways to produce some interesting designs. When viewing your image, the sparkles originate from the Luminosity Threshold setting. Sliders and input boxes allow you to set values.

You can work within the preview pane to find where sparkle will work best to adjust the natural lighting aspects of your picture. You will see big differences in how sparkling an image works with different pictures, even those with similar lighting. You can also create some interesting border effects on your images.

Check the Add Border check box in the Sparkle filter dialog box to select this option. This creates a border around the image instead of creating sparkle on the image's radiant pixels.

Supernova

The Supernova filter (Filters ➤ Light and Shadow ➤ Supernova) can be used to apply a light source to your image when one is not present. You can use this effect to apply a glowing light or brilliance effect such as the sun.

Figure 14-13 shows the use of this filter to make it appear as though the sun is out and directly located behind the foreground image. This simulates interesting shadows and adds some shine to your composition.

Using the Supernova effect to adjust the lighting in your digital image

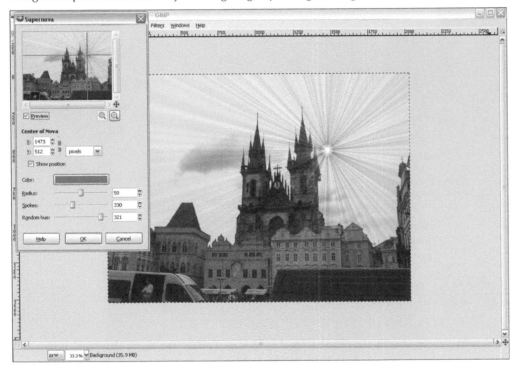

To apply the effect, you can zoom in and adjust the specific location of the center spot for the supernova. Use the preview pane options to zoom, as well as place the crosshairs on a general location. You can then zoom in closer and use the Center of Nova X and Y options and adjust granularity. You can click the menu selector and change the Pixels option to a more precise unit of measurement, using percentages for more accuracy.

Drop Shadow

When you need to apply a border around your image, or apply a shadowing effect to make part of your image appear to float over the rest of it, Drop Shadow (Filters ➤ Light and Shadow ➤

Drop Shadow) is your tool. Figure 14-14 shows the Drop Shadow dialog where you can apply the Drop Shadow filter.

This filter adds a drop shadow to the current selection or to the image if there's no active selection. You can adjust the color (by clicking the color bar), position (with X and Y), and size (Blur Radius) of the shadow and apply it to your image or current selection. You can use the Layers dialog to create a layer, or the script will do it for you. The right side of Figure 14-14 shows the creation of a layer (or a few of them) to help create the desired effect.

FIGURE 14-14

From the drop Shadow dialog (left) you can apply border effects to your picture. In the Layers dialog (right), Drop Shadow effects directly relate to active layer. Select what is viewable and what is not to check multiple layers of effects, as well as adjust opacity

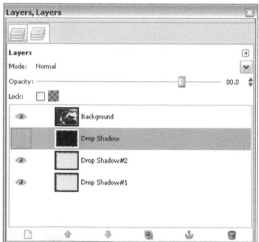

Once you click OK, your final images have new borders, as shown in Figure 14-15.

FIGURE 14-15

The new borders

Perspective

The Perspective filter (Filters ➤ Light and Shadow ➤ Perspective) is used to adjust lighting so that your picture has a new point of view. It does this by adding a perspective shadow to the alpha channel and can be seen in the Layers dialog. It can help to change the aspect of the image, giving it a different frame of reference and making your selection or layer appear to be standing on a floor that's perpendicular to the image view.

You can adjust the color, length, and direction of the background layer, which you can see in Figure 14-16.

FIGURE 14-16

Viewing both layers created by Perspective. This can be used to give your image a perspective shadow.

Xach-Effect

If you need a drop shadow on your image, this is a great script that basically gives you the ability to apply perspective with a color gradient. The Xach-Effect filter is found by going to (Filters ➤ Light and Shadow ➤ Xach-Effect).

Using this filter is simple. You can apply a drop shadow and adjust the blur radius for different three-dimensional effects, or control highlights of the effect. You can adjust the offset with X and Y coordinates as well. The effect may not appear at first if you select similar colors for the drop shadow, so consider using lighter colors to add lighter shadows.

Lens Effect

To render your image in a way to mimic a spherical camera lens, use the Lens Effect filter (Filters ➢ Light and Shadow ➢ Lens Effect). Figure 14-17 shows the Lens Effect dialog box where you can adjust the surroundings and lens refraction index. Although this is a very simple-to-use tool, it applies a powerful effect.

FIGURE 14-17

Using the Lens Effect filter to distort your image

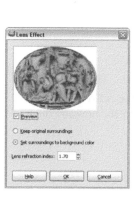

You can adjust the active layer by making it transparent. The two radio buttons for surroundings allow you to adjust how the lens affects the image inside the lens, as well as outside. You can use the preview pane to see how the Lens Effect filter makes your final image distort and bend. Find a good setting and click OK.

Glass Tile

If your image needs to be tiled, the Glass Tile filter (Filters ➢ Light and Shadow ➢ Glass Tile) is extremely helpful. It's simple to use and does what it says. If you can imagine looking through a shower door, or other type of glass tile, you can apply that same effect to your digital images. Figure 14-18 shows the application of tiling on a rock surface to make it appear like glass.

FIGURE 14-18

You can use the Glass Tile filter to apply the glass tiling effect on just about any surface.

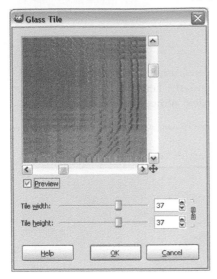

This filter works on your entire image, or within a selection of it through the active layer. You can use the preview pane to zoom in on particular sections of your image to see how the tiling will work with it.

Noise Filters

In Chapter 13 you learned how to add blur to your work. Now, if you need to add noise to your active layer, you can use GIMP's deep noise-based filter set. It includes Scatter HSV, Hurl, Random Pick, RGB Noise, Slur, and Spread. These plug-ins offer many different graining effects that can enhance your work and make it look porous. The filter adds defects to the image and makes it imperfect by modifying different elements of your color model and distorting them.

Noise filters are great for breaking up solid colors to give a more natural or dirty feeling. Noise filters can be combined with motion blur or wind filters to generate a brushed aluminum look. Basically, their best use is for generating random grit on an image. Used creatively, these filters can be used to do everything from generate fog to work as the base for pores in a skin texture to apply to a 3D model. Noise filters are also great for generating bump maps.

Scatter HSV

You can use the Scatter HSV filter effect to apply noise to your image. It does this by allowing for specific adjustments in your color map. You can adjust the hue, saturation, and luminosity of your composition or work as shown in Figure 14-19. This filter is located in the image window menu under the Light and Shadow menu. Run it by going to Filters ➤ Noise ➤ HSV Noise. Figure 14-19 shows how a glossy map surface can be turned into a porous-looking surface when applying a large saturation number with the adjustment slider.

FIGURE 14-19

Pixels can be adjusted with different settings based on hue, saturation, holdness, and value (luminosity) levels.

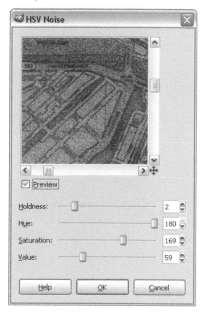

Hurl

When you need to apply random noise effects to your image, use Hurl (Filters ➤ Noise ➤ Hurl). The Hurl filter allows you to apply noise to random sections of your image and adjust seed randomization, randomization percentages, and repeat ratio.

Random Pick

Just like Hurl, Pick can be used to apply random noise to your image. The Pick filter within GIMP takes each pixel in your graphic and replaces them randomly by taking a baseline sample from itself and with its eight neighbor pixels. The percentage of affected pixels is determined by the Randomization (%) input or slider option. This filter is located in the image window menu under the Noise menu. Run it by going to Filters ➤ Noise ➤ Pick. Figure 14-20 shows the Pick filter in use.

FIGURE 14-20

Using the Pick filter to create noise elements within your image

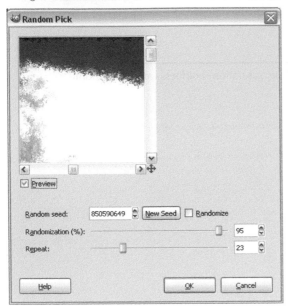

RGB Noise

When looking to apply noise to your image and find and use the noise that is most natural look-ing on an RGB image, you should select RGB Noise. In contrast, you can use the HSV Noise filter, which works on a different color model. Both produce subtle results.

The RGB Noise (Filters ➤ Noise ➤ RGB Noise) filter works by applying more of the effect in some areas of the image and less in others to give the noise value a more natural look and feel. You can apply it to a layer or a selection. Figure 14-21 shows the RGB Noise filter dialog box where you can adjust your effect settings.

You can configure correlated noise by selecting the associated check box option. This option allows channel values to determine where the noise effect will be distributed. Independent RGB allows you to adjust the red, green, and blue values for the image. The RGB Noise filter does not work with indexed images.

Note

When discussing digital images, it is important to remember that the main property of an image is its mode. The three possible modes are RGB, grayscale, and indexed. When working with an indexed image, only a limited set of 256 colors or less are used to make up the image's color map. Images of this type were used primarily when system hardware had not caught up to the software's technology. Now that systems are relatively faster, these files are not used often and GIMP's filter sets do not work well with them. It's recommended that you make an RGB file out of your image and then convert it to an indexed image if you need to or for compatibility. ■

FIGURE 14-21

Using the RGB Noise filter to enhance a background, or distort an image with random values

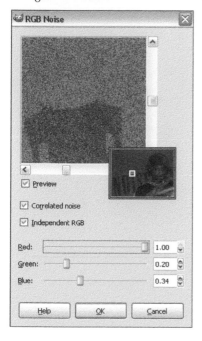

Slur

When you need a noise filter that produces a slurring motion, you should use GIMP's Slur filter (Filters ➢ Noise ➢ Slur). This filter samples the pixels in your image and then pushes the pixel color in a downward motion to slur the view. You can use the Randomization (%) option to adjust the affected pixels. Figure 14-22 shows how a glowing light at night can be converted to a blurry distortion, making it appear as it is were neon.

Spread

You can use the Spread filter (Filters ➢ Noise ➢ Spread) to swap each pixel in the active layer or selection with other randomly chosen pixels. Figure 14-23 shows how to use Spread to move your pixels.

FIGURE 14-22

The Slur filter lets you randomize pixels on your image.

FIGURE 14-23

Using the Spread filter to move pixels vertically and horizontally

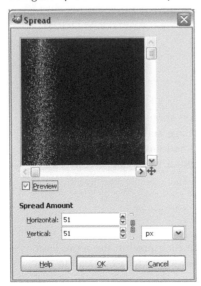

You can use this filter to adjust color transitions. Similar to Slur, its main difference is that it disperses the pixels that are present, whereas slur copies the color and reapplies it downward. This filter does not introduce any new coloring effects.

Render Filters

When considering GIMP's toolset for image creation, no better toolset is found than within the Filters menu. Here, you can work with Render filters to create some crazy-looking images — some psychedelic, some distorted, but all purely mathematical as you will soon see. Because most of GIMP's tools covered earlier in the chapter affect the underlying image, this section focuses solely on how specific filters are used to create new images. Most of the filters in this submenu completely cover the active layer that you apply them to. The exception to this is the Gfig filter, which allows you to draw directly on the image. In general, though, if you want to use filters from this submenu, it's a good idea to apply them to a new empty layer.

Clouds

When you open up the Render filters, the first menu item you will find is Clouds. Within it you find other cloud-like effects you can add to your image, or use to create a new image completely.

Difference Clouds

The Difference Clouds filter (Filters ➤ Render ➤ Clouds ➤ Difference Clouds) is used to adjust the lighting of the image and apply solid noise to create a pattern on the image. Figure 14-24 shows the Solid Noise filter effect dialog box where X and Y adjustments can be made, as well as options to make Turbulent and Tileable selections.

FIGURE 14-24

The Difference Cloud filter creates a "fog" around your image that gives the appearance of a low-flying cloud.

Note

This filter provides the same effect as creating a layer of clouds with the Solid Noise filter and then setting that layer's blend mode to Difference. ■

When working with the image, you can alternate the placement of the effect using the Random Seed function. By applying a new seed you can set different placement values for your cloud effect.

Plasma

You can use the Plasma rendering effect to saturate your image with color. You can also download an enhanced version of the Plasma plug-in from the GIMP Plug-in Registry (Plasma2) found at http://registry.gimp.org, which offers a deeper option toolset to work with. This filter is located in the image window menu under the Render menu. Run it by going to Filters ➤ Render ➤ Clouds ➤ Plasma.

Use adjustments such as Random Seed and Turbulence to alter the appearance of the Plasma effect until you have a pattern you are happy with, then click OK to apply the effect. A brand-new image appears with your Plasma filter settings applied.

Solid Noise

Like the other cloud effects, Solid Noise (Filters ➤ Render ➤ Clouds ➤ Solid Noise) is useful for creating a new distorted image. Solid Noise can be used to create background images that need a textured look and feel. Figure 14-25 shows how plasma-like effects can be manipulated to create a solid image in the image window, and to simulate fog like the Difference Clouds filter.

FIGURE 14-25

Using Solid Noise to create a Plasma-like effect (left) or a Difference Clouds-like effect (right). You can adjust the detail, X and Y components, or add turbulence to your effect.

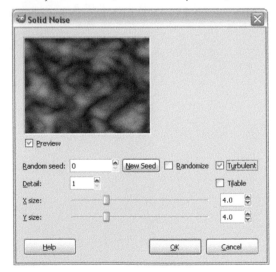

Nature

Nature effects let you create images that relate to the environment. For example, flame relates to fire and how a fire burns and peaks, and so does the Flame filter plug-in effect.

Flame

You can use natural effects to enhance your image. For example, if you had a picture of a fireplace and wanted to enhance the center of it with more detail in the flames emitting from it, you could apply the Flame filter.

This filter is located in the image window menu under the Render menu. Run it by going to Filters ➤ Render ➤ Nature ➤ Flame. Figure 14-26 shows how the Flame filter can be used to create a new flame effect in the preview pane of the Flame filter dialog box. This will then be applied to your image.

FIGURE 14-26

Creating, loading, or editing a new flame filter item in the Flame filter dialog box

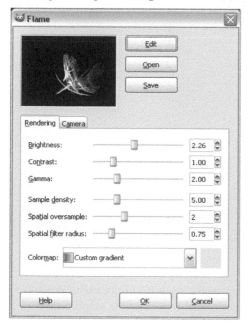

Warning

GIMP users should be warned that issues are posted on GIMP's web site (http://registry.gimp.org) regarding using this filter with large images. Shortcuts and workarounds are also posted on there if more problematic behavior takes place. You can save your creations and then load them when needed. If you use the Edit button, you can open an editor that allows you to further refine the flame image. You have multiple preset themes to choose from for different pattern types. ∎

IFS Fractal

When seeking more nature-like filters, consider applying the Iterated Function System (IFS) Compose filter (Filters ➤ Render ➤ Nature ➤ IFS Fractal) to your image. This tool creates nature shapes such as flowers, leaves, and tree branches. It works by making small changes to your image to apply this effect with finesse. Figure 14-27 shows the IFS Fractal filter dialog box where you can make adjustments to your image.

FIGURE 14-27

Using the IFS Fractal editor to create natural-looking designs within your image

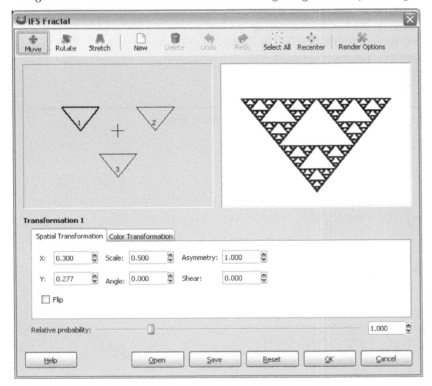

The main interface is a little dense and takes some getting used to, but it's full of useful presets and tools. For example, you can adjust coloring, as well as spatial aspects of the graphic effect. When you find an interesting pattern, click OK to apply the effect.

Pattern

The Pattern effects in the Render filter menu are useful when you want to create new images from a blank background or a pre-existing image file. For example, you can use the

CML Explorer (covered next) to apply texture to a graphic to adjust coloring aspects such as hue.

CML Explorer

The Coupled-Map-Lattice (CML) filter is used to apply a mathematical equation (Cellular Automata) to your image to produce a complex (and colorful) pattern. This filter is located in the image window menu under the Render menu. Run it by going to Filters ➤ Render ➤ Pattern ➤ CML Explorer. Figure 14-28 shows the CML Explorer filter dialog box where you can make adjustments to your image.

Using the CML Explorer to make color and pattern changes to your image, or to create a new image entirely from scratch

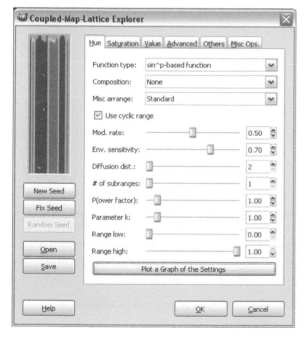

Checkerboard

You can use the Checkerboard filter to create a checkerboard effect on your image, or create a new layer with only the Checkerboard on it as a background or to manipulate into a pre-existing image. The Checkerboard filter (Filters ➤ Render ➤ Pattern ➤ Checkerboard) is used to create this pattern on the current layer of your image.

Figure 14-29 shows the Checkerboard filter dialog box where you can make adjustments to your image.

You can try the Psychobilly option for a different look. This option gives an eiderdown look to the checkerboard and you select it by placing a check in the check box. Click OK to apply the effect, viewable in the image window.

Using the Checkerboard filter

Diffraction Patterns

When you need a filter that can create wave-like interference, or diffracted textures, use the Diffraction Patterns filter (Filters ➢ Render ➢ Pattern ➢ Diffraction Patterns). This effect can be used to change frequency, contours, and sharp edges of images you load or want to create. Figure 14-30 shows the Diffraction Patterns filter dialog box where you can make adjustments to your image.

You can use this filter to create psychedelic backgrounds as well as very colorful distortions.

Grid

The Grid filter can be used to apply a grid feature to the top layer so you can adjust it to make many different types of enhancements to your work. This filter is located in the image window menu under the Render menu. Run it by going to Filters ➢ Render ➢ Pattern ➢ Grid. Figure 14-31 shows the Grid filter dialog box where you can make adjustments to your image.

You have three separate options for controlling the horizontal and vertical grid lines and intersections. The chain icon locks the horizontal and vertical settings together. This is done so that any changes applied to one option are reflected in the other option. Click the chain icon to unchain them and work with them independently if needed.

FIGURE 14-30

Using the Diffraction Patterns filter to apply psychedelic-looking imagery to your graphic

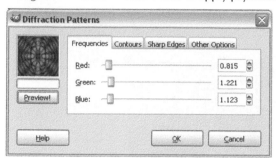

FIGURE 14-31

Using Grid to apply a grid to your image

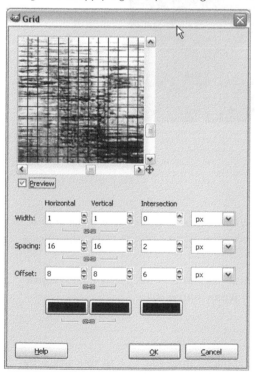

Once you set your colors of the grid lines and intersection marks you can apply the filter, as shown in Figure 14-32.

FIGURE 14-32

Using the Grid effect on your image and viewing it within the image window of GIMP. Notice how the Grid filter effect applies a mathematical grid directly over your original image.

Jigsaw

The Jigsaw filter (Filters ➢ Render ➢ Pattern ➢ Jigsaw) can be used to turn your image into a jigsaw puzzle. Figure 14-33 shows the Jigsaw filter dialog box where you can make adjustments to your image.

You can make adjustments to the horizontal and vertical placement of the puzzle pieces, adjust the beveled edges, or pick between square and curved jigsaw puzzle styles.

Maze

The Maze filter (Filters ➢ Render ➢ Pattern ➢ Maze) applies a maze-like look to your image by completely overwriting the previous contents of the active layer and replacing the information with a random black-and-white maze pattern. Figure 14-34 shows the Maze filter dialog box where you can make adjustments to your image.

FIGURE 14-33

Creating a jigsaw-like pattern on your original image with the Jigsaw filter plug-in

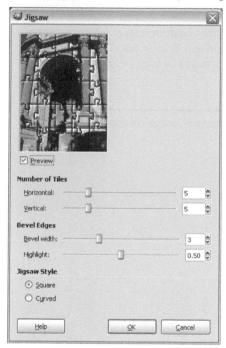

FIGURE 14-34

Using the Maze render effect to create a maze on your image

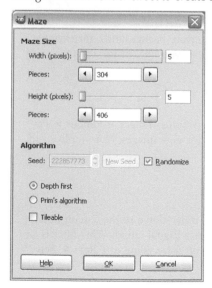

By selecting between multiple algorithms, you can choose among different types of maze overlays.

Qbist

The Qbist filter (Filters ➢ Render ➢ Pattern ➢ Qbist) generates random texture information that is used to create interesting color gradients on preexisting images or new ones. Figure 14-35 shows the Qbist filter dialog box where you can make adjustments to your image.

FIGURE 14-35

Using the Qbist filter effect to generate random patterns and textures for new image creation

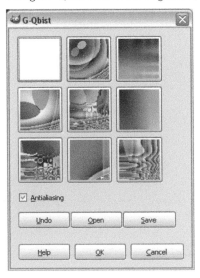

The Qbist filter generates random textures that you can use to create backgrounds, for example. You can use the presets found within the dialog box to select ones you like, or use the Open and Save buttons to load and create new ones.

Sinus

The last effect in the Pattern section of the Render filter menu is Sinus (Filters ➢ Render ➢ Pattern ➢ Sinus). The Sinus effect lets you create striped textures for new images, or to replace old ones.

Circuit

Once you have finished looking at the Render menu's patterns, move down to the Circuit option. Here, you can apply and/or create a new pattern that looks like a digital circuit. This filter is located in the image window menu under the Render menu. Run it by going to Filters ➢ Render ➢ Circuit.

Fractal Explorer

With this filter, you can create fractals and multicolored pictures verging on chaos. Unlike the IFS Compose filter, with which you can fix the fractal structure precisely, this filter lets you perform fractals simply.

This filter is located in the image window menu under the Render menu. Run it by going to Filters ➤ Render ➤ Circuit. Figure 14-36 shows the Fractal Explorer dialog box where you can make adjustments to your image.

Using the Fractal Explorer to create new images with GIMP

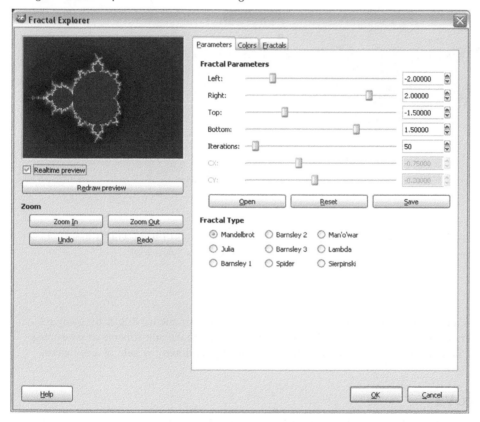

Gfig

The Gfig filter (Filters ➤ Render ➤ Gfig) allows you to edit an image directly and gives you drawing tools for editing. The filter is more of a toolbox filled with things you can use with your composition. Figure 14-37 shows the Gfig filter dialog box where you can make adjustments to your image.

FIGURE 14-37

Using Gfig to create lines and other shapes on your drawing

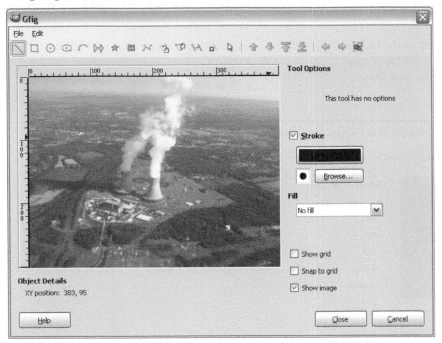

You can make lines, circles, and other geometric shapes. You will find using Gfig a more convenient process than trying to draw vectors and shapes with GIMP's Paths tool.

Lava

This filter is located in the image window menu under the Render menu. Run it by going to Filters ➤ Render ➤ Lava. In the Lava Filter dialog box you can make adjustments to your image and apply a flow-like blur, much like the effect of lava dripping down the side of a mountain.

Line Nova

This filter is located in the image window menu under the Render menu. Run it by going to Filters ➤ Render ➤ Line Nova. Figure 14-38 shows the Line Nova dialog box where you can make adjustments to your image. You will also notice the image window with a preview of the image being rendered.

FIGURE 14-38

Applying the Line Nova filter to an image and watching the application of it while rendering

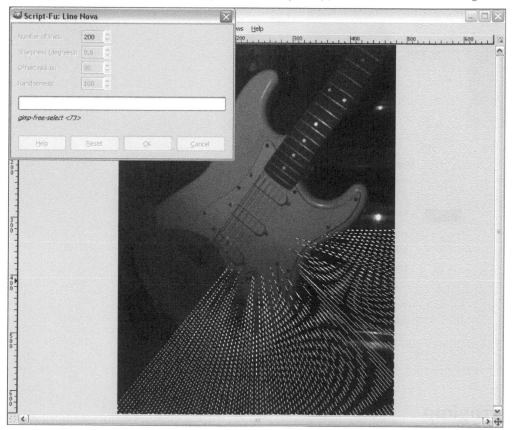

Sphere Designer

The Sphere Designer filter (Filters ➤ Render ➤ Sphere Designer) allows you to design and create images with 3D spherical designs and textures. Figure 14-39 shows the Sphere Designer filter dialog where you can make adjustments to your image.

You can use the Preview section to view your setting changes before you make them. You have many options to select from within the Sphere Designer, such as texture and light settings, as well as X and Y placement on the screen.

Using the Sphere Designer filter effect to create 3D images

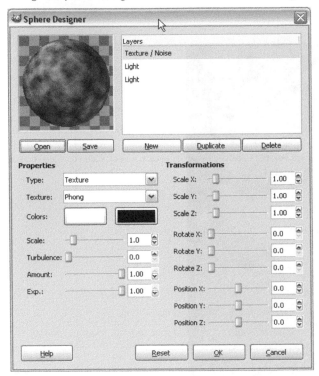

Spyrogimp

This filter is located in the image window menu under the Render menu. Run it by going to Filters ➢ Render ➢ Spyrogimp.

You can select between many options such as Type and Shape of effect, as well as where the effect can be placed on the image. This is useful if you are trying to create a fence or grating effect in front of an image.

You can also adjust the coloring if needed by clicking the color bar and clicking OK to apply the effect. In Figure 14-40 you can see the Spyrogimp filter creating a chain-link fence look in front of the current image.

FIGURE 14-40

FIGURE 14-40

Create a chain-link fence in front of your image.

Summary

This chapter covered many of GIMP's filters available for enhancing your digital images. Most of them, whether for lighting, noise, or rendering images from scratch, showed you how powerful GIMP can be under the hood. The next chapter covers more of GIMP's filter menu options, plug-ins, and filters for compositing effects.

Using Compositing Filters

Because it is an image editor with an advanced layers system, one of GIMP's primary uses is that of a compositing tool. In computer graphics, *compositing* is the art of mixing multiple graphic elements together to attain a specific visual look. A simple example of compositing would be if you take a picture of your friend and overlay text that says "Friend for Sale." You might not be friends for long after doing such a stunt, but you'd have a good example of compositing in your hands. In advanced compositing examples, you can mix an image with itself to give it an ethereal glow or you can change a daytime scene to look like it was taken at night.

IN THIS CHAPTER

Using edge detection for advanced compositing

Taking advantage of GIMP's sadly misnamed "Generic" filters

Using one image to create another

Compositing consists of using a series of small steps and processes to influence the final look of your image. The filters described in this chapter play into that process because they're small, generally simple tools that can be used at each step to achieve the final composited result. Being as simple as they are, these tools are also often used for tasks that aren't directly related to compositing. I'll try to point out where a filter can be used as more than just a tool to help mix graphical elements together.

That said, the filters in this chapter offer some of GIMP's greatest abilities to dramatically influence the look of your final image, often completely changing it from the original. Filters are easy to use and really quite fun. And when you use them effectively, you get some very powerful results.

Working with Edge-Detect Filters

Edge detection is a means of automatically generating a contour line to differentiate the various features of an image. At its simplest, you can use edge detection to generate an image that looks like a line drawing of your original, as shown in Figure 15-1. The results of these filters can look pretty odd and may seem useless, and as such these are some of the most overlooked filters by people who are new to image editing, particularly when it comes to compositing. This is a bit ironic considering the fact that a lot of computer scientists and mathematicians consider edge detection to be one of the fundamental elements of image processing. In fact, the math behind edge detection is used heavily in research on artificial sight because it's helpful in visually separating one object from another.

You can use edge detection to quickly create a line drawing from a photograph. (Photo credit: Chris Hoyer)

The most common use for edge detection is to mix two images cleanly by overlaying one over the other. As an example, say you have a photograph of someone; perhaps it's the same friend you used earlier at the beginning of this chapter and you're making up for your mean poster by digitally putting a kitten in the photo. With GIMP's existing selection tools, you can generate a mask for cutting the kitten out of its source image. The difficulty here, though, is that the kitten is a fuzzy creature and selecting around the outer edge of it can be tedious. In fact, even if you did go through and create a selection mask for the kitten, the edges are likely to be rough and aliased. You could try to alleviate this by feathering the selection by only one or two pixels, but the results aren't always reliable.

This is where edge detection can help save the day. Using an edge detection filter, the outline of this kitten's features can be obtained. Using this outline image as the basis for a fine mask, you can then quickly define the rest of your mask by painting on the outline image or using it as the starting point for selection and moving forward from there. The basic process goes something like this (assuming you've already opened your image and are ready to work on it):

1. **Duplicate your base layer (Shift+Ctrl+D).** This is a good idea in general so you don't destroy your original image, but it's also important because of the next step.

2. **Run an edge detection filter on your new layer (Filters ➤ Edge-Detect).** Exactly which filter you choose depends on the specific image. For this example (see Figure 15-2), I used Filters ➤ Edge-Detect ➤ Edge and chose the Sobel algorithm.

3. **Use the functions in the Colors menu to increase contrast and desaturate the result.** The idea here is to really pull out fine details that would be tedious to select by

hand and give yourself a decent selection base. My weapons of choice are Colors ➢ Levels and Colors ➢ Desaturate. When you're done, you need to convert this to a selection mask. I prefer to use custom channels for this.

FIGURE 15-2

Using edge detection to get a cleaner selection mask for compositing part of one image with another (Photo credit: Tina Keller, www.flickr.com/photos/earthandeden/395466458/)

4. **Convert your edge-detected layer into a channel.** There are a couple ways to do this. You could try the Select by Color tool (Shift+O) to get a good selection and then use Select ➢ Save to Channel, but the faster way is to go to the Layers dialog, click your edge-detected layer, and drag it into the Channels dialog. This creates a custom channel that you can convert to a selection whenever you want. Besides being faster, the other advantage of this method is that you don't have to play with the Threshold slider in the Select by Color tool to make sure the not-completely-white pixels are selected. This way a gray pixel means a specific semi-transparent value. At this point, you may also want to change the color of your channel from the default semi-transparent black to something that shows up a little better on your image.

5. **With your new channel active and visible, use the Paintbrush tool (P) to refine the selection.** For a quick review on painting selections on a custom channel, check out Chapter 7. While you're working, it's probably a good idea to briefly pop over to the Layers dialog and hide your edge-detected layer since you no longer need it and it's more helpful to see your base image for this step.

6. **Add a layer mask to your base layer using your custom channel.** Do this by right-clicking your base layer in the Layers dialog and selecting Add Layer Mask. Then, on the dialog that pops up, click the Channel radio button and choose your custom channel from the drop-down beneath it. You can find out more on layer masks in Chapter 6.

7. **With your layer mask active, use the Paintbrush tool (P) to do any final clean-ups on the mask.** And with that, you're done. You have a nice cut-out of an object that might otherwise be tedious to do by hand.

Figure 15-2 shows some progress images of this technique in action.

You can find all of the filters covered in this section at Filters ➤ Edge-Detect. Getting into the raw mathematical details of how each edge detection algorithm works will likely bore you and fill these pages with mountains of formulas and Greek symbols. So rather than doing that, what follows are basic descriptions of how each filter affects images and the settings you can use to adjust and refine them.

The Difference of Gaussians Option

This method of edge detection involves taking two duplicates of your source image and applying a different Gaussian blur to each of them. Then one image is subtracted from the other. That difference reveals the edges in the image. This method is really attractive because the Gaussian blur algorithm is very well known and can be optimized to run very quickly. That makes it ideal for large images or for applying this filter to a whole batch of images. On the downside, it's not as accurate as some other techniques, yielding broken lines on some images and really fuzzy contours when you use large blur radii. To use this filter, choose Filters ➤ Edge-Detect ➤ Difference of Gaussians. Upon doing so, you get a window like the one in Figure 15-3.

The most effective way to use this filter is to take advantage of the small preview at the top of the window. This interactively updates as you adjust your settings so you can get a really good idea of what your resulting image looks like. The parameters available to you in this window are as follows:

- **Radius 1/Radius 2** — These are the radii of the two Gaussian blurs that this filter performed. Their default units are in pixels, but you can easily use different units by clicking the drop-down menu to the right of these text fields. If you want to experiment with higher blur radii while keeping one blur radius proportional to the other, click the chain-link icon, and changes in one influence the other. In most cases, setting Radius 2 smaller than Radius 1 gives you the best results, but experiment to figure out what works best for your particular image.

- **Normalize** — Enable this check box to increase the contrast between outlined parts and non-outlined parts. Not only does this make edge detection more visible, but it also makes the edges easier to select when building masks.

- **Invert** — Nearly all edge detection algorithms result in a dark image with the outlines defined by light-colored lines. However, if you want an image that looks like a dark line drawing on white paper, you can enable this check box to get that result. Something to note here is that on some copies of GIMP, the preview window may just show all black if you have this check box enabled. For these situations, it's best to tweak your radius settings with Invert disabled and then re-enable the Invert check box before you click OK to run the filter.

FIGURE 15-3

The settings window for the Difference of Gaussians edge detection filter

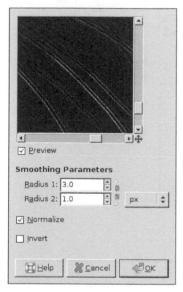

Note

If you enable the Normalize option in this filter, what shows in the preview window isn't completely accurate. This is because it only normalizes what's visible in the preview area instead of normalizing the whole image, which is what happens when you click OK. This means the contrast might be higher or lower in the preview than it is in the final processed image. ■

The Difference of Gaussians filter is very fast and works pretty well for most circumstances. And if you play with the radius values, you can get some really interesting results. Figure 15-4 shows a handful of results that you can get on a single image when using different radius values on this filter.

Edge

The Edge filter is kind of a dumping ground for a bunch of different edge detection methods. In fact, it actually implements some of the edge detection algorithms that have their own filters in GIMP, such as Sobel and Laplace, which I cover later in this section. The difference, though, is that the Edge filter doesn't offer the same options on these techniques as their direct counterparts. That said, the Edge filter tends to give you more refined control. Call up this filter by going to Filters ➢ Edge-Detect ➢ Edge. When you do this, you get the window that appears in Figure 15-5.

FIGURE 15-4

The results of playing with radius values for the Difference of Gaussians filter

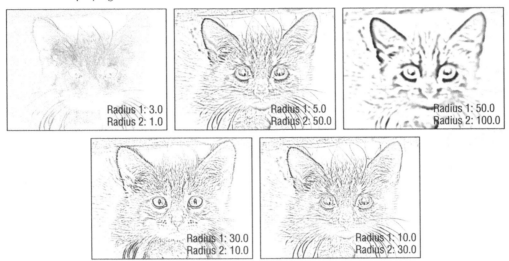

FIGURE 15-5

The settings and parameters available for the Edge filter

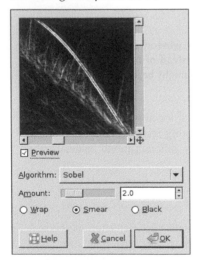

Like the window for the Difference of Gaussians filter, this also features a preview window to give you an idea of what the resulting image looks like with this filter applied. The settings, of course, are different. Following is a description of each one:

- **Algorithm** — This is a drop-down menu that gives you the choice of six different edge detection algorithms. What follows is a brief description of each one.

  - **Sobel** — Described in more detail at the end of this section, the Sobel edge detection algorithm actually checks the image vertically and horizontally and then combines the results. Splitting the image in this way uses fewer computational resources, but it does so at the expense of accuracy.

  - **Prewitt Compass** — The Prewitt Compass edge detection algorithm is really good at not only determining where edges are, but also how defined the edge is and even its orientation. It uses a similar technique to the Sobel algorithm, but rather than evaluate just vertically and horizontally, it evaluates by rotating in 45-degree increments (north, northwest, west, etc.; like a compass). The only disadvantage to using it is that because of the additional steps, it can often work more slowly than other methods.

  - **Gradient** — This is one of the simplest edge detection algorithms. It treats the color variations in your image as gradients. When there's a dramatic change past a certain threshold, it considers that to be an edge. Although it's a bit of a naive approach, it works rather well. When compared to the Sobel method, the edges produced by this technique are thinner and lighter.

  - **Roberts** — Also known as the Roberts Cross edge detector, this method is older than some of the others. That said, it's still very fast when compared to these methods because it doesn't require a lot of computational power. This algorithm tends to work best on source images that are grayscale.

  - **Differential** — The Differential edge detection algorithm is basically the same as the Difference of Gaussians method, although the method here uses a different blur and you don't have the control that Difference of Gaussians gives you. It usually results in lighter edges than those produced by the Sobel technique.

  - **Laplace** — Like Sobel, this edge detection algorithm has its own filter. It's described in more detail in the next section, but the biggest difference between this method and others in the Edge filter is that Laplacian edges are more crisp, though the overall edge detection image tends to be more noisy.

- **Amount** — This slider controls the accuracy of your edge detection. Lower values return darker images that only show the main edges in your image, whereas higher values detect more edges but tend to get noisy.

- **Warp/Smear/Black** — The results of these radio buttons are tough to perceive visually, but they deal with the pixels that are at the image boundary. Edges that go beyond the boundary can be tricky to calculate. You typically get the best results by choosing the default option of Smear.

Figure 15-6 shows the same image with each of the six edge detection algorithms applied to it.

FIGURE 15-6

Top row: Sobel, Prewitt, Gradient; bottom row: Roberts, Differential, and Laplace

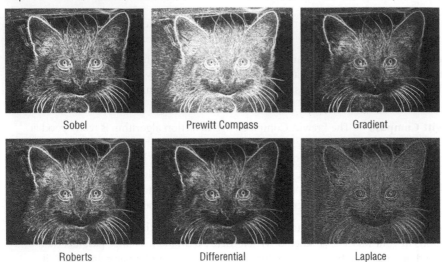

Sobel	Prewitt Compass	Gradient
Roberts	Differential	Laplace

Laplace

This edge detection filter is the only one that doesn't have any additional features for you to adjust. Just choose Filters ➢ Edge-Detect 22 ➢ Laplace and let it cook. When it's done, the result is an image with thin, one-pixel-wide edges. The edges in this resulting image may be a bit light, so you can quickly increase contrast by choosing Colors ➢ Auto ➢ Equalize and then Colors ➢ Auto ➢ Stretch Contrast. You could also load Colors ➢ Levels and click the Auto button. Either way, be careful when you do this because although you get nice, crisp edges, one of the side effects of the Laplace edge detection algorithm is that it can be noisier than other methods. Without getting too heavy into the math of it all, it's because Laplacian edge detection uses the second derivative of the color gradients in your image. This gives you more refined results than the pure gradient method, but results in a greater number of "false edges." Figure 15-7 shows the results of applying the Laplace filter on an image and stretching out its contrast. Without doing so, the result looks a lot like a solid black image.

FIGURE 15-7

The result of using the Laplace edge detection filter and applying Colors ➢ Auto ➢ Equalize followed by Colors ➢ Auto ➢ Stretch Contrast

Neon

The Neon edge detection filter produces some of the most unique results of all the ones available in this menu. The results are typically thicker, blurrier lines and Neon doesn't necessarily find as many lines as the other edge detection algorithms. What it does offer, however, is a very interesting effect that appears a bit like a neon sign. To use this filter go to Filters ➤ Edge-Detect ➤ Neon and GIMP gives you a window like the one that appears in Figure 15-8.

The parameters window for the Neon edge detection filter

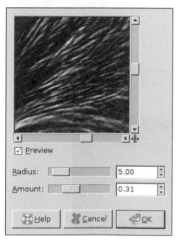

Like the windows for all of the other edge detection filters, this one features a preview window of the result to give you an idea of what the completed filter looks like. Beyond that, this filter offers only two settings for you to adjust:

- **Radius** — Adjust this value to control the width of the edges this filter produces. At very high values, this produces an interesting result that looks like edge detection with motion blur applied horizontally and vertically. This is particularly cool when used with text.

- **Amount** — This slider controls the brightness and intensity of the neon edges.

The really neat thing about this filter is that it has a tendency to highlight edges rather than merely outline them. This means that you can use the Neon filter to create an ethereal glow around the objects in your images. It's not a true bloom effect because edge detection doesn't really account for the brightness in an image, but if you're looking for an interesting glow rather than a bloom, this filter can be quite helpful.

The basic steps to producing such a glow are as follows:

1. **Duplicate the layer that you want to make glow (Shift+Ctrl+D).** This is your working layer.

2. **Apply the Neon edge detection filter (Filters > Edge-Detect > Neon).** You can play with the parameters here to get your edges highlighted the way you'd like.

3. **Apply a Gaussian Blur to the edge detection results (Filters > Blur > Gaussian Blur).** Using horizontal and vertical values of around 15 pixels tends to work nicely, but it really depends on your image size and what your image content is.

4. **Change this layer's blending mode to Addition, Dodge, or Screen.** As described in Chapter 6, you do this from the Layers dockable dialog. When you change it to one of these modes, the brighter parts of your edge detection results increase the intensity of those portions of the original image.

Figure 15-9 shows the results of this method compared to the original image, as well as the results of a more true bloom effect.

FIGURE 15-9

From left to right: the original image, a glow effect using the Neon filter, and a bloom effect made by adjusting colors with Curves

Sobel

Sobel edge detection and Laplace edge detection tend to be two of the most popular edge detection algorithms. This is largely because they are fast and accurate. Sobel differs from Laplace in a couple of ways, though. Most obviously, the results from Sobel edge detection are not edges with a width of one pixel. They tend to be a bit softer. The advantage is that Sobel edge detection isn't subject to some of the issues of "false edges" that the Laplacian method has. It achieves this advantage this by independently evaluating the image horizontally and vertically, and then mixing the results. When you use the Sobel edge detection filter by going to Filters > Edge-Detect > Sobel, you get a window like the one in Figure 15-10.

Aside from enabling and disabling the preview window, this filter offers three options:

- **Sobel Horizontally** — By default, this check box and the Sobel Vertically check box are both enabled, allowing you to get the full Sobel effect. However, if you only want to detect the edges that are mostly horizontal, disable this check box.

- **Sobel Vertically** — Disable this check box if you want to detect mostly vertical edges.

- **Keep Sign of Result (One Direction Only)** — If you disable either of the previous check boxes, the resulting effect looks a bit like you've used an emboss effect on the image. To get an actual edge detection result when evaluating in only one direction, disable this check box as well. If you have both the horizontal and vertical check boxes enabled, then enabling or disabling this check box has no effect.

FIGURE 15-10

The Sobel edge detection parameters window

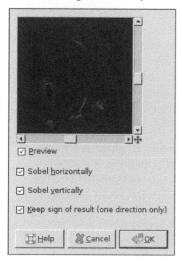

Figure 15-11 shows the results of all three of the Sobel edge detection possibilities: horizontal, vertical, and both.

FIGURE 15-11

From left to right: Sobel edge detection horizontally, vertically, and in both directions

Sobel horizontal   Sobel vertical   Sobel both directions

Using the Filters in the Generic Menu

As an unfortunate side effect of the way that the GIMP developers organized the Filters menu, a few filters don't really fit any of the existing filter menu options. Those filters have found their way to the catch-all menu at Filters ➢ Generic. Interestingly enough, all of the filters in this category are quite useful for compositing (hint, hint to any GIMP developers who may be reading this). The next few sections detail for you why this is the case.

Convolution Matrix

Of all the filters that GIMP has, this is the most versatile and flexible. At the same time, it's also the most technical of filters and the most confusing to use for people who aren't mathematicians with specialized study in image processing. The simple truth is that most image processing filters involve a convolution step. Because of that, you can actually re-create the effect of nearly any other filter using just this one. In fact, you can actually build a complete custom filter of your own using the Convolution Matrix filter. Of course, to do that, you need to understand how these things work. The next bit gets a touch technical, but trust me, it's worth it.

Everything starts with the terminology. As described earlier in this book, an image is nothing more than a two-dimensional grid, or *matrix*, of pixels. Mathematically speaking, a matrix can be defined as a mathematical function. *Convolution* is the mathematical combination of two functions, resulting in a third. So basically you're combining your original image matrix with another matrix to generate a new image. Of course, images can be really large and computers prefer to work on small chunks of data at a time. So to help with that, GIMP breaks down your image into a series of matrices that are 5x5 or 3x3 pixels. Each matrix is defined by looking at each pixel and using the pixels around it to define the matrix. Figure 15-12 illustrates this for a 3x3 matrix and a 5x5 matrix.

Now, these matrices get a little tricky when you get to the border of your image. If you're evaluating the pixel that's the farthest to the left, there are no more pixels to the left of that one that you can use to generate your matrix. In these cases, you have three possible choices:

- **Extend** — Simply put, this is just taking the pixels that you have at the border and copying them beyond the border so you can complete the matrix.

- **Wrap** — Rather than just copying the same pixel over and over, you could try to use the pixels that are on the opposite border to complete your matrix.

- **Disregard the pixel and crop it** — Your last option is to simply disregard these border pixels and crop them off after you finish processing.

Figure 15-13 illustrates how each of these methods works on that example with the pixel on the left border. Since it's a bit difficult to see with just one or two pixels, I've exaggerated it a bit in this figure.

Great. Now that you have a whole set of matrices for your image, now what? Well, start with one matrix. Each pixel in this matrix is defined by a value. On an RGB image in GIMP, you actually have three values per pixel; one each for the red, green, and blue channels. Convolution is the combination of one matrix with another, so you need another matrix. This is where the real magic happens. Each filter effect that uses a convolution matrix is really defined by this second matrix, called a *kernel*. By multiplying the two matrices together, you get a result that is a single value, called a *dot product*. That's the new value for that pixel in the final resulting (convolved) image. Figure 15-14 illustrates this concept by applying a 3x3 kernel to a 3x3 pixel matrix. Incidentally, the kernel shown in this figure produces a simple edge detection effect.

FIGURE 15-12

GIMP uses 3x3 (top) and 5x5 (bottom) matrices defined by the pixels that surround any one pixel in your image (Photo credit: Melody Smith)

3 × 3 Matrix

5 × 5 Matrix

FIGURE 15-13

Generating a matrix for a pixel sitting on the far left border of the image; from left to right: extending, wrapping, and disregarding/cropping

Extend   Wrap   Crop

So that's the technical background behind the Convolution Matrix filter. And really, unless you're studying image processing, that's the most you need to know about how these things work. You can actually go on the Internet and find a ton of predefined kernels that other people have already figured out and you can just plug them directly into this filter. To do that, first run the filter by going to Filters ➤ Generic ➤ Convolution Matrix and you'll get a window like the one in Figure 15-15.

FIGURE 15-14

Multiplying a pixel matrix (an image) by a kernel matrix to determine the value of a pixel in a new image

Pixel matrix

85	93	118
95	119	155
122	138	185

×

Kernel

0	1	0
1	−4	1
0	1	0

=

Dot product

	5	

$(85 \times 0) + (93 \times 1) + (118 \times 0) + (95 \times 1) + (119 \times -4) + (155 \times 1) + (122 \times 0) + (138 \times 1) + (185 \times 0) = ⑤$

FIGURE 15-15

The Convolution Matrix parameters window

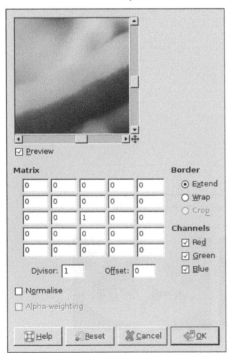

Aside from the preview window, the biggest feature here is the numerical entry fields that define the kernel matrix that you want to use. If you find a kernel that you like online, you just need to plug the values in here and let it rock. You may notice that the matrix fields define a 5x5 matrix and you might wonder, "How would I do a 3x3 matrix in this?" The answer to that is pretty simple. Set all of the outer text fields to zero and define your 3x3 matrix with the text entry fields in the center.

Tip

GIMP uses only 3x3 and 5x5 matrices for its kernels. As you hunt for kernels on the Internet, you may come across kernels that are larger, such as 9x9. Unfortunately, the Convolution Matrix filter isn't capable of handling kernels that large. ■

Below the text fields that comprise your matrix are a few more values that directly control your kernel's influence on the resulting image. These parameters are described here:

- **Divisor** — The Convolution Matrix filter works by sequentially applying a kernel to each pixel in your image. Each pixel calculation (dot product) is divided by the value in this field. Leaving the value at 1 keeps the result unchanged, whereas increasing it has the overall effect of reducing the influence of your kernel. Values less than 1 but greater than zero tend to intensify the result. Negative values invert the result, but setting the divisor to zero gives you a blank image because division by zero is undefined.

- **Offset** — The number you enter in this field is added to the dot product result at each pixel. If the resulting image from your chosen kernel is dark, increasing this value may help make the results more apparent.

- **Normalize** — Of course, if you have no interest in manually fiddling with the Divisor and Offset, you can have GIMP normalize your results, automatically trying to make your effect as visible as possible.

- **Alpha-weighting** — This option is available only if you're working on an image that has an alpha channel. Typically you want to keep it enabled, because if you disable it the Convolution Matrix filter may generate some artifacts in the resulting image. This is particularly true when using a kernel that blurs your image.

To the right of the matrix fields are some more controls. The radio buttons under the Border label determine how GIMP creates matrices at the border of your image. As described earlier in this section, your options are Extend, Wrap, and Crop. The cool thing here is that thanks to the preview window, you can see exactly what each of these options does to your image.

Note

The Crop option is available only if you're using an image that has an alpha channel and you have the Alpha-weighting check box enabled. ■

Beneath the Border options are a series of check boxes that correspond to the channels in your image. If you don't have an alpha channel, the only options available are red, green, and blue. However, if you do have an alpha channel on your image, there's a check box for that channel as well. Enabling a check box here tells the Convolution Matrix filter to apply the kernel to the value corresponding with that channel. This way you can choose to filter only a couple of the available channels, or perhaps just one of them. This, of course, makes the Convolution Matrix filter even more flexible.

So that's the Convolution Matrix filter. You have an immense amount of flexibility to create your own filters or borrow some neat ones that you find online. Figure 15-16 shows what you can do to an image by simply changing the kernel matrix.

FIGURE 15-16

Oh, the fun things you can do with the Convolution Matrix!

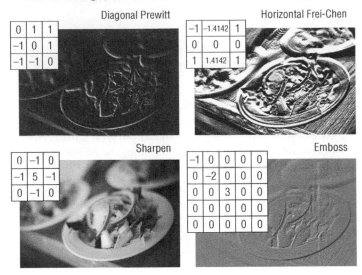

Dilate and Erode

The remaining two filters in the Filters ➢ Generic menu are related and are particularly useful when it comes to compositing. In addition, neither one of them has any parameters or options. You simply select Filters ➢ Generic ➢ Dilate or Filters ➢ Generic ➢ Erode and let each filter do its thing. The easiest way to remember what these filters do is to think about how eyes or cameras work. When your pupil dilates, it gets wider, letting more light into your eye, making things brighter so you can see them. The Dilate filter does something similar. When you run it, the brightest parts of your image get brighter and larger. In contrast, the Erode filter cuts away at these bright sections by increasing the size of the darker portions of your image as well as making them darker. Figure 15-17 shows what happens when you run the Dilate and Erode filters a couple times in a row on a single image. Notice the stripes on the band around the hat. When dilated, the stripes almost become a single white band whereas when the image is eroded, the stripes in the hat band nearly disappear altogether.

At first glance, these two filters may not appear to be useful on their own. However, when used in the context of compositing, they become much more valuable. As an example, assume you've shot a photograph of a person in front of a green screen, like what's used for special effects in films. But also assume that person is being suspended by some wire rigging and you want to remove those wires. Now, you could go in with the Healing tool or the Clone tool and paint that rigging out by hand, but there's an easier way, and it's only a couple steps:

1. **Select the area around your subject consisting of just the green screen and the wires.** You can do this with any of the selection tools at your disposal, but the Free Select tool works pretty well for this.

2. **Run Filters ➤ Generic ➤ Dilate on this selection.** Assuming that your wires are dark, this should effectively expand the green screen area enough to get rid of those wires. If the wires were light, choosing Filters ➤ Generic ➤ Erode would get you a similar result.

FIGURE 15-17

From left to right: the original image, the image with the Dilate filter applied, and the same image with the Erode filter applied (Photo credit: Melody Smith)

Original   Dilated   Eroded

And that's it. You can also use the same technique to refine edge detection, localize highlights for a bloom effect, or quickly make text thicker or thinner. These unassuming little filters are very useful when you know where to use them. And now you do.

Using the Combine Filters

As the menu name implies, the filters you find in Filters ➤ Combine are used to take a couple images (or more) and combine them in interesting ways. It'd be tough to get closer to the definition of "compositing" than that. There aren't many filters in this menu because they are pretty specialized. They don't get used often in straight image editing, but they're great to have when you need them. This is particularly true if you're using GIMP to batch process a sequence of images in a video or animation project, as covered in Part V of this book.

Depth Merge

The Depth Merge filter is an incredibly useful compositing filter and it's used extensively in special effects compositing as well as 3D animation. To use it effectively, you need to understand the concept of z-depth. When a 3D animation tool renders a still image, all of the three-dimensional data is flattened into a two-dimensional image. This means that if you create an image of a tree and you want to go in later and composite a character sticking out from behind that tree, you typically need to use a lot of clever selections and masking to get it to look right. This can be a tedious and time-consuming process. To get around this, most 3D applications give you the ability to render a depth map. A *depth map* is basically a grayscale image that defines how far away from the camera an object in the scene is. Depending on the program, the generated depth map may define white pixels as farthest from the camera or black pixels as the farthest ones, but in GIMP, the whiter the pixel, the farther it is from the camera. Figure 15-18 shows an example of an image and its associated depth map, both generated with the open source 3D animation suite Blender.

FIGURE 15-18

On the left is an image of a scene rendered with Blender and on the right is that image's corresponding depth map.

Now take the example of the character and the tree and imagine that you generated depth maps when you rendered both of them. Because you have the depth map defining how far away each thing is from the camera, and therefore from each other, your compositing world gets all sorts of easier. The first thing you need to do is load all of the necessary images, including their depth maps, into GIMP with File ➢ Open to make sure that the Depth Merge filter is aware of them. You can use separate images or a single image with multiple layers. Depth Merge is capable of handling both instances. With the images loaded, choose Filters ➢ Combine ➢ Depth Merge to get the Depth Merge parameters window, shown in Figure 15-19.

Beneath the large preview window you have four drop-down menus where you define your source images and their corresponding depth maps. Each possible image is listed in the format [image_name]/[layer_name]. Just click each drop-down and choose which image goes where. As you do this, the preview window updates to give you an idea of what the final composite image looks like.

Tip

An important thing to remember here is that to use this filter properly, all of the images you use, including the depth map, must have the exact same dimensions. So if one image is 1024x768, all of them need to be. ■

Now if your two images are using the same scale for their depth maps, you can just click OK to accept this as your composited result. However, oftentimes depth maps aren't on the same scale and you need to tweak the composite. This is what the four sliders at the bottom of the Depth Merge window are for. The following is a brief description of what each value does:

- **Overlap** — The default value of 0.000 in this field makes the transition from one image to the next very sharp and crisp. This is usually a very good thing. However, on complex depth maps, keeping this value at zero can leave nasty aliased edges where the images composite together. By slightly increasing the Overlap value, you can soften that edge a bit and get rid of the aliasing.

- **Offset** — This value is best when you're dealing with two depth maps that aren't on the same scale. This means that your character may look like he's standing in front of the tree rather than behind it. Adjusting this slider back and forth helps you put the character behind the tree and get the composite you want.

- **Scale 1/Scale 2** — Like Offset, these values also control how the depth maps position the content relative to the camera. The difference, though, is that because each Scale value adjusts one depth map independently of the other, you have more control. Lowering the Scale value for one of the depth maps makes that map darker, thereby giving its content priority and effectively saying it's closer to the camera than the other one.

FIGURE 15-19

The Depth Merge filter's parameters window

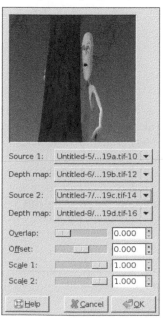

Figure 15-20 shows an example of how you can use depth maps with the Depth Merge filter to effectively composite two separate images together.

Across the top, two images and their corresponding depth maps. Below them is the result of compositing them together with the Depth Merge filter (Tree model credit: Blender Foundation, www.bigbuckbunny.org; character model credit: Bassam Kurdali)

Filmstrip

If you need an effect that makes your image (or a set of images) look like a film print, as shown in Figure 15-21, this filter is what you're looking for. Like the Depth Merge filter, this one has a very specific use, so you may not use it very frequently. However, when you need it, this filter is really helpful. You can use it just as the effect that it is and you get a result that looks like a series of photos taken with an old-school film camera. However, you can also very easily use it to generate a texture to use for mapping to an object for use in a 3D animation. Surprisingly, this happens more than you might expect when creating motion graphics for television programs, particularly entertainment shows.

The Filmstrip effect can make one or more images look like they're part of a film print (Image credit: Hand Turkey Studios)

Tip

The Filmstrip effect doesn't really produce a result that's exactly like a film negative or the film prints used in movies. For example, in a real film negative, the colors in all of the images are inverted. And in movie film, the images are rotated 90 degrees because the film records vertically rather than horizontally. To get either of these effects, you first need to process your source images, inverting their colors (Color ➤ Invert) or rotating them (Image ➤ Transform ➤ Rotate 90° counter-clockwise). If you're using the Filmstrip filter on multiple images, you can use the Filtermacro filter from the GIMP Animation Package plug-in to help automate the process. You can find more on Filtermacro in Chapter 18. ■

To use this filter, open the images you want to use and go to Filters ➤ Combine ➤ Filmstrip in any of their image windows. What you get when you do that is a window like the one shown in Figure 15-22. This window has two tabs full of parameters and settings for you to adjust: Selection and Advanced. The bulk of your time with this filter is spent in the Selection tab.

FIGURE 15-22

The Filmstrip filter's parameter window

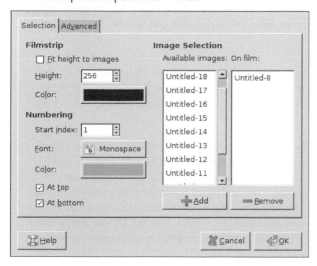

Selection

The controls in this tab control the overall look and content of the final output of this filter. Unlike many of GIMP's filters, this one does not actually give you a preview window, so you do have to utilize a bit of imagination (or guesswork, depending on your perspective) when adjusting the values here. The most important controls in this window are on its right side under the Image Selection label. There are two panels with lists of image names. The left column lists the images you currently have open in GIMP. The Filmstrip filter only has access to those images. The panel on the right lists the images you want to use in this effect in the order you want them to appear. By default, the only image in the right-side list is the one that you used to call the Filmstrip filter.

To add images to the list of ones that this filter uses, first select them in the left panel. Like most lists in GIMP, you can use Ctrl+click to select multiple random items and Shift+click to select a series of items. With your images selected, click the Add button underneath the Available Images panel and they're added to the list on the right. You also have the ability to add the same image multiple times if that's something that you need.

An important thing to notice here is that if you select multiple images, they are added to the right panel in the order that they appear in the left one. This means that if you want these images to appear in a specific order that's different than the one they use in the Available Images list, you need to manually add them one at a time in the desired order. And if you have an item out of order, you need to select it as well as all of the images below it and click the Remove button below the right-side panel to get them out of the list. Then you can add images back where they belong. It's a bit inconvenient this way, but until GIMP developers (or you!) modify this filter to provide controls for rearranging the order of items on these lists, we'll have to deal with doing it this way.

Note

The Filmstrip filter cannot load all of the images from a directory and use them for you. The only images that the Filmstrip filter is aware of are the ones that are currently open in GIMP. Keep this in mind, especially if you're using a lot of large images. If you have an older computer, this can quickly use up all of your available RAM. ■

On the left side of this tab are parameters to control how your series of images appear in the final filmstrip image, as well as how the filmstrip itself looks. Under the heading of Filmstrip, you have the following settings controlling the size and appearance of the filmstrip, relative to your source image(s):

- **Fit Height to Images** — Enable this check box to fit the filmstrip effect to wrap around your original image's size, resulting in an image that is larger than your original image. If you're using a series of images with different sizes, the filmstrip is fit to the height of the largest of these images. All other images are scaled up to fill the remaining space. This is important to remember because enabling this option may cause small images to look pixelated in the final result. Also, when you enable this check box, the Height option below it is disabled and grayed out, but it shows the pixel size that the result image will be after you run this filter.

- **Height** — If you leave the Fit Height to Images check box disabled, this value gives you control of the exact height in pixels of your final image. Your selected images are scaled to fit this size. Note that unlike the Fit Height to Images setting, this is the actual height of the resulting image, not the height of your source images within the filmstrip frame.

- **Color** — This is the color of the film portion of your filmstrip. By default this is set to the standard black color, but you can adjust it to be anything you'd like. Do note, however, that you cannot control the color of the filmstrip "holes." Those are always white.

The Filmstrip filter also gives you the ability to number each frame in the series of images, like what's commonly seen on photographic film negatives. The parameters that control the look and location of these numbers are beneath the Filmstrip parameters, under the Numbering heading. What follows is a brief description of what each parameter does:

- **Start Index** — This is the value of the first number on the generated filmstrip. The numbers count up from left to right, so this is the left-most number in your resulting image. You can set this value to any positive integer value you want, even if you're only applying the Filmstrip effect to a single image.

- **Font** — This drop-down menu allows you to choose the font you want to use for the numbers on the strip.

- **Color** — The standard color of these numbers in photographic film is the default orange color. However, you can click this color swatch to change it to any color you want it to be.

- **At Top/Bottom** — By default, these check boxes are enabled to have the numbering appear both above and below the source images. However, you can disable either of them to have the numbering only above or only below each frame. To remove numbering altogether, disable both options.

Advanced

The Advanced tab for this filter, as shown in Figure 15-23, provides you with a series of sliders that more directly control the final look of the generated filmstrip. All of the parameters here are relative to the Height value set in the Selection tab, normalized to a scale from 0 to 1. So setting any value to 0.500 makes that attribute half the size of the strip's height and setting it to 1.000 makes that attribute the exact same size as the strip's height.

FIGURE 15-23

The parameters available in the Advanced tab of the Filmstrip filter

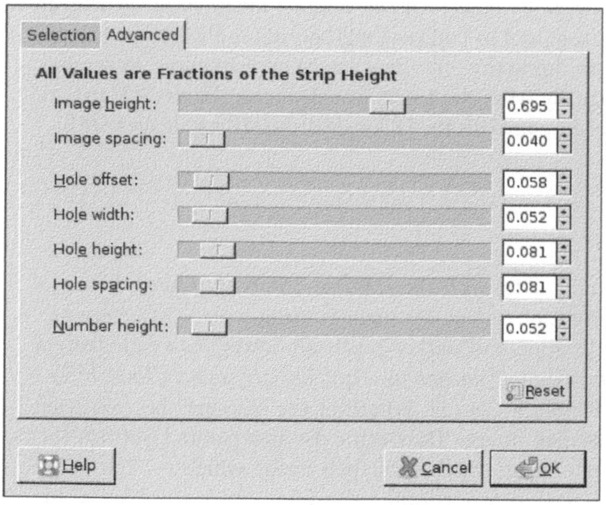

The following list is a short description of each of the values in this tab:

- **Image Height** — This is the height of your source images relative to the overall height of the final result. The default value of 0.695 sets the image to be 69.5% of the overall height.

- **Image Spacing** — This value controls how wide the space is between the images in the strip. Set this value to zero if you want each image to butt right up to the next one.

- **Hole Offset** — Increase this value to push the holes inward from the top and bottom borders of the final image.

- **Hole Width/Height** — These sliders control the dimensions of the holes in the final strip. If you want square holes, make sure these values are the same.

- **Hole Spacing** — This value controls how far apart each hole is from its neighbor, horizontally.

- **Number Height** — If you're using numbering on your filmstrip, adjust this value to change the height of your numbers. Their width is adjusted proportionally.

Note

The values in the Advanced tab are still relative to the Height value you set in the Selection tab. Furthermore, it's good to remember that all of the filmstrip objects like holes and numbers are secondary to the source images in the strip. This means that if, for example, you set the Number Height value to 1.000, it will be the full height of the strip, but it will also be obscured by the image itself. This also means that if you set Image Height to 1.000, you effectively maximize the height of the source images and hide features like numbering and the filmstrip holes. The filmstrip holes *won't* appear to cut holes in your image. ∎

Taking Advantage of Mapping Filters

Mapping is a process of distorting the pixels on your image by using a source object of some sort. That source object could be a separate image, a 3D object, or the original image itself. Whatever the specific filter may be, mapping is a valuable tool in compositing because it allows one graphical element to be manipulated by another. In doing this, the final image appears more integrated, unified, and (hopefully) interesting. That's really what the filters in this menu (Filters ➤ Map) are for. You can use them as an additional tool in compositing or for creating strong images with these filters alone.

Bump Map

One of the most common forms of mapping is done with the humble Bump Map filter. It works by using a grayscale image to define the height of surface features. Starting with a 50% gray as your baseline, lighter pixels are higher in elevation and darker pixels are lower. You can create a good bump map with everything from hand-painted images to a quickly generated Cloud filter from the options available under Filters ➤ Render ➤ Clouds. Whatever the case may be, you need two images: your source image and a bump map image. They can exist as separate layers on the same GIMP image file or they can be separate images with their own image windows. You need to have both images open and available to GIMP before running this filter. Once you have your two images, you activate this filter by going to the image or layer where your source image data lives and choosing Filters ➤ Map ➤ Bump Map to get a window like the one in Figure 15-24.

FIGURE 15-24

The Bump Map filter's parameters window

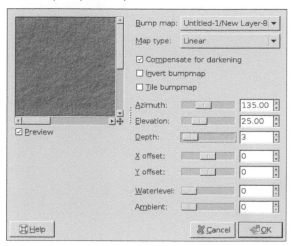

The Bump Map dialog has a preview window on the left side and a series of control parameters along the right side. These values are designed to control what you're using for the bump map as well as how that bump map influences the final look of your output. The following list describes each setting in more detail:

- **Bump Map** — The drop-down menu here is a list of all the images and layers that were open when you launched the filter. Choose your grayscale bump map from this list. Note that you have the ability to choose color images from this drop-down as well. In those cases, the bump map filter deals only with the brightness of each pixel and disregards color information.

- **Map Type** — This parameter offers you a drop-down with a choice of three options to control how your bump map influences your image. Figure 15-25 shows the results of each map type on the same circular gradient used as a bump map.

  - **Linear** — This has the bump work on a linear scale, so the simulated height of a pixel changes evenly as you move through gray levels from black to white.

  - **Spherical** — Choosing this map type results in a more abrupt change in height when moving from dark to light. This setting most noticeably makes low elevations darker. Notice how the example in Figure 15-25 looks like a sphere is protruding from the surface.

  - **Sinusoidal** — This map type is the least abrupt of all; it smoothly eases in and out of the darkest and lightest values. And the mid-tone grays are treated almost linearly.

- **Compensate for Darkening** — Because bump mapping involves mixing your image's pixels with the brightness of another set of pixels, it tends to darken an image overall. Enable this check box to compensate for that and try to retain the original image's brightness.

451

FIGURE 15-25

At the top is the source image (a flat color) and a bump map. Along the bottom from left to right are the applied bump map with linear, spherical, and sinusoidal map types

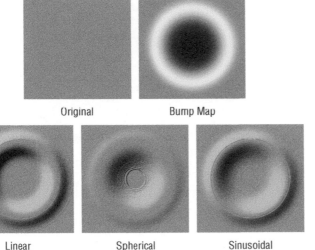

Original   Bump Map

Linear   Spherical   Sinusoidal

- **Invert Bumpmap** — If you have a bump map that's backwards from GIMP's light-high, dark-low convention (or you're like me and you get those two mixed up on occasion), enable this check box.

- **Tile Bumpmap** — If your bump map image is smaller than your original image or you're using an Offset value, enabling this check box repeats the bump maps as a tile throughout your image so the entire image gets the same bump mapped appearance.

- **Azimuth** — Consider this to be the direction that your source light is shining from to reveal the bumps, measured in degrees. An Azimuth of 0° has the light shining from the right side of the image. Increasing the Azimuth moves counterclockwise, so 90° shines from the top, 180° shines from the left, and 270° shines from the bottom.

- **Elevation** — This value, measured in degrees, is a control of how the bump's height is perceived, starting from a horizon value of 0.50° to a zenith, or highest point, at 90°. The easiest way to remember this value is to think of it as controlling the intensity of the bump map.

- **Depth** — This value controls how much variation there is between the highest point (white) and the lowest point (black) on your bump map. Lower values make your bumps shallow whereas higher values make them steeper.

- **X/Y Offset** — These values, measured in pixels, shift your bump map left and right or up and down, respectively.

- **Waterlevel** — This value has an influence only when your bump map has transparency. By default, transparent areas are treated as solid black, as if they're the lowest part of the bump. However, by increasing this slider you can manually control how high on the bump transparent areas are considered. If you have the Invert Bumpmap check box enabled, this treats transparent areas as if they were white and the opposite behavior is true.

- **Ambient** — Increasing this value simulates an increase in *ambient light*, or light that bounces around from the environment. This effectively takes the shadows that your bump map generates and makes them softer.

Once you're done playing with the settings, click OK and GIMP applies your bump map for you.

Displace

Where the bump map adjusts the brightness of pixels to simulate a raised 3D surface in an image, a *displacement map* is a grayscale image that actually moves pixels around. Like the bump map, you start with a value of 50% gray, which indicates that the pixel is not shifted. Now, values that are lighter than 50% gray shift the source image's pixels in the negative direction. Values that are darker than 50% gray shift pixels in the positive direction. These are the basic mechanics behind what makes displacement maps work. If you use a color image as a displacement map, GIMP only accounts for the brightness, or *luminosity*, of those pixels.

Tip

The Displace filter is unique from the Bump Map filter in another way as well; for the displacement map to work, it *must* be the exact same width and height as the image you intend on displacing. This is an extremely important consideration to make, because unlike the bump map, you can't stipulate that the displacement map is tiled. ■

To use the Displace filter, select the image and layer that you want to apply the filter to and go to Filters ➤ Map ➤ Displace. GIMP provides you with a dialog like the one that appears in Figure 15-26.

The most important option is in the bottom-left corner, Displacement Mode. There are two different ways, or better stated, two different kinds of coordinate systems that your displacement map can use to influence the pixels on your source image:

- **Cartesian** — This is the standard coordinate system with which most people are familiar. You have a horizontal x-axis and a vertical y-axis. The Displace filter allows you to distort the pixels along these axes independently. If you enable them, light gray values shift pixels left and down and dark gray values shift pixels right and up.

- **Polar** — Another commonly used coordinate system is polar coordinates. Rather than use the typical x- and y-axes, for a grid-based system, polar coordinates locate points by saying how far away they are in a straight line from the center and at the angle that line is from horizontal. The interesting thing here is that if your displacement map is a solid color other than 50% gray, setting the Displacement Mode to polar coordinates makes this filter behave just like the Whirl and Pinch filter described in Chapter 13.

The default behavior of the Displace filter is to use Cartesian coordinates. When this is the case, the dialog gives you two directions that you can displace independently: the x direction and the y direction. Check boxes next to each of these values enable or disable whether the displacement map influences them. Each of these displacement directions is associated with a numerical value that controls the strength of the displacement used. You can also enter negative numbers for these values and cause the displacement map to have an inverted influence. And not only can you control the displacement of each direction independently, but each displacement direction can have its own separate displacement map, allowing you to distort pixels vertically in a different manner than the way you distort them horizontally.

The parameters available in the Displace filter's dialog

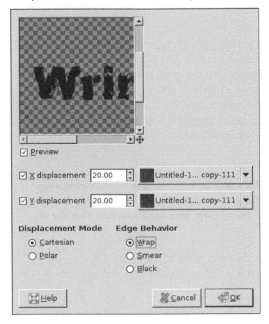

If you choose the Polar Displacement Mode, the x and y directional values are swapped for Pinch and Whirl values. The following bullets describe how the displacement map influences these settings. As with the Cartesian mode, setting the intensity values to negative numbers inverts the expected behavior or the map.

- **Pinch** — Values lighter than 50% gray cause the corresponding pixels in the source image to pinch in toward the center, whereas values darker than 50% gray cause pixels to push or balloon outward from the center.

- **Whirl** — If your displacement map is a solid color, the Whirl parameter only rotates the colors around the source image's center. However, on a map that has multiple gray values, it whirls pixels about the center. Values lighter than 50% gray rotate pixels in the clockwise direction; values darker than 50% gray cause their corresponding pixels to rotate in the opposite direction.

The only other settings in the Displace filter's dialog are the radio buttons for Edge Behavior. Like with the edge detection filters described earlier in this chapter, the Displace filter has to deal with the pixels at the border of the source image or the edge of your selection. Specifically, you need to tell the Displace filter what to do when a pixel along the border is pushed away from its location and there's no pixel to fill the remaining void. In this situation, you have three choices:

- **Wrap** — Fill the empty area with the value of pixels from the opposite side of the image or selection.

- **Smear** — Use the colors near the empty area and use those samples to choose a color to fill the gap.

- **Black** — Don't do any guessing for the new color. Simply fill in the empty area with black pixels.

Once you get all the parameters set to the values you want, click OK and the Displace filter does its magic. In terms of practical application, you can use this filter with a cloud image as the displacement map to distort an image with crisp, clean lines and make them look more natural and messy. Alternatively, in some more compositing-related examples, you could use this filter with a gradient to arc text or you can use it along with the Bump Map filter to make a logo appear like it's on some rumpled-up cloth. Figure 15-27 provides a few examples of how you can apply this filter.

FIGURE 15-27

From top to bottom: using the Displace filter to "sketchify" perfect lines, arc text, and apply a logo to wrinkled cloth (Cloth texture from cgtextures.com)

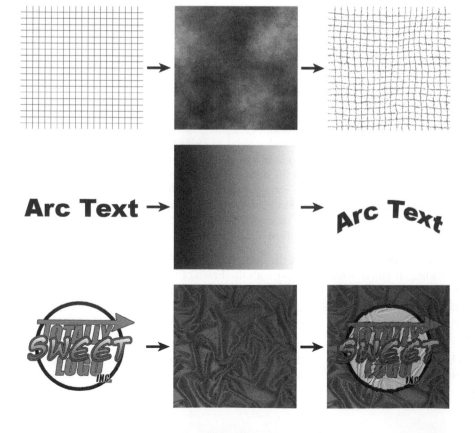

Fractal Trace

This interesting little filter maps your source image to the Mandelbrot fractal. In fact, this filter is similar in many ways to the Fractal Explorer filter covered in Chapter 14. The difference here is that rather than just showing the fractal with some interesting colors, the Fractal Trace filter actually takes your image and makes it work in the Mandelbrot set. Launch this filter by going to Filters ➤ Map ➤ Fractal Trace. This brings up a dialog like the one in Figure 15-28 where you can adjust the parameters to control how your image is mapped to the fractal.

FIGURE 15-28

The Fractal Trace dialog

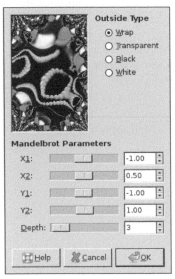

At the top of this dialog are a preview window and a series of radio buttons that control how Fractal Trace handles empty areas around the central Mandelbrot fractal. You have four choices: Wrap, Transparent, Black, and White. Wrap is the default behavior and is also the most interesting to look at, filling in empty sections with corresponding pixels that appear on the opposite side of the fractal. If you choose Transparent, Black, or White, the empty areas are simply left transparent or filled with black or white pixels, respectively. Figure 15-29 shows the resulting image when you choose each of these Outside Type values on the same image.

The real controls for this filter, however, are at the bottom of the dialog under the Mandelbrot Parameters heading. If you're already familiar with the Fractal Explorer filter, these values behave similarly to the Left, Right, Top, Bottom, and Iterations parameters. They're not exactly the same, though, so the following list offers more detailed descriptions of each parameter. To interactively practice with these settings, set the Outside Type to Black or White and push the sliders around.

- **X1** — Lowering the value in this parameter squashes the Mandelbrot fractal to the right of the image. Increasing it stretches it out to the left, often leaving you with nothing but blank space.

- **X2** — This parameter works somewhat in reverse to X1. Increasing it squashes the fractal to the left and decreasing it stretches it to the right. Curiously, setting these two values to their extreme opposite limits results in a squashed fractal right down the center of your image space.

- **Y1/Y2** — The Y1 and Y2 parameters behave like the X1 and X2 ones, but vertically instead of horizontally. Decreasing Y1 squashes the fractal to the bottom of the image and increasing Y2 squashes it to the top.

- **Depth** — This parameter controls how detailed the fractal is. Increasing this value maps your image to a more detailed fractal with a greater number of iterations. The higher this value, the more your result resembles the actual Mandelbrot fractal.

FIGURE 15-29

From left to right, using Fractal Trace with outside types of Wrap, Transparent, Black, and White (Photo credit: Melody Smith)

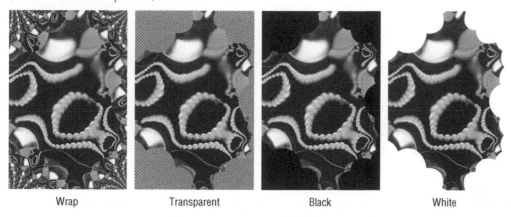

Wrap　　　　　　Transparent　　　　　　Black　　　　　　White

Note

If you're using the Outside Type of Wrap, and you increase the Depth parameter beyond a certain threshold, the preview window makes the result look like you're using Transparent as your Outside Type. However, when you click the OK button, the parts that appeared transparent in the preview have vertical stripes based on the last color at the edge of the fractal. ■

Illusion

This filter is similar to Fractal Trace in that it maps your image to a predefined pattern. In the case of this filter, though, the pattern is as if you're looking at your source image through a kaleidoscope. When you run this filter by going to Filters ➤ Map ➤ Illusion, the dialog that you get, shown in Figure 15-30, has a remarkably minimal set of controls.

One of the first things to notice is that unlike a lot of the preview windows in some of GIMP's other filters, this one actually gives you the ability to zoom in and see how the filter affects your image at a more detailed level. The Illusion filter works by slicing your image radially, duplicating those slices, and mixing them back with your source image. The filter has two different patterns you can use, indicated by the Mode 1 and Mode 2 radio buttons. The Mode 1 version makes the slices appear to spin about the image's center. Mode 2 pushes the slices outward from the center. By adjusting the Divisions value, you can control the number of slices that the Illusion filter uses as well as the direction of the kaleidoscope's rotation. You can set this value to any integer value from −32 to 64. Negative values spin the kaleidoscope in the reverse direction. Figure 15-31 shows the difference between using Mode 1 and Mode 2 on the same image.

FIGURE 15-30

The Illusion filter's dialog

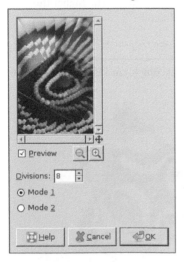

FIGURE 15-31

From left to right: the original image and that same image with the Illusion filter applied in both Mode 1 and Mode 2

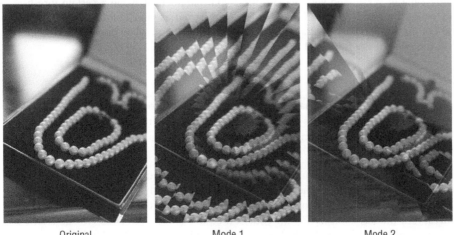

Original   Mode 1   Mode 2

Make Seamless

Although this filter, run by going to Filters ➤ Map ➤ Make Seamless, has no parameters, it's an extremely useful filter. It takes any image input that you give it and modifies it so it can be tiled seamlessly. You can use this to create a tiled background for a web site or if you do 3D modeling, you can use it to create a texture that you can map to the surface of your model without showing any seams. Figure 15-32 shows the results of running this filter on an image.

FIGURE 15-32

Running Filters ➤ Map ➤ Make Seamless creates an image that can easily be tiled without showing any seams.

Original   Make Seamless

Pattern fill with seamless version

The Map Object Filter

When compositing an image, you may need to map your image to a three-dimensional object. This filter is for that exact purpose. Before getting into it, though, be aware that this filter doesn't map your image to any arbitrary 3D model. The filter provides a handful of primitive objects that one or more source images can be mapped to. It's really quite cool. To run it, go to Filters ➤ Map ➤ Map to Object and GIMP provides you with a window like the one in Figure 15-33.

Everything with this filter starts with the preview window on the left side. Unlike the preview window in most other filters, this one doesn't always update immediately. This is because GIMP has no 3D acceleration, so when you adjust a parameter in this filter, it may take time to update the preview window. So rather than have a laggy preview window for these parameters, the preview simply doesn't update for them until you click the Preview button below it. It can be a bit confusing to see the preview window update immediately for some parameters and not for others, but fortunately the parameters that update immediately are pretty obvious. They're also in the minority. One of them is the Show Preview Wireframe check box beneath the preview window. If you enable this check box, a wireframe of the 3D object is drawn in the preview window to help you better visualize the orientation of the object your image is being mapped to.

The Map to Object dialog

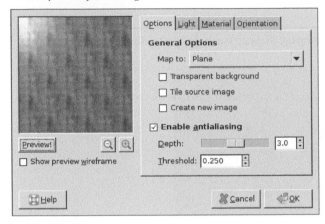

Options

To the right of the preview window is a series of tabs that give you detailed control over which object to use, how it's oriented, how your image is applied to that object, and how the whole thing is lit. You start with the Options tab. The following list describes the parameters in this tab:

- **Map to** — This drop-down gives you the list of available 3D objects that you can use.
  - **Plane** — This is the default object; a flat plane that you can position and rotate in 3D space however you like.
  - **Sphere** — Choose this object and your image is wrapped around a sphere like a world map is wrapped around a globe.
  - **Box** — This box object's default is a cube, but if you choose this option, an additional tab, named Box, appears. In that tab, you can not only stretch the box to a non-cube box, but you can also define a different image for each of the box's six faces.
  - **Cylinder** — Choose this object to get a cylinder to map your image to. Like the Box option, this gives you another tab named Cylinder where you can adjust the attributes of the cylinder object as a well as control what images get mapped to it. The Box and Cylinder tabs are covered more later in this section.
- **Transparent Background** — When you map your image to one of these objects, there's very often a lot of blank space around it. By default, GIMP paints this empty space as white. However, if you want to composite your mapped object into another scene it makes more sense to leave this background transparent. Enable this check box to do just that.

- **Tile Source Image** — This option is valid only if you choose the Plane as your object to map to. If you do choose the Plane, your source image is tiled indefinitely in all directions. This is most apparent when you rotate the plane's orientation.

- **Create New Image** — Rather than applying the filter directly to your source image, you can enable this check box and GIMP creates a completely new image with the result of this filter.

- **Enable Antialiasing** — This is a feature that you almost always want to keep enabled. If you disable it, the edges of your mapped result are jagged and aliased.

  - **Depth** — Increasing this value increases the quality of antialiasing that the filter does. The only downside is that higher values make the filter run slower when you click OK.

  - **Threshold** — Like depth, this parameter controls the quality of your antialiasing. If the difference between pixels is less than this value, the antialiasing algorithm stops. Basically, lower values increase quality, but can drastically increase the processing time when the filter runs.

Light and Material

The next two tabs, Light and Material, control how the 3D object is lit and how your image reflects light when it's applied to that object, respectively. Figure 15-34 shows these tabs.

FIGURE 15-34

In the Map to Object dialog, you have a Light tab (left) and a Material tab (right) for controlling the look of your image mapped to the chosen object.

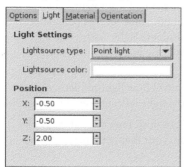
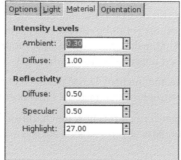

In the Light tab, you have two primary controls:

- **Lightsource Type** — This drop-down menu gives you the choice of one of three options:

  - **Point Light** — This is a singular point of light, which you can control the location of using the X, Y, and Z position values that appear at the bottom of this tab. Also, if X and Y are positive values, a blue dot appears in the preview window. You can click and drag this blue dot around to interactively position your light in the X and Y axes. To change its z-axis position, though, you need to use the numeric entry field.

  - **Directional Light** — Rather than use a single point to define the origin of light for your object, you can instead define the direction from which that light is coming by choosing this option. When you do so, the parameters at the bottom of the tab dictate the direction that the light is pointing. There's no visual reference for this vector in the preview window, but you can click the Preview button after making changes to see how your changes affect the object.

- **No Light** — This name is a bit misleading because if there were truly no light, the resulting image would be black. Instead, it's better to think of this option as being "no shadows" because that's its ultimate effect. Your source image is stretched to fit the surface of the 3D object, but no shadows are really generated. This is helpful if you just want to warp your image and don't want to have additional light information added to it.

- **Lightsource Color** — Clicking this color swatch should change the color of the source of light shining on your object. When you change the color, the difference is most apparent in the highlight on the 3D object.

In the Material tab, you control how your source image reflects light when it's applied to your chosen 3D object. With these settings, you can make the object shiny, dull, bright, or dark. The following list describes each parameter in more detail:

- **Intensity Levels** — These parameters control how the light affects your image when mapped to the 3D object.

  - **Ambient** — A bright light bounces off of every object in any environment, providing an even tone that gives a base light to everything. This is called *ambient light* and you can increase or decrease how much of it shines on your object by adjusting this value.

  - **Diffuse** — The diffuse light is the light that's explicitly generated from your light source. The default value of 1.00 is the standard full strength value for this parameter. Dropping it to zero causes your object to be lit by only ambient light. Increasing it to values greater than 1.00 makes your source light more intense and can easily cause details in your mapped image to be lost or obscured.

- **Reflectivity** — Whereas the Intensity Levels parameters control how light influences your image, these settings control how that material influences the light reflected off of it.

  - **Diffuse** — This parameter controls how much diffuse light your material reflects back into the environment. Basically, if you increase this value, your mapped image appears brighter.

  - **Specular** — In 3D lighting, *specularity* is the brightness of a highlight on a material. So if you want your object to appear shiny, increase the specular value. If, however, you prefer a more matte appearance, drop the specularity down to zero.

  - **Highlight** — This parameter controls the size of your specular highlight. By increasing it, you make the specular highlight smaller and more focused. Lowering it disperses the highlight over a greater area of your 3D object.

Orientation

The sliders in this tab, shown in Figure 15-35, control where your mapped object appears in your image window and how it's rotated in that space. The X, Y, and Z values under Position control where your object is located in 3D space. This uses image coordinates, so X values work as expected, with lower values moving the object left and higher X values moving it right.

However, Y values are inverted from the standard y-axis you're taught in grade school math, so higher Y values actually push the object down instead of up. For the Z parameter, increased values bring the object closer to you and decreased values push it farther away. The Rotation values all work as expected, rotating your object in degrees about each of the three axes. For any of the changes you make in this tab, you need to click the Preview button to see what the results are in the preview window.

The Orientation tab of the Map to Object dialog

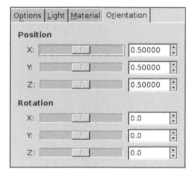

Extra Tabs: Box and Cylinder

If you choose Box or Cylinder from the Map to drop-down in the Options tab, an additional tab corresponding with either one of these objects is added to the Map to Object dialog. Figure 15-36 shows what each tab looks like. Whichever tab you get, the parameters available in it are there to control the dimensions of your box or cylinder object as well as the images that get mapped to its surface. When you change any of these options, be sure to remember to click the Preview button so you can see their effects.

For the Box tab, the bulk of it is devoted to determining which image goes on each of its six faces. Each face (Front, Back, Left, and so on) has a drop-down menu associated with it where you can select any layer from any of the images that were open when you launched this filter. By default, all drop-downs are set to use the layer that you launched the filter from. Below that, the Scale X, Y, and Z sliders give you control over the box's width, height, and depth, respectively. Something to note here is that when you choose an image to be mapped to a face, that image is scaled to fit the face. So unless you use proportions that match the dimensions of your image, it may appear to be stretched or squashed.

The same basic controls exist in the Cylinder tab, although there are fewer of them. When you choose to use the cylinder object, the filter assumes that the layer selected when you launched this filter is the one to map to the cylinder's surface. The Cylinder tab doesn't change this. However, it does give you control over what layers to map to the top and bottom caps of the cylinder. The Radius and Length sliders at the bottom of the tab give you control over the cylinder object's dimensions.

FIGURE 15-36

The Box tab (left) and the Cylinder tab (right) give you control over mapped images and object dimensions.

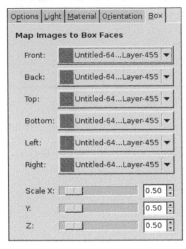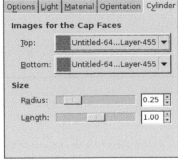

Tip

When you use this filter, it's a good idea to use it on a layer with square dimensions. If you don't do that, the resulting image ends up distorted. For example, if you run this filter on an image with dimensions 480x640 pixels and choose the Cylinder object for mapping, the resulting cylinder is stretched vertically even though it appears properly scaled in the square-shaped preview window. ■

Paper Tile

The Paper Tile filter is a pretty interesting way to add some randomness to your image. What it does is divide your image into a grid of rectangular tiles and then shift them around so you get overlapping tiles and gaps between them. To run this filter, go to the image window and choose Filters ➤ Map ➤ Paper Tile. Figure 15-37 shows the dialog that appears and gives an example of what an image looks like after you run this filter on it.

The parameters in the Paper Tile dialog are organized into four sections: Division, Fractional Pixels, Movement, and Background Type. The parameters in the Division section control how the filter breaks up your image. The X and Y values control the size of the grid that chops up your image, dictating how many divisions there are across and down. When you set these values, with Width and Height parameters are automatically adjusted to show how large in pixels each tile is. At the same time, if you know how large you want each tile to be, you can stipulate that in the Width and Height parameters and the X and Y values are automatically adjusted to match.

Of course, because you have arbitrary control of how large each tile is, there's a good chance that some pixels could be left hanging. For example, if you have an image that's 100 pixels wide and you choose to set the X division parameter to 3, then technically the width of each block should be 33.333 pixels. However, because a pixel can't really be divided, each block is 33 pixels wide and you're left with an extra pixel floating at the end. The Fractional Pixels options give you control over what to do with that leftover pixel. You have three choices:

- **Background** — Replace the leftover pixel with whatever Background Type you choose.

- **Ignore** — Don't do anything with the pixel and just let it stay there unaffected.

- **Force** — This option forces the remaining pixel to stick to one of the blocks even if it means that block won't be the same size as the others.

When you run the Paper Tile filter (center) on your source layer (left), it chops up your image and shifts those blocks around to get a result like the one on the right.

 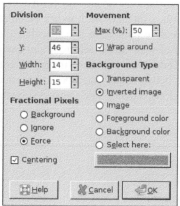 

The Centering check box below the Fractional Pixels options really belongs in the Movement section. It tells the filter that the majority of the tiles should be grouped around the center of the resulting image. If you disable this check box, the tiles are shifted around randomly without any grouping. Aside from the Centering check box, you have two other controls for the movement of each tile:

- **Max (%)** — This is the maximum distance any one tile can move, relative to its size. The default value of 25 means that if you have a tile that's 40 pixels tall, the maximum distance it can travel in the vertical direction is 25% of that height, or 10 pixels.

- **Wrap Around** — This check box is specific to tiles around the outer border of your image layer. If it's disabled, the tiles just run off of the edge of the layer and that's all she wrote. However, if you enable this check box, the tiles that get shifted over the border appear on the opposite side of the layer.

The options for Background Type give you control over what is done with the gaps that remain between tiles after they're shifted around. For this, you actually have a lot of choices:

- **Transparent** — The space between tiles is rendered as transparent. Be aware that if you're applying this filter to a Background layer that doesn't have transparency, this option makes the background pixels black instead of transparent.

- **Inverted Image** — This option takes the original layer, inverts its colors, and sets that result to fill the gaps between tiles.

- **Image** — This is the same as the Inverted image option, except it doesn't invert colors first. It results in a really interesting, noisy version of your source image.

- **Foreground/Background Color** — These options replace the gap pixels with whatever you have chosen for your foreground or background color, respectively.

- **Select Here** — Choose this option and you can use the color swatch below it to dictate the specific color you want to use to fill the spaces left by shifted tiles.

Small Tiles

The Small Tiles filter is a quick way to take an image and fill it with small tiles of itself. You can use this with the Make Seamless filter to see how the seamless image would look tiled. You can also use this filter to replace part of an image with a tiled version of itself. For instance, if you have the background of your image selected, you can run this filter and the background is replaced with a tiled version of the whole image. This can create some really interesting results that sit somewhere between kaleidoscope and mosaic. Run this filter by going to Filters ➤ Map ➤ Small Tiles and you get a dialog like the one shown in Figure 15-38.

FIGURE 15-38

The parameters in the Small Tiles dialog

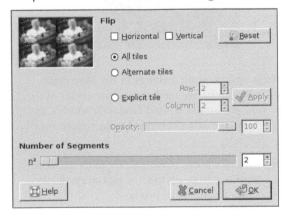

The Small Tiles dialog provides you with some interesting controls that you might not expect to see. Of course, the most important and most obvious of these controls is the Number of Segments slider at the bottom of the window. This gives you control over the size of the final grid. And as you adjust this value, you can see the preview window update to show you what the result looks like.

Note
It's worth noting that this Number of Segments value has a maximum of six segments, so if you want to have more divisions than that, you need to run this filter multiple times. ■

The really interesting stuff happens with the controls at the top of the window, though. The Small Tiles filter gives you controls for flipping your duplicated tiles. The default behavior is to leave them as is, but you can choose to flip them horizontally, vertically, or in both directions. Furthermore, with the radio buttons below these check boxes, you can actually control which tiles get flipped:

- **All Tiles** — As the name implies, every one of the small duplicated tiles is flipped according to the Horizontal and Vertical check boxes.

- **Alternate Tiles** — This creates an interesting checkerboard pattern where every other tile is flipped.

- **Explicit Tile** — This is the really interesting option. You can pick arbitrary tiles to be flipped with this. Once you enable this radio button, one of the tiles in the preview window is highlighted around its border. By clicking in the preview window or adjusting the Row and Column parameters, you can select individual tiles. Click the Apply button to tell the filter to flip that specific tile. If you want to flip more than one tile, simply select another one and click Apply again. Using this method, you can even have some tiles flipped horizontally and others flipped vertically. It's really an incredibly powerful feature. If you want to clear everything and start over, just click the Reset button at the top of the window.

You also have control over the opacity of the tiles that this filter generates, with the Opacity slider. This slider is available only if you're applying the filter to a layer that's capable of having transparency. So if you're applying Small Tiles to a background layer, this slider is grayed out. Figure 15-39 shows an example image created with the Small Tiles filter.

FIGURE 15-39

On the left is the source image and on the right is that same image after the Small Tiles filter is applied (Photo credit: Melody Smith)

Tile

This filter is similar to the Small Tiles filter, but quite a bit simpler. Rather than create duplicated tiles at reduced size to fit within the dimensions of your original image, the Tile filter creates tiles of your original image to fill the space of a new image with larger dimensions. Also, unlike the Small Tiles filter, this one does not give you any controls for arbitrarily flipping individual tiles. As Figure 15-40 shows, the dialog for controlling this filter is pretty simple. Launch it by going to your image window and choosing Filters ➤ Map ➤ Tile.

The controls here are pretty limited. Using the Width and Height values, you can dictate the size of your newly tiled image in whatever units you like. The default behavior is to use pixels, but the drop-down menu to the right allows you to choose other units. Also by default, the Width and Height values are linked to maintain the same proportion, but you can disable this behavior by clicking the chain-link icon to the right of them.

The dialog for the Tile filter

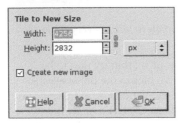

Note

For the Tile filter to work properly, you need to make the new image size larger than that of your original. If you don't, you're only going to see one (or part of one) tile. ∎

Below the dimension settings is a check box for creating a new image. With this enabled, the Tile filter creates a new image from the layer that you're tiling. If you disable this check box, the filter is applied directly to the layer you launched it from, resizing it to the dimensions you enter. This is important because the Tile filter applies to only the currently selected layer. So if you have other layers in your image and you want them to keep working with them, you need to run the Tile filter on them as well with the Create New Image check box disabled. Otherwise, you may want to flatten your image prior to running this filter. Figure 15-41 shows an example of running the Tile filter.

On the left is the source image and on the right is the result after running the Tile filter.

Original

Tiled

Warp

The easiest way to think of the Warp filter is to consider it as an advanced version of the Displace filter with one very important distinction. Although both the Displace filter and the Warp filter use a grayscale image as a displacement map, the Warp filter treats it a bit differently.

Whereas the Displace filter treats each gray value as a different height, the Warp filter only deals with the change in values. This means that for the Warp filter, a solid color — whether it's black, white, or turquoise — the result is the same: no displacement. The Warp filter is all about gradients. To help you get a clearer picture of this, Figure 15-42 shows the difference between using the Displace filter and the Warp filter on the same image with the same displacement map.

When you use the Displace filter (bottom left) and the Warp filter (bottom right) on the same image (top left), the result is different, even if when using the same displacement map (top right).

Original   Displacement map

Displaced   Warped

The applications for the Warp filter are roughly the same as for the Displace filter, but because it relies on the change in pixels rather than their explicit value, the Warp filter is more useful when your displacement map is generated from an image. For example, you could have a photograph of some cloth and you want to map a logo to appear like it's on that cloth. Now you could take that photo, desaturate it (Colors ➤ Desaturate) and meticulously adjust its contrast levels to get it to get a displacement map that works properly with the Displace filter. However, it's often faster to use the Warp filter on the same desaturated photo and get roughly the same results. To run the Warp filter, select the layer you want to warp and go to Filters ➤ Map ➤ Warp. Upon doing so, you get a window like the one that appears in Figure 15-43.

Basic Options

The Warp filter works iteratively. That is, it runs through your image multiple times, displacing the pixels in that image with each pass. The parameters under Basic Options let you control how many passes the filter uses and how much displacement happens with each pass. The most important parameter here is the Displacement Map drop-down menu. With this menu, you choose which of the available image layers you want to use as your displacement map.

FIGURE 15-43

The parameters available in the Warp filter's dialog

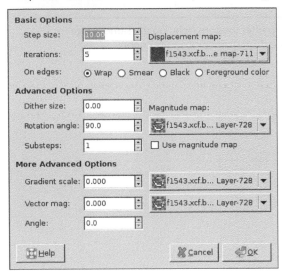

Warning

Your displacement map must have the exact same dimensions as the layer that you want to warp. To protect you from inadvertently selecting a layer that's the wrong size, the Displacement Map drop-down menu includes only layers that share the exact dimensions of your warped layer. If your displacement map doesn't appear in this menu, cancel the Warp filter and resize that layer to match. ∎

Besides the Displacement Map drop-down, you have three other controls under Basic Options:

- **Step Size** — With each iterative pass, the Warp filter looks at the difference between adjacent pixels in the displacement map. If the difference is greater than this value, the pixel is displaced proportionally. The default value of 10.00 means that there must be a difference of 10 to get one pixel of displacement. If you use a negative value here, the displacement is inverted.

- **Iterations** — This value controls how many times this filter runs through your image.

- **On Edges** — Like many filters, the pixels around the border of your image are a special case because they don't have as many adjacent pixels as any of the others. These options allow you to tell the filter what to use for those missing pixels:

  - **Wrap** — Use the pixels on the opposite side of the image.

  - **Smear** — Copy the border pixels; extending them outward as much as necessary for the filter to finish.

- **Black** — Just use black pixels for the missing ones.
- **Foreground Color** — Similar to the Black option, but instead using whatever color is set as the foreground color to fill in for these missing pixels.

Advanced Options

The parameters in this section give you fine control over how the Warp filter moves pixels around, and even which pixels that may be. The following list describes each option:

- **Dither Size** — Because the Warp filter is iteratively pushing individual pixels around, it can quickly pixelate the image and make it look grainy. To compensate for this, you can increase the dithering in the displacement. Increasing this value reduces the grain that the Warp filter produces.

- **Rotation Angle** — The biggest thing to remember about this parameter is that this is an angle against the vertical axis. So the default value of 90° is a horizontal line. Use this value to control the direction of displacement by the Warp filter.

- **Substeps** — The Warp filter works iteratively, but by adjusting the dithering and rotation angle, you may need to have more detailed calculation than you can get in a single iteration. By increasing this value you can get smoother results, but it takes longer for the filter to finish processing.

- **Magnitude Map** — This drop-down menu has an influence only if you enable the Use Magnitude Map check box beneath it. A *magnitude map* is another grayscale image that controls how much influence the displacement map has on your source image. In the magnitude map, black pixels indicate zero influence and white pixels mean that the displacement map has full influence. This is helpful if you need to mask off an area of your image so it doesn't get displaced by the Warp filter. Like the displacement map, you want to make sure that this layer is the same size as the layer you're warping. Figure 15-44 shows how you can use a magnitude map to mask the influence of your displacement map.

FIGURE 15-44

Using a magnitude map to control that part of your image that the displacement map warps

| Original | Displacement map | Magnitude map | Warped image |

More Advanced Options

The options in this section allow you to define two additional grayscale maps that you can use to influence the displacement of the Warp filter. By default, these maps have no influence because their corresponding parameters are zeroed out. The following is a description of what each map does:

- **Gradient Scale** — Unlike the displacement map, where the Warp filter uses the difference in pixel values to dictate how many pixels are displaced, the *gradient map* is a grayscale image where the difference in pixels dictates the direction of displacement. Like other maps in this filter, your only available layers are the ones that are the exact same size as your source image. Adjusting the Gradient scale parameter, to the left of the Gradient Map drop-down, controls how much influence this map has in a range from −1000 to 1000.

- **Vector Mag** — The vector mag also controls the direction of displacement from the Warp filter, but in a slightly different way. It uses the vector map to control the intensity and general direction of displacement, but you can also use an additional Angle parameter to tweak that direction. The Vector Mag parameter, to the right of the Vector Map drop-down, controls the intensity of this effect. Using the vector map, you can actually use this effect to achieve a bit of motion blur.

- **Angle** — The value here is relevant only if you're using a vector map. 0° is directly up and angle values increase in a counterclockwise direction. So if you set this parameter to 90°, the Warp filter uses the vector map to push pixels left.

Note

Both the gradient scale and vector mag operations work on the entire image layer, so your results when using these maps may appear to be blurry. ■

Tip

Although the vector mag and gradient scale are capable of using complex grayscale images as your maps, you can often get good results with a simple gradient from black to white. This is particularly true with the vector map because you can control the overall angle with the Angle parameter. ■

Using Warp to Map a Logo to a Photo of Rumpled Cloth

To accomplish the logo-mapping example at the beginning of this section, use the following basic steps:

1. **Duplicate your cloth layer (Layer ➢ Duplicate Layer or Shift+Ctrl+D) and desaturate it (Colors ➢ Desaturate).** This new layer is both your displacement map as well as your bump map for shadows. To make things easy, rename this layer to something memorable, like "displacement."

2. **Open your logo image as a new layer (File ➢ Open as Layers or Ctrl+Alt+O).** You're applying the image to the cloth, so it makes sense to do all this work from the same image layer. For clarity, name this layer "logo."

3. **Using Scale Layer (Layer ➢ Scale Layer) and Layer Boundary Size (Layer ➢ Layer Boundary Size), adjust the logo layer to be the exact same size as the displacement layer.** The Warp filter requires that the displacement map be the same size as the layer you're warping.

4. **Select the logo layer and launch the Warp filter (Filters ➢ Map ➢ Warp) and adjust to taste.** Be sure to set the displace layer as your displacement map.

5. **With the Warp filter applied, run the Bump Map filter (Filters ➤ Map ➤ Bump Map) on the logo layer and adjust to taste.** This uses your displacement map to get the lighting and shadows right on your logo so it more accurately matches the cloth. You may want to disable the Compensate for Darkening check box here.

6. **Finish by hiding the displacement layer and revealing the cloth layer beneath.** With these steps complete, you should have something like the example in Figure 15-45.

FIGURE 15-45

Using the Warp filter to map a logo to some cloth

      Logo   Cloth   Warped logo

Summary

So there you have it. This chapter covered a whole chunk of filters that can help you when compositing multiple images together. You got to play with all of the different edge detection filters that GIMP offers. You read about how the filters under the Generic menu are really helpful for compositing and how the Convolution Matrix can be used to create most of the other filters GIMP uses, as well as custom filters of your own. By going over the filters in the Combine menu, you figured out how to use filters to directly mix images together and by going through all of the Map filters, you found out how to make one image or object influence the look of another. All in all, this was very cool stuff. Of course, the next chapter takes things a step further with a whole slew of artistic filters. Now it's time to have even more fun.

Enhancing Images with Artistic Filters

When applying your editing skills and focusing on creativity, no set of filters rivals the Artistic filters found within GIMP. You can now focus on artistry and imagination while enhancing your digital images. Your creative options expand greatly once you learn and know how to use GIMP's Artistic filter set. The purpose of these filters is to simulate the effect of a few different traditional art media and techniques and apply them to photographs.

IN THIS CHAPTER

Mimicking pencil and paint with artistic filters

Creating borders for your images

Using filters to make quick automated effects

Creating artistic images using specialized filters

Applying decorative elements to your images

Artistic Filters

In the following sections, you will learn how to apply effects like cubism and oil painting, create old-looking photos, use the GIMPressionist toolset, and apply textures such as canvas.

Apply Canvas

If you are looking for a filter to apply a canvas-like texture to your image, you need the Apply Canvas filter. This filter gives your picture or composition the same texture as the canvas an artist paints on.

This filter is located in the image window menu under the Filters ➤ Artistic menu. Figure 16-1 shows the Direction and Depth options within the Apply Canvas filter dialog. Applying a deeper depth creates (and sometimes distorts) the canvas effect through your image.

Within the Apply Canvas filter options are a zoom-capable preview pane, and sliders for horizontal and vertical adjustments. As you will find with most Artistic filters, they are processor-intensive and require a few seconds to process.

FIGURE 16-1

Using Apply Canvas to get different effects. You can create an interesting pattern on a wood surface (left). You can apply more depth to achieve a deeper canvas-look, although it will distort (or destroy) the original image (right).

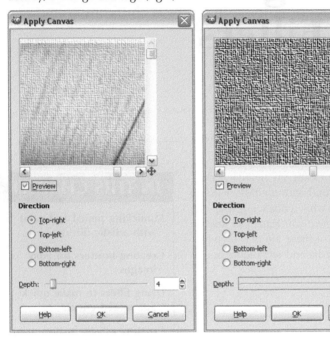

You can also specify the direction of the filter's effect, using the Top-Right, Top-Left, Bottom-Right, or Bottom-Left options. This will also specify where the light source is originating from to give the filter more effect. This filter is basically a shortcut bump map filter with a specific bump map for a canvas texture.

Note
A canvas is what an artist uses to paint or draw on, and what makes it unique is the image that resonates from the embedded textures of the fabric the canvas is made of. Usually, a canvas is made of high-quality plain-woven fabric and is extremely durable. Typically, canvas is used with oil-based paint. It is commonly stretched over and held in place by a wooden frame. When working in the digital realm, the filters used within this chapter simulate the look of an image printed or painted on a canvas surface. ■

Cartoon

For those of you who are into comic books, this filter is for you. There is a specific look and feel to a comic book, based on how it's designed, penned, and printed. The Cartoon effect does something similar. The effect is basically used to soften the image to solid colors (similar to what GREYCstoration does combined with outlines like those produced by edge detection) to produce a comic book look and feel.

The Cartoon filter can produce the same results by using the active layer or selection and creating a shadow around other object elements. This filter is located in the image window menu under the Filters ➤ Artistic menu.

Mask Radius is adjustable via the slider bar, or by the configurable input box. If you are looking to blacken certain areas of your image completely, you can use a larger number in the input box. If you are looking for something more subtle, consider using a lower number.

The Percent Black option allows you to control the specific amount of black coloring used around object elements. As with Mask Radius, Percent Black, when set to a higher number, produces thicker and more detailed coloring and lower numbers create thinner, less detailed color areas.

Cubism

Artists have many effects to choose from when thinking of how to create the right look for their work. When working with GIMP, you can select the Cubism filter to make your image appear cubed. This effect looks like small dice fragments when applied to your image. The Cubism filter is meant to emulate the style of the Cubist art movement, which included Picasso and Braque. The way it works is the filter emulates what a painter would paint, such as a scene or portrait, as if he or she were looking at it from multiple angles simultaneously. In that context, this filter is a bit of a misnomer because it doesn't do that; it simply gives that impression by duplicating and rotating parts of the image geometrically.

This filter is located in the image window menu under the Filters ➤ Artistic menu. Run it by going to Filters ➤ Artistic ➤ Cubism. Figure 16-2 shows the Tile Size and Tile Saturation options within the Cubism filter dialog.

Just like with most other filters in GIMP, you can use the preview pane to zoom in, scroll, and pinpoint how this filter impacts specific portions of your image.

You can adjust the Tile Size slider and input box options to create deeper-looking tiles by adjusting the pixel size to be used. You can also adjust Tile Saturation, which allows you to blend the colors together for a blur effect. This slider and input box option set the opacity and intensity levels of the filter. Higher numbers specify more intensity; lower number render less intensely.

You can also check Use Background Color to set your image to black. If the box is unchecked, it sets it to whatever the background color of the image may be. Once you apply the effect, you will create a distorted image, as shown in Figure 16-3.

FIGURE 16-2

Viewing the Cubism filter dialog, where you can make adjustments to your image. You can use Tile Size and Tile Saturation to distort your current image, or create a new one from the pattern you design.

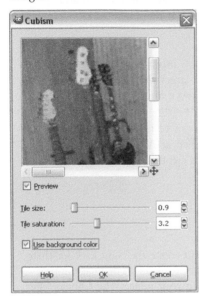

FIGURE 16-3

Viewing the Cubism effect on an image within the image window. This filter is handy if you are looking for a patterned blur effect.

GIMPressionist

GIMPressionist is a complete toolset of different preset effects. If the Cubism filter didn't cut it, this will surely do the trick. For example, you can work with multiple presets, load others, or make new ones entirely. This filter is specific to simulating the look of impressionist period (Monet, Degas, and Renoir).

This filter is located in the image window menu under the Filters ➢ Artistic ➢ GIMPressionist. Figure 16-4 shows the Presets tab options within the GIMPressionist filter dialog.

GIMPressionist offers presets to give your image painting-like effects such as Smash and Weave.

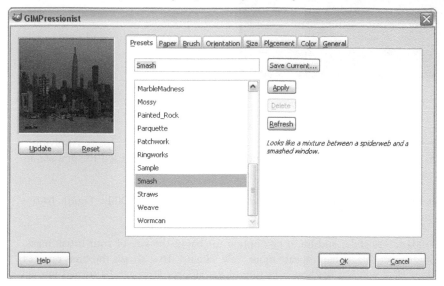

At first it may be difficult to learn and work within GIMPressionist because it has a lot of presets, and a lot of parameter adjustments you can make. For example, you can load a preset, update it, and then save it. Save Current allows you to keep a record of your parameter changes and you can then reuse them.

Other tabs, such as the Paper tab, allow you to change the texture of your effects. Much like Apply Canvas, this tab enables you to preview multiple texture presets. The Brush tab allows you to select between painting brushes. The Orientation tab provides you options to adjust brush strokes. The Size tab contains options to set the brush sizes that are available. You can specify how the strokes are distributed, what the stroke color is, and the background and relief of your brush strokes. The Placement tab allows you to configure where strokes are placed on the image. You can adjust the color of the stroke in the Color tab. The General tab is where you can set the background and the relief of brush strokes.

Lastly, you can configure a drop shadow. Figure 16-5 shows application of the GIMPressionist filter to create a "smashed" view of the city with an image drop shadow effect.

Using the Smash filter preset within GIMPressionist

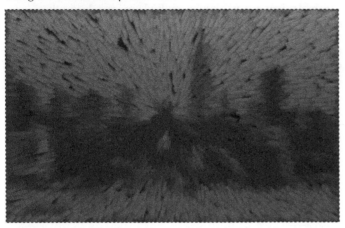

Oilify

If you are a traditional artist, you may have worked with oil-based paints on canvas. Applying this filter produces much of the same effect. The Oilify filter within GIMP is used to simulate an oil painting from your original image or selection.

This filter is located in the image window menu under Filters ➤ Artistic ➤ Oilify. Figure 16-6 shows many options within the Oilify filter dialog.

You can adjust the Mask Size slider and input box option to change the size of your brush mask. Larger numbers produce an image that appears more "oily." Figure 16-7 shows the final product in the image window. Here you can see how a picture of the Hoover Dam can be turned into an oil painting with one filter.

Photocopy

You can use the Photocopy filter within GIMP to create a black-and-white photocopy out of your original image. The filter darkens lighter areas in the image based on an average taken of the current pixel colors and then sets the other pixels to white.

This differs from changing the image's mode to Grayscale or simply desaturating the image or using the Threshold feature from the Colors menu. This filter basically combines these effects with some edge detection to reproduce the effect of using an old copy or fax machine on an image.

This filter is located in the image window menu under the Filters ➤ Artistic ➤ Photocopy. Figure 16-8 shows the many options within the Photocopy filter dialog, such as Mask Radius and Sharpness adjustments.

FIGURE 16-6

When looking to turn your image into an oil painting, this effect is for you. All you need to do is load your image and adjust the Mask Size slider, select a map if necessary, and adjust the Exponent settings to create your desired effect.

FIGURE 16-7

Creating an oil painting out of the Hoover Dam

FIGURE 16-8

Using the Photocopy filter to create a black-and-white image from the original image

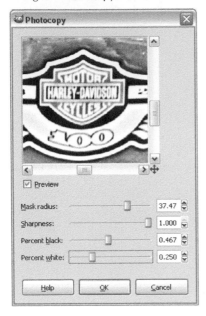

You can adjust your settings and review them in the Preview section of the dialog. Here, you can adjust the Mask Radius, Sharpness, Percent Black, and Percent White slider and input box options to get your desired results.

Figure 16-9 shows the final image within the image window. Here you can see that Photocopy took a standard color image and applied black and white pixel percentages to the entire image to create this effect. The black-and-white copy can also be adjusted to be sharper if needed. You can also adjust the opacity within the Layers dialog to create a sharper image.

Predator

This may be a silly question, but have you seen the movie *Predator*? If not, you will likely have no clue as to what this filter does. This filter gives off the same thermo-based effects that the Predator used to hunt its prey. Although the filter is much simpler in design than the equipment this hunter used, it's still helpful when you find its hidden gems. The Predator used a form of thermal vision as well as infrared. These are the specific outlines you see when you apply this filter.

When applied, this filter uses edge detection to simplify the image to a few colors and apply it to the edges to provide the same effect that the Predator used in his hunting goggles.

This filter is located in the image window menu under the Filters ➤ Artistic ➤ Predator. Figure 16-10 shows the options within the Predator filter dialog.

FIGURE 16-9

Using the Photocopy filter to create sharp black-and-white images out of full-color images

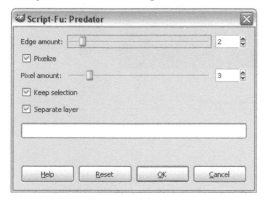

FIGURE 16-10

Using the Predator filter to give effects similar to the ones seen in the *Predator* movie

In the Predator filter's dialog, you can adjust the Edge Amount, Pixelize, Pixel Amount, Keep Selection, and Separate Layer options.

The Edge Amount slider and input box option allow you to perform edge detection. The higher the number, the more edges will be detected. The lower the number, the fewer edges will be detected. You can also select the Pixelize check box, which allows you to make adjustments with the Pixel Amount slider and input box option. Using this slider option dramatically changes the effect within the final image. Unfortunately, there isn't a preview pane option to check the result because the filer is a group of combined filters run by Script-Fu.

You can check the Keep Selection option to use the effect on the active selection. If unchecked, this effect is not applied to the active layer. The Separate Layer option, when checked, creates a copy of the active layer for the filter to be applied to. Figure 16-11 shows the final settings when applied to the photo of a well's bottom.

FIGURE 16-11

Viewing the Predator filter on an image of the bottom of a well. On the right, you see the bottom of the well with the Predator effect applied.

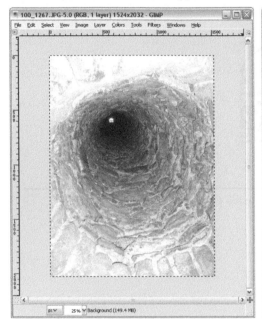
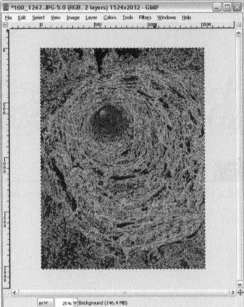

Softglow

The Softglow filter is handy when you are trying to apply interesting lighting effects to your digital image. Basically, the filter produces a light (soft) glow on the image by finding the bright areas on the image and making them brighter, also sometimes referred to as a *bloom* effect. This filter can also produce images that look like photographic double-exposures.

This filter is located in the image window menu under the Filters ➤ Artistic ➤ Softglow. Figure 16-12 shows the Softglow filter dialog. Here you can use the preview pane to zoom in on a specific part of your image to test effects.

Whether your aim is to intensify particular segments of the image or the entire image, what really matters is the original image. If you use a lighter image to start with, the Softglow filter may brighten the image too much. If you use a darker image, the Softglow filter enhances the dark spots and makes the entire image lighter by comparison.

To do this, you can adjust the Glow Radius slider, which serves as a sharpness tool. If you adjust the slider and input boxes, you can see the sharpness adjust in the Preview section of the dialog.

If you adjust the Brightness slider and input box options, you increase the intensity of the brightness in darker sections of the image. The Sharpness slider and input box options allow you to increase the overall sharpness of the image. Figure 16-13 shows Softglow filter in action, where a dark image is made lighter for better viewing.

FIGURE 16-12

Using the Softglow filter to apply brightness on a particularly dark image

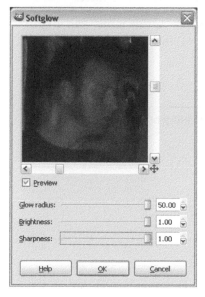

FIGURE 16-13

Viewing the final effect of the Softglow filter. Here you can see that specific sections of the image were made brighter for better viewing, or you can enhance the brightness for a more distorted effect.

Van Gogh (LIC)

The Van Gogh (LIC) filter is used to apply blurring and textures to your image. For those unfamiliar with Dutch painter Vincent Van Gogh, a quick Internet search of "Starry Night over the Rhone" will give you an idea of the general effects of this filter. It emulates many of Van Gogh's stylistic art pieces.

LIC stands for Line Integral Convolution, a mathematical computation used to create the texture and blurring effects. The Van Gogh (LIC) filter uses a blur map to achieve these effects.

This filter is located in the image window menu under the Filters ➤ Artistic menu. Run it by going to Filters ➤ Artistic ➤ Van Gogh (LIC). Figure 16-14 shows the Van Gogh (LIC) filter dialog.

FIGURE 16-14

The Van Gogh (LIC) filter dialog is used to create textures and blurring reminiscent of Van Gogh's famous paintings.

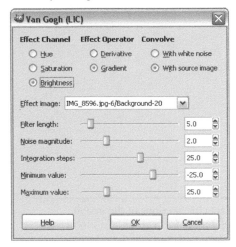

The Van Gogh (LIC) filter has many different configuration settings within it. For one, you can configure the Effect Channel items. Here, you can select between Hue, Saturation, and Brightness. You can also adjust the Effect Operator items and use the Derivative or Gradient options. You can use these options to apply a derivative to your image, or to change (reverse) the gradient of your image.

You can also select from a predefined Effect Image option. Here you can set your background for your image. You can then adjust the Filter Length, Noise Magnitude, Integration Steps, Minimum Value, and Maximum Value slider and input box options. These options allow you to adjust the amount of effect you apply to your image. White noise is nothing more than all frequencies operating at the same amplitude. You can adjust the Noise Magnitude control to achieve a higher white noise effect if desired.

Decor Filters

Decor filters are located under the Filters menu within GIMP. These filters are mainly script-fu scripts, which are multiple effects tied together under one command. For example, if you were to use the Add Bevel filter, this would call on other effects you have already learned about and used in other chapters, as well as this one. Decor filters are used mainly to create decorative borders on your images, but can be used in many other ways to create interesting effects.

Add Bevel

You can use the Add Bevel filter (Filters ➤ Decor ➤ Add Bevel) to create a bevel (otherwise known as a slant, pitch, or grade-change) on your image. It does this by utilizing a bump map. Figure 16-15 shows the Add Bevel filter dialog.

FIGURE 16-15

Using the Add Bevel filter to create a beveled edge on your images surfaces

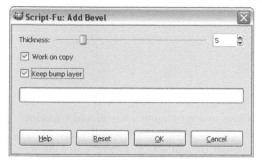

In the Add Bevel dialog, you can adjust the thickness by using the slider and input box options. The maximum thickness is 30 pixels. You can also select the Work on Copy check box, which creates a copy of the original image so that you can always fall back on it, instead of reverting from the edited one.

Caution

If you are trying to add a bevel using the Add Bevel filter and are unable to, you may be trying to apply a bevel to an image that already has a bevel integrated into it. Some images are already set with an incline (for example) and if so, aren't affected by Add Bevel. You may encounter this while editing and become confused as to why this particular filter doesn't work on specific images. ■

The Keep Bump Layer option enables you to generate a new layer in the Layers dialog. This is what the bump map will be used with, keeping your original image intact. Figure 16-16 shows the Layers dialog, which shows the additional layers that are created with this option.

FIGURE 16-16

Multiple layers are created when using the Keep Bump Layer option. By doing this, you can always revert to the original image, which is currently the background image.

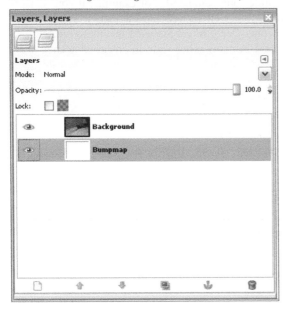

Add Border

When looking to apply a simple (or not so simple) border to your graphic, you should consider using the Add Border filter (Filters ➤ Decor ➤ Add Border) within GIMP's filter offerings. The Add Border effect does exactly what is says: it adds a border to your image. Figure 16-17 shows the Add Border filter dialog.

FIGURE 16-17

Using the Add Border filter to create a colorful border around your image. You can also adjust the border's size and thickness.

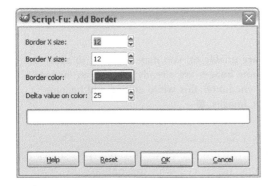

Within the Add Border filter dialog, you can adjust the border thickness in the horizontal (X) and vertical (Y) directions by using the Border X Size and Border Y Size settings, as well as adjust the border color for colorizing effects. Once the border is applied, your Layers dialog is affected. Figure 16-18 shows the Layers dialog where the border layer is created in the Layers dialog.

FIGURE 16-18

When creating a border around your image, take note that it's created in the Layers dialog.

After you create your border, you can apply the effect by clicking OK in the Add Border filter dialog. Figure 16-19 shows the bordered image within GIMP's image window.

Note
An obvious question about the Add Border filter would be "Does the border increase my image size?" The answer is yes. Because the original image is not covered by the border, the border is added "around" the image, thus creating a larger image. If you are looking to create specific sized images (perhaps for slicing in sections of a web site), be aware that this filter increases the size of your overall image once the border effect is applied. ■

Coffee Stain

How many of you are laughing as you read this? Why someone would want to add a coffee stain to their image seems ridiculous, but for a select few, it's a mainstay component in their artist's toolbox. It's particularly helpful if you want to make an image look aged and worn by time. When applied, the Coffee Stain filter adds realistic-looking coffee stains to the image without the need for your own spillage!

FIGURE 16-19

The final image with a new border wrapped around it. This border resides on its own layer in the Layers dialog.

If you do have a need to create stains on your artwork, you can do so by going to Filters ➤ Decor ➤ Coffee Stain. Figure 16-20 shows the Coffee Stain filter dialog.

FIGURE 16-20

Using the Coffee Stain filter to create staining effects on your digital image

Within the filter, you can adjust the number of stains (1 to 10) and apply the Darken Only option to merge multiple layers (multiple stains) into one.

Knowing how to work within the Layers dialog is essential to working with your coffee stains once applied. Because each stain creates its own layer, you need to activate the layer that contains the stain you want to work on. Figure 16-21 shows the Layers dialog where each coffee stain created on your image is created on its own layer in the Layers dialog.

FIGURE 16-21

Each coffee stain has its own layer in the Layers dialog.

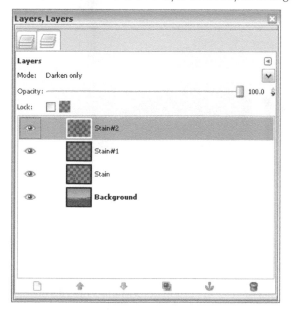

Fuzzy Border

The Fuzzy Border filter (Filters ➤ Decor ➤ Fuzzy Border) can be used to create more border effects to your image. Different from the Add Border filter, this effect gives you more options than just adding a simple border effect. Here you can adjust other options, such as shadowing effects. Figure 16-22 shows the Fuzzy Border filter dialog.

Within the dialog, you can adjust the image's border by tweaking the Color, Border Size, Add Shadow, and Shadow Weight options, to name a few. By using the slider and input boxes, you can create shadow effects around your image's border.

Effects you can generate include fuzziness and blurring within the image's border. Adjusting the border's granularity (in pixels) gives the border a jagged effect. Adding a shadow is easy to do; simply check the box and a shadow appears when you click OK. As with other Decor filters covered in this section, you can select Work on Copy, which creates a new image with the filter applied, protecting your old image from any editing changes.

FIGURE 16-22

Working with the Fuzzy Border filter to create border effects that contain blurring elements. You can select between border size and color as well as create shadow effects around your image, as shown on the right.

Old Photo

When working with color photos, especially those taken from a digital camera, likely you are taking full-color pictures. Reminiscent of old flash photography and old cameras, black-and-white photos (or sometimes seen as sepia) aren't very common anymore. But, if you don't want to get specialized photography equipment to take an "old photo," you can take a preexisting one and re-create this effect. How? Use GIMP's Old Photo filter (Filters ➤ Decor ➤ Old Photo). This filter also applies slight deterioration and discoloration effects to make the picture look like it's been around for a while and perhaps even exposed to the elements. For additional wear and tear, you could also use this filter in combination with the Coffee Stain filter, covered earlier.

Figure 16-23 shows the Old Photo filter dialog. The Old Photo filter dialog has multiple options. For one, you can check the Defocus check box to apply a Gaussian blur to the image. You can also adjust the Border Size option. Adjusting the Mottle option marks up your image with spots for a more distorted look and feel. The Old Photo filter is a really great filter because it does the work of many other treatments, masks, and filters for a specific purpose. The Mottle option creates image noise that ages the photo in a way that would require you to use several other filters and mask applications. Also the Sepia tone preset option on this filter is one of the best ones out there, giving you many choices to enhance your work.

You can do other things with this filter by working with your layers in the Layers dialog box. Here, you can create the layers you need to apply your tone effect. If needed, you can duplicate the original image and save it so that you have a backup copy.

FIGURE 16-23

Use the Old Photo filter to turn a new color photograph into a discolored photo so that it looks aged.

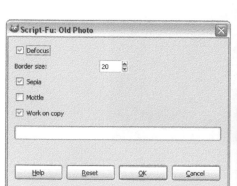
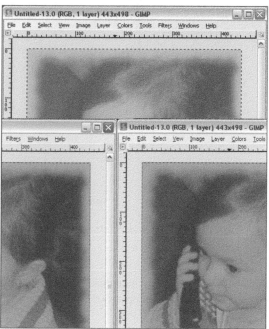

Note

Sepia is a dark brown and gray color mix, which when applied to your work produces an older-looking photo from your image. Sepia is a color that matches the coloring of the cuttlefish.

When using sepia, you are applying a process to your image called *sepia-toning*. This is a traditional method (or technique) used in darkrooms to unevenly apply sepia coloring to sections in your image that are darker or lighter. If you adjust your RGB image to grayscale, make sure that you convert it back (change the mode) to RGB for best results; otherwise, no color can be applied to your image at all. ■

Round Corners

At times while you are editing your digital images you may want to apply an effect to take corners in your image and make them rounded. This is an effect commonly used for people creating web sites with photo galleries. It's an interesting way to present the image that isn't the same old square-corner look. It can be used to create a drop shadow behind the primary image. The Round Corners filter works on RGB as well as grayscale images that contain only a single layer.

This filter is located in the image window menu under the Filters ➢ Decor menu. Run it by going to Filters ➢ Decor ➢ Round Corners. Figure 16-24 shows the Round Corners filter dialog.

FIGURE 16-24

Use the Round Corners filter to round off the corners on your image.

Within the Round Corners filter dialog, you can adjust the Edge Radius option. This option allows you to set (with the input box) a radius setting, where the rounding of corners will originate from.

You can add a drop shadow to your image by checking the Add Drop-Shadow check box. You can then adjust the X and Y Offsets for that shadow and use a Blur Radius option to define the shadow's softness.

Slide

Old film footage and slide-like film are created (or emulated) by the Slide filter within GIMP's myriad filter options. This one is extremely handy if you are looking for the "old film" effect. This is a simplified version of the Filmstrip filter (Filters ➤ Combine ➤ Filmstrip) covered in Chapter 15.

This filter is located in the image window menu under the Filters ➤ Decor menu. Run it by going to Filters ➤ Decor ➤ Slide. Figure 16-25 shows the Slide filter dialog.

You have a few things to consider when using this filter. For one, it encases the original image into a slide. Because of the size restrictions, your image may be cropped to fit. Second, this filter (script) works only on specific image types. For example, only RGB and grayscale images that contain one layer will work. Third, you should consider using the Work on Copy check box selection. By doing so, you can protect the original image and create a slide out of a new one.

FIGURE 16-25

Using the Script-Fu: Slide filter to create images that look as if they are part of a film reel

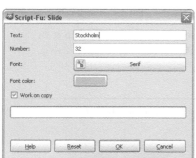

Other options to configure include the following:

- **Text** — Once you apply the filter, the slide created can be tagged by a name. If you add a description within the Text section of the dialog, you can mark your slide with a title (for example).

- **Number** — Just like true film footage, the segments run in numerical order. You can add a number here to denote where this slide fits into a group of multiple slides.

- **Font** — You can select and adjust the different font options that appear within the text and numbering of your slide.

- **Font Color** — You can also adjust what color scheme your font selection adheres to. If you choose orange, all of the text and numbering in your slide are colored as such.

Stencil Carve

The Stencil Carve filter creates a carving effect on your image. The carving effect is basically performing edge detection on your image and using that to attempt to generate silhouettes that could be cut from the image. The carving effect is applied to a carve layer. Therefore, you must use a second layer when applying this filter. If you do not have a multilayer setup, this option appears grayed out.

If you do not have a second layer configured, you can create a new one easily. The simplest way to do this is to create a new image by going to File ➤ New.

This prompts the Create a New Image Wizard and a new dialog appears. Create a carve layer by specifying the size and dimensions of the secondary image (the image you want to affect). Click OK to create the new layer, also called the source. Then, load in the image you want to carve, which will be the target — the image you will carve.

There are a few rules you must follow. The source image must be a grayscale image and it must be a single-layer alpha channel. The image you want to affect (carve), needs to be a single-layer RGB or grayscale image. The image layers must also be the same size.

This filter is located in the image window menu under the Filters ➤ Decor menu. Run it by going to Filters ➤ Decor ➤ Stencil Carve. Figure 16-26 shows the Stencil Carve filter dialog.

FIGURE 16-26

Running the Stencil Carve filter on an image with the Carve White Areas selection applied. Here the Stencil Carve filter shows the outline and image of a black cat

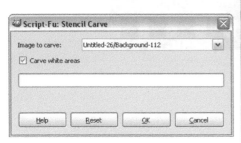

To load the target, select Image to Carve and browse to the image you want to edit. If you did not load an image into the image window, you will not find your image listed in the drop-down list. You can select the Carve White Areas option by selecting the check box to apply one of two effects:

- **Carve White Areas (enabled)** — A stencil must be selected to carve with. If this option is selected, the source (background) layer is used as the stencil.

- **Carve White Areas (disabled)** — A secondary stencil can be selected. If you uncheck this option, the source images colors are inverted. This is then used as the stencil to carve with.

Stencil Chrome

The Stencil Chrome filter (Filters ➤ Decor ➤ Stencil Chrome) creates a chroming effect on your image. It is very similar to the Stencil Carve filter. It is nearly identical in operation as well. All of the same rules apply, but the effect is completely different as it produces a chrome look instead.

Figure 16-27 shows the Settings tab options within the Stencil Chrome filter dialog.

FIGURE 16-27

Using the Stencil Chrome filter within GIMP, you can apply chroming effects to your images based on specific settings to saturation, lightness, and coloring.

You can run the Stencil Chrome filter and configure multiple options:

- **Chrome Saturation** — When the slider or input boxes are adjusted, the level (or amount) of saturation is increased or decreased to apply more or less chroming effect to your image.

- **Chrome Lightness** — When the slider or input boxes are adjusted, the level (or amount) of lightness is increased or decreased to apply more or less lighting effect to your image.

- **Chrome Factor** — When the slider or input boxes are adjusted, the level (or amount) of chrome applied is increased or decreased to apply more or less overall chroming effect to your image.

- **Environment Map** — When the drop-down list is selected, you can choose an image (environmental map) that will supply the chroming effect.

- **Highlight Balance** — You can click the color bar to select the highlight color to be used.

- **Chrome Balance** — You can click the color bar to select the chrome color balance to be used.

- **Chrome White Areas** — When this check box is selected, the white areas in your image will be chromed, as opposed to the darker areas in your image.

Note

You can download chroming effects at the GIMP Plugin Registry. As mentioned in other chapters, one of the nice things about GIMP is that you can expand it using additional scripts and plug-ins. For example, you can download Chromonium (http://registry.gimp.org/taxonomy/term/315), which is a script that applies chroming effects to your work easily once installed. More on plug-ins and the GIMP Plugin Registry can be found in Chapter 21. ■

Summary

This chapter has covered the use of many GIMP filters, including those found within the Artistic and Decor filter menus. Each set of filters provides quite a few means of enhancing your image, from lighting effects to blurring to distorting and chroming.

The next chapter covers the use of specialized filters. These filters include web filters, animation filters, photo filters, as well as other layer effects and Alpha to Logo. We cover how to use filters to speed up web design as well as how to work with filters to aid animation. The chapter also looks at the art of creating quick 'n' dirty logos. You learn how to work with layer effects as well as how to use filters to simplify photo editing in multiple ways. All of this up next!

Working with Specialized Filters

S pecialized filters are useful when you want to apply your work to the
web. The Internet and the servers that provide the pages you view
host your art. To get the best possible view of your work, and fast
load times, you can apply GIMP's Specialized filter set. For example, Web
filters in GIMP optimize the size, functionality and appearance of an image
for use on for the web.

IN THIS CHAPTER

**Using filters to speed up web
design**

**Working with filters to aid
animation**

Creating quick 'n' dirty logos

Understanding layer effects

Web Filters

These filters are mostly used on images used for web sites with tables, as
well as for quicker loading of pages, hyperlinking and so on. The filters
themselves work with your image to make them "web-ready".

The Image Map filter is used to add linkable hot-spots on your digital image.
Often called "slicing", this function will take an image too large for the
screen and break it up into smaller segments in order to load faster. It is
also used to apply hyperlinks to specific sections of the image. This is done
through HTML table code. You can also use the Semi-Flatten filter, which is
used for images without an alpha channel and can create semi-transparent
images.

You can use web filters for most of your slicing and dicing needs. The
Slice filter is helpful when you want to create tables in HTML for your
sliced work.

Image Map

When looking to create a hyperlink from an image source, you can use the
Image Map filter. This filter is used to create a link from an entire image, or
with the grid, you can select a single portion of your image to be linkable.
When you hover your mouse pointer over the final image, you will be able
to open a new page, file, or other component you decide to link up to it.

You should take note that because this filter is extremely hardware resource intensive (particularly the CPU), it may be difficult to use the filter as the preview may take up to a minute to refresh based on your adjustments. If running GIMP on a system with few resources, using the Image Map filter may take some time and lead to some frustration on the artist's part.

This filter is found in the image window menu under the Filters ➢ Web menu. Run it by going to Filters ➢ Web ➢ Image Map. Figure 17-1 shows the image map found within the Image Map filter dialog box.

FIGURE 17-1

Using the Image Map filter to specify linkable sections of your graphic, which, when clicked, will select a hyperlinked web site, file, or other component you choose

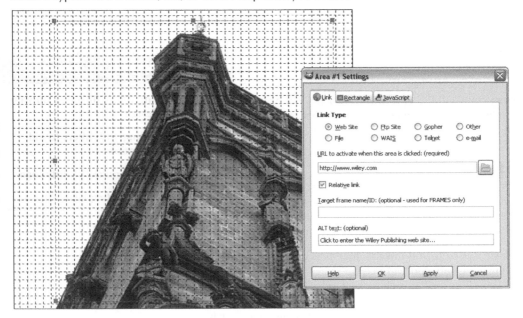

The Image Map filter can be confusing to use at first because you have to select to use the grid from the menu options, as well as use the toolbar on the top-left side of the filter's dialog box. Here you can make selections based on your grid elements.

Once you make your selection, you can open the Area Settings dialog. To do this, use the right-hand side section/pane of the dialog box and double-click on the active selection within the pane.

You can now make adjustments on the Link, Rectangle, and JavaScript tabs. Each tab offers many options for you to select when defining a selection on your map. The Link tab is useful for selecting the link type. In this section you can choose from many options to include: Web Site, File, FTP Site, WAIS, Gopher, Telnet, and e-mail, as well as Other, which you can specify manually.

You can also select the URL to activate when your selection is clicked (or selected). You can type in the target location, or specify via the file/folder Browse button. Once you select your URL, you can choose how it will interact with the site when clicked on. For example, you can specify that the target be a new window, so that when your image is clicked on, a new web browser will open with the URL you wanted to use.

On the Rectangle tab, you can choose the dimensions manually — this way you can adjust your selection based on exact height, width, and X and Y settings of your choosing. The JavaScript tab is helpful when you want to create the most commonly used JavaScript commands, such as onMouseover, onMouseout, onFocus, and onBlur.

Semi-Flatten

The Semi-Flatten filter effect is helpful when you are attempting to create a background color blend with your foreground image selection. For example, if you have a web page with green or red coloring, you can blend some of those coloring aspects into the image when you flatten it. Not to be confused the with Layer dialog box Flatten command, which fully flattens all layers to one, this will simply merge (or blend) the coloring together to create a visual effect for the viewer of the page (or image).

This filter is found in the image window menu under the Filters ➤ Web menu. Run it by going to Filters ➤ Web ➤ Semi-Flatten. Figure 17-2 shows the flattening of the background image with the foreground image, found within the Semi-Flatten filter dialog box. It is available if your image holds an Alpha channel. Otherwise, it is grayed out.

If your image does not have an Alpha channel, you can create one (or associate one) within the Layers dialog box. You can also adjust your color schemes (for background and foreground layers) in GIMP's toolbox; click on the color section and adjust the coloring as you would like to see it.

Image Slice

The Image Slice filter is similar in function to the Image Map filter, except it creates only the actual slices that you can then work on within the Image Map filter (as an example). Here, you can create exact slices based on the original dimensions of the image you want to edit.

This filter is found in the image window menu under the Filters ➤ Web menu. Run it by going to Filters ➤ Web ➤ Slice. If you find that you do not have this option available, then you need to download and install the Image Slice (http://registry.gimp.org/node/14953) plug-in from the GIMP registry. Figure 17-3 shows the Script-Fu: Image Slice filter dialog box where you can make adjustments to the rows and columns you will slice. You will be able to use this filter only if your image holds an Alpha channel. Otherwise, it is grayed out.

Tip

If you slice up your work, you can do the opposite and join the slices to create a single image from multiple ones. How? Well, in Figure 17-4, you can see the File Selection dialog box from within the Image Slice dialog. You can load these so that you can then create a single image. Figure 17-5 shows how GIMP will create multiple layers for each image slice. This way, you can adjust each slice per layer as you need to. ■

FIGURE 17-2

Using the Semi-Flatten filter effect to blend background colors into foreground images. In this figure, the background was black. Black is then added to portions of your image when duplicating the background image color.

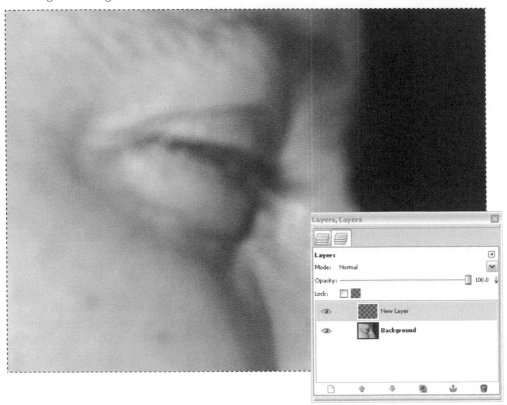

FIGURE 17-3

Using Script-Fu: Image Slice to create multiple chunks out of a single image. It does this by slicing along the Rows and Columns adjustments you select and then saves it where you specify, as the file type you want.

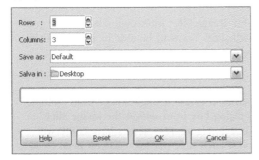

FIGURE 17-4

Using Script-Fu: Image Slice to create multiple chunks out of a single image. It does this by creating files out of each slice you create.

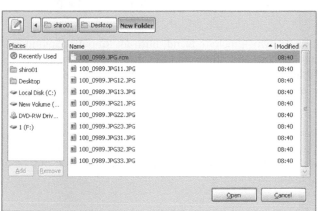

FIGURE 17-5

When viewing the Layers dialog box, you can see how each slice is created as a single layer for easy editing.

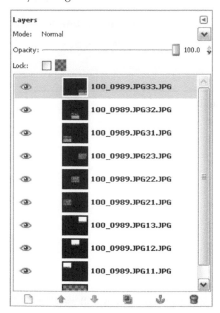

Animation Filters

When working with digital images within GIMP, there may come a time when you wish to animate specific items of your work. GIMP provides a set of filters to allow you to create such animations, as well as to enhance the look and feel of your work or composition. GIMP's animation filters are specialized filters that help add animated effects as well as give you a platform to edit and test them.

You can choose between GIMP's default filters, which include Blend, Burn-in, Rippling, Spinning Globe, and Waves. There are many filters available and others you can download and install from the GIMP registry (http://registry.gimp.org/node/19555). When you use the animation filters, you will be able to create animated GIFs, optimize them for the Web, and much more.

One of the main reasons you need to test (and optimize) your work is because many times the Web offers limited resources and your work may take a long time to load in a user's web browser. When you enhance and optimize images for the Web, they tend to look better, but overall, they load faster and are easier to use in web format.

Blend

When looking to create one image out of multiple images, you can use the Blend filter. The Blend filter will take multiple images or selections and allow you to create one from a mixture of pictures.

To use the filter, you will need to use multiple layers. If you do not use at least three, GIMP will produce an error message letting you know that you do not have enough layers to use this effect.

This filter is found in the image window menu under the Filters ➤ Animation menu. Run it by going to Filters ➤ Animation ➤ Blend. Figure 17-6 shows the Blend filter dialog box.

FIGURE 17-6

Using the Script-Fu: Blend filter effect to create an image out of multiple images

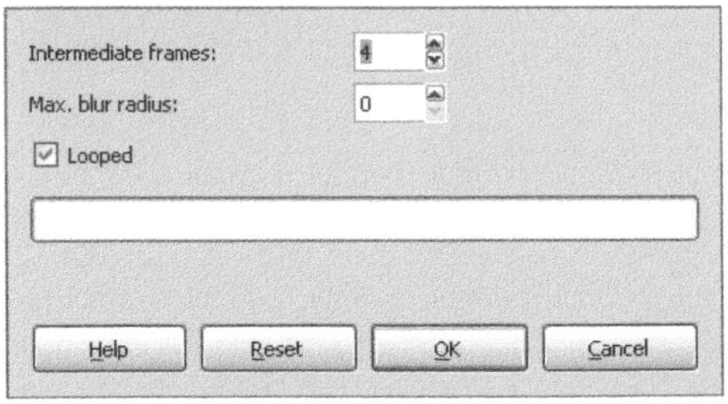

You can adjust the Intermediate Frames input box option, which allows you to select the number of frames that will exist in your animation. This is the number of frames that will exist in

between your images. A general rule of thumb to employ here is to use more intermediate frames for smoother transitions between images. This will also increase your file size and make your animation longer. You can also adjust the Max (maximum) Blur Radius option input box. This will adjust the blurring between images and the radius in which it will be affected. If you select the Looped check box, it will loop your animation when you save it. In Figure 17-7, there are three separate images blended together.

FIGURE 17-7

Using three images to create one. Here, there are two waterway images with a city landscape in the background. You can make some interesting pictures out a few by thinking about which ones would look good together and testing out a few samples until you find something you like.

Rippling

Just like the Blend filter, the Rippling filter will provide an animated effect using ripples, like those seen in moving water. You can use this filter to create interesting wave effects when applied to your digital imagery.

This filter is found in the image window menu under the Filters ➤ Animation menu. Run it by going to Filters ➤ Animation ➤ Rippling. Figure 17-8 shows the Rippling filter dialog box.

In the Script-Fu: Rippling effect dialog box, you can adjust the rippling strength (which is self-explanatory), the number of frames, and the edge behavior. The Rippling Strength slider and input box options allow you to adjust the strength of the ripple within your image.

The Number of Frames input box option is similar to the one you configured while working with the Blend filter previously. Since animations work off of frames, you can select the number of frames to place in your animation here.

FIGURE 17-8

Using the Script-Fu: Rippling filter found within GIMP's filters to create animated ripples on your image

You can also adjust the edge behavior. For example, since the edges of your image will have the ripple effect applied to them, you may want to adjust how that looks by setting the edge behavior. For example, here the Wrap setting is used, which will do just that – wrap the effect around each edge of the graphic to produce a clean effect.

Just like any other animation, you can test it to see if it's working as advertised. Within the image window, click Filters ➤ Animation ➤ Playback. In the Animation Playback dialog box, click the Play button to test your animation. Then stop the animation if it appears to work as you wanted it to work.

Once you finish your tests, close the Animation Playback dialog box.

Spinning Globe

Another filter you can create animations with is the Spinning Globe. The Spinning Globe filter effect is used to take your image and spin it like the planet Earth spins on its axis. A globe that represents a planet (like Earth) spins on an axis as well, which is the basis of what this effect provides when applied. If you want to produce a spinning globe effect on your image, then launch this animation effect and apply it to your images within the image window.

This filter is found in the image window menu under the Filters ➤ Animation menu. Run it by going to Filters ➤ Animation ➤ Spinning Globe. Figure 17-9 shows the Spinning Globe filter dialog box.

In the Spinning Globe filter dialog box, you can adjust the Frames section. Here you can adjust the number of frames used in between images to create your animation, provide smoother transitions and provide direction to the effect – such as turning right to left or left to right. The Turn from Left to Right check box, when selected, will turn your image left to right. If unchecked, it will turn from right to left. You can also set the Index to n Colors option, which will alternate your color patterns, whether grayscale or RGB.

Lastly, you can select the Work on Copy check box, which will create a backup copy for your to work on, which keeps your original image safe if you want to revert your changes back and remove the effect.

FIGURE 17-9

Using the Script-Fu: Spinning Globe filter effect found within GIMP's filters to create a spinning animation on your image

Waves

The Waves filter is almost identical to the Ripple filter. Here, you will produce waves instead of mere ripples. Although the Ripple filter will create what look like small waves, the Waves filter will create bigger-resemble actual waves in the ocean.

This filter is found in the image window menu under the Filters ➤ Animation menu. Run it by going to Filters ➤ Animation ➤ Waves. Figure 17-10 shows the Waves filter dialog box.

FIGURE 17-10

Using the Script-Fu: Waves filter found within GIMP's filters to create animated waves on your image

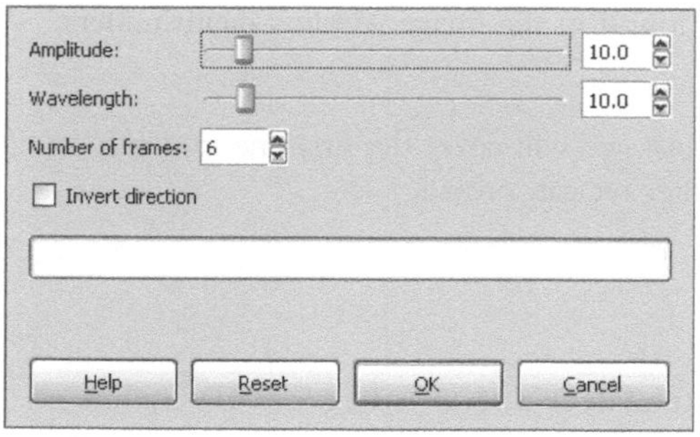

Just like any other animation, you can test it to see if it's working as advertised. Within the image window, click Filters ➤ Animation ➤ Playback. In the Animation Playback dialog box, click the Play button to test your animation. Then stop the animation if it appears to work as you wanted it to work. Once you finish your tests, close the Animation Playback dialog box.

Optimizing Filters

Other animation effects you can use include Optimize, Playback, and Unoptimize. Optimize comes in two different flavors: Optimize (Difference) and Optimize (for GIF). Once you have finished your animations, you can optimize them, or test them. This is done with the Optimizing filters found within GIMP's Filters menu.

Each setting will optimize your animation, but both in different ways. For one, Optimize (Difference) will generally optimize your animation using the full extent of its power, whereas Optimize (GIF) is used to reduce layers size. This subsequently reduces file size as well. Unoptimize can be used to remove all optimization settings.

Playback will play the animation as you would see it before being saved as a file or multi-layer file. You can view the results in the preview pane, and use the Play/Stop buttons to play or stop the animation. You can also select Rewind to restart the animation and use the Step option to play the animation frame by frame.

If you are satisfied with your work you can click File ➤ Save As. Here, you can adjust the file type and choose GIF, for example, if making an animated GIF. Once you save it, you can export it. Within the Export File dialog box, choose the Save as Animation option.

Alpha to Logo

The Alpha to Logo filters menu contains many filters you can choose from to generate logos. Most of these filters (like many of the ones you just learned about) are Script-Fu based. Alpha to Logo filter effects add different effects to the Alpha channel of the active layer. This means that if you do not have an active layer with an alpha channel. You can create one easily in the Layers dialog box if needed.

Also, it's important to note that these filters reflect the Script-fu's available through File ➤ Create ➤ Logos. The Alpha to Logo filters are found in the image window menu under the Filters ➤ Alpha to Logo menu.

Although we will not cover each of these filters in depth, we will cover the first one in depth so that you can get an idea of what the Alpha to Logo filter set can provide.

3D Outline

You can access this filter in the Filters menu, or use the File ➤ Create ➤ Logos ➤ 3D Outline option. The 3D Outline effect will change your image so that colors are inverted, new colors are used, and an outline is applied to your entire image. Then, with blurring effects, the filter will make the image appear as if it's a 3D image.

It does this by outlining all non-transparent areas of the active layer, which is determined by the Alpha channel and then uses the Sobel edge detect filter to get the Alpha channel's outline.

This filter is found in the image window menu under the Filters ➤ Animation menu. Run it by going to Filters ➤ Alpha to Logo ➤ 3D Outline. Figure 17-11 shows the 3D Outline filter dialog box.

As with other filters you learned about in this chapter, the 3D Outline filter will work only if the active layer has an Alpha channel. If it doesn't, then the menu entry will be grayed out and unusable.

Using the Alpha to Logo – 3D Outline effect to create interesting patterns, outlines, and 3D effects with your image

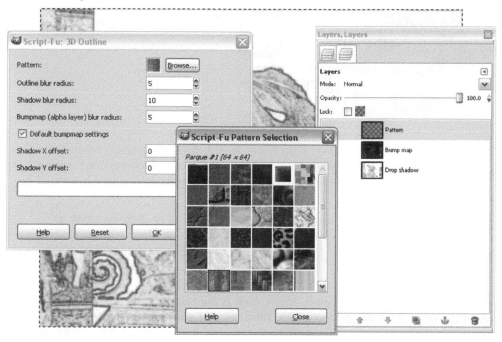

Once you open and launch the 3D Outline filter, you can adjust the pattern applied to the graphic, the outline blur radius, the shadow blur radius, the bumpmap settings, and X and Y shadow offsets.

You can also select from many default patterns found in the Script-Fu: Pattern Selection dialog box. Once you change your settings and select your pattern, you can apply your effect. Figure 17-12 shows the application of the 3D Outline filter on a historical statue.

FIGURE 17-12

Using the 3D Outline filter effect to create bold outlines, new patterns, and much more within your digital image

Other filters you can try are Alien Glow, Alien Neon, Basic I, Basic II, Blended, Bovination, Chalk, Chip Away, Chrome, Comic Book, Cool Metal, Frosty, Glossy, Glowing Hot, Gradient Bevel, Neon, Particle Trace, and Textured. They resemble many of the effects already covered through the past four chapters.

Continue to use preset filters, or adjust and make your own as you need them. GIMP is as flexible as it is powerful, so apply what you need and see how it affects your digital images.

Tip

Remember, the Layers dialog box also contains many effects, such as the Opacity slider, and the drop-down menu that contains many other filters you can work with. There are also many options that you can select in the Layers menu within the image window. These effects include Add Border (Stroke), Bevel and Emboss, Color Overlay, Drop Shadow, Gradient Overlay, Inner Glow, Inner Shadow, Outer Glow, Pattern Overlay, Satin, and more.

These filters are provided by a plug-in that may not come with GIMP by default, so you may need to download and install them.

Check what you can use by going to Layer ➤ Layer Effects, or by going to the right-clickable menu on the top of the Layers dockable dialog box. ■

Note

If you are looking to use more filters, you can also choose photo filter effects. These filters are provided by the Exposure Blend plug-in. Refer to Chapter 12's coverage of filter plug-ins to learn more. ■

Summary

In this chapter we covered the use of specialized filters. You learned about using filters to work on web design and to aid animation. We covered how to create basic animations using filters such as Blend, Rippling, and Waves, and how to use the Alpha to Logo filters for creating quick 'n' dirty logos and other interesting effects.

Whether you're a photographer, a filmmaker, an animator, or even a web designer, chances are good that you're going to run into situations where you need to run the same set of operations on a whole batch of images. You may want to apply standardized color correction on a series of photos. The next chapter covers the methods that are available through the Filters menu.

In the next chapter, "Batch Processing with Automating Filters," we cover the processing of multiple images all at once, how to apply multiple filters to your workflow, as well as how to filter all layers in a single image.

Summary

18

Batch Processing with Automating Filters

Whether you're a photographer, a filmmaker, an animator, or even a web designer, chances are good that you're going to run into situations where you need to run the same set of operations on a whole batch of images. You may want to perform standardized color correction on a series of photos of a single location. Or you may want to take a folder of images and quickly generate thumbnail previews of each one. Or perhaps you have a sequence of images from an animation and want to do a gradual blur-out effect. These are examples of *batch processing* and GIMP allows you to perform these kinds of actions in a few different ways. This chapter covers the methods that are available through the Filters menu. The other way to get this sort of automation is by way of scripting. That, however, is covered in Chapter 22.

Something to note, though, is that the features covered in this chapter aren't shipped with the default installation of GIMP. They're provided by plug-ins, or programmed extensions to GIMP. Chapter 21 covers plug-ins in a more thorough manner, including where to find plug-ins and how to install them. As I go through this chapter, I'll indicate which plug-in provides the feature I'm covering. From there, you can either track them down online or download them directly from this book's companion web site at www.gimpbible.com.

Batch Processing Multiple Files

So you want to perform the same operation on a whole bunch of images. They may or may not all be in the same folder, but you know you want to perform the same actions on all of them. This is the essence of batch processing; the files you want to work on are the *batch* and the actions you want to perform are the *processing*. GIMP offers you the ability to do this by hand with its scripting interfaces, but as an artist — and especially for relatively simple actions — it's a bit friendlier to have a graphical interface to work with. The two filters covered in this section, Batch Process and Contact Sheet, give you exactly that. This way you can work on a whole chunk of images without having to know how to code anything at all. Woohoo!

Note

If you're running GIMP in Debian or Ubuntu Linux the two plug-ins discussed in this chapter are part of the `gimp-plugin-registry` package. If you have this installed, both of these options appear in Filters ➢ Batch. On nearly every other Linux and non-Linux operating system, they're separated into Filters ➢ Batch Process and Filters ➢ Batch ➢ Contact Sheet. ∎

Using the Batch Process Plug-in

"David's Batch Processor," or DBP — named for its developer, David Hodson — is a graphical interface for performing one or more simple operations on an arbitrary set of images. If you have the DBP plug-in installed, then you can launch it by going to Filters ➢ Batch Process. This should provide you with a window like the one in Figure 18-1. It's a pretty slick plug-in and definitely comes in handy as a great time-saver. Rather than spend your entire day manually perfoming any of these tasks one image at a time, you can use this interface to choose which images you want to modify and what operations to perform on them. Then you can go get a cup of coffee while it cooks. Hooray for computers!

FIGURE 18-1

The window that appears for David's Batch Processor, which you find at Filters ➢ Batch Process

Tip

If you're using the `gimp-plugin-registry` package on a Debian or Ubuntu Linux distribution, David's Batch Processor is at Filters ➤ Batch ➤ Batch Process. ∎

Using the Input Tab to Select Images

To use DBP, the first thing you need to do is select the images you want to operate on from the Input tab, which displays by default the first time you load this plug-in. To add images for the processor to work on, click the Add Files button near the bottom of the window. This brings up a File Chooser, allowing you to go through your hard drive and pick the images you want to process. When you're in a folder, you can use the following shortcuts to select more than one file:

- **Click** — Selects a single file. If any files are currently selected, it deselects them in favor of the file you click.

- **Ctrl+click** — If you've already selected a file, Ctrl+clicking other files highlights them, adding them to the list of selected files. If you Ctrl+click a file that's already been selected, it is deselected.

- **Shift+click** — If you've already selected a file, you can then scroll up or down the list of files and Shift+click another file. When you do this, all of the files between those two files are selected.

- **Ctrl+A** — This keyboard shortcut selects all files in the folder.

- **Start typing** — You can also just start typing. If you do that, the File Chooser searches the folder you're in for files that start with the characters you've typed.

After you select your files, click the Add button and they are added to the list of images to be processed. Note, however, that clicking the Add button does not automatically close the window. This allows you to go to other folders and add images in them to your list of processed files as well. If you want the File Chooser window to close after you make your selection, click the Open button instead. Alternatively, you can use the Add button and click the Close button when you're done choosing your images.

If you've mistakenly added images that you don't want to include in the batch, you can select those images from the list of files under the Input tab using the same selection shortcuts mentioned previously and then click the Remove Files button. If you decide that you foolishly chose the entirely wrong set of images, click the Clear List button.

After you choose your images, you can begin to choose the operations you want to perform on them. Each of the tabs in this window is an operation that DBP can do. To activate an operation, click the Enable check box at the top of each tab. You can actually enable multiple operations at once. If you do that, though, it's important to remember the order in which these functions happen. They happen in the order of the tabs. So if you enable Turn, Blur, and Resize, DBP does the processing in that order. Also, at the bottom of each tab is a button called Test. Basically, if you select a file in the Input tab and click the Test button, DBP performs all enabled operations and shows the result in an image window. When it does this, it activates the Show Images button on the bottom right of the window. This button is a toggle. If it's enabled when you click the

Start button, you can see the selected images get processed as DBP goes through them. If it's not enabled, DBP just silently does its thing without showing the images. If your images are large, keeping Show Images disabled will improve the plug-in's performance.

Tip

It's certainly possible to choose the operations you want to perform *before* selecting your files, but it usually makes more sense if you know what you're working with from the start. This is especially true if you're scaling or cropping. ■

Using the Turn Tab

This tab, shown in Figure 18-2, is a simple rotate operation. You have three choices:

- **Clockwise** — Rotates your image 90° to the right
- **Anti-Clockwise** — Rotates your image 90° to the left, or counter-clockwise
- **Upside-Down** — Rotates your image 180°

FIGURE 18-2

The Turn tab on the DBP plug-in

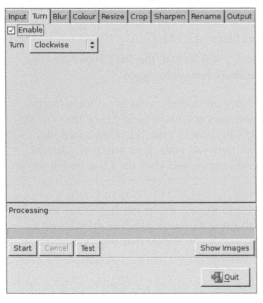

Use the drop-down menu to select the type of rotation you want. Once you do that, you can either click Start or move on to the next operation you want DBP to perform.

Note

If you're in the U.S., you may notice that some of the terminology and spelling (for example, "anti-clockwise" or "colour") may be unfamiliar. This is because the plug-in is written by an

Australian developer and it currently doesn't have localization support for other languages or even other forms of English. This means that no matter what language you have your computer set to use, this plug-in displays Australian English. ■

Using the Blur Tab

As the name implies, this tab blurs your selected images. As Figure 18-3 shows, the only control for this operation is a radius for the blur, measured in pixels. The type of blur that's used for this operation is actually GIMP's Gaussian Blur, using the IIR method. This is the same as opening each of your images and choosing Filters ➢ Blur ➢ Gaussian Blur and then enabling the IIR radio button under the Blur Method label.

FIGURE 18-3

The Blur tab in DBP

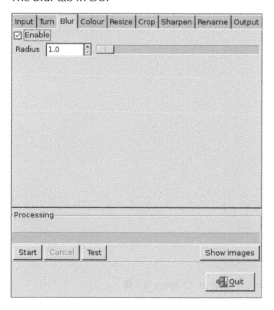

Using the Colour Tab

This tab, as shown in Figure 18-4, gives you a handful of controls for adjusting the coloring of your images. The settings available are as follows:

- **Auto Levels** — If you enable this check box, DBP does the same operation that happens when you choose Colors ➢ Levels and click the Auto button at the bottom.

- **Manual** — Three sliders in this section control brightness, contrast, and saturation. There actually isn't a single color tool in GIMP's menus that gives you an interface to control all three, so it's pretty handy to have all three here.

- **Invert** — Enabling this check box performs the same operation as Color ➢ Invert.

517

- **Convert to Gray** — This option makes your image grayscale. If you enable this option, though, be aware of two things. First, this does not change the image's mode to the Grayscale colorspace. It's still an RGB image. The other thing to note is that this operation is not the same as simply dropping the image's saturation to zero. This operation generally ends up with a grayscale image that is somewhat brighter than one you'd get if you zero out the saturation.

FIGURE 18-4

The Colour tab in DBP

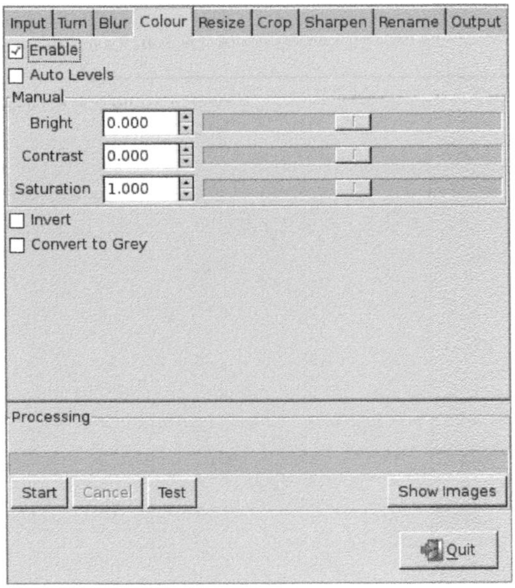

Tip

For more information on how these color operations work, have a look at Chapter 9. ∎

Using the Resize Tab

The Resize tab on DBP, shown in Figure 18-5, has some pretty unique and powerful capabilities.

Radio buttons at the top of the window allow you to control whether you're using relative or absolute resizing. The differences between the two are outlined here:

- **Relative** — By choosing this option you're adjusting the size of your images relative to their current size. For instance, if you want all of the images to be half as large as they currently are, you choose this option and set the X and Y sliders both to 0.50. To make things easier, select the check box that locks the X and Y aspects together so you can be sure your images are scaled proportionally. The only limitation here is that the maximum scale you can increase any image to is twice its original size.

- **Absolute** — Choosing this option allows you to set an explicit size in pixels to which you can scale your images. You may notice that this option doesn't have a Keep Aspect check box like Relative does. Instead, it offers a Fit drop-down menu with four options:

  - **Exactly** — As the name implies, this scales your image to the exact pixel dimensions for width and height that you set with the sliders. Of course, this means that your image may end up disproportionately scaled to match the pixel sizes you've chosen.

  - **Padded** — If you choose this option, your image is scaled maintaining its aspect, but in order to make the image match the width and height you stipulate, DBP pads the empty space with the current background color you have set in GIMP. So if you have a vertically tall image and you resize it to a square, padding will be added on the left and right of your image.

  - **Inside** — Choosing this option scales your image proportionally, but keeps it within the dimensions you set. Using the same rectangular image example, if you set the width and height to the same values, you still get a rectangular image that's exactly the height you stipulate, but with whatever the proportional width is calculated to be.

  - **Outside** — This option uses the same basic principles as Inside, except in reverse. Whereas the Inside option scales your image to fit inside the sizes you set, the Outside option scales your image to wrap outside those dimensions. So to reuse the same rectangular example, its width is set to exactly what you set and the height is proportionally calculated to a value larger than the height setting you entered.

Figure 18-6 illustrates the differences between each of the Fit settings.

FIGURE 18-5

The Resize tab in DBP

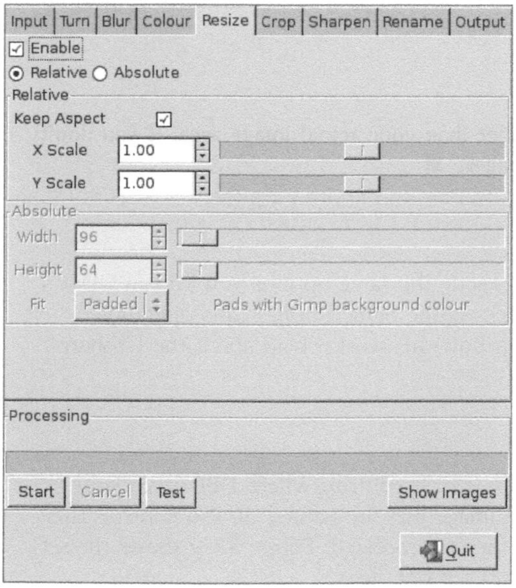

FIGURE 18-6

On the far left is a rectangle that represents the original image dimensions. From left to right are how each of the Fit settings adjust that image to an absolute square size. For Inside and Outside, the dashed line represents the boundaries of the square.

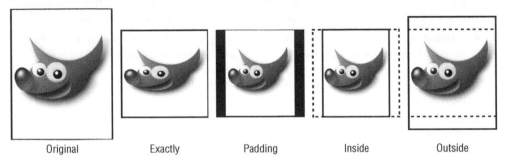

| Original | Exactly | Padding | Inside | Outside |

Note

The scale operation on this tab uses the interpolation type stipulated in your preferences as the Default Interpolation. To change this, go to Edit ➤ Preferences and click Tools. Under Scaling there's a Default Interpolation drop-down menu. Change this to get DBP to use a different interpolation. ■

Using the Crop Tab

The values in this tab crop your images to the size and location that you specify. Remember that image coordinates are a bit unlike the X-Y coordinate system they teach in high school geometry. The standard is that the X value increases from left to right and the Y value increases from bottom to top. However, when dealing with images, the Y value is backwards: the origin coordinate (0,0) is in the top-left corner and the Y value increases as you move downward from top to bottom. Figure 18-7 shows the settings in the Crop tab.

Warning

If you use this option make sure that your crop region is smaller than your actual image area. If you don't do this, DBP chokes and errors out while working on your images. ■

Using the Sharpen Tab

The options in this tab, shown in Figure 18-8, are exactly the same options you find in GIMP's Unsharp Mask (Filters ➤ Enhance ➤ Unsharp Mask). As the name implies, this operation reduces the blurriness of images. For information on how this works, read about the Unsharp Mask in Chapter 13.

Using the Rename Tab

This tab, like the Input and Output tabs, is always active. It controls where DBP saves your images once it completes processing and how those image files are named. It also controls the image mode that's used for saving the images once they're processed. Figure 18-9 shows the settings for this tab and the following list explains what each one does.

FIGURE 18-7

The Crop tab in DBP

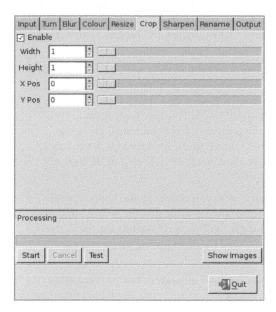

FIGURE 18-8

The Sharpen tab in DBP

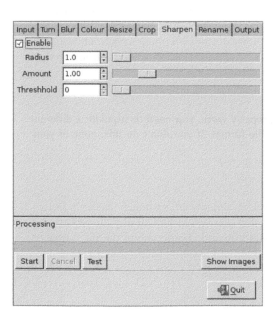

- **To Directory** — This controls where the processor saves files. By default, your images are saved in exactly the same folder they came from. However, you may want to have a separate folder where you want all processed files to go. For that, click the Select Dir button and choose the folder you want to use from the File Chooser that appears. If you decide that you would instead rather use the default setting, just click the Source Dir button. As you make these changes, the values next to the Original and Becomes labels change to reflect the modifications you've made.

- **Prefix/Add Postfix** — If you're saving these images back to their source folder, it makes sense to differentiate your processed images from the originals. One of the best ways to do this is to append something to the beginning (prefix) or end (postfix, or suffix) of the filename. You can use these two fields to specify what you may want them to be. For instance, if you're batch resizing all of your images to have thumbnail previews, you may want to have a postfix with the value -thumb so the file becomes, for instance, image-thumb.jpg. Any changes you make to these fields are reflected in the example values next to Original and Becomes as well.

- **Before Writing** — Depending on the image format you choose in the Output panel, you may want to remove layers or convert the image to a mode that the format supports. For example, if you're saving your processed files as GIFs, you'll want to use the Convert Indexed option. The choices you have are described in the following list. If you need a review of what these options do, refer to Chapter 2.

  - **Flatten** — If the images that you're processing have any layers and you're saving to a format that doesn't support layers, enable this option to automatically flatten the image to a single layer.

  - **Convert Grey** — Enabling this check box converts the image mode to grayscale. This is different than the Convert to Grey option in the Colours tab because it actually does change the image mode, whereas the other option keeps the image in RGB mode.

  - **Convert Indexed** — Enabling this check box converts the image to an indexed palette. If you do enable this option DBP also uses the values you set for Dither and Colours. As explained in Chapter 2, the Dither drop-down options control how GIMP converts color gradients in an indexed palette and the Colours value controls exactly how many colors are used in the images' palettes.

Note

DBP won't overwrite any existing file. So in order for it to properly work, you need to stipulate a different folder to save to, modify the filename, or save to a different file format. If you don't do this, none of your batch operations will work. ■

Using the Output Tab

This is the very last tab, and, as Figure 18-10 shows, its options are extremely basic. In fact, there's only one option and that's the image format that you would like all of your processed images to be saved in. Simply click the drop-down button and choose one of the file formats listed there.

FIGURE 18-9

The Rename tab in DBP

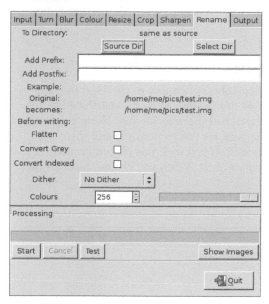

FIGURE 18-10

The Output tab in DBP

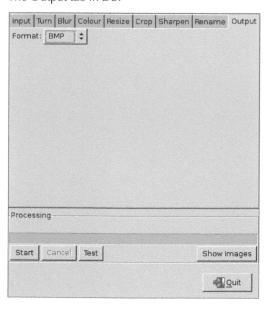

One thing to be aware of is that there's a chance that you may not have the plug-in installed to support some image formats in that list, such as MIFF. So it's a good idea to make sure you can save to that format first in GIMP by itself before trying to do it with DBP. Of course, if you choose a format that is supported, everything should work smoothly. Just click the Start button at the bottom of the window and let things cook.

Using the Contact Sheet Plug-in

A *contact sheet* is a page of preview images that photographers often give to clients so they can choose which image they would like to purchase. Now, it's possible to create something like this by hand, or even use the DBP plug-in to generate thumbnail previews for you. However, DBP doesn't put all of these thumbnail images on a single page for you to print out and share. It's for this reason that the Contact Sheet plug-in was created. If you have this plug-in installed, it appears in the Filters menu as Filters ➤ Batch ➤ Contact Sheet. When you choose this from the menu, the window shown in Figure 18-11 appears.

FIGURE 18-11

The window for the Contact Sheet filter

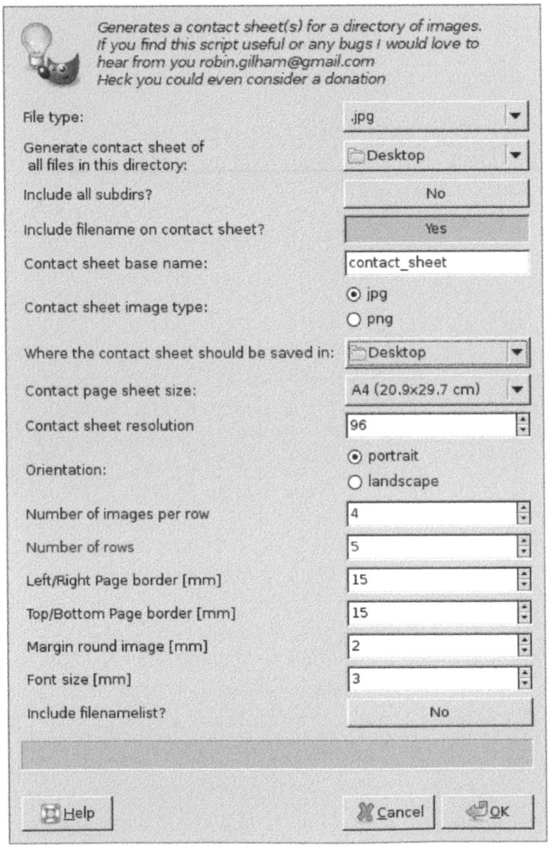

To use this filter, you need to select the folder where your source images live. Unlike with DBP, you cannot choose arbitrary images from all over your hard drive. All the images for your contact sheet must already be in the same folder, or a subfolder of that folder. After adjusting the rest of the settings, described in the following list, click the OK button and your contact sheet is generated for you.

- **File Type** — This drop-down menu gives you the option of limiting the Contact Sheet filter to only use files in the selected folder that are one of the following image formats: JPEG, PNG, TIFF, PCX, or XCF. You can also just have this filter use all image formats that it recognizes in the folder you choose.

- **Generate Contact Sheet of All Files in this Directory** — This is where you choose the folder that your source images live in. It attempts to use one of a set of potential defaults, but if the folder you want to use isn't in that list, just click the Other option and pick a folder from the File Chooser that appears.

- **Include All Subdirs?** — If the folder you choose has other folders inside it, you can click this button to enable the Contact Sheet filter to enter those subfolders as well to find images for populating your contact sheet.

- **Include Filename on Contact Sheet?** — Enable this option to make the filter print the name of each file under its thumbnail on the contact sheet.

- **Contact Sheet Base Name** — This filter generates an image file for your contact sheet. If you have enough images to fill multiple pages of contact sheets, each sheet gets its own file. The base name is what each contact sheet file starts with. After the base name, a number is appended to indicate which page it is. So if your base name is `contact_sheet` your first contact sheet's filename will be `contact_sheet_000.png`.

- **Contact Sheet Image Type** — Because you're creating an image for your contact sheet, you need to choose the format that the filter will save it in. Your options here are either JPEG or PNG.

- **Where the Contact Sheet Should Be Saved in** — Like the source directory setting, this lets you specify where your contact sheet images are saved. You can choose a default directory or pick a custom one.

- **Contact Page Sheet Size** — Because contact sheets are intended to be printed, you need to tell the filter the physical size of the paper that you intend on using for the contact sheet. This drop-down menu gives you the choice of some standard paper sizes.

- **Contact Sheet Resolution** — Again, contact sheets are intended to be printed, so use this value to control how many pixels per inch the contact sheet files are. If you want to have a high-quality print, use a value of 300ppi.

- **Orientation** — As the name indicates, you can control whether the images on your contact sheet are displayed horizontally (landscape) or vertically (portrait).

- **Number of Images per Row** — Unlike DBP, you don't explicitly control the size of each thumbnail. Instead, the Contact Sheet filter calculates the size that best fits these values. For example, this setting controls how many images are in a row on your contact sheet.

- **Number of Rows** — Here you control the number of rows. Higher row numbers make your thumbnails smaller, whereas larger row numbers usually increase the number of individual contact sheets that get created.

- **Left/Right Page Border [mm]** — This value, in millimeters, controls how much space is used for the left and right margins on the whole contact sheet.

- **Top/Bottom Page Border [mm]** — Like the previous setting, this value controls the margin at the top and bottom of your contact sheets.

- **Margin Round Image [mm]** — Each image needs a little bit of breathing room to separate it from the other images around it in the contact sheet. This value, in millimeters like the others, controls how much empty space you have around each image in your contact sheet.

- **Font Size [mm]** — If you decide to include filenames on the contact sheet, this value controls the size of the font used when the text for those filenames is added.

- **Include Filenamelist?** — Enable this option if you want the filter to generate a text file that lists all of the files included on your contact sheet. This is a pretty handy organizational tool. The text file gets saved to the same folder that the contact sheets do and includes the full path to where each image in the sheet lives on your hard drive.

Figure 18-12 shows an example contact sheet that the Contact Sheet filter creates.

FIGURE 18-12

An example contact sheet automatically created by the Contact Sheet filter (Photo credit: Chris Hoyer)

Automating Tasks with GAP's Filtermacro

Chapters 19 and 20 cover GIMP features that you can use to make changes across a sequence of images for video or animation. This functionality is added to GIMP with a plug-in package called the *GIMP Animation Package*, or GAP. With this package, you find all kinds of ways to perform batch operations on a series of images. One of the ways GAP allows this is by adding a filter called Filtermacro. For most filters provided by GAP, images need to be sequentially numbered like the individual frames in a movie. However, Filtermacro doesn't require this. So even if you don't have sequentially numbered images and you don't work in animation or video, it's worth it to install GAP for Filtermacro and some other useful automated processing filters.

Tip
If you don't already have this plug-in installed on your system, Chapter 21 walks you through the process of getting it installed and working on your machine. ∎

In many programs, there exists the concept of *macros*, or a recorded sequence of operations that the user (that's you) performs on a file. You see this concept put to use in everything from word processors and spreadsheets to raster image editors and 3D modeling software. In graphics programs particularly, they often have the concept of a *construction history* or *action list* that sequentially lists all of the operations you've performed on an image in the order you performed them. With this, you don't even really have to record your macro, you can just pull a sequence of operations from the history and specify that as your macro.

Now for the bad news: GIMP does not currently have any sort of construction history or action list or even a means of recording macros. There is the Undo History dialog, but it currently has no facility for saving or replaying actions. It's something under consideration for future versions, but the current version of GIMP doesn't give you a graphical way of creating macros. The only way to do anything like this in the default (GAP-free) installation is to write a script. Though that's certainly the most powerful way to automate processes in GIMP, it's not necessarily "artist-friendly." Incidentally, I'm really not a fan of the term "artist-friendly" used in this way because it gives the false impression that artists are incapable or unwilling to work with code. Some of the most talented artists have extremely technical minds and are more than willing to bang out a few lines of code to get a specific effect or make it easier or faster for them to create. If you can relate to this, definitely have a look at scripting, covered in Chapter 22 of this book.

The Filtermacro Window

If you've installed GAP, you can automate some operations without using any code at all. To do this, you use the Filtermacro filter, available at Filters ➤ Filtermacro. Figure 18-13 shows the window that appears when you choose this option.

As the figure shows, the window consists of two distinct parts:

- **Filename** — This is the filename your macro is saved and loaded from. It's a plain text file that stores the filter operations you choose. You can't do anything with the Filtermacro until you create this text file and point to it from this field. To create a new macro file or load one that you've already created, click the button on the far right of the Filename field labeled with the ellipsis (...). This pops up a basic file chooser where you can pick a previously created macro or type in the name of a new one. Because these are just text files, you can use just about any extension for the filename that you want (or no extension at all). I like to use .macro at the end of my filenames, so I can have something like beautify.macro and createthumbs.macro. However, you can just as easily call them beautify.txt and createthumbs.txt if you prefer.

- **Operation list** — This next block in the Filtermacro window is where you can see your macro's list of operations. Once you have a file named for your macro, use can use the buttons at the bottom of this window to add or remove operations from the list.

FIGURE 18-13

The Filtermacro window appears when you choose Filters ➤ Filtermacro

Warning

The Filtermacro documentation warns that "filtermacro scriptfiles are machine dependent, plug-in version dependent, and may not work in the expected way or even crash at execution on other machines or on execution with newer versions of the recorded filter plug-ins." It's a bit like operating a motorcycle without a helmet, but as long as you're careful, you won't run into any catastrophic errors. This is a good time to remind you that when working with computers, keep backups of your originals and work on copies of those files so you don't make unrecoverable mistakes. ■

Adding Operations

If you have your macro file created, you can begin adding operations to it. To do this, click the Add button at the bottom of the Filtermacro window. When you click this button, GIMP gives you a Filtercall Browser window like the one in Figure 18-14. This window lists the filters you've used in the current GIMP session in the list on the left. Click any of these filters and the panel on the left displays some helpful information on what the filter does and what sort of parameters it uses.

Now, if you run Filtermacro and try to add a filter operation as the first thing you do after opening an image file, you'll notice that this browser window appears markedly desolate. The reason for this is that this browser shows only the filter operations that you've used in this session. So if you haven't done anything to your image yet, there are not going to be any filter operations listed here. The idea here is that you perform a series of filter operations on an image and decide that this produces an interesting effect that you'd like to retain and use again in the future. So *then* you click Filters ➤ Filtermacro and start re-creating the sequence of filter operations.

The Filtercall Browser that appears when you click the Add button in the Filtermacro window to add filter operations to your macro

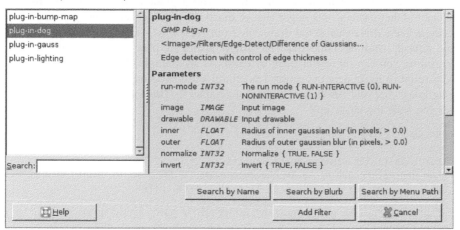

Adding an operation is a snap. Just click the filter you want to add in the filter browser and then click the Add Filter button. Note that when you do this, Filtermacro doesn't prompt you with any settings for that filter. This is because it just uses the last settings you used on that filter. Though this is incredibly convenient, two ramifications to this exist:

- If the effect that you've created uses the same filter multiple times, but with different settings, you're going to use a slightly different method for creating your macro. Rather than produce the full effect and then run Filtermacro, you have to be a bit more interactive. That is, you need to perform your filter operation, add it to the Filtermacro script, and then perform the next filter operation and subsequently add it and so forth. The good news here is that you can keep the Filtermacro window open while you're working on the image so you don't have to constantly open and close it through the Filters menu.

- Filtermacro is able to load these filter operations without prompting you for input because it uses something called a LAST_VALUES variable. This variable is something in GIMP that stores the settings from the last time you used a particular filter. The catch is that not all filters in GIMP actually utilize this variable. You can tell which ones they are because you won't be able to use Filters ➤ Repeat Operation on them. Because these filters don't use LAST_VALUES, it's impossible for Filtermacro to figure out what settings you used when you last used them. For that reason, those filters are unable to be added to a Filtermacro script.

Note

When you click the Add Filter button from the Filtercall Browser, that filter is automatically added to the Filtermacro script file you created and that file is automatically saved. There's no "save script" functionality here because it all happens seamlessly. The same thing happens when you select a filter operation for removal and click the Delete or Delete All button in the Filtermacro window. ∎

Once you have your Filtermacro script created, you can reuse it at any time and on any image that you can load in GIMP. Pay attention to your scripts if you upgrade GIMP or any plug-ins because the values in Filtermacro scripts might change drastically if filter parameters get modified. However, most filters don't change too drastically from version to version, so modifications shouldn't be too difficult. And the scripts that Filtermacro creates are plain text, so if you're feeling really adventurous, you can try to edit them by hand. As an example, the following lines are a Filtermacro script to implement the simple smoothing and denoising operation described in the "Changing Image Size and Resolution" section of Chapter 2. This Filtermacro script does steps 2–4 (after you scale the image up):

```
# FILTERMACRO FILE (GIMP-GAP-1.3)
# lineformat:
# 1.st item plug-in PDB name in double quotes
# 2.nd item decimal length of lastvalue data plug-in PDB name in double quotes
# 3.rd until N items hex bytevalues of lastvalue data buffer
#
"plug-in-despeckle"   16   03 00 00 00 01 00 00 00 07 00 00 00 f8 00 00 00
"plug-in-greycstoration" 112   00 00 00 00 04 00 00 00 00 00 00 00 00 00 24 40
0 0 00 00 00 00 00 2e 40 07 00 00 00 00 00 00 00 00 00 00 00 00 00 4e 40 66 66
66 66 66 66 e6 3f 33 33 33 33 33 33 d3 3f 33 33 33 33 33 33 e3 3f 9a 99 99 99
99 99 f1 3f 9a 99 99 99 99 99 e9 3f 00 00 00 00 00 00 3e 40 00 00 00 00 00 00
00 40 00 00 00 00 01 00 00 00 01 00 00 00 01 00 00 00
"plug-in-unsharp-mask"   24   00 00 00 00 00 00 14 40 00 00 00 00 00 00 e0 3f 00
00 00 00 00 00 00 00
```

Pretty slick, huh?

Note

The Filtermacro is a feature provided by GAP, but it may be removed from future versions if GIMP begins to support a proper construction history or macro system. It's pretty helpful for what it does, but as GIMP improves, there's a chance that it may be superseded by a better system. ∎

Filter All Layers

GIMP Animation Package provides another pretty slick piece of filtered automation in the Filter All Layers tool. Where DBP works across multiple images and Filtermacro works with multiple filters on a single image, Filter All Layers applies the same filter to all the layers in an image. In fact, it's even cooler than that. If you want to run a sequence of multiple filters on all the layers of an image, you can actually use Filter All Layers to call Filtermacro. On top of that, because this feature is a component of GAP, you can actually animate the change in values of a filter across your layers. This is useful if, for example, you want your image to get progressively more blurry over time.

Using Filter All Layers

To take advantage of this feature, the first thing you need is an image with multiple layers. This could be an image that you've done a lot of work on and you have multiple working layers or it could just be a single image where you've repeatedly clicked the Duplicate Layer button in the Layers dockable dialog. If you're starting with an animation from a sequence of still images, you can use the Video ➤ Frames to Image feature of GAP to make each still image a separate layer on a new image window. You can actually use Filter All Layers on a single layer image, but in that case it's not really any different from directly running the filter you want.

Assuming you have your multi-layer image, the next step is to choose Filters ➤ Filter All Layers. When you do this, GIMP provides you with a window like the one shown in Figure 18-15. The window looks like the one that appears when you click the Add button in the Filtermacro window, except it has more items available. In fact, both Filtermacro's Filtercall Browser and the Filter All Layers browser window are very similar to GIMP's Procedural Database (PDB) window (Help ➤ Procedure Browser). All three buttons feature a list on the left side with procedures that GIMP can do, and clicking any procedure in the list updates the panel on the right with information pertinent to that procedure. The difference is that, unlike Filtermacro's Filtercall Browser, Filter All Layers doesn't limit its list to the filters you've used in your current session. And unlike the PDB, which lists all procedures and plug-ins in GIMP, the Filter All Layers window shows only the roughly 50 filters that support it.

Note
To find out more about the PDB, have a look at Chapter 22. ∎

FIGURE 18-15

The Filter All Layers browser window

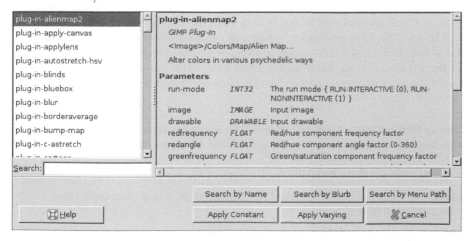

Another thing that differentiates the Filter All Layers browser window from the others is the buttons along the bottom. The first row of buttons, Search by Name, Search by Blurb, and Search by Menu Path, give you very specific controls that allow you quickly and easily to find the filter you're looking to apply to all layers. To use these buttons, type a search term in the Search field on the left of the window and then click the button that corresponds to the type of search you'd like to make. However, the real power of Filter All Layers is in the next row of buttons, specifically the Apply Constant and Apply Varying buttons. Basically, these buttons let you decide whether you want to apply the same filter settings consistently to each layer or if you'd like to iteratively change filter settings from the bottom layer to the top one. Here's how it works.

Apply Constant

This is the most straightforward feature and it's available for each and every filter listed in the Filter All Layers window. As you might expect, you first pick the filter you want to apply by clicking it in the list. Then, when you click the Apply Constant button, a dialog appears for that particular filter. In this dialog, choose the settings you would like to apply to all layers and click OK when you're done. Upon doing so, Filter All Layers proceeds to apply the filter to all of your image's layers, starting with the bottom-most, or *background layer* and working its way up. However, there's one more step. After applying the filter to the background layer, Filter All Layers pops up an Animated Filter Apply dialog as shown in Figure 18-16.

FIGURE 18-16

The Animated Filter Apply dialog appears after Filter All Layers processes the background layer

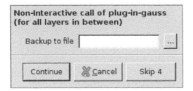

This handy little dialog gives you a few helpful little features. The first of these features is a backup file. Type in a filename and path in this field or click the browse button indicated with the ellipsis (. . .) to get a File Chooser window where you can pick where to save your backup and what name to use. By choosing this option, at every step in the process Filter All Layers saves a backup file so you don't lose image data or undo levels. This feature is optional, though, so if you don't feel the need to create a backup file, simply leave this field empty.

Tip

Filter All Layers saves backup files in GIMP's native XCF format. This maintains layer information and gives you the most complete backup of your image prior to running the Filter All Layers filter. ∎

Below the backup file field are three buttons:

- **Continue** — Click this button to make Filter All Layers process all remaining layers in your image without further prompting.

- **Cancel** — If you don't want Filter All Layers to process any more layers in your image, click this button and it will stop. Layers that have already been filtered won't be reverted to their previous state. To get that, you either need to use Undo (Ctrl+Z) or a backup file, if you created one.

- **Skip N** — This option is really interesting. Assume N is the layer that Filter All Layers is going to work on next. So if Filter All Layers just worked on the background layer, this button says "Skip 2." Click this button and that layer is omitted from being processed by the filter. Filter All Layers just goes to the next layer above that and re-prompts you with a new Animated Filter Apply dialog for that one. This feature is very helpful if you want to use the power of Filter All Layers, but need to exclude one or more layers from being processed.

After Filter All Layers works its way through all the layers in your image, it's done and you're ready for the next step.

Warning

Filter All Layers is kind of a meta-filter. This means that once it's done, if you try to use GIMP's Undo feature (Ctrl+Z), it won't undo the application of the filter to all layers. It will only undo the last application. To completely undo the full effect of Filter All Layers, you need to Undo the same number of times as the number of layers you have. This is actually why the backup file feature exists. If you have more layers than you have levels of undo, you may not be able to completely reverse the Filter All Layers effect. ■

Tip

You can use Filter All Layers to run multiple filters if you need to. In order to do this, you need to have Filter All Layers call Filtermacro. It's in the filter list as plug-in-filter-macro. Because you're calling multiple filters, though, you're limited to only using Apply Constant. All layers are processed by all filters in the Filtermacro with the same settings. Make sure that this is what you want to do. ■

Apply Varying

The Apply Constant button is really useful, but the real awesomeness lies with Apply Varying. Clicking this button goes through the same basic process as Apply Constant, but with some important differences:

1. **The dialog for the filter you've chosen appears.** Adjust the settings here for where you want your filter settings to start. When you've picked the settings you want to use, click OK.

2. **Filter All Layers processes the background layer.** When it finishes, a new dialog as shown in Figure 18-17, appears. Click Continue to proceed to the next step.

3. **A new dialog for the filter you've chosen appears.** This dialog has all the settings you used in step 1. Take this opportunity to adjust the settings for where you want your filter settings to end and click OK when you finish. For example, if you chose plug-in-gauss from the list and initially set your blur radii to 5.0, you can now set them to 50.0. If you do this, Filter All Layers applies the second filter settings to the top layer and then figures out what the settings need to be for the interim layers.

4. **Filter All Layers processes the top layer.** From this point, it then starts calculating the necessary filter settings for all the layers in between so you get a smooth transition from the background image's filter settings to the top layer's filter settings.

5. **Filter All Layers prompts you with the Animated Filter Apply dialog.** This is the same window that you see if you click Apply Constant and it has all of the same features and options. If you want to process all of the remaining layers automatically, simply click Continue.

FIGURE 18-17

The confirmation dialog to continue to the next step in the Apply Varying feature of Filter All Layers

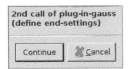

When this process is complete, you basically have an animation across your layers that smoothly transitions the settings of your chosen filter from the background layer to the top layer. From here you can proceed with further editing on your project, generate an animated GIF from these layers, or kick the layers out to a sequence of still images with Video ➤ Split Image to Frames. Figure 18-18 shows a sequence of images created with Filter All Layers to transition from a regular image to an incredibly blurry one.

FIGURE 18-18

You can use Filter All Layers to make interesting transitions on your image, such as going from clear to unrecognizably blurry. (Photo credit: Chris Hoyer)

Note
The Apply Varying option isn't available for all filters supported by Filter All Layers. You can tell which filters don't currently support Apply Varying because the button is grayed out and unselectable. If you're not afraid of a little bit of code, the GAP documentation gives some helpful information on how to get filters to support the Apply Varying feature. ■

A Quick Shortcut: Selection to AnimImage

Occasionally you may want to apply the Filter All Layers feature to the selected part of a particular image. In and of itself, this is not a difficult task, but it can involve a lot of clicking or keyboard shortcuts. In fact, you would have to use the following steps:

1. Make a selection.
2. Copy the selection (Ctrl+C).
3. Paste as a new image (Shift+Ctrl+V).
4. Duplicate the background layer a desired number of times (Shift+Ctrl+D x number of times).
5. Filter All Layers (Filters ➤ Filter All Layers).

It's only five steps, but it's five steps that could be easily consolidated by taking advantage of a GAP feature that uses Filter All Layers, called Selection to AnimImage. To use it, take the following steps:

1. Make a selection.
2. Choose Filters ➤ Animation ➤ Selection to AnimImage. Doing this pops up a dialog like the one shown in Figure 18-19, which automates the rest of the process for you. From this window, you decide how many duplicated layers you want in the new image, and two other options:

   - **Fill with BG Color** — Enable this option to fill space that's not part of the selection with whatever the current background color is. If this option is disabled, the background is just transparent.

   - **Anim-Filter for all Copies** — Enable this option and the next thing this filter does is call the Filter All Layers filter. From here, it's the same process as if you ran Filter All Layers directly. The only difference is that you didn't have to call it yourself this time, making you click fewer times. Hooray for efficiency!

FIGURE 18-19

The Selection to AnimImage dialog

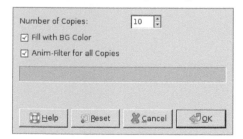

Figure 18-20 shows the results of using Selection to AnimImage and varied application of the Oilify filter on a selected portion of Figure 18-18.

Using Selection to AnimImage on a selected portion of an image to create a separately animated piece

Summary

This chapter introduced you to the variety of ways that GIMP and GAP can help you automate repetitive tasks. You can use these tools to process multiple images, run multiple filters, or even filter all of the layers in an image. By using these automated tools, you save heaps of time over doing it manually or trying to write a script for some of this basic functionality. These are powerful tools and when they're wielded by your very capable hands, an incredible amount of work can be done in a negligible amount of time.

This chapter has served as a bit of a taste of how you can use GIMP with the very cool GAP plug-in. The next section of this book should take that taste and mature it into a full-blown hunger for using GIMP on video and animation tasks. Onward!

Using GIMP Animation Package

G IMP can do animation. It's one of the things that many people don't realize about it. Even without any additional extensions, the official release of GIMP has been able to generate animated GIF files for years. But when you add on the tools and features provided by GIMP Animation Package (GIMP-GAP or GAP for short; it's a lot easier than saying the GNU's Not Unix Image Manipulation Program Animation Package), the animation possibilities with GIMP become even broader. This chapter covers the use of GIMP to create those simple animated GIFs as well the use of GAP for more advanced animation projects. The next chapter covers how you can use GAP's features to let you use GIMP's tools on videos and animations that have already been produced. That means to get the most use out of this part in the book, you need to make sure you have GAP installed on your computer. It doesn't ship with GIMP by default. If you don't already have it, flip ahead to Chapter 21 and read the section on installing GAP. Once you have it installed, come on back to this chapter and have some fun.

Be aware that this chapter covers topics and terminology specific to traditional hand-drawn animation.

Note

It's not the intent of this chapter to teach you the basic principles of animation. Volumes and volumes of books covering this topic have been written by animators far more experienced and talented than I. If you're interested, you may want to check out Preston Blair's *Cartoon Animation* (Walter Foster, 1560100842) or Richard Williams' *The Animator's Survival Kit* (Faber & Faber, 0571238343). ■

Although GAP has some features to help you automate some parts of the animation process, GAP's tools work best to facilitate the traditional hand-drawn animation workflow. The cool part, however, is that it makes GIMP's features, like advanced layers and paint dynamics, available to an animator. Not only that, but because you're working digitally, GAP can provide you with instant feedback on the progress of your animation and you don't have to use multiple sheets of paper or go through the time-consuming process of scanning or photographing each of those drawings to get them into the computer. It's a much faster way to produce animation.

Using Still Image Sequences and Layers for Animation

An animated sequence, like those in film and video, consists of a series of individual images, referred to as *frames*. In GAP, you have two ways to define frames. You can either use multiple layers in a single image file where each layer is a frame in your animation, or you can use a series of individual image files as a sequence where each image file is a frame. The official vanilla release of GIMP only has the ability to use layers. GAP provides the facilities to handle image sequences.

Creating a Simple GIF Animation with Layers

The useful thing about using layers as the frames in your animation is that your entire animation project is contained within a single image file. If you want to copy, move, or even delete your animation project, you only have to worry about that one file. GIMP supports this feature out of the box. Its native XCF format isn't read as animation, but GIMP does support exporting layers as frames in an animation to two file formats: GIF and MNG (pronounced "ming"). Of the two, only GIF is well-supported in other programs. In fact, as of this writing, GIMP has difficulty reading back MNG files that it creates. For that reason, this section focuses primarily on exporting to the GIF file format. That said, the process for creating an animated MNG uses the same steps as generating a GIF, so if you need to create a MNG file, all is not lost.

Using layers to create an animated file is incredibly simple. Consider each layer in your project as a frame of animation. Your bottom layer is the first frame of the animation and each layer above it is a subsequent frame in the animation. Now, you can leave it at that and go through the export process outlined later in this section, but often you want more control over the nature of your animation. GIMP provides you with two such controls. You can control the duration of each frame and you can control how subsequent frames influence preceding frames.

The timing control for each frame is read from the layer name itself. At the end of the layer name, include the duration of the frame in milliseconds. So if your layer is named frame01 and you want that frame to be up for 50 milliseconds, you would change the layer's name to frame01 (50ms). This way you can control the duration of each frame in your animation. This is actually a pretty unique feature for animation. In film and television, there's a fixed frame rate, so the only way that you can keep a frame up for longer is to repeat it the number of times required to keep it on-screen for your desired duration. For instance, film runs at 24 frames per second, so each frame is on screen for 1/24th of a second, or roughly 42 milliseconds. If you want a frame displayed for 100 milliseconds, you can choose to display the frame twice in a row (84 milliseconds) or three times (126 milliseconds). The disadvantage of traditional media is that you can't stipulate an exact duration for a frame, whereas with GIF animation, you have explicit control over that timing.

GIMP also lets you control how subsequent frames affect frames that have already been shown. This is referred to as the *frame disposal method*. You have two options:

- **Replace** — This is the most common behavior. After a frame is displayed, it is discarded and replaced with the next frame. This is the equivalent of using a completely new drawing for each frame of animation. For all intents and purposes, this is the default behavior that GIMP uses for animated files.

- **Combine** — This method is like having each frame on a sheet of transparent acetate. You see frames that have already appeared as well as the latest frame. This is valuable if you have an animation where you want to add on to previous frames, such as if you're animating a line being drawn. You can also mix this with the Replace behavior and do *limited* or *layered animation* where you have some static drawings that don't change mixed with the changing drawings that actually give the animated effect. Not only does this reduce your workload per frame, but it also reduces the overall file size of your finished animated file.

To stipulate whether you want a frame to use the Replace or Combine behaviors, use the same layer-name method used for adjusting timing per frame, but use either `replace` or `combine` in the parentheses. As an example, if you have a layer named `frame02` and you want to ensure that it uses the Combine method, you would change the name to `frame02 (combine)`. Furthermore, you can mix and match your controls. If you have a layer named `frame03` and you want it to be up for 200 milliseconds and use the Replace frame disposal method, you would change that layer's name to `frame03 (200ms) (replace)`. Figure 19-1 shows the Layers dialog for a simple bouncing ball animation.

FIGURE 19-1

Working from the bottom of the layer stack to the top, each layer is treated as a frame in your animation. By modifying the name of each layer, you can control its duration and frame disposal method.

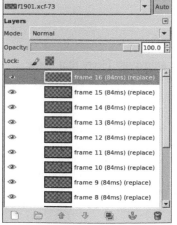
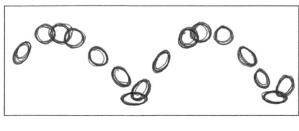

After you have your layer structure set up, it's time to generate your actual animation file. To initiate this process, go to File ➢ Export (Shift+Ctrl+E) and in the file chooser that appears, make sure you're saving the image with .gif as the image's file extension. When you click the Save button, GIMP presents you with one of two dialogs, shown in Figure 19-2.

FIGURE 19-2

When exporting an RGB image to be an animated GIF, you get the dialog on the left. Otherwise, you get the dialog on the right.

Recall that the GIF file format doesn't use the full RGB color spectrum. Instead, it uses an indexed color palette or a grayscale palette. If your image is in RGB mode, GIMP gives you the dialog on the left. If you've set the image mode to Indexed (Image ➢ Mode ➢ Indexed) or Grayscale (Image ➢ Mode ➢ Grayscale), you see the simpler dialog on the right. The difference between the two is that the left dialog asks whether you want to convert your image to be either indexed or grayscale. Though working in RGB gives you more flexibility with your color choices, converting your image to an indexed palette ahead of time allows you to fine-tune your colors with a bit more control. This is particularly valuable if you're trying to optimize your image's file size.

Tip

If you want to further optimize your animated file, you can use the Optimize animation filters that come with GIMP. You can access these filters from Filters ➢ Animation ➢ Optimize (Difference) and Filters ➢ Animation ➢ Optimize (for GIF). You can read up more on these filters in Chapter 17. ∎

The consistent thing between both dialogs in Figure 19-2 is the first set of radio buttons to determine what you want to do with your layers. You have two options: either flatten the image to a single layer and save that as your GIF image or use each layer as a frame of animation. Because this chapter is devoted to animation, you should probably choose the second option. Once you choose Save as Animation and click the Export button, GIMP provides you with a second dialog to give you final control over the behavior of your animation. Figure 19-3 shows this dialog.

FIGURE 19-3

When exporting an animated GIF, this dialog gives you final control over how your animation behaves.

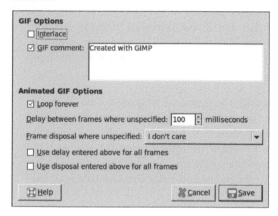

For animation, the controls you're interested in are on the lower half of the dialog. The following describes each of these five options:

- **Loop Forever** — When your animation reaches the last frame you can control whether it stops there or repeats, or *loops*, the full sequence. By default, this check box is enabled, causing your animation to loop.

- **Delay between Frames where Unspecified** — Whether or not you stipulate a duration for each frame as described earlier in this chapter, each frame *must* have a duration. This value is the duration used for all frames that you don't provide an explicit duration for.

- **Frame Disposal where Unspecified** — As with the previous option, this drop-down menu lets you control how frames are handled if you don't specify it in each layer name. The default value of I Don't Care works identically to the Replace behavior.

- **Use Delay Entered above for All Frames** — If you enable this check box, GIMP uses the duration stipulated in this dialog regardless of what you've used as the duration in the layer name of each frame.

- **Use Disposal Entered above for All Frames** — If you want all frames to be disposed of the same way, regardless of how you stipulate in the layer name, enable this check box.

And there you have it. Click the Save button at the bottom of this dialog and you have an animated GIF file that can be uploaded to a web site for the amusement of all people.

Tip

If you want to watch your animation play back before exporting to a GIF file, you can use GIMP's handy Playback filter, as covered in Chapter 17. To use it, go to Filters ➢ Animation ➢ Playback and use the VCR-style controls on the window that appears. ■

Images to Layers and Layers to Images

Despite the simplicity of working with one file, you quickly find that there are disadvantages to building animations this way. Working with layers is great — especially for very short animations — but for longer animations or more complex animations, using layers as frames can start becoming a management nightmare. Not only that, but if you have a lot of frames in your animation or you want to animate at higher image sizes like those used for television or film, you'll also start to notice your project file explode in size. What was a convenience for small and simple animations can easily become a liability.

To deal with those issues, there's a better way to manage the frames of your animation. It's better to use a lot of still images rather than pile your animation in to a single image with hundreds of layers. Not only do you get the benefit of smaller individual files, but you can also take advantage of GIMP's layering system to match its intended purpose. It's much easier this way to do animated line drawings on one layer and then animate the color for your drawings on another layer. Furthermore, your final output isn't limited to the paltry 256-color indexed palette of the GIF format.

Note
GAP uses the convention of referring to image sequences as frames and referring to layers as layers regardless of whether they're used as frames in an animation. This can be a bit confusing. To help a bit, in this chapter (and the next one), I refer to frames as the individual components of an animation, and I refer specifically to layers and image sequences by those names. ■

Splitting a Layer Image into an Image Sequence

Of course, without experience and planning, it's difficult to know ahead of time how long or complex an animation may end up being. You may start your animation using layers as frames as described earlier in this chapter and come to realize that the project is more involved than that technique can adequately handle. For this situation, it's valuable to have a convenience function that can convert your project from the layer-based method to the technique that uses an image sequence. Fortunately, such a beast does exist and it's provided when you install GAP. To access it, go to the image window of your project and select Video ➤ Split Image to Frames. You should get a dialog like the one in Figure 19-4.

As the dialog says, this features takes each layer and produces a separate image with the naming format of [basename]_[frame].[extension]. The dialog that guides this process gives a few options on the nature of each image that's produced. The following describes each option:

- **Extension** — This is the file format that you are using for each image in the sequence. The default is GIMP's native XCF format. You should be able to use any format here, but to take full advantage of GIMP's features, it's recommended to stick with XCF while working and then if you need to export the sequence to another format, you can do that as a batch process.

- **Inverse Order** — The default behavior of the layer-based animation method is to use the bottom layer as the first frame and work up the stack. However, if you produced your layers in the reverse order, you can enable this check box.

- **Flatten** — This check box is important only if your layers have any transparency. If they do and you want to retain their Alpha channels, leave this box unchecked. Otherwise, enable this check box and the alpha channel is removed from each of the image files this feature produces.

- **Only Visible** — Enable this check box to convert only visible layers to individual images in your sequence.

- **Copy Properties** — If the image you are working on has channels, paths, or guides, you can have those elements included in each image file that's created by this feature. Note that this is true only if the file format you choose in the Extension option actually supports these elements. This is another reason to stick with the XCF format while you work.

- **Digits** — This is the number of digits used to indicate the frame number that each image corresponds to. By default, the value is 6, so your frame number in the image name for the first frame would be 000001. If you set the value to 3, the frame number would be 001.

FIGURE 19-4

GIMP's Split Image to Frames dialog, provided by GAP

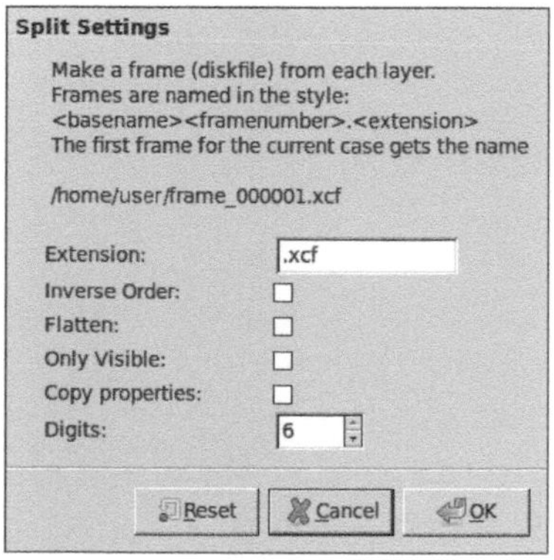

Note
If your image already has a number at the end of its name, this feature may not work for you. To get around that, duplicate the image (Ctrl+D or Image ➢ Duplicate) and run Split Image to Frames on your duplicated image. ∎

Tip
The Split Image to Frames feature dumps your image sequence in the same folder as the original image. This can mean having a lot of images in a single folder. If your original image is in a folder mixed with other projects, this can make file management difficult. For that reason, it's highly recommended that you create a separate folder to hold the individual images in your image sequence and copy your original layered image to that folder prior to calling Video ➢ Split Image to Frames on it. ∎

Converting an Image Sequence into a Single Layered Image

On the flipside, you may have a clip from a complex animation or a short sequence of video that you want to share on the Internet. However, it's hard to guarantee that everyone is capable of viewing in the video file format you choose. The animated GIF has been around for a long time and all major web browsers support it. So it's often useful to generate a quick animated GIF from a short image sequence. GAP has a convenience function to facilitate this need as well. To run it, open any image in your sequence and choose Video ➤ Frames to Image. This gives you a dialog like the one in Figure 19-5.

FIGURE 19-5

GAP's Frames to Image dialog controls how you convert a sequence of images into a single multi-layer image.

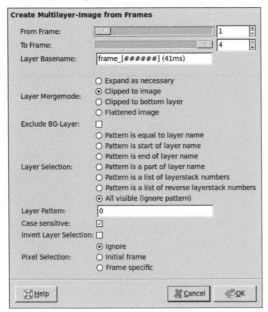

Compared to the Split Image into Frames dialog, this one is quite a bit more involved. However, despite its size, it's actually not too difficult to wrap your head around. The following list describes each option:

- **From Frame** — GAP is pretty smart about recognizing the names and numbers of images in your image sequence. This slider and the text field next to this label indicates where in your sequence you want to start converting images into layers. The default value is the first image in the sequence (typically 1).

- **To Frame** — This slider and text field control where GAP stops converting images into layers. The default value is the last image in the sequence.

- **Layer Basename** — Using the naming structure defined by your image sequence, GAP tries to use a similar structure for naming the layers in your single-image project. This is also where you can predefine how you want GIMP to treat the duration of each frame and the frame disposal method for each frame, as described earlier in this chapter. The default timing is 41 milliseconds per layer.

- **Layer Mergemode** — The images in your sequence of images may each have multiple layers. These radio buttons control how those layers are merged to create your single-image project. These options are the same ones you have if you choose Merge Visible Layers from the Layers dialog's context menu.

- **Exclude BG-Layer** — The layers in all the images of your image sequence may have the same bottom layer as a stack background image. You can exclude this image from being included in the merging process and just include the layers that are being animated if you enable this check box.

- **Layer Selection** — As the preceding option shows, when using an image sequence to produce an animation, not all layers in an individual image may contain the actual frames of your animation. They could be helper layers that include guides, backgrounds, or — as covered later in this chapter — onion skinning. When converting your image sequence into a single-image animation project, you need to isolate your animation layers from the helper layers. In a perfect world, you've worked in a way that all of your helper layers are hidden and your animation layers are visible. Then the default option of All Visible (Ignore Pattern) is all you need. However, that's not always the case. Fortunately, if you use a regular naming pattern to differentiate your animation layers from your helper layers, you can leverage that here. The pattern, which you type in the next text entry field, labeled Layer Pattern, can be handled in the following ways:

  - **Equal to Layer Name** — If in every image you have only one layer that's for animation and that layer has a consistent name like Frame or Drawing, choose this radio button and enter that name as the Layer Pattern.

  - **Start/End of Layer Name** — Often you have multiple layers in each image that are used for animation. If you use a prefix or suffix like anim- or -animated on each layer that's used for the final animation, you can use one of these options to select those layers when converting to a single-image project.

  - **A Part of Layer Name** — In another scenario where you have multiple frames in each image of your sequence, you could be using each layer to animate part of a single character or object. This happens frequently in limited animation where part of the character is static and you only animate the mouth and eyes. In these situations, you may have layer names that include your character's name as your pattern. So if you have layers with names like left_Fred_arm, right_Fred_arm, and Fred_mouth, you can use this radio button and type Fred as your pattern in the Layer Pattern field.

  - **A List of Layerstack (or A List of Reverse Layerstack Numbers)** — Another way to organize layers in each image of an animated sequence is to stipulate that the layers at the top (or bottom) of the stack are your animation layers while the other layers are just helpers. So, for example, if you know that the top three layers on the stack in each image is where your animation lies, you can enter 0-2 as your Layer Pattern. The Reverse Layerstack option is if you've stipulated that your bottom layers are the animation layers.

- **All Visible (Ignore Pattern)** — If you know that in each image the only layers used for animation are the ones that are currently visible, you can skip the pattern process altogether and just choose this radio button.

- **Layer Pattern** — Type in this text entry field the pattern you want to use for selecting your animation layers in each image of your sequence. If you're using the All Visible (Ignore Pattern) option, the content of this field is disregarded.

- **Case Sensitive** — If you don't want GAP to pay attention to whether you've used uppercase or lowercase letters in your Layer Pattern, disable this check box.

- **Invert Layer Selection** — If you actually want to use the opposite layers — layers *not* stipulated by your Layer Pattern — enable this check box. This is useful if, for example, you know that all of your helper layers have a consistent pattern (like a prefix of onionskin-) and your animation layers don't. Then you can use the Layer Pattern to choose those layers. With this check box, you invert that selection and import the actual animation layers.

- **Pixel Selection** — When using GAP, one of the interesting features is its ability to remember what pixels you have selected in each image of a sequence. These radio buttons allow you to ignore or use those selections. You have three options:

  - **Ignore** — This ignores your selections altogether and includes the full combined layers of each image in your sequence.

  - **Initial Frame** — Choose this option, and the region selected in the first image of your sequence is used in each of the images in your sequence when converting to a single-image project. This is helpful if you want to mask off a portion of your animation.

  - **Frame Specific** — This is similar to the preceding option except it utilizes the selection (if any) in each image of your sequence. This is great if you want to have an animated mask separating part of your animation from the rest.

Managing the Frames of Your Image Sequence with GAP

When working on a complex animation, using an image sequence is undeniably the more powerful and flexible method compared to a single-image layer-based method. However, one of the advantages of using layers is that you have the Layers dialog right there to act as a rudimentary timeline. Using the features of that dialog you can easily delete, add, duplicate, and move layers, which in this case are frames, in an understandable and visual way. When working with an image sequence, you can't use the Layers dialog this way. Fortunately, some features provided by GAP help mitigate this problem.

The Easy Way: GAP's Video Navigator

GAP provides some quick navigation controls in the Video ➤ Go To submenu. You have a handful of choices that allow you to move from one frame to another in your sequence. The Any Frame menu item randomly opens an image from you to work on, whereas the First Frame, Last

Frame, Next Frame, and Previous Frame items give you more regular control. This menu is great for moving through your animation sequentially or for skipping to the start or end of it. However, if you have a long sequence of images, this can be a very tedious way to navigate through your animation. Fortunately, GAP includes a Video Navigator to alleviate this very issue. Bring up the navigator dialog by going to Video ➤ VCR Navigator and you get a dialog like the one shown on the right of Figure 19-6.

FIGURE 19-6

To navigate the frames of your animation, you can use the controls in Video ➤ Go To (left), but it's much easier to use GAP's integrated Video Navigator (right).

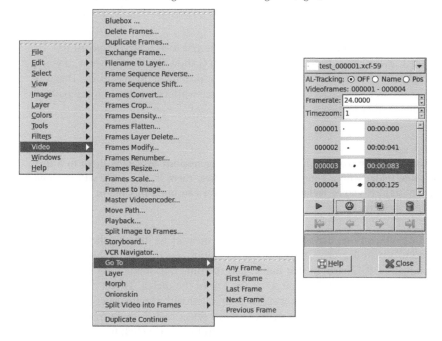

With GAP's Video Navigator, you not only have the ability to see the frames of your animation in a global overview like you would if you were doing a single-image animation project, but you also get some very valuable controls. Starting at the top of the navigator is a set of radio buttons next to the label AL-Tracking, which is short for *Active Layer Tracking*. What this does is attempt to keep you working in the same layer as you navigate from image to image in your animation. That way you don't have to switch layers each time you change images. By default this feature is turned off, but you can turn it on by selecting one of the two ways it identifies your current active layer:

- **Name** — Use this radio button and when you switch images, GAP compares the name of the active layer in your original image to the names of each of the layers in your destination. The closest match is set as your active layer.

- **Pos** — Use the Pos (Position) option if you don't care about layer names (although you really should) and you just want to use layer position to determine which layer is active. So if you're working in the third layer from the bottom in your origin image, GAP activates the third layer from the bottom in your destination image when you switch to it.

Beneath the AL-Tracking controls is a simple information area labeled Videoframes that tells you the start and end frames of your image sequence. The text fields below that control the play-back speed of your animation and how the frames of your animation are displayed in the Video Navigator:

- **Framerate** — This controls the playback frame rate of your animation. By default it's set to 24 frames per second: the standard used in film. Increase this value and your animation plays back faster. Reduce it and each frame is on-screen longer, making the animation play more slowly.

- **Timezoom** — In other programs, this is sometimes referred to as a Step value. At its default value of 1, every single frame of your animation is shown in the navigator. If you increase this value, GAP skips that number of frames for display in the navigator. This way you can get a good overview of a long animated sequence without loading a thumbnail for every single frame in that sequence.

Tip

GAP actually retains the Framerate and Timezoom values between editing sessions by saving them to a text file on your hard drive. In the same folder where your image sequence lies, there is also a file with a name structured like [basename]_vin.gap. If you're feeling adventurous, you can open this file in your text editor and modify the values there directly. ■

The list of frames at the center of this dialog is where the real meat of its functionality lies. Most obviously, it allows you to see an overview of your entire animation. Each frame is shown with its frame number, a thumbnail of the image in that frame, and the time that frame is shown in your animation, according to the Framerate value you set at the top of the dialog. If you double-click any one of the frames in this list, GIMP's image window is updated with the image corresponding with that frame so you can edit it. The list also enables you to select one or more frames. If you just click a frame, that selects it without updating the image window. Ctrl+click frames in the list to select frames in an arbitrary order. If you want to select a range of frames, click the first frame and Shift+click the last frame in the range. All of the frames in between are selected.

With frames selected, you may be tempted to try and drag them around to re-order them as you would in the Layers or Channels dialogs. Unfortunately, this is not yet a feature of the Video Navigator window. However, that's not to say it isn't possible. If you right-click in the frame list area, you get a context window that allows you to perform some functions on your selected frames:

- **Copy** — GAP maintains a video buffer on your hard drive so you can copy and paste frames as you need them. By right-clicking your selected frames and choosing Copy, those frames are placed in the buffer for you to reuse elsewhere in your project.

- **Cut** — As expected, this performs the same behavior as Copy, except it also removes the copied frames from the list. This is useful if you want to move a frame to a different location.

- **Paste Before/After/Replace** — Once you have one or more frames copied to the video buffer, you can paste them back to the sequence. Paste Before and Paste After are relative to the first selected frame, regardless of how many frames you have selected. If you choose Paste Replace, all of the selected frames are replaced with the frames in the video buffer.

- **Clear Video Buffer** — If you are done with your copied selection or you just need to save some hard drive space, you can clear the video buffer by selecting this menu item.

- **Select All/None** — These functions select all or none of the frames in the list, respectively.

Below the frames list are two rows of buttons. The buttons on the bottom row correspond to the same functionality as the last four items in the Go To submenu (First, Previous, Next, Last), giving you control over where you're working in your animation. The top set of buttons is a bit more specialized. The following list describes the function of each one:

- **Playback** — Click this button to bring up the Videoframe Playback window. This feature is described in more detail in Chapter 20, but it allows you interactive control over animation playback. Alternatively, you can Shift+click this button and the selected frames are converted into a single-image animation project with layers as frames, and then automatically the Filters ➢ Animation ➢ Playback window comes up so you can preview your animation as if it were an animated GIF.

- **Smart Update Thumbnails** — Click this button to update thumbnails from frames whose images have changed. Shift+click this button and GAP updates the thumbnails for all frames in your animation.

- **Duplicate Selected Frames** — Treat this as a shortcut for the Video ➢ Duplicate Frames function described later in this chapter. Basically, it immediately copies and pastes the selected frames in your animation without the interim step of loading them to the video buffer.

- **Delete Selected Frames** — As advertised, click this button, and your selected frames are removed from the image sequence.

Warning

Because you're working with multiple images, GAP has no good way of maintaining a proper undo history for functions like deleting, pasting, and duplicating frames. This means that you need to be extra careful around these features. If you delete a frame, then POOF, it's gone. Save frequently, save multiple copies, and keep good backups. ■

Additional Frame Management Functions in the Video Menu

In most situations, using GAP's Video Navigator is the quickest and easiest way to manage the frames in your animated image sequence. That said, there are a few situations that the navigator isn't ideal for handling. These are typically large sweeping changes or functions that you want to apply to each frame. For these functions, there's a veritable smörgåsbord of them in the Video menu that GAP adds to the image window. The following list gives you a quick run-down of the items in this menu:

- **Bluebox** — Bluebox is a feature that provides a *chroma key* feature for GAP. This allows you to define a single color in each image as being transparent. The typical usage for this is in compositing for combining special effects with live footage. A character is shot in front of a wall or cloth backing with a specific color (typically blue in film or green in digital footage). If you can pick that exact color, you can separate the character and place her in a virtual world. See the "Using the Bluebox Feature" sidebar later in this chapter for more information on the controls in the Bluebox dialog.

- **Delete Frames** — You can delete frames from the Video Navigator, but if you want to delete a large set of them, the dialog that this menu item brings up gives you that ability. It allows you to choose a number of frames after your current image to permanently delete.

- **Duplicate Frames** — The dialog that this menu item pops up enables you to choose a range of frames to duplicate and place after your current frame. The advantage this feature has over the Copy/Cut/Paste features of the Video Navigator is that it allows you to stipulate how many times you'd like to duplicate that chosen range of frames.

- **Exchange Frames** — This convenient feature gives you a quick way swap your current frame with another frame in the animation.

- **Filename to Layer** — When generating previews of your animations, it's often useful to generate a *burn-in* or *timestamp* that's superimposed over your animation. This way if you're showing the preview to someone, they can tell you specifically which frames they're critiquing. The dialog that this menu item produces allows you to choose how much of the filename is used, what font to use, and where in the frame the filename should be rendered.

- **Frame Sequence Reverse** — On some occasions you need to reverse the order of some or all of the frames in your animation. This feature allows you to choose a range of frames and have their order reversed. This is sometimes helpful if you're looping an animation.

- **Frame Sequence Shift** — If you need to make room in your sequence for additional frames or — more commonly — you need to sync the frame numbers of one animated sequence with those of another, you can use this feature to adjust the numbering on your image sequence in either the positive or negative direction.

- **Frames Convert** — When working by yourself, it's definitely best to work in GIMP's native XCF file format. However, if you're working in an environment with other teams, those teams may need you to deliver your image sequence in another file format. This feature enables you to choose a range of your animation and convert those files to another format, like PNG or JPEG.

- **Frames Crop** — The problem with using the Crop tool (Shift+C) or Canvas Size (Image ➢ Canvas Size) feature on an individual image in your sequence is that the cropping isn't extended to the other images. This feature bridges that gap, allowing you to crop all of the images in your animation en masse.

- **Frames Density** — Occasionally you may find that you've miscalculated how many frames are necessary to animate a specific action and therefore you need to increase or decrease the number of frames for some or all of your animation. This feature lets you pick a range of frames and stipulate a multiplication (for increasing density) or division (for decreasing density) factor for adjusting the number of frames in that range.

- **Frames Flatten** — You can use the Layers dialog to flatten an individual image in your sequence, but that can be tedious if you have to do that for more than one image in your animation. This feature gives you a convenient way to flatten a range of frames or all frames in your animation.

- **Frames Layer Delete** — Like the Frames Flatten function, this feature gives you a quick way to modify the layer structure of each image in the sequence. The dialog that appears allows you to choose a range of frames and which layer in each image you want to delete. You choose that layer by its position in the stack.

- **Frames Modify** — The Frames Layer Delete is a quick feature, but it doesn't give you very much control. If you want to delete layers based on a pattern in their name, that function can't do it. Furthermore, there's no way to adjust other attributes of arbitrary layers. The Frames Modify feature is the tool that meets that need. In the dialog that appears, you can choose a function or layer attribute to change and then stipulate which layers to perform that function on, based on a pattern in the layers' names. This feature can be applied to all images in the sequence or just the ones within a specific range.

Tip

The Frames Modify feature enables you to run any arbitrary filter on layers in every image of your animated sequence. To do this, use the Apply Filters on Layers(s) function in the Frames Modify dialog. This causes GIMP to pop up a filter selection dialog when you click the OK button. From this dialog, you can choose any filter. Among those filters are a few additions included with GAP — in particular, the items available in the Video ➤ Layer submenu. This also explains why the items in that submenu seem to work only on the current frame's image. Use those functions only within the bounds of the Frames Modify feature. ■

- **Frames Renumber** — As you're adding frames to your animation, you may find that you've got more frames than you have digits. For instance, if your naming structure uses two digits for each frame number (01, 02, 03, and so on), you may run into problems if you create more than 99 frames. This feature gives you a convenient way to tweak the numbering in your frames and increase the number of digits used to express what frame you're on.

- **Frames Resize** — This feature extends the Image ➤ Canvas Size feature to all of the frames in your animation. Unlike the Frames Crop feature, it does not modify the size of individual layers in each image.

- **Frames Scale** — This feature extends the Image ➤ Scale Image feature to all frames in your animation. This way you can increase or decrease the size of each image at once. Just remember that there's no undo for this function.

- **Duplicate Continue** — When you're animating, this menu at the bottom of the Video menu is the fastest way to add new frames. It takes your current frame, duplicates it, and sets it as the current image in your sequence.

This list covers the bulk of frame management features that GAP provides you. The remainder of items in the Video menu are discussed later in this chapter or in Chapter 20.

Using the Bluebox Feature

One of the really desirable features of GAP is Bluebox, which you can access by going to Video ➢ Bluebox on an RGB image (Bluebox does not work on indexed or grayscale images). As described elsewhere in this chapter, this feature enables you to do simple chroma keying for compositing live action footage. Getting a good chroma key result is not an exact science. It's a combined consequence of good lighting when shooting, an artistic eye, and a clear understanding of the controls provided by a feature like Bluebox. The following is a brief description of each of the controls in the Bluebox dialog:

- **Keycolor** — Click this large color swatch to pick the color in your footage that you would like to be transparent. Typically this is a fully saturated blue for film or a fully saturated green for digital footage.

- **Threshold sliders** — When working with footage that needs to be composited with keyed color, it's understood that even in the best of circumstances, it's unlikely that the color background is shot as a perfectly even color. This means that you need to use threshold controls to account for tones near to your chosen Keycolor value. Depending on what you choose for the Threshold Mode (described next), these sliders give you that control for each channel you have available.

- **Threshold Mode** — You have four choices for this setting. While each mode works on the RGB color gamut, they all give you different levels of control when relating to the Keycolor value. Although the RGB radio button is the first one listed, HSV is typically the more useful mode because it's easier to compensate for uneven lighting by adjusting Saturation and Value thresholds while keeping Hue largely unchanged. The Value mode is useful if you're keying on the luminosity of the image rather than a specific color. This is often referred to as luma keying. If you want absolute control, you can use the All mode and have access to threshold sliders for RGB and HSV values.

- **Alpha Tolerance** — The primary purpose for this slider is to help account for aliasing artifacts where your key color meets the threshold values you set. A value of zero for Alpha Tolerance uses hard pixel selection whereas higher values increase how many pixels get selected.

- **Source Alpha** — This slider is useful only if your image is already using an alpha channel. If a pixel in your image has an alpha value less than the one stipulated by this slider, then Bluebox ignores it altogether.

- **Target Alpha** — The Target Alpha slider dictates the alpha value you want to assign to pixels that match your chosen key color. Typically you want this to be at zero, or full transparency.

- **Feather Edges** — If you have to increase the Alpha Tolerance slider, you may inadvertently pick up some pixels with your key color. You can smooth the results and hide these unwanted pixels by feathering. Enable this check box to take advantage of this.

- **Feather Radius** — If you enable the Feather Edges check box, then you can use this slider to control the influence of the feathering effect. The value in this slider is in units of pixels.

- **Shrink/Grow** — This slider behaves like the Shrink and Grow features accessible from the Select menu in the image window. Negative values shrink the transparent area dictated by your key color whereas positive values grow that area.

- **Automatic Preview** — Enable this check box and Bluebox generates an image window with a preview of the resulting image. With this check box enabled, the preview image is updated any time you adjust a setting in the Bluebox dialog. If you do not have this check box enabled, you need to click the Preview button to the right in order to generate a preview image.

- **Previewsize** — To reduce processing time, you can adjust the size of the preview image that Bluebox generates. This slider, using percentage units, gives you that control.

And there you have it. Once you choose your desired key color and get the threshold settings and other controls adjusted to give you the best keyed image, click OK. Bluebox then performs the keying operation on your image. To use Bluebox on a full sequence of images, use the Video ➤ Frames Modify feature and choose Apply Filter on Layer(s) as your function. Then you can pick `plug-in-bluebox` from the filter selection dialog that appears next.

Convenience Features to Improve Workflow

Up to this point, the features covered in this chapter are geared toward the assumption that you're producing animation using a more traditional workflow that requires animators to not only draw key frames, but also all of the in-between frames. Of course, we live in the future and you're working on these extremely powerful calculators that some people call computers; surely there's a way to leverage the power of these machines to do some of the work for you. As a matter of fact, there is. GAP includes some features that automate some parts of the animation process. In particular, creating in-between frames can be a time-consuming and tedious process that it would be nice to automate.

Tip

Although the features covered in this section are helpful, I wouldn't recommend leaning on them too heavily for generating in-between frames. No matter how helpful these automating features are, computer-generated in-betweens are still typically stiff and robotic-looking. The best option would be to use these features as starting points and then go in afterwards to add life to the computer-generated motion. ■

Working with the Move Path Feature

One of the coolest features of GAP is Move Path. This feature allows you use a path to control the motion from one frame to the next. Need to animate a logo moving across the screen? Have a character with a static walk cycle that you want to move from one side of the frame to another?

These processes can be automated with Move Path. Call up Move Path by going to Video ➤ Move Path in the image window. Upon doing so, you get the dialog that's shown in Figure 19-7.

FIGURE 19-7

Using Move Path to add a moving platform to the bouncing ball example used earlier in this chapter

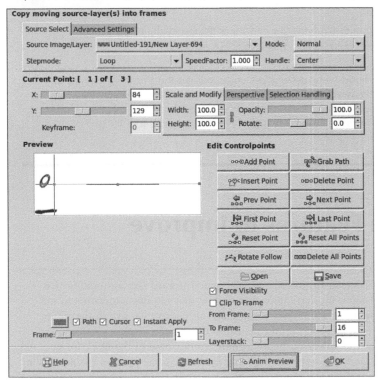

Tip

To use the Move Path feature, you must already have a sequence of images for it to work with. If you don't already have an image sequence, the quickest way to generate one is to create a new blank image and use the Frames Duplicate (Video ➤ Frames Duplicate) feature for the number of frames you want your animation to use. ■

As an example, imagine you're taking the bouncing ball example from earlier in this chapter (as a sequence rather than a single image with layers) and using the Move Path feature to add a sliding platform for the bouncing ball to bounce off of. To do this, you need to have two images open. First you need any image from your animated sequence. This is the destination in which Move Path will create layers. The second image you need is an image for the platform. For the purposes of the Move Path feature, this image is considered the source image or layer. That image could be a member of its own sequence of images or a layered image where each layer is a frame of animation. With both images open, go to the image window for your destination image and choose Video ➤ Move Path.

In the Source Select tab at the top of the dialog, you can choose which open image and layer to use as the source for Move Path. The other options in this tab control how this source layer is blended with your existing animated frames and the Stepmode setting to use if you're using a multi-layer animated source image. The Handle drop-down menu controls the location of the control point in the source layer. That handle can be at any corner of the image or at the center. Typically using Center gives you the most expected controls, particularly for rotation. It generally looks more natural for a layer to rotate about its center rather than an extreme corner. However, if you want a more orbit-like rotation, then using one of the corners may work better for you. In the Advanced Settings tabs, you have some additional controls for the nature of the in-betweens, or *tweens*, that Move Path creates, including the ability to use Bluebox on those frames.

Back on the Source Select tab, let's temporarily skip over the next sliders and tabs down to the preview image that takes up the largest portion of the Move Path dialog, this is where the fundamental motion controls for your source live. If you click in the preview image, it creates the first control point in your motion path, marked with a set of crosshairs. That control point corresponds with the current frame that you're in, indicated by the Frame slider at the bottom of the dialog. You can add, modify, and delete points using the array of buttons to the right of the preview. The last two buttons in this array allow you to import a previously saved motion path or save your current path to your hard drive for future use.

Above the Frame slider is a set of check boxes that control the visibility of the path, its color, and the crosshairs. There's also a check box labeled Instant Apply. Enable this to cause the preview image to update each time you change the Frame slider. If you don't have this check box enabled, you need to click the Refresh button at the bottom of the dialog each time you change the Frame settings.

Above the Preview image are a set of tabs with sliders and options for adjusting the location of individual points on the motion path as well as the state of your source at each of those points. You can control the opacity, rotation, scale, and perspective values of the source. This gives you a lot of control over how your source moves along the motion path. And if you have any pixels selected in your source layer (or layers, if animated), you can use the Selection Handling tab to control if and how those selected pixels are used by the Move Path feature.

The workflow for using Move Path consists of first creating your motion path and then going back to adjust the state of your source at each control point. Once you do this, use the sliders at the bottom right of the dialog to define the range of frames to apply the Move Path feature. By adjusting the Layerstack slider, you can control where in the stack Move Path places the layers it generates. By default, this is set to zero, meaning the top of the stack.

One last helpful feature of Move Path is the Anim Preview button at the bottom of the dialog. This allows you to see what Move Path is going to produce without making any irreversible changes to your image sequence. When you click this button, you get a dialog like the one in Figure 19-8.

FIGURE 19-8

Move Path's Anim Preview Options dialog

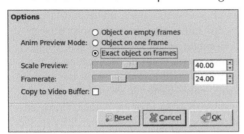

The Anim Preview button generates a layered animated image and automatically opens the Filters ➤ Animation ➤ Playback window so you can preview its motion. The dialog allows you to scale down the preview and explicitly specify the frame rate that you want the preview to play at. Of the Anim Preview Mode radio buttons, the Exact Object on Frames option gives you the most accurate results at the potential expense of real-time performance. To see the results of this filter, check out its files on this book's companion web site (www.wiley.com/go/GIMPBible.com).

Morphing

Move Path is a handy tool for moving, rotating, and animating objects. The disadvantage of this tool, though, is that it moves around a static image. While it gives you some flexibility with rotation, perspective, and scale, more often than not transitions from one frame to another appear a bit stiff and robotic. There's not a lot of room to deform your image dramatically from one frame to another. This is where morphing can be a huge benefit to animators.

Warning

The Morph feature in GAP is still a bit experimental, so the interface for it may change in the near future. That said, the principles behind the way it works should be pretty consistent and future interfaces should be similar. ∎

In the 1990s morphing technology took off and was used extensively in music videos and television commercials. If you were alive then, you might remember these videos where one person's face would transform into another person's. GAP's Morph is certainly capable of this, but there are more benefits for someone pursuing traditional animation. Morphing works by taking a pair of images and marking corresponding points on each image. In the face example, corresponding markers might be the eyes or the corners of the mouth on two faces. The morph algorithm then produces the necessary in-between frames to transition from one image to the next.

As a traditional animator, the benefit of this is the ability to draw key frames and mark the similar points on each key frame. Then you can use the Morph feature to generate your in-between frames for you. Granted, these in-betweens may not be perfect. Although the Morph tool is great at deforming pixels from one key frame to the next, the motion is largely linear. That means you may have to go in afterwards and do some clean-up on each frame. However, it's a great way to generate a set of rough in-betweens that you can use as a starting point. Alternatively, if you've animated on 2's or 3's, then you can use the Morph feature to smooth the animation out and give the impression that you've animated on 1's.

Note

Animating on 1's (or 2's or 3's) is traditional animation terminology meaning that if your frame rate is 24 frames per second, you have one drawing for each frame. By extension, animating on 2's means that you only make a drawing every other frame, essentially halving your frame rate. ■

The Morph feature works between any two layers you have open in GIMP. The only real requirement is that those layers have an alpha channel. For simplicity, it's typically best to use two layers within the same image. To use the Morph feature, open your images and go to Video ➤ Morph ➤ Morph. This brings up a dialog like the one in Figure 19-9.

GAP's Morph feature allows you to create smooth transitions from one image to another.

Using the Morph dialog, you choose the Source and Destination layers from their corresponding dialogs. With the images loaded, you can proceed to place and edit points on each image.

Below the image windows is a series of radio buttons that define your Edit Mode. You have the following options:

- **Set** — From this edit mode, if you click one of the images, the Morph feature tries to guess where the corresponding point on the other image is located. By default most points are green and the active point in each image is yellow. You can customize these colors with the color swatches at the bottom of the dialog. You can try to move around points from this mode, but it requires very accurate clicking. For moving, a better option would be to switch your Edit Mode to Move.

- **Move** — Using this mode you can click near any point you've set in either image and move it to a new location. Clicking a point changes it to the active point color (yellow by default).

- **Delete** — In this mode, you can delete points from your image. Be aware, though, that you're not necessarily deleting points that you click near. To be absolutely sure which point you're deleting, use the Point text entry field at the top right of the Destination image. The Point field is helpful, too, because it also shows how many points you're using.

- **Zoom** — With this Edit Mode active, clicking either the Source or Destination image zooms in on that location.

- **Show** — Think of this mode more as a test mode than anything else. With the Show mode active, clicking in one image places a red dot on the other image where the Morph feature guesses the corresponding pixel is. This mode is influenced by the Quality check box on the lower right of the dialog. Enabling the Quality check box makes picking points slower, but more accurate.

Along the lower-left side of the Morph dialog are three numeric entry fields that are invaluable in controlling the behavior of the morph effect. The best, most controlled way to add points to your image is to do it manually. However, if you're working with images that have defined silhouettes, the Morph tool can actually attempt to place points for you around the outline of that shape. The ShapePoints value controls how many points GAP uses when making this guess. Click the Shape button to automatically place those points. Shift+clicking the Shape button adds more points to your image instead of replacing the ones in place.

Below the ShapePoints numeric entry field is a field labeled Radius. Each control point controls a set of pixels with a radius around it. That radius, measured in pixels, is controlled from this numeric field. The default value of 100 is pretty good on smaller images or if you have a pretty dense set of control points. However, for larger images or sparse control points, you may need to increase the Radius value. Beneath the Radius value is a numeric field labeled Steps. This is the number of frames that you want the Morph tool to use to animate the transition from one image to the next.

The next most influential options in the Morph tool's dialog are the Render Mode radio buttons. These buttons control how the Morph tool calculates and creates the transition between images. By default, the Morph option is enabled and it produces the best results because it not only shifts pixels based on your control points, but it also crossfades and mixes those pixels to produce smooth results. If you instead use the Warp option, GAP does only the pixel shifting operation and doesn't smooth it out for you. This is great for debugging, but its results are typically less than desirable.

After your points are placed and your settings configured, it's definitely a good idea to use the Save button on the right of the dialog to save your settings for reuse later. This is especially helpful if the Morph operation doesn't go as nicely as you want and you need to go back in and tweak your points and settings. If you re-open the Morph feature, all points and settings are gone. You need to use the Open button to reload your settings.

Figure 19-10 shows results of using the Morph feature. The top part of the figure shows the transitioning of one face to another and the bottom shows using the Morph feature to smooth out the in-betweens in the earlier bouncing ball example.

FIGURE 19-10

At the top, morphing from one ape to another; at the bottom, the results of using the morph tool to generate smooth in-between frames in animation

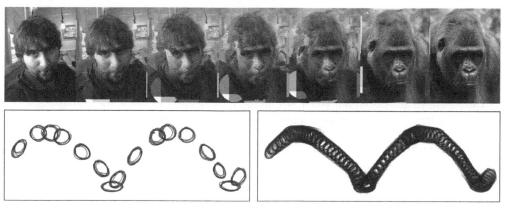

Onionskinning

In traditional hand-drawn animation with pencil and paper (yes, people do actually still work this way; and a lot of them are very talented), animation is done on a light table. The drawings for previous frames are stacked beneath the paper used to draw the current frame. With the light table and sufficiently thin paper, the previous drawings shine through so the animator can know where he's coming from to draw the next frame. This process is sometimes referred to as *onion skinning* and it's incredibly useful for creating good motion. GAP re-creates this feature by taking advantage of GIMP's layer system. It can sometimes take a little time to set up, but once in place, it's an invaluable aid for drawing the frames of your animation. All of the controls for GAP's onion skinning features are in the Video ➤ Onionskin submenu. To set up onion skinning for your animation project, click Video ➤ Onionskin ➤ Configuration. This gets you a dialog like the one in Figure 19-11.

FIGURE 19-11

GAP's Onionskin Configuration dialog gives you controls for setting up onionskin layers in each image of your animation project.

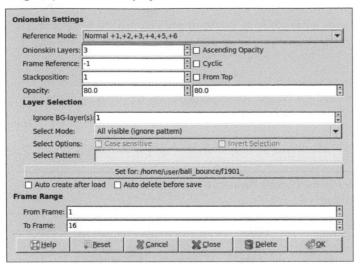

The default values in the Onionskin Configuration dialog generally give you results that work well for hand-drawn animation, but you're free to use these settings to tweak the onionskins more to your liking. The following list is a quick run-down of the settings in this dialog:

- **Reference Mode** — The options available from this drop-down menu control which frames GAP uses to create onionskins. You have the following three options:
  - **Normal** — This option creates onionskin layers based solely on frames coming from a single direction. Your onionskin layers are only from previous or next frames, depending on what you enter for the Frame Reference setting. It most closely matches the process used in traditional animation. The $+1, +2, +3, +4, +5, +6$ sequence refers to the initial reference offset. The value in the Frame Reference field is multiplied by the values in this sequence to determine which frames are copied as onionskin layers.
  - **Bidirectional (Single)** — Rather than pulling frames from only previous or only next frames, this option pulls frames from both sides of your current frame. This option is a bit unique, though. Rather than pulling frames symmetrically (one frame forward and one frame back), this option pulls frames that are progressively farther from your current frame. This is what the strange $+1, -2, +3, -4, +5, -6$ sequence means.
  - **Bidirectional (Double)** — This option is similar to Bidirectional (Single), but rather than progressively pulling frames, it pulls frames symmetrically using the pattern $+1, -1, +2, -2, +3, -3$.
- **Onionskin Layers** — This numeric field controls how many layers get created for onionskins in each image file of your sequence. Note that this is the total number of created layers, so if you choose one of the Bidirectional reference modes and have the default value

of two onionskin layers, GAP creates only one onionskin layer on either side of your current frame.

- **Frame Reference** — This number gets multiplied by the values in the reference sequence. This is useful if you have tight motion with frames that don't differ from one another by too much. You can change this value to increase the number of frames between each onionskin layer. Note that if you're using the Normal reference mode and you want to see previous frames, this value must be negative.

- **Stackposition** — This numeric value controls where onionskin layers start being placed in the layer stack. A value of zero puts onionskins on the bottom of the stack. The default value places onionskin layers one level above the bottom layer. If you want to enter numbers that relate to the top of the stack, enable the From Top check box to the right of this field.

- **Opacity** — There are actually two numeric entry fields for this setting. The first value is the opacity of the first onionskin layer. The second value is the opacity of subsequent onionskin layers relative to their prior onionskin layer. That is, using the default values of 80 in both fields, the first onionskin layer is at 80 percent opacity and the second onionskin layer is 80 percent of that opacity, or 64 percent. A third onionskin layer would be 80 percent of the second onionskin's opacity, or roughly 51 percent.

- **Ascending Opacity** — On a few rare occasions, it's useful to have onionskins that are farther from your current frame to be more opaque than onionskins nearer to the current frame. Enable this check box if you need this feature.

- **Cyclic** — If your animation is a cycle where the first and last frames are the same, you can enable this check box and onionskins can wrap from the first and last frames of your animation.

- **Layer Selection** — Like many of the functions provided by GAP, you can define which layers are used to create onionskin layers. Unlike the interface of the Frames Modify feature, this dialog uses a drop-down menu rather than radio buttons. Hopefully in the future the other dialogs are changed to match this one. The Select Mode/Options/Pattern options should be familiar to you, but the Ignore BG-Layers feature is a bit unique. Basically, this field is used to tell GAP how many layers from the bottom of the layer stack to disregard when creating onionskins. By default, it has a value of 1, meaning that the bottom-most layer is ignored. If you change this value to zero, no background layers are ignored.

- **Set For** — Click this large button and GAP edits or creates a _vin.gap text file in the same folder as your image sequence, storing your onionskin values for future use.

- **Auto Create after Load** — Enable this check box and each time you change frames using GAP's Video Navigator, the onionskin layers for the image you're moving to are automatically updated.

- **Auto Delete before Save** — Enable this check box and each time you change frames using GAP's Video Navigator, the onionskin layers for the layer you're leaving are deleted. Use this feature along with the Auto Create on Load check box and you have a double benefit: thumbnails that don't display onionskin layers, and small individual file sizes. Your onionskins are generated on the fly each time you change frames with the Video Navigator.

- **Frame Range** — With these values you can control which frames in your image sequence get onionskin layers.

After you configure your onionskin settings to your liking, click OK and GAP generates onionskin layers for the relevant layers of your animation project. Looking at the Layers dialog, you can see that each onionskin layer's name is prefixed with onionskin_ followed by the number of the frame it's representing. Figure 19-12 shows a frame and the Layers dialog for the bouncing ball example with visible onionskin layers.

FIGURE 19-12

On the left is the Layers dialog for a frame of animation with onionskin layers. On the right is that specific frame.

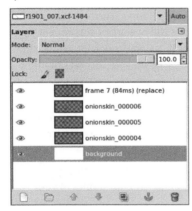
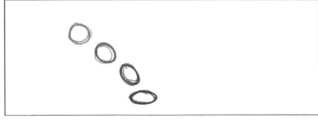

After you configure your onionskin layers, GAP provides you with a few additional options for managing those onionskins once they're created. They're all in the Onionskin submenu, found in Video ➤ Onionskin. Three options are available to you here:

- **Create or Replace** — If you've configured your onionskins without Auto Create after Load, then as you change frames in your animation, it doesn't automatically update your onionskin layers. Click this option to generate or update them for you.

- **Delete** — As advertised, clicking this menu item removes onionskin layers from your current frame's image.

- **Toggle Visibility** — Showing or hiding all of the onionskin layers in your image can be tedious if you do it manually. Use this option to show or hide them all at once.

Creating a Storyboard

One of the unique features of GAP is the ability to generate what it refers to as a storyboard. In animation and film production, storyboards are commonly used to plan the production. In that context storyboards are typically drawings organized in a sequence to describe the action happening on-screen. They're almost like a comic book version of the film. The idea here is that it's easier and cheaper to make changes in the planning stages with storyboards than to spend lots of time and money reshooting or redrawing footage that's already been produced. In GAP, the storyboard concept is extended a little bit because it includes more than just a series of static drawings. The storyboard in GAP is more akin to an *animatic*, or storyboard set to time. Animatics are used extensively in animation production because it's much easier to judge timing with them than by imagining the timing while staring at static storyboard drawings on a wall. GAP storyboards are defined by a text file, which stipulates various clips that get included in the storyboard and the sequence in which those clips appear. A clip can be virtually any form of media, including still images, image sequences, video footage, and audio files.

If you're feeling really spry, you can hand-generate a storyboard file in any text editor using the format specifications that come with GAP's documentation. However, for artists, it's much nicer to have a visual means of generating the storyboard file. Fortunately GAP includes just such a utility. Call it up by going to Video ➤ Storyboard and you get the GAP Storyboard Editor. It consists of a window like the one shown in Figure 19-13.

FIGURE 19-13

GAP's Storyboard Editor is similar to a very basic non-linear video editing suite.

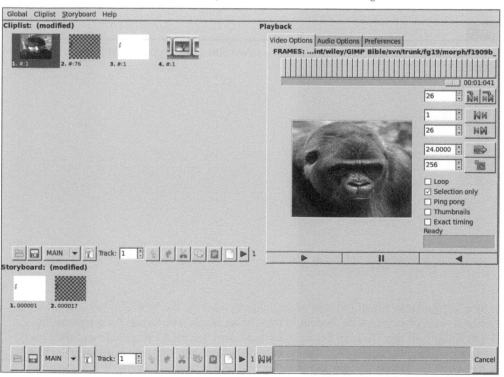

Warning

The Storyboard Editor is a powerful feature of GAP, but it's not perfect. For some media formats it can be pretty unstable and crash-prone. Crashes in the Storyboard Editor don't often bring down GIMP with it, but there is the possibility that this may happen. Be sure to save your work frequently. ■

If you've worked with a non-linear editor (NLE) like Final Cut Pro or Adobe Premiere for video production, the Storyboard Editor should look familiar to you. If you've never dealt with a program like that before, don't worry: it's not too complex. The whole point of an NLE is that it allows you a lot of freedom to mix and match media to create a final sequence. An important feature of this is that the source media (images, video, sound) are not directly modified by the editor. The Storyboard Editor merely points to this data while you work and you can use GAP's video encoder (covered in the next chapter) to generate a separate video file that you can share with others.

Looking at the editor window in Figure 19-13, you can break it down into three primary sections. In the upper-left corner of the Storyboard Editor is a Cliplist section, where you can keep a list of the assets, called *clips*, available for use on your storyboard. You can actually have multiple cliplists in the Storyboard Editor. Before adding clips, you need to first create a new cliplist. To do this go to Cliplist ➤ New. This brings up a dialog like the one in Figure 19-14 where you can stipulate general size and frame rate information that your clips should conform to.

FIGURE 19-14

The Master Properties dialog comes up when you create a new cliplist or storyboard file through the Storyboard Editor.

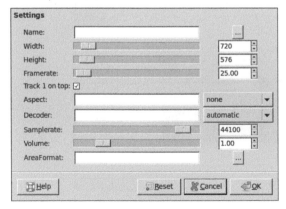

With your cliplist created, you can start adding clips by clicking the New Clip icon, which looks like a blank sheet of paper, at the bottom of the Cliplist block. This brings up a separate dialog for defining your clip. You can browse your hard drive for media to include and then use that dialog to define the length of it. After you load the clip, you can always update the clip's properties by right-clicking the clip and bringing up the dialog again. That dialog is shown in Figure 19-15.

FIGURE 19-15

The Clip Properties dialog that appears when loading a new clip to either the Cliplist or Storyboard sections

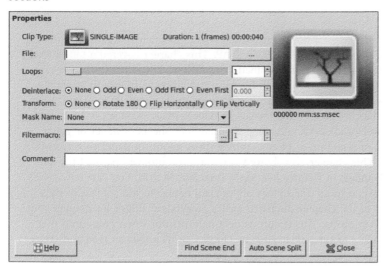

To the right of the Cliplist section in the Storyboard Editor is the Playback window. This section allows you to play back a rough version of any clip as well as your storyboard. Any clip can be sent directly to the Playback section by double-clicking it. Alternatively, a set of selected clips (you can select multiple clips by Ctrl+clicking them) can be sent to the Playback area by selecting them and clicking the gray Play button at the bottom of either the Cliplist or Storyboard section of the editor. The controls for the Playback section are pretty involved and covered in detail in Chapter 20.

The entire bottom section of the Storyboard Editor is dedicated to creating your storyboard. Like in the Cliplist area, you have to create a new storyboard file before you can add clips to it by going to Storyboard ➤ New at the top of the editor window. The Master Properties window that appears is identical to the one used for the Cliplist. With the storyboard file created, you can start adding clips. You can either pull these from the Cliplist section or add them explicitly by clicking the New Clip button at the bottom of the Storyboard section. Here you can load clips and adjust their location in the storyboard by cutting, copying, or pasting individual clips. You can even drag and drop clips in the storyboard to re-order them. The Storyboard Editor also supports multiple tracks so you can overlay clips atop one another. This is particularly important if you have audio like music or sound effects that you want to sync with other clips in your storyboard. You also have the ability to generate transitions from one clip to the next, although as a storyboard, it's often better to keep things simple. If you want to do full video editing, you're better served using an NLE that's designed to fulfill that task.

After you create your storyboard, you can click the Save button at the bottom of the Storyboard Editor or choose Storyboard ➤ Save As from the menu at the top of the editor. This saves your storyboard text file for future use. You can come back later and add more clips to it or use GAP's video encoder to generate a video file that you can play and share on other computers.

Summary

And that's an introduction to animating in GIMP using GAP. This chapter covered a ton of information on using GIMP to facilitate a traditional animation workflow. You started off by seeing GIMP's built-in ability to generate an animated GIF file by using layers as frames in an animation. Then this chapter showed how images sequences allow for more complex animation than layers and how GAP makes the process of using images sequences easier. You get to take advantage of the traditional look and process without using thousands of sheets of paper or going through the tiresome process of scanning or photographing those pieces of paper to get your drawings into the computer. This chapter also showed you ways to automate parts of the animation process by taking advantage of features like Move Path and Morph. You saw how GAP's onion skinning feature allows you to see the frames of your animation in the context of their surrounding frames. The end of the chapter discussed GAP's Storyboard Editor for helping you with planning your animation projects. This feature is definitely helpful when going into the next chapter, which covers GAP's features that relate specifically to its ability to read and create video files.

Working with Video-Specific Functions in GIMP

I n Chapter 19, you were introduced to the GIMP Animation Package, or GAP, an extension that adds animation functionality to GIMP's already broad set of features. Because GAP can handle the multiple frames of animation, it's logical to assume that it can also handle some basic video functions as well. It wouldn't make much sense to use GIMP to create an animation if there's not a way to play back that animation to test timing and check the fluidity of a character's movement. Fortunately, GAP provides these basic video features as well.

Using GAP, you have the ability to play back the frames of your animation or video on the fly. For a more accurate sense of timing, you can also use GAP to encode the video to one of a variety of supported video formats via the incredibly powerful FFMPEG library. And because you can encode your still image sequences into video files, it makes sense that you can also take video files and extract individual frames from them. This gives you the ability to do everything from video cleanup to replacing your friend's head in a home movie with a picture of a paper bag (mean, I know, but your friend will laugh, I'm sure).

This chapter focuses on using the features of GIMP — and more specifically, the GAP plug-in — to give you the chance to create and modify video files. GAP does not, by any stretch of the imagination, make GIMP a video editing package like Final Cut or Avid. Those tools, called *non-linear editors*, or NLEs, are designed to let you edit the sequencing of multiple shots of a full video. What GAP gives you is fine-grained control over the content of each individual frame. If you keep that in mind, you'll be able to use this tool very effectively.

IN THIS CHAPTER

Playing video with GIMP

Creating video and movie files from within GIMP

Pulling a range of frames from a video file for editing in GIMP

Playing Back Video

Whether you're working with a hand-drawn animation or editing frames from a video, one of the critical things that you need to do is see how your work looks in motion. You could simply encode the sequence of frames into a video file as described in the next section, but this can be a time-consuming process and if you just need to do a quick check, waiting for a video file to encode can quickly become tedious. To get around this and provide you with a quick alternative to encoding, GAP includes a video playback feature.

At its most basic, the video playback feature loads the individual frames from your sequence and displays them one by one. On large files, though, this can make playback really choppy as GIMP struggles to quickly open each file in sequence at the correct speed. To allow for real-time playback, the video playback feature caches smaller thumbnail images of each frame that load much faster. This allows you to get a really clear understanding of the timing in your sequence. You can even load an audio file with the video to make sure they are synchronized.

Assuming you have GAP installed (if you don't, see Chapter 21), you can use the video playback feature by navigating to Video ➤ Playback. The Video menu is pretty long and organized a bit oddly, so Figure 20-1 shows where Playback shows up there. When you choose this item from the menu, the Videoframe Playback window (also shown in Figure 20-1) appears. In this interface, you can watch all or part of your sequence and interactively control how you view it.

Note

As of this writing, when you use GAP 2.6.6 with the latest version of GIMP (GIMP 2.7) all of your still images need to be in GIMP's native XCF format for many of GAP's features to work. Hopefully in future versions of GAP, you'll be able to load image sequences of any format. In the meantime, you may need to resave your sequence images in XCF. Fortunately, if you have the David's Batch Processor (DBP) plug-in installed, this is a relatively quick and painless endeavor. For more on DBP, check out Chapter 18. ■

Video Options

The Videoframe Playback window has three tabs across the top: Video Options, Audio Options, and Preferences. As Figure 20-1 shows, when this window opens, the default behavior is to show the Video Options tab. This tab is where the bulk of your playback controls live. It loads with its own set of defaults, allowing you to start playing with your sequence immediately. Probably the most interesting feature of this window is across the top of this tab. GAP provides a pretty unique interface to allow you to interactively *scrub*, or shuffle back and forth, through your video sequence. Figure 20-2 shows this interface.

There are actually two controls for this. The topmost control that looks like a series of thin buttons is called a *Button Array* and it's your fine scrubbing control. Each of these 51 little buttons represents a single frame in your sequence. If you hover your mouse over one of these buttons, the frame that corresponds to it appears in the window's playback preview. So by simply running your mouse back and forth across these buttons, you can interactively control a sequence of 50 frames with extremely fine-grained control. Clicking any of these buttons loads that frame into the GIMP image window.

FIGURE 20-1

On the left, choosing Playback from the Video menu; on the right, the Videoframe Playback window

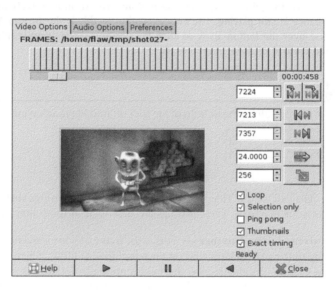

FIGURE 20-2

The video playback's unique interface for scrubbing and shuttling through your video sequence

Of course, there's a good chance that your video sequence is longer than 51 frames. To get to those other frames, you have the shuttle slider, called the *Position Scale*, beneath the fine scrub buttons. Click this slider and drag it left or right to view another segment of your sequence. After you move the shuttle to the segment you're interested in, the button array spans 51 frames around that segment.

Along the bottom of the Videoframe Playback window, between the Help and Close buttons, are three buttons that give you VCR-like controls for playback. Figure 20-3 shows these buttons, which are actually persistent across all three tabs in this window. The first button, with the traditional triangular Play icon, runs forward through your sequence in real time when you click it. You can pause playback by clicking the middle Pause button. Clicking the third button in this set, featuring a backward-facing play icon, does a reverse real-time playback of your video sequence.

Tip

If you click the Play or Reverse Play buttons, you can still change the options and settings in the playback window. This feature is really quite helpful because it allows you to interactively make changes and adjustments while the sequence is still playing. The only exception to this is the Button Array and Position Scale. If you run your mouse over the button array or click the position scale's shuttle, playback stops and you get the more fine-grained control of these interfaces. ■

FIGURE 20-3

The playback control buttons along the bottom of the Videoframe Playback window

Along the right side of the Video Options tab is a series of settings that you can use to get more control over your playback. These settings are described in the following list:

- **Current Frame Number** — This is the frame of your sequence that is currently on display in the playback preview on the left of this window. When you're scrubbing or allowing GAP to continually play, this field continually updates its value. You can also manually type in a number here and the playback window takes you directly to that frame when you press Enter. To the right of this number field are two additional buttons which can help you define your playback range:
  - **Set Start Frame** — Click this button to take the current frame number and define it as the start frame for your preview. This is helpful if you have a long video sequence and you're interested in previewing only a section of it.
  - **Set End Frame** — Clicking this button performs a similar operation, except it sets the end frame of your preview sequence.
- **Start Frame** — This numeric value defines the frame number at which your playback preview starts. You can set it by clicking the Set Start Frame button mentioned previously or by explicitly typing in the value you want. Clicking the button to the right of this field doesn't do anything in the GIMP interface. Instead, it sends the start value to *standard out*. That is, if you start GIMP from a terminal window, you can see this number get printed there when you click that button. It's helpful for debugging, but not of much use to regular users.
- **End Frame** — Like the Start frame field, this value defines the last frame number in your playback preview's range. Also like the Start Frame field, the button to the right of this one sends the end frame value to standard out for debugging purposes.
- **Playback Speed** — This defines the playback speed, or *frame rate*, of your sequence. By default, the value for this is the standard film frame rate of 24fps, or *frames per second*.

If you're working in video, you need to change this value to the frame rate your source video uses. If you're in a country using the NTSC standard, like the U.S., you'll probably use 29.97fps. Other parts of the world tend to use the PAL standard of 25fps. The cool thing, though, is that you also have the ability to set this to whatever arbitrary frame rate you want. This is particularly helpful for hand-drawn animation work, which can often happen at non-standard frame rates. Clicking the button to the right of this field reverts the frame rate value to its previous setting.

- **Video Preview Size** — As mentioned earlier in this section, GAP's video playback feature can create an interim cache of smaller thumbnail versions of each frame in your sequence. This improves the performance of the playback preview, allowing for a preview that plays in real time. Depending on how powerful your computer is, you may have to adjust the size of these cache images. This is the field where you make those adjustments. By default, the value is set to 256 pixels. This defines the maximum width of the cache images. You can type in this field to define any arbitrary width that you want and the height will be scaled proportionally. If you click the button to the right of this field it toggles the value in this field between 128 and 256. Also, if you Shift+click this button, it sets the cache previews to full size, up to a maximum value of 800 pixels.

- **Loop** — This option, enabled by default, causes your video sequence to play continually. If you click the play button with this option enabled, as the playback reaches the last frame in its range, it jumps back to the beginning and keeps playing. The same is true if you click the Reverse Play button.

- **Selection Only** — Also enabled by default, this ensures that the playback plays only the range defined by the Start Frame and End Frame fields. With this option disabled, the preview shows all the frames in the entire sequence.

- **Ping Pong** — This option is similar to Loop, but with one major difference. Instead of jumping to the beginning of the preview when it gets to the end, the Ping Pong option causes the animation to play in reverse when it gets there. If you watch the Position Scale's shuttle move while the preview plays, you'll notice that it bounces back and forth like the "ball" in that magnificently old-school video game, Pong. This option is disabled by default. Also note that if both Loop and Ping Pong are enabled, Ping Pong takes precedence.

- **Thumbnails** — Keep this option enabled to allow the playback preview to use image caching. If you disable this feature, GIMP needs to load and dynamically scale each frame of your sequence on the fly. Enabling this check box saves RAM usage, but can be a serious impediment to playback performance.

- **Exact Timing** — By keeping this option enabled, the playback preview tries to maintain the frame rate you defined as much as possible. To guarantee that the correct frame gets shown at the correct time, the preview may skip loading a few frames. If you absolutely need to see each frame in your sequence and you're not concerned with it running at the correct frame rate, disable this option.

At the very bottom of these settings is a short status message for feedback. Typically it just says Ready; however when playing your sequence, it lets you know if any processing is being done, such as generating or regenerating thumbnails for the image cache so you can have real-time playback.

Tip

The playback feature of GAP does not currently retain your settings after you close the window. So for example, if you're using a frame rate other than the playback default of 24fps, the next time you choose Video ➤ Playback, you need to remember to change the frame rate back to what you need it to be. ■

Audio Options

If you click the Audio Options tab in the Videoframe Playback window, you get a series of settings like the ones shown in Figure 20-4. In a nutshell, this tab gives you the ability to load an audio file or extract audio from a video file and play it along with your video sequence. This is a very powerful feature for animation because it helps you ensure that your images synchronize with the audio of the piece. In particular, if you have a character speaking dialogue and you're animating lip sync, this capability is absolutely critical.

FIGURE 20-4

The Audio Options tab of the Videoframe Playback window

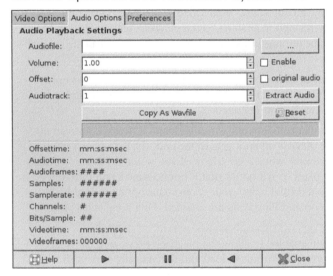

Following is a description of each of the fields and buttons in this tab:

- **Audiofile** — This field shows the path to your chosen sound file. The file you choose does not necessarily have to be a pure audio file. It can also be a video file that has audio *multiplexed*, or mixed into it. By default this field is empty. If you know the exact path to your file, you can type it directly into this field. Alternatively, you can click the Browse button to the right of the field, indicated with ellipses (...), to get a File Chooser where you can navigate through your hard drive to find the file you need.

- **Enable** — This is a quick toggle to enable or disable audio playback with your video preview. If you don't have a file loaded or you want to see your sequence without audio, simply make sure this check box is disabled.

- **Volume** — This controls the playback volume of your audio. Think of the value in this field as a scaling value. That is, if you keep Volume at its default value of 1.00, the playback uses the original volume of the sound file. If you increase the value to 2.00, the playback will be twice as loud as the original. On the flip side, setting the Volume value to 0.50 sets the playback volume to be half as loud.

- **Offset** — On the chance that your video sequence doesn't start in the same place as your audio, you need to offset either the video or the audio so they can be synchronized. That is why this field exists. This value, measured in frames, nudges the video sooner or later relative to the audio. The thing to note, though, is that the *audio is trimmed to fit the video*. As an example, imagine you have a video sequence set to play back at 24fps. If you set the offset value to −24, then when you start playing the preview, there is one second (24 frames) of silence before the audio starts to play. However, if you set the offset value to 24, the audio starts playing immediately with the video, but it starts one second into the audio file.

- **Original Audio** — This check box works in concert with the offset value. By default, it's disabled, meaning that whatever you have in the Offset field takes precedence. However, if you enable this check box, the playback preview assumes that the audio and video sequence both start at the same point. This is functionally equivalent to setting the offset to zero. The advantage of this toggle, though, is that you can quickly switch it to zero if you need to and you won't lose anything you've entered as the Offset.

- **Audiotrack** — If you're pulling audio that's been multiplexed into a video file, this option can be quite useful. Many video file formats support having multiple audio channels. For example, there may be a channel for dialogue and a separate channel reserved for music or sound effects. If you have one of these types of video files, you can stipulate which audio channel you want to use. If not, the default value of 1 works just fine.

- **Extract Audio** — This button works with the previous setting. If you want to use audio that's been multiplexed into a video file, you need to extract that audio before the playback preview can recognize it. So once you've picked your file and stipulated which audio track to pull from it, click this button and GAP liberates your audio from its video-encoded prison so you can use it with your video sequence.

- **Copy As Wavfile** — Decoding audio can be a nasty business. If it's multiplexed with a video file or compressed in a format like MP3 or Ogg Vorbis, it can be computationally expensive to decode these files to raw audio. You can usually get better playback performance in the preview if you're using a file in WAV format. To facilitate this, you can click this button and GAP transcodes your encoded or extracted audio to a WAV file and saves it to your hard drive. When you click this button, a dialog like the one in Figure 20-5 appears. Use this dialog to choose where your new WAV file is saved as well as what sample rate you want this new audio file to use. When it's done transcoding, the new file is listed in the Audiofile field at the top of the Audio Options tab.

- **Reset** — If you need to knock the volume and offset values back to their defaults of 1 and 0, respectively, click this button.

The lower half of the tab provides numerical values and information about your chosen audio file. In particular, the Audiotime and Videotime values are really helpful for getting tight synchronization between your video sequence and your sound.

FIGURE 20-5

The file dialog for saving a WAV file for use with the video playback

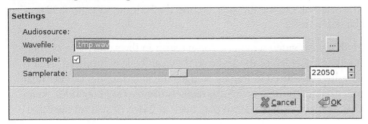

Preferences

The third tab in the Videoframe Playback window, shown in Figure 20-6, provides you with a set of options to control the playback's performance and its interface.

FIGURE 20-6

The Preferences tab in the Videoframe Playback window

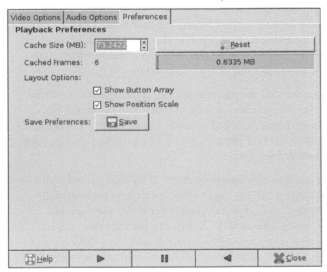

The first set of options in this tab deals with how the video playback feature handles its image cache. You may find that while you're playing your sequence, the playback preview skips or pauses to regenerate the cache. The reason for this is that the cache is too small for the number of preview images you have at that size. Of course, you could try to fix things by reducing the preview image size or shortening the playback range. However, if you need the larger preview images and you need to see the longer sequence, the only remaining thing that you can do is increase the amount of memory used to store your image cache. You do this by adjusting the value in the Cache Size field.

Beneath the Cache Size field is a numerical value that shows how many frames are currently cached and how much memory those frames are taking up. You can use these two values to get a pretty good idea of how much space you need for your cache. To do this, click the Reset button at the top of the tab. This empties out the frame cache. Once you do that, click the Play button at the bottom of the window and your cache should start to get populated. After a few frames get cached (maybe 10–30), click the Pause button and take a look at the values for Cached Frames. By seeing how much space these few cached frames take up, you can extrapolate how much space you need for the full sequence.

The next two options in this tab are entirely interface-related. These two check boxes toggle the visibility of the Button Array and Position Scale on the Video Options tab. By default, they're both turned on, but if you want to play back your sequence without inadvertently stopping it by running your mouse over the Button Array, it may be helpful to disable it here.

The last thing available in this tab is a Save button. Clicking this button saves the preferences for video playback so they're available the next time you run Videoframe playback. Bear in mind, though, that this only stores the information from the Preferences tab. Settings from Video Options, like frame rate, are not saved at all. Hopefully this gets resolved in a future version of GAP, but in the meantime, that's just how things are.

Encoding Video

Not only can you use GAP to create quick playback previews of your videos or animations, but GAP is also capable of producing an actual video file as well. This is particularly useful if you have a long sequence that you want to play at full size. However, full-sized frames may be larger than the 800-pixel limit of the Videoframe Playback window and you may not have enough memory to create a cache large enough to hold your full sequence. Of course, it's also good for generating deliverable content. Since the release of GAP 2.6.6, which includes support for the FFMPEG video encoding and decoding library, I've started using GAP to generate short video clips from sequences of still frames, rather than typing an FFMPEG command from the terminal window with a lengthy string of switches and options.

To get started with this, load up a frame from your image sequence and choose Video ➤ Master Videoencoder. When you do this, you get a window like the one in Figure 20-7 offering multiple tabs for video and audio, plus some additional features to aid the encoding process.

The first thing to note about this window is the Output field and Status bar at the bottom. Because these things don't change regardless of what settings you choose, they're persistent across all tabs. Output controls where your encoded video file goes on your hard drive, as well as what its filename is. You can either explicitly type a path and name here, or you can click the Browse button to the right of the field to get a File Chooser window for graphically picking where your encoded file goes. The Status bar remains empty and blank until you actually hit OK and start encoding. Then it gives you a progress indicator to show how long you have to wait until the encoded video is complete.

FIGURE 20-7

The Master Videoencoder feature of GAP opens a multi-tabbed window that lets you control how your image sequence becomes a video file

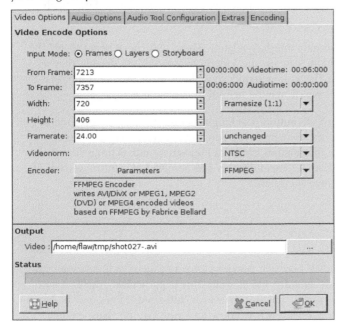

Setting Video Options

Video encoding is a highly technical topic that could be a book unto itself. As such, this chapter can't cover all the nuanced terminology and definitions involved with that topic. However, it does walk you though how to access these options and what options work well for a few specific situations. The following list covers the settings available to you through the Video Options tab.

- **Input Mode** — This series of radio buttons controls what type of input you're feeding to the encoder. As covered in Chapter 19, GAP can recognize, and therefore encode, one of three input types:
  - **Frames** — Frames are a sequence of still images that represent each frame in a video or animation. This is the most typical format for large projects.

- **Layers** — GIMP natively supports creating animated GIF images by using layers as each frame in the animation. GAP also supports this feature for encoding video files.

- **Storyboard** — Storyboards are interesting beasts in GIMP terms. As covered in Chapter 19, they're text files that can point to still-frame images as well as video files. If you want to take the input from a storyboard file and encode a video file to produce an *animatic*, or storyboard set to time, this is the way to do it. Something to remember here, though, is that if you choose this option, you *must* load the storyboard file in the Extras tab of this window. This is explained more later in this chapter, but it's worth mentioning now.

- **From Frame** — Whether you're using frames, layers, or storyboard items, you need to stipulate which unit the encoded video starts at. GAP does its best to guess this for you, but if you need a custom value, this is what you modify.

- **To Frame** — Like the From Frame setting, this designates where the animation ends. By default, GAP guesses for you and loads the highest-value frame, layer, or storyboard element it can find. However, if you need a custom value, you enter it here.

- **Width/Height/Framesize** — You're probably working on your animation or video at full size. However, if you're just producing a quick preview or you're generating a video file to go online, you may want to encode to a smaller size. The Width and Height fields allow you to set an explicit size in pixels, but you can also use the Framesize drop-down to the right of these fields to choose from a handful of standard sizes.

- **Framerate** — This value, set in frames per second, controls how fast your animation or video plays back. For convenience, the drop-down menu to the right of this field provides you with some standard frame rates so you can avoid typing.

- **Videonorm** — If you're encoding video that's intended for television, you definitely want to pay attention to this setting. It actually controls the shape of the pixels in your video file. Up until this point, everything you've done in GIMP has involved square pixels. However, some television standards like NTSC actually use rectangular pixels. The options in this drop-down menu let you control your pixel aspect to match a given standard. If you want to keep using square pixels, just set this to Undefined.

- **Encoder** — This is where the really technical part of video encoding comes in. The latest version of GAP gives you four options to choose from when you click on the drop-down menu next to this label:

  - **FFMPEG** — FFMPEG is a Free Software library for encoding and decoding video. It's extremely powerful and renowned for its reputation to convert nearly any video format to another by leveraging a variety of third-party libraries. Although FFMPEG is an excellent and powerful library, it's worth mentioning that some of the codecs it supports — namely H.264 and MPEG-4 — place this library in a somewhat gray legal area with respect to patent and intellectual property laws. You can read more detailed information on the FFMPEG web site at http://www.ffmpeg.org/legal.html. The short version is this: if you're using FFMPEG for personal, non-commercial purposes, you're not likely to run into any trouble.

- **Single Frames** — This option does as its name implies; it generates a sequence of still images rather than a single video file. This setting is most useful if you're encoding a GAP Storyboard that has a variety of video input types. Using this option unifies the storyboard to a single project that you can edit further.

- **Raw Frames** — This option behaves exactly like the Single Frames option in all cases except for one very specific case. If your output is stipulated as JPEG images and you're using the Storyboard input mode with source footage that is JPEG images, JPEG-encoded video, MPEG1 video, or Motion JPEG video, GAP copies those frames directly to the output without recompressing them. This makes the encoding process faster and allows you to forgo any generational loss due to recompressing in the lossy JPEG format.

- **AVI1** — This is an older encoding setting that ships by default with GAP. If you don't have FFMPEG installed on your computer, you should at least be able to encode with this format. It doesn't support the diverse codecs that FFMPEG does, but the files it creates should be universally readable.

Video Formats and Video Codecs

It's worth pausing here to cover the difference between a video format and a video codec. The definitions of these two things are actually pretty straightforward. Think of a *video format* as a container. Inside this container is video data and audio data. The video data that's stored in whatever video format you choose is compressed with a *video codec*, an algorithm that encodes and decodes your video to and from its compressed format. For example, AVI is a container format that can hold video encoded in a variety of codecs, including DV, MPEG-4, or JPEG compression. Pretty simple, huh?

Where things start getting complicated is that some formats share names with codecs. For instance, you can have MP4 file. This file uses the MPEG-4 video format, and within that format, you can encode your video to a number of different types of MPEG-4 implementations, such as H.264, "standard" MPEG-4, or one of three different kinds of Microsoft MPEG-4 codecs. Additionally, some codecs behave as their own containers. For instance, the DV, or digital video, format used in many digital video cameras is often stored and read in its own raw DV format rather than being wrapped in an AVI or QuickTime container.

Regardless of these bits of confusing naming conventions, the differentiation between a format and a codec remains the same. For instances where you're discussing codecs and formats that share the same name, you're best off asking the other person to specify which one they're talking about.

Setting FFMPEG Parameters

The default encoder that the Master Videoencoder presents you with is FFMPEG and by all accounts it's the best option. It gives you the most flexibility and the most choices of codecs to use for compressing your video file. If you choose FFMPEG from the Encoder drop-down menu, the next thing you should do is click the Parameters button to the left of it. Upon clicking it, GAP opens the window shown in Figure 20-8.

FIGURE 20-8

The FFMPEG Video Encode Parameters window is where you control how FFMPEG encodes your video file

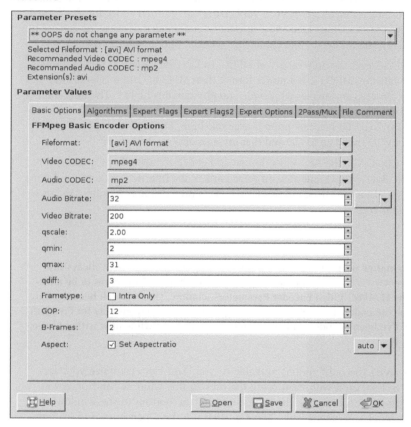

FFMPEG's flexibility is a bit of a double-edged sword. Though you have virtually limitless control of the encoding process at your fingertips, this also means that there's a potential for a mind-bogglingly large number of choices and decisions. Fortunately, GAP attempts to simplify the process by offering you a set of presets in the drop-down menu at the top of the window. Specifically, you're given four separate codec choices and different quality levels associated with each one. They are as follows:

- **DiVX** — Of the presets listed here, the DiVX options are the most Internet-friendly, offering the best quality video at the smallest file sizes. Your choices here are Default, High Quality, Low Quality, and Windows. For most situations, Default should work fine. However, if you want to have the greatest chance of your video playing on Windows, the Windows option may be better for you.

- **MPEG1** — The MPEG-1 video standard has been around for a long time and as such, is recognized and playable just about everywhere. The only downside is that the quality of MPEG-1 compression is not all that great, especially when compared to more modern codecs like H.264 and DiVX. One thing that you do need to use MPEG-1 for, though, is if you intend on creating a Video CD, or VCD. MPEG-1 is the required codec for that format. Alternatively, if you're encoding video and you want to guarantee that everyone can see it, regardless of quality, the MPEG-1 High Quality preset is an option you can use.

- **MPEG2** — MPEG-1 isn't the only variety of MPEG. In fact, the variety of MPEG formats can get pretty confusing. MPEG-2 is a newer format than MPEG-1 and it offers better compression, so file sizes are smaller while video quality remains higher. The important thing to remember is that MPEG-2 is the video codec that's used on DVDs. It's for this reason that the MPEG-2 (DVD) Presets option is available here. MPEG-2 is also used for an enhanced type of VCD called an SVCD and that preset is also available here.

- **Real Video** — Like DiVX, the Real Video format and codec are actually proprietary formats. Real is a bit older, but it's still used on some parts of the Internet, so there's still some value in having the ability to encode to this format. This preset option simplifies the process of encoding for you.

Note

You may be alarmed to see that no matter what preset you choose, the drop-down menu may always say "** OOPS do not change any parameter **." You shouldn't worry too much, though. This seems to be a display bug in the interface code of the FFMPEG Video Encoder Parameters window. (You can tell because you can read GAP's source code and see the code comment listing this bug as a "todo" item. Hooray for Free Software!) It's anecdotal evidence, but I've been encoding video with these presets for a while now without issue, so it *should* work fine for you, too. ∎

Of course, these presets aren't the only options available to you. You can customize your formats, codecs, and options associated with each using the tabs in this window. And once you set your own custom settings, you can click the Save button at the bottom of the window to save your custom parameters to an external file. You can then use the Open button to load any of your stored custom settings and quickly get to the actual encoding process. Of course, to do that, you first have you go through and set those parameters. Most of the general controls can be set in the Basic Options tab. Following are descriptions for each of the settings here:

- **Fileformat** — This drop-down menu gives a full choice of the different formats that FFMPEG supports. The most helpful aspect of this menu is that based on what you select here, GAP attempts to choose sensible video and audio codecs to match it. The options in this menu are too numerous to list here, but the one I favor the most for delivering video content to the Web is [ipod] iPod H.264 MP4 Format. Not only will this play on an iPod, but it also works online in most Flash-based video players using Flash Player 10 or later.

- **Video Codec** — This drop-down menu gives you the full list of video codecs supported by FFMPEG. It would be nice if this list were culled according to the codecs supported by the format you choose in the Fileformat option, but currently that's not the case, so you need to know which codecs fit in which containers. This list is really valuable, however, if you choose an AVI container and you want to explicitly specify which codec to use.

- **Audio Codec** — Like the Video Codec drop-down, this setting controls which audio codec to use for any audio that you're encoding. When you pick an option from the File-format drop-down, it tries to choose the best audio codec here to suit that selection, but you still have the ability to customize.

- **Audio Bitrate** — This value, measured in kilobits per second, controls how much memory is used to encode each second of audio. Higher values give you better results. To the right of this field is a drop-down menu with a series of preset bitrates that are typical standards for audio.

- **Video Bitrate** — Like the Audio Bitrate setting, this value controls how many kilobits are used to encode each second of video. Higher values increase the quality of your video. The default value of 1500 kbps is a pretty high-quality setting. When encoding video for the Web or a mobile device like an iPod, using the H.264 codec with an 800 kbps video bitrate yields a good compression ratio.

- **Qscale** — This is the *quantizer scale* used for encoding your video. That is, this value controls how detailed the compressor is when it looks at the frames in your video. Smaller values indicate that it's looking at smaller chunks and therefore being more detailed. For simplicity, think of this value as "quality scale." Lower values yield higher-quality files, but larger file sizes. Typically values over 13 are of unacceptable quality, with large obstructive compression artifacts. For content destined for the Internet, setting Qscale to 5 or 9 tends to work well.

- **Qmin/Qmax** — FFMPEG allows you to do *variable bitrate encoding*, meaning it can adaptively adjust the video bitrate to get the best compression for each portion of your video. To do this, it adjusts the Qscale value described previously. The Qmin and Qmax settings tell FFMPEG what range to stay within. Because higher values of Qscale are of really low quality, good settings to use are a Qmin of 2 and a Qmax of 11.

- **Qdiff** — When encoding at a variable bitrate, FFMPEG may determine that the best Qscale setting for one part of your video is 2 and the next part's best Qscale value is 10. Though it's perfectly acceptable to do this, that large of a jump in quality might be disorienting to your audience. To prevent such large jumps, you can control how wide of a difference in Qscale values FFMPEG allows between sequential parts of your video with this value. The default value of 3 is good for most situations.

- **Frametype** — The next few settings require a bit of knowledge about how video files are encoded. Early video compression techniques were pretty simple. They involved taking each frame of video and just performing image compression on each of those frames, regardless of how different it was from its previous or following frames. This method yields good quality, but file sizes tend to be pretty large. Most modern codecs have an advanced technique that saves more space. However, on some types of video, particularly video that features fast motion, modern techniques may generate too many compression artifacts. For this kind of video, you have the option of enabling this Intra Only check box to compress only the data internal to each frame, like with early techniques, rather than accounting for temporal *inter-frame* data. If you enable this check box, the GOP and B-frames values become grayed out and aren't used by the compressor.

- **GOP** — Modern video compression techniques involve taking a sequence of frames from a video and classifying them as a *group of pictures*, or GOP. Within this GOP the compressor deals only with finding the changes from one frame to the next and throws out all extra data to save space. This method can make video files dramatically smaller with very little loss in quality. The value in this field controls how many frames long each GOP block in your video is. The default value of 12 should work well.

- **B-frames** — A B-frame is a *bi-directional predicted frame*. This is a fancy way of saying that within a GOP, when the compressor gets to a frame, it needs to decide what information to keep and what information to toss out. Earlier techniques relied on information available in previous frames. However, modern compression does basic motion prediction to guess following frames as well, thus saving even more space. The value in this field controls how many frames in each direction the compressor looks or predicts. The default value of 2 is fine in most cases.

- **Aspect** — If you enable this check box, a drop-down menu to the right of it is activated to allow you to manually control your output video's aspect ratio. The default value of Auto is best for most circumstances. However, this setting is helpful if you want to do *anamorphic widescreen*, which consists of video encoded to a 4:3 size, like the NTSC 720×480 size, but played back at 16:9 widescreen. This is used frequently for widescreen DVD videos. To do this use the following steps:

  1. Work on your video or animation in a 16:9 widescreen width and height, such as the HD image size of 1920×1080 pixels.

  2. When you load the Master Videoencoder (Video ➤ Master Videoencoder), set the width and height values of the video to a 4:3 aspect, such as the NTSC framesize of 720×480 pixels.

  3. When you click Parameters for FFMPEG encoding, enable the Set Aspectratio check box and use the drop-down menu to choose 16:9.

  4. Now when you have your parameters set and you click OK in the Master Videoencoder window, it scales your video to fit 720×480 pixels (if you were to view it without aspect adjustments, it looks vertically stretched). However, when played back by a player that understands aspect ratio settings — like a DVD player — your video regains its widescreen appearance.

The other tabs in the FFMPEG Video Encode Parameters window offer you a full series of advanced encoding controls. Some of these controls are specific to particular codecs that FFMPEG offers, whereas some are more general. Discussing all of these settings in detail is out of the scope of this book, but if you're interested in this kind of information, check out the full set of documentation available on the FFMPEG web site, www.ffmpeg.org.

Warning

Be careful when setting your options here. FFMPEG allows you to create video files using nearly any combination of format, codec, and compression settings. Though FFMPEG may happily create this file for you, there's a possibility that the file won't play in standard video players like QuickTime Player or Windows Media Player. Resources are available online that can help you generate the magical incantation to get universally playable files. That said, the defaults that the Media Videoencoder provides should yield good results for you. ∎

The last tab in this window is File Comment. The contents of this tab, shown in Figure 20-9, allow you to add metadata to your video file in the form of comments. It's a small thing, but it's a good way to let the world know some information about your video, who made it, and what kind of license you want to cover it.

FIGURE 20-9

The File Comment tab in the FFMPEG Video Encode Parameters window allows you to add metadata to your video.

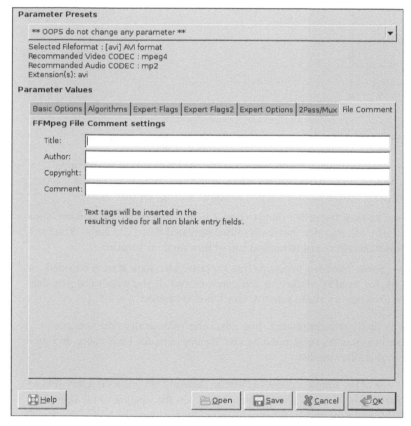

Setting AVI1 parameters

The AVI1 parameters are much simpler than ones available through FFMPEG, but they still offer a surprising amount of control over the nature of your final video file. If you choose AVI1 as your encoder and then click the Parameters button in the Master Videoencoder window, GAP provides you with a window like the one in Figure 20-10.

FIGURE 20-10

The AVI Video Encode Parameters window

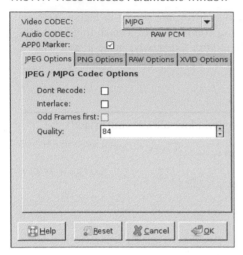

The first things worth mentioning about this window are the three options at the top:

- **Video Codec** — This drop-down menu gives you the choice of five different video codecs — JPEG, Motion JPEG (MJPG), PNG, RAW, and XViD. When you choose a codec, its corresponding tab is activated, allowing you to adjust settings for that codec.

- **Audio Codec** — The most important thing to notice here is that regardless of what video codec you choose, the AVI encoder always uses uncompressed Raw PCM audio. You can't change this, so this item is here just to remind you of how audio is handled.

- **APP0 Marker** — Some Windows programs that support video look at each encoded frame in an AVI file for an APP0 Marker, or *application marker*. If you want to be sure that your file will play in Windows, make sure this check box is enabled.

Working in this window is pretty straightforward. Just select the video codec that you want to use and then adjust the values in its corresponding tab. Descriptions for each codec and its parameters are included in the following list:

- **JPEG** — This is one of the simplest codecs available. Basically, all it does is apply JPEG compression to each frame of your video. It doesn't give you the smallest of file sizes, but the quality is reliable and predictable. When you choose this option, the JPEG Options tab appears. The different parameters available to you are as follows:

  - **Don't Recode** — Only enable this option if your source frames are JPEG files encoded in YUV 4:2:2 colorspace. Because you're working in GIMP, which is limited to RGBA colors, this is unlikely, so you're best off leaving this check box disabled.

- **Interlace** — Interlacing is a video technique used mostly in television where a frame is split into two fields containing alternating horizontal lines from the frame. If your source video is interlaced or you intend to send your video for standard definition television, enable this check box. Otherwise, leave it disabled.

- **Odd Frames first** — If you choose to use interlacing, you have the option of starting with odd-numbered lines or even-numbered ones. The default is even numbering, but some video systems require odd frames first and that's what this option is for.

- **Quality** — Like the quality setting for a regular JPEG image, this value controls how compressed each frame of your video is.

- **Motion JPEG (MJPG)** — Motion JPEG is an adaptation of the JPEG codec that accounts for temporal data. That is, similar to the modern codecs discussed in the FFMPEG parameters, Motion JPEG attempts to look at the differences between a frame and the ones surrounding it to see what kind of redundant data can be removed to save space. This format gives you roughly the same quality as JPEG encoding, but also a smaller file size. The parameters available for Motion JPEG are identical to the ones for the JPEG codec.

- **PNG** — As described earlier in the book, PNG is a lossless image compression algorithm. Like the JPEG codec, it does not account for temporal data, so file sizes tend to be larger. In fact, because PNG is lossless, a PNG-encoded video file is even larger than a JPEG-encoded one. The difference, though, is that PNG doesn't have the compression artifacts that JPEG does. Parameters for the PNG codec are as follows:

  - **Don't Recode** — If all of your source images in your frame sequence are PNGs, you can save some time by not recoding and recompressing them. To do that, enable this check box. However, if your source footage is in any other format than PNG, leave this disabled.

  - **Interlace** — Like the Interlace parameter for JPEG and Motion JPEG encoding, this option enables interlacing for your PNG frames.

  - **Compression** — PNG is a lossless format, so image quality remains the same regardless of how much you compress it. However, higher compression values take longer for computers to decode. If you have an older computer and you need the file to play back in real time, use a lower compression value. This setting has a range from 0 to 9.

- **Raw** — The PNG codec is great when you want to have a high-fidelity video file that's compressed to a smaller file size, but doesn't have any video compression artifacts. Unfortunately, not all video players know what to do with a PNG-encoded video file. If you want to guarantee that your high-quality file is playable elsewhere, you may need to resort to the Raw codec. As its name implies, it consists of the raw image data in each frame. This means that it's the best possible quality you can get, but the file sizes for videos in the format are *huge*, so make sure you have spare hard drive space. Because this codec is completely uncompressed, it has no encoding options, with one exception. You have the option to write the raw frames vertically flipped. This is a setting that makes the Raw AVI playable on programs like WinDVD. If you want to have your file playable on systems other than Linux, it's a good idea to leave this check box enabled.

- **XViD** — XViD is a Free Software implementation of the popular DiVX video codec. You have the option to use this codec in this window. When you select this codec, its corresponding tab appears with the following options:

  - **Kbitrate** — Like the Video Bitrate value in the FFMPEG settings, this value controls how many kilobits are used to store each second of your video file.

  - **Reaction Delay** — When encoding frames XViD uses a variable bitrate. This value controls how quickly the bitrate is allowed to change from one frame to the next. It's similar to the Qdiff value covered in the FFMPEG parameters. You want this value to be smaller when you're dealing with video content that features fast motion.

  - **AVG Period** — Like the Reaction Delay factor, this value — the averaging period — controls the fluctuation of compression in time as you go through your video. If you recall the Qscale value discussed in the FFMPEG parameters, XViD encodes similarly. However, rather than using an explicit Qscale value, it uses the average quantization values over a range of frames. This value controls how many frames are used to compute that average.

  - **Buffer** — This setting is similar to the B-frames parameter for FFMPEG. It's the number of frames that the XViD codec uses to determine the average deviation from one frame to the next. Higher values can give you better compression, but may reduce quality.

  - **Max Quantizer** — This value is identical to the Qmax setting for the FFMPEG parameters. It's the maximum quantization value that any frame in your video can use. For good quality video, keep this value below 15.

  - **Min Quantizer** — This is the corresponding minimum quantization value that you want XViD to use. Smaller values yield better results at the expense of larger sizes. This is the same as the Qmin setting in the FFMPEG parameters.

  - **Key Interval** — This value is similar to the GOP setting used in the FFMPEG parameters. Rather than defining a GOP, XViD stipulates a particular frame as a reference, or *key frame*. This value defines how many frames are between each key frame.

  - **Quality** — This quality value is like the Compression parameter for PNG encoding. Higher values give you better compression and smaller file sizes, but the resulting video files are slower for your computer to decode. Lower values decode faster, but your file sizes are larger.

Setting Audio Options

With your video options set, the next thing you need to do is configure your audio options. So access these options, click the Audio Options tab in the Master Videoencoder window. Doing so gives you a window like the one shown in Figure 20-11.

If you don't have any sound for your video, the options in this window are easy: leave them blank. Of course, assuming you do have sound for your video, the options here are important. Everything is driven from the Audiofile text field at the top of the window. At its simplest, you click the Browse button to the right of the field and pick your audio file from the File Chooser that appears.

After picking the audio file, you can manually control the sample rate that the audio in your finished video file will have. Ideally, you should use the same sample rate as the source audio. However, some video format specifications require that you use a specific sample rate. For instance, the DV standard requires 16-bit audio to be at a 48 kHz sample rate. The value in the Samplerate text field is set in Hertz, so you can either manually type in the sample rate you want to use or you can use the drop-down menu to the right of the field to choose from a set of standard presets. Something to remember here is that if you increase the sample rate to be greater than that of your source file, the sound quality of the new file is the same as that of the original. However, if you reduce the sample rate, the output audio has lower sound quality than the original.

Note

The preferred audio format that the encoder likes to use is a 16-bit RIFF WAV file with the .wav file extension. You can use other audio formats if you have an audio converter program installed. You tell GAP where that converter is in the Audio Tool Configuration tab and get it to convert to the 16-bit RIFF WAV by clicking the Audioconvert button. ■

FIGURE 20-11

The Audio Options tab in the Master Videoencoder window lets you choose one or more audio sources to multiplex with your video.

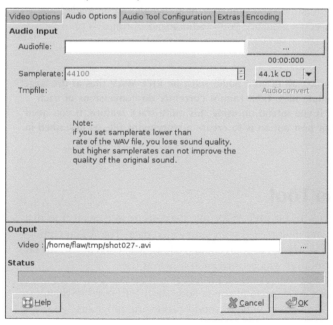

If your original audio file is in a format other than the preferred RIFF WAV format, you need to have GAP convert that file to something it understands. You do this by clicking the Audioconvert button. When you click this button, GAP uses the converter stipulated in the Audio Tool

Configuration tab to create a temporary audio file, which the encoder uses to multiplex with your video data.

That's basically all there is to the audio options. However, there is a neat trick that this tab allows if you use the FFMPEG encoder. You can actually load multiple audio files as individual tracks in your completed video file. As an example, say you have one audio file for character dialog and separate files for music and sound effects. Rather than mix down these files to a single RIFF WAV before encoding, you can tell GAP to encode each of these files as separate tracks in the final video. To do this, you need to create a text file that has the path to each audio file as a separate line of text. The path to these files can be either an absolute path from the root of your file system (/ in Linux and Mac; C:\ in Windows) or a path relative to the location of your text file (using ./ to indicate the current folder and ../ to indicate the parent folder). You can even use comment lines by starting them with the # character. An example text file might look like this:

```
# This is a comment line.
./dialog.wav
../music/music.wav
/data/soundfx/effects.wav
```

After you create this text file, load it into the Audiofile field at the top of the window. GAP handles it from there. Note that this feature gives you only the ability to create multiple tracks of audio. It does not give you the ability to stipulate a sequence of audio files to be loaded one after the other. This means that you need to sequence your audio ahead of time.

Warning

If you use this technique to load multiple audio files, all of your audio *must* be RIFF WAV files at the target sample rate of your output video file. With multiple files, GAP cannot currently do conversions of each file and store them temporarily. Keep this mind if you intend on using this multi-track feature. If you need the ability to load a sequence of audio files, your best option is to create a storyboard file, as described in Chapter 19. ∎

Configuring the Audio Tool

If you're loading an audio file that isn't a 16-bit RIFF WAV file, GAP needs to convert it to that format so it can be properly encoded and multiplexed with your video data. The Audio Options tab, described previously, lets GAP know where the source audio file is. The contents of this tab, shown in Figure 20-12, give you control over which conversion tool you use.

The default sound conversion tool that GAP expects to use is SoX, short for Sound eXchange. The SoX web site describes it as "the Swiss Army knife of sound processing programs." Available on Linux, Mac OS X, and Windows, SoX is capable of converting to and from nearly 40 different audio formats. Like GIMP, SoX is Free Software, released under the GNU General Public License. It ships by default on most Linux distributions, so if you're running Linux, chances are good that you already have it installed. If you're running Mac OS X or Windows, however, you may not have it installed. Fortunately, you can easily get it from the SoX web site at `http://sox.sourceforge.net`. All of the default settings that are in the Master Videoencoder window under the Audio Tool Configuration tab should then work just fine for you.

Of course, if you have another program that you prefer to use for audio conversion, you can still do that. Simply type the name of the program's executable in the Audiotool field at the top of the window. If you want to be even more explicit, you can type the full path to where that executable lives on your hard drive. Unfortunately, there's not a Browse button next to this field, so if you do that, you need to enter the path manually or copy and paste it from the address bar in your file browser (Explorer in Windows, Finder on Mac OS X).

Note

The Master Videoencoder expects that the audio conversion tool can be run from the command line. If your conversion tool of choice requires that you use a graphical interface to set options, the Audioconvert button may not work with it. In those cases, you're best off manually converting your audio file to a 16-bit RIFF WAV with your preferred tool ahead of time. ■

FIGURE 20-12

The Audio Tool Configuration tab gives you control over the tool you use to convert your audio files from their original format to the RIFF WAV format required by GAP.

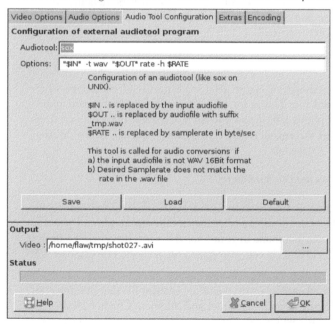

If you do choose to use a different tool, chances are good that its command-line options are quite different than the ones that SoX uses. This is why the Options field exists. Here is where you enter the options that your conversion tool uses to get that 16-bit RIFF WAV file. Even if you're using SoX, you can still use this field as way to customize SoX settings if you want. When customizing these options, there are some variables that you should be sure to include. They're briefly covered in this tab, but the following list includes descriptions that should be a bit more clear:

- **$IN** — This is the audio file that you enter in the Audiofile field of the Audio Options tab. You need to include this or the Audioconvert function won't know what the original file is.

- **$OUT** — As its name implies, this is the temporary output file in RIFF WAV format that the Audioconvert feature creates. It should be the value of $IN with _tmp.wav appended to the end of it.

- **$RATE** — This is the sample rate that you specify in the Samplerate field of the Audio Options tab. If you want your converted file to have the same sample rate as the original file, then it's not critical that you include this variable in the Options field.

After you have your customized conversion tool and its options (or just customized options for SoX) entered, the Master Videoencoder gives you the ability to store these settings to your hard drive for future use. To do this, click the Save button at the bottom of this tab. This brings up a File Chooser window where you can save a text file that maintains these settings for you. Then the next time you want to use GAP to encode video, you can reload these settings by clicking the Load button and finding the file that you saved. If you want to use just the default SoX tool and its settings, click the Default button and those settings are reloaded for you.

Using the Extras Tab

The options available in the Extras tab, shown in Figure 20-13, are mostly for situations where you're encoding video from a storyboard file. This is for when you click the Storyboard radio button for Input Mode in the Video Options tab. If you choose Storyboard, the Video Options tab doesn't give you any controls to tell the encoder where your storyboard file is. To do this, you need to use the parameters in the Extras tab.

Descriptions of each of these parameters are provided here:

- **Macrofile** — This is one of the few options in this tab that isn't directly associated with encoding from a storyboard file. Use this if you've created a Filtermacro file and you want to use the filters in that macro on each frame in your final video file. Just click the Browse button to the right of the text field and choose your macro file with the File Chooser window that appears.

- **Storyboard File** — As described earlier, a storyboard file is a text file that describes various image, video, and audio elements and their order and duration. Chapter 19 goes into more detail on creating storyboards with GAP. This field is where you tell the encoder where your storyboard file is on your hard drive.

- **Storyboard Audio** — GAP's encoder isn't capable of sequencing audio files while it's encoding, so it cannot dynamically load audio files named in your storyboard file and encode them on the fly. You can get around this by doing a *mixdown*, or a single audio file with all audio mixed together in the proper sequence. You can create the mixdown directly in this tab by clicking the Create Composite Audio button here. This creates a single RIFF WAV audio file that you can point to in the Audio Options tab for encoding and multiplexing.

- **Monitor Frames while Encoding** — If you're using a Filtermacro it's often helpful to monitor the progress of the encoder while it works. When you enable this check box, GAP generates an image window that loads each frame of your video as it gets processed. The only disadvantage to this option is that it may make your encoding process take slightly longer because GIMP has to load and display each frame in sequence. While encoding, if you no longer want to monitor the encoding process, you can close the image window and the encoder continues happily.

- **Debug Flat File** — This option is designed to help you sort out encoding errors, but it's actually a lot more helpful than that. What it does is create a JPEG file of each frame of your video prior to sending it to be encoded. If you run a Filtermacro, this is helpful in determining if the encoder got a properly filtered frame. However, you can also use this to reproduce a video file without running any filters. Just load these frames in the Master Videoencoder and create a new video file.

- **Debug Multilayer File** — This parameter is similar to Debug Flat File, except it's earlier in the process. If you're generating your video file from a sequence of multilayer files, this takes each file prior to filtering or encoding and saves it as an XCF file. This helps you ensure that the Filtermacro and encoder are getting good data from GIMP.

FIGURE 20-13

The Extras tab in the Master Videoencoder window

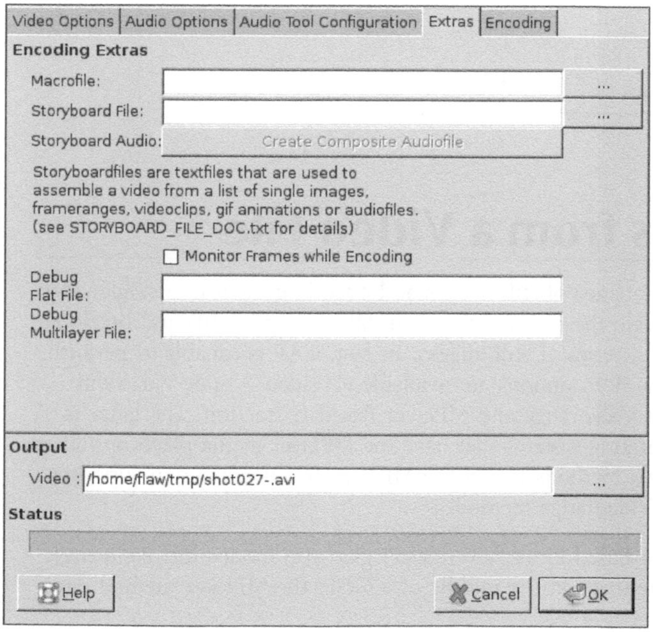

The Encoding Tab

This tab, shown in Figure 20-14, has no options available for you to set. What it does is show the status of your encoding job as it's processed. When you click the OK button at the bottom of the window, the Master Videoencoder window automatically makes this tab active so you can actively monitor the encoder's progress.

The Encoding tab of the Master Videoencoder window shows the progress of your encoding job as it works.

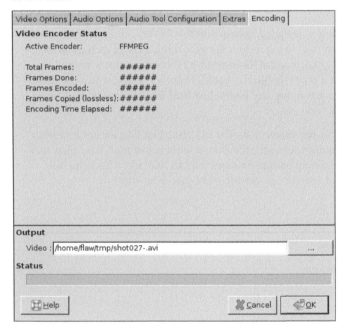

Extracting Frames from a Video File

Because GAP is capable of taking a sequence of still images and encoding them to a single video file, it makes sense that GAP can also do the reverse operation: taking a video file and breaking all of it or a segment from it out into a series of still images. In fact, GAP is capable of performing this operation in one of two ways. Both options are available at Video ➤ Split Video into Frames. The two methods are Extract Videorange and MPlayer Based Extraction. The latter is available only on Linux and Unix operating systems that have the MPlayer media player installed. The biggest difference between the two methods is that the MPlayer Based Extraction supports more video formats than the Extract Videorange method.

However, the trade-off is that MPlayer Based Extraction doesn't give you *frame-exact positioning*. This means that if you choose a frame that's in the middle of a GOP, the MPlayer method does not give you accurate frame data until it reaches the start of the next GOP. There are ways to deal with this, but it's definitely something worth remembering.

Using Extract Videorange

If at all possible, always try to extract frames with this method first by choosing Video ➢ Split Video into Frames ➢ Extract Videorange. When you pick this menu item, GAP provides you with a window like the one in Figure 20-15.

FIGURE 20-15

The Extract Videorange window is a reliable way to pull a range of frames from a video file.

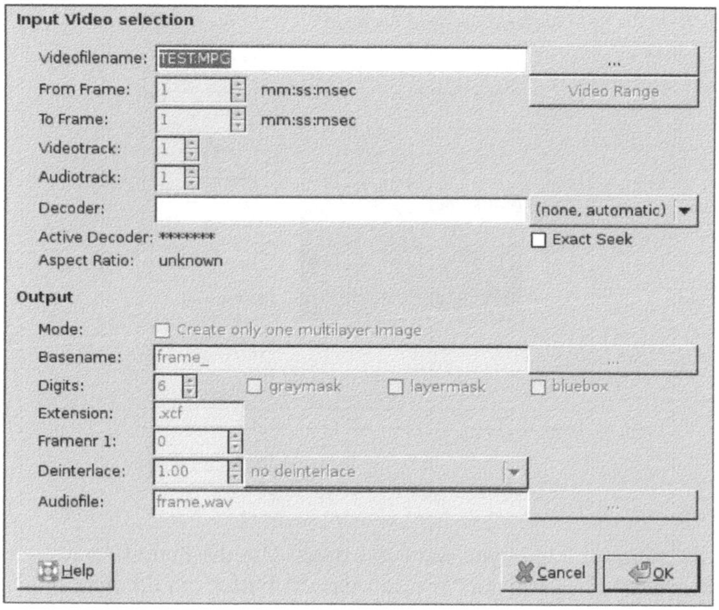

This method uses a few specialized libraries for reading video files, so although it doesn't support as many formats as MPlayer, it does give you more reliable extraction. Furthermore, if you're running Windows or Mac OS X, this is the only sure way of performing this operation. The window is split into two sections: input options at the top and output options at the bottom.

Setting Input Options

The most important field in this entire window is the Videofilename field. This is your source video file. If you know the exact path to this file, you can type it directly; however, it's easier to click the Browse button to the right of the text field and pick your file using the File Chooser. Once you choose your source video file, all of the other options in this window become active and "un-grayed," allowing you to control their values. With your video file chosen, the next thing you need to do is define the range of frames from your video file that you want to extract. If you know the actual frame numbers you want to use to define the start and end of your range, you can enter them directly into the From Frame and To Frame fields. However, chances are good that you won't know this information off the top of your head. To help with that, GAP gives you an interactive means of defining your start and end frames. To do this, click the Video Range button on the right of the window. When you do this, the window is extended to the right, revealing the exact same interface used when you select Video ➤ Playback. Figure 20-16 shows what the Extract Videorange window looks like after you click the Video Range button.

FIGURE 20-16

Using the Video Playback interface to interactively define the video range for your frame extraction

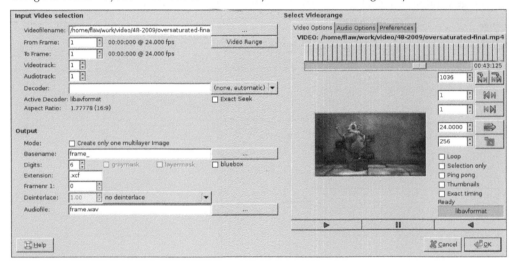

Use this interface to determine the range of frames you want to extract. Use the Button Array and the Position Scale to see the content of each frame. You can use the buttons to the right of the window to set the start and end frames for your range. Alternatively, you can just look at the frame number and manually type the From Frame and To Frame values on the left side of the window.

If your video file features multiple video or audio tracks, such as DVD footage that has alternate camera angles or dialog recorded in a different language, you can stipulate which track you want to use using the Videotrack and Audiotrack parameters. Most video files feature only one of each, so typically you'll keep both of these values set to 1, but it's handy to have the option available if you need it.

When you choose your file, GAP tries to determine which decoding library to use for extracting your frames. The one it chooses is shown next to the Active Decoder label. However, if GAP guesses incorrectly or you just know that you want to use a different decoding library, you can set it manually in the Decoder field. Click the drop-down to the right of the field to choose from one of the libraries GAP has access to. Typically, the choices will be Libmpeg3, Libavformat, and Quicktime4linux. More often than not, Libavformat — provided by FFMPEG — is the choice that GAP makes automatically. If none of these libraries work, you may need to try using MPlayer Based Extraction instead. If you have troubles extracting frame data from compressed video files, you may want to enable the Exact Seek check box. This is particularly useful if you click the Video Range button to interactively set your start and end frames for your extraction range.

Setting Output Options

The lower half of this window is devoted to what happens to the frames that you extract from the video file. Each of these parameters is described here:

- **Mode** — By default, the video extract feature creates a sequence of still images from the range you defined. However, if you enable this check box, GAP creates a single image where each frame has its own layer on the image. This is useful if you want to turn a segment of a video into a short animated GIF. However, if you're extracting a large number of frames or the size of each frame image is large, you're better off using a sequence of stills. This prevents you from having an unreasonably large single file.

- **Basename** — This parameter and the next few ones beneath it control the name of each frame that gets extracted. By default, frames follow the pattern of `frame_000001.xcf`, `frame_000002.xcf`, and so on. This value controls the front of the filename, including the full path, up to the number of the frame. To make things easier, you can click the Browse button to the right of this field and use the File Chooser to control where the frame files go and what their names start with.

- **Digits** — Put simply, this value controls how many digits are used to define the frame number that's extracted. By default this value is 6, but if you're extracting less than 1000 frames, you may prefer to use a value of 3 instead.

- **Bluebox** — As described in Chapter 19, Bluebox is a feature provided by GAP that acts like a chroma key, allowing you to define a single color as transparent. This is used often in effects footage where actors are placed in front of a blue or green screen. Enable this check box if you're working with this kind of footage. When defining what's transparent, you have two additional options of how GAP gives you that transparency:

  - **Graymask** — If you enable this option, Bluebox generates a grayscale image that works as a mask, defining what portions of the frame are transparent and what portions are opaque. That grayscale image is what gets extracted as each frame, rather than the full content of each frame. This is useful if you want to extract just the transparency mask of effects footage rather than the footage itself.

  - **Layermask** — If you have Bluebox enabled, the extractor generates transparency in each frame for you. However, you have control over how that transparency is saved. The default behavior is to generate an alpha channel for the frame. This works well, but it makes it difficult for you to select those transparent pixels. So you may prefer to have transparency defined by a layer mask instead. Enabling this check box is what sets that behavior.

- **Extension** — This parameter not only controls the three-letter extension at the end of each image file extracted, but it also controls the format of that file. The default behavior is to use GIMP's native XCF format so you have full access to GIMP's features like layer masks and alpha channels. However, if you want the extracted frames to be in a different format that takes up less disk space, you can set that by typing in another extension, like .jpg or .png.

- **Framenr 1** — This value defines what number your extracted frames starts with. This is helpful if your extraction range starts partly through your video file. You can define this value to be the same value used in the From Frame field and your extracted frames remain consistent with the frame numbers in the source video.

- **Deinterlace** — If you're extracting frames from standard definition television or a DV video camera, the footage that you get is interlaced. The nature of interlaced footage makes it difficult to edit frame by frame or apply filters and effects. To compensate for this, you can deinterlace the frames as they're extracted. GAP provides you with a handful of options, each with their advantages and disadvantages:

  - **No Deinterlace** — If your input footage isn't interlaced or you want to deinterlace with another process later on, choose this option.

  - **Deinterlace (Odd/Even Lines Only)** — As explained earlier in this chapter, interlacing is the process of taking a frame and splitting it into two fields, each consisting of alternating horizontal lines of the originating image. These two options let you choose either the odd lines or the even lines as your basis. Then the missing lines are interpolated from the lines you choose. You can control the smoothness of this interpolation with the numeric field to the left. A value of 0.00 gives you no interpolation whereas a value of 1.00 gives you the smoothest possible interpolation.

  - **Deinterlace Frames x 2** — The disadvantage of the odd/even lines only method is that it completely throws out half of the image information for each frame. To account for this, you have the option of using both the even and the odd sets of lines. What this does is take each frame of video and generate two still images; one for each set of lines. This way no information is lost, but to properly play back the video, you need to double your frame rate.

- **Audiofile** — If your source video file has audio in it, that audio is extracted to its own 16-bit RIFF WAV file. This field allows you to control where that file is created.

Using MPlayer-Based Extraction

If your source video file cannot be read by any of the libraries available in the Extract Videorange feature, and you're running Linux, you may want to try using MPlayer Based Extraction. To run it, navigate to Video ➤ Split Video to Frames ➤ MPlayer Based Extraction. When you select this menu item, you should get a window like the one in Figure 20-17.

FIGURE 20-17

The MPlayer Based Extraction window

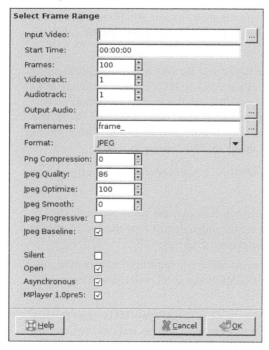

The first few options in this window are just like the ones in the video range extraction feature:

- **Input Video** — This is your source video file. Either type in the full path to this file or use the Browse button to the right of this field to pick your file with the File Chooser.

- **Start Time** — This value is similar to the From Frame setting in Extract Videorange. The difference, though, is that this value is set in standard SMPTE time. That is, it uses the format hours:minutes:seconds. This is partially because MPlayer can't give you frame-exact positioning. This also means that you may need to view your file in an external player to see the start time you want to use.

- **Frames** — Rather than define an explicit end frame for your extraction range, MPlayer Based Extraction has you stipulate how many frames you want to extract with this setting.

- **Videotrack/Audiotrack** — Like the Extract Videorange feature, MPlayer Based Extraction recognizes video files with multiple video and audio tracks. These parameters let you control which tracks to pull from your source footage.

- **Output Audio** — This is the full path and filename where MPlayer saves the 16-bit RIFF WAV file that it extracts from your video file.

- **Framenames** — Like the Basename parameter for the Extract Videorange feature, this value controls what each frame's filename starts with, as well as where on your hard drive it's stored.

- **Format** — MPlayer Based Extraction gives you the ability to save still frames into one of three image formats: XCF, PNG, or JPEG. This drop-down menu gives you the choice of which format to use.

The options below the Format drop-down menu are dependent on which format you choose. If you choose to use GIMP's native XCF format, none of the PNG or JPEG options have any influence over the final extracted image frame. If you choose PNG, the only relevant option is the PNG compression parameter. Choosing the JPEG image format then takes advantage of the five subsequent JPEG settings to control the compression of each generated frame file. Those settings are the exact same settings you find if you save any image in JPEG format in GIMP.

The last four check boxes in this window control how MPlayer behaves when it goes through the extraction process:

- **Silent** — The MPlayer extractor's default behavior is to play the video and audio files while it's extracting. If you would rather not see the video data or hear the audio playing, enable this check box and your frames will be extracted silently.

- **Open** — If this check box is enabled, then when MPlayer completes the extraction process, GAP opens the first extracted image in a GIMP image window for you to begin editing.

- **Asynchronous** — Keep this option enabled to make sure GAP runs MPlayer as an asynchronous process. This means that MPlayer runs as its own process and only periodically checks in with GAP while it's extracting to give notification of its progress.

- **MPlayer 1.0pre5** — If you're running an older version of MPlayer — specifically version 1.0pre5 or earlier — enable this check box. If you're running a newer version of MPlayer, make sure this check box is disabled.

Once you've set the options you need in this window, click OK and GAP goes through the process of extracting each frame of your video file within the range you've defined. Neat, huh?

Summary

This chapter was packed with a ton of information that you wouldn't normally expect to read about in a standard raster image editor. GAP has provided GIMP with the ability to work with animation and video since before GIMP hit version 1.0. And with the information in this chapter, you can now use GAP's features to create a video playback preview, encode video files for distribution, and rip individual frames from a video file for future editing. It's all incredibly cool stuff and certainly makes GIMP shine as an excellent tool in the toolbox for animation and video touch-ups.

Of course, all of these video and animation features are made possible because of GIMP's advanced ability to use scripts and plug-ins. This is the topic of the next section of this book. It's time to find out some excellent ways to bend GIMP to your will!

Part V

Advanced Topics

IN THIS PART

Chapter 21
Finding and Installing Plug-ins

Chapter 22
Creating Custom Effects with Scripting

Advanced Topics

Finding and Installing Plug-ins

One of the attractive aspects of GIMP is its extensibility. That is, anyone with a bit of coding experience can add features and functionality to GIMP in one of two ways. The most obvious way is by directly modifying GIMP's source. It's one of the real, tangible benefits of GIMP's Free Software status. However, taking this route has a couple disadvantages. GIMP is a *big* program, consisting of more than 600,000 lines of code spread across around 2,600 individual files. Figuring out where your feature fits in can be a daunting task. And if your code doesn't get included in the official release, it can be difficult to maintain across multiple versions of GIMP.

To help alleviate that pain, GIMP developers cooked up the ability to allow *plug-ins*, or small programs that can be tightly integrated into GIMP's interface. To facilitate this, GIMP has a few plug-in application programming interfaces, or APIs, depending on whether the plug-in is written in the C programming language or a scripting language like Python or Scheme. The API is basically a means of allowing plug-ins to access some of the data structures and functions in GIMP. The API is a lot less volatile than the main codebase and by using it, coders can maintain their plug-ins independently of the main GIMP developers. In fact, quite a few features that you might consider to be "core functionality" of GIMP, like importing or exporting files, are actually plug-ins that ship with GIMP.

This chapter does not cover the process of writing plug-ins. For that, have a look at Chapter 22. Instead, this chapter covers where you can get plug-ins on the Internet and the process involved with installing them. At the end of the chapter, I also cover a handful of plug-ins that many GIMP artists find useful. In fact, the usage of quite a few of these plug-ins has been covered elsewhere in this book. This chapter is focused on what they do, how to get them, and any "gotchas" that you may run across when installing them.

IN THIS CHAPTER

Using the GIMP Plugin Registry to find plug-ins

Understanding some of the most useful plug-ins

601

The GIMP Plugin Registry

The first place to go looking for plug-ins is the online GIMP Plugin Registry at http://registry.gimp.org. This web site features an exhaustive list of user-created GIMP plug-ins, both old and new. You may wonder, "Why would I have any interest in plug-ins for older versions of GIMP?" Truth be told, you might not be interested at all. Newer versions of GIMP may natively implement the feature that plug-in provided or perhaps implement it better. However, if you still find that feature useful, the plug-in and its source code are available to you through the registry. You can contact the original developer of it to make an updated version or modify it yourself (or hire someone to do that).

The GIMP Plugin Registry houses a large variety of plug-ins ranging in functionality from image manipulation shortcuts like automated timestamp removal or giving photos that vintage duo-tone look, to giving GIMP whole new features like rotating brushes or a more Photoshop-like interface. Because the registry relies on plug-in creators to submit their plug-ins, it's not comprehensive. A few plug-ins don't get submitted by their creators, but the majority of useful ones can be found here.

When you visit the GIMP Plugin Registry, you're greeted with a page like the one shown in Figure 21-1. If you want to upload a new plug-in or create new posts in the registry's forums, you need to create an author login. However, creating a login isn't absolutely necessary. You can read nearly all of the content on the registry and post comments without logging in at all.

FIGURE 21-1

The GIMP Plugin Registry web site

If you're looking for a specific plug-in, use the keyword search on the right sidebar. This returns any plug-ins or forum posts that include the keyword you've typed. Alternatively, if you would like to look through the registry and get an idea of what's available, you can use the links in the center of the page under the Browse the Registry heading. You can often quickly find interesting plug-ins by using the tag cloud. Each plug-in that's added to the registry can be *tagged* with a word or phrase that pertains to it, just like you can tag resources in GIMP's Brushes dialog. The tag cloud, shown in Figure 21-2, shows all the tags that have been used on the registry with a weighting that matches the font size of the tag to how often it's used. In Figure 21-2, the tags *Plugins & Scripts* and *2.6* are associated with more plug-ins than the tags *vignette* and *astronomy*.

FIGURE 21-2

The tag cloud for the GIMP Plugin Registry shows which tags have been associated with more plug-ins.

Of course, if you just want to look through a list of what's available, click the List All Plugins, Scripts, Images, and Files link to get a paginated list of everything uploaded to the registry. When you click a plug-in entry, it brings up a page with a simple description of the plug-in provided by whomever uploaded it. Some plug-ins have more detailed entries than others, ranging from a simple link to the plug-in or script itself to detailed usage instructions with accompanying images. The really cool thing, though, is that each entry in the registry allows for user feedback and commentary. So if you have a question about a plug-in or you want to share a usage tip or trick with other users, you can make a comment directly on the plug-in's page. This kind of feedback is not only valuable to other people who may use the plug-in, but it also helps plug-in authors improve their work by notifying them of bugs, offering enhancement suggestions, or even sharing code improvements. Figure 21-3 shows an example plug-in registry entry.

FIGURE 21-3

Plug-ins that have been uploaded to the registry can have detailed descriptions with images, and each entry allows user feedback via comments.

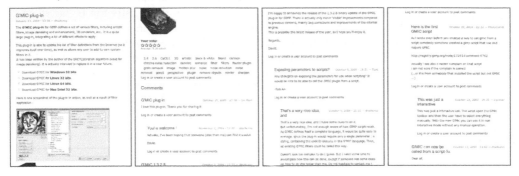

Installing Plug-ins

When you decide that you want to use a plug-in from the registry, you have to download it and install it so GIMP can recognize it. For most plug-ins, this is a fairly straightforward process. To be safe, though, if the plug-in includes a README file or any sort of installation instructions, it's *highly recommended* that you read through them and do what they suggest. When it comes to plug-ins, you'll encounter two main types: *scripts* and *plug-ins*. "But wait," you might say, "I thought all of these things were called plug-ins. What gives?"

Generally speaking, a plug-in is a small program that extends the functionality of another program. When writing programs, developers can write in all sorts of programming languages. These languages can be split into two main categories: scripting languages and compiled languages. Scripting languages are human-readable and interpreted by the computer on the fly, line-by-line, much as you would read a cooking recipe. They are very effective at quickly developing programs that perform relatively simple tasks, but because they're run on the fly, scripts aren't necessarily optimized and can take a while to process. GIMP natively supports the Python, Perl, and Scheme scripting languages, but there have been user extensions that allow support for other languages like Ruby. You can find out more about scripting in GIMP in Chapter 22.

Note
A GIMP script written in Scheme is referred to as a Script-Fu. ∎

In contrast, a compiled programming language is converted to the computer language of ones and zeros before you run it. Although this conversion process, called *compiling*, makes the code no longer human-readable, it's much easier for your computer to understand and is often optimized to perform better. Compiled languages are often used for more processor-intensive tasks that benefit from the speed increase you can get from taking the extra compiling step. GIMP itself is written in a compiled language called C.

Although the GIMP Plugin Registry and even some GIMP documentation use the term "plug-in" as a generic umbrella term, for configuration and installation purposes a plug-in written in a scripting language is called a script, and a plug-in written in a compiled language is actually a plug-in. To help differentiate a bit, I'll call the latter type "compiled plug-ins."

Warning

To complicate things further, even though plug-ins written in Python are technically scripts, you actually install them with compiled plug-ins rather than with scripts. The reasons for this aren't made entirely clear, but just remember to install Scheme plug-ins (with the .scm file extension) with your scripts and Python plug-ins (with the .py file extension) with your compiled plug-ins. ■

Installing Scripts

Of the two types of plug-ins, scripts are the simplest to install. If you download them from the registry, they should be pretty easy to pick out. The script file usually has a .scm extension at the end of the filename. Installing them is as easy as copying that file to your GIMP scripts folder. You can actually have more than one and it varies a bit depending on whether you're using GIMP in Linux, Mac OS X, or Windows. To see where your scripts folder is, check your preferences (Edit ➤ Preferences) under Folders ➤ Scripts. You should have something like what's shown in Figure 21-4.

FIGURE 21-4

Look in GIMP's Preferences to see where your script folders are.

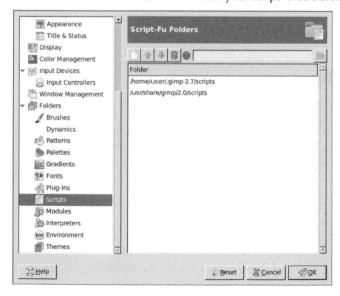

In most systems, two folders are shown here: one is a global folder available to all users on your computer and the other is only for your current user. On Linux systems, the global folder is usually something like /usr/share/gimp/2.0/scripts and the current user folder is /home/[user_name]/.gimp-2.8/scripts.

To install the script, copy the .scm file to one of these folders and restart GIMP. When you restart GIMP, the name of this new script shows up in the loading splash image. Of course, this often goes by too fast for anyone to see, so the best way to see if the script was properly installed is to navigate to wherever it's supposed to be accessed in GIMP's interface. This information should be available with the documentation that came with the script.

Tip

When you install a script-fu script, you actually don't have to restart GIMP. You can navigate to Filters ➤ Script-Fu ➤ Refresh Scripts and the list of available scripts will be reloaded for you. ■

If you can't find the new feature that the script is supposed to add, there's a chance that there was a problem loading it. To determine this, you can try starting GIMP from the command line. To do this, you'll need a terminal window. In Linux, this is usually GNOME-Terminal or xterm.

On a Mac, launch the terminal by going to Applications ➤ Utilities ➤ Terminal. In Windows, go to Start ➤ Run, type cmd in the dialog that appears, and press Enter. From there, launching GIMP should be as easy as typing gimp at the prompt and pressing Enter.

Starting GIMP this way allows you to see any errors that may happen as GIMP loads. If you see an error message that mentions your plug-in, you've found your problem. From here you can either try to debug the situation yourself, or report the problem on the script's page in the GIMP Plugin Registry. You can also use the error as a search term on a search engine such as Google to see if anyone else has run into this same problem.

Installing Compiled Plug-Ins

This process is used for compiled plug-ins as well as plug-ins written in Python. Generally speaking, you install these plug-ins in much the same way that you would install a Script-Fu script. The GIMP Preferences dialog (User ➤ Preferences) lists one or more folders where compiled plug-ins are installed, as shown in Figure 21-5. For simple compiled plug-ins or Python scripts, the installation process is often as easy as copying the plug-in to one of these folders and restarting GIMP.

Typically, though, GIMP plug-ins are a bit more complex and sometimes involve installing helper libraries that they use to accomplish their task. For that reason, many compiled plug-ins come with their own installers for Mac OS X and Windows or are supplied as separate packages for some Linux distributions. It's for this reason that you should really pay attention to any documentation that comes with a compiled plug-in. If there's a web site for the compiled plug-in, definitely check it for the proper installation procedure.

Note

As mentioned before, when a program is compiled, it's translated from human-readable code to computer-readable ones and zeros. This compiling process doesn't just translate to any computer language; it translates to a very specific processor type, or *architecture*, such as 64-bit Intel processors. It's for this reason that you should make sure that, unless you're compiling the plug-in yourself, you download the right compiled plug-in that matches your operating system and processor architecture. ■

FIGURE 21-5

The Preferences dialog shows where GIMP's compiled plug-ins and Python scripts are installed.

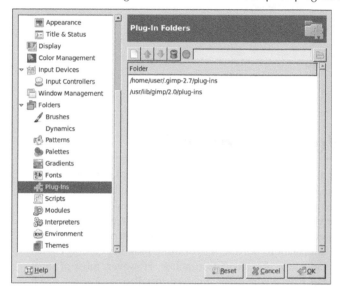

Once you have the compiled plug-in installed, it's actually much easier to determine if the installation went smoothly. Obviously you can do the same as with scripts and just see if it shows up in GIMP's interface where the plug-in's documentation indicates, but there's a slightly better way: GIMP's Plug-in Browser, shown in Figure 21-6. To bring up this browser, navigate to Help ➢ Plug-in Browser in the image window.

From this window you can search for your new compiled plug-in by name using the Search field, or you can hunt for it manually using either the List or Tree views on the left of the browser. If you click a plug-in name, the panel on the right of the window shows some basic information about what the compiled plug-in does, who wrote it, where it can be found in GIMP's interface, and some technical information about the input parameters the plug-in accepts. This is also a fun way of seeing just how much of GIMP's functionality is implemented as a compiled plug-in.

FIGURE 21-6

GIMP's Plug-in Browser lets you search installed plug-ins and find out basic information about each one.

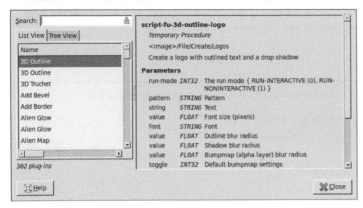

A Few Plug-ins Worth Mentioning

What would this chapter be if I didn't actually share some of the cool GIMP plug-ins that can make your life easier or give you additional features that don't ship with the official version of GIMP? This section has a short alphabetical list of GIMP plug-ins that are certainly worth sharing. In fact, some of these plug-ins are valuable enough that I've covered their usage in depth in other chapters of this book. When I come across those plug-ins I'll give you a cross-reference of which chapters hold this additional information. For the rest of these plug-ins I'll cover a little bit of usage, but most of them have adequate documentation online. However, most of these plug-ins are compiled plug-ins, which can have a somewhat involved installation process, so I'll definitely go into detail on how to get them installed and working for you.

Tip

Many of these plug-ins are maintained independently of the main GIMP development and often have their own release cycles. It's a good idea to check periodically with the Plugin Registry and, if it exists, the plug-in's web site. You can also follow the web site that accompanies this book for links and updates on each of these plug-ins, as well as others that get released after this book is published. ■

Exposure Blend

At the end of Chapter 12, there's in-depth coverage of the usage of the Exposure Blend plug-in, a plug-in designed to give your digital photographs the appearance of having a higher dynamic range. This section covers the installation of that plug-in so GIMP can make use of it. First, though, you have to download the actual plug-in. It's listed in the GIMP Plugin Registry and you can find the most recent version and detailed documentation on its web site. From there, Installation is pretty simple. Just download the Exposure Blend .scm file (exposure-blend .scm), copy it to your GIMP scripts folder, and restart GIMP or refresh your scripts (Filters ➤

Script-Fu ➤ Refresh Scripts). If you're running the Ubuntu Studio Linux distribution, you may have the gimp-plugin-registry package already installed. If that's the case, you already have Exposure Blend installed. Just be aware that it's actually a slightly older version than the one that you can find on the Exposure Blend web site.

The biggest difference between the two versions is where you find the Exposure Blend functions in the Filters menu. In the older version, you would find them at Filters ➤ Photo ➤ Exposure Blend, whereas in the newer version they're directly at Filters ➤ Exposure Blend. For the purposes of this section, I'm going to assume that you have the most recent version installed. After installation, you should have the set of menus shown in Figure 21-7 at Filters ➤ Exposure Blend.

FIGURE 21-7

The Exposure Blend menu that appears once you have the script installed

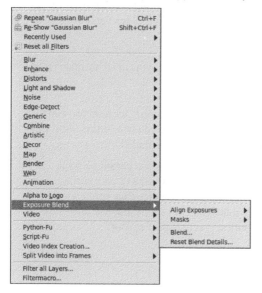

GIMP-GAP

The majority of this book covers using GIMP in the capacity of editing and creating still images. The exceptions to this are Chapters 19 and 20, which discuss how GIMP can be used to work with video and animations. The plug-ins that provide nearly all of these features are bundled into the GIMP Animation Package, or GIMP-GAP (usually called simply GAP). GAP provides you with a whole array of features for working with video and animation, including onionskinning, motion tweening, and video encoding. Chapters 19 and 20 go into heavy detail on how to take advantage of all these features. Before doing that, though, you're going to have to get GAP installed.

Strangely, aside from a few forum posts and a link to a Windows binary of GAP 2.4.0, you won't find GAP on the GIMP Plugin Registry. It's actually distributed directly from the main GIMP web site. You can find the latest version on the download page.

Installing GAP on Linux

Like most programs in Linux, the easiest way to install GAP is to use your distribution's package management system. On Ubuntu, OpenSUSE, and Mandriva, GAP is included as an independent package called gimp-gap. You should be able to fire up your package manager (Synaptic in Ubuntu; YaST in OpenSUSE; Rpmdrake on Mandriva), do a search for a package by this name, and enable it for installation. On distributions where it's not maintained as its own package, you need to download it from www.gimp.org, compile it yourself, and install it manually. In fact, as of this printing, the current version of GAP is 2.6.0, released in early June of 2009. If this updated version hasn't quite found its way into the main Linux distribution repositories, you'll have to install it manually. However, if you're okay with using a slightly older version and waiting until the new version has been thoroughly vetted, you can install that older version of GAP with your distribution's package manager.

If you're going to compile and install the latest version of GAP yourself, you need to make sure you have the following packages:

- **GIMP 2.6.0 (or higher)** — This should probably go without saying because you can't actually use GAP without first starting GIMP. Fortunately, if you've made it this far in this book, there's a pretty good chance that you already have GIMP installed.

- **GIMP development package** — Most Linux distributions have a separate package for files that developers usually need to compile their code if it links to an existing program. GIMP is no exception. On most distributions, the package that you're looking for is gimp-dev. Look for it with your package management tool or just use one of the following commands (depending on the distribution you're using) as root:
  - For Debian/Ubuntu:

    ```
    apt-get install gimp-dev
    ```
  - For Fedora:

    ```
    yum install gimp-devel
    ```
  - For OpenSUSE:

    ```
    yast -i gimp-devel
    ```

    or

    ```
    zypper in gimp-devel
    ```
  - For Mandriva:

    ```
    urpmi gimp-devel
    ```

- **GLib 2.8 (or higher)** — GLib is a core library that GIMP requires to work. Chances are good that you already have this installed. Depending on your distribution, you may also have to install its developer package, glib-dev, as well.

- **Encoding and decoding libraries for ffmpeg and libmpeg3** — If you can play and encode video on your system already, you may already have these libraries installed. They're largely optional, depending on how much you want to be able to encode or decode video from GIMP. However, it's a good idea to have the following libraries installed: libbz2, libfaac, libfaad, libmp3lame, libx264, and libxvid. Most of these packages and their respective developer (-dev) packages should be easy to install from your package manager. If not, consult your distribution's documentation.

- **A full build environment** — This means the basic tools necessary to compile the code from GAP into something that both GIMP and your computer processor can understand. To have a full build environment for compiling GAP, you'll need at least the following three tools:

  - **GCC** — The GNU C compiler. This translates code written in the C programming language to the computer language that your processor understands. On nearly all distributions, the name of the package to install it is simply gcc. In fact, most distributions come with it already installed.

  - **Make** — Make is a tool that helps the compilation process, especially when a lot of files are involved. The package for this tool is called automake on most Linux distributions.

  - **NASM** — Another commonly used programming language that's closer to your processor's native language is called *assembly language*. NASM, or Netwide Assembler, is a type of compiler that translates the assembly code into the native processor language. On most Linux distributions, the package to install this tool is simply nasm.

With the proper requirements met, it's time to actually compile GAP. The first step after downloading it from www.gimp.org is to decompress it somewhere on your hard drive. This is where you compile the source code. I like to have a directory called src in my home directory, but you can do this nearly anywhere. Open a terminal window and go to this directory by typing the following command (assuming you also have created a src directory for yourself):

    cd ~/src

Once you're in your source directory, decompress the GAP file you downloaded by using the following command (assuming you downloaded the file to your src directory):

    tar -xvjf gimp-gap-2.6.0.tar.bz2

This creates a directory (gimp-gap-2.6.0 in this example) where all of GAP's source code is. Get into this directory by typing the following:

    cd gimp-gap-2.6.0

Now you're almost ready to compile. Run the following command:

    ./configure

This prepares the source to be compiled. You can specify some options here, but the defaults generally work fine. Basically this is a short script that checks your system to make sure that you have all of the required libraries and files necessary to compile GAP. If you're missing something, this script errors out and gives you a message to let you know what the problem is (usually a missing library). Once you rectify that situation, re-run the `./configure` command and make sure it completes without any errors. Once that happens, run the following command:

```
make
```

Like its name indicates, this makes GAP for you, compiling all of the necessary files to create an installable executable that both GIMP and your computer will understand. Occasionally this may error out because of a library dependency that the configure script didn't catch. If that happens, try to resolve the dependency issue and then re-run `make`. If the problem persists, search for the error online and see if other people have run into it. Chances are good that they have and also have a solution. The compiling process will definitely take some time, so be patient. However, assuming that it finishes without errors, you have one final step. You need to install GAP. To do this, though, you'll need to be the root, or administrator user. Depending on your distribution, you do this with either the `su` or `sudo` command. Either way, once you're root, you need to run the following:

```
make install
```

This should run without any errors at all, copying the compiled files to a directory on your hard drive where GIMP will know to look for GAP. Once this is done, you should be able to fire up GIMP and see that GAP is installed. The quickest way to see this is to look in the image window. If there is a menu called Video, then GAP is installed, recognized, and running in GIMP.

Installing GAP on Mac OS X

The easiest way to install GAP on Mac OS X is to use MacPorts. This is covered in a bit more depth in Appendix A on how to install GIMP on Mac OS X. However, assuming you have Ports already installed, the process is relatively straightforward. Open up the terminal app by going to Applications ➤ Utilities ➤ Terminal. Once you have a terminal window open, change directories to the folder where the GAP MacPorts file lives by typing the following:

```
cd /opt/local/bin/portslocation/dports/gimp-gap
```

From here you can install GAP by typing the following command and entering your administrative password when prompted:

```
sudo port install gimp-gap
```

Wait until Ports finishes doing its thing and once it's done, you should be able to start GIMP and see the Video menu in the image window, letting you know that GAP has been installed properly.

Installing GAP on Windows

Aside from the Linux distributions that cleanly include a version of GAP in their package repositories, the GAP installation process on Windows is the most painless. There's actually an installer for GAP available on the GIMP Plug-in Repository. You can go there directly at http://registry.gimp.org/node/3700 or you can use the search feature on the registry and type in GAP. One of the first few search results will be an entry called GAP 2.4 (Windows Installer). Go here to download the zip file of the installer and the bugfix file that fixes one of the bundled GAP plug-ins for Windows. When you have the files downloaded, decompress them and have a look at the file called HOW TO INSTALL.txt. This will give you information on how to use the installer. Basically all you have to do is double-click the Gimp-GAP-2.4.0-Setup.exe file and follow the installation wizard.

Once the installer finishes, you should be able to fire up GIMP and play with all of the fun new features that GAP gives you.

Note

At the time of this writing, GAP 2.6.0 was not yet available for Mac OS X or Windows in an easily installable form. You do have the ability to compile them yourself, but because setting up a build environment on these platforms is a bit more involved than it is in Linux, I've decided to omit that information from this chapter. Until the installer package for GAP on these platforms has been updated to the latest version, you're best off making do with GAP 2.4.0. ■

GIMPshop and GimPhoto/GimPad

Quick disclaimer: most of what I cover in this section aren't really plug-ins per se. They're actually hacks on the GIMP source, which may involve one or two external plug-ins. That said, the topic is covered often enough that it's worth mentioning here.

GIMPshop

When Photoshop users first encounter GIMP, one of the things that they often criticize is the GIMP interface and how different it is from the Photoshop interface. This is particularly true for users on the Windows platform. The reason for this is that prior to GIMP 2.6, it used to litter the Windows taskbar with each window in GIMP's interface. So if you had an image window, a Toolbox, and a Layers dialog, that would be three GIMP items in the taskbar rather than just one. In March of 2005 a "proof of concept" hack of GIMP called GIMPshop was released. Utilizing a plug-in called Deweirdifyer, GIMPshop took all of the separate GIMP windows and made them part of a more Photoshop-like *multiple document interface*, or MDI, where there's one large parent window containing all of GIMP's individual component windows. In addition to that, GIMPshop renamed and moved around menu items in GIMP to make them more familiar to Photoshop users. According to the original developer, Scott Moschella, the idea was to "convert a Photoshop *pirate* into a GIMP *user*." Figure 21-8 shows a screenshot of what GIMPshop looks like.

Unfortunately for users who enjoyed GIMPshop, the last release was in May of 2006 and it was tied pretty closely to the GIMP 2.2 series. Given that, it doesn't work as well on the current GIMP source tree and exhibits some pretty buggy behavior. In fact, it's even difficult to find the Deweirdifyer plug-in on the GIMP Plugin Registry. However, if you're still interested in playing with GIMPshop, you can download working versions for Mac OS X, Linux, and Windows from the "Home of the 'Original' GIMPshop," www.plasticbugs.com. There seems to be a slight resurgence of development energy around GIMPshop happening at www.gimpshop.com, but the original developer doesn't seem to be involved with that project and it appears to still be based on the GIMP 2.2 series.

FIGURE 21-8

Behold! GIMPshop!

GimPhoto/GimPad

If you're interested in having a more Photoshop-like interface on more recent version of GIMP — though not quite the 2.6 series yet — you may want to take a look at GimPhoto. GimPhoto is a modified version of GIMP 2.4.3 that, like GIMPshop, adjusts GIMP's menus to be more like Photoshop and includes a bundle of plug-ins that former Photoshop users may find useful. On Windows machines, you can use GimPhoto with another package, developed by the same people, called GimPad to give GIMP an MDI. You can get GimPhoto installation files for Windows and Linux at www.gimphoto.com. If you're a Windows user, you can also get GimPad here. Figure 21-9 shows what GimPhoto/GimPad looks like on a Windows system.

FIGURE 21-9

FIGURE 21-9

GimPhoto working with GimPad on Windows to give you a more Photoshop-like experience

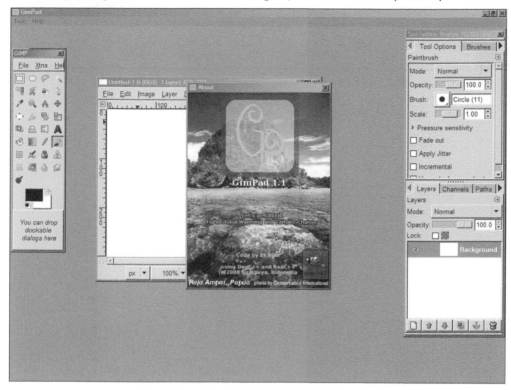

Of course, GimPhoto is built based on the GIMP 2.4 series, so you won't have access to a lot of the new features available in the latest versions of GIMP, and in fact, GIMP 2.6's implementation of Utility Window hints for the Toolbox and dockable dialogs went a long way to alleviate the problems Windows users had with GIMP's lack of an MDI. That said, the beauty of Free Software is that you're free to use GimPhoto or GIMPshop if you want and development still continues on both of these modified versions of GIMP. The last release of GimPhoto was in late 2008 and there's still active development going on with it. So in the future Photoshop migrants may be able to have the comfort of their formerly favorite tool with the cool features and benefits of Free Software that GIMP has.

GREYCstoration and G'MIC

The GREYCstoration plug-in has been mentioned elsewhere in this book, particularly in Chapter 2 when discussing the process of cleanly scaling up a small digital image. Specifically speaking, GREYCstoration is an *image regularization algorithm* that you use for doing noise reduction in your images. For example, if you take a photograph in low light conditions, the result is often a really grainy image. The GREYCstoration plug-in helps clean up this grain for you. This plug-in does not ship with GIMP by default, but fortunately, it's easy to find on the GIMP Plugin Registry. After you download it, decompress the zip file to your GIMP plug-ins folder and restart GIMP. If everything goes well, you can navigate to Filters ➤ Enhance ➤ GREYCstoration and you'll be greeted with a dialog like the one in Figure 21-10.

FIGURE 21-10

The interface for the GREYCstoration GIMP plug-in, used to reduce noise in images

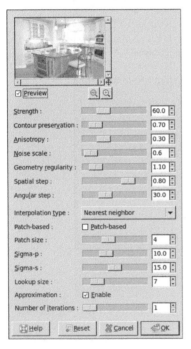

However, as of late 2008, the developers of GREYCstoration have integrated its functionality into a new plug-in called G'MIC, or GREYC's Magic Image Converter. G'MIC is actually a suite of tools and filters that you can use to apply all kinds of customized effects on images, some of which overlap functionality with features already present in GIMP. Because G'MIC supersedes GREYCstoration, it's recommended that you install it instead of GREYCstoration. That said, you can actually have both installed at the same time and they won't interfere with each other, so the choice is really yours. The G'MIC plug-in is also available on the GIMP Plug-in Repository, but you can find more detailed documentation for it on the G'MIC web site at http://gmic.sourceforge.net/gimp.shtml.

Once you have the G'MIC plug-in for your operating system downloaded, installation is as simple as decompressing the zip file in your GIMP plug-ins directory as described near the beginning of this chapter. With G'MIC installed, can fire up GIMP and play with it by going to Filters ➤ G'MIC for GIMP. Doing this brings up the G'MIC Toolbox, shown in Figure 21-11, with its incredibly diverse set of filters.

FIGURE 21-11

The G'MIC Toolbox is where an insanely large number of image filters live, including the functionality of the GREYCstoration plug-in.

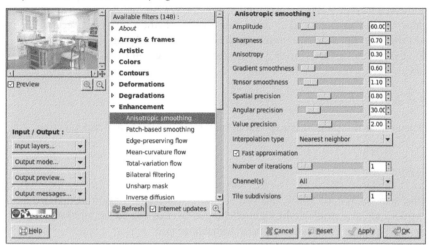

To use the features of the GREYCstoration plug-in from G'MIC, navigate through the available filters to the ones under the heading of Enhancement. In particular the filters you're looking for are Anisotropic Smoothing and Patch-Based Smoothing. Both of these filters are actually part of the GREYCstoration framework and between them, the options are very similar to the ones available for GREYCstoration, particularly the ones for Anisotropic Smoothing.

G'MIC is a fully involved toolset that can do everything from simple noise reduction to generating a 3D animated relief from a single image. It's definitely worth your time to sit down and play with all of the available filters and options it gives you. The best thing about this plug-in is that it integrates a preview window so you can get a good idea of what the final result will look like before actually applying the filter. Unfortunately, covering every single one of the 126 filters that ship with G'MIC is outside the scope of this book, but the G'MIC online documentation is very helpful and the interface for the plug-in itself is very discoverable, giving you the ability to play with it and play the "what does this button do?" game. Have fun!

Layer Effects

Another one of the features that some Photoshop users miss when migrating to GIMP are *layer effects*. Some examples of layer effects are drop shadows, glows, and embossing. GIMP does not currently support Photoshop-style layer effects where the effect is bound to a specific layer, but the Layer Effects plug-in can give you comparable features, though not exactly the same interface. You can find Layer Effects on the GIMP Plugin Registry at `http://registry.gimp .org/node/186`. You get pretty detailed installation instructions there, but the biggest thing to pay attention to is the fact that you can get the Layer Effects as either a Script-Fu script or a Python script. Both plug-ins offer the same functionality, but the one written in Python is more tightly integrated with GIMP's interface, offers an interactive preview, and should be slightly more familiar to Photoshop users.

To install the Python version of this plug-in, download it from the repository and copy it to your plug-ins folder, as indicated in Edit ➤ Preferences under Folders ➤ Plug-ins. If you're running GIMP on Linux or Mac OS X, you may need to make sure that the Python script is executable. The easiest way to do this is to open up a terminal window and go to the plug-in folder where you copied layerfx.py by issuing the following command (assuming you installed the plug-in in your home directory):

```
cd ~/.gimp-2.8/plug-ins
```

Once you're there, ensure that the plug-in is executable by typing the following and pressing Enter:

```
chmod +x layerfx.py
```

Once you've done this, start (or restart) GIMP and you should notice a new option in the Layers menu. Those same options are also available by right-clicking a layer in the Layers dockable dialog. Figure 21-12 shows the Layer Effects options now available to you.

FIGURE 21-12

The Layer Effects plug-in gives you quick access to some handy features that are similar to what you might find in Photoshop's layer effects.

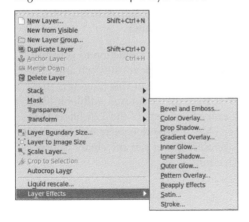

Layer Effects gives you the following effects to apply to a selected layer:

- **Bevel and Emboss** — This is actually a series of effects to bevel or emboss the contents of a layer. It's often used with text to give it some form of depth or dimension. The options for this effect give you control over the type of bevel or embossing you want to use, as well as color choices and angle control for highlights and shading.

- **Color Overlay** — As the name implies, the contents of your layer are overlaid with the color of your choice. This is a quick way to generate a mask or make a layer seem muted by overlaying it with a semi-transparent white.

- **Drop Shadow** — A staple effect used in all sorts of designs, the drop shadow helps give an image a sense of depth and can be effectively used to visually separate a layer from the layers beneath it.

- **Gradient Overlay** — This effect is similar to the Color Overlay effect, but rather than using a flat color, this effect allows you to use one of the many gradients available in GIMP or one that you've custom created yourself.

- **Inner Glow** — This effect produces something like what you may see on a sign or in a room with recessed lighting. Rather than glowing outward from the layer's alpha mask, the effect puts the glow over the contents of the layer you apply it to.

- **Inner Shadow** — This effect is like the Drop Shadow effect, but instead of making the layer appear to lift above the layers beneath it, this effect gives the illusion that your layer is actually inset into the layers beneath it instead.

- **Outer Glow** — If you want to give a layer or text a glow that radiates outward from its alpha mask, covering some of the content in the layers below, use this effect. Like the Drop Shadow effect, this can be an effective means of separating a layer from the ones beneath it.

- **Pattern Overlay** — Like the Color Overlay and Gradient Overlay effects, this effect covers the contents of your layer according to its alpha mask. However, instead of using a flat color or a gradient, this effect allows you to use one of the patterns built into GIMP or one that you've created yourself.

- **Reapply Effects** — Probably one of the coolest and most useful options in the Layer Effects menu, this takes any effects that you've applied to your layer and automatically reapplies all of them. This is extremely helpful if, for example, you're adding effects to a text layer and you decide to change the text. After changing the text, you can click this menu item and all of your layer effects will be adjusted and applied to your modified text.

- **Satin** — This is a quick effect that's somewhat similar to the Bevel and Emboss effect, but instead of beveling your layer, the Satin effect creates a kind of crumpled satin effect over your layer.

- **Stroke** — This handy little shortcut effect is the same as doing the following steps on a layer: Layers ➤ Transparency ➤ Alpha to Selection, Layers ➤ New Layer (Shift+Ctrl+N), Edit ➤ Stroke Selection. The good thing, though, is that all of your settings are in one place with this effect and it's a huge time saver.

When you select one of these options, with the exception of Reapply Effects, you get a dialog with a series of options that you can use to customize the effect that you're applying. Near the bottom of each dialog is a Preview check box. Click this check box and as you adjust the values and sliders in this dialog, the image window interactively updates to show you what the final effect looks like. This is left as an option because if you apply one of the Layer Effects filters to a really large layer, the image window might be too slow to update interactively. Figure 21-13 shows the Drop Shadow dialog with the Preview check box enabled.

FIGURE 21-13

The Python version of the Layer Effects plug-in allows for interactive previews.

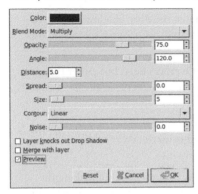

After you choose the options you want for the layer effect that you've selected, click OK to apply the effect. GIMP then generates one or more layers to get that effect applied to your layer. Figure 21-14 shows the Layers dockable dialog after a few layer effects have been applied to some text. One of the really cool things about this plug-in is that it remembers the layer effects you've applied to any particular layer. So if you add a drop shadow to some text and you later decide that the drop shadow is too dark, you can select this layer and choose Layers ➢ Layer Effects ➢ Drop Shadow and reduce the shadow's opacity. Then when you click OK, the Layer Effects plug-in regenerates the drop shadow layer for you.

FIGURE 21-14

Unlike Photoshop's layer effects, the Layer Effects plug-in generates additional layers to apply each layer effect that you select.

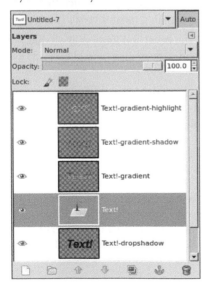

Note

With each layer effect, you also have the option to use the Merge with Layer check box. This reduces the overall number of layers in your GIMP project and can ultimately reduce the amount of system memory used when you load the file. However, if you do this, you lose the ability to take advantage of the Reapply Effects option if you make a change to this layer or one of the layer effects you've already applied. ■

Liquid Rescale

As I mentioned in Chapter 8, this is probably one of my favorite plug-ins to come out for GIMP in a long time. The Liquid Rescale plug-in implements a *seam carving* algorithm that was presented in a paper at the 2007 SIGGRAPH conference in San Diego. What this algorithm basically allows you to do is resize your images in a logical way without losing the most important content. The technique also allows you to manually control what content in your image is more important than other content. This gives you the power, for example, to more cleanly remove objects or people from an image as well as protect certain parts of an image from getting scaled. The paper and accompanying video presentation were presented at SIGGRAPH in August of 2007 and within about a month the concepts from that paper were implemented as the Liquid Rescale plug-in. In contrast, it took until Photoshop CS4, released in October of 2008, until this feature made it in there under the name of Content Aware Scale. Hooray for the power of Free Software!

I cover the use of the Liquid Rescale plug-in in Chapter 8, so this section is primarily devoted to installing Liquid Rescale and getting it running in your copy of GIMP. You can find the Liquid Rescale plug-in on the GIMP Plugin Registry, but the official web site at `http://liquidrescale.wikidot.com` usually gets updated before the registry entry does, so that's the best place to check for the most current version. To get Liquid Rescale working, you actually need two things, both available through the Liquid Rescale web site:

- **Liquid Rescale Library (liblqr)** — This library is what actually does the heavy lifting and implements the seam carving algorithm. The plug-in talks with this library, sending it image data to be processed and returned. Most installation processes handle downloading and installing this library automatically.

- **Liquid Rescale GIMP plug-in** — Think of this as the glue between GIMP and the Liquid Rescale Library. The plug-in gives you an interface from GIMP to allow you to tweak settings that get sent with the image data to the library.

Installing Liquid Rescale on Linux

Because this plug-in has had a lot of popularity, it's actually included in the package repositories of most Linux distributions. For most of these, it's as simple as opening your package management tool (Synaptic in Ubuntu, PackageKit in Fedora, YaST in OpenSUSE) and doing a search for `gimp-lqr-plugin`. The package manager will handle downloading the Liquid Rescale Library dependency for you. In fact, in Debian or Ubuntu, if you have the `gimp-plugin-registry` package installed, you already have Liquid Rescale installed. If you prefer to use the command line to install, open up a terminal window as root and run one of the following commands (depending on the distribution you're using):

- **Debian/Ubuntu:**

```
apt-get install gimp-plugin-registry
```

- **Fedora:**

```
yum install gimp-lqr-plugin
```

- **OpenSUSE:**

```
yast -i gimp-lqr-plugin
```

or

```
zypper in gimp-lqr-plugin
```

- **Mandriva:**

```
urpmi gimp-lqr-plugin
```

- **Gentoo** — The GIMP Liquid Rescale plug-in isn't included by default in Portage, but it is available in the sunrise overlay. To take advantage of this, you need to have the layman package installed and the sunrise overlay added. Assuming you have layman installed, you can add the sunrise overlay with the following command:

```
layman -a sunrise
```

Once the overlay is added, you can install the Liquid Rescale as you would expect with the following command:

```
emerge -av gimp-lqr-plugin
```

For the ease of maintenance and integration with your distribution, it's definitely recommended that you stick with the package that your distribution provides. Of course, if your distribution doesn't provide packages or you simply prefer to build the plug-in from source, you need to download the source packages for the Liquid Rescale Library and Liquid Rescale GIMP plug-in from their respective sites and follow these steps. (These instructions assume that you already have a working build environment set up with GCC, GIMP development headers, Make, gettext, and intltool.)

1. Compile and install the Liquid Rescale Library:

   a. Decompress the Liquid Rescale Library sources (as of this writing, the latest version of the library is version 0.4.1):

   ```
   tar -xvjf liblqr-1-0.4.1.tar.bz2
   ```

   b. Go into the directory that gets created:

   ```
   cd liblqr-1-0.4.1
   ```

   c. Configure the sources for compiling and compile them (this is actually two commands, configure and make. Typing it this way runs make after configure successfully completes without errors:

   ```
   ./configure && make
   ```

> **d.** Install the Liquid Rescale Library as root (using `su` or `sudo`, depending on your distribution):
>
> ```
> make install
> ```
>
> **e.** Change directories back to the parent directory:
>
> ```
> cd ../
> ```

2. Compile and install the Liquid Rescale GIMP plug-in:

> **a.** Decompress the Liquid Rescale plug-in sources (as of this writing, the latest version of the plug-in is version 0.6.1):
>
> ```
> tar -xvjf gimp-lqr-plugin_0.6.1.tar.bz2
> ```
>
> **b.** Go into the created directory:
>
> ```
> cd gimp-lqr-plugin_0.6.1
> ```
>
> **c.** Configure the sources and compile them:
>
> ```
> ./configure && make
> ```
>
> **d.** Install the Liquid Rescale GIMP plug-in as root:
>
> ```
> make install
> ```

Whether you install by compiling the sources yourself or by using the recommend packages that your distribution provides, you can start up GIMP and you should notice the neat little Liquid Rescale item at the bottom of your Layers menu in the image window. Game on!

Installing Liquid Rescale on Mac OS X

Installing the Liquid Rescale plug-in on Mac OS X is the easiest of all. Why? Because you already have it installed! By default, it's included with the GIMP on OS X bundle as well as the GIMP that you can install if you use MacPorts. How's that for easy?

Installing Liquid Rescale on Windows

For Windows users, there's a nice installer package available that installs and configures everything for you on the Liquid Rescale plug-in's web site. On the download page in the Windows section, click the Standard GIMP Installation link to download the installer. Assuming you installed GIMP in the default location (`C:\Program Files\GIMP-2.0`), after you download the file, double-click it to launch the installer. You should get a window like the one in Figure 21-15.

If everything meets your approval, click the Extract button in this window and the installer handles the rest. Once you do that, start up GIMP and you'll have Liquid Rescale goodness available to you in your Layers menu.

Separate+

If you intend to use GIMP with images you'll be sending to a printer, having some manner of support for the CMYK (cyan, magenta, yellow, and black) color profile is critical. As discussed in

Chapter 2, GIMP does not currently have this functionality natively. This plug-in provides you with rudimentary CMYK support as well as color management preferences support for CMYK. When you have the Separate+ plug-in installed, it's pretty tightly integrated into GIMP's interface. Chapter 9 goes into the usage of this plug-in's features, so here I'll just go into getting it installed on your system.

The installer window that appears when you run the Standard GIMP installation file for the Liquid Rescale plug-in

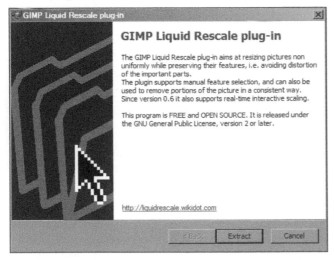

Installing Separate+ on Linux

Unfortunately, Separate+ isn't included in most distribution repositories, so unless you're running Debian or Ubuntu, you have to build it yourself. If you do happen to be running Debian or Ubuntu, the Separate+ plug-in is included with the `gimp-plugin-repository` package. You can install it by searching for it with the Synaptic package manager or opening a terminal as root and typing the following command:

```
apt-get install gimp-plugin-registry
```

If you're using a different distribution, you need to compile Separate+ yourself. To do so, first make sure you have a proper build environment that includes GCC, GIMP development headers, and Make. If you've built any of the other plug-ins listed in this chapter, you should already be golden. You also need to have a library called Little CMS (Color Management System) installed along with its development libraries. This *is* included in most distributions and can be found pretty easily with the graphical package management tool (PackageKit in Fedora, YaST in OpenSUSE). If you prefer using the command line, open a terminal as root and type one of the following commands (depending on your distribution):

- **Fedora:**

  ```
  yum install lcms lcms-devel
  ```

- **OpenSUSE:**

  ```
  yast -i liblcms liblcms-devel
  ```

  or:

  ```
  zypper in liblcms liblcms-devel
  ```

- **Mandriva:**

  ```
  urpmi lcms lcms-devel
  ```

- **Gentoo:**

  ```
  emerge -av lcms
  ```

Once you have your environment set up, it's time to get to compile the Separate+ plug-in. Open a terminal window and go to the folder where you want to do your compiling. As mentioned previously, I have a directory named src in my home directory, but you can do this step just about anywhere. Assuming the Separate+ zip file from the GIMP Plugin Registry is here (the latest version at the time of this writing is version 0.5.5), perform the following steps to get it compiled and installed:

1. Decompress the zip file that you downloaded from the registry:

   ```
   unzip separate+-0.5.5.zip
   ```

2. Go into the directory that was created:

   ```
   cd separate+-0.5.5
   ```

3. Compile the sources for Separate+:

   ```
   make
   ```

4. When it finishes compiling, type the following command as root:

   ```
   make install
   ```

5. Separate+ is now compiled and installed, but you should also install some additional color profiles like the Adobe ICC profiles and the included sRGB profile. By default, Separate+ and Little CMS look for color profiles in the following three directories:

   ```
   /usr/share/color/icc/
   /usr/color/icc/
   ~/.color/icc/
   ```

   So this is where you want to install your color profiles. The easiest is the sRGB color profile that's included with Separate+. As root, copy it to one of the aforementioned directories. Typing the following command should do the trick:

   ```
   cp sRGB/sRGB\ Color\ Space\ Profile.icm /usr/share/color/icc/
   ```

6. To get the Adobe ICC profiles, you can download them from the following web address:

   ```
   www.adobe.com/support/downloads/iccprofiles/iccprofiles_win.html
   ```

7. The profiles will be in a zip file. You can decompress them by typing the following:

```
unzip AdobeICCProfilesCS4Win_end-user.zip
```

8. Go into the directory that this just created:

```
cd Adobe\ ICC\ Profiles\ \(end-user\)/
```

9. Now, as root, you can install all of these color profiles by copying them to one of the preceding directories with a command like this one:

```
cp RGB/* CMYK/* /usr/share/color/icc/
```

Once you have completed all of these steps, you should be able to start GIMP and have access to the features that Separate+ provides. The quickest way to tell if GIMP recognizes it is to try to navigate to Image ➤ Separate in the image window. If you can do that and you see something like what's shown in Figure 21-16, it's working. Congratulations!

FIGURE 21-16

The options available in Image ➤ Separate when you have the Separate+ plug-in properly installed

Installing Separate+ on Mac OS X

As of this writing, there's unfortunately not an official compiled version of the Separate+ plug-in for Mac OS X. Hopefully in the future it will be bundled with GIMP like Liquid Rescale is. However, in the meantime your only option is to compile the plug-in yourself from the sources provided on the GIMP Plugin Registry. Setting up a build environment in Mac OS X is a bit more involved than in doing it in Linux, so it's unfortunately outside of the scope of this book.

Installing Separate+ on Windows

To install Separate+ on Windows, you actually need to download two files. Both of these files are provided on the Separate+ plug-in's main web site, http://cue.yellowmagic.info/ softwares/separate.html, at the bottom of the page under the Downloads heading. One file is the same Separate+ zip file that you need to download for installing on all the other platforms, but the other is a file called `liblcms-1.dll.zip`. This gives Separate+ access to Little CMS functionality in Windows. Once you've downloaded both files, the installation is basically as simple as copying and pasting:

1. **Open the** `separate+-0.5.5.zip` **file by double-clicking it.** This will show you the contents of the zip file, as shown in Figure 21-17.

FIGURE 21-17

Double-clicking the Separate+ zip file reveals the content within it.

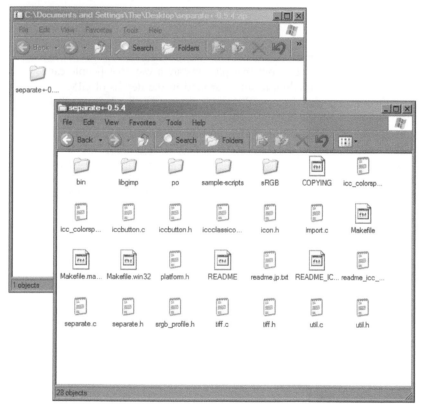

2. **Double-click the folder named** `bin` **to go into it. Inside, there should only be one folder named** `win32_gimp2.4`. Double-click this folder, too, to see what's inside it. Inside you find the following three files:

    -   `icc_colorspace.exe`

    -   `separate.exe`

    -   `separate_import.exe`

3. **Copy all three files to your plug-ins folder, as indicated in GIMP under Edit ➤ Preferences in Folders ➤ Plug-ins.** It should be something like `C:\Program Files\GIMP-2.0\plug-ins\`.

4. **Separate+ is now installed, but you still need to install the Little CMS library so Separate+ and GIMP know where to look for it.** To do this double-click the `liblcms-1.dll.zip` file that you downloaded. Inside, you should find just one file, `liblcms-1.dll`. Copy it to the same folder where you have the GIMP executable. By default, it should be in `C:\Program Files\GIMP-2.0\bin\`.

With that, you should have the Separate+ plug-in installed and ready to rock with all its beautiful CMYK goodness. Check out Chapter 9 for more information on how to use it. Enjoy!

Summary

So there you have it. In this chapter you found out that plug-ins are a way that people can extend the capabilities of GIMP without needing to muck around in the depths of GIMP's more than 600,000 lines of code. You also discovered that plug-ins can either be compiled as separate programs or written in scripting languages like Scheme (Script-Fu) or Python, but you only install Script-Fu scripts in GIMP's scripts folder, and all other plug-ins get installed to the plug-ins folder. You were exposed to the very awesome GIMP Plugin Registry, where you can hunt for new plug-ins or provide feedback on existing ones. Through the last part of this chapter, you were shown a handful of plug-ins and extensions to GIMP that increase its capabilities in a really substantial way. Some of these plug-ins are a bit of a bear to get installed, but once you have them in, they're totally worth it.

Now for some more advanced fun: extending GIMP's capabilities yourself by writing your own scripts. Here we go!

Creating Custom Effects with Scripting

O ne of the most useful features of GIMP is its extensibility. You have ultimate control over GIMP's features because you have the ability to automate them or add new ones if necessary. For instance, quite a few examples in this book are given as a sequence of discrete steps that you have to perform in GIMP. If you find yourself repeatedly performing the same sequence of steps to get a specific effect, you can write a script to automatically perform those steps for you. It may be a bit of a cliché, but think of a script as a recipe. It's a sequence of steps used to produce a final result. In cooking, that final result might be a pie. In computer graphics, the final result may be an improved image.

To facilitate the scripting process, the developers of GIMP have included a scripting *Application Programming Interface* (API). A scripting API is a set of operations and tools that can be accessed from a higher-level scripting language like Scheme or Python. With an API as your specification, you don't have to dig through lines and lines of source to find the function you're looking for and you don't have to do any guesswork to figure out how your code fits in the overall source tree. You find the operations that you need and can then write a little script that automates some useful task for you. That script can then be saved for re-use later or you can share it to benefit other artists.

This chapter covers GIMP's scripting capabilities and shows you how you can take advantage of them in your work. Even if you've never had any programming experience before, you should be able to work through this chapter and come out on the other side with a firm grasp of what can be achieved with scripting. That said, it's beyond the scope of this chapter (and even this book) to teach you the fundamentals of programming or the specific idiosyncrasies of the scripting languages covered herein. If you've never coded before, think of this chapter as a means of whetting your appetite. You can find more detailed information on scripting languages such as Scheme and Python online. In particular, you can find good Scheme resources at www.schemers.org, and the official Python documentation at www.python.org/doc is remarkably helpful.

Multi-Lingual GIMP: Scripting Languages GIMP Understands

Whether you're writing your own program or augmenting one like GIMP, one of the first things to understand is the difference between a programming language and a scripting language. Programming languages and scripting languages are human-readable instructions written in code that a computer must perform. However, computers don't understand human-readable languages and that code must be translated into the raw ones and zeros that the computer actually understands. In a *programming language*, that translation process is called *compiling* and it happens well in advance of the program being executed. In *scripting languages*, that translation happens on the fly; each line of code is *interpreted* for the computer. The advantage of compiled languages is that they execute a lot faster, but it takes more time to make changes and they're generally a lot stricter about their syntax. In contrast, interpreted languages are more flexible to code in, but typically don't perform as fast as compiled languages.

To visualize the difference between these two, imagine you have to give a message to someone who speaks a different language. If you know what you want to say ahead of time, you can have an expert translate your words in advance and you can play that recording for the other person. This is like the compiling process. It happens in advance, so the other person can understand more quickly. In contrast, the interpreting process would be like having a person translate your words to the other person as you speak them. This affords you more flexibility in what you can say, but the process takes a bit more time because the translator has to wait for you to finish speaking before transmitting your message.

GIMP itself is written in the C programming language. Because it's Free Software, you and everyone else on the planet has access to source code, so not only can you see what goes on under the hood, but this also offers you a potentially limitless ability to extend and customize GIMP to your needs. Of course, to take advantage of the source code, you really need a decent background in C programming. C is a pretty involved, low-level language and as digital artists, programming in C isn't a typical skill we pick up in pursuit of our craft. That's not to say that programming isn't something that digital artists are interested in; far from it. Artists are often great problem-solvers and typically excel at programming once they understand its value and how it's done. No, as valuable as having access to GIMP's source is, as an artist you often want to solve technical problems quickly so you can get back to creating. GIMP's source is hundreds of thousands of lines of code and even with prior understanding of how it's organized, it can take quite a bit of time to figure out where your code fits in.

This is where scripting languages and GIMP's scripting API come in. With these tools, you can do everything from creating simple macros to prototyping full-blown extensions to GIMP. To get an idea of how powerful this feature is, consider that nearly all of the filters in Part IV are implemented as scripts. Not only that, but quite a few "built-in" features that ship with GIMP are actually scripts written in GIMP's default scripting language, Scheme.

Scheme and Python – GIMP's Primary Scripting Languages

By default, the main scripting language for GIMP is the deceptively simple Scheme language. GIMP actually implements a subset of Scheme called TinyScheme. It's a lightweight Scheme interpreter that uses fewer system resources than many other Scheme implementations. Scheme itself is a derivative of the popular LISP programming language and shares much of the same syntax and structure. The valuable thing to know about Scheme is that it has relatively few commands and it's particularly good when it comes to mathematical operations and operating on lists — a common data structure used throughout GIMP. The syntax for Scheme is fully *parenthesized*, meaning that all of its operations are enclosed within parentheses. Scheme also uses a *prefix notation* for its functions, meaning that the function is written before the values that it operates on. For example, to write the equivalent of "two plus two" in Scheme, you would type (+ 2 2). "Two plus four" would be written (+ 2 4) and "two plus four plus seven hundred" would be written (+ 2 4 700). When written well, Scheme scripts are easy to read and understand. However, it can be pretty easy to get lost in all the parentheses that Scheme uses.

As previously mentioned, many of the default features of GIMP are actually Scheme scripts, known as *script-fu*, that ship with the official release. To get an idea of just how many of GIMP's built-in features are Scheme scripts, have a look in GIMP's default scripts folder on your hard drive. If you don't know where this folder is located, look in the Folders section of GIMP's Preferences window (Edit ➤ Preferences; Folder ➤ Scripts). All the files in that folder with the .scm extension are script-fus that provide many of GIMP's basic features. The following list shows the files you should see when looking in this folder:

3d-outline.scm	crystal-logo.scm	plug-in-compat.init
3dTruchet.scm	difference-clouds.scm	predator.scm
add-bevel.scm	distress-selection.scm	pupi-button.scm
addborder.scm	drop-shadow.scm	rendermap.scm
alien-glow-arrow.scm	erase-rows.scm	reverse-layers.scm
alien-glow-bar.scm	flatland.scm	ripply-anim.scm
alien-glow-bullet.scm	font-map.scm	round-corners.scm
alien-glow-button.scm	frosty-logo.scm	script-fu-compat.init
alien-glow-logo.scm	fuzzyborder.scm	script-fu-set-cmap.scm
alien-neon-logo.scm	gap-dup-continue.scm	script-fu-util.scm
basic1-logo.scm	gimp-headers.scm	script-fu.init
basic2-logo.scm	gimp-labels.scm	sel-to-anim-img.scm
beveled-button.scm	gimp-online.scm	select-to-brush.scm

beveled-pattern-arrow.scm	glossy.scm	select-to-image.scm
beveled-pattern-bullet.scm	glowing-logo.scm	select-to-pattern.scm
beveled-pattern-button.scm	gradient-bevel-logo.scm	selection-round.scm
beveled-pattern-heading.scm	gradient-example.scm	slide.scm
beveled-pattern-hrule.scm	grid-system.scm	sota-chrome-logo.scm
blend-anim.scm	guides-from-selection.scm	speed-text.scm
blended-logo.scm	guides-new-percent.scm	spinning-globe.scm
bovinated-logo.scm	guides-new.scm	spyrogimp.scm
burn-in-anim.scm	guides-remove-all.scm	starscape-logo.scm
camo.scm	i26-gunya2.scm	swirltile.scm
carve-it.scm	images	swirly-pattern.scm
carved-logo.scm	land.scm	t-o-p-logo.scm
chalk.scm	lava.scm	text-circle.scm
chip-away.scm	line-nova.scm	textured-logo.scm
chrome-it.scm	mkbrush.scm	tileblur.scm
chrome-logo.scm	neon-logo.scm	title-header.scm
circuit.scm	news-text.scm	truchet.scm
clothify.scm	old-photo.scm	unsharp-mask.scm
coffee.scm	palette-export.scm	waves-anim.scm
comic-logo.scm	paste-as-brush.scm	weave.scm
coolmetal-logo.scm	paste-as-pattern.scm	xach-effect.scm
copy-visible.scm	perspective-shadow.scm	

The other scripting language that's frequently used in GIMP is Python. Python is an incredibly easy-to-learn scripting language that continues to grow in use and popularity. One of the really nice features of Python is that it's an *object-oriented* language. In an object-oriented language, you can create complex data structures (objects) with their own methods, variables, and internal logic. Once created, these objects can easily be used and re-used in scripts to perform specific tasks. To use an abstract example, imagine you have a cup of water. If you were to treat that cup of water as an object in Python, it would have internal data, such as a `quantity` variable that stores how much water is in the cup. That object would also have methods associated with it such as `empty_cup()` and `fill_cup()`, which would adjust the value of the `quantity` variable accordingly. Furthermore, once you have your `cup_of_water` object defined, you could very easily create multiple *instances*, or copies, of it to share with your friends. This is a very rough explanation of how object-oriented languages work, but the idea is that you can create libraries of objects that can do complex processing for you. Thanks to the continually rising popularity of Python, hundreds, if not thousands, of Python libraries have been created to aid in performing all kinds of tasks. And often these libraries are also released under a Free Software license like the GPL, so you're free to take advantage of them in your GIMP scripts.

Python's increased popularity has had another tangential benefit. Many graphical programs, in the commercial and Free Software worlds, have already or are beginning to include Python as a scripting option. This means that the Python knowledge you gain for use in GIMP can also be applied, in part, for use in these other applications.

Note
If you're working in a Linux or Mac OS X environment, your copy of GIMP should support Python by default. However, if you're using Windows, chances are good that you may be missing Python support. The reason for this is that, unlike Mac OS X and most Linux distributions, Windows does not have the Python scripting language installed by default. To add Python support to GIMP, go to www .python.org and download the Windows installer for Python on your machine. There's an excellent tutorial for installing Python for GIMP on Windows on GIMPusers.com (www.gimpusers.com/ tutorials/install-python-for-gimp-2-6-windows.html). If you're going to write or use Python scripts on your Windows machine, you need to go through this process. ∎

As a user, the main difference between the Scheme-based script-fu and Python scripts is that Python scripts are actually treated as plug-ins. In fact, to get a Python script recognized by GIMP, you have to save it in GIMP's plug-ins folder rather than the scripts folder. This was covered briefly in Chapter 21 when covering the Layer Effects plug-in.

Other Scripting Languages Supported by GIMP

Scheme and Python aren't the only scripting languages that have their hooks embedded in GIMP. One of the funny things about people who write code is that everyone seems to have their personal favorite language to work in, and with a Free Software program as popular as GIMP, one of the side effects is that people tend to add scripting support for their language of choice. It's for this reason that although GIMP speaks Scheme and Python natively, it's also fluent in other popular languages like Perl and Tcl. There's even experimental support for the Ruby scripting language. Unfortunately, I don't have the space to address how to script for GIMP in all of these languages, so this chapter sticks to working with Scheme and Python. That said, the way these other languages interface with GIMP is largely consistent with how Scheme and Python do it, so most of the knowledge in this chapter should be transferable.

Taking Advantage of the Procedure Browser

The single biggest help that GIMP provides you as a script writer is its Procedure Browser. The Procedure Browser is an interactive reference to GIMP's scripting API that you can access from directly within GIMP. To see the Procedure Browser go to Help ➤ Procedure Browser in an image window. When you do this, you should get a window like the one in Figure 22-1.

FIGURE 22-1

The Procedure Browser is an interactive reference to GIMP's scripting API.

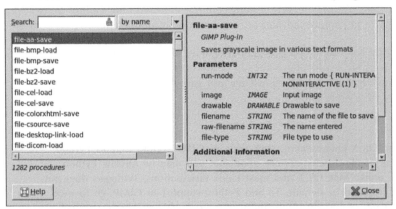

The left side of the Procedure Browser shows a list of the procedures that you can call from a script that you write for GIMP. Clicking any of these procedures updates the panel on the right of the browser, displaying information about that procedure. The information in the right panel includes a description of what the procedure does, the parameters that you need to feed to it, what kind of values (if any) the procedure returns, and additional information about the procedure, such as the name of its author and when it was created.

When writing your own scripts, the Procedure Browser is an invaluable tool because it lets you know exactly what features of GIMP you have available. For example, if your script is a macro (a series of frequently performed actions), you can type each operation that you do in the Search field at the top of the Procedure Browser and find out the name of its associated scripting procedure. Armed with this information, you can quickly cobble together the script you need in whatever language you want.

Using the Scripting Console

Besides the Procedure Browser, the second most valuable tool for script writers in GIMP is the Scripting Console. The Scripting Console provides you with a quick way to test procedures and see their results before committing to writing an actual script. If you're just learning how to write in Scheme or Python, the Scripting Console is also a great way to test the language and get comfortable with its syntax.

Both Scheme and Python have their own scripting consoles and they look pretty similar to one another, so be sure that you're aware of which one you call up. Both consoles are available from the Filters menu. For the Scheme console go to Filters ➤ Script-Fu ➤ Console and for the Python console, use Filters ➤ Python-Fu ➤ Console. Figure 22-2 shows both consoles side-by-side, each performing the same mathematical operation.

FIGURE 22-2

On the left is the Scheme Console and on the right is the Python Console. Both scripting consoles are showing how you would write "two plus four plus seven hundred" in their respective languages.

As the figure shows, both consoles are very similar to one another. The primary difference between the two is that the Python Console includes a Browse button at its bottom. If you click this button, GIMP pops up a Python Procedure Browser. This browser looks and behaves like the Procedure Browser you can call from the Help menu, but with one major exception: after selecting a procedure, you can click the Apply button at the bottom of the browser and the Python Console is updated with the Python version of that procedure. This is a great way to see what GIMP expects you to type when creating your own scripts.

Writing a Custom Script for GIMP

Now that you've got a handle on the tools that GIMP provides you for script writing, it's time to build a custom script. As a practical example, I'm going to provide you with a scenario that I've come across where scripting can be a help. One of the things that I use GIMP for is creating and cleaning up graphics and logos for use in television commercials. Although HDTV is gaining more and more ground each day as a television standard, many media outlets still continue to produce in older standard-definition formats like NTSC. Even modern DVDs (regular DVDs, not Blu-ray) are produced using the NTSC (or PAL if you're not in the United States) standard.

For an image to look decent on an NTSC display, some specific conventions should be adhered to. The script that I want to write is going to process an incoming logo to match those specifications. I'll get into the exact specifications in a moment.

Tip

When writing scripts, avoid using word processing software like OpenOffice.org or Microsoft Office. These programs may add unwanted and unnecessary formatting hints to your script files. Instead, use a raw text editor or a text editor that has features to aid the scripting process, such a syntax highlighting. ■

Building a Structure for Your Script

First, though, a basic template needs to be set up for the script. I'm writing this example in Python, but the process is very similar if you're working in Scheme. The first step is to fire up your text editor of choice with a new text document and type these lines at the top of the file:

```
#!/usr/bin/env python
from gimpfu import *
```

The first line defines your script as a Python script so GIMP's interpreter knows what language it needs to be using. The second line imports gimpfu, the Python library that holds the procedures in GIMP's Python scripting API. This makes all the procedures in the Procedure Browser available for use in your script. The next thing you need to do is build your scripting template. A GIMP script has two primary parts: the function definition and the registration. The function definition is the actual meat of your script. It's the part that does the heavy lifting and image processing that you want done. The registration makes GIMP aware of your script, providing descriptive information about it as well as where the script should appear in GIMP's interface. When scripting in Python, you want to do the function definition first. The following code is a stand-in template that you can use as a generic placeholder until you have the meat of your script in place:

```
def python_script_template(img, layer):
    # This is where the code for your Python script goes
    return
```

When defining a script's function, the convention is to prefix it with the scripting language that you're using. If this script were being written as a script-fu, the function would be named `script-fu-script-template`. An important distinction to note between Scheme and Python is that Scheme prefers that you use dashes to separate words in a function name, whereas Python prefers underscores. The second line of the function definition is just a comment. This is the placeholder for your script's actual code. The third line, simply saying `return`, marks the end of your script's function definition. Customizing this template for use in the TV preparation script, the function definition looks like so:

```
def python_ntsc_prep(img, layer):
    # This script preps an image for use in NTSC television
    return
```

You come back to filling this function with actual code momentarily. In the meantime, this script needs to be registered with GIMP. The following code listing should serve as a generic template for registering any Python script with GIMP:

```
register(
    "python_fu_script_template", #Procedure Name
    "Short description",
    "Long description of what your script does",
    "",                          #Author Name
    "",                          #Copyright-holder Name
    "2009",                      #Copyright Date
    "",                          #Name in Menu
    "*",                         #Image Types
    [                            #Parameters
    (PF_IMAGE, "image", "Input Image", None)
    ],
    [],                          #Return Values
    python_script_template,      #Work Function
      (function definition)
    menu="<Image>/Filters/")     #Menu Location

main()
```

This is really two functions, `register()` and `main()`. The `register()` function takes a series of parameters as input and uses those to make GIMP aware of your script. If you think these parameters look familiar, you're right. This is the actual information that gets displayed in the Procedure Browser. Once your script is registered with GIMP, any other script can be made to take advantage of it. This also makes it easy to share your script with other GIMP users who may find it useful. The `main()` function is a requirement for Python scripts in GIMP. Without it, your Python script won't work at all.

Most of the parameters of the `register()` function are self-explanatory. The only exceptions are the last few:

- **Image Types** — This is where you can define the color modes that your script works on. You can choose RGB, Grayscale, Indexed, or All. By using an asterisk (*) here, you're telling GIMP that your script is suitable for images that use all color modes. If you want this to be a specific color mode, type that color mode here in lowercase (for example, "grayscale").

- **Parameters** — This is a list of parameters that may be presented to the user. Typically a good one to include here is a parameter for the image you want to apply the script to. Each parameter is shown in the script's dialog box when you run it. For a complete list of available parameters, check out GIMP's official Python documentation at `www.gimp.org/docs/python`.

- **Return Values** — Like the Parameters list, this is a list of values that the script can return for use if it's called by another script. Most Python scripts don't return anything, so it's fine to leave this blank as well.

- **Work Function** — This is the name of the function that you defined at the top of this script. Theoretically you could use the name of another function that's defined in another script, but that's really not recommended.

- **Menu Location** — This string defines where in GIMP's interface your script is going to appear. It uses a path format like what is used when telling GIMP where various folders are in the Preferences window. The first element in this string is always the window or dialog that the menu appears in. In this case, <Image> indicates the image window. So if you wanted your script to appear in the image window at Layer ➤ Transform, you would type "<Image>/Layer/Transform".

With the register() function's parameters filled in for the TV preparation script, the entire script looks like this:

```
#!/usr/bin/env python
from gimpfu import *

def python_ntsc_prep(img, layer):
    # This script preps an image for use in NTSC television
    return

register(
        "python_fu_ntsc_prep",
        "Preps an image for NTSC",
        "Prepares an image to match conventions for NTSC television",
        "Jason van Gumster",
        "Jason van Gumster",
        "2009",
        "NTSC Prep",
        "*",
        [
        (PF_IMAGE, "image", "Input Image", None)
        ],
        [],
        python_ntsc_prep,
        menu="<Image>/Filters/Video")

main()
```

At this point, it's worth it to save your script and see if it shows up in GIMP. To do this, you have to do two things. First, save the script in a location where GIMP is looking for it. Because this example is a Python script, you need to save it in GIMP's plug-ins folder. You can see where this is by going to the Preferences window (Edit ➤ Preferences; Folders ➤ Plug-ins). If you were writing this script in Scheme, you would save it to the scripts folder (Edit ➤ Preferences; Folders ➤ Scripts). Save your Python script with the .py extension. If you're saving a Scheme script, save it as .scm.

Because this particular script is written in Python, there's one additional step that you must take. The file must be made executable. In Linux and Mac OS X, the easiest thing to do is open a terminal window and navigate to the folder where you saved your script and run chmod 755 on that file. As an example, assume that the TV preparation script is named `ntsc_prep.py`. You would go to the plug-ins folder and type the following command:

```
chmod 755 ntsc_prep.py
```

In Windows, all files can potentially be treated as executable, so you don't have to go through this process. Once you have your script in the correct folder and made sure that it's executable, start up (or restart) GIMP. Your script should appear in the Procedure Browser as well as the image window menu. Figure 22-3 shows the TV preparation script in both of these locations

FIGURE 22-3

With your script template properly created and saved, a menu item (left) should be available for your script and it should be visible in the Procedure Browser (right).

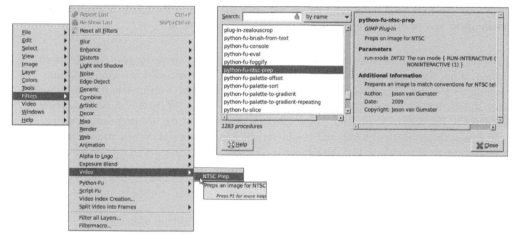

Writing the Meat of Your Script

With GIMP properly recognizing the existence of your script, now you can do the fun part of actually building a functional tool with your script. As I mentioned earlier in this chapter, my script performs a set of convenient operations to prepare an image or logo for use on standard-definition NTSC television. In particular, I want my script to make any image I pass to it conform to the following specifications:

- **NTSC-safe colors** — NTSC does not handle colors at full saturation very well. It's recommended that colors have luma and chroma values less than 100%. Fortunately, as seen in Chapter 9, GIMP already has a feature to help with this with the Hot function from the Colors menu.

- **Title-safe and action-safe guides** — It's recommended that any action in NTSC video happen within 10% of the image border and that any text, logos, or titles be within 20% of the image border. I want my script to add guides to my image to make it easy for me to see where the title-safe and action-safe regions are.

639

- **A final resolution of 720x480 pixels with an aspect ratio of 4:3** — The NTSC specification uses rectangular pixels. By default, GIMP uses square pixels. A little bit of trickery will be necessary for this to work right.

Now that you have some specifications to work with, it's time to write the script. The first thing to do is determine the order in which you want to achieve these specifications. Logically speaking, it doesn't make any sense to add the guides for title-safe and action-safe regions until after the image is set to the right size. Likewise, scaling an image can introduce pixels that aren't exactly the colors in the original image, so it would be best to wait on running the Hot plug-in until after the image is the proper size. Based on this, the order you want to use is first to resize the image, then run the Hot plug-in and finally add safe guides.

Tip

When writing scripts for GIMP that you intend on testing, it's a good idea to launch GIMP from a terminal window. This way you can have your script print debug and error messages to the terminal window when it runs. It's a really good way to make sure your script is working as planned. ∎

First things first: getting an arbitrary image to be the proper size. There are two complications here. First of all, the image that's being passed to the script is of an unknown size, so before any scaling or resizing takes place the script needs that information. Fortunately the Procedure Browser shows that the gimp_image_width() and gimp_image_height() functions return those values to the script. Going back to the function definition of the TV preparation script, you can assign these values to width and height variables in your script. When you do this, your function definition should look like the following code listing:

```
def python_ntsc_prep(img, layer):
    # This script preps an image for use in NTSC television

    # Get the active layer in this image (assuming one layer)

    layer = pdb.gimp_image_get_active_drawable(img)

    width = pdb.gimp_image_width(img)
    height = pdb.gimp_image_height(img)

    return
```

Now that the script knows the width and height of the incoming image, it can generate an image of the proper size. Remember, though, that the final image needs to be suitable for use with NTSC rectangular pixels. GIMP naturally works with square pixels. To compensate for this disparity, this script is going to work with the square-pixel size before doing the final resize to 720x480 pixels. This means that the target working size for the image is going to be 720x540 pixels. With the target working size known, it's just a matter of getting any image to fit that size without being distorted. The process for doing this is pretty simple. The following is some basic *pseudocode* to explain the process:

```
if image is smaller than target working size:
    increase image canvas size to 720 x 540; keep image centered
```

```
    else if image is portrait or square:
        scale image proportionally to a height of 540 pixels
        increase image canvas width to 720 pixels; keep image centered

    else: #image is landscape
        scale image proportionally to a width of 720 pixels
        increase image canvas height to 540 pixels; keep image centered
```

That's the basic workflow. The idea is to test the size of the image and if it's smaller than the target size, just increase the canvas size to fit. If the image is larger than the target size, the script has to determine if the image is square or if it's a tall (portrait) or wide (landscape) rectangle. Based on those determinations, the image is scaled down to fit the space and then the canvas is adjusted to fit the missing area. In Python, the actual code looks like so:

```
    target_width = 720.0
    target_height = 540.0

    width = pdb.gimp_image_width(img)
    height = pdb.gimp_image_height(img)

    # Scale or resize image to fit target work size
    if ((width < target_width) & (height < target_height)):
        # Determine offsets so the image stays centered
        offx = (target_width - width) / 2
        offy = (target_height - height) / 2
        pdb.gimp_image_resize(img, target_width, target_height, offx,
                                offy)

    elif ((width == height) | (width < height)):
        # Determine new width in a proportional scale operation
        new_width = (target_width / target_height) * height
        pdb.gimp_image_scale_full(img, new_width, target_height, 2)

        # Determine x offset so image stays centered
        offx = (target_width - new_width) / 2
        offy = 0
        pdb.gimp_image_resize(img, target_width, target_height, offx,
                                offy)

    else: # Image is landscape
        # Determine new height in a proportional scale operation
        new_height = (target_height / target_width) * width
        pdb.gimp_image_scale_full(img, target_width, new_height, 2)

        # Determine y offset so image stays centered
        offx = 0
        offy = (target_height - new_height) / 2
        pdb.gimp_image_resize(img, target_width, target_height, offx,
                                offy)
```

Once the image is properly sized to fit the square-pixel sizing for NTSC video, you can scale the image to fit the proper NTSC dimensions. Be aware that after you run this portion of your script, your image will be slightly distorted. That's okay, though, because that's the way it's supposed to be. When the image is shown on an NTSC television with its rectangular pixels, everything in the image appears at the proper proportions. Scaling the image to fit NTSC dimensions is a simple one-liner:

```
pdb.gimp_image_scale_full(img, 720, 480, 2)
```

The 2 at the end of this function call is actually a numeral defining the interpolation mode that the scale procedure uses. Instead of using the number 2, you could also use the INTERPOLATION-CUBIC constant value.

Excellent! Now the image is properly sized for NTSC video. The next step is to adjust the colors in the image to fit within NTSC's recommended color gamut. If you were doing this manually, you would go to Colors ➤ Hot in the image window and configure the dialog that appears there. In scripting, it's actually easier than that. If you do a search for the term "hot" in the Procedure Browser, it shows a procedure named plug-in-hot. To get your image to be within the proper luma and chroma values, you need to run this plug-in twice: once to fix luminance values and once to fix saturation values. So adding this to your script is two lines of code:

```
pdb.plug_in_hot(img, layer, 0, 0, False) # Reduce luminance
pdb.plug_in_hot(img, layer, 0, 1, False) # Reduce saturation
```

You're on the home stretch now. All that remains is adding the safe-region guides. To do this, you can use a little trick that's provided by the scripting API. There's a function in Procedure Browser named script-fu-guides-from-selection. If you make a rectangular selection that's centered on the image and 90% of the image's size, you can use this procedure to generate your guides based on that selection. That gets you your action-safe guides. Then you can use the same process to make a selection that's 80% of your image's size and get your title-safe guides. After that, you clear your selection and your script is complete. The following is the code to produce those results:

```
# Add Title-safe and Action-safe guides
#   Action Safe
safe_width = 720 * 0.9
safe_height = 480 * 0.9
offx = (720.0 - safe_width) / 2
offy = (480.0 - safe_height) / 2
pdb.gimp_rect_select(img, offx, offy, safe_width, safe_height, 2,
                     False, 0)
pdb.script_fu_guides_from_selection(img, layer)

#   Title Safe
safe_width = 720 * 0.8
safe_height = 480 * 0.8
offx = (720.0 - safe_width) / 2
offy = (480.0 - safe_height) / 2
```

```
pdb.gimp_rect_select(img, offx, offy, safe_width, safe_height, 2,
                    False, 0)
pdb.script_fu_guides_from_selection(img, layer)

pdb.gimp_selection_none(img)
```

And there you have it: a simple procedural script to take any image and bring it to work within the constraints of NTSC video specifications. The following listing is the script in its entirety:

```python
#!/usr/bin/env python

from gimpfu import *

def python_ntsc_prep(img) :
    # This script preps an image for use in NTSC television

    # Get the active layer in this image (assuming one layer)
    layer = pdb.gimp_image_get_active_drawable(img)

    target_width = 720.0
    target_height = 540.0

    width = pdb.gimp_image_width(img)
    height = pdb.gimp_image_height(img)

    # Scale or resize image to fit target work size
    if ((width < target_width) & (height < target_height)):
        # Determine offsets so the image stays centered
        offx = (target_width - width) / 2
        offy = (target_height - height) / 2
        pdb.gimp_image_resize(img, target_width, target_height, offx,
                             offy)

    elif ((width == height) | (width < height)):
        # Determine new width in a proportional scale operation
        new_width = (target_width / target_height) * height
        pdb.gimp_image_scale_full(img, new_width, target_height, 2)

        # Determine x offset so image stays centered
        offx = (target_width - new_width) / 2
        offy = 0
        pdb.gimp_image_resize(img, target_width, target_height, offx,
                             offy)

    else: # Image is landscape
        # Determine new height in a proportional scale operation
        new_height = (target_height / target_width) * width
        pdb.gimp_image_scale_full(img, target_width, new_height, 2)
```

```python
        # Determine y offset so image stays centered
        offx = 0
        offy = (target_height - new_height) / 2
        pdb.gimp_image_resize(img, target_width, target_height, offx,
                              offy)

    # Scale image to NTSC dimensions
    pdb.gimp_image_scale_full(img, 720, 480, 2)

    # Get NTSC-safe colors
    pdb.plug_in_hot(img, layer, 0, 0, False) # Reduce luminance
    pdb.plug_in_hot(img, layer, 0, 1, False) # Reduce saturation

    # Add Title-safe and Action-safe guides
    #    Action Safe
    safe_width = 720 * 0.9
    safe_height = 480 * 0.9
    offx = (720.0 - safe_width) / 2
    offy = (480.0 - safe_height) / 2
    pdb.gimp_rect_select(img, offx, offy, safe_width, safe_height, 2,
                         False, 0)
    pdb.script_fu_guides_from_selection(img, layer)

    #    Title Safe
    safe_width = 720 * 0.8
    safe_height = 480 * 0.8
    offx = (720.0 - safe_width) / 2
    offy = (480.0 - safe_height) / 2
    pdb.gimp_rect_select(img, offx, offy, safe_width, safe_height, 2,
                         False, 0)
    pdb.script_fu_guides_from_selection(img, layer)

    pdb.gimp_selection_none(img)

    return

register(
        "python_fu_ntsc_prep",
        "Preps an image for NTSC",
        "Prepares an image to match conventions for NTSC television",
        "Jason van Gumster",
        "Jason van Gumster",
        "2009",
        "NTSC Prep",
        "*",           [
        (PF_IMAGE, "image", "Input Image", None)
        ],
        [],
        python_ntsc_prep,
        menu="<Image>/Filters/Video")

main()
```

Summary

Woohoo! That's all she wrote. This chapter covered one of the most powerful and advanced features in GIMP: scripting. You discovered the main scripting languages that GIMP recognizes and got a strong handle on the advantages of having an integrated scripting API in a graphics program. The chapter also showed that even as a non-coder you can create simple scripts by looking through GIMP's Procedure Browser and finding the functions that you want to utilize in your scripts. You saw that you could play with both Scheme and Python through their interactive consoles. At the end of the chapter was an example of a relatively simple script to constrain any given image to the recommended specifications for standard-definition video. Hopefully, with these examples of the kind of power scripting gives you, your appetite is whetted for code and you'll find more ways to take advantage of it in your work.

Part VI

Appendices

IN THIS PART

Appendix A
Downloading and Installing GIMP

Appendix B
Setting Up External Input Devices

Appendix C
Customizing GIMP

Appendix D
Additional Resources

Appendix E
What's on the Web Site

Downloading and Installing GIMP

O ne of the really cool things about GIMP is that its free nature makes it incredibly easy to get a copy installed on your computer. The only requirement — besides a computer — is an Internet connection. GIMP works on Unix-based operating systems like Linux and FreeBSD as well as Microsoft Windows and Apple's Mac OS. There's even a community of users at PortableApps.com who distribute a version of GIMP that will run from a USB flash drive. There's a direct URI and a bit more information on them in Appendix D, but basically they've made it so you can literally run GIMP on nearly any computer available. How's that for cool?

The most direct route to getting GIMP is by going to www.gimp.org and clicking the Download button. Depending on which operating system you're using, the GIMP web site automatically loads a page with information on installing GIMP for your particular machine. Although that's usually enough to get you going, there are a few "gotchas" that this appendix should help mitigate.

IN THIS APPENDIX

Downloading GIMP

Installing GIMP on Linux, Windows, and Macintosh platforms

Installing GIMP on Linux

If you're using one of the many Linux distributions out there, such as Fedora from Red Hat, chances are good that you may already have GIMP installed and you can probably find it under Graphics in your Applications menu. In fact, rather than going to www.gimp.org to download and install GIMP yourself, it's recommended that you install it using the package management tool that your distribution uses, such as yum in Fedora. GIMP is available in the main package repositories for all of the main Linux distributions. Depending on how much you've adjusted or customized your installation, some of the graphical frontends that are mentioned in this section may not be used. Fortunately, each of these distributions offers package management from the terminal window as well.

Debian/Ubuntu

Probably one of the most popular Linux distributions right now is Ubuntu (www.ubuntu.com) and its variants, including Ubuntu Studio, Kubuntu, Edubuntu, and Linux Mint. Ubuntu is actually based on another distribution called Debian, and they share the same basic package management system, based on the .deb file format. Ubuntu ships with a graphical package management tool called Synaptic Package Manager. To launch it from a standard Ubuntu system, go to the menu and choose System ≻ Administration ≻ Synaptic Package Manager. Upon doing so, you might be prompted to enter a password to allow you to install software. After doing that, you get a window like the one in Figure A-1.

FIGURE A-1

Synaptic Package Manager

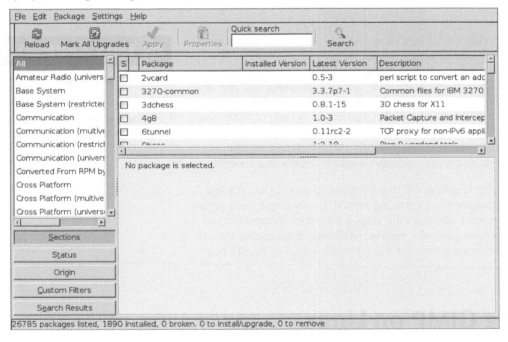

The quickest way to get GIMP installed with this tool is to click the Search button and type **gimp** in the Search field of the dialog that pops up. After a quick hunt through the list of packages in your repositories, Synaptic should provide you with results that list the most recent version of GIMP available. Click the check box next to the GIMP package to mark that package for installation. There's a chance that installing GIMP will also require that you install one or more *dependencies*, or other packages that GIMP requires to run. If that's the case, Synaptic pops up a dialog to let you know what these dependencies are and requests your approval to install them. Click the Mark button on this dialog, and Synaptic knows to install these packages as well. Once you've done that, click the Apply button in the toolbar, and Synaptic pops up another dialog to confirm installation. Click Apply once more, and Synaptic goes through the process of downloading all of the required packages and automatically installing them for you. Depending on your Internet connection speed, this may take a little bit of time to complete, but when it's done, you'll have GIMP happily running on your computer. Figure A-2 shows this installation process.

FIGURE A-2

Installing GIMP using Synaptic Package Manager

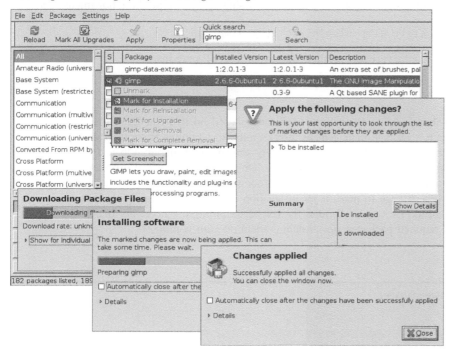

Debian doesn't ship with Synaptic by default. You can choose to install it if you'd like, but there's another way to install GIMP without using the graphical interface — using the apt-get command. This method actually works in Debian as well as all of its derivatives, including Ubuntu. To use it, you'll have to get access to the command line. You can easily do this by opening a terminal window. Type **su** to become the administrator, or *root* user. At the next prompt type the following:

```
apt-get install gimp
```

An important thing to note here is that the Ubuntu distribution and its derivatives do not ship with a root user by default. If you're on an Ubuntu machine and you want to use apt to install GIMP, you need to use sudo to perform administrative tasks. To do that, type the following text at your terminal window prompt:

```
sudo apt-get install gimp
```

After you press Enter, apt tracks down all dependencies required for GIMP and prompts you to confirm their installation. At that prompt, type **Y** and hit Enter. Apt will take it from there, downloading and installing all of the necessary packages for you.

For some of the additional functionality in this book, you may want to install some GIMP plug-ins such as G'MIC, Liquid Rescale, and the GIMP Animation Package. Each of these plug-ins can be pulled from the GIMP Plugin Registry, mentioned in Chapter 21, but you can also install them directly using Synaptic or apt. If you're using Synaptic, do a search for the following terms: gimp-plugin-registry and gimp-gap. Using apt, just type the following as root:

```
apt-get install gimp-plugin-registry gimp-gap
```

Doing so will get you the veritable motherload of useful GIMP plug-ins.

Fedora

The Fedora distribution (`www.fedoraproject.org`), based on Red Hat Enterprise Linux (RHEL), ships with a package management utility similar to Ubuntu's Synaptic, called PackageKit. As Figure A-3 shows, PackageKit works very similarly to Synaptic. Open it by clicking System ➤ Administration ➤ Add/Remove Software. Once it appears, type **gimp** in the search field on the left and click Find. From there, the process is about the same. You click the check box next to GIMP's package to mark it for installation and then click the Apply button in the lower-right corner. PackageKit handles the rest, determining the necessary dependencies, downloading all required packages, and installing them on your computer.

FIGURE A-3

Fedora's PackageKit package manager

Installing from the command line in Fedora is also slightly different than in Debian or Ubuntu. Fedora is based on another package format called RPM and uses a tool called yum for command-line package management. To use this in Fedora, open up a terminal window and, as the root user, type the following:

```
yum install gimp
```

Yum finds all of the package dependencies that GIMP requires and prompts you to confirm their installation. Type **Y**, press Enter to confirm, and wait for yum to download and install each package. When it's done, you'll be treated to a world of GIMP awesomeness. As with Ubuntu, there's a large package of plug-ins for GIMP called gimpfx-foundry. To install that package as well as the additional GREYCstoration, Liquid Rescale, and GIMP Animation Package plug-ins, use PackageKit or type in the following in the terminal window:

```
yum install gimpfx-foundry greycstoration gimp-lqr-plugin gimp-gap
```

Once you press Enter and confirm any additional dependencies, you should be ready to rock. If you want to install additional plug-ins, you can also use PackageKit as a quick way to search for them by name.

OpenSUSE

OpenSUSE (`www.opensuse.org`) is like Fedora in that it's an RPM-based distribution. However, it uses a different tool for managing those packages. Graphically, it uses a tool called YaST, which is short for Yet another Setup Tool. OpenSUSE installations typically use either the KDE or Gnome desktop environments and each environment has a slightly different way of getting to YaST. In KDE, click the "geeko," which is the kickoff-applet tool, and click Computer ➤ YaST. You are prompted for your root password and then YaST opens. In GNOME, start YaST by choosing Control Center ➤ YaST from the main menu. In doing this, you are also prompted for your root password before continuing. YaST then opens with a window like the one in Figure A-4.

FIGURE A-4

The YaST interface

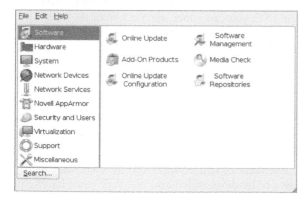

Once YaST is up, click the Software tab in the Control Center. The window that pops up, called YaST2, is very similar to the Synaptic Package Manager. If you're using the KDE release of Open-SUSE, you can actually also access this window directly from the geeko menu by clicking Computer ➤ Install Software. On the left panel, type **gimp** in the Search field and press Enter. This should find GIMP in your OpenSUSE repositories. Click the check box next to GIMP to mark it for installation. When you're done with that, click the Accept button at the bottom right of the window. YaST hunts down the dependencies you need and requests your confirmation. After you confirm, you'll have GIMP and be ready to go. Figure A-5 shows the YaST2 package manager interface.

FIGURE A-5

Installing GIMP with the YaST graphical interface

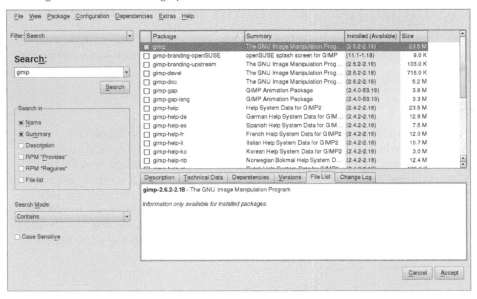

Like the other distributions, OpenSUSE provides you with a way to install GIMP from the command line. Depending on your version of OpenSUSE, you can either use YaST from the command line or use its intended replacement, zypper, which appeared in OpenSUSE 10.3 and has since matured. So if you're installing from the command line, open a terminal window, become root user, and type the following:

```
zypper in gimp
```

If you're using an older copy of OpenSUSE, use YaST by typing the following, again as root:

```
yast -i gimp
```

In either case, the tool finds all the necessary dependencies and prompts you for their installation. After you confirm and wait for the packages to be downloaded and installed, you'll have GIMP goodness to work with.

Installing G'MIC and Liquid Rescale in OpenSUSE is a bit more difficult because they don't appear in the package repository. For those, it would be best to download them from the GIMP Plugin Registry. The GIMP Animation Package, however, is in the repository, so you should be able to install it with YaST or zypper. You can search for it in the YaST2 interface or, in a terminal window, type:

```
zypper in gimp-gap
```

Or, for older versions of OpenSUSE, type the following:

```
yast -i gimp-gap
```

Gentoo

Gentoo (www.gentoo.org) is called a *source-based* Linux distribution, meaning that all of the programs and libraries are compiled on your computer directly from their source code before installation. This means installation can take much longer than on the *binary-based* distributions mentioned in this section. It also offers a somewhat more unique challenge when it comes to package management. To deal with this task, Gentoo uses a system called portage, which is accessed from the terminal with the command emerge. Installing GIMP is as straightforward as opening a terminal window, becoming the root user, and typing the following:

```
emerge -av gimp
```

The -av flag isn't necessary, but it helps give you a much clearer understanding of the dependencies that portage will download, compile, and install on your system. Gentoo also provides access to the GREYCstoration, Liquid Rescale, and GIMP Animation Package plug-ins. For GREYCstoration, it's as simple as typing:

```
emerge -av greycstoration
```

However, for the other two, you'll have to use an *overlay repository*, a package repository that's not part of the official Gentoo distribution, but instead managed by the community. You're looking for two overlays: sunrise and ibormuth. To use overlays, you'll need to install a program called layman (overlay manager). The entire process goes as follows (each line is a separate command you type at the terminal prompt as root and wait for it to complete):

```
emerge -av layman
layman -a sunrise ibormuth
emerge -av gimp-lqr-plugin gimp-gap
```

And with that, you'll have GIMP installed, along with some very handy plug-ins.

Mandriva

Like Fedora and OpenSUSE, Mandriva (www.mandriva.com) is an RPM-based distribution, but it too comes with its own package management software. As a graphical frontend, Mandriva uses Rpmdrake. To launch Rpmdrake, open the Mandriva Linux Control Center, choose Software Management, and click the icon for Install & Remove Software. This launches Rpmdrake, shown in Figure A-6.

Rpmdrake, Mandriva's package manager

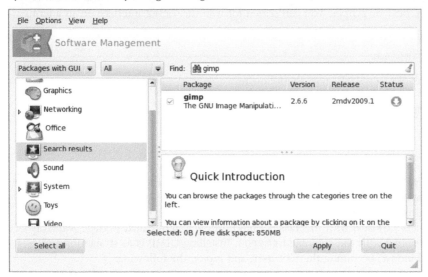

This tool works similarly to Synaptic and YaST2. Type `gimp` in the Find field at the top, and Rpmdrake shows GIMP in its list of available packages. Click the check box next to GIMP's package to mark it for installation and then click the Apply button at the bottom of the window. Rpmdrake tracks down all of the necessary dependencies and asks for your confirmation before downloading and installing them. And then, *poof!*, you have GIMP. Mandriva also supplies you with packages for GREYCstoration, Liquid Rescale, and the GIMP Animation Package. You can find them with the search terms `greycstoration`, `gimp-lqr-plugin`, and `gimp-gap`, respectively.

You can also use the command line to install GIMP, if you're more inclined to manage your software that way. You do this with the `urpmi` command. If you open a terminal window and become root, you can install GIMP along with the additional plug-ins covered in this book by typing the following:

```
urpmi gimp greycstoration gimp-lqr-plugin gimp2-gap
```

When you press Enter, `urpmi` shows you all the necessary dependencies and asks for confirmation before installing. Once you confirm and wait for the installation to complete, you'll have GIMP at your fingertips. Sweet.

Installing GIMP on Windows

Of course, not everyone can or wants to run Linux on their computers. It's still very much a Windows world out there. Fortunately, GIMP runs just fine on this operating system. Be aware, though, that the number of GIMP developers who actively work on and write code for Windows is far fewer than the number of GIMP developers working in Linux, so occasionally it takes a little bit longer for some GIMP updates to reach Windows users. That said, GIMP on Windows works, and works well.

Regular Installation on Windows

Installing GIMP on Windows is extremely easy. The GIMP web site at www.gimp.org gives you a direct download link for the latest version of GIMP for Windows at the top of the page. It also gives you a link to the main GIMP for Windows web site at http://gimp-win .sourceforge.net. This site has a bit more information that's specific to running GIMP on Windows. The Download page for this site is shown in Figure A-7; the first link is to an installer executable that includes everything you need to run GIMP. Click that link to download it and save it to your hard drive. Unless you have a designated folder where you download files, it's probably easiest just to download this file straight to your desktop.

FIGURE A-7

The GIMP for Windows download page

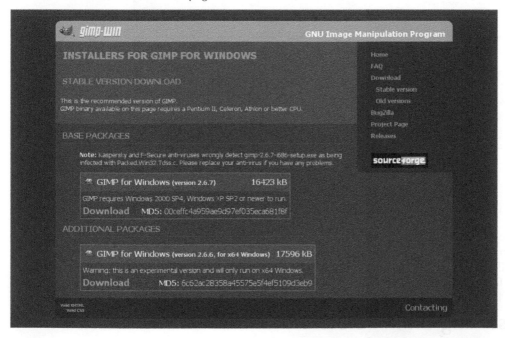

Note

Older versions of GIMP in the 2.0 series run on old versions of Windows, like Windows 95 and Windows 98. The newer (and cooler!) versions of GIMP, however, are not supported on these older operating systems. Current versions of GIMP require Windows NT, 2000, XP, or Vista. ■

When you have the GIMP installer downloaded, navigate to it on your hard drive (likely your downloads folder or your desktop) and double-click the installer icon. This launches the installer application, which walks you through the installation process. There aren't too many decisions you have to make. In fact, the Express install should adequately cover all your bases. Figure A-8 shows the GIMP installer in action.

FIGURE A-8

Installing GIMP on Windows

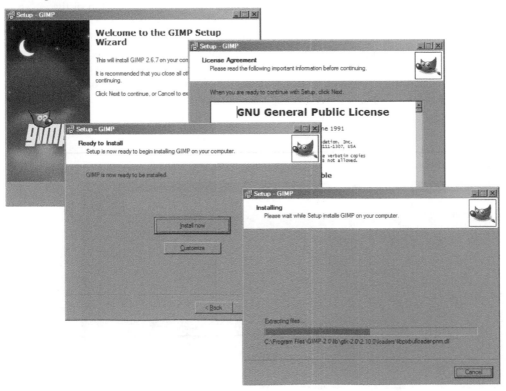

Once GIMP is installed, you should be ready to go. If you want to install any of the plug-ins covered in this book, like GREYCstoration, Liquid Rescale, and the GIMP Animation Package, you'll need to head over to the GIMP Plugin Registry web site at `http://registry.gimp.org` and follow the Windows installation instructions that are listed there for each of these plug-ins.

Installing GIMP Portable

Being completely free gives GIMP some advantages in the realm of portability. You never have to worry about whether or not some license allows you to have extra copies of GIMP or what computers you can run it on. If you're at a library or a friend's house or an Internet kiosk and you need to edit an image, you're completely allowed. And the very cool people at `PortableApps.com` have made this even easier for everyone by releasing GIMP Portable. GIMP

Portable is a special release of GIMP for Windows that you can install and run from a USB thumb drive. To get GIMP Portable, go to the web site at `www.portableapps.com/apps/graphics_pictures/gimp_portable` and click the large download button. Figure A-9 shows the GIMP Portable web site.

The GIMP Portable web site is where you go to get a copy of GIMP that you can run virtually anywhere

After you download the GIMP Portable installer, double-click it to launch it. The installation process is nearly identical to the regular GIMP for Windows installation, with one major exception: the GIMP Portable installer explicitly asks you where you want to install it. This is where you click the Browse button and navigate to the USB drive where you want to install. Once you pick that location, the installer handles the rest. Then any time you want to edit images with GIMP, you can plug in your USB drive and have at it.

Tip

USB thumb drives can often take a long time to write data to and occasionally USB ports will flake out. A trick you may want to do is temporarily install GIMP Portable directly to your hard drive; perhaps on your desktop. This ensures that the installation process goes as quickly and smoothly as possible. Then, once you have GIMP Portable installed, you can simply copy the GIMP Portable folder from your hard drive to your USB drive. Sure, this is an extra step and it doesn't speed up your installation time, but it's typically easier to recover from an error that happens when copying files than an error that happens while installing. This also gives you the ability to burn GIMP Portable to a CD, in case you find yourself in front of a computer that doesn't have an available USB port. ■

Installing GIMP on Apple Macintosh

Installing GIMP on Apple Mac OS X is a bit unique. In order for GIMP to work on OS X, you need to first have an X Window System installed. The X Window System (or X11 for short) is a means of getting graphical windows on a computer screen that dates back to the early Unix days and is still actively used in Linux today. Since Mac OS X is built on top of a Unix kernel, Mac users can often get Linux and Unix programs to run on their machines without much additional work. To take advantage of this yourself, you can use the XQuartz project. XQuartz is an open source project to implement the X.org form of X11 on Mac OS X. Apple has shipped XQuartz with OS X since version 10.5 (Leopard), so there's a good chance you already have it installed. However, if you're running Mac OS X 10.4 (Tiger), then you have an older version of the X Window System and you may need to upgrade to use GIMP.

To find the X Window System in Mac OS X, go to the Applications folder found on your system's main hard drive. Here, in the Utilities folder, you will find the X11 icon that you can either click and launch, or drag into your dock for easy access later.

However, if you're running an earlier version of Mac OS X and do not see XQuartz installed on your system or you want to install the newest version of XQuartz, the download page on www.gimp.org provides you a direct link to the XQuartz web site (http://xquartz .macosforge.org/trac/wiki). Pay special attention here and notice that all of the .dmg installer files for XQuartz are for Leopard. If you're running Tiger, then the only way to get XQuartz is to install via MacPorts. MacPorts is a package management utility for Macs like the ones commonly used in Linux. In fact, MacPorts is based on Ports, a package management utility used in BSD Unix. Ports is actually the inspiration for Gentoo's very powerful package management tool, Portage.

To install MacPorts, visit the MacPorts web site (www.macports.org), as shown in Figure A-10 and download the .dmg disk image for your version of Mac OS X from the Installing MacPorts link. The .dmg files are installers and they're available for Leopard, Tiger, and even the much older Panther version of Mac OS X.

Note
In order to successfully use MacPorts, you need to have Apple's Xcode Developer Tools installed. If you don't already have this installed, you can find it on your Mac OS X installation disks. Alternatively, you can download the most recent version from the Apple Developer Connection web site at http://connect.apple.com. ∎

With MacPorts installed, getting XQuartz on your Mac is quite simple. Open a terminal window and type the following command:

```
sudo port -v install xorg-server
```

You may be prompted for an administrative password here, but this command automatically looks for all of the dependencies that XQuartz requires and then downloads and installs everything for you. Once it completes, you should have XQuartz at Applications ➢ MacPorts ➢ X11.app.

FIGURE A-10

The MacPorts web sites is where you can get the latest version of MacPorts

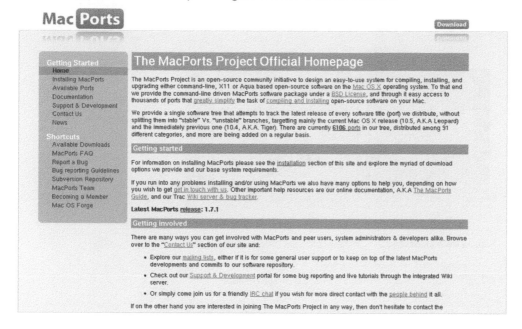

Once you are sure that you have XQuartz on your Mac, you have two choices for how to install GIMP, as shown on the GIMP web site: you can use GIMP on OS X, or you can install GIMP via MacPorts.

Installing GIMP on OS X

Of the two ways of installing GIMP on a Mac, the first one — GIMP on OS X — is the most straightforward and simple to do. If you click the GIMP on OS X link from www.gimp.org, you will be directed to the site shown in Figure A-11.

When you click the Download GIMP on OS X button, you are given the choice of universal binaries for different versions of OS X, either Leopard or Tiger. Click the one that applies to you, and the .dmg application bundle will be downloaded to your computer. Once that file is on your hard drive, you can simply run GIMP by double-clicking its icon. This automatically causes XQuartz to launch, and then executes GIMP within it. Then you're off to the races!

Included with the GIMP on OS X package are a handful of plug-ins, including GREYCstoration and Liquid Rescale. To install any additional plug-ins, such as the GIMP Animation Package, you need to go to the GIMP Plugin Registry web site at http://registry.gimp.org and follow the Mac OS X installation instructions for each of those plug-ins.

FIGURE A-11

The GIMP on OS X web site

Installing GIMP from MacPorts

The MacPorts system is a bit more involved than the GIMP on OS X project, but it has some very distinct advantages. For example, since it's a package management tool in the same vein as the ones used by Linux distributions, it shares many of the same features. For example, it's much easier to stay up to date with the latest and greatest version of GIMP because package management tools make it quick and painless to do software upgrades. Additionally, MacPorts is a repository for a much wider array of programs than the ones that you have to hunt down online by yourself. Not only that, but many GIMP plug-ins are also available to you. The kind maintainers at MacPorts have done all of that legwork for you.

If you do not yet have MacPorts installed on your Mac, review the previous section about installing XQuartz via MacPorts. It gives you a set of simple directions for downloading and installing MacPorts. Once you have it installed, that's where all the fun starts to take place. To get GIMP plus a few handy plug-ins like GIMP Animation Package, Liquid Rescale, and GREYCstoration, open up a terminal window and type the following command:

```
sudo port -v install gimp gimp-gap gimp-lqr-plugin greycstoration
```

Press Enter after typing, and MacPorts will do its installation magic and gift you with GIMP and this full set of goodies.

Setting Up External Input Devices

The bulk of this book is focused on dealing with image data that's already been digitized — whether it started as a digital photograph or was scanned from a paper source — and is in your computer. Eventually, though, you're going to have GIMP interact with the meatspace world a bit. This means scanning photos or drawings to digitize them or taking your digital works and creating tangible copies printed on paper. It also includes the use of drawing tablets like the ones made by Wacom (www.wacom.com) to use a more familiar pen interface to draw directly in GIMP rather than using a mouse or trackball.

Getting these external devices to play nice with GIMP can be a bit daunting, depending on the operating system that you're using. This is especially true if you're using GIMP in a Linux environment. There used to be a time when I wouldn't even consider seriously using scanners, tablets, or printers with GIMP simply because of the hassle involved with getting them set up. Fortunately, things have improved quite a bit since then.

This appendix walks you through making sure these devices work well with GIMP and points out ways to get around common potential snags you might hit along the way.

Acquiring Images with a Scanner

No matter how cool and flexible working digitally is, good reasons still exist to create things in the old-school, analog method. Some artists are just more comfortable working in traditional media, or you may have some old photographs that need retouching or restoration. Whatever the reason may be, getting these images digitized and in GIMP is the same: you have to use a scanner. Once connected to a computer (with modern scanners, this is typically via USB) a scanner device works by interfacing with some sort of program that controls it. Usually that program gives you the ability to make a preview scan, crop the part of the image you want, and even do some basic color correction. In almost all situations, you can run this scanner utility program independently. Just run the program, scan your image, and then you can use GIMP or some other image editor to open and modify it. Though this process works, it's an inconvenient and clunky workflow. Fortunately, there's a way to launch this scanner utility directly from within GIMP and get your scanned image loaded directly into an image window.

That's the good news. The bad news is that every operating system handles scanners a little bit differently, and in Windows and Mac OS X, the program to control the scanner can vary depending on manufacturer. This section of the appendix is dedicated to getting your scanner working and getting GIMP to "play nice" with it.

Linux

Of the three primary operating systems that are supported by GIMP, the most difficult one to get scanners to work in is Linux. The exact reasons for this vary, but they're generally related to the fact that some scanner manufacturers don't release Linux drivers or specifications for how their scanners work that would allow anyone else to code adequate Linux drivers themselves. Fortunately, as Linux has grown in user base and popularity, more and more scanners are being supported, and on some of the more user-friendly Linux distributions like Fedora and Ubuntu, most scanners work right out of the box. Most of the time, you don't have to do anything more than plug your scanner in, and you're ready to rock.

The nice thing about scanning in Linux is that the interface is consistent, regardless of who makes the scanner. Linux uses a library called SANE, or Scanner Access Now Easy, and a graphical interface for that library called XSane. It basically works like this:

1. Get SANE to recognize your scanner by configuring it with the proper *backend*, or driver, for your scanner. Most modern distributions have this step done for you.

2. Once you have the proper backend configured, launch XSane to make sure everything works.

3. Scan as much as you want from within GIMP.

That's basically it. You normally run into hiccups on only old parallel port scanners or one of those printer/copier/scanner all-in-one devices. In these cases, things can get a bit dicey. Usually there's a SANE backend that offers some support for your scanner, but it might not be complete. To get a clear idea of whether your specific scanner is supported, visit the Support Devices page of the SANE web site (www.sane-project.org/sane-mfgs.html). In Ubuntu, these "incomplete" drivers are sequestered into their own package. You can install them by firing up the Synaptic Package Manager and searching for a package named libsane-extras. Alternatively, if you're comfortable with the command line, you can launch a terminal and type the following:

```
sudo apt-get install libsane-extras
```

Another thing that you might run into is that some scanners will only work if you're *root*, or the admin user. In these cases, you'll have to open a terminal and launch XSane by typing the following:

```
sudo XSane
```

You could also launch GIMP as root, but running regular applications as root can be a security risk and it's not recommended. For these wacky scanners, it's better just to scan with XSane as root and open the image separately in GIMP.

Whether you scan from GIMP (File ➤ Create ➤ XSane ➤ Device Dialog) or by calling XSane directly, the actual scanning process is the same. Once XSane recognizes your scanner, it loads up its interface, which consists of a few windows, as shown in Figure B-1. The two most important ones are the main window with scanning options in it, shown on the upper left, and the large preview window, shown on the right.

FIGURE B-1

The standard windows that appear when you launch XSane

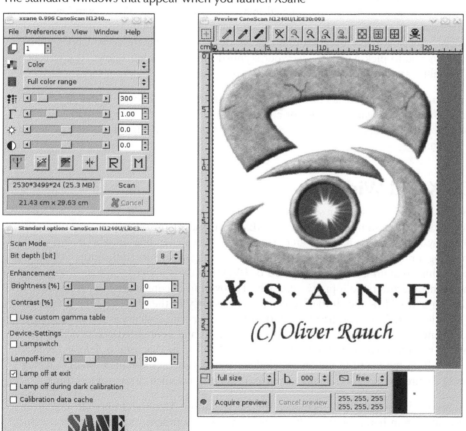

Now, you could simply scan by clicking the Scan button in the main window. However, you may want to do some color adjustments or cropping before scanning. To do that, first click the Acquire Preview button in the preview window. This prompts the scanner to create a low-resolution scan of your image. With the preview created, XSane automatically does a few things. It tries to determine where your image is in the scanned space, specifying that as the scanning area. Then XSane performs some color adjustments to try to maximize contrast and the color balance of your image. If you want to define a different specific area to scan, use your mouse in the preview window to resize the existing, auto-generated area by clicking and dragging the dashed line that defines it. If you don't like the automatic color and contrast adjustments that XSane does, you can use the sliders in the Main window to adjust it to better suit your tastes. Another setting in the main XSane window that you probably want to adjust is the scan resolution. This defaults to 100ppi. The actual limits of this value are determined by your scanner. However, I typically try to scan at 300 or 600ppi.

Once you've made all the adjustments you want, click the Scan button in the main window and XSane scans the area that you've chosen in the preview window. If you launched XSane from within GIMP, the scanned image result automatically appears in a GIMP image window. If you launched XSane separately, it brings the scanned image in its own XSane Viewer window, as shown in Figure B-2. You can save the image — and later modify it in GIMP — by clicking the save icon or choosing File ➤ Save As from this window. This brings up a File Chooser dialog, which allows you to pick where to save your scanned image and what format to save it in. To maintain quality, saving in TIFF or PNG is your best option.

XSane offers you several more advanced options, which are outside the scope of this appendix, such as *optical character recognition* (OCR) for automatically detecting text in your scans. You can find out more about these options by using the Help menu or by checking the documentation at www.XSane.org.

Mac OS X and Windows

In Mac OS X and Windows, scanner software is much more diverse than in Linux. Rather than having a single unified scanning interface like SANE, Apple and Microsoft rely on scanning software provided by the scanner's manufacturer. This means that, depending on who makes your scanner, the program that actually does the scanning will look and behave differently. When you buy a scanner, this program is included on a CD or DVD that the scanner is packaged with. Fortunately, most manufacturers do a pretty good job of providing documentation for their own software, though it would be nice if there was more consistency in the interface from one to the other. The upside, though, is that driver support in these operating systems is generally more up-to-date. So once you have your scanner properly installed and configured according to the instructions the manufacturer provides, scanning in GIMP is a snap. Navigate to File ➤ Create ➤ Scanner/Camera from the menu in the image window. When you click the menu item, a dialog like the one in Figure B-3 appears. If your scanner is properly installed, it appears in this list.

Click the name of your scanner and then click the Select button. This starts up your scanner's scanning program. From here, use this software to scan your document. When the scan is complete, it is automatically loaded into a GIMP image window.

Tip

If you have a webcam installed on your computer, you can also use this interface to pull images from that. This is especially helpful on newer laptops that have a webcam integrated into the bezel of the LCD screen. ■

FIGURE B-2

The XSane Viewer window appears after scanning if you run XSane by itself instead of launching it from within GIMP.

Size 2530 x 3499 pixel, 8 bits/channel, 3 channels, 300 dpi x 300 dpi, 25.3 MB

FIGURE B-3

The dialog for choosing your scanner device

Printing Images

Inevitably, there's going to come a time when you need to get digital work out of your computer and into a medium that people can put their hands on. This means that you're going to have to deal with printing and using a printing device. Of course, the easiest solution is to export your image to a flat image format like PNG, JPEG, or TIFF and take that file to a print shop and let them handle it from there. Print shops give you excellent quality and can generally print out a high volume of prints in a much shorter time than you could on your own. That said, print shops can be expensive and can sometimes take days to actually get a print back in your hands. Additionally, modern inkjet printers have come a long way in terms of print quality and they've actually lowered in price (thank you, Moore's Law!). If you're not printing volumes of high-color images, printing them yourself is an extremely attractive option.

Of course, that means you need to work with configuring GIMP to properly communicate with your printer. Two basic print systems are available for you to use: GIMP's bundled print function that uses the familiar print interface from GTK+, or a plug-in that uses the Gutenprint print system. Of the two, the GTKPrint interface is more standardized. If you've printed from other GTK+ applications like OpenOffice.org or Mozilla Firefox, you're probably already familiar with it. Gutenprint, on the other hand, though not as commonly used as GTKPrint, gives you more power over the printing output, with more refined controls for color management, page setup, and printer-specific features. Fortunately, you can actually have both systems installed at the same time, using GTKPrint for basic printing jobs and Gutenprint for cases where you need higher quality output.

Using the Bundled GTKPrint Module

Despite its simplicity, the Print function that ships with GIMP is pretty full-featured and works well on all platforms that GIMP runs. However, before you go rushing to print something, it's a really good idea to set up your print environment ahead of time. Do this by going to File ➤ Page Setup. If you do this from Windows, you get the default system dialog for page setup. If you do this from within Linux or Mac OS X, you get a much simpler dialog. Despite the cosmetic differences, these dialogs allow you to adjust two basic things: the paper size you're printing on and the orientation (portrait or landscape) of your image on that paper. Figure B-4 shows these dialogs side by side.

The reason why you want to do this first is because the built-in Print module doesn't offer you the facilities to adjust orientation, and although it provides you with the ability to adjust sizing, it doesn't provide you with default sizes like the Page Setup dialog does. However, once you've set up your page for printing, you can call up the Print dialog by going to File ➤ Print from the image window you want to print. Again, if you're running Windows, this menu item calls the default print system dialog. Within Linux, you get the GTKPrint module discussed previously. Figure B-5 shows the default view of each of these dialogs.

I'm not going to go all that heavily into the standard print dialogs because they are something you should already be familiar with. However, the GTKPrint interface requires a bit of attention. As Figure B-5 shows, this interface basically gives you two choices for printing:

FIGURE B-4

When you call File ➤ Page Setup you get a standardized dialog for setting your print job's size and orientation. On the left is the Windows dialog and on the right is what you see in Linux or Mac OS X.

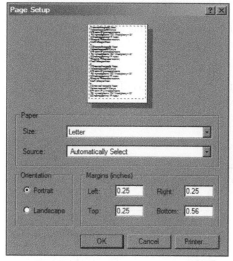
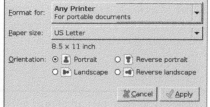

FIGURE B-5

Depending on your operating system, when you call File ➤ Print, you get either the system print dialog (left) or the GTKPrint dialog (right).

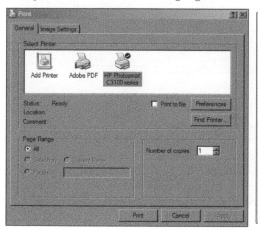
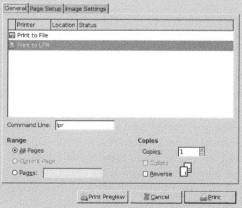

- **Print to File** — As advertised, this allows you to produce a "printer-friendly" file from your image in either PostScript (.ps) or PDF format. Typically this is unnecessary because most decent print shops can handle regular image formats like JPEG and TIFF. However, in the event that you have very specific dimensions that you want to print to, printing to a file is a good way to guarantee that. It's also a good quick way to get your image into PDF format if you don't have the PDF export plug-in installed.

- **Print to [*Printer*]** — Here [*Printer*] is either the name of your installed printer or LPR, or *Line Printer Daemon*, an older print system used on Unix and older Linux distributions. If you want to send your file to your printer, this is the option to choose. Depending on what print driver you're using, choosing this option may reveal some additional tabs in this dialog that assist in managing the print job or taking advantage of advanced features of your printer.

Regardless of whether you choose Print to File or Print to [*Printer*], the GTKPrint dialog from GIMP provides you with two tabs for controlling your printer's output: Page Setup and Image Settings. These two tabs are shown in Figure B-6.

FIGURE B-6

When using the GTKPrint dialog, you have two additional tabs for controlling output from your printer: Page Setup (left) and Image Settings (right).

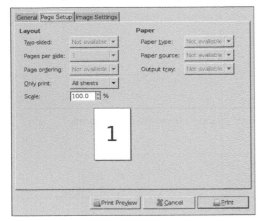
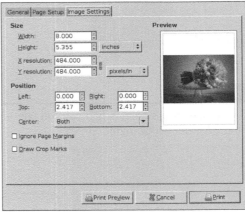

The Page Setup tab allows you to take advantage of some additional setup options if your printer supports them. If those features aren't supported, they're grayed out in the interface. The main thing that you should note about this tab is that you have the ability to adjust the scale of the image going to the printer. This is particularly useful if you need to print out a small draft version of your image before printing out a full-sized copy. Also notice that there is nothing in this tab that allows you to control the orientation of your image on the paper or the size of the paper itself. If you need to change either of these things, close this dialog and go back to the File ≻ Page Setup dialog to get it properly arranged first.

The Image Settings tab controls how the printer applies your image to paper you designate in the File ≻ Page Setup dialog. The Width, Height, and X/Y Resolution fields are what the print system intends on using. Pay special attention to this because the default behavior of GTKPrint is to fit your image to the full extent of the available paper size. This means that it does not use the resolution stipulated by your file. If you want to be sure that your desired resolution is used, go to your image window and click Image ➤ Print Size to verify the resolution you want. Then manually enter that value in the X/Y Resolution fields of the Image Settings tab in the Print dialog. You can also use the controls under the Position heading to precisely place your image on the paper. For faster control, simply click your image in the Preview area and drag it to the desired location. If you just want to center it, use the options available from the Center drop-down menu.

Note

If you adjust the Scale value in the Page Setup tab, that size is *not* reflected in the Image Settings tab. The dimensions in the Image Settings tab are actually what get scaled. So if your Image Settings dimensions are 8"x5" and you set the scale in Page Setup to 50%, your printer produces an image that's 4"x2.5". ∎

Once you're satisfied with your page layout, you can go ahead and print your image by clicking the Print button on the bottom right of the dialog. Of course, it's probably a smarter idea to test your print settings ahead of time. Fortunately, you can do this using the Print Preview button that's also at the bottom of the dialog. When you click this button, your distribution's default PDF reader — usually Evince or GPDF — is called to open a temporary PDF file of your image as it should appear coming from your printer. Assuming everything is good to go, you can either print from the preview program or close the preview and click Print on the GTKPrint dialog.

Printing with Gutenprint

The GTKPrint module gets the job done, but it doesn't always address all of the advanced features that are available on your printer, such as printing on special paper or refined color correction by controlling ink output. For these features, you need to use a specialized print driver and plug-in called Gutenprint. Gutenprint started as Gimp-Print and was the original print plug-in for GIMP, dating back to the 1.2 series. As Gimp-Print matured, it started taking on features that made it valuable to other applications that required the use of advanced printer settings. Because its scope had grown much larger than a simple print plug-in for GIMP, it was renamed to Gutenprint when it hit version 5.0. You can find more history and additional documentation on Gutenprint on its official web site at http://gimp-print.sourceforge.net.

Installing Gutenprint

Installing Gutenprint from its source code can be a bit of a bear. Fortunately, pre-built installation packages are available for Windows, Mac OS X, and nearly every modern Linux distribution.

Installing on Linux

Each distribution tends to package Gutenprint a little bit differently. Typically, though, you can simply fire up the package management tool (Synaptic on Ubuntu, PackageKit on Fedora, YaST on OpenSUSE, and so on) and search for packages using the term gutenprint. Choose the packages you need from the search results and the package manager should track down any additional dependencies you need. The only thing to note is that some distributions separate Gutenprint from its GIMP plug-in, so you'll need to make sure that gets installed as well. If you don't want to mess around with searching for the right packages, the following are commands for installing Gutenprint on each distribution from the command line:

- **Debian/Ubuntu** — `apt-get install gimp-gutenprint`
- **Fedora** — `yum install gutenprint-plugin`
- **OpenSUSE** — `zypper in gutenprint-gimpplugin`
- **Mandriva** — `urpmi -i gutenprint-gimp2`
- **Gentoo** — `USE="gimp" emerge -av gutenprint`

Once everything is properly installed, you should be able to launch GIMP and see a new menu item at File ➤ Print with Gutenprint.

Installing on Mac OS X

On Mac OS X, the installation instructions are a bit simpler. In fact, if you have GIMP installed, there's a good chance that you already have Gutenprint up and available. You can check by launching GIMP and looking for File ➤ Print with Gutenprint. If that's there, you're done and you can go to the next section. Otherwise, visit the download page at `http://gutenprint.sourceforge.net/p_Download.php` and follow the links and instructions there to download the `.dmg` file with the Gutenprint installation package. From there, it's a simple matter of double-clicking the `.dmg` file wherever you downloaded it and letting the install process go from there. Once that's done, you should be able to fire up GIMP and be ready to rock.

Installing on Windows

Installing Gutenprint on Windows is a bit different from the other operating systems because there's no official download link for it on the Gutenprint web site. To get Gutenprint and its accompanying GIMP plug-in for Windows, you need to visit the GIMP Plugin Registry at the following address: `http://registry.gimp.org/node/14567`. Download the zip file from that page and open it once it's on your computer. Within the zip file is a subfolder named `plug-ins`. Copy the contents of that subfolder to the folder where GIMP looks for plug-ins. By default, this should be `C:\Program Files\GIMP-2.0\lib\gimp\2.0\plug-ins\`. If you get confused, look through the other files in the zip. You'll find some very clear installation instructions, complete with GIF illustrations. Once you copy the necessary files, the Print with Gutenprint option should appear in the File menu the next time you run GIMP.

Using Gutenprint

When you initially run Gutenprint by clicking File ➤ Print with Gutenprint, you get a dialog like the one in Figure B-7, including a large preview area and a bevy of settings and controls.

Unfortunately, if you try to print immediately from this window, it will error out and fail. This is because you first need to set up a printer. By default, the Gutenprint plug-in is completely unaware of your printing configuration. To get things properly configured, click the Setup Printer button. This gets you a second dialog, like the one that appears in Figure B-8. Using this dialog, find the make and model of your printer.

FIGURE B-7

The default view of the Gutenprint dialog

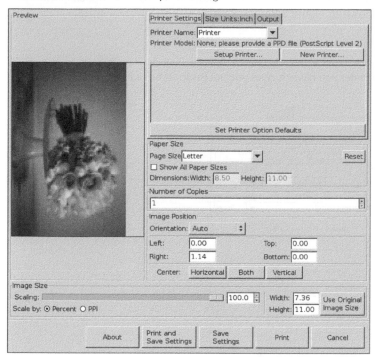

FIGURE B-8

The Setup Printer dialog for Gutenprint

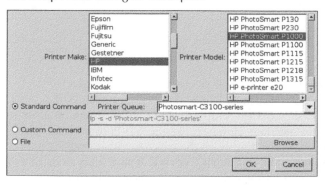

If you don't see your printer's exact make and model, try finding a similar model and using its settings. This may require you to open your web browser and do a little bit of Internet kung fu to hunt down a printer model that matches. Of course, although Gutenprint supports more than 700 different printers, there's always the possibility that your specific printer isn't supported yet.

If that ends up being the case, your only resort is to use the built-in Print module or take your file to a professional print shop. However, if your printer is in the list, pick it out and click the OK button. Once you do that, you should see some additional settings and options back in the Gutenprint dialog, as shown in Figure B-9.

FIGURE B-9

Once you tell Gutenprint what kind of printer you have, it gives you access to some of that printer's advanced features.

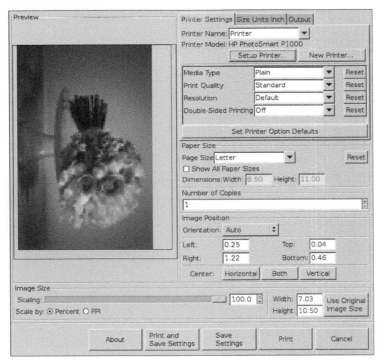

From here, you can adjust those advanced options as well as tweak some of the more conventional controls such as paper size and orientation. Unlike the GTKPrint module, the Gutenprint plug-in doesn't require you to do any Page Setup operations ahead of time. You can do everything directly from within this interface. However, like the GTKPrint interface, Gutenprint does allow you to position your image directly on the paper by either dragging it around the preview space or entering values in the Left, Right, Top, and Bottom entry fields near the bottom of the dialog. You define the units for these dimensions by clicking the Size Units tab at the top of the dialog and choosing the units you want to use. Gutenprint is set to use inches by default. Also, Gutenprint gives you more immediate feedback if you adjust the scaling of your image relative to the paper. As you adjust the Scaling slider, the preview updates in real time.

Not only can you tweak the positioning of your image on the paper with great precision, but Gutenprint also gives you very refined control over the color output of your printer. To adjust these controls, click the Output tab at the top of the dialog. This reveals a deceptively simple panel. The two radio buttons at the top, labeled Output Type, determine whether you're printing in color or grayscale (unless your printer is incapable of printing color; then it should just show grayscale). Once you determine your Output Type, click the large Adjust Output button. This should pop up a window similar to the one in Figure B-10.

FIGURE B-10

Gutenprint's Print Color Adjust dialog

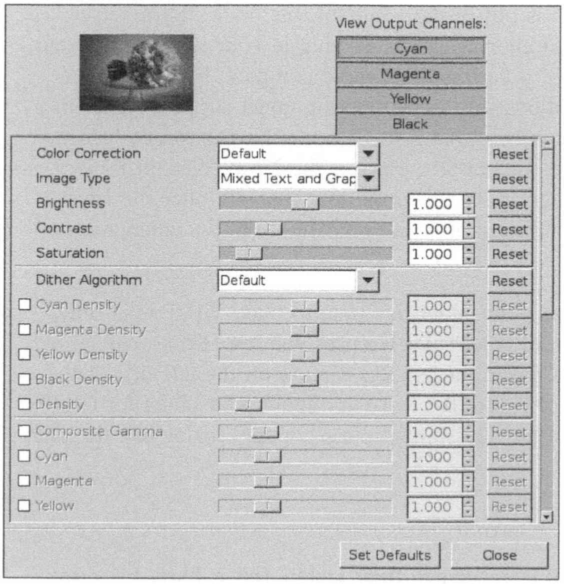

The exact content of this window varies depending on the type of printer you have. Gutenprint recognizes everything from simple black-and-white printers to highly advanced printers that use six or more different inks. From this window you do color correction by tweaking how much of each ink is used to print your images, so you can match what you see on your monitor as closely as possible.

Once you finish tweaking, click the Close button and you're ready to print. Because you're required to set up your printer each time you launch Gutenprint, it provides you with the facility to save your printer settings and layout by clicking the Save Settings button. After that, you can click Print and let your printer do the rest of the work.

Tip

For efficiency, the Gutenprint interface also offers a single Print and Save Settings button so you don't have to click as much. ■

Configuring a Drawing Tablet

Whether you're using GIMP for photo editing or generating custom digital artwork from whole cloth, your life can be made infinitely easier and more productive with a drawing tablet. These tablets leverage the years of training that most artists already have under their belts by using a pen-like pointing device on a pressure-sensitive surface. Not only does this allow you to draw more natural lines, but it also puts less strain on your wrist than working with a mouse does. Even tools like the Free Select tool are made faster and more comfortable when using a tablet.

The most ubiquitous tablets (and arguably the best) on the market are made by Wacom. That being the case, GIMP offers the most support for tablets of this brand. Getting into the full details of installing and configuring your tablet is out of the scope of this book. If you're on Windows or Mac OS X, installation and configuration is easy; just plug in your tablet and install the software that came with it. For Linux users, it can be a bit more complex. However, the good news is that most modern Linux distributions ship with working tablet support right out of the box (or installed from the Internet, as it were). That said, if you're having trouble getting your tablet to work in Linux, the best resource and starting place is the Linux Wacom Project web site at http://linuxwacom.sourceforge.net. Not only does that site offer the latest production version of the Linux Wacom drivers, but it also has very thorough documentation on how to install and configure them.

Once your operating system properly recognizes your tablet, it's time to make GIMP take notice of it. You do so from the Input Devices section of GIMP's Preferences window. Bring that up by clicking Edit ➤ Preferences and going down to the Input Devices section on the left side of the dialog. You should see something like the left of Figure B-11. To configure your tablet for GIMP, click the Configure Extended Input Devices button. This pops up a secondary dialog like the one shown on the right of Figure B-11.

Tip

Mac OS X users may have some difficulties getting GIMP to recognize their tablet. This is likely because GIMP works through X11 rather than the native Mac OS X interface. To ensure everything is working properly, make sure that your copies of Mac OS X and XQuartz are up-to-date. ■

Tip

If you're using Windows and GIMP isn't recognizing your tablet device, you may not have DirectInput as an active input controller. To make sure this is the case, go to the Input Controllers section of the Preferences window and make sure that the DirectX DirectInput controller is in the Active column. If you have to do this, make sure you restart GIMP so it can finally recognize your tablet. ■

The Device drop-down menu at the top of the configuration dialog has a list of devices that GIMP recognizes. Not all of them will belong to your tablet, especially on newer versions of Linux. You're primarily interested in four specific devices:

- **Stylus** — This device may also just simply be the name of your tablet device (for example, "Wacom Intuos3 6x8"). This device and its settings control the tip of your pen, including its location, tilt angle, and the pressure you're applying to the tablet with it.

FIGURE B-11

Get GIMP to recognize your drawing tablet by going to the Input Devices section of the Preferences window (left) and clicking Configure Extended Input Devices to get the configuration dialog (right).

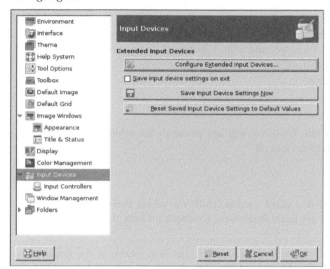 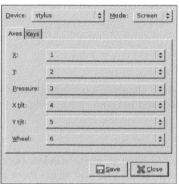

- **Eraser** — You may see your tablet's name in front of the word *eraser* (for example, "Wacom Intuos3 6x8 eraser"). This is the back of your pen. It has the same basic settings and attributes of the stylus device.

- **Cursor** — As with the eraser, this device may be prefixed with your tablet's name. The cursor device is technically the mouse device provided by the tablet. Some tablets actually come with a separate mouse that feeds directly to this device. Otherwise, the cursor is the position of your pen when it's not touching the surface of your tablet.

- **Pad** — Not all tablets have this device. It's more common on higher-end Wacom tablets like those in the Intuos series. This device is really for the additional buttons and scroll strips that many tablets come with.

To configure your tablet to work with GIMP, you need to configure each of these devices. Of the settings to configure, the most important one is the Mode drop-down menu. By default, each device may be set to Disabled. With this setting, you can probably control the location of your mouse cursor with the tablet, but none of the extra goodies like tilt and pressure sensitivity work. To get those to work, you need to set the mode to either Screen or Window. The Screen setting maps the drawing area of your tablet to the full screen area of your monitor. Alternatively, the Window setting maps the drawing surface to the image window in which you're currently working. Everyone has their personal preferences, but generally speaking, most digital artists set style, eraser, and cursor to Screen. A few artists like to have more precision in the image window, so they set style and eraser to Window and leave the cursor set to Screen. Play with it a bit and see which way works best for you.

Note

If you have a tablet that has a pad device, leave it disabled. The buttons from the pad device are controlled either through X11 on Linux and Mac OS X or through the driver software on Windows, so GIMP really doesn't have anything to do with this device. ■

Once you choose the mode for each device on your tablet, go through and, on the devices you enabled, adjust the Axes keys for each one. These keys bind the hardware on your pen to a function within GIMP such as X/Y Location, Pressure, and Tilt. Typically, the default settings work just fine here. However, if you want to customize your tablet to your unique working style, you can do it through these drop-down menus.

Note

Don't worry about changing anything in the Keys tab. Those settings are primarily for other devices such as MIDI controllers and have no real bearing on tablet devices. ■

Tip

It's a good idea to have an image window open with a blank canvas while you adjust these settings. That way you can test them while you adjust them and get some immediate feedback on how they work. ■

Once you have your tablet configured to your satisfaction, click the Save button at the bottom of the dialog to store your configuration for future use. Also, feel free to play around with these settings and really find out what works for you. There's virtually no risk. If you set your tablet to do something really wonky, you can always click the Reset Saved Input Device Settings to Default Values button and put everything back to where they were before you started mucking around with them.

The coolest thing, though, is now that you have your tablet configured, you can really take full advantage of the Brush Dynamics settings for each of the painting tools described in Chapters 11 and 12. Have at it!

Customizing GIMP

Chapter 1 contains information about how to customize GIMP's behavior and workflow to make it work the way you want. You can customize keyboard shortcuts, the appearance of the image window, and even the different kinds of mouse cursors that GIMP uses to give you feedback on the tool you've selected. You can control these options from the Edit ➤ Preferences dialog. However, some changes that can go a long way toward enhancing your experience require you to do some work outside of GIMP's standard Preferences window. These changes may seem largely aesthetic, but they can help GIMP feel like it's more integrated with the rest of the programs on your computer and more pleasant to use for long stretches of time.

IN THIS APPENDIX

Customizing how GIMP starts

Tweaking GIMP's appearance

Fixing an annoying bug

Changing the Splash Image

Probably the easiest thing to change in GIMP is the splash image that appears when you first start the program. This is Free Software. You're allowed to take ownership of the program and make it feel like it's yours. First things first: you have to create an image to use as your splash. Splash images have only a couple specifications:

- Make the size of the image 300 × 200 pixels or more. Smaller images still work, but the text for the modules being loaded will be cut off.

- Splash images can be in any image format that GIMP can understand. However, for the best combination of quality and small file size, it's recommended that you use the PNG or JPEG file formats.

That's it. After you create your image, save it where GIMP will be looking for it. This is your "personal GIMP directory." For Unix and Unix-like operating systems such as Linux and Mac OS X, this is normally /home/[username]/.gimp-2.8, where [username] is your login name. In Windows, this is typically C:\Documents and Settings\[username]\.gimp-2.8. Because these are configuration files that you don't need to see frequently, they're often set as hidden folders. On Linux and Mac OS X, the simple fact that the folder name starts with a dot indicates that it's a hidden folder. If you don't see this folder, you should be able to make it visible by right-clicking and choosing Show Hidden Files. In Windows, you may have to enable the Show Hidden Files option in Tools ➤ Folder Options under the View tab. Figure C-1 shows what the contents of the folder look like in Windows.

FIGURE C-1

The personal GIMP directory as you may see it on Windows

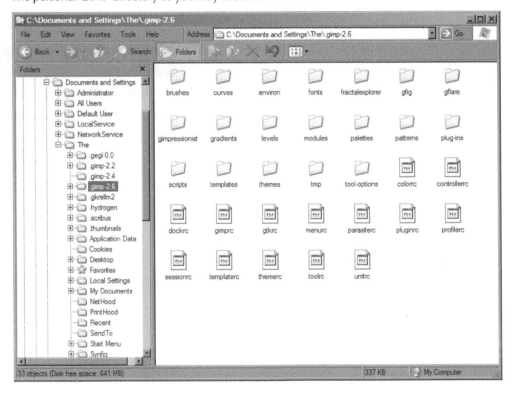

Once you're in this directory, look for a folder named splashes. If this folder does not already exist, create it. This is where you save your customized splash image. Once you save your image to this folder, restart GIMP and you'll see your image come up as the new splash instead of the default one. Figure C-2 shows a couple of custom splash images that I created for my copy of GIMP.

If you put more than one image in this splashes folder, GIMP randomly cycles through them each time it starts. So you could save a handful of different splash images to this folder and every time you start GIMP, you'll see a different one. How's that for sweet?

FIGURE C-2

Custom splash images for GIMP

Using a Different Theme

Now that you have a taste for customization, it's time to bite into something more substantial. A more valuable part of GIMP to customize is the theme that it uses for buttons, widgets, and even the overall interface color. Not only does this help integrate GIMP into your desktop environment so that it feels like part of the tools in your digital toolbox, but depending on the theme you use, it can also make GIMP easier to use for long periods of time. As an example, dark interfaces tend to put less strain on the eye. A dark, neutral base color for an interface is a great way to keep the program out of your way and let you focus more directly on your work. It's for this reason that many graphic artists prefer a dark gray or even a straight black for the programs they use.

As explained early in this book, GIMP is the basis for the GIMP toolkit, or GTK+, the widget set used for a large number of Free Software programs. If you're interested writing programs using GTK+, you can have a look at www.gtk.org. However, from a user's perspective the really valuable thing about GTK+ is that it's completely themeable, allowing you to change colors, icons, mouse cursors, and even the look of widgets like scrollbars. The default appearance for GTK+ is the "standard" middle gray color that's nearly become the de facto standard for most interfaces. Although this is a neutral color, it's still pretty bright.

Note
Some Linux distributions like Ubuntu Studio already ship with a dark gray GTK+ theme. In these cases, the default is usually quite nice. However, you still have the flexibility to change the theme to anything else you may prefer. ∎

Figure C-3 shows the GIMP Toolbox with the default gray GTK+ theme compared to a darker theme that I like to use called Marble Look.

FIGURE C-3

On the left, the GIMP Toolbox with the default gray GTK+ theme; on the right, the same Toolbox, but using the Marble Look theme

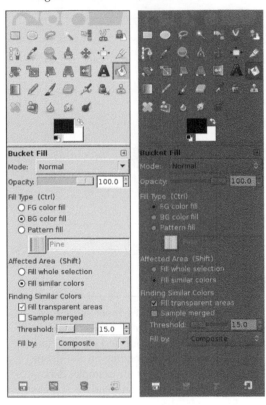

You can find a whole variety of GTK+ themes at http://art.gnome.org and www.gnome-look.org. The process for making GTK+ — and by extension, GIMP — aware of these themes once you download them varies a bit depending on which operating system you're using. However, in all cases you start by downloading the theme you like and extracting the compressed file to somewhere on your hard drive. After that, use one of the following sets of instructions based on the operating system you're using.

Linux

Because GTK+ was originally built in Linux and Unix, getting themes to work in it is the most straightforward. Of course, it can vary a bit depending on which distribution you're using. However, if you're running the GNOME desktop environment, it's pretty consistent because it has an integrated theme manager. To access it, go to the main menu and choose System ➤ Preferences ➤ Appearance, and you'll get a window like the one in Figure C-4.

FIGURE C-4

The GNOME theme manager

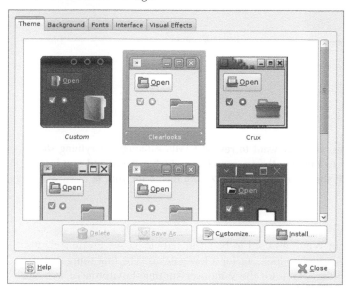

To add a custom theme to the theme manager, drag your downloaded theme into this window and it will be instantly added as one of your available choices. From there, it's just a matter of clicking the theme you want to use. This automatically updates your theme across all GTK+ applications. Once you have the theme you want, click Close. That's all there is to it!

If you aren't running GNOME or can't find the theme manager for some reason, you can still install themes manually and use a different tool to switch between them. In these cases, the process is similar to setting up your custom splash image in GIMP. In your home directory, usually /home/[username], there should be a directory named .themes. If there isn't one already there, go ahead and create it. This .themes directory is where you need to decompress the theme archive that you downloaded.

Once you have the theme (or themes) you want decompressed to that directory, you need to run a program to switch between themes. This is a small program called gtk-switcher2. The actual name of the program varies from one distribution to the other, but if you use the package manager to search for the term "switcher," it should be easy to find. When installed, the executable is typically named switch2 and if you can't find it in your application menus, you can launch it from the command line by typing the following:

```
switch2
```

This loads a small interface that looks like a simple dialog box, as shown in Figure C-5. This simple tool has a drop-down button that lists the themes you have installed in your .themes directory. Select the theme you're interested in using and click the Preview button to see what it looks like. If that's the theme you want, click Apply, and all of your programs that use GTK+, including GIMP, will be updated to use that theme. If you want, you can also use this interface to install themes as well by clicking the plus sign on the right and clicking Install New Theme. That will get you a file chooser to pick where the compressed archive of your theme is.

FIGURE C-5

The interface for the gtk-switcher utility

Tip

If you have GIMP open while changing themes, you may want to restart GIMP. Although everything *should* roll along smoothly with an instant transition to the new theme, sometimes glitches occur and you lose menu items or other widgets. Restarting GIMP should properly initialize the theme for you. ∎

Windows

Getting GTK+ themes to play nice in Windows used to be an incredible hassle. Fortunately it's gotten a lot easier. That said, you still need to look out for a few gotchas. The first thing that you need to do is point your browser to the GTK+ for the Windows Runtime Environment web site (http://gtk-win.sourceforge.net), shown in Figure C-6. What you're specifically looking for here is the GTK+ Preference Tool.

FIGURE C-6

The GTK+ for Windows Runtime Environment web site is where you find the GTK+ Preference Tool for changing your GTK+ themes

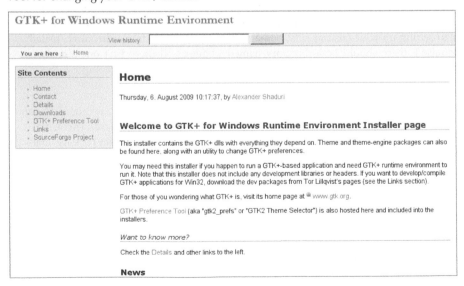

From this web site, go to the download page to get the GTK+ Preference Tool. I recommend that you download the theme package, named gtk2-themes-[release_date]-ash.exe. Not only does this installer include the Preference Tool, but it also packs a variety of themes and theme engines for you to choose from. You can always download more themes from sites like gnome-look.org, but this package gives you a good start. More importantly, it includes some of the different GTK+ theme engines, like the Pixbuf engine, which is necessary for some themes.

Once you've downloaded the themes package, run the installer. When doing this, it's *very* important to pay attention to the installation path. The GTK+ for Windows Runtime Environment web site gives a recommendation for this path that is actually not up to date with the latest GIMP installer. The current GIMP installer packs GTK+ along with it. So, assuming you used the default settings when installing GIMP, the actual path that you want to use is C:\Program Files\GIMP-2.0. Figure C-7 shows the installer prompt with the path that you need to use.

FIGURE C-7

The proper install path for the GTK+ themes package that includes the Preference Tool

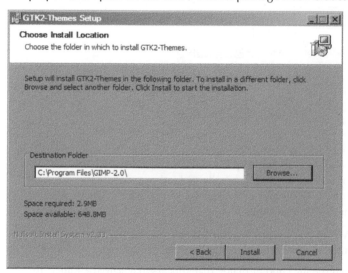

Upon installation, if you try to run the GTK+ Preference Tool, you'll find that it still doesn't work, complaining that it can't find one or more missing .dll files. A quick fix for this is to copy the executable file into GIMP's bin folder. However, a better option is to update the shortcut in the Start menu. To do this, use the following steps:

1. Go to Start ➤ All Programs ➤ GTK2 Runtime and right-click Change GTK2 Appearance.

2. From the context menu that pops up, click Properties. This brings up a properties window where you can edit the shortcut.

3. In the Start In field, change the value to C:\Program Files\GIMP-2.0\bin. This assumes that you installed GIMP with default settings. If you installed GIMP somewhere

else, you should be able to get away with adding bin to the end of whatever path is already in that field.

4. Click OK when you are done.

If you run the GTK+ Preference Tool (Start ➢ All Programs ➢ GTK2 Runtime ➢ Change GTK2 Appearance), you should be able to pick and choose any of the themes that came in the GTK+ themes package. Figure C-8 shows what the dialog might look like. If you click the Show Preview button, you can get a clearer idea of how the theme looks before applying it.

FIGURE C-8

The GTK+ Preference Tool

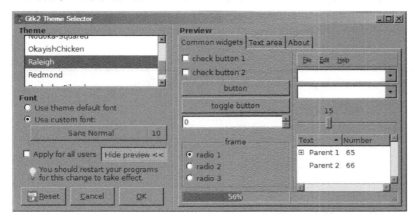

One thing you should notice, though, is that the full theme won't look like it's being properly applied. Buttons and other interface widgets might keep the standard Windows appearance. This can clash with what the actual theme looks like and generally make things ugly. The reason for this is that GIMP, by default, uses the GTK-Wimp, or "Windows Impersonator" theme engine. To get around this, you need to make a quick change to a text file. Use the following steps:

1. Open a text editor, like Wordpad. You may be tempted to use Notepad, but the GTK+ configuration files look funky in Notepad and maintain better formatting in Wordpad.

2. Click File ➢ Open and from the file chooser dialog that appears, navigate the folders to open the file C:\Program Files\GIMP-2.0\etc\gtk-2.0\gtkrc. This is the GTK+ configuration file where you can control the default theme engine that GIMP will use.

3. In the file, search for a line with the following code:

```
engine "wimp"
```

4. Change this line to be this instead:

```
engine "default"
```

5. Save this file (File ➢ Save) and close it. Now when you open the GTK+ Preference Tool, it will use the proper widgets and buttons from each theme, rather than the standard Windows ones. Figure C-9 shows an example of this using the Aurora-Midnight theme.

FIGURE C-9

The GTK+ Preference Tool, using proper theme widgets on the Aurora-Midnight theme

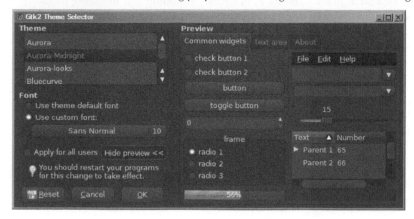

Once all of this is done, pick the theme that you want to use and click OK. You'll be prompted to say that this will write to a .gtkrc file in your user folder. Click Yes to confirm and the next time you start up GIMP, it will use your chosen theme. If you download additional themes from the Internet, extract them in C:\Program Files\GIMP-2.0\share\themes and the GTK+ Preference Tool will automatically add them to the list of possible GTK+ themes to choose from.

Mac OS X

Running GIMP in Mac OS X is a bit unique because, as explained in Appendix A, it requires you to run the X Windows System via XQuartz on top of the standard Mac OS X user interface. While this makes porting Unix and Linux applications to Macs easier, it occasionally causes some visual glitches to happen on applications that have been ported. So prior to customizing your theme, it's best to fix bugs.

Fixing the "Yellow Cursor" Bug

One of the things that you may find bothersome when using GIMP on Mac OS X is the cursor. On some Intel-based Macs, XQuartz may render the cursor to be a transparent yellow outline rather than the full-color cursor that you expect. This is caused by a bug in XQuartz. Fortunately, it's easy to work around. On the companion web site for this book (www.gimpbible.com), there's a link to a file named xfix.tar.gz. Download this file. Once it's downloaded, open Terminal.app and change directories to wherever you downloaded the file. From there, run the following command:

```
sudo tar xvzf xfix.tar.gz -C /
```

Once you do this, restart XQuartz and when you run GIMP, your cursors should be fixed.

Changing Your GTK+ Theme

Because the underlying infrastructure in Mac OS X is based on Unix, many of the same tools for changing GTK+ themes are also available. The trick, of course, is finding and installing them. Fortunately you can use MacPorts. As explained in Appendix A, MacPorts is a command-line tool for downloading and installing software from a central repository. It's very similar to apt or yum on Linux distributions. Unfortunately, it doesn't ship by default with Mac OS X, so you'll have to download and install it. To do this, visit the MacPorts web site (www.macports.org).

As part of the installation process, MacPorts updates its internal list of available programs in the repository. However, to ensure that you have the recent version of any software you install with MacPorts, it's a good idea to update this list periodically along with MacPorts itself manually. You do this from the command line by opening Terminal.app and typing the following command:

```
sudo port -v selfupdate
```

Now that you have MacPorts installed and updated, you can install the GTK+ theme switcher mentioned in the Linux section. To do this, use Terminal.app again and type the following command:

```
sudo port -v install gtk-theme-switch
```

This downloads and installs the GTK+ theme switcher for you. Once it's installed type the following:

```
switch2
```

This launches the same theme switcher program covered in the Linux section. Figure C-10 shows the standard and expanded versions of the switcher program. If you download one of the many GTK+ themes from gnome-look.org — perhaps one that more closely matches the Mac OS X colors and widgets — you can install it by clicking the plus (+) symbol to expand the switcher program and then clicking the Install New Theme button. Then use the File Chooser to track down where you downloaded the theme, select it, and install it. Once installed, you can pick that theme from the list of themes in the drop-down box.

FIGURE C-10

The standard and expanded views of the GTK+ theme switcher in Mac OS X

You can also install themes using MacPorts. To see what's available, type the following command in Terminal.app:

```
port search gnome-themes
```

This gives you a list of the various GTK+ themes available through MacPorts. The unfortunate downside here is that there aren't any preview images that show what the themes look like before installing them. The nice thing, though, is that if the theme ever gets updated, you can automatically do upgrades using MacPorts. That being the case, some people like to hunt through theme sites like `gnome-look.org` and find a theme that they like. Then you can check MacPorts to see if that theme is in there, and if so, install it that way.

Regardless of the method you use, you now have the capability to customize GIMP to more comfortably fit your work environment. Have fun!

Additional Resources

This book is designed to be as comprehensive as possible and give you everything you need to have a complete understanding of GIMP. That said, GIMP development happens quickly and it's good to have additional resources to allow you to more effectively track new features as they get added. Also, the GIMP user community is an indispensable source of not just technical information on using GIMP, but also immediate feedback and valuable critiques of your work.

This appendix shares some of the resources on the Internet that I've personally found useful and I hope will be useful for you.

On the Web

Seeing as how GIMP is distributed almost entirely via the Internet, it's natural that the first place anyone is going to look for more information is the World Wide Web. Now, your Internet kung fu may be strong, but this list should work as a great supplement to give you a good head start.

- **The official GIMP web site** (www.gimp.org) — I would be remiss if I did not include the official GIMP web site in a list of valuable Internet resources. Not only is this the place to go to download the latest version of GIMP and find out about any new developments with it, but it's also a well-organized portal to the entire GIMP community. Probably the most valuable part of this is the official documentation at http://docs.gimp.org. Aside from that, though, there is a variety of good tutorials to get you started with using GIMP. If you're interested in programming, this site also gives you the resources to get involved with GIMP's development.

- **This book's companion web site** (www.wiley.com/go/GIMPBible) — It's a bit of a shameless plug, but this web site was designed specifically to accompany and supplement this book. It hosts example files for you to work on and also provides you with web links to GIMP resources available online, including the ones listed in this appendix. I will also periodically post video tutorials to help show off specific features in GIMP, in case you're the sort of person who learns better by seeing a tool in action. The entire site is organized blog-style, so you can subscribe to the RSS feed that the site generates to get updated whenever I add new content.

  Also, in the (hopefully) rare event that there's an error in this book, corrections will be made immediately and posted to the Errata page.

- **GIMP Plugin Registry** (http://registry.gimp.org) — One of the really cool things about GIMP is its extensibility. Using either scripting or writing custom C code with GIMP's internal plug-in API, anyone can quickly add powerful new features to GIMP. This web site is the best place to find new plug-ins for GIMP. Most of the additional features you might want in GIMP have been implemented as some sort of plug-in and that plug-in is available here. Chapter 21 names a few plug-ins worth looking into.

- **GIMPusers.com** (www.gimpusers.com) — This site, the GNU Image Manipulation Portal, is exactly that. It's a user portal to the world of GIMP: kind of a virtual storehouse for all of the GIMP-related information around the Internet. This site syndicates content from other GIMP resources online and puts them in a central place where you can see all of it. One of the things about this site that's particularly nice is its forums. These forums actually tie in directly with the official GIMP e-mail discussion lists. So all of the posts in their For GIMP Users forum are actually e-mails that were sent to the gimp-users e-mail list. If you post a new thread in this forum, it's automatically sent for the list for all subscribers to see. It's a great way to get your question in front of the full user community.

- **Meet the GIMP** (http://www.meetthegimp.org) — This blog-style web site houses a full series of video tutorials and news about GIMP. The site is updated pretty regularly and even periodically holds challenges where you can test your skills for fun GIMP-related prizes.

- **Gimper.net** (www.gimper.net) — Gimper.net is an active GIMP user community forum where users share their experiences as well as their work. It's a great place to go to ask questions about using GIMP and it even has a dedicated section for Mac users. This community is also a fantastic resource for feedback on the work you create in GIMP. You can get feedback on the content of your work and suggestions for improvement (or a bunch of "oohs" and "ahhs" if your work is *really* good). This way you can not only improve as a GIMP user, but also as a digital artist in general.

- **GIMP-tutorials.net** (www.gimp-tutorials.net) — This site is actually a sister site to Gimper.net and features a blog-style format that gives you an incredibly wide variety of tutorials for GIMP. The tutorials are broken down by category and each one has comments to allow user feedback so you can ask the tutorial author specific questions or offer improvement suggestions. The tutorials here are of a really high quality, but that isn't all that's available here. GIMP-tutorials.net also has some high-quality resources like custom gradient packs and brushes that you can download for free.

- **GimpTalk** (www.gimptalk.com) — Like Gimper.net, GimpTalk is a community web site with an active forum where users share GIMP tips and critique each other's work. A nice thing about GimpTalk is that it features a dedicated set of "official" tutorials created by forum members that can help you become familiar with specific features and techniques. There's also a news section on the front page that gives you updates on GIMP development as well as provides you with helpful tips and tutorials.

- **GIMP Paint Studio** (http://code.google.com/p/gps-gimp-paint-studio) — GIMP Paint Studio is a collection of brushes and presets assembled by the very talented Ramón Miranda. These presets were specifically put together to make GIMP more friendly for digital painting and illustration work. The best part about them, though, is that they provide you with a good starting point and you can pick and choose which presets work well for you.

- **GIMP Portable** (www.portableapps.com/apps/graphics_pictures /gimp_portable) — One of the beautiful things about Free Software is the cool and novel ways that people end up using these programs. For instance, because GIMP is freely available for anyone to use and redistribute, the excellent people at PortableApps.com have kindly packaged it so you can use GIMP anywhere. They have created a version of GIMP for Windows that runs from a USB thumb drive. This means that you're able to edit and create digital images from nearly any computer you stumble across. This is the very definition of awesome.

- **GIMP UI brainstorm** (http://gimp-brainstorm.blogspot.com) — GIMP's user interface is incredibly powerful, but it's far from perfect. If you come up with an idea that can enhance the workflow within GIMP, use this web site to share your idea with the rest of the community. Who knows: the developers may find it useful and interesting enough to add it for you. And because ideas are posted publicly, you also have the opportunity to have a look at ideas from other GIMP users and evaluate them for yourself.

- **Gnome-look.org** (www.gnome-look.org) — If you want to customize GIMP with a specialized GTK+ theme to match your operating system's look or be more comfortable to work in, this is the site you want to check out. In particular, you want to use its section devoted to GTK 2.x to find themes that you may like. The site features a nice rating system, so you can sort themes by the ones that are rated highest and find the most complete ones that match the look you want. Also, if you happen to create your own GTK+ theme, you can submit it here for other users to take advantage of. Welcome to the community!

- **CGTalk** (http://forums.cgsociety.org) — This site isn't specifically dedicated to GIMP, but it's incredibly valuable to GIMP users nonetheless. CGTalk is a community web site for computer graphics artists of all types: 2D artists like photographers and digital painters as well as 3D modelers and animators. Skill levels on this site cover the gamut, ranging from students and hobbyists to well-paid professionals. There's a section dedicated to 2D digital art where there's a preponderance of work done in Photoshop. However, there's still high-quality GIMP work that's shown and many of the tips and techniques discussed for other software packages are directly translatable for use in GIMP. This is a larger computer graphics community, but it's an invaluable resource for improving your skills.

Internet Relay Chat

Internet Relay Chat, or IRC, is a technology that's nearly as old as the Internet itself. Despite its age, IRC has surprisingly not gone the way of similarly aged, but less-frequently used technologies like gopher and newsgroups. It's alive and well, and used extensively with the Free Software communities. IRC gives you an open chatroom, called a *channel*, where you can get real-time help and feedback. Jump in a channel and ask a question, and if there's someone signed in who knows the answer, you can have an answer in a matter of minutes, sometimes even seconds. This is a great way to handle quick questions that are too short to bring up in a user forum or if you need an answer as fast as possible. Also, if you think you've stumbled upon a bug in GIMP, you can use the IRC channel to talk with GIMP developers and find out if it really is a bug or if you're just doing something wrong. GIMPNet, the GIMP community's dedicated IRC server, was a huge help to me while writing this book and it should be just as helpful to you.

To access it, you'll need a chat *client*, like mIRC in Windows or XChat in Linux and Mac OS X. You can also use a web-based client like the one available at www.mibbit.com. Point your client to irc.gimp.org and log in. You'll need to pick a user name for yourself when you do this. Once you're logged in, you have a few choices for channels that you can enter. There's an extensive list on www.gimp.org, but these are the two I find the most useful:

- **#gimp** — This is the primary GIMP channel and it's also where most of the GIMP developers hang out. Nearly any question about GIMP is fair game here, but because this is where developers are, discussion tends to be more technical and code-related.

- **#gimp-users** — If you have a question about using GIMP, this is the best channel for you to ask it. Because the discussion is centered on actually using GIMP, there's less technical discussion about programming here. There's actually a shortcut to access this channel via Mibbit on the GIMPusers.com web site.

Note
A lot of the sites referenced in this appendix, and especially IRC channels, involve interactive discussion with real people around the world. The kinds of personalities that you're likely to interact with will run the gamut from kind, helpful, and articulate to rude, obtuse, and incomprehensible. Such is the nature of the Internet. Just remember that you're more likely to get what you want if you're polite and respectful. ■

What's on the Web Site

As a Free Software application developed completely by volunteer programmers across the globe, GIMP is a constantly evolving piece of software. It's tough enough to keep track of all the changes, let alone document them all in a single printed reference. Also, this book is designed primarily as a comprehensive reference to all of the features available within GIMP. References are great, but I completely understand that some people learn better when they have a little bit more tutorial-based information in their hands. It's for these precise reasons that this book has a companion web site at www.wiley.com/go/GIMPBible. It is the purpose of this appendix to describe what you can find on this web site and how to get the most out of it.

IN THIS APPENDIX

A description of content on this book's companion web site

How to take advantage of the companion web site

How the Site Is Organized

To make the companion web site as useful as possible, it's organized in two ways: chapter by chapter and blog-style. When you first visit the site, you're greeted with the main page. This page gives a brief description of the book and immediately proceeds to give you a chapter-by-chapter breakdown.

Not only does this chapter-by-chapter breakdown provide you with the table of contents to this book, but beneath most chapters in the list are links to supplemental material. This supplemental material may be files that you can open, dissect, and reuse. They can also be video tutorials to show useful and interesting ways to take advantage of some of GIMP's features. And in the event that something changes in GIMP or that there's a mistake in the book (hopefully that's a rarity), it will be noted on an errata page for that chapter. The chapter-by-chapter organization is a great way to work your way through the book while staying up to date with the latest and greatest changes and additions to GIMP.

However, since GIMP is continually being updated and improved, it only makes sense that *GIMP Bible's* web site also stay current. This is the reason for the blog-style organization. You can access the blog by clicking the link to it on the side bar. The blog format gives you access to all the same files available in the chapter-by-chapter organization, but instead of being listed per chapter, the supplemental material is posted in chronological order as I get it uploaded. The blog format also features an RSS (Really Simple Syndication) feed that you can subscribe to with a feed reader like Google Reader so you can immediately know when there's new content on the site. This way, as I add more tutorials and files and perhaps share an interesting bit of GIMP-related news, you're the first to know.

Getting the Most out of the Site

You should be able to use this book's companion web site with any modern web browser, such as Firefox, Safari, Internet Explorer, or Opera. To view any of the supplemental video tutorials directly from the site, you'll also need to have Flash Player 10 or greater installed on your computer. However, if don't have Flash installed, don't worry too much. Each video tutorial is also available for you to download directly and play locally from your home computer. Most video players should work just fine, but in case you have troubles, try viewing the video with the very cool multi-platform open source video player VLC. You can download it for your operating system of choice at `www.videolan.org/vlc`.

It's also worth noting that in the spirit of Free Software, all of the supplemental material that gets posted to `www.wiley.com/go/GIMPBible` is available to you under a Creative Commons Attribution license. This means that you're free to download, copy, modify, and share any of the files or video tutorials posted there, so long as you give me a little credit for creating the original material. Also, if you make something cool with these files (or even without the files), please share it with me. I love seeing when people make awesome work.

Happy GIMPing!

Index

3D animation, Depth Merge filter, 443
3D Outline filter, 508–510

A

action list, 527
active layer, 137
Active Layer Tracking, 547
Add Bevel filter, 487–488
Add Border filter, 488–489
Add Tab, 12
Addition blending mode, 157–158
Adobe Photoshop, 5
Adobe Premiere, 564
Airbrush tool, 301–302
AL-Tracking, 547
Alias Pix format, 87
aliasing, 173
Alien Map effect, 257–258
Align Exposures option, 344
Align Threshold, 117
Align Visible Layers dialog, 149–150
alignment
    Clone tool and, 334
    layers, 149–152
Alignment tool, 209–212
    pixels, transparent, 210
    transparency and, 211
Alpha channel, 173–175
    Eraser tool, 175
    lock, layers, 138
    XCF format, 174
Alpha to Logo filters, 3D Outline,
        508–510

Alpha Trimmed Mean, 364
anchors, 110, 111
    components, 112
    floating selections, 139
    handles, 112
animated brushes, 308–313
animated GIMP brush format, 88
animatic, 563
animation, 537
    AL-Tracking, 547
    controls, 541
    Framerate, 548
    frames, 538
    IWarp filter, 374–377
    layers, 538
        GIF animation, 538–541
    loops, 541
    Move Path, 553–556
    Video Navigator, 546–553
    XCF format, 538
Animation filters
    Blend, 504–505
    Optimizing filters, 508
    Rippling, 505–506
    Spinning Globe, 506–507
    Waves, 507
antialiasing lines, 126
Antialias filter, 361
antialiasing, 287–288, 361
    Mosaic filter, 378–380
API (Application Programming Interface),
        629
APP0 marker, 584

Index

Apple Macintosh, GIMP installation, 660–662
Apply Canvas filter, 475–476
artifacts, compression, 57
Artistic filters, 475
    Apply Canvas, 475–476
    Cartoon, 476–477
    Cubism, 477–478
    GIMPressionist, 479–480
    Oilify, 480
    Photocopy, 480–482
    Predator, 482–484
    Softglow, 484–485
    Van Gogh (LIC), 486
aspect, 582
audio
    bitrate, 581
    codec, 581
    multiplexed, 562
    options, 586–588
    video playback, 562–564
audio tool, configuration, 588–590
Auto Follow Active Image, 12
Autocrop, 191–193
AutoDesk FLIC format, 87
automated adjustments, color, 243–249
AVI1 parameters, 583–586

B

B-frames, 582
background, replacing, channels and, 179–183
batch processing, 513–526
    plug-in, 514–524
Behind mode, 300
Bevel and Emboss effects, 618
Bézier curves, 109, 110
bi-directional predicted frame, 582

binary transparency, 173
bitmap brushes, 307–308
bitmaps, 44
black point limits, 234
Blair, Preston (*Cartoon Animation*), 537
blank images, 68–69
Blend filter, 504–505
blending modes, 156–161
Blinds filter, 368–369
bloom effect, 484
Bluebox, 550, 552–553
Blur filter, 349, 353
    Gaussian Blur, 353–354
    Motion Blur, 354–356
    Pixelize, 357–358
    Selective Gaussian Blur, 359
    Tileable Blur, 359–360
Blur/Sharpen tool, 324–326
bookmarks, 63
Border Average, 267
boundary size, layers, modifying, 146–147
bracketing, 43, 341
    Align Exposures option, 344
breadcrumbs, 63
Brightness-Contrast tool, 230–231
Brush Editor, 305–307
brushes, 298–299
    adjusting, 299–303
    angle, 306
    animated, 308–313
    aspect ratio, 306
    bitmap, 307–308
    direction, 128
    duplicating, 306
    hardness, 306
    Ink tool, 316
    new, 303–313
    preset starter, 306
    pressure, 127

procedural, 305–307
radius, 306
random, 128
settings, Image window, 302–303
shape, 306
spacing, 307
spikes, 306
tilt, 128
velocity, 127–128
Brushes dialog, 14, 298, 299–303
color, 304
Bucket Fill tool, 320–321
Buffer submenu, 81–82
buffers, copy/paste, 81–82
Buffers dialog, 14
Bump Map dialog, 451
Bump Map filter, 450–453
Burn blending mode, 159
burn-in, 550
Button Array, Videoframe Playback window, 558
buttons
Create Folder, 84
Image Window Resize toggle button, 18
Refresh, 22
bzip format, 87

C

C programming language, 630
C source code, saving as, 86, 87
calligraphic brush, 306
calligraphic lines, Ink tool, 315–317
canvas, 18–21
Fit Canvas to Layers, 188–189
snapping to edge, 98
cap style of lines, 125
Cartoon Animation (Blair), 537
Cartoon filter, 476–477

centered text, 289
chaining channels, 137–138, 178
chaining paths, 119
Channel Mixer, 249–252
channels, 50, 171
Alpha channel, 173–175
attributes, 177
background replacement and, 179–183
chaining, 137–138, 178
creating, 176–177
default, 172–173
deleting, 177
duplicating, 176, 177
Quick Mask, 176
raising/lowering, 177
RGB, 172–173
as selection masks, 178
Channels dialog, 13, 171–172
channel attributes, 177
deleting channels, 177
duplicating channels, 177
New Channel Options dialog, 176
raising/lowering channels, 177
Checkerboard filter, 415–416
chroma key, 550
Circuit filter, 420
clipboard, 70
Clone tool, 331–338
alignment, 334
options, 333–334
cloning, 331–338
Perspective Clone tool, 335–338
Close Tab, 12
closing windows, 9
Clouds filter
Difference Clouds, 411–412
Plasma, 412
Solid Noise, 412
clustered-dot dithering, 380

CML Explorer filter, 415
CMS (color management systems), 275
CMYK (Cyan, Magenta, Yellow, Black), 6, 51, 275
CMYK TIFF, image creation, 72–73
codecs, 56
Coffee Stain filter, 489–491
color
    automated adjustments, 243–249
    Brushes dialog, 304
    channels, 50
    Color Enhance operation, 245–246
    depth, 50
    dithering, 54
    Equalize operation, 244
    filters, plug-ins, 269–275
    gamut, 33
    ICC (International Color Consortium), 33
    indexed, 53
    Info submenu
        Border Average, 267
        Colorcube Analysis, 267–268
        Histogram, 266–267
        Smooth Palette, 268
    inverting values, 243
    Normalize operation, 246–247
    Padding Color submenu, 98
    remapping, 255–256
        Alien Map effect, 257–258
        Color Exchange, 258–260
        color maps, 256–257
        Gradient Map, 260
        Palette Map, 260
        Rotate Colors operation, 260–263
        Sample Colorize, 263–265
    separations, exporting, 275–279
    Stretch Contrast operation, 247–248
    Stretch HSV operation, 248–249
    subcolors, 265

    text, 288–289
    White Balance operation, 245
Color Balance tool, 226–227
Color blending modes, 160–161
color components, separated, Channel Mixer, 249–252
color correction, 221
    Display Filters, 96
Color Enhance operation, 245–246
Color Erase mode, 300
Color Exchange operation, 258–260
color management, 32–34
color maps
    defining, 256–257
    rearranging, 256–257
Color menu, 223
color modes, 52–55
Color Overlay effect, 619
color profiles, 33
color spaces, 51–52
Color to Alpha filter, 269
Color tools, 106
    Brightness-Contrast tool, 230–231
    Color Balance, 226–227
    Colorize tool, 229–230
    Curves tool, 236–239
    Desaturate tool, 241–243
    Hue-Saturation tool, 227–229
    layers, 225
    Levels tool, 232–236
    Posterize tool, 239–241
    presets, 224
    Threshold tool, 231–232
Color Tools menu, 223–242
Colorcube Analysis, 267–268
Colored HTML format, 87
Colorify filter, 269
Colorize tool, 229–230
Colormap dialog, 13

Colors dialog, 14
Colors menu, 9
compiled plug-ins, 606–608
compiled programming languages, 604
components, 112
    anchors, 112
Compose operation, 255
compositing, 419
compression
    artifacts, 57
    compression ratios, 56
    generation loss, 57
    lossless, 55–56
    lossy, 57–58
construction history, 527
Contact Sheet plug-in, 524–526
contact sheets, 524
controls, snapping, 98
convolution matrix, 438–442
Convolve tool, 324–326
copy, 284
copying, 79
    buffers and, 81–82
copyleft license, 4
copyrights, 67
Corner Always Threshold, 117
Corner Surround, 117
Corner Threshold, 117
Create Folder button, 84
Create submenu, 70
Crop to Selection, 191
Crop tool, 213–215
cropping, 190
    Autocrop, 191–193
    Crop to Selection, 191
    frames, 550
    Guillotine, 194
    Zealous Crop, 193–194
Cubism filter, 477–478

Current Folder panel, 64
    file types, 65
Curve Bend filter, 369–371
curves, 109
    Bézier curves, 110
Curves tool, 236–239

D

Darken blending modes, 158–159
dash pattern of lines, 126
dash preset of lines, 126
DBP (David's Batch Processor), 514
    Blur tab, 517
    Colour tab, 517–518
    Crop tab, 520
    Input tab, 515
    Output tab, 522–524
    Rename tab, 520–522
    Resize tab, 518–520
    Sharpen tab, 520
    Turn tab, 516–517
Decompose dialog, 253–254
decomposing, 252–255
Decor filters
    Add Bevel, 487–488
    Add Border, 488–489
    Coffee Stain, 489–491
    Fuzzy Border, 491–492
    Old Photo, 492–493
    Round Corners, 493–494
    Slide, 494–495
    Stencil Carve, 495–496
    Stencil Chrome, 496–498
Default Image Grid settings, 28–29
default image preferences, 28
Deinterlace filter, 361–362
depth map, 444
Depth Merge filter, 443–446

depth of color, 50

depth of field (DOF), 325–326

Desaturate tool, 241–243

desktop link, saving as, 87

Despeckle filter, 362–363

Destripe filter, 363–364

Detach Tab, 12

detaching items in interface, 9

Device Status dialog, 13

dialog-specific context menus, 12

dialogs, 9–16

    Align Visible Layers, 149–150

    Brushes, 14, 298, 299–303

    Buffers, 14

    Bump Map, 451

    Channel Mixer, 249–252

    Channels, 13, 171–172

    Colormap, 13

    Colors, 14

    Decompose, 253–254

    detaching, 11

    Device Status, 13

    Document History, 14

    Enter Location, 67

    Error Console, 14

    Export Image as Brush Pipe, 309–310

    File Chooser, 84

    Fonts, 14

    GEGL Operation, 222

    Gradients, 14, 317–320

    GTKPrint, 670

    Histogram, 13

    Images, 14, 75–77

    Layers, 13

    Lighting Effects filter, 397

    Navigation, 13

    New Image, 68, 69

    non-blocking, 8

    Open Image, 62

Paint Dynamics, 298, 333

Palettes, 14

Paths, 13, 118–121

Patterns, 14, 320–321

Pointer, 13

Preferences, 22

Sample Points, 13

Scale Image, 20

Screenshot, 71

Selection Editor, 13

Small Tiles, 466

Stroke Path, 124

Templates, 14, 68

Text Color, 289

Tool Options, 13, 298, 299–300

Undo History, 13

DICOM format, 88

Difference blending mode, 160

Difference Clouds filter, 411–412

Diffraction Patterns filter, 416

digital images *versus* traditional photographs, 41–44

Dilate filter, 442–443

direction of brushes, 128

dispersed-dot dithering, 380

Displace filter, 453–455

displacement map, 453–455

Display Filters, color correction, 96

Display preferences, 32

Dissolve blending mode, 157

distortion, mapping, 450

Distortion filters, 368

    Blinds, 368–369

    Curve Bend, 369–371

    Emboss, 371–372

    Engrave, 372–374

    Erase Every Other Row, 374

    IWarp, 374–377

    Lens Distortion, 378–379

Mosaic, 378–380
Newsprint, 380–381
Pagecurl, 381–382
Polar Coordinates, 382–383
Ripple, 383–384
Shift, 384–
Value Propagate, 384–386
Video, 386
Waves, 386–388
Whirl and Pinch, 388–389
Wind, 389–390
Distorts submenu, filters, 349
dithering, 54, 380
Divide blending mode, 160
DiVX, 579
docks, 9–16
    resizing, 10
Document History dialog, 14
Dodge blending mode, 157
Dodge/Burn tool, 329–331
DOF (depth of field), 325–326
Dot for Dot, 94
dot products, 439
dpi (dots per inch), 49
dragging images, 78
dragging segments, 112
drawable elements, 331
drawing
    Path tool, 111–114
    straight lines, 299
drawing tablets, configuration, 676–678
Drop Shadow effect, 619
Drop Shadow filter, 402–403
duplicating
    channels, 176, 177
    layers, 141
    paths, 120
dynamic range, 330

E
Edge Detect filters, 419–437
edge detection, 419–422
Edge Enhancement, 365
Edge filter, 423–434
Edit menu, 8
Ellipse Select tool, 101–102
Emboss filter, 371–372
encapsulated Postscript, 88
Encoding tab (Videoframe Playback
    window), 592
Engrave filter, 372–374
Enhance filters, 349, 360
    Antialias, 361
    Deinterlace, 361–362
    Despeckle, 362–363
    Destripe, 363–364
    NL Filter, 364–365
    Red Eye Removal, 365
    Sharpen, 365–367
    Unsharp Mask, 367–368
Enter Location dialog, 67
Environment preferences, 23
Equalize operation, 244
Erase Every Other Row filter, 374
Eraser tool, 301
    Alpha+ channel, 175
Erode filter, 442–443
Error Console dialog, 14
Error Threshold, 117
Export Image as Brush Pipe dialog,
    309–310
Export Settings to File, 225
exporting, 86
    color separations, 275–279
    paths, 123
Exposure Blend, 330, 341, 608–609
    Auto-Trim Mask Histograms, 342
    Blend Mask Blur Radius, 341

Exposure Blend, *(continued)*
   Blur Type/Edge Protection, 341–342
   Dark/Bright Mask Grayscale, 342
   Dark Takes Precedence, 342
   Scale Largest Image Dimension to, 342
extensibility, 629
external images, 70
Extract Videorange, 592, 593–596
Extras tab (Videoframe Playback window),
      590–591

F

faking ink drawing, 129–132
feature discard mask, 200
feature preservation mask, 200
FFMPEG library, 557, 575, 577
   parameter setting, 578–583
File Chooser dialog, 84
file formats
   supported by GIMP, 87–90
   XCF, 85
File menu, 8, 61
file types, 65–66
files
   hidden, 64
   maximum size, 64
   opening, 61
   path, 62
   printing to, 669–670
   saving, 84–80
      options, 85
Fill Window, 94
filled justification, 289
Filmstrip effect, 446–450
Filter All Layers tool, 530–534
   Selection to AnimImage, 535–536
Filter Alternative Surround, 117
Filter Epsilon, 117

Filter Iteration Count, 117
Filter Pack filter, 269–272
Filter Percent, 118
Filter Secondary Surround, 118
Filter Surround, 118
filtering resources, 304
Filtermacro, 527
   operations, 528–530
   window, 527–528
filters
   Alpha to Logo, 3D Outline, 508–510
   Animation
      Blend, 504–505
      Optimizing filters, 508
      Rippling, 505–506
      Spinning Globe, 506–507
      Waves, 507
   Artistic, 475
      Apply Canvas, 475–476
      Cartoon, 476–477
      Cubism, 477–478
      GIMPressionist, 479–480
      Oilify, 480
      Photocopy, 480–482
      Predator, 482–484
      Softglow, 484–485
      Van Gogh (LIC), 486
   Blur, 349, 353
      Gaussian Blur, 353–354
      Motion Blur, 354–356
      Pixelize, 357–358
      Selective Gaussian Blur, 359
      Tileable Blur, 359–360
   Bump Map, 450–453
   color, plug-ins, 269–275
   common features, 350–352
   Decor
      Add Bevel, 487–488
      Add Border, 488–489

Coffee Stain, 489–491
Fuzzy Border, 491–492
Old Photo, 492–493
Round Corners, 493–494
Slide, 494–495
Stencil Carve, 495–496
Stencil Chrome, 496–498
Depth Merge, 443–446
Dilate, 442–443
Displace, 453–455
Distortion, 368
Blinds, 368–369
Curve Bend, 369–371
Emboss, 371–372
Engrave, 372–374
Erase Every Other Row, 374
IWarp, 374–377
Lens Distortion, 378–379
Mosaic, 378–380
Newsprint, 380–381
Pagecurl, 381–382
Polar Coordinates, 382–383
Ripple, 383–384
Shift, 384
Value Propagate, 384–386
Video, 386
Waves, 386–388
Whirl and Pinch, 388–389
Wind, 389–390
Distorts submenu, 349
Edge, 423–434
Edge Detect, 419–437
Enhance, 349, 360
Antialias, 361
Deinterlace, 361–362
Despeckle, 362–363
Destripe, 363–364
NL Filter, 364–365
Red Eye Removal, 365

Sharpen, 365–367
Unsharp Mask, 367–368
Erode, 442–443
Filmstrip, 446–450
filter abuse, 350
Fractal Trace, 456–457
Illusion, 457–458
introduction, 349
Laplace, 434
Light and Shadow, 391–392
Drop Shadow, 402–403
Glass Tile, 405–406
Gradient Flare, 392–395
Lens Effect, 405
Lens Flare, 395–396
Lighting Effects, 397–400
Perspective, 404
Sparkle, 400–401
Supernova, 402
Xach-Effect, 404–405
Make Seamless, 459
Map Object, 459–464
Neon, 435–436
Noise, 406
Hurl, 407
Random Pick, 407–408
RBG Noise, 408–409
Scatter HSV, 406–407
Slur, 409
Spread, 409–411
overuse, 350
Paper Tile, 464–466
preview window, 352
Render
Circuit, 420
Clouds, 411–412
Fractal Explorer, 421
Gfig, 421–422
Lava, 422

filters *(continued)*
    Line Nova, 422–423
    Nature, 413–414
    Pattern, 414–420
    Sphere Designer, 423–424
    Spyrogimp, 424–425
  Small Tiles, 466–467
  Sobel, 436–437
  Tile, 467–468
  Warp, 468–473
  Web
    Image Map, 499–501
    Image Slice, 501
    Semi-Flatten, 501
Filters menu, 9
  Re-show Last, 350
  Recently Used, 351
  Repeat Last, 350
  Reset All Filters, 351
Final Cut Pro, 564
Fit Canvas to Layers, 188–189
Fit Image in Window, 94
Flame filter, 413
Flexible Image Transport System, 88
Flip tool, 219–220
flipping, 195–196
floating selection, 80–81, 139
  anchoring, 139
Floyd-Steinberg, 54
focus of window, 12
folders
  hidden, 64
  preferences, 36–37
fonts
  edging, 287–288
  hinting, 288
  text editor, 286
  Text panel, 286–287

Fonts dialog, 14
Foreground Select tool, 103–104
Fractal Explorer, 421
Fractal Trace filter, 456–457
frame disposal method, 539
frame-exact positioning, 592
Framerate, 548
frames. *See also* text frames
  animation, 538
  Combine behavior, 539
  extracting from video, 592–598
  GAP and, 546–553
  number, video, 560
  Replace behavior, 539
Frametype, 581
Free (Lasso) Select tool, 102
Free Software, 4
freeware, 4
Fullscreen option, 95
Fuzzy Border filter, 491–492
Fuzzy Select tool, 102, 114

G

G3 Fax, 88
GAP (GIMP Animation Package), 527, 537, 557
  Bluebox, 552–553
  chroma key, 550
  frames management, 546–553
  installation
    Linux, 610–612
    Mac OS X, 612
    Windows, 612–613
  morphing, 556–559
  Move Path, 553–556
  onion skinning, 559–562
  Storyboard Editor, 564
  storyboards, 562–576
  Video Navigator, 546–553

Gaussian blur, 422
Gaussian Blur filter, 353–354
   Selective Gaussian Blur filter, 359
GEGL (Generic Graphics Library),
     222–223
GEGL Operation dialog, 222
generation loss, lossy compression, 57
Gfig filter, 421–422
GIF animation, layers, 538–541
GIF format, 88
GIMP Animation Package (GAP), 527
GIMP (GNU Image Manipulation Program),
     3
   abilities, 6–7
   brush format, 88
   pattern format, 88
GIMP Paint Studio, 314–315
GIMP Plugin Registry, 602–603
   searching, 603
GIMP XJT compressed format, 88
GimPhoto/GimPad, 614–615
GIMPressionist filter, 479–480
GIMPshop, 613–614
Glass Tile filter, 405–406
G'MIC, 615–617
GNU (GNU's Not Unix), 4
GOP (group of pictures), 582
GPL (GNU General Public License), 4
Gradient Editor, 318
Gradient Flare filter, 392–395
Gradient Map operation, 260
Gradient Overlay effect, 619
gradients, 317–320
   vector, 317
Gradients dialog, 14, 317–320
Grain Extract blending mode, 160
Grain Merge blending mode, 160
grayscale, 52
   Bump Map filter, 450

Desaturate tool, 242
   displacement map, 453–455
grayscale images, layer masks, 162
GREYCstoration, 615–617
GREYstoration, 477
grid
   showing/hiding, 97
   Snap Distance setting, 26
Grid filter, 416–418
group layers, 193
grouping layers, 144–146
GTKPrint dialog, 670
GTKPrint module, 668–671
guides
   adjusting, 17
   removing, 17
   showing/hiding, 97
   Snap Distance setting, 26
Guillotine, 194
Gutenprint, 672–675
   installation
      Linux, 671–672
      Mac OS X, 672
      Windows, 672
gzip format, 88

H

halftones, Newsprint filter, 380
Hand tool (Photoshop), 78
handles, anchors, 112
hanging indent, 289
hardware, image generation, 69
HDR (high dynamic range), 43, 66, 341
HDRI (high dynamic range image), 330
Healing tool, 338–340
Help menu, 9
Help System preferences, 25
hidden files, 64
hidden folders, 64

hidden images, 43
highlights with Dodge/Burn tool, 330
hinting, 288
histogram, 231–232, 266–267
Histogram dialog, 13
History Brush, 334
horizontal/vertical alignment of layers, 150
horizontal (X) resolution, 68
Hot filter, 272
HSV (hue, saturation, value), 51
HTML table format, 88
Hue blending mode, 161
Hue-Saturation tool, 227–229
Hurl filter, 407

I

ICC (International Color Consortium), 33
IFS Fractal filter, 414
Illusion filter, 457–458
Image, brush settings, 302–303
Image Map filter, 499–501
Image menu, 8
    transformations, 187
image regularization algorithm, 615–617
Image Slice filter, 501
Image Thumbnails settings, 23
image tools
    Informational tools
        Color Picker, 104–105
        Measure, 105
        Zoom, 105
    Transform tools, 106
image window, 16–18, 77–79
    navigation shortcuts, 79
    showing/hiding, 99
    View menu, 93–95
Image Window Resize toggle button, 18
Image Windows, 30

images
    Auto Follow Active Image, 12
    fidelity, 55
    formats supported by GIMP, 87–90
    generating with scripts, 74–75
    increasing size, 43
    layers, splitting into image sequences, 542–543
    new blank, 68–69
    pixelated, 44
    raster images, 44
    sequences, converting to single layered image, 544–546
    Show Image Selection, 12
    size
        changing, 47–49
        resolution and, 46–50
    vector images, 44–46
Images dialog, 14, 75–77
Import Settings from File, 224
importing
    images
        Mac, 73
        Windows, 73
    paths, 121–122
indentation, 289
    hanging, 289
indexed color, 53
ink drawing, faking, 129–132
Ink tool
    brushes, 316
    calligraphic lines, 315–317
Inner Glow effect, 619
Inner Shadow effect, 619
input devices, preferences, 34–35
input levels
    black point limits, 234
    mid point limits, 234–235
    white point limits, 234

Input Mode, 576–577
installation
    on Apple Macintosh, 660–662
    GAP
        Linux, 610–612
        Mac OS X, 612
        Windows, 612–613
    on Linux, 649–656
    plug-ins, 604–608
    scripts, 605–606
    on Windows, 656–659
instances, Python, 633
Intelligent Scissors Select tool,
        103
intensity, 265
interface, 5
    detaching items, 9
    menus, 7–9
    startup, 7
    windows, 7–9
Interface preferences, 24
inverting values, 243
IRC (Internet Relay Chat), 694
IWarp filter, 374–377

J

Jigsaw filter, 418
join style of lines, 125
JPEG 2000 format, 56
JPEG format, 88
justified text, 289

K

Keep Knees, 118
kernel, 4, 439
kerning text, 290
keyboard commands, Curves tool,
        239

keyboard shortcuts
    customizing, 37–38
    text, 284
Kimball, Spencer, 3
KISS CEL format, 88

L

languages. *See also* programming languages;
        scripting languages
    compiled, 604
    object-oriented, 632
Laplace filter, 434
Lava filter, 422
Layer Effects plug-in, 617–620
layer masks, 162–163
    modifying, 163–165
Layer menu, 9, 136
    Liquid Rescale, 199
    transformations, 187
Layer to Image Size, 189–190
layers, 80
    active layer, 137
    adding, 139
    AL-Tracking, 547
    alignment, 149–152, 209–212
    animation, 538
        GIF animation, 538–541
    arranging in stack, 142–143
    boundary size, modifying, 146–147
    collecting, 150
    color tools, 225
    creating, 140–141
    deleting, 142
    duplicating, 139, 141
    Filter All Layers tool, 530–534
    Fit Canvas to Layers, 188–189
    floating selection, 139
    frames, 538

layers, *(continued)*
  group layers, 193
  grouping, 144–146
  Guillotine and, 194
  images
    converting sequences to single layered
      image, 544–546
    splitting into image sequence,
      542–543
  introduction, 135
  Layer to Image Size, 189–190
  locks, 138
  management, 136–146
  merging, 143–144, 193
  moving, 142–143
  offsetting content, 148–149
  removing, 139
  resizing, 146–149
  rotating all, 198
  scaling, 147–148
  solid, 141–142
  temporary, 193
  text, 294–296
    outlines, 190
  transparency
    Color to Alpha, 152–153
    selections and, 154–156
    Semi-Flatten, 153
    Threshold Alpha, 153–154
  transparent, 141–142
  visibility, 138
Layers dialog, 13, 136–139
leading, 290
Lens Distortion filter, 378–379
Lens Effect filter, 405
Lens Flare filter, 395–396
Levels tool, 232–234
  all channels, 235–236

  input levels, 234–235
  output levels, 235
Libavformat, 595
Libmpeg3, 595
libraries, GEGL (Generic Graphics Library),
    222–223
LIC (Line Integral Convolution), 486
licensing
  copyleft license, 4
  GPL, 4
Light and Shadow filters, 391–392
  Drop Shadow, 402–403
  Glass Tile, 405–406
  Gradient Flare, 392–395
  Lens Effect, 405
  Lens Flare, 395–396
  Lighting Effects, 397–400
  Perspective, 404
  Sparkle, 400–401
  Supernova, 402
  Xach-Effect, 404–405
Lighten blending modes, 157–158
Lighten Only blending mode, 157
lighting
  Emboss filter, 371
  Softglow filter, 484–485
Lighting Effects filter, 397–400
Lighting Effects filter dialog, 397
Line Integral Convolution (LIC), 486
Line Nova filter, 422–423
Line Reversion Threshold, 118
Line Threshold, 118
Line tool, 299
line width, stroking and, 125
linear bump map, 452
linear segments, 112
lines
  antialiasing, 126
  calligraphic, 315–317

cap style, 125
dash pattern, 126
dash preset, 126
edge detection, 419–422
join style, 125
miter limit, 126
paths, 110
Linux, 5
GAP installation, 610–612
GIMP installation, 649
Debian/Ubuntu, 650–652
Fedora, 652–653
Gentoo, 655
Mandriva, 655–656
OpenSUSE, 653–655
Gutenprint, 671–672
Liquid Rescale, 621–623
scanners and, 664–666
Separate+, 624–626
themes, 682–684
XSane, scanning, 73–74
Liquid Rescale plug-in, 198, 620–623
Advanced tab, 204–206
Height, 199
interactive mode, 206–208
output options, 202–204
seam carving, 199
seam map, 199
seams, 199
smart zoom, 208–209
Width, 199
LISP programming language, 631
Lock Tab to Dock, 12
locks
layers, 138
paths, 120
loops, 541
lossless compression, 55–56
lossy compression, 57–58

M
Macintosh
GAP installation, 612
GIMP installation, 660–662
Gutenprint, 672
Liquid Rescale, 623
scanners, 666–667
scanning images, 73
Separate+, 626
themes, 687–689
macros, 527
magnifying glass, 18
Main Toolbox, 7
Make Seamless filter, 459
Manage Settings, 225
Mandelbrot fractal, 456
Map Object filter, 459–464
mapping, 450
displacement map, 453–455
Marching Ants Speed, 30
mascot, Wilbur, 7
masks
feature discard, 200
feature preservation, 200
introduction, 135
layer masks, 162–163
modifying, 163–165
Master Videoencoder, 589
Mathematical/Mixing blending modes,
159–160
matrixes, 438–442
Mattis, Peter, 3
Maximum RGB filter, 272–273
Maze filter, 418–420
MDI (multiple document interface),
613
measurement units, 17
megapixels, 43

menus, 7–9
  Color, 223
  Color Tools, 223–242
  Colors, 9
  dialog-specific context menus, 12
  Edit, 8
  File, 8, 61
  Filters, 9, 350–351
  Help, 9
  Image, 8
  Layer, 9
  Select, 8
  Tools, 9
  Video, 9
  View, 8, 93–95
  Windows, 9
merging
  layers, 143–144, 193
  paths, 121
mid point limits, 234–235
minimizing, bug, 35
miter limit of lines, 126
MJPG (Motion JPEG), 585
MNG format, 538
Module Manager, 21–22
modules, information about, 22
morphing, 556–559
Mosaic filter, 378–380
Motion Blur filter, 354–356
Motion JPEG (MJPG), 585
mouse commands, Curves tool, 239
Mouse Pointers settings, 31
Move Path, 553–556
Move to Screen, 12
moving
  layers, 142–143
  with Transform tool, 217
MPEG1, 580
MPEG2, 580

MPlayer Based Extraction, 592, 596–598
MS Windows Icon, saving as, 89
MS WMF format, 89
MSRCR (MultiScale Retinex with Color
      Restoration) algorithm, 273
MTA (mail transfer agent), 87
multi-dimensional arrays, animated brushes,
      311–312
multiple document interface (MDI), 613
multiplexed audio, 562
Multiply blending mode, 159

N

naming, Paths dialog, 119
napkin analogy, 56
Nature filters
  Flame, 413
  IFS Fractal, 414
navigation, shortcuts, 79
Navigation dialog, 13
Neon filter, 435–436
New Image dialog, 68
  Advanced Options, 69
new images, 68–69
Newsprint filter, 380–381
NL Filter, 364–365
NLEs (non-linear editors), 557, 564
Noise filters, 406
  Hurl, 407
  Random Pick, 407–408
  RBG Noise, 408–409
  Scatter HSV, 406–407
  Slur, 409
  Spread, 409–411
non-blocking stroke path, 125
non-blocking windows and dialogs, 8
non-linear editors. *See* NLEs
Normal blending mode, 156

Normalize operation, 246–247
NTSC, 635

O

object-oriented languages, 632
offsetting content of layers, 148–149
Oilify filter, 480
Old Photo filter, 492–493
onion skinning, 559–562
Open as Layers, 66
Open Image dialog, 62
Open Location, 66
Open Recent, 67
opening files, 61
opening images, 62–67
Optimal Estimation, 364
Optimizing filters, 508
Outer Glow effect, 619
outlines on text layers, 190
output levels, 235
Overlay blending modes, 159

P

Padding Color submenu, 98
Pagecurl filter, 381–382
paint dynamics
    activating, 313
    Smudge tool and, 327
Paint Dynamics dialog, 298, 333
Paint Shop Pro format, 89
Paint tools, 106
painting, 297
    Airbrush, 301–302
    along a path, 124–125
    angle, 300–301
    Apply Jitter, 301
    aspect ratio, 300
    brushes, 298–299, 300

adjusting, 299–303
    Image window and, 302–303
Eraser tool, 301
fade out, 301
GIMP Paint Studio, 314–315
gradients and, 301
incremental option, 301
modes, 300
opacity, 300
scale, 300
tools, 297
Palette Map operation, 260
Palettes dialog, 14
panels
    Current Folder, 64
    Places, 63
Pantone color, 6
Paper Tile filter, 464–466
Paste, 79–80
Paste Into, 80–81
pasting, 79–81
    buffers and, 81–82
Path tool
    drawing with, 111–114
    Polygonal option, 113
    Shift key, 111
    shortcuts, 113
paths, 62, 109
    advantages, 109–110
    chaining, 119
    creating, 110–118
        with text, 292–293
    deleting, 121
    duplicating, 120
    exporting, 123
    importing, 121–122
    locking, 120
    merging, 121
    naming, 119

paths, *(continued)*
  painting along, 124–132
  scaling, 122
  selecting with, 129
  from selections, 114–118
  stroking, 121
    antialiasing, 126
    brushes, 127–128
    cap style, 125
    dash pattern, 126
    dash preset, 126
    join style, 125
    line width, 125
    miter limit of lines, 126
    Paint Tool, 126–128
    patterns, 125
    solids, 125
  text along, 290–292
  vectors, 109–110
  visibility, 119
Paths dialog, 13, 118–121
  chaining, 119
  deleting paths, 121
  Duplicate Path, 120
  Lock label, 120
  Merge Visible Paths, 121
  Name, 119
  new paths, 120
  Paint Along the Path, 121
  Path to Selection, 120
  Preview, 119
  Raise/Lower Path, 120
  Selection to Path, 121
  visibility, 119
pattern fills, 320–321
Pattern filters
  Checkerboard, 415–416
  CML Explorer, 415
  Diffraction Patterns, 416

  Grid, 416–418
  Jigsaw, 418
  Maze, 418–420
  Qbist, 420
  Sinus, 420
Pattern Overlay effect, 619
Patterns dialog, 14, 320–321
PBM format, 89
PDB (GIMP's Procedural Database), 531
PDF format, 89
Pen tool, 110
Perl scripting language, 633
perspective, Transform tool, 218
Perspective Clone tool, 335–338
Perspective filter, 404
PGM format, 89
Photocopy filter, 480–482
photographer tools, 323–331
photographs, *versus* digital images, 41–44
Photoshop, 5
  file format, 89
pixel lock, layers, 138
pixel matrix, 440
pixel units in Pointer Coordinates box, 17
pixelated images, 44
Pixelize filter, 357–358
pixels, 357
  binary transparency, 173
  dimensions, 357
  inverting values, 243
  resolution, 357
  transparent, Alignment tool and, 210
pixels per inch (ppi), 46, 49, 357
Places panel, 63
  searches in, 63
Plasma filter, 412
Plug-in Browser, 608

plug-ins, 601
  color filters, 269–275
  compiled, installation, 606–608
  Exposure Blend, 608–609
  GIMP-GAP, 609–613
  GimPhoto/GimPad, 614–615
  GIMPshop, 613–614
  G'MIC, 615–617
  GREYCstoration, 615–617
  image generation, 69
  installation, 604–608
  Layer Effects, 617–620
  Liquid Rescale, 620–623
  scripts and, 604
  Separate+, 623–628
PNG format, 56, 89, 585
PNM format, 89
Pointer Coordinates box, 16–17
Pointer dialog, 13
Polar Coordinates filter, 382–383
polygons, 113
post production, 221
Posterize tool, 239–241
Postscript format, 89
  Encapsulated Postscript format, 89
ppi. *See* pixels per inch
PPM format, 89
Predator filter, 482–484
preferences
  color management, 32–34
  default image, 28
  Default Image Grid settings, 28–29
  Display, 32
  Environment, 23
  folders, 36–37
  Help System, 25
  Image Windows, 30–32
  input devices, 34–35
  Interface, 24
  setting, 21–36
  Theme, 24–25
  Tool Options, 26–27
  Toolbox, 27–28
  Videoframe Playback window, 564–575
  Window Management, 35–36
Preferences dialog, 22
  Theme settings, 25
prefix notation in Scheme, 631
premultiplied alpha, 174
presets, Color Tools, 224
pressure, brushes, 127
preview, Paths dialog, 119
Preview Size, 12
preview window, filters, 352
previewing images, 75–76
printing images, 668
  to file, 669–670
  GTKPrint module, 668–671
  Gutenprint, 671–675
  to printer, 670
procedural brushes, 305–307
Procedure Browser, 634
processors, number used, 23
programming languages, 630
  compiling, 630
PSD files, 6
Python scripting language, 631–633
  instances, 633

Q

Qbist filter, 420
Qdiff, 581
Qmin/Qmax, 581
Qscale, 581
Quick Mask, 18
  channels and, 176
Quicktime4linux, 595

Index

R

RAM (random access memory), 17
Random Pick filter, 407–408
Random setting for brushes, 128
raster images, 44
Raw image format, 89, 585
RBG Noise filter, 408–409
RBG (red, green, blue), 50, 51, 52
RBGA (red, green, blue, alpha), 6
Real Video, 580
Reapply Effects effect, 619
Recompose operation, 255
Rectangle Select tool, 100–101
Red Eye Removal filter, 365
Refresh button, 22
remapping colors, 255–256
   Alien Map effect, 257–258
   Color Exchange, 258–260
   color maps, 256–257
   Gradient Map, 260
   Palette Map, 260
   Rotate Colors operation, 260–263
   Sample Colorize operation, 263–265
Render filters
   Circuit, 420
   Clouds
      Difference Clouds, 411–412
      Plasma, 412
      Solid Noise, 412
   Fractal Explorer, 421
   Gfig, 421–422
   Lava, 422
   Line Nova, 422–423
   Nature
      Flame, 413
      IFS Fractal, 414
   Pattern
      Checkerboard, 415–416
      CML Explorer, 415

      Diffraction Patterns, 416
      Grid, 416–418
      Jigsaw, 418
      Maze, 418–420
      Qbist, 420
      Sinus, 420
   Sphere Designer, 423–424
   Spyrogimp, 424–425
reparameterization, 117
Reparameterize Threshold, 118
replication, drawable elements, 331
resizing
   docks, 10
   layers, 146–149
resolution, 68
   changing, 47–49
   image size and, 46–50
   misuse of term, 50
   Newsprint filter, 380
   pixels per inch, 46, 357
Resource Consumption, 83
Retinex filter, 273–275
Revert, 83. *See also* Undo
RGB channels, 172–173
Ripple filter, 383–384
Rippling filter, 505–506
Rotate Colors operation, 260–263
rotation, 196–198
   Transform tool, 217
Round Corners filter, 493–494
Ruby scripting language, 633

S

Sample Colorize operation, 263–265
sample points, showing/hiding, 97
Sample Points dialog, 13
Satin effect, 619
Saturation blending mode, 161

saving
exported paths, 123
files, 84–90
as C source code, 86
options, 85
XCF format, 84
Scale Image dialog, 20
scaling
layers, 147–148
paths, 122
Transform tool, 218
scanners
acquiring images, 663–664
Linux, 664–666
Mac OS X, 666–667
Windows, 666–667
importing images
Mac, 73
Windows, 73
Linux Xsane, 73–74
Scatter HSV filter, 406–407
Scheme scripting language,
631–633
prefix notation, 631
Screen blending mode, 157
screen grabs, 71
Screenshot dialog, 71
Screenshot tool, 70–71
Macintosh, 71
screenshots, images from, 70–72
script-fu, 74–75, 631
scripting, 629
Scripting Console, 634–635
scripting languages, 630
interpreting, 630
Perl, 633
Python, 631–633
Ruby, 633
Scheme, 631–633

Tcl, 633
text editors, 636
writing custom script, 635–644
scripts
image generation, 74–75
installation, 605–606
plug-ins and, 604
structure, 636–639
scrollbars, 77
seam carving (Liquid Rescale), 199, 620
seam map (Liquid Rescale), 199
seams (Liquid Rescale), 199
searches
GIMP Plugin Registry, 603
Places panel, 63
Subdivide Search, 118
segments
dragging, 112
linear, 112
Select by Color tool, 103, 114
Select menu, 8
selection creation functions, 166
selection modification functions,
166–168
Select to Path feature, 116
selecting, with paths, 129
Selection Editor dialog, 13
selection masks, channels as, 178
Selection to AnimImage, 535–536
selection tools
Ellipse Select, 101–102
floating selections, 139
Foreground Select, 103–104
Free (Lasso) Select, 102
Fuzzy Select, 102
Intelligent Scissors Select, 103
Mode, 99
Rectangle Select, 100–101
Select by Color, 103

selections
  Crop to Selection, 191
  layer transparency, 154–156
  paths from, 114–118
Selective Gaussian Blur filter, 359
Semi-Flatten filter, 501
Send By Email, 87
Separate+, 275–279
separated color components, Channel
    Mixer, 249–252
SGI IRIS format, 90
shadows. *See also* Light and Shadow filters
  Dodge/Burn tool, 330
  Drop Shadow filter, 402–403
shallow depth of field, 326
shapes, paths, 110
Sharpen filter, 365–367
shearing, Transform tool, 218
Shift filter, 384
Shift key, Path tool, 111
shortcuts
  navigation, 79
  Path tool, 113
Show Button Bar, 12
Show Image Selection, 12
Show Preview Wireframe check box,
    460
showing/hiding, 99
Shrink Wrap option, 95
shrink wrapping, 78
Sinus filter, 420
sinusoidal bump map, 452
sizing
  Fit Canvas to Layers, 188–189
  Layer to Image Size, 189–190
Slide filter, 494–495
Slur filter, 409
Small Tiles dialog, 466
Small Tiles filter, 466–467

smart zoom (Liquid Rescale), 208–209
Smooth Palette, 268
Smudge tool, 326–328
Snap Distance setting, 26
snapping control, 98
Sobel filter, 436–437
Softglow filter, 484–485
software, free, 4
solid layers, 141–142
Solid Noise filter, 412
SoX (Sound eXchange), 588–589
Space Bar option, 31
Sparkle filter, 400–401
Sphere Designer filter, 423–424
spherical bump map, 452
Spinning Globe filter, 506–507
splash image, 679–681
Split Image to Frames feature, 542–543
Spread filter, 409–411
Spyrogimp filter, 424–425
stack, layer arranging, 142–143
Stallman, Richard, 4
startup, interface, 7
Stencil Carve filter, 495–496
Stencil Chrome filter, 496–498
storyboards, 562–576
straight lines, drawing, 299
Stretch Contrast operation, 247–248
Stretch HSV operation, 248–249
Stroke effect, 619
Stroke Line option, 125–126
Stroke Path dialog, 124
  non-blocking, 125
Stroke Path function, 124
stroking paths, 121, 124
  antialiasing, 126
  brushes
    direction, 128
    pressure, 127

random, 128
tilt, 128
velocity, 127–128
cap style, 125
dash pattern, 126
dash preset, 126
join style, 125
line width, 125
miter limit of lines, 126
Paint tool, 126–128
patterns, 125
solids, 125
subcolors, 265
Subdivide Search, 118
Subdivide Surround, 118
Subdivide Threshold, 118
Subtract blending mode, 160
SUN Rasterfile, 90
Supernova filter, 402
SVG format, 90, 122

T

Tab Style, 12
tags, 304
GIMP Plugin Registry, 603
Tangent Surround, 118
Targa format, 90
Tcl scripting language, 633
templates, 86–87
Templates dialog, 14, 68
temporary layers, 193
text
along paths, 290–292
antialiasing, 287–288
color, 288–289
copy, 284
indentation, 289–290
justification, 289–290

keyword shortcuts, 284
layers, 294–296
path creation, 292–293
spacing, 289–290
kerning, 290
leading, 290
tracking, 290
Unicode, 285
uses for, 281
Text Color dialog, 289
text editor, 283
fonts, 286
scripting, 636
Text Editor window, 285
text frames
creating, 282
resizing to fit text typed, 282–283
text layers, outlines, 190
Text panel, 286–287
color, 288–289
fonts, 286–287
edging, 287–288
indentation, 289–290
justification, 289–290
Size, 286–287
spacing, 289–290
Text tool, 282
The Animator's Survival Kit (Williams),
537
Theme preferences, 24–25
themes, 681–682
Linux, 682–684
Mac OS X, 687–689
Windows, 684–687
Threshold tool, 231–232
thresholds
align, 117
corner, 117
corner always, 117

thresholds *(continued)*
  error, 117
  line, 118
  line reversion, 118
  reparameterize, 118
  subdivide, 118
thumbnails
  Image Thumbnails settings, 23
  maximum size, 64
  video playback, 561
TIFF format, 90
TIFF images, 72–73
tile cache size, 23
Tile filter, 467–468
Tileable Blur filter, 359–360
tilt of brushes, 128
timestamp, 550
TinyScheme, 631
tone mapping, 43, 330, 341
Tool Options dialog, 13, 298, 299–300
  preferences, 26–27
Toolbox preferences, 27–28
Tools menu, 9
tooltips, 25
Torvalds, Linus, 4
tracking text, 290
Transform tool, 215–219
  moving with, 217
  perspective, 218
  rotating, 217
  scaling, 218
  shearing, 218
transformations, 187
  cropping, 190–194
  Flip tool, 219–220

  flipping, 195–196
  Liquid Rescale, 198–202
  rotation, 196–198
transparency
  Alignment tool and, 211
  layers
    Color to Alpha, 152–153
    selections and, 154–156
    Semi-Flatten, 153
    Threshold Alpha, 153–154
transparent layers, 141–142

U

Undo, 82. *See also* Revert
Undo History, 82
  increasing/decreasing number, 83
Undo History dialog, 13
Unicode, 285
units of measure, 17
Unsharp Mask filter, 367–368
URI (uniform resource identifier), 62, 66
Utility Window, bug in, 35

V

Value blending mode, 161
Value Propagate filter, 384–386
values of pixels, inverting, 243
Van Gogh (LIC) filter, 486
vector images, 44–46
vectors, 109–110, 317
velocity of brushes, 127–128
venetian blind effect, 368–369
vertical (Y) resolution, 68

video
   aspect, 582
   B-frames, 582
   bitrate, 581
   codecs, 578, 580
   encoding, 575–592
   extracting frames, 592–598
   formats, 578
   frame number, 560
Video filter, 386
Video menu, 9
Video Navigator, 546–553
   frames
      converting, 550
      cropping, 550
      deleting, 550
      density, 551
      duplicating, 550
      exchanging, 550
      flattening, 551
      layer delete, 551
      modifying, 551
      renumbering, 551
      resizing, 551
      scale, 551
      sequence reverse, 550
      sequence shift, 550
video playback, 558–575
   audio, 562–564
   looping, 561
   options, 576–586
   preview size, 561
   thumbnails, 561
Videoframe Playback window,
     558
   Audio Options, 562–564
   Encoding tab, 592
   Extras tab, 590–591
   playback control buttons, 560
   preferences, 564–575
View as List/Grid, 12
View menu, 8, 93–95
visibility for layers, 138

W

Warp filter, 468–473
Waves filter, 386–388, 507
Web filters
   Image Map, 499–501
   Image Slice, 501
   Semi-Flatten, 501
web sites
   companion to book, 221,
     695–696
   resources, 691–693
Whirl and Pinch filter, 388–389
White Balance, 245
white point limits, 234
Wilbur, 7
Williams, Richard (*The Animator's Survival Kit*), 537
Wind filter, 389–390
window blind effect, 368–369
window decorations, 71

Window Management, 35–36
Windows
   GAP installation, 612–613
   GIMP installation, 656–659
   Liquid Rescale, 623
   Macintosh, 672
   scanners, 666–667
   scanning images, 73

Windows *(continued)*
    Separate+, 626–628
    themes, 684–687
windows, 7–9
    closing, 9
    image window, 16–18
        View menu, 93–95
    non-blocking, 8
Windows BMP format, 90
Windows menu, 9
WYSIWYG (what you *see* is what you get),
        292

X

X bitmap format, 90
x window dump format, 90

Xach-Effect filter, 404–405
XCF format, 85, 87
    animation, 538
    saving in, 84
XViD, 586

Y

YUV (luma, chrominance), 52

Z

Zealous Crop, 193–194
Zoom tool, 77–78
zooming, 94
    wheel mouse, 94
ZSoft PCX format, 90

The books you read to succeed.

Get the most out of the latest software and leading-edge technologies with a Wiley Bible—your one-stop reference.

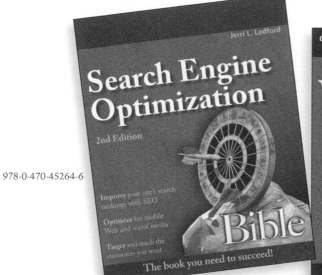

978-0-470-45264-6

978-0-470-50909-8

978-0-470-43640-0

978-0-470-47191-3

WILEY
Now you know.
wiley.com

Printed and bound by CPI Group (UK) Ltd, Croydon, CR0 4YY

27/10/2024

14580182-0005